Charles T. Brues

Psyche

I0085846

Charles T. Brues

Psyche

ISBN/EAN: 9783741163234

Manufactured in Europe, USA, Canada, Australia, Japa

Cover: Foto ©Klaus-Uwe Gerhardt /pixelio.de

Manufactured and distributed by brebook publishing software
(www.brebook.com)

Charles T. Brues

Psyche

PSYCHE

A Journal of Entomology

- - -

Volume XLIV

1937

EDITED BY CHARLES T. BRUES

Published by the Cambridge Entomological Club
Biological Laboratories
Harvard University
Cambridge, Mass., U.S.A.

PSYCHE

A JOURNAL OF ENTOMOLOGY

Established in 1874

VOL. XLIV   MARCH - JUNE, 1937   Nos. 1- 2

TABLE OF CONTENTS.

CAMBRIDGE ENTOMOLOGICAL CLUB

OFFICERS FOR 1937-1938

President .	. C. A. FROST
Vice-President	J. C. BEQUAERT
Secretary	V. G. DETHIER
Treasurer	RICHARD DOW
	THOMAS BARBOUR
Executive Committee {	F. M. CARPENTER
	C. H. BLAKE

EDITORIAL BOARD OF PSYCHE

EDITOR-IN-CHIEF
C. T. BRUES, HARVARD UNIVERSITY

ASSOCIATE EDITOR
F. M. CARPENTER, HARVARD UNIVERSITY

CONSULTING EDITORS

NATHAN BANKS,
Harvard University.

A. E. EMERSON,
University of Chicago.

THOMAS BARBOUR,
Harvard University.

A. L. MELANDER,
College of the
City of New York.

RICHARD DOW,
New England Museum of
Natural History,
Boston, Mass.

J. G. NEEDHAM,
Cornell University.

PSYCHE is published quarterly, the issues appearing in March, June, September, and December. Subscription price, per year, payable in advance: $2.00 to Subscribers in the United States; foreign postage, 25 cents extra, Canada 15 cents. Single copies, 65 cents.

Cheques and remittances should be addressed to Treasurer, Cambridge Entomological Club, Biological Laboratories, Harvard University, Cambridge, Mass.

Orders for back volumes, missing numbers, notices of change of address, etc., should be sent to Professor F. M. Carpenter, Biological Laboratories, Harvard University, Cambridge, Mass.

IMPORTANT NOTICE TO CONTRIBUTORS
Manuscripts intended for publication, books intended for review, and other editorial matter, should be addressed to Professor C. T. Brues, Biological Laboratories, Harvard University, Cambridge, Mass.

Authors contributing articles over 8 printed pages in length will be required to bear a part of the extra expense, for additional pages. This expense will be that of typesetting only, which is about $2.00 per page. The actual cost of preparing cuts for all illustrations must be borne by contributors; the expense for full page plates from line drawings is approximately $5.00 each, and for full page half-tones, $7.50 each; smaller sizes in proportion.

AUTHOR'S SEPARATES
Reprints of articles may be secured by authors, if they are ordered before, or at the time proofs are received for corrections. The cost of these will be furnished by the Editor on application.

Printed by the Eliot Press Inc., Jamaica Plain, Mass., U. S. A.

PSYCHE

VOL. XLIV   MARCH-JUNE, 1937   Nos. 1-2

THE SCIENTIFIC WORK OF ALBERT PITTS MORSE

BY RICHARD DOW

New England Museum of Natural History

Albert Pitts Morse, best known for his work on the Orthoptera of New England, was born in Sherborn, Massachusetts, on February 10, 1863. He was a direct descendant of Samuel Morse of Dedham, whose son Daniel became one of the incorporators of the town of Sherborn in 1674. His father, Leonard Townsend Morse, was prominent in town affairs for many years.

As a boy, Mr. Morse attended the local schools, graduating from the Sawin Academy of Sherborn in 1879. He was unfortunately prevented from acquiring additional schooling by lack of robust health and the need of his services at home. Early attracted by the beauty of nature and endowed with an inquiring mind, he began to collect specimens, study taxidermy, and become acquainted with the wild life in his vicinity, a district rich in natural resources. He was encouraged and aided in these pursuits by several local naturalists and collectors, among whom should be mentioned Amory L. Babcock and Edgar J. Smith of Sherborn, and William Edwards of South Natick.

At the age of 23 he abandoned farming as a livelihood and took up draughting, a vocation which he followed for several years. After the death of his parents in 1886 and 1888, he accepted a position as assistant in the Zoölogical Department of Wellesley College, with which institution he was connected in different capacities for more than 45 years (until 1933). As collector and instructor, he served the students and teachers in various ways, developed the museum, and lectured on elementary and systematic zoölogy and entomology. During the first part of this period he attended the summer school of the Marine Biological Laboratory at Woods Hole, took a long summer course in entomology at Cornell University under Professor J. H. Comstock, and made extensive collections of New England insects, paying particular attention to the Orthoptera and Odonata, in which orders he discovered and described many new species.

In 1893 Mr. Morse married Miss Annie McGill of Dover. They lived in Sherborn until 1900, and then moved to Wellesley.

In 1897, with the encouragement of Mr. S. H. Scudder, Mr. Morse undertook a summer's trip to the Pacific Coast to collect the Orthoptera of that region. He returned with several thousand specimens including representatives of many new species most of which were described by Mr. Scudder.

In 1901, at the request of Professor Alpheus Hyatt, he reorganized the instruction in zoölogy of the Teachers' School of Science of the Boston Society of Natural History, combining a series of field trips each spring and fall with a winter term of laboratory work, in a four year course. This was successfully conducted for two periods of four years, each of which included a year of entomology. The purpose of these lessons was to equip the teacher of biology in secondary schools with a practical as well as theoretical knowledge of the subject. Their success was attested by the numbers which attended and the affection and loyalty of the students.

In 1903 and again in 1905, Mr. Morse was appointed Research Assistant by the Carnegie Institution of Washington and awarded a fund to be expended in the study of the Orthoptera of the southern United States. With this assistance he made two field trips covering the region from Virginia to Texas, as a result of which he wrote two reports on the grasshopper fauna and its ecology.

During a portion of the summer vacations from 1909 to 1912, Mr. Morse taught natural history to the boys, girls, and teachers of Woodstock, Vermont, under the patronage of Miss Elizabeth Billings of that town, and then, at her suggestion and with her support, devoted his spare time for several seasons to the preparation of an excellent monograph on the New England Orthoptera. This volume of 350 pages was published by the Boston Society of Natural History in 1920.

In January, 1911, Mr. Morse became connected with the Peabody Museum of Salem, at first in charge of insects only, and later (December of the same year) as Curator of Natural History, though devoting only part of his time to that institution until 1926. In 1920 he spent a month in field work on the Orthoptera of Maine, subsequently preparing a report on this subject for the Maine Agricultural Experiment Station. From 1919 to 1923, at least a part of his summer vacation was spent, mainly in Nebraska, in a study of the food habits of grasshoppers with reference to their attacks on binder-twine. In 1926 he became a trustee of the Ropes Memorial of Salem, serving on the committee on grounds and as chairman of the committee on botanical lectures, which during his incumbency were largely arranged by him.

In 1934 his health began to fail, and after February, 1935, he was forced to give up his regular work at the Peabody Museum. His death occurred at Wellesley on April 29, 1936. He is survived by his wife, two children, and four grandchildren.

Mr. Morse was a fellow of the American Association for the Advancement of Science and of the Entomological Society of America, and a member of the following organizations: the Boston Society of Natural History, Morse Science Club of Salem (twice President), American Association of Economic Entomologists, Cambridge Entomological Club (President 1898, 1914, 1923, 1933-34), American Ornithologists' Union, Essex County Ornithological Club (Vice-president from its inception until 1934, then President until his death), Massachusetts Audubon Society, New England Bird-banding Association, Nuttall Ornithological Club, American Fern Society, New England Botanical Club (Vice-president 1928-1931), and the Massachusetts Horticultural Society.

Mr. Morse's private collection of insects, which contained more than fifty thousand specimens and included many types, was acquired by the Museum of Comparative Zoölogy at

Harvard College during the academic year 1920-21. The museums at Boston and Salem also possess many specimens which he collected personally. Some of his material bears one or more of the following printed labels:

Coll. A. P. M.	Essex Co.	Coll. P. M.
Lot	Lot	Lot
No.		No.

The numbers to be found on the first of these labels are explained in a manuscript notebook at the Museum of Comparative Zoölogy. The key to those on the second and third labels is contained in another notebook at the Peabody Museum of Salem. The data for all of the lots is available at both of the above museums, and also at the Boston Society of Natural History. It should be noted that these labels sometimes indicate only the authority who determined the material, and that the Essex County label does not necessarily mean that the specimen with which it is pinned was collected in that locality.

Mr. Morse was above all a lover of nature with a remarkable knowledge of natural history. The members of the Cambridge Entomological Club, at whose meetings he was a constant and welcome attendant, greatly miss his presence and his interesting, often humorous, contributions. He was an accurate observer and meticulous in attention to detail. Few men with as little formal training are able to command so much respect for their scientific work.

The following bibliography contains most of Mr. Morse's published writings. It does not include the articles which he contributed to newspapers, or a record of the many notes and exhibits which he presented at meetings of the Cambridge Entomological Club. The latter may be found in various issues of PSYCHE.

[Letter concerning the orchid fly.] Insect Life 2: 250. 1890.

[Letter concerning orchid pests.] Insect Life 3: 22. 1890.

A suggestion to lepidopterists. Ent. News 3: 121-122. 1892.

A melanistic locust. Psyche 6: 401-402. 1893.

A new species of Stenobothrus from Connecticut, with

remarks on other New England species. Psyche 6: 477-479, figs. 1-6. 1893.

Wing-length in some New England Acrididæ. Psyche 7: 13-14. 1894 (mailed in December, 1893). Ibid.: 53-55. 1894.

A preliminary list of the Acrididæ of New England. Psyche 7: 102-108. 1894.

Notes on the Orthoptera of Penikese and Cuttyhunk. Psyche 7: 179-180. 1894.

Notes on the Acrididæ of New England. 1. [Tettiginæ.] Psyche 7: 147-154, 163-167, pl. 6. 1894.

On the use of bisulphide. Journ. N. Y. Ent. Soc. 2: 191. 1894.

Spharagemon: a study of the New England species. Proc. Boston Soc. Nat. Hist. 26: 220-240, figs. 1-9. 1894.

[Review of preceding article.] Psyche 7: 138, figs. 1-9. 1894.

New North American Odonata. Psyche 7: 207-211, 274-275. 1895.

Revision of the species of Spharagemon. Psyche 7: 287-299, figs. 1-6. 1895.

Enallagma pictum Morse. Psyche 7: 307. 1895.

New North American Tettiginæ. 1. Journ. N. Y. Ent. Soc. 3: 14-16. 1895.

New North American Tettiginæ. 2. Journ. N. Y. Ent. Soc. 3: 107-109. 1895.

Notes on the Acrididæ of New England. 2. Tryxalinæ. Psyche 7: 323-327, 342-344, 382-384, 402-403, 407-411, 419-422, 443-445, pl. 7. 1896.

Some notes on locust stridulation. Journ. N. Y. Ent. Soc. 4: 16-20. 1896.

Both sides of butterflies. Journ. N. Y. Ent. Soc. 4: 20-22. 1896.

Illustrations of North American Tettiginæ. Journ. N. Y. Ent. Soc. 4: 49, pl. 2. 1896.

Notes on New England Acrididæ. 3. Oedipodinæ. Psyche 8: 6-8, 35-37, 50-51, 64-66, 80-82, 87-89, 111-114, pl. 2. 1897.

Birds. In *A history of Dover, Massachusetts* [etc.] by Frank Smith: 336-348. Dover, Mass. 1897.

List of birds of Dover. [Reprint of preceding article.] pp. [i-ii], 1-13. 1897.

Annotated list of birds of Wellesley and vicinity, comprising the land-birds and most of the inland water-fowl of eastern Massachusetts. pp. 1-56, frontispiece. Wellesley, Mass. 1897.

Pacific Coast collecting. Psyche 8: 160-167, 174-177. 1898.

Notes on New England Acridiidæ. 4. Acridiinæ. Psyche 8: 247-248, 255-260, 269-273, 279-282, 292-296, pl. 7. 1898.

The distribution of the New England locusts. Psyche 8: 315-323, pl. 8. 1899.

New North American Tettiginæ. 3. Journ. N. Y. Ent. Soc. 7: 198-201. 1899.

A new method of pressing plants. Plant World 2: 114-115. 1899.

Subfam. Tettiginæ. Biol. Centrali-Amer., Insecta, Orth. 2: 3-16, 6 figs. 1900. Ibid.: 17-19, 2 figs. 1901.

Variation in Tridactylus. Psyche 9: 197-199, figs. 1-5. 1901.

[Translation of *Ebauche sur les mœurs des fourmis de l'Amérique du Nord* by Auguste Forel (Riv. di Scien. Biol. 2: 180-192. 1900.).] Psyche 9: 231-239, 243-245. 1901.

New North American Orthoptera. Can. Ent. 33: 129-131. 1901.

The Xiphidiini of the Pacific Coast. Can. Ent. 33: 201-205. 1901.

A new Xiphidium from Florida. Can. Ent. 33: 236. 1901.

Dichopetala brevicauda—a correction. Psyche 9: 380-381. 1902.

[Review of *A nature wooing at Ormond by the sea* by W. S. Blatchley.] Psyche 10: 43. 1903.

New Orthoptera from Nevada. Psyche 10: 115-116. 1903. Reprinted in Invertebrata Pacifica 1: 14-16. 1903.

Amory Leland Babcock. Psyche 10: 187. 1903 [1904].

New Acridiidæ from the southeastern states. Psyche 11: 7-13. 1904.

[Review of *The Orthoptera of Indiana* by W. S. Blatchley.] Psyche 11: 23-24. 1904.

A faunal and floral tabulation-scheme. Psyche 11: 25-28, pl. 4. 1904.

Diestrammena unicolor in North America. Psyche 11: 80. 1904.

Researches on North American Acridiidæ. Carnegie Institution of Wash., Publ. 18: 1-55, figs. 1-13, pls. 1-8. 1904.

Some Bahama Orthoptera. Psyche 12: 19-24. 1905.

New Acridiidæ from the southern states. Psyche 13: 119-122. 1906.

Melanoplus viridipes in New England. Psyche 13: 135. 1906.

Nemobius palustris Blatchley. Psyche 13: 158. 1906.

The ecological relations of the Orthoptera in the Porcupine Mountains, Michigan. Rept. State Board of Geol. Survey of Michigan for 1905: 68-72. 1906.

Paratylotropidia beutenmuelleri sp. nov. Psyche 14: 14. 1907.

Podisma australis nom. nov. Psyche 14: 57. 1907.

Further researches on North American Acridiidæ. Carnegie Institution of Wash., Publ. 68: 1-54, fig. 1, frontispiece, pls. 1-9. 1907.

Tettigidean notes, and a new species. Psyche 15: 25. 1908.

Melanoplus harrisii n. sp. Psyche 16: 12. 1909.

Report on the Isle Royale Orthoptera of the 1905 expedition. An Ecological Survey of Isle Royale, Lake Superior, published as a part of the Rept. of the Board of Geol. Survey of Mich. for 1908: 299-303. 1909.

A hopperdozer for rough ground. Psyche 17: 79-81, fig. 1. 1910.

Lucilia sericata as a household pest. Psyche 18: 89-92, fig. 1. 1911.

The orthopterological work of Mr. S. H. Scudder, with personal reminiscences. Psyche 18: 187-192. 1911.

A pocket list of the birds of eastern Massachusetts with especial reference to Essex County. pp. 1-92 + 13 (chart), frontispiece. Salem, Mass. 1912.

Leptura emarginata in New England. Psyche 22: 212. 1915 [1916].

[With Morgan Hebard as joint author.] Fixation of single type (lectotypic) specimens of species of American Orthoptera. Division 3. Species of North American Orthoptera described by Albert Pitts Morse. Proc. Acad. Nat. Sci. Philadelphia 67: 96-106. 1915.

A New England orthopteran adventive. Psyche 23: 178-180. 1916 [1917].

[Review of *The Blattidæ of North America, north of the Mexican boundary* by Morgan Hebard.] Ent. News 28: 430-431. 1917.

List of the water-color drawings of fungi by George E. Morris in the Peabody Museum of Salem. pp. 1-70, frontispiece (portrait). Peabody Museum, Salem, Mass. 1918.

Amaranthus Powellii and *Digitaria lanata* in New England. Rhodora 20: 203. 1918 [1919].

New records of Orthoptera in New England. Psyche 26: 16-18. 1919.

A list of the Orthoptera of New England. Psyche 26: 21-39. 1919.

Manual of the Orthoptera of New England, including the locusts, grasshoppers, crickets, and their allies. Proc. Boston Soc. Nat. Hist. 35: 197-556, figs. 1-99, pls. 10-29. 1920.

At a food-shelf. Bull. Essex Co. Ornith. Club 2: 12-14. 1920 [1921].

Sympetrum corruptum in Massachusetts. Psyche 28: 7. 1921.

Monecphora bicincta (Say) in New England. Psyche 28: 27-28. 1921.

Orthoptera of Maine. Grasshoppers and related insects. Bull. Me. Agric. Exper. Sta. 296: [i-ii], 1-36, figs. 1-25. 1921.

Grasshoppers and related insects. pp. 1-6. [Circular Me. Agric. Exper. Sta. 541. 1921.]

A sheld duck (*Tadorna tadorna* L.) from Essex County, Mass. Bull. Essex Co. Ornith. Club 3: 68, 1 pl. 1921 [1922].

Franklin's gull in New England. Bull. Essex Co. Ornith. Club 3: 69. 1921 [1922].

The seal of the Cambridge Entomological Club. Psyche 29: 42. 1922.

The European house cricket; hearth cricket. Psyche 29: 225. 1922 [1923].

Another Essex County record for the blue-gray gnatcatcher. Bull. Essex Co. Ornith. Club 5: 25. 1923 [1924].

Lepidium latifolium in New England. Rhodora 26: 197-198. 1924.

Some rarities from Essex County, Mass. Psyche 32: 298. 1925 [1926].

Two vagrant grasshoppers and a moth. Psyche 33: 53. 1926.

Protective tubes for birdskins. Bull. Essex Co. Ornith. Club 8: 57-59. 1926 [1927].

An interesting butterfly capture. Psyche 34: 10. 1927.

Another vagrant grasshopper. Psyche 34: 134. 1927.

"Data is" or "data are": which? Science n.s. 65: 355. 1927.

The way of a snake with a gopher. Copeia 164: 71-72. 1927.

John Robinson, botanist, of Salem, Massachusetts. Rhodora 31: 245-254, 1 pl. (portrait). 1929.

Grasshoppers vs. salt. Journ. Econ. Ent. 23: 465. 1930.

A window-print. Bull. Essex Co. Ornith. Club 11: 74, 1 pl. 1929 [1930].

The American lotus at West Peabody, Massachusetts. Rhodora 33: 230. 1931.

The insect collections of a public museum. Psyche 41: 158-163. 1934.

Another kingfisher and a goldfish. Bull. Essex Co. Ornith. Club 16: 18. 1934 [1935].

[Bibliography of the scientific writings of E. S. Morse in *Biographical memoir of Edward Sylvester Morse, 1838-1925* by L. O. Howard.] National Acad. Sci., Biogr. Mem. 17 (1): 20-29. 1935.

NEW SPECIES OF EXOTIC SYRPHID FLIES

By Frank M. Hull

University of Mississippi

Some time ago, Professor Nathan Banks placed in my hands for study an interesting collection of Syrphid flies that had accumulated in the collections of the Museum of Comparative Zoölogy. These flies have come from many sections of the world and, as was to be expected, include a number of new species, the descriptions of which are presented in this paper. Notes on the occurrence and distribution of other species will perhaps be published at a later date. I wish to thank Prof. Banks for the opportunity of studying this interesting assortment of Syrphids as well as for the facilities for study in the Museum which he so kindly placed at my disposal.

Meromacrus melmoth n. sp.

Male. Eyes narrowly joined. Vertex slightly raised, black. Face and front black, conspicuously yellowish white pilose along the sides of the front, on the eye margins, running down the sides of the eyes and thence to the oral margin as a diagonal facial stripe. This leaves the face obscurely shining black, the black as a V-shaped wedge below antennæ, reaching to oral margin, its widest part at the base of the antennæ. Cheeks shining blackish. The facial stripe beneath the sparse pile is whitish pruinose and much more conspicuous than the pile. The pile on the sides of the front assumes the curious appressed character typical of the genus. Occiput and lower part of vertical triangle below the ocelli, similarly colored, pilose and pruinose. Face somewhat carinate. Antennæ blackish brown, the third joint lighter brown, extraordinarily truncated dorso-apically and coming to a rounded point, the arista basally thickened, yellow, quite pale at tip, and twice as long as the third joint.

Thorax, pleuræ, and scutellum dull black, except that the

latter has a brownish rim. The markings unfortunately obscured by poor preservation but a yellow tomentose spot on the inner medial angles of humeri, a vertical narrow similar stripe on the middle of pleuræ, and some evidence of the same on the posterior calli. Halteres brownish; stalk darker.

Abdomen black, very dark brown laterally and on the posterior half of the last segment and the hypopygium, covered with microscopically short, black bristles, some scattered short pale pile, and a transverse narrow band of pale tomentum on the post border of first segment.

Legs black, tarsi brown, the femora covered with thick, quite long, pale, very fine hair. Hind femora extraordinarily thick.

Wings with a strong black anterior border, the black keeping to the configuration of the third longitudinal vein, but filling the anterior part of the first basal and the first posterior cells, and the loop of the third longitudinal vein is filled, but bears a small clear spot.

Length 15mm.

One male. Bolivia. Province of Sara (Steinbach). Type in the Museum of Comparative Zoölogy.

This peculiar species is very close to *Meromacrus niger* Sack, from which it differs in the extraordinarily thickened hind femora besides other characters. The dull black color and femora serve to distinguish it.

Velocimyia n. gen.

Small flies. Eyes bare, touching in male for a short distance. Face and front heavily pubescent and with some longer pile on the former. Face with a very low weak tubercle on bump in the middle, the lower face bluntly conical. Antennæ of the simple Eristaliform type; arista bare, basally thickened. Thorax simple. Scutellum small, two or three times as wide as long, and without margin. Abdomen tapering posteriorward, but four segments and tip of hypogynium visible. The last segment of the abdomen together with the hypopygium wide, round, exceptionally prominent and conspicuous. In this respect the form resembles the new world *Meromacrus*.

Legs except for thickened hind femora largely simple. The hind femora apicoventrally possesses a low setæ-beset tubercle. Hind tibiæ basally incised.

Wings Eristaliform. The kink of third vein is formed like that of *Eristalis* rather than *Protylocera* and there is no spur on the kink.

Genotype: *Velocimyia velox*, new species.

Velocimyia velox n. sp.

Plate II, Figs. 1, 2, 3

Male. Eyes narrowly touching for less than distance of posterior ocelli. Front, face, vertex black, the latter covered with dark brown pollen, the front with grey pubescence, the face thickly covered with white pubescence. A small shining bare space above the antennæ without trace of wrinkles. No shining median stripe on face, but an obscure bare, shining stripe on cheeks. Antennæ black, third segment grey pollinose or pubescent. Arista two and one-half times length of oval third joint, light brown in color, bare.

Thorax black, with a bluish cast, dully shining, heavily dark grey pollinose. Scutellum wide, translucent, yellowish brown, without pile, except on the corners, although its punctate surface indicates that it was pilose. Pile of thorax thick, erect, moderately long, pale in color. Squamæ and fringe pale yellow, very large. Abdomen with venter and hypopygium entirely bright orange with one exception. The base of the second segment with a broad basal triangle, its apex reaching less than one half of the length of the segment, the triangle continued to the first segment, where it is bluish black, leaving only the lateral corners of that segment pale. Abdomen practically opaque except for the last segment. Last two segments and third and fourth with parallel sides, narrower than the second. Hypopygium very large. Pile of abdomen pale, rather long terminally.

Legs black, base of face and mid tibiæ yellowish brown, mid basitarsi dark brown. Hind femora very thick, but confined to anterior surface, posterior surface straight, a nodular prominence beset with bristles near the apex. Hind tibiæ opposite nodule of femora noticeably incised, its apex spurred.

Wings hyaline, stigma brown. A deep loop of third longitudinal vein into first posterior cell; the marginal cell closed before the apex of first longitudinal vein, and the first posterior cell closed before apex of third longitudinal vein.

Length 10 mm.

Three co-types. Males. One is from Mandritsara, Madagascar (Wulsin) whose type no. is 2270 in the Museum of Comparative Zoölogy. The two others, Antananarivo, Madagascar, were discovered in the collections at the Museum für Naturkunde, Berlin. Dr. G. Enderlein has kindly presented me with one of them, which is in my own collection. The third is in his collection.

The first specimen studied, from the Museum of Comparative Zoölogy, curiously bears no evidence of the spotted eyes, and I was inclined to view this species as nearest to *Protylocera*. The discovery of subsequent specimens reveals that the eyes are generously spotted. Nevertheless, the distinctive type of abdomen, much enlarged hypopygium, as well as the excised tibia and nodulate hind femora show that it is not an ordinary *Lathyrophthalmus*. Another species which Speiser placed under *Lathyrophthalmus, myiatropinus*, agrees in these peculiarities and differs from the present species in its dark terminal segments, etc. The two forms may very well be grouped under the name given, since besides the other distinctions mentioned, they lack either the metallic color or the characteristic stripes of *Lathyrophthalmus*. It may be remarked that the spotted nature of the eyes probably shows no close relationship to *Lathyrophthalmus* whatever, since at the present no less than five genera show such spots. Three genera show the enormous hypopygium: *Meromacroides* of Curran (Africa), *Meromacrus* Rondani (S. America) and the present group of species.

Lathyrophthalmus vitrescens n. sp.

Plate II, fig. 4

Female. Eyes distant by one and one-half times width of posterior ocelli; side of front diverging considerably towards antennæ. Front yellow and grey-brown pollinose, varying according to direction, but apparently with a constant, pale, narrow eye stripe, a large pale region above antennæ surrounding a brown central elevation. Middle of lower front with a narrow dark brown streak. Face with pale yellow brown pubescence, except for bare central knob. Face rippled. Antennæ light or orange brown, darker dorsally on third joint. Arista very long, pale brown. Cheeks more or less bare shining light brown. Eyes spotted, of which it may be said that the spots are very numerous, small, mostly regularly spaced, rarely confluent, and usually separated by from one to two times their own diameter.

Thorax blue black, shining, five vittate, the vittæ dull grey but being obscurely shining posteriorly. Scutellum strongly shining greenish blue. Squamæ dark brown, halteres lighter.

Abdomen shining, greenish or bluish black, except that the first segment and base of second is dark brown, and the second, third and fourth segments are crossed by opaque black bands, first barely interrupted, the latter two well interrupted medially and laterally.

Legs dark brown, apices of femora very narrowly, basal half or third of tibiæ, and all the tarsi light yellow or brownish yellow, palest on the tibiæ. Wings very hyaline. Stigma quite small.

Length 12 mm.

One female. Fiji; Lomoti. (W. M. Mann.) Type in the Museum of Comparative Zoölogy.

I should be inclined to place this species in *L. nitidus* Wulp, did not specimens I have seen from Samoa agree better with the notes and interpretation of the species by Herve-Bazin and Bezzi. These I have commented on in my paper on Samoan Syrphidæ. The more totally blue black coloration, entire opaque bands of abdomen, and minor differences convince me that the two forms are at least quite different species.

Korinchia simulans de Meij.

Originally described by de Meijere as a Milesia, but should probably be placed in *Korinchia*.

Two females in the Museum of Comparative Zoölogy. Java; Tijboda (T. Barbour).

Eumerus obtusiceps n. sp.

Male. Eyes touch for the short length of front. Vertical

triangle is therefore long, acute in front, its sides parallel behind. Occiput remarkably thick, pale brownish polinose, black punctate. Vertex similarly pollinose and punctate, anterior ocelli far removed, lying in brown pollen, the posterior pair in a black area. Eyes bare. Pile of the vertex largely blackish except just in front. Front and face covered with brilliant silver scalose pubescence and some erect white pile. Occiput punctate white scalose, short white pilose. Antennæ situated slightly below middle, black. Third joint large, ventrally pointed. Arista basally thickened, yellow, remainder very wiry, slender and dark.

Dorsum of thorax black, obscurely shining, thickly punctate, pile short, thick, black with some pale hairs, the suture narrowly pale whitish or greyish pollinose. Scutellum concolorous, flat, its edge with a conspicuous narrow yellowish brown pollinose border, its apex with outwardly directed short pile of the same color, and its erect surface pile longer than that of the thorax and entirely pale. Moreover, the bulk of the pile is also on the rim and directed upward at an angle of forty-five degrees. Squamæ and halteres brownish yellow.

Abdomen decidedly flared basally; abdomen shining black, thickly black punctate, bearing thick appressed black bristles most prominent on terminal segment, and considerable fine white pile, particularly on the sides of the abdomen. First segment with a narrow V of white punctate pollen, barely interrupted medially, the angle anteriorly directed, and the ends continued (narrowly) into the corners of the third segment. Third segment similarly marked, and fourth similar except that the pollinose spot spreads out posteriorly and is largely broken by black punctate spots. Fore and middle legs brown, apices of the femora, of the tibiæ and their base and all the tarsi brownish yellow. Hind femora and tibiæ black, except narrow apex of former, and base of latter; both thickened, the femora greatly enlarged. Hind tarsi brown, basi tarsi greatly dilated.

Wings with terminal segment of fourth longitudinal vein oddly angulated, just before reaching the third longitudinal vein, it forms an acute V-shaped angle; the angle of the V is spurred. Wings slightly fumose.

Length 8.5 mm.

One male. Neumannis Boma, British East Africa (Allen and Brooks). Type in the Museum of Comparative Zoölogy. This species traces to *Eumerus scaber* in Bezzi's key. That species is said to have a bare bluish front; its genitalia are reddish. The occiput of this species cannot be described as black pilose, etc. In Herve-Bazin's key it traces to *Eumerus feæ* Bez. with which it could hardly be confused.

Microdon argentinae n. sp.

Plate II, fig. 5.

Male. Front narrowed sharply above antennæ. The narrowest width slightly better than one-half width at vertex measured from upper eye angles. The narrowest portion marked by a prominent groove on its front side obtusely widened and leading down to a point between antennæ. Front and vertex and face rich shining brown. Cheeks a little darker brown. Face strongly convex, both from the side and from above. Vertex slightly raised. First joint of antennæ light shining brown, as long as front from vertex to depression. Remainder of antennæ wanting. Pile of face and head everywhere pale yellow, sparse, shorter on the front, rather long and thicker on the sides of face below antennæ. Middle of face nearly bare, possibly due to denudation.

Dorsum of thorax, pleuræ, scutellum, and legs rich shining brown, the abdomen pale brown. Pile of thorax short, pale, appressed, with a few scattered darker hairs. Scutellum quite wide, trapezoidal, the small but slender, sharp, bare points, quite far apart, slightly diverging. Middle of scutellum not emarginate. Halteres dark brown.

The abdomen is of the short broad form, pointed apically, with ventral flexure at the edges of the flared second segment.

Piles of legs dark brown, becoming golden brown on lower surfaces of tarsi and apical portions of tibiæ. Hind basitarsi not remarkably thickened, its greatest thickness basally, twice its distal thickness, perhaps a little more than twice as thick as the second tarsal segment.

Wings tinged rather uniformly with brown. Veins dark brown. Last section of fourth longitudinal vein very angulated, emitting a stump on each side toward margin of wing, and trace of an inward stump on one wing. Lower terminal section of vein closing first posterior cell and one closing discal cell remarkably rounded. An extensive spur is present from the third longitudinal vein almost reaching spurious vein.

Length 10.5 mm.

One male, Cordova, Argentina (Davis). Type in the Museum of Comparative Zoölogy.

Microdon digitator n. sp.

Plate II, fig. 6.

Male. Head rounded in profile; similar to *Microdon investigator*. Front narrowest above antennæ, but the sides nearly parallel, diverging toward the vertex. Antennæ, face, front and vertex black, the latter shining. Antennæ short, the first joint and third subequal, either twice the length of second. Arista short, much thickened basally, reaching just past third joint. Pile of head everywhere pale yellowish to whitish, sparse.

Thorax and scutellum everywhere shining black. Pile sub-appressed, sparse, yellowish to golden. Scutellum evenly rounded, a little more pointed centrally, without spines, margins, déntations, etc. Halteres brown.

First and fourth abdominal segments brown to black, obscurely shining; second and third pale brownish yellow, the second the palest, subtranslucent. Pile very short except on the outer edges of the second segment where it is long and golden. Pile black or brown elsewhere, except on the posterior lateral angles of the third segment where it is golden. Legs light brown except for the middle of all the femora, and quite small spots in the middle of each tibiæ. Hind basitarsi not at all thickened.

Wings rather uniformly suffused with brown, lighter in the first posterior, discal, first basal cells. Termination of fourth longitudinal vein straight, nearly rectangular, angle of discal cell rounded. Spur of third longitudinal present, spurious vein not prominent. Angle of first posterior cell spurred to near by wing margin.

Length 9 mm.

One male, Tjibodas, Mt. Gede, Java. 1909, 4500 ft. (Bryant and Palmer). Type in the Museum of Comparative Zoölogy.

Microdon investigator n. sp.

Plate II, fig. 7 and 8.

Male. Sides of front nearly parallel, slightly converging to vertex, narrowest just across ocelli. Front smooth, shining brownish black, punctate. Antennæ situated just below upper point of middle third of profile. Profile of head evenly rounded, remarkably convex. Cheeks very narrow, invisible in profile. Face widest just below antennæ. Sides nearly parallel. No antennal prominence. Antennæ light orange, first joint twice length of second, third equal to first and second concave dorsally, drawing out to a sharp point, suggesting a thumb. Arista pale, slightly longer than third joint. Face shining brassy brown, with a suggestion of violaceous color. Pile of face, front, vertex sparse brassy yellow, appressed on face.

Thorax and scutellum dark, moderately shining brown, pile golden, thick and markedly appressed. Pleuræ similarly colored with a conspicuous patch of dense golden pile. Pile of scutellum erect. Squamæ and halteres light yellow.

Abdomen pale yellowish brown, third and fourth with basal halves and nearly the whole of the fifth segment dark brown. Pile of light area exceptionally dense and appressed, golden; of dark area black. Venter pale brownish yellow, sub-translucent, the lateral edges continuously black.

Legs light brownish yellow, except for a dark brown spot about the middle of antero-ventral surface of each femur and the basal third of the tibiæ, paler yellow. Hind femora with anterior diagonal scar or cicatrix on basal half. Hind basitarsi nearly as long as remaining segments inclusive; twice their thickness.

Wings palely but uniformly brownish; termination of fourth longitudinal vein sharply rectangular, its angle emitting a spur; an angle of discal cell rounded. Spurious vein quite faint. Spur from third longitudinal vein prominent.

Length 13.5 mm.

One male, Galog River, Mt. Apo, Mindanao, Philippine

Islands, Sept. 12 (C. S. Clagg). Type in the Museum of Comparative Zoölogy.

Hypselosyrphus n. gen.

Plate II, fig. 9.

Small flies, related to *Microdon* with the weak and flattened abdomen somewhat longer than broad. Face round convex, with the vertex produced into a curved jutting knob. Scutellum sulcate, tumid, angularly directed upward. Hind basitarsi and forebasitarsi swollen. Hind tibiæ convex, with a swollen ornament suggesting a load of pollen, heavily pilose. Hind femora not greatly thickened. No trace of spur from third vein is directed into the first posterior cell. Terminal (bent up) portions of fourth and fifth longitudinal veins, that is, subapical and posterior cross veins, nearly straight, bulging at their basal corners and making angles of approximately seventy-five to eighty degrees with the veins they join.

Genotype: *Hypselosyrphus trigonus* n. sp.

This fly suggests very strongly a trigonid bee, as do the species of *Ubristes* of the *Microdontini*. *Microdon scutellaris* Shannon, described from the Amazon, seems to fall into *Hypselosyrphus*, but differing in the differently colored abdomen.

Hypselosyrphus trigonus n. sp.

Plate II, fig. 9.

Male. Front enormously swollen as a shining knob, the ocelli on top. Front excavated, flat, leaving a considerable concavity in profile. Face in profile convex, evenly rounded. Antennæ situated at upper third. First and third joints subequal, the latter pointed, second quite short. Arista slender, as long as third joint. Color of antennæ dark brown. Face, front and vertex shining dark mahogany red or brown, almost black.

Thorax very dark brown, almost black, a row of white pile across at suture, and on base of scutellum, remainder densely erect short black pilose. Pleuræ shining dark brown, sparsely pilose. Halteres and squamæ dark blackish. Scutellum dark blackish, prominent, directed upward at an angle of forty-five degrees, deeply sulcate medially, the sides swollen, rounded, without spines.

Abdomen short oval, flat, vitreous, dark reddish brown on first, second and narrowly on base of third segment. Remainder bright orange.

Legs dark shining purplish or reddish black, tarsi except hind basitarsi light yellowish brown. Fore basitarsi swollen anteriorly. Hind basitarsi considerably swollen. Hind tibiæ greatly swollen and dorsally arcuate, a curious crease running around it, below the part of greatest swelling. Tibiæ heavily long black pilose.

Wings brownish especially basally, with a faint pale yellow spot beginning past the stigma. Last section of fourth longitudinal vein straight, not angular, no spurs present, not even from the angle of the fourth longitudinal vein.

Length 7 mm. or about 8 mm. with the antennæ.

One male. Barro Colorado, Panama, July 16, 1924 (Nathan Banks). Type in the Museum of Comparative Zoölogy.

This remarkable species suggests *Microdon panamensis* Curran, which lacks the interesting structural characters of this form. It is a handsome and peculiar species, that like *Ubristes* resembles *Trigonid* bees, but differs from that genus in the development of the vertex and scutellum, etc.

Paramicrodon novus n. sp.

Plate II, figs. 10 and 11.

Female. Head very globular, front wide, almost horizontal, sides nearly parallel diverging slightly to vertex. Vertex from corner of eyes very suddenly and sharply widened so that the post optical vertex is wide and deep. Front and vertex slightly convex, their color shining brownish or black, with short abundant, upright, golden pile. Ocelli set far down the middle of the front, more than half way down from vertex (extreme) to antennæ. Face more narrow than front, sides almost parallel, similar in color and similarly pilose. Antennæ set a little above middle of face, wholly brownish orange, first and second joints short, subequal, third equal to first and second. Arista dark, thickened basally, half again as long as third joint. Eyes bare.

Thorax shining brown, slightly brassy, covered with dense golden pile, highly appressed, a vertical pilose band on the pleuræ. Scutellum brown, simple. Margin evenly rounded, surface but little convex. Halteres and squamæ brownish yellow.

Abdomen dark brown, base of first segment with a yellow band, incised on its posterior border, a convex yellow band on the posterior border of second segment, a narrow similar border on the posterior edge of third segment and the narrow corners posteriorly of fourth and extreme tip of fifth segments. The posterior margins of second, third, fourth and fifth segments with a fringe of thick long, appressed golden pile. Abdomen quite elongate, over twice the length of thorax. Second segment nearly as long as third and fourth; fifth segment almost as long as fourth. Third and fourth segments subequal. Abdomen but little, if at all, constricted basally.

Legs light brownish yellow, golden appressed pilose, a brownish median band on the hind femora, a trace of same on mid femora.

Wings quite elongate; first posterior cell five to six times as long as wide at widest point. Third longitudinal vein without protruding spur. Spurious vein faint. Wings uniformly pubescent, tinged with pale brown.

Length 13.5 mm.

One female. Galog River, 6500 ft. Sept. 12, Mt. Apo, Mindanao, Philippine Islands (C. S. Clagg). Type in the Museum of Comparative Zoölogy.

This species must certainly be very close to Herve-Bazin's genotype, *Syrphinella miranda* H. B. Nevertheless, a careful comparison of the specimen before me with his very excellent figure, shows this form to have the third antennal joint a little shorter, the body narrower at base or more spatulate, and there are a fused pair of sub-translucent windows at the base of the second segment. The posterior golden pilose band of the fourth segment appears widely interrupted in *novus* (and there is in fact no light colored ground color), though it may be denudate. The wings are less generally infuscated, being really darkened only about the extreme tip. The veins over the wing are clearly not margined with brownish. I have seen other specimens from the Philippines agreeing with Herve-Bazin's figure of *Syrphinella* in that the veins are markedly infuscate. Moreover they agree in the lack of translucent window to abdomen, and in having the fourth abdominal segment yellowish posteriorly and more or less golden pilose over the whole width. Thus they are very close to *Syrphinella* if not identical. But they have the third antennal joint distinctly pointed. *P. novus*, and the figure of *miranda* in nowise agree in this particular. De Meijere has described three other species in this genus from Java, New Guinea and Borneo, so that there may be many species. Sack has described what is probably a synonym of *miranda* under the name *Mixogaster cinctella* Sack.

Paramicrodon delicatulus n. sp.

This species differs from *Microdon flukei* Curran in the general bluish purple color, as well as other particulars. Pile above antennæ on vertex and occiput silvery, narrowly black below ocelli in the front. The antennæ are wholly orange, whereas they are brown in *flukei* with a black third joint. Abdomen unicolorous purplish, with the basal red color of *flukei*.

Two males. Soledad (Cienfuegos), Cuba, August 6, 1920 (N. Banks). Type in the Museum of Comparative Zoölogy. Paratype in the author's collection.

Pseudomicrodon n. gen.

Head short to quite short. In profile, occiput above moderately or considerably thickened. Antennæ situated above the middle of the head in profile, quite elongate in form. The first joint about as long or longer than remaining two, though obviously proportions in length must vary over some latitude in *Microdontine* antennæ. Face gently convex. Cheeks inconspicuous. Vertex rarely protuberant. Abdomen rather strongly pedunculate; the segments after the second fused into a beautiful, oval, cylindero-convex body, which is widest on the fourth segment, rounds off posteriorly, tapers gently forward anteriorly, and is strongly flexed downward at the second segment, practically held at right angles. Scutellum usually bears two fairly well developed teeth or points. Hind femora usually only moderately thick-

ened. First posterior cell with an adventitious vein, the
subapical cross vein is straight.

Genotype: *Microdon beebei* Curran.

I have seen a number of species which fit with tolerable
accuracy and certainty into the concept above; among them
may be mentioned *Microdon nigrispinosis* Shannon, *illucens*
Bezzi and probably *bellula* Williston.

Ceriomicrodon n. gen.

Head in profile not very long but extremely wide, practically twice as wide as thorax between the humeri. Occiput
and vertex moderately developed, in nowise conspicuous.
Front and face of average width. In profile the face bulges
out below, much as in *Rhopalosyrphus* Gig.-Tos. Antennæ
quite elongate, the third joint quite wide and flat and about
two and one-half times as long as the first joint. Eyes bare
on either side opposite antennæ with a curious narrow
crease margined with grossly enlarged facets. This may be
an abnormality, but as it is perfectly symmetrical on both
sides, it may be normal. Occipital fringe reduced to a single
row of long collar like hairs, much as in *Asarcina* or *Baccha*.
Abdomen extremely petiolate, the first segment small, apparently completely fused with second segment, at any rate
the first and second segments together are nearly ten times
as long as wide in the middle. The second segment expands
on its extreme posterior edge rather suddenly to some three
or four times its narrowest width. Remaining segments
fused into an oval bulging club. Scutellum quite short,
broad and rounded, without spurs. Wings with a spur descending into the first posterior cell. Angles of the first
and second posterior cells broadly rounded, without a trace
of spurs.

Genotype: *Ceriomicrodon petiolatus* n. sp.

Cerioimicrodon petiolatus n. sp.

Face pale yellow, a wide median stripe, the cheeks, front,
vertex, dorsum of thorax and scutellum fully shining bluish
black. Abdomen obscurely shining black, second segment
sub-translucent yellowish brown. Pile of thorax and dorsum microscopically short, save for white flecky pile on

transverse suture and at junction of third and fourth abdominal segments.

One male. West border Matto Grosso, Brazil, May, 1931 (R. C. Shannon). Type in the U. S. National Museum.

Stenomicrodon n. subgen.

Head in profile not especially long, the occiput above not more than normally developed, the front quite flat, of moderate width. Ocelli in a small, nearly equilateral triangle. Antennæ situated near the top of head, elongate, first joint at least as long as remaining joints. Cheeks inconspicuous and eyes bare. Abdomen elongate, several times as long as wide. The first segment flattened and excavated on each side. A deep constriction at the junction of the third and fourth segments and in the female slightly between the fourth and fifth segments. Scutellum without spines. Femora slightly thickened, with more than usually strongly developed patches of bristly setæ on the base of the third femora in both sexes as well as on the others. This extensive setiferous patch is quite differentiated from the surrounding pile. Third vein sends an adventitious vein down into the first posterior cell. Corners of first and second posterior cells broadly rounded, without spines apically. Wings in the known species are dark purplish brown.

Subgenotype: *Stenomicrodon purpureus* n. sp.

Stenomicrodon purpureus n. sp.

Differing from *Microdon stenogaster* Curran in the thicker third antennal joint, silvery pile, deeper scars on the hind femora and lighter colored pile.

One female, Tainan, Formosa (Rolle). Type in the author's collection.

Oligeriops n. gen.

Head very broad from above; vertex enormously developed. ‹ Ocelli situated on the summit in an equilateral triangle. Front in consequence quite broad, deeply punctate, eyes reduced in size, bare; cheeks bulging, together with the wide, slightly diverging face, densely long pilose. Head in profile more or less smoothly and evenly round. Antennæ set about the middle. First and third joints elongate, the latter thick, particularly so at base, on its upper surface curved, with a short massive arista. Abdomen broad, oval, about one and one-half times as long as broad. The margins of the segments rolled, but in no way massively developed. Terminal portion of abdomen fused, gradually rounded, curved downward, the sides particularly convex towards the tip. Scutellum without points. Hind femora moderately thickened, femora and tibiæ without cicatrices or furrows. Subapical crossvein erect, almost straight, meeting the third vein at right angles quite far back from the margin. First basal cell with an adventitious vein descending into first posterior cell.

Genotype: *Microdon chalybeus* Ferguson.

Papiliomyia n. gen.

Head hemiglobular in profile, post occiput above tumid and vertex protruding as a conspicuous bump, but otherwise the front and vertex are quite narrow. Ocelli situated at top of the protuberance. Antennæ situated near top of head, the first joint quite elongate, in fact being considerably longer than remaining two together. Arista weak and delicate. Face narrower from the front, converging from below the antennæ. Eyes bare. Cheeks practically absent. The enormous eyes seem to cover almost the whole head. Abdomen elongate, over two times as long as wide. Widest at junction of second and third segments, but very little wider here. Fourth segment most deeply transversely concaved as far as the anterior two-thirds, leaving a convex rim posteriorly. The concave portion most oddly covered with centrally converging, flat lying hair from the base and sides. Metanotum exceedingly conspicuous and deep. Scutellum without points. Hind femora slender, basally spindled. Hind tibiæ thickened apically and with a deep shallow groove separating the apical fifth. Hind tibiæ very brushy as in *Trigonoid* bees. Wings long and slender. No trace of adventitious veins descends into the first posterior cell. Subapical cross vein straight and recurrent as well. Postical cross vein sigmoid in the genotype species. Costa deeply beaded with setigerous tubercles. Wings banded in both the known species. Weakly chitinized, delicate species, that suggest moths or scorpion flies.

Genotype: *Papiliomyia sepulchrasilva* n. sp.

Papiliomyia sepulchrasilva n. sp.

Differing at once from *Microdon maculatus* Shannon in the possession of only a single basal wing spot; apical half of thorax largely yellow, with two round spots and a wedge shaped spot; posterior half with two L-shaped spots. Abdomen past second segment almost wholly dark. Yellow wing border extended across wing as a stripe.

Two males. Rio Grand do Sul (Stieglmayr). Type in the Natural History Museum of Vienna. Paratype in the author's collection.

Syrphus cinereomaculatus n. sp.

Plate II, fig. 12.

Female. Front rather wide, nearly twice as wide at antennæ as at vertex, with the slightly raised vertex shining black, long blackish pilose, a dull grey pilose spot in the shallow depression of front, on either side about midways. Antennæ black. First and second subequal, the third three times as long as first, decidedly pointed at outer dorsal end. Arista black, thickened on basal two-thirds; no longer than the third joint. Face with a small shining black bare tubercle, gently concave beneath antennæ. Cheeks brownish, white pollinose, with a small bare diagonal stripe. Face heavily pollinose. Occiput to just above middle, long white pilose, thickly so. Pile of face long, thin, white, a conspicuous tuft before wing base. Scutellum yellowish brown, very shining long sparse black, pilose. Squamæ nearly white, tinged with brown, bare on lower lobe surface. Plumula snow white, halteres dark brown; knob paler.

Abdomen oval, shining black, a band on second segment interrupted in middle, quite narrow bands on third and fourth, narrowly interrupted in middle, are noticeable only for the gray pollen which covers them, though careful examination shows the underlying surface to be dark brown. Traces of smaller narrow spots are on the fifth segment. Abdomen very flat, emarginate. Venter shining black, with obscure grey pollinose bands.

Legs with the femora black, except the narrow yellow or

brown apices, white pilose. Tibiæ yellowish brown, darker in the middle. Tarsi dark brown to black. Hind femora very slender. Wings quite hyaline, stigma yellow, with proximal brown spot.

Length 9.5 mm.

One female. Mt. Kenia, British East Africa, Sept. 8 (G. M. Allen and G. Brooks). Type in the Museum of Comparative Zoölogy.

This interesting species is characterized by the highly vitreous black color, flat abdomen, remarkably narrow, slender grey pollinose bands or spots.

Pipunculosyrphus n. gen.

Head hemispherical. Eyes very large. Vertex small, compressed until knife like, the anterior ocellus not much remote and the vertex not swollen. Occiput narrowly visible in profile, except near the top, its collar of hairs short, but conspicuous, single rowed, and *Baccha*-like. The eye margins strongly concave in the middle, their facets enlarged above in the male. Antennæ set in middle of head in profile. Short, third joint orbicular. Arista slender, longer than the antennæ. Front swollen, face below antennæ rather concave, tubercle conspicuous, abruptly rising and declining. Face retreating past the tubercle. The cheeks inconspicuous. Sides of face parallel and close together. Thorax slightly longer than broad, convex. The humeri hidden by the head, bare. The mesopleuræ and dorsum practically without pile. Scutellum is long with long bristles on its rim and a ventral fringe is present.

Abdomen long and slender, about five times as long as wide with parallel sides. First segment short, laterally inflated and strongly convex. Its extreme base equipped with a vertical fringe of erect hairs against the metanotum which is inconspicuous. Abdomen dark with yellow bands or pairs of spots. Hind femora very slender and long. Hind tibiæ equally slender, not quite as long. The basi tarsi more than half as long as tibiæ. The mid femora flattened basally. Wings very elongate, being more than three times as long as wide. Alulæ absent. The marginal cross veins quite sigmoid. Vena spuria prominent.

Genotype: *Pipunculosyrphus globiceps* n. sp.

I consider this genus to be amply well founded since it represents an extreme as far as the known species are concerned, in at least four or five particulars. Unrelated to *Baccha* to which it bears a superficial resemblance, but it is noteworthy in the enormous eyes, hidden humeri, narrowly reduced face, knife-like vertical triangle, the shortened non-petiolate, abdomen, exceedingly elongate wing and lost alulæ, to say nothing of the erect basal metanotal fringe.

Pipunculosyrphus globiceps n. sp.

A slender light yellowish fly, which is brown on the upper part of the third antennal joint, upper half of front, disc of thorax, hind femora except basally, and the abdomen, except for pairs of yellow spots which are bordered by black. Front with a small round black spot above antennæ. Vertex black, paired spots of abdomen obliquely directed forward, their black posterior borders like confluent V-shaped marks. Last segment vitate. The middle stripe broad and black. Wings pale brownish. Stigma a little darker.

Two males, San Bernardino, Paraguay (Fiebrig). Type in the Museum of Natural History, Vienna, paratype in the author's collection.

Oligorhina n. gen.

Eyes bare, the vertex narrow, rapidly widening to the level of the antennæ, where the face is parallel-sided and rather narrow. In profile the head slants down from the vertex quite straight to the low tubercle shortly below the antennæ and is then still further produced to the epistoma, though not quite so sharply. Face, because of the narrowness, with a pinched out aspect. Antennæ set very far apart, short. The third joint a little longer than wide. Arista as long as the antennæ. Occiput not visible from the side below the middle of the eyes. Thorax as wide as head, quite convex, both from the front and from the side very sparsely pilose. Humeri bare, scutellum large, semicircular, somewhat flattened, a few large bristles on the margin, a few downward projecting hairs, but scarcely any fringe. Abdomen slender, spatulate, about five times as long as its greatest width, which begins on the fourth segment. Fourth and fifth segments with practically parallel sides. Second segment apically about two-thirds as wide as the fourth segment. Sides of the short first segment convex with stiff bristles. Margins of the abdomen curling over, especially posteriorly, where they decrease the width some. Femora short, straight, scarcely thickened. Tibiæ distally a little thickened and a little pinched, every bit as long as the femora. Wings considerably longer than abdomen. Alulæ reduced. Subapical cross veins close to wing margin, but very sigmoid. Third vein and costa carried down somewhat deeply at the end of the wing. Vena spuria heavily chitinized. Stigma dark.

Genotype: *Oligorhina anea* n. sp.

Oligorhina aenea n. sp.

A curious species characterized by the very brown wings, darkened apically with a dark brown stigma. The rusty orange front, the black spot above antennæ and facial strip black. Vertex bright yellow, pleuræ, humeri, sides of pronotum calli, scutellum and anterior pairs of legs and the base of hind femora. The cheeks pale brownish yellow, the sides of the face bright shining yellow. Abdomen reddish brown, basal and apical borders of the remaining segments broadly shining, but preceded by opaque bands, which are produced forward as a slender triangle as far as the base of the segment.

Two females. Desbarriere, Mt. La Hotte, Haiti (4000 ft.), October 12, 1934 (Darlington). Type in the Museum of Comparative Zoölogy. Paratype in the author's collection.

EXPLANATION OF PLATE II

1. *Velocimyia velox* n. sp. (abdomen)
2. *Velocimyia velox* n. sp. (hind femora)
3. *Velocimyia velox* n. sp. (wing)
4. *Lathyrophthalmus vitrescens* n. sp. (abdomen)
5. *Microdon argentinæ* n. sp. (wing)
6. *Microdon digitator* n. sp. (antennæ)
7. *Microdon investigator* n. sp. (antennæ)
8. *Microdon investigator* (wing)
9. *Hypselosyrphus trigonus* n. sp. (profile of head; 9 a is scutellum)
10. *Paramicrodon novus* n. sp. (wing)
11. *Paramicrodon novus* n. sp. (profile of head)
12. *Syrphus cinereomaculatus* n. sp. (abdomen)

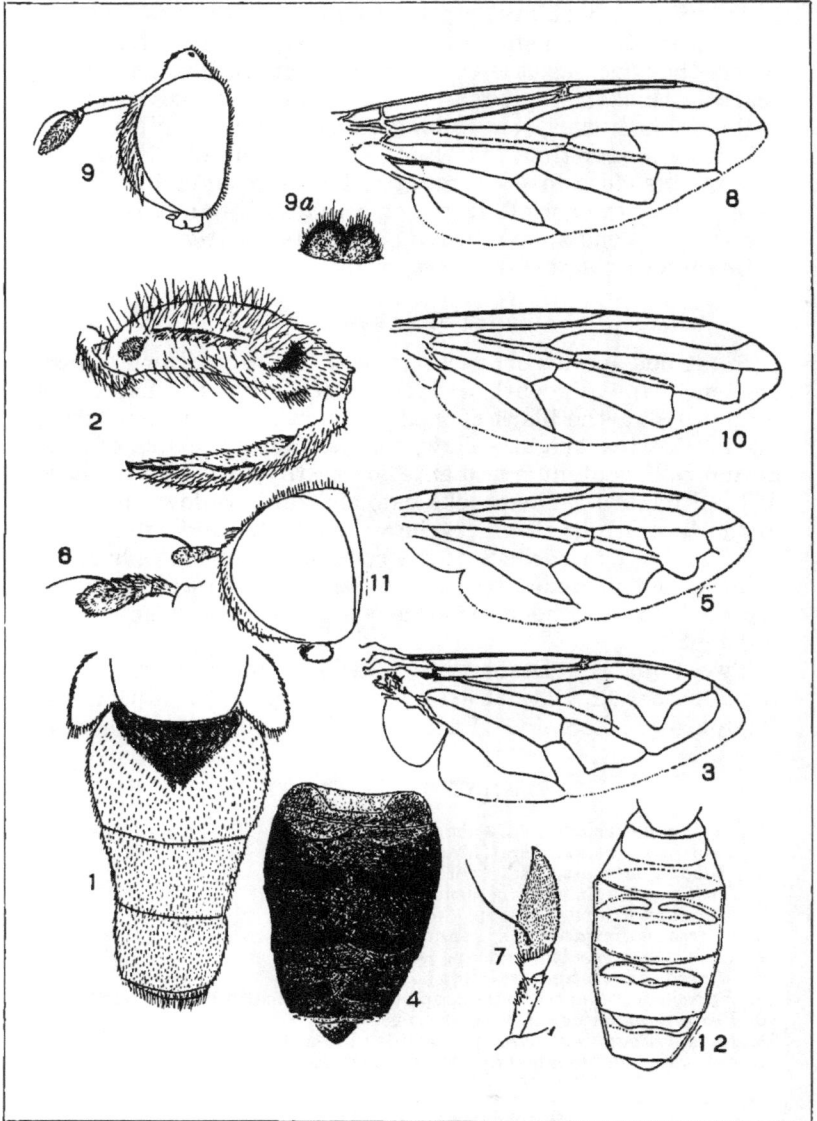

Hull — Syrphid Flies

NEW BUPRESTID BEETLES COLLECTED IN THE
SOLOMON ISLANDS AND FIJI ISLANDS BY DR. W. M.
MANN, WITH DESCRIPTIONS OF SOME OTHER NEW
INDO-MALAYAN SPECIES

By A. Théry

Attaché au Muséum National d'Histoire Naturelle de Paris

The present paper contains descriptions of new species of
Buprestidæ collected, for the most part, by Dr. W. M. Mann
in the Solomon Islands and the Fiji Islands. I have to thank
my colleague, Dr. P. J. Darlington, of the Museum of Comparative Zoölogy, Harvard College, Cambridge, U. S. A., in
whose care Dr. Mann's insects are at present placed, for
lending me the specimens here described.

Genus *Paracupta* H. Deyr.

Paracupta meyeri Kerr., Ann. Soc. Ent. Belg. XLIV, 1900,
p. 63.

This species is still very rare in collections; one ♀ specimen only was captured by Dr. Mann, at Mt. Victoria, Viti
Levu, Fiji Islands; I have compared this specimen with the
unique type in the collection of the British Museum to which
it is exactly similar.   Kerremans' description is not quite
exact; the author states that the five furrows of the pronotum are uninterrupted; as a matter of fact only the two external and the median furrows are so, the two others are
lightly interrupted at the middle.   The Kerremans Collection
at the Paris Museum contains a specimen of this species.[1]

Paracupta evansi n. sp. (Pl. III, Fig. 1)

Length: 19 mm.; breadth: 6.5 mm.—♂.   Elongate, navicu-

[1]The first collection of the late Mr. Kerremans was sold to the
British Museum in the year 1903.   A new collection containing the
species described by this author from 1903 to 1915 was divided after
his death; the African species except those of Madagascar have been
purchased by the Musée du Congo, at Tervueren (Belgium), the rest
of the collection by the Muséum National d'Histoire Naturelle at Paris.

lar, rather convex, narrower behind than in front, feebly gibbous above. Head and pronotum green, with the bottoms of the depressions coppery red; scutellum reddish; elytra brown with a slight greenish tinge. Beneath, shining green with cupreous reflexions, the extreme tip of the last segment reddish, the ground of all the depressions, above and beneath, clothed with deciduous, short pubescence, intermixed with a brownish secretion. Antennæ, apex of the tibiæ, and tarsi entirely of a bright yellow color; the rest of the tibiæ and the femora castaneous.

Head triangularly impressed in front, the summit of this impression reaching the vertex; front separated from the eye by a shallow groove interrupted at the middle of its length and communicating with the frontal impression. Eyes large, a little more widely separated in front than on the vertex. Antennæ reaching the level of the intermediate coxæ.

Pronotum nearly once and a third as wide as long; as wide at the anterior margin as long. Anterior margin arcuately emarginate. Greatest width at about posterior two sevenths of length; sides nearly straight from the anterior angles to middle, then arcuate, and feebly narrowed quite near the base. The base nearly transversely truncate; the posterior angles feebly acute; the lateral margin with lateral carina not well defined, coarsely punctate. Disk with an entire, narrow, longitudinal stria at middle; a broad irregular depression along the lateral margin on each side extending from near the anterior margin to the base, and widest at the base, narrowed anteriorly, with the bottom very finely rugose. Behind the anterior margin, on each side, there is a little, finely punctured area. The disk is coarsely punctured.

Scutellum small, smooth, shining, wider than long.

Elytra wider at the shoulders than the pronotum at the base, truncate at the humeral angles; the sides nearly parallel to the apical third, then straight and narrowed to apex, with sides strongly serrate from the apical third to the tip, the serration becoming obsolete at the apex, the sutural angles feebly acute. The side of the disk with a large depression along the lateral margin, extending from the humerus to the tip, this depression very finely and very densely punctate, limited exteriorly by the epipleural carina. Each elytron with three elevated, parallel, shining costæ, not including the scutellar one which is short, extending only from the base to anterior third and then united to the sutural one; the intervals between the costæ very finely and densely punctate, less shining than the costæ. The first costa only is entire; between the second and third costæ, near the humerus, there is a short obsolete costula. Beneath very shining on the smooth spaces, and sparsely punctured. Prosternal episterna and a broad depression on each side of the abdominal segments finely and densely punctate and covered with a very fine recumbent pubescence. The last segment with a small triangular emargination at the apex. Prosternum feebly convex; the prosternal process strongly grooved, strongly punctured in the region of the sulcus.

Described from a single specimen (type, Museum of Comparative Zoölogy no. 22,507) collected at Taviuni, Somo Somo, Fiji Islands, by Dr. W. M. Mann. There is also, in the British Museum's collection, a specimen of this new species captured in the Fiji Islands by Mr. Evans. This specimen is a little smaller.

The description of this species agrees pretty well with that of *Paracupta dilutipes* Fairm., Pet. Nouv. Ent. II., 1878, p. 278, from the same region; the type of this species seems to be lost. Fairmaire's description is so short that it is quite useless; the author says: *"Elongata, antice posticeque fere æqualiter attenuata, modice convexa, fusco-ænea, metallica; foveis duabus prothoracis vittaque elytrorum marginali cupreis griseo-sericeis; subtus dense luteo sericans, medio fere lævis; antennis pedibusque flavo-testaceis, femoribus paulo obscurioribus; elytris post medium attenuatis,* parum profunde striatis, intervallis fere planis, *strigosis."* P. *evansi* is evidently "bicolor" above. The expressions in Roman type in Fairmaire's description, above, seem not to agree with the description of P. *evansi* mihi.

Paracupta manni n. sp. (Pl. III, Fig. 2)

Length: 19 mm.; breadth: 6 mm.—♂. Elongate, rather acuminate posteriorly. Above uniformly golden green with reddish tinge at the tips of the elytra. Beneath light cupreous; antennæ and legs light brown.

Head rather wide, with a triangular depression in front,

the bottom of this depression very finely punctate and clothed with an inconspicuous pale pubescence. The epistoma separated from the front by a swelling. Eyes elliptic, feebly convex, converging to the occiput; antennæ reaching the level of the anterior cotyloid cavities.

Pronotum a little more than once and one third as wide at base as at the anterior margin, and a little more than once and a half as wide as long; widest at the base; the anterior margin strongly arcuately emarginate; the sides feebly attenuate from the base to the anterior third, then arcuately narrowed to the anterior angles, the posterior acute and rather prominent; the base nearly tranversely truncate. Disk coarsely sculptured, the punctures becoming more distinct near the sides and the anterior angles; the middle of the surface narrowly furrowed; each side with a deep, wide depression, finely punctured, occupying half of the length and reaching the posterior margin.

Scutellum small, rounded posteriorly and straight anteriorly, smooth.

Elytra as wide as the pronotum at base, slightly expanded and truncate at the shoulders, then nearly parallel to behind the middle, and straight and strongly acuminate to the tips, strongly and sharply serrate along the margin from the middle to apex; the sutural angle toothed. Surface with eight punctate striæ, the juxtasutural stria reaching only from the base to the basal quarter of the length; the intervals between the striæ very slightly convex.

The prothoracic episterna, and the sides beneath, very finely punctate and clothed with very inconspicuous recumbent pubescence; the middle of the body shining, glabrous, very sparsely punctate. Prosternal process deeply furrowed and coarsely punctate at middle; first abdominal segment flattened at middle; last abdominal segment brownish, constricted at apex, angularly and feebly emarginate. Legs and tarsi long.

A single specimen (type, M. C. Z. no. 22,508) of this very beautiful species was captured by Dr. W. M. Mann at Nadarivatu, Viti Levu, Fiji Islands.

It seems to me that this species is very unlike all others in the genus.

Genus *Haplotrinchus* Kerr.

Haplotrinchus manni n. sp. (Pl. III, Fig. 3)

Length: 12 mm.; breadth: 4.5 mm.— ♂. Wide, very attenuate posteriorly, the elytra tailed at apex. Green above, with violaceous reflexions; beneath green, the tarsi bright brown.

Head as wide as the anterior margin of the pronotum; eyes slightly convex, regularly elliptic, and very much closer on the vertex than in front. Front with a rounded depression near the epistoma occupying its entire breadth, and a longitudinal one above the first and separated from it by a smooth and shining transverse swelling; this second depression reaches the upper level of the eyes and is separated from the anterior margin of the eyes by a narrow, smooth, and shining carina; the bottom of this depression is clothed with inconspicuous pubescence. Epistome emarginate. Antennal cavities subtriangular. Antennæ reaching to base of the pronotum, serrate from the fifth joint, the fourth and fifth subequal, the third joint a third shorter than the fourth, and the second a third shorter than the third.

Pronotum widest at base, about once and a half as wide at base as in front, nearly once and three quarters as wide as long. The anterior margin slightly bisinuate; the sides rather regularly rounded, with a little notch near the anterior angles produced by a small transverse furrow which runs along the anterior margin; the posterior angles rectangular; the sides bordered by a sharp carina, feebly sinuous, which reaches to the anterior transverse furrow already mentioned. Base slightly bisinuate. Surface bounded on each side by a broad cariniform swelling which runs along the lateral margin for two thirds of length from base; this swelling limited outside by an impression, very finely punctured at bottom, occupying the whole length of the pronotum. The middle of the disk smooth, shining, irregular, coarsely punctured, with a median, longitudinal, obsolete, finely punctate sulcus.

Scutellum cordiform, convex, smooth, shining.

Elytra once and a quarter as wide at the shoulders as the pronotum at base, outlined by a narrow smooth carina at the base, the shoulders expanded and forming a rounded lobe with a little notch behind; slightly enlarged to the posterior third, then sinuously constricted, ending in a trispinous tail each side of the suture, the external spine of each elytron longer and more acute than the median one but not reaching the level of the median one. Disk shining, punctate-striate, the intervals convex and punctate. Each elytron with seven large, finely punctate, and inconspicuously pubescent areas, arranged as follows: one in the humeral depression; another one, large and rounded, at the middle of the length of the elytra, nearer the margin than the suture; a third one marginal, elongate, in the posterior third; and a juxta-sutural one at the posterior fifth; the other areas less marked, disposed between the humeral and the median areas.

Anterior margin of the prosternum angulately prominent on each side, with a little triangular notch at the middle; the prosternal process densely punctate, pubescent, not mar-gined. Prothoracic episterna strongly and rather densely punctate on the outer sides, smooth and sparsely punctate on the inner sides. Abdominal segments strongly but sparsely punctate, the anterior angles finely and densely punctate and inconspicuously pubescent. The last sternite rounded at apex, with an acute spine on each side. Aedeagus narrow, its sides furnished with some little, erect, spaced denticles. Parameres angulate at tip.

The ♀ is generally larger than the ♂; the last sternite is the same at apex; the prosternal process is strongly and sparsely punctate, not pubescent.

Six specimens of this new species (type ♂, M. C. Z. no. 22,509) were captured by Dr. W. M. Mann at Vanua Ava, Fiji Islands; a paratype stands in my own collection at the Museum National d'Histoire Naturelle at Paris, and another in the British Museum.

Genus Nosotrinchus Obb.

Nosotrinchus solomonensis n. sp. (Pl. III, Fig. 4)

Length: 12 mm.; breadth: 4 mm.—(? ♀). Elongate, at-tenuate posteriorly, the apex of the elytra not forming a tail, as in *N. cœruleipennis* Fairm.; blue, elytra olive green with a longitudinal purple band, this band very narrow near the scutellum, enlarged behind and covering the apical third of the elytra; apex black; the last two segments of the abdomen blackish.

Head moderately large, with a feeble tranverse depression between the eyes; occiput finely striate, finely and sparsely punctate; the part of the front between the eyes wider than long, its sides converging toward the vertex; epistoma not distinctly separated from the front, slightly emarginate. Antennal cavities wide, triangular, with a little oblique carina above. Antennæ reaching nearly to the middle of the length of the pronotum, serrate from the fourth joint, the first joint rather long, the second subglobular, the third nearly twice and a half as long as the second and equal to the fourth.

Pronotum widest at base, nearly once and a fifth as broad at base as at apex, and once and a half as wide as long; the anterior margin nearly transversely truncate, with a swollen margin, latter feebly obliterated at middle; the sides feebly arcuate, sinuate before the posterior angles, which are acute; the marginal carina arcuate, interrupted at the anterior quarter; the prothoracic episterna nearly smooth; the base widely and somewhat deeply bisinuate. Disk feebly and sparsely punctate, more strongly and rugosely at the sides; on each side of the median line, not far from the base, a very deep impression the bottom of which is crossed by an oblique stria inclined outward and forward at an angle of 45°.

Scutellum small, transverse, nearly cordiform.

Elytra once and a fifth wider than pronotum, long, sinuate at sides from shoulders to middle, and arcuately attenuate from middle to apex; strongly tridentate at tips, the posterior half strongly serrate; surface punctato-striate, the striæ stronger on the sides, the intervals flat, equal, and obsoletely punctate. Punctures of the striæ of the sides anteriorly transverse and forming some wrinkles.

Anterior margin of the prosternum slightly emarginate, finely margined; prosternal process smooth, with swollen margin. Beneath, aciculately punctate, the last abdominal segment tridentate at apex, with a little denticle on each side. (The ♂♂ in the genus *Nosotrinchus* generally have the last abdominal segment emarginate between two spines, among the ♀♀ it is bi-emarginate, with three spines.) Tarsi half as long as the tibiæ; claws short and rather strong.

A single specimen of this new species (type, M. C. Z. no. 22,510) was captured at Malaita, Auki, Solomon Islands, by Dr. W. M. Mann.

This species is very like *N. coeruleipennis* Fairm.[1] from the Fiji Islands, but is specifically distinct by the following characters.

1. The front without a depression.
2. The depressions of the base of the pronotum.
3. Sides of the pronotum sinuate before the anterior angles.
4. The color is different. *N. coeruleipennis* Fairm. has the head, the pronotum, and the lower surface, except the last segment at apex, cupreous, the elytra purplish with apex blackish.

Genus *Melobasis* C. & G.

Melobasis albertisi Théry

I described this species in the *Ann. Mus. Civ. Stor. Nat. Genova*, LI. (1923), p. 7, from four ♀ ♀ specimens captured at Kataw, N. Guinea, by M. d'Albertis. A specimen of this species in the Museum of Comparative Zoölogy (Harvard College Collection), captured at Humboldt Bay by Dr. Thomas Barbour, is a ♂; it differs from the ♀ type in its slender form, the frontal punctures very close and confluent, the pubescence thicker on the occiput, the posterior angles of the pronotum less divergent, the intervals between the elytral striæ slightly convex, the anterior femora dull, the abdomen less pubescent and with green reflections, and the last abdominal segment longitudinally wrinkled. Perhaps this form is a new variety.

Subgenus *Diceropygus* H. Deyr.

Diceropygus stevensi n. sp. (Pl. IV, Fig. 8)

Length: 15 mm.; breadth: 5 mm.— ♀. Aeneous, the punctures green and shining; tarsi bluish, claws steel blue and more shining; labrum green. Elongate, distinctly more attenuate posteriorly than in front. Elytra as wide at the shoulders as at the posterior third of their length.

---

[1] *Nosotrinchus simondsi* Obb., Sbornik II., 1924, p. 13, is a synonym of *N. coeruleipennis* Fairm.

Head narrower than the anterior margin of the pronotum, very feebly convex in front, flat on the vertex, finely, densely, and irregularly punctate; front with a narrow, smooth, longitudinal carina reaching nearly to the epistoma; latter emarginate, not distinctly separate from the front. Anterior margins of the eyes converging posteriorly. The space separating the eyes, on the vertex, equal in width to the width of the eyes. Antennæ not reaching the base of the pronotum, serrate from the fourth joint, the first joint elongate, the second twice as long as wide, the third as long as the second and slightly longer than the fourth.

Pronotum widest at base, a little more than once and a half as wide at base as at apex, and once and two thirds as wide as long; the anterior margin rather broadly and deeply bisinuate, finely margined; the sides straight and nearly parallel at base, then rounded and feebly convergent in front, each margined laterally by a regularly arcuate, sharp carina, slightly bent in front and reaching the anterior margin a little below the anterior angle; the posterior angles acute and slightly divergent; the base feebly bisinuate; the surface regularly convex, feebly flattened in the middle, punctate, the punctures green, slightly oval, larger, denser, and more oval on the sides than in the middle, and with an irregular, impunctate, longitudinal space at middle, and with a little impressed fovea in front of the scutellum.

Scutellum wide (0.8 by 0.5 mm.), rounded laterally and posteriorly and truncate in front, smooth, shining, sometimes reddish.

Elytra as wide as pronotum at base, subtruncate at the shoulders, widest at the shoulders, nearly parallel to apical third, then straight and attenuate to the tips, which are separately rounded and acutely serrate, the denticles becoming very small at apex. Sutural edge margined in apical third of its length. Surface with nine striæ, the bottom of each with a line of very transverse punctures, the intervals between the striæ very convex, the third and fourth striæ feebly divergent at the base, leaving a coarsely punctured space, the fifth abutting a mass of shining punctures; the intervals becoming obsolete at base, except the fifth, which is prolonged in front.

Prothoracic episterna finely and regularly punctate,

pubescent; prosternal process flat, acute at apex, finely and regularly punctate, clothed with long, very sparse greyish hairs; the last abdominal segment with four strong spines at end, the lateral not so strong as the median, which are very long, acute, and limit a small semicircular emargination. Tarsi rather long, the first two joints narrow, the two following expanded, claws rather long and thickened at the base.

Three specimens of this new species, all of which are females (type, M. C. Z. no. 22,511), were captured at Mt. Misim, Morobe District, New Guinea, by Mr. Herbert Stevens. A paratype stands in my own collection at the Muséum National d'Histoire Naturelle, Paris.

I do not know any *Diceropygus* with which I may compare this; it is so much like *Briseis curta* Kerr. that it seems possible to confuse the two species. They can be distinguished by the scutellum, which is twice as broad in *Diceropygus stevensi* as in *Briseis curta* Kerr., and by the lack of a lateral protuberance on the prosternal margin of *Diceropygus stevensi*. The latter will be placed next to *Briseis curta;* it appears that the characteristics given for the subgenus *Briseis* are without value.

Diceropygus brevicollis n. sp. (Pl. IV, Fig. 10)

Length: 12 mm.; breadth: 4 mm.—♂. Bronzy green above, the elytra with three steel blue spots and with some slightly purplish reflections; lower surface brownish, with bluish and purplish tinges. Legs brownish, the femora green anteriorly, tarsi and antennæ greenish blue; prosternal process and middle of the metasternum green. Elongate, distinctly more attenuate posteriorly than in front.

Head slightly convex on the vertex, nearly flat in front, very finely and confluently punctate, clothed with rather long greyish pubescence. Eyes broad and regularly elliptic, their anterior edges slightly convergent toward the vertex; the interval between the eyes a fifth wider than the breadth of the eyes. Epistoma not distinctly separated from the front, very slightly emarginate. Antennæ reaching the base of the prothorax below, serrate from the fourth joint, all joints except the first nearly equal in length, the first joint yellow at base, apex of the last joints brownish; palpi brownish.

Pronotum short, widest at the middle, twice as wide as

long, scarcely once and a fifth as wide at base as at the anterior margin. The anterior margin nearly straight in the middle, bordered by a stria; the anterior angles projecting forward; the sides slightly converging from middle to the anterior angles, sinuate from middle to the posterior angles, which are slightly divergent. The sides margined in basal two thirds of their length by a smooth, straight carina. The base tranversely truncate. Surface sparsely and unequally punctate, the punctures well separated on the middle, but becoming much denser and very confluent at the sides, which are clothed with long recumbent pubescence.

Scutellum very wide, straight in front, nearly semicircular posteriorly, the disk with a few punctures in the middle.

Elytra a little wider at the humeral angles than the pronotum at the base; the shoulders slightly expanded and rounded; the sides nearly parallel from the shoulders to behind the middle, then feebly attenuate to the tips, which are separately narrowly rounded; the sides in the posterior marginal half very acutely serrate, the denticles closer apically but also strong laterally. Sutural margin bordered by a sharp carina in the apical half of its length. Surface unequal, with a narrow and deep depression between the base and the humerus, striate-punctate, the striæ obsolete, the punctures well marked but irregular, becoming stronger toward the sides. The intervals slightly and irregularly convex, becoming quite obsolete at base. The steel blue spots arranged thus: the first on the first third, not reaching the base; the second behind the middle, reaching the suture and the lateral margin; the third covering the apex; these spots rather indistinct, as in *Diceropygus maculatus* H. Deyr.

Prothoracic episterna very finely and regularly punctate, clothed with recumbent pubescence. Prosternal process very wide, trifid at apex, finely and regularly punctate, flat, shining. Abdomen pubescent toward the sides; the abdominal segments finely longitudinally strigose; the last segment much more strigose, emarginate at apex between two long and acute spines which are prolonged on the disk of the segment, forming little carinæ; the emargination with a little stria parallel to the edge. Posterior tibiæ rather long; posterior tarsi rather short and distinctly enlarged at apex.

A single ♂ specimen of this new species (type, M. C. Z.

no. 22,512) was captured at Nadamvatu, Viti Levu, Fiji Islands, by Dr. W. M. Mann. This species is colored like *D. maculatus* H. Deyr., but differs from all previously known *Diceropygus* in the very short pronotum.

Diceropygus variegatus n. sp. (Pl. IV, Fig. 5)

Length: 9.75 mm.; breadth: 3.6 mm.— (?♂). Elongate, distinctly more attenuate posteriorly than in front; elytra slightly widened at the posterior third; color purple above, with the suture, a narrow band reaching from the humeral depression to the anterior fifth, and another submarginal one at the middle of the elytra, green. Beneath purplish black; tarsi cyaneous.

Head less wide than the anterior margin of the pronotum, nearly flat in front, very densely and strongly punctured. Epistoma slightly emarginate, not distinct from the front; eyes large; antennæ rather long, the base of the first joint yellow.

Pronotum widest at the middle, nearly twice as wide as long, and a little less than once and a fourth as wide at base as the anterior margin. Anterior margin strongly bisinuate, margined; the sides feebly rounded, sinuate in front of the posterior angles, which are acute and slightly divergent. The base slightly bisinuate, without distinct median lobe. The sides bordered by a smooth, curved carina, reaching from the base to the anterior angles, which are rounded, the posterior angles acute and feebly divergent. Disk regularly convex, slightly flattened at middle, with a little depression in front of the scutellum, strongly and sparsely punctured, the punctures more sparse at middle.

Scutellum wide, twice as wide as long, rounded posteriorly, truncate in front, very finely strigose.

Elytra a little wider at the shoulders than pronotum at base, widest at apical third; the sides straight and diverging from the shoulders to apical third, then arcuately attenuate to tips, the sides very strongly and sharply serrate from the middle to apex, where the serration is less strong. Disk with a close punctuation disposed in longitudinal series, without distinct striæ; the intervals scarcely convex, the ground microscopically sculptured.

Anterior margin of the prosternum nearly tranversely

truncate, slightly swollen; the prosternal process rather convex, very sparsely and rather strongly punctate, margined at the sides and very acutely narrowed at the apex. Abdomen covered with sparse aciculate punctuation; the last abdominal segment broadly emarginate apically, between two long spines. Posterior legs long, the tarsi more than half as long as the tibiæ; first joint of the posterior tarsi as long as the second, the fourth joint very short.

A single specimen of this new species (type, M. C. Z. no. 22,513) was found, in good condition, in the stomach of a bird, *Pœcilodryas albonotata* Hart., at Mt. Misim, Morobe District, New Guinea, by Mr. Herbert Stevens.

Genus *Sambus* H. Deyr.

Sambus manni n. sp. (Pl. IV, Fig. 6)

Length: 3.9 mm.; breadth: 1.7 mm.— ♀. Small, short, subparallel at middle; æneous above, with purplish reflections. The front and the two first joints of the antennæ reddish purple; beneath, black, with the legs more or less blackish æneous. Entirely clothed above with regular, whitish pubescence which does not conceal the ground; two lateral elytral impressions, and the scutellum, glabrous.

Head very convex in front, deeply grooved, the groove becoming less distinct on the front and quite obsolete behind the middle; finely punctate and clothed with silvery pubescence. The portion of the front between the eyes rectangular and slightly longer than wide; epistoma separated from the front by a carina, emarginate in front, depressed in the middle. Eyes very convex, elliptic, more than twice as long as wide. Antennæ black, serrate from the fifth joint, short, reaching the middle of the pronotum.

Pronotum nearly twice as wide as long, distinctly narrower in front than behind; anterior margin bisinuate, with the median lobe feebly prominent and broadly rounded; the sides flattened and nearly regularly arcuate, with the lateral margins finely crenulate, particularly behind the middle; base strongly bisinuate with median lobe broadly rounded in front of the scutellum; lateral carinæ entire, slightly sinuate; posterior angles entirely rounded, angular carinæ very arcuate, reaching from the posterior angles to the apical fourth;

disk convex anteriorly, broadly concave posteriorly, with a rather deep longitudinal depression inside of the angular carina on each side, reaching from the base to the middle of the length. Surface rather strongly punctate, sparsely clothed with long, white, semi-recumbent pubescence.

Scutellum subtriangular, without transverse carina.

Elytra nearly as wide at the shoulders as the middle of the pronotum, rather convex; sides arcuately constricted from the shoulders to basal third, expanded at posterior third, then arcuately attenuate to tips, which are separately rounded; the sutural angles rounded, without denticle; the sides of the elytra finely serrate at the shoulders and along the posterior third; surface finely granulate; each elytron with a shallow depression reaching from the base to the suture at basal fourth and another along the lateral margin behind the humerus.

Chin piece straight in front, bordered by a little swelling, separated from the prosternum by a very deep and narrow groove. Prosternum convex, granulate. Inner posterior angles of the posterior coxæ rounded. Abdomen finely punctate and regularly clothed with sparse, white, recumbent pubescence. Disk of the last segment separated from the pleural margin by a deep and narrow groove; this groove curved inward onto the disk on each side, curving away from the basal angles of the segment. Lamellæ of the tarsi yellow.

A single specimen of this new species (type, M. C. Z. no. 22,514) was captured at Marova L., Fiji Islands, by Dr. W. M. Mann.

Sambus darlingtoni n. sp. (Pl. IV, Fig 7)

Length: 4.3 mm.; breadth 1.9 mm.—♂. Small, short, very feebly narrowed from the shoulders to the middle. Blackish æneous above; elytra pubescent, marked with designs forming transverse bands and spots of white pubescence mixed with yellow hairs. Head and antennæ green. Beneath, blackish, clothed with short, greyish, recumbent pubescence.

Head convex, more convex and bituberculate at the summit of the front, deeply grooved, the groove reaching nearly to the epistoma; slightly rugose and distinctly punctate, with white, sparse, rather long pubescence forming a rosette; the

portion of the front between the eyes longer than wide, feebly
constricted at middle, and distinctly expanded before the
epistoma, from which it is separated by an entire carina.
Epistoma a little wider than long, emarginate in front.
Eyes prominent, more than twice as long as wide. Antennæ
very short, serrate from the fifth joint, reaching the middle
of the pronotum.

Pronotum more than twice as wide as long, distinctly narrower in front than behind; anterior margin bisinuate, with
the anterior angles prominent, the median lobe slightly
prominent and broadly rounded; the sides expanded and very
regularly arcuate, with the lateral margins feebly crenulate;
base strongly bisinuate, with the median lobe rounded in
front of the scutellum; lateral carinæ entire, feebly sinuate
when viewed from side; posterior angles entirely rounded;
angular carinæ very arcuate, reaching from the posterior
angles to the apical fifth, where they are abruptly terminated.
Disk convex anteriorly, broadly concave posteriorly, with a
rather deep depression on each side, reaching from the posterior margin to near the anterior angles. Surface distinctly
and regularly punctate, semicircularly and finely striate,
sparsely clothed with white, semi-recumbent hairs.

Scutellum wide, subtriangular, finely transversely strigose,
with a very distinct transverse carina.

Elytra a little wider at the shoulders than at the middle,
slightly wider at the shoulders than behind the middle (a
little wider behind the middle than at the shoulders in the
female), rather convex; the sides slightly, arcuately constricted from the shoulders to posterior third, arcuately attenuate apically, tips nearly conjointly rounded, but with
sutural angles rounded, without denticles; the sides of the
elytra very finely, almost indistinctly serrate behind the
shoulders and in the posterior third. Surface finely imbricate, indistinctly punctate, each elytron with a shallow depression at the base and another behind the shoulders along
the lateral margin. Disk of the elytra clothed with a very fine,
semi-recumbent pubescence; this pubescence blackish and
inconspicuous on the ground between the designs of silvery
and yellow (mixed) hairs, which are disposed as follows: the
basal quarter except the humeri nearly covered with intermixed silvery and yellow hairs; a lateral spot at the middle

of the lateral margin, united with a discal one at the anterior third; a juxta-sutural spot behind the middle; and two transverse, very sinuous, ante-apical bands, which are more or less confused.

Chin piece indistinctly emarginate in front, finely margined, separated from the prosternum by a deep, narrow groove. Prosternum convex, granulate, clothed with sparse hairs; the prosternal process rather wide; internal posterior angle of the posterior coxa acute. Abdomen finely punctate and clothed with sparse, whitish, recumbent pubescence. Disk of the last segment clothed with long recumbent hairs, emarginate at apex, separated from the pleural margin by a deep narrow groove, which is curved onto the disk on each side, the curve tending away from the basal angles.

A ♂ specimen of this species (type, M. C. Z. no. 22,515) was captured at Yandina, Russell Islands, by Dr. W. M. Mann; a ♀ specimen was captured at Marowa L., Fiji Islands, by Dr. Mann, and is now in my own collection. The ♀ differs from the ♂ by having the front reddish.

Genus *Agrilus* Steph.

Agrilus mannianus n. sp. (Pl. IV, Fig. 11)

Length: 6.6 mm.; breadth: 2 mm.—♂. Elongate, rather broad, subopaque, feebly convex above; cupreous, with a purplish tinge, the front and the antennæ smaragdinous green, the anterior and median femora with a greenish tinge, each elytron ornamented with a poorly defined longitudinal pubescent vitta along the posterior quarter of the suture, this vitta narrowed posteriorly and not reaching the apex. The whole surface clothed with a fine, greyish, recumbent pubescence. Beneath, cupreous, clothed with a very short, regular, greyish, recumbent pubescence, not concealing the ground.

Head with the front rather wide, very feebly convex, vaguely wider basally than anteriorly, with lateral margins feebly sinuate; the vertex and front finely furrowed, the furrow reaching the epistoma but nearly obsolete in front. The color of the vertex sharply defined from that of the front. The front transversely impressed anteriorly, with a little pore at each side, separated from the epistoma by a narrow carina; the surface regularly punctured, more or less rugose, the intervals between the punctures convex. Surface covered with a sparse but distinct whitish pubescence. Vertex finely punctate, the punctures becoming more longitudinal near the front. Eyes large, subelliptic; the temples clothed with silvery, rather long, dense pubescence. Antennæ extending nearly to base of pronotum, serrate from the fourth joint, the second and third joints subequal, longer than the fourth.

Pronotum widest near the anterior margin; obliquely widened, with sides straight, from base to the anterior third, then feebly, arcuately narrowed to the anterior angles. The anterior margin slightly bisinuate, bordered by a stria interrupted at middle, with the median lobe feebly produced. The posterior angles feebly expanded and distinctly obtuse; when viewed from the side, the marginal carina is nearly straight, feebly sinuate, to the anterior angles; the lower carina is connected at base with the lateral carina, and the two are nearly parallel on the anterior half of the pronotum. The angular carinula extends from near the posterior angle to near the middle of the lateral carina, but does not reach the angle or the lateral margin. Base trisinuate, the median lobe feebly produced and broadly, arcuately emarginate in front of the scutellum. Disk broadly transversely depressed in front and near the base, with a suboval longitudinal depression in front of the scutellum; surface very feebly pubescent, finely and subtransversely rugose, with the intervals between punctures slightly convex.

Scutellum wide, transversely carinate.

Elytra somewhat wider at the shoulders than the pronotum at the base, nearly equal in width at base and behind the middle, then obliquely and arcuately narrowed to the apices, which are separately and rather narrowly rounded and very finely serrulate. Disk slightly flattened, without costæ, feebly depressed posteriorly along the suture. Suture moderately elevated posteriorly. The base of each elytron with a broad, deep depression between the humerus and the basal margin, which is distinctly carinate. Surface finely imbricate.

Abdomen wider than elytra, narrowly exposed at sides. Chin piece slightly emarginate at middle; prosternum rugose; prosternal process wide, depressed at middle, rounded at apex. Abdomen very finely punctate; disk of the last segment arcuately emarginate at apex, the pleural margin feebly emarginate at middle, separated from the disk of the segment by a deep, narrow, entire groove; the apex bordered by some long erect hairs. The suture between the first two segments not distinct. Tibiæ slender, the anterior nearly straight; tarsi elongate.

Seventeen specimens of this new species (type, M. C. Z. no. 22,516) were captured at Yandina, Russell Islands, by Dr. W. M. Mann; paratypes of this species are in my own collection and in that of the British Museum.

Agrilus levuensis n. sp. (Pl. IV, Fig. 12)

Length: 11 mm.; breadth: 3 mm.— ♀ . Shining bluish black with a violaceous tinge above, of the same color below; elongate, rather robust; elytra sinuate laterally from the shoulders to behind the middle, then sinuously narrowed to the tips, which are separated, each ending in a strong spine. Elytra with a wide sulcus along the suture, the surface finely and irregularly punctate and clothed with short, greyish, recumbent pubescence which is scarcely distinguishable. The front with a large white spot. Abdominal segments with, on each side, little depressions not reaching the margin, and clothed at bottom with recumbent white pubescence.

Head rather wide, with the front strongly concave between the eyes, the excavation carinate at the sides along the eyes, finely grooved at middle; the sides of the front, between the eyes, are at first parallel, then abruptly convergent toward the epistoma; the surface covered with transverse and slightly oblique wrinkles. Eyes elliptic, large, reaching the anterior margin. Antennæ extending nearly to the middle of the pronotum, serrate from the fourth joint, the second joint wider than, and once and a half as long as, the third.

Pronotum trapezoidal, scarcely once and three quarters as wide as long, widest at the base; the anterior margin scarcely bisinuate; the sides straight, a little angulose at middle; the base deeply bisinuate, with the median lobe truncate in front of the scutellum. The posterior angles obtusely angulate; the marginal carina feebly sinuate; the lower carina obsoletely indicated, interrupted at middle, and forming a smooth swollen area anteriorly; the angular carina sharply defined, extending arcuately from the posterior angles to the lateral carina at middle. Surface with a wide longitudinal sulcus, narrowed in front, the bottom of this sulcus with some little wrinkles; the sides of the pronotum each with a wide, oblique, strong depression at the middle of the margin and reaching the anterior angle, the bottoms of these depressions also with some wrinkles, the rest of the surface with some coarse punctures on a nearly smooth ground.

Scutellum large, cordiform, the anterior margin straight, the apex strongly acuminate.

Elytra scarcely wider at the base than the pronotum, nearly twice and three fifths as long as wide, slightly sinuate behind the shoulders, then narrowed and nearly straight, and again slightly sinuate laterally before the apex, where each is produced in a strong spine; the sutural angles slightly spinose; the sides without any serration. Disk very finely sculptured, the punctures triangular and rather sparse; a strong sulcus along the suture, widened on anterior third, attenuate near apex, and very rugose at bottom.

Chin piece of the prosternum straight at middle, short. Prosternal process wide, rounded at apex, shining, smooth, and sparsely punctate. Last abdominal segment separated from the pleural margin by a groove; the pleural margin finely striate; surface of the last segment with a series of spiniform granulations intermixed with rigid, black, erect hairs. Abdomen slightly punctate, shining. First joint of the posterior tarsi as long as the second.

Described from a single specimen (type, M. C. Z. no. 22,517) collected at Nadarivatu, Viti Levu, Fiji Islands, by Dr. W. M. Mann.

This species will be placed next to *Agrilus taveuniensis* mihi (Ann. Soc. Ent. Belg. 1934, p. 145). It is distinguishable by its violaceous black color, its smooth prosternal process, the first joint of the posterior tarsi not longer than the second, etc.

Agrilus fidjiensis Obb. (Arch. f. Nat. 1924, p. 119)

After a careful examination of the description of this species, it appears to me that it agrees with that of *A. fissifrons* Fairm. from the Fiji Islands. *A. fidjiensis* is a syno-

nym of *A. fissifrons* Fairm., and the name *tetrastictus* Obb.
(*l. c.*) must apply to a variety of *A. fissifrons* Fairm., the
type of which has each elytron marked with a single spot.
Fairmaire's species is represented in my own collection by
a paratype.

Genus *Trachys* F.

Trachys darlingtoni n. sp. (Pl. IV, Fig. 9)

Length: 2.5 mm.; breadth: 1.6 mm. Oval, rounded in
front, attenuate posteriorly, broadest at the shoulders,
rather flattened above, with the scutellar region slightly
convex and glabrous; the rest of the surface ornamented
with designs of whitish pubescence forming two ante-apical,
very sinuous fasciæ which join in several places, and a transverse, very irregular, inconspicuous band in the middle; the
space between the designs clothed with yellow, sparse, semierect pubescence. Above, of a bright brassy color; beneath,
dark bronze; the four first joints of the tarsi, and the palpi,
yellow; the last joint of the tarsi, and the antennæ, black.
The scutellar region appears to be normally glabrous (it is
so in the four specimens examined).

Head very wide, shining, obsoletely punctate, with the
front and vertex furrowed, the furrow reaching a wide, well
marked impression above the epistoma; the latter rugose,
distinguishable from the front only by the sculpture, emarginate in front. Eyes small, regularly elliptic, very oblique,
and not prominent. Antennæ very short, serrate from the
seventh joint, with a few long, rigid hairs.

Pronotum widest at the base, short; anterior margin
emarginate, with a median, feebly projecting lobe; the
anterior angles acute and feebly projecting, blunted at apex;
sides moderately arcuate; the posterior angles slightly
obtuse. Base narrowly margined, with a feebly projecting
median lobe which is broadly subtruncate in front of the
scutellum. Disk regularly convex, impressed along the base,
shining, indistinctly sculptured at middle, the sides marked
with distinct circles.

Scutellum small, equilaterally triangular.

Elytra widest at the shoulders, the humeri rather prominent, the sides arcuately attenuate from the base to the tips,

which are conjointly and broadly rounded.   Disk feebly
reticulate.

Plate of the prosternal process narrowed in front, obsoletely punctate, clothed with more or less erect hairs.   All
the abdominal segments separated from the pleural margin
by an uninterrupted, narrow groove, the first segment with
only a half groove.   Last segment rounded at the apex, with
the pleural margin very narrow.   Claws bifid, the inner
branch quite as long as the outer.

Four specimens of this species were captured at Coimba-
tore, S. India, by Mr. P. S. Nathan, and received by the
Museum of Comparative Zoölogy from the Nicolay Collec-
tion.   The type (no. 22,518) and a paratype are in the
M. C. Z.; there is a paratype in my own collection at the
Muséum National d'Histoire Naturelle in Paris.

Psyche, 1937 VOL. 44, PLATE III.

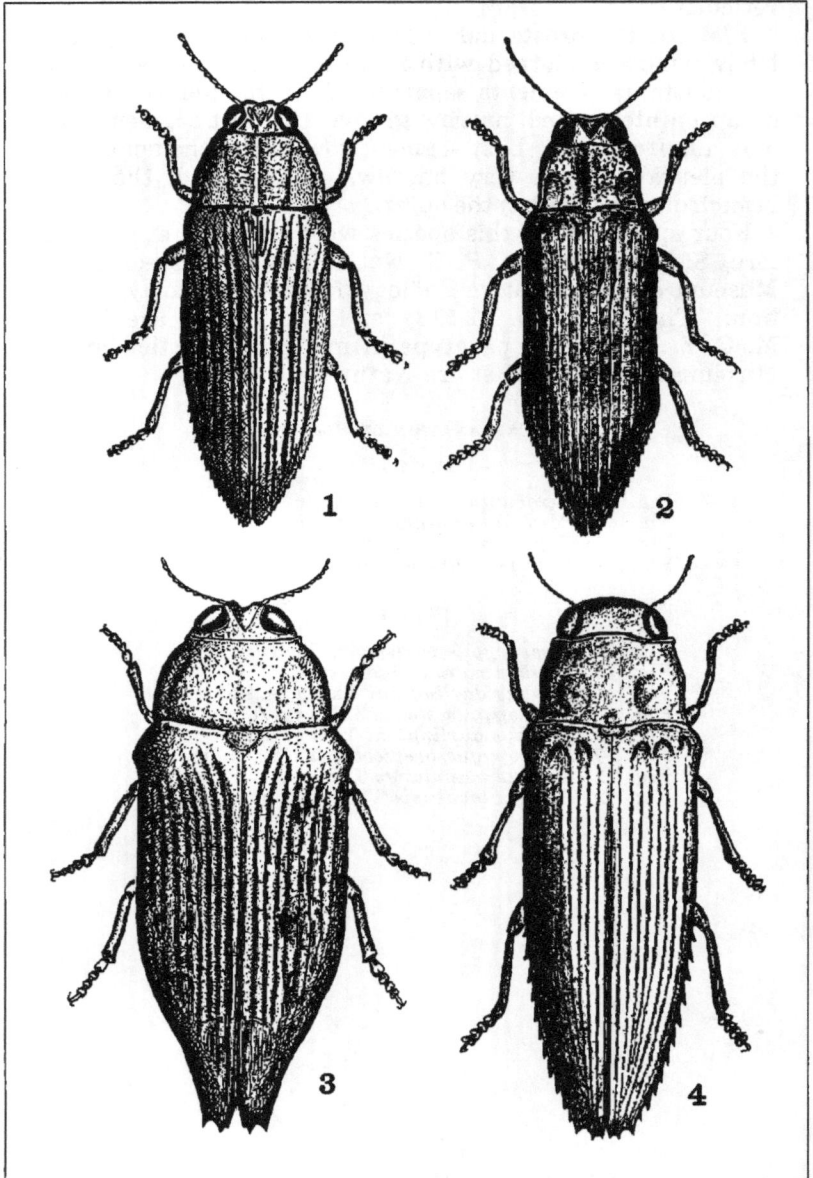

Théry — Buprestid Beetles

Psyche, 1937 VOL. 44, PLATE IV.

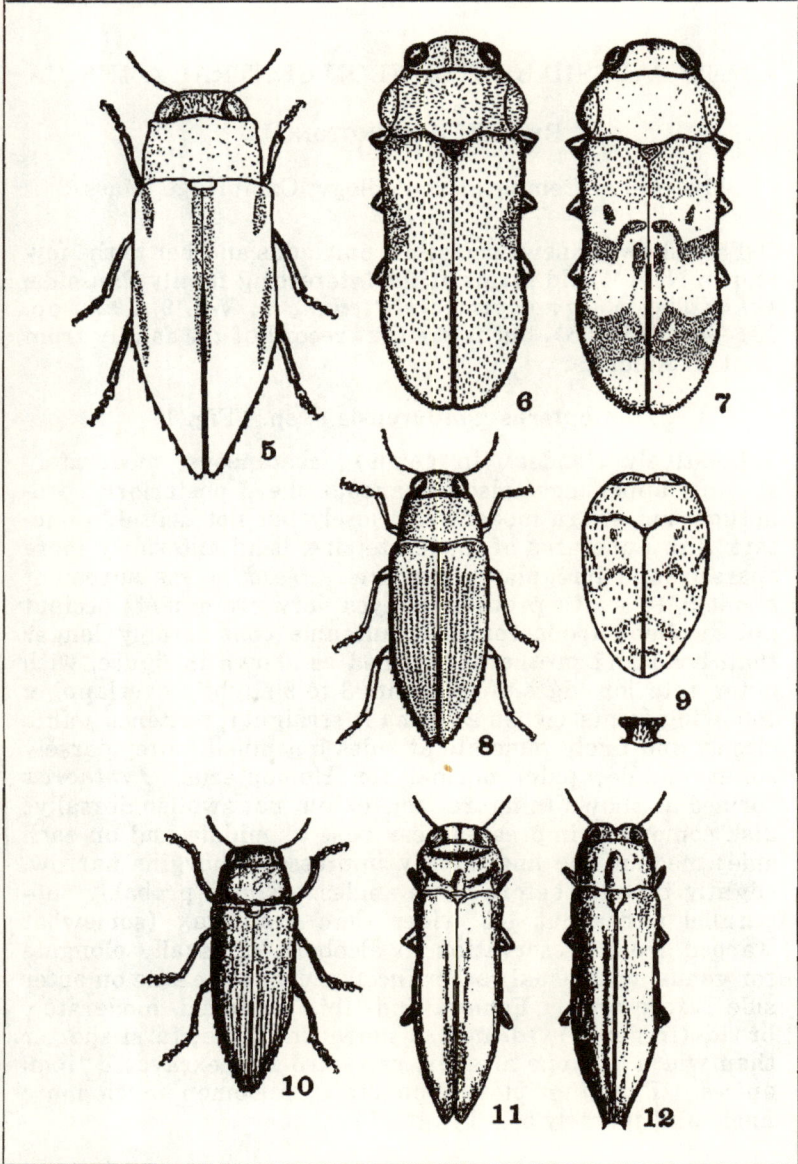

Théry — Buprestid Beetles

A NEW PAUSSID BEETLE FROM CENTRAL AMERICA

By P. J. Darlington, Jr.

Museum of Comparative Zoölogy, Cambridge, Mass.

The following new species not only adds another to the few known New World forms of the interesting family Paussidæ (*cf.* Kolbe, *Entomologische Mitteilungen*, Vol. 9, 1920, pp. 131-141; 145-156), but is the first record of the family from Central America.

Homopterus hondurensis n. sp. (Fig. 1)

Relatively slender (in genus); castaneous, moderately shining, appendages also castaneous; head posteriorly, pronotum, and elytra moderately closely but not densely punctate with punctures of moderate size, head anteriorly more sparsely and irregularly punctate. *Head* by measurement about 9/10 width prothorax; eyes very prominent; occiput not swollen; front concave; antennæ considerably longer than head and prothorax, formed as shown in figure, with outer anterior edges of segments 3 to 9 slightly overlapping following joints (when antenna is straight), flattened joints closely and finely punctate at sides but much more sparsely so at middle; palpi normal for Homopterus. *Prothorax* formed as shown in figure; convex but not swollen dorsally; disk somewhat impressed near base at middle and on each side; median line fine, lightly impressed; margins narrow, slightly broader before basal angles. *Elytra* probably subparallel and about 1/3 wider than prothorax (somewhat warped from preservation in alcohol), unusually elongate for genus, with usual rather inconspicuous tubercle on outer side before apex. Femora and tibiæ flattened, moderately broad (in genus), formed as shown in figure; tarsi shorter than width of tibiæ at apex, retracted into excavated tibial apices. Pygidium closely punctate; abdomen much more finely and sparsely so. Length 7¾ mm.

Type a unique (M. C. Z. no. 22,502) from Lancetilla, Honduras, collected by Dr. Marston Bates.

Lack of an occipital swelling apparently distinguishes this from the three previously described species of Homopterus. Otherwise the relatively narrow form and elongate antennæ ally the new species to *brasiliensis* Westw. and *bolivianus* Kolbe, although it differs from both in having a more nearly quadrate (less cordate) prothorax with more weakly arcuate sides. *Hondurensis* differs further from *brasiliensis* (but resembles *bolivianus*) in the overlapping of the edges of the antennal segments. I do not know either *brasiliensis* or

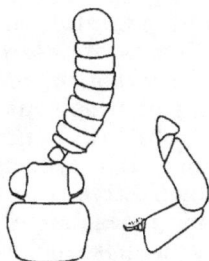

Fig. 1. *Homopterus hondurensis* n. sp. (type) : outlines of pro-thorax, head, and right antenna, and of left middle leg from in front; from camera-lucida drawings.

bolivianus except from the literature, but the former has been figured in detail several times, and the latter is care-fully compared with it by Kolbe. I have, however, seen a specimen of *Homopterus steinbachi* Kolbe, from Colombia. A sketch of the important segments of one antenna of this specimen has been compared with the type of *steinbachi*, and pronounced the same, through the kindness of Prof. Kolbe and the good offices of Dr. Walther Horn.

SOCIAL BEHAVIOR IN HOMOPTERA

BY AUGUST P. BEILMANN

Missouri Botanical Garden, St. Louis, Missouri

The literature relating to parental solicitude in the sub-social insects began, according to Bequært, with the writings of Herbst and Modeer in 1764. Most observations, however, have been reported during the last forty years. Bequært (1) lists but one case of parental care in the Homoptera. The following observation is of interest, since it concerns the terrapin scale (*Eulecanium nigrofasciatum*) ; hardly a promising subject for the development of social habits.

During the spring of 1932 heavy infestations of this scale were found on hawthorn and sycamore. Since dormant spraying had proven ineffective, these insects were being watched to learn the emergence date of the young. For this purpose one small undernourished hawthorn was selected, since its convenient location permitted frequent observations. On three successive mornings in June the young were seen to emerge in a body at 10 o'clock and move upward toward the new growth. When an examination toward evening failed to disclose their destination, it was assumed that these individuals were experiencing an unusual mortality rate. However, more young made their appearance the following morning, and continued to move about during the sunny hours. About 4 o'clock very few could be found, although some had settled on the foliage. It was then observed that a few stragglers were returning to the adult scales and after slight hesitation were crawling underneath. Again on the third morning, the nymphs appeared at one time and began their journey up the branch toward the new growth. Observations were more frequent during the afternoon and an additional number were found permanently located on the leaves. However, about 3 :30 P. M. the general movement of the larvæ was reversed. They began to come down the branch—for some of them a journey of three feet— and to disappear beneath the adult females. Within twenty minutes all had returned to remain safely covered for the night.

Simanton (2) has published a very comprehensive account of this scale as it occurs on the peach in Pennsylvania. He has noted the well timed emergence in the morning, but does not mention having seen any evidence of a return in the evening. This performance may have been due solely to the de-vitalized condition of the tree upon which the observations were made. The total new twig growth did not exceed two inches per year, and hardly more than four scrawny leaves grew from each branch tip. Thus, suitable locations for feeding and growth were reduced to a minimum. The apparently aimless wanderings and the return during the night, may have been due solely to the restricted choice of feeding sites.

LITERATURE CITED

1. BEQUAERT. J., 1935. Presocial behavior among the Hemiptera. Bull. Brooklyn Ent. Soc. XXX, pp. 177-191.
2. SIMANTON, W. A., 1916. U. S. D. A. Bull. 351.

BOOK REVIEW. — A Monograph of the British Neuroptera, Vol. I, by Frederick J. Killington. Pp. 1-269, 68 text-figures and 15 plates. Printed for the Ray Society and sold by Bernard Quaritch, Ltd., London. This is the first comprehensive account of the British Neuroptera since MacLachlan's "Monograph" in 1868. The book is divided into six chapters. The first deals with the morphology of the families of British Neuroptera with special reference to the genitalia; the second, third, and fourth are concerned with the metamorphosis of the British species; the fifth deals with the bionomics; and the sixth with the systematics of the Coniopterygidæ, Osmylidæ, Sisyridæ and a few genera of Hemerobiidæ. The second volume will apparently consist of a systematic account of the rest of the Hemerobiidæ and the Chrysopidæ, as well as the entire bibliography. Although the systematic part of this book is of interest only to the specialist in the Neuroptera, the first five chapters should be of general interest to entomologists, since they contain much new information on the structure and biology of these insects.

F. M. CARPENTER.

OBITUARY

Professor William Morton Wheeler, for many years an active member of the Cambridge Entomological Club and its most distinguished member, died suddenly on April 19th. The forthcoming issue will contain an account of Professor Wheeler's biological career and a list of his many and highly important entomological publications.

PIN-LABELS IN MULTIPLES OF 1000, ALIKE

One Dollar Per Thousand

Smallest Type. Pure White Ledger Paper. Not over 4 Lines nor 30 Characters (13 to a line) Additional Characters, 3 cents each, in total and per line, per 1000. Trimmed so one cut makes a label.

C. V. BLACKBURN, 7 Emerson St., STONEHAM 80, MASS.

CAMBRIDGE ENTOMOLOGICAL CLUB

A regular meeting of the Club is held on the second Tuesday of each month (July, August and September excepted) at 7.45 p.m. in Room B-455, Biological Laboratories of Harvard University, Divinity Ave., Cambridge. Entomologists visiting Boston are cordially invited to attend.

WARD'S ENTOMOLOGICAL SERVICES

Entomological Supplies and Equipment
Carefully designed by professional entomologists. Material of high quality at low prices. **Send for Supply Catalog No. 348.**

Insect Preparations
Life Histories, Type Collections, Collections of Economic Insects and Biological Insect Collections. All specimens are accurately determined.

Insects for the Pest Collection
We have in stock over three hundred species of North American Insect Pests. **Send for Price List No. 349.**

Ward's Entomological Bulletin
A monthly publication sent free to all entomologists requesting it.

Information for the Beginner
Send for "**Directions for Collecting and Preserving Insects**" by Dr. A. B. Klots. A mine of useful information. Price 15 cents.

WARD'S NATURAL SCIENCE ESTABLISHMENT, Inc.
P. O. Box 24, Beechwood Station
Rochester, N. Y., U. S. A.
The Frank A. Ward Foundation of Natural Science of the University of Rochester

BACK VOLUMES OF PSYCHE

The Cambridge Entomological Club is able to offer for sale the following volumes of Psyche. Those not mentioned are entirely out of print.

Volumes 2, 3, 4, 5, 6, 7, 8, 9, 10; each covering a period of three years, $5.00 each.

Volumes 12, 14, 17, each covering a single year, $1.00 each.

Volumes 18, 19, 20, 21, 22, 23, 24, 25, 26, each covering a single year, $1.50 each.

Volumes 27, 28, 29, 30, 31, 32, 33, 34, 35, 36, 37, 38, 39, 40, 41, 42, 43, each covering a single year, $2.00.

Orders for 2 or more volumes subject to a discount of 10%.

Orders for 10 or more volumes subject to a discount of 20%.

A set of all the volumes available (39 in all) will be sold for $77.00.

All orders should be addressed to

F. M. CARPENTER, Associate Editor of Psyche,
Biological Laboratories,
Harvard University,
Cambridge, Mass.

PSYCHE

A JOURNAL OF ENTOMOLOGY

ESTABLISHED IN 1874

| VOL. XLIV | SEPTEMBER, 1937 | No. 3 |

TABLE OF CONTENTS.

CAMBRIDGE ENTOMOLOGICAL CLUB

OFFICERS FOR 1937-1938

President .	. C. A. FROST
Vice-President	J. C. BEQUAERT
Secretary	V. G. DETHIER
Treasurer	RICHARD DOW
	. THOMAS BARBOUR
Executive Committee	. F. M. CARPENTER
	C. H. BLAKE

EDITORIAL BOARD OF PSYCHE

EDITOR-IN-CHIEF
C. T. BRUES, HARVARD UNIVERSITY

ASSOCIATE EDITOR
F. M. CARPENTER, HARVARD UNIVERSITY

CONSULTING EDITORS

NATHAN BANKS,
Harvard University.

THOMAS BARBOUR,
Harvard University.

RICHARD DOW,
New England Museum of
Natural History,
Boston, Mass.

A. E. EMERSON,
University of Chicago.

A. L. MELANDER,
College of the
City of New York.

J. G. NEEDHAM,
Cornell University.

PSYCHE is published quarterly, the issues appearing in March, June, September, and December. Subscription price, per year, payable in advance: $2.00 to Subscribers in the United States; foreign postage, 25 cents extra, Canada 15 cents. Single copies, 65 cents.

Cheques and remittances should be addressed to Treasurer, Cambridge Entomological Club, Biological Laboratories, Harvard University, Cambridge, Mass.

Orders for back volumes, missing numbers, notices of change of address, etc., should be sent to Professor F. M. Carpenter, Biological Laboratories, Harvard University, Cambridge, Mass.

IMPORTANT NOTICE TO CONTRIBUTORS
Manuscripts intended for publication, books intended for review, and other editorial matter, should be addressed to Professor C. T. Brues, Biological Laboratories, Harvard University, Cambridge, Mass.

Authors contributing articles over 8 printed pages in length will be required to bear a part of the extra expense, for additional pages. This expense will be that of typesetting only, which is about $2.00 per page. The actual cost of preparing cuts for all illustrations must be borne by contributors; the expense for full page plates from line drawings is approximately $5.00 each, and for full page half-tones, $7.50 each; smaller sizes in proportion.

AUTHOR'S SEPARATES
Reprints of articles may be secured by authors, if they are ordered before, or at the time proofs are received for corrections. The cost of these will be furnished by the Editor on application.

Printed by the Eliot Press Inc., Jamaica Plain, Mass., U. S. A.

PSYCHE

VOL. XLIV   SEPTEMBER, 1937   No. 3

PROFESSOR WILLIAM MORTON WHEELER

WITH A LIST OF HIS PUBLISHED WRITINGS

Professor Wheeler was born in Milwaukee, Wisconsin on March 19, 1865 and died suddenly in Cambridge, Massachusetts on April 19, 1937 shortly after passing his seventy-second birthday. He had retired from active teaching in 1934, but was still energetically engaged in the continuance of his biological investigations which had extended, without interruption, over a full half century.

Young Wheeler was educated in Milwaukee, for a time in the public schools and afterwards in the Englemann German Academy. He was later graduated in 1884 from the German-American College, a remarkably efficient school, with ideals based on those of the fine group of early German immigrants whose culture dominated Milwaukee during the latter part of the last century. He always attributed much to the training received at the Academy; perhaps too much, for he was certainly their star pupil of all time. There he received a broad education, and developed his first interest in the classics, which he read extensively, never forgot and referred to frequently in his later writings. At this point his formal education ended for a period of six years.

Wheeler had always been much interested in Natural History, and was greatly delighted when in 1884 Professor H. A. Ward of Rochester brought to Milwaukee a collection of stuffed animals, skeletons, and other natural history specimens, with the idea of selling them in that city as the nucleus for a public museum. Ward was so pleased with Wheeler that he offered him a position in the Ward's Natural Science Establishment at Rochester. This was accepted and Wheeler spent a year arranging zoölogical material of all kinds and identifying specimens for Professor Ward. At that time he prepared a check-list of shells, so well done that it is still useful to conchologists after the lapse of more than fifty years! At the Ward Establishment he met Carl Akeley, later famous taxidermist. Concerning their early association and life-long friendship Wheeler has written interestingly in his obituary of Akeley, published in 1927. This contains also reminiscences of Wheeler's own early youth.

He left Ward's in 1885, returned to Milwaukee and at the invitation of the well-known entomologist, Dr. G. W. Peckham, who was then principal of the Milwaukee High School, accepted a position to teach German and physiology there. After he had taught in the high school for two years, he was made custodian of the newly established Milwaukee Public Museum where he remained until 1890. During this period there was established nearby the Allis Lake Laboratory, a biological station, to which Professor C. O. Whitman came as director. From contact with this laboratory and especially through the interest of one of its staff, Dr. William Patton, Wheeler was induced to undertake a study of insect embryology. With the help of Dr. Patton he mastered the necessary microscopical technique, procured a microtome and set to work, utilizing such time as he could spare from his duties at the museum.

Professor Whitman was then called to Clark University, and recognizing young Wheeler's genius in the problem he had undertaken, offered him a fellowship at Clark. This he accepted in 1890 and two years later was granted the degree of Doctor of Philosophy for this "Contribution to Insect Embryology" which had its inception in the happy circumstance of the establishment of the Allis Laboratory. The next year Wheeler spent in Europe, first at Würzburg, then at the Naples Zoölogical Station and finally at Liège before returning to America. He then went to the University of Chicago, where he remained for five years, first as instructor in embryology and after 1896 as assistant professor. During this period his interest in insect embryology was waning, and he became more interested in other phases of entomology.

In the autumn of 1899 he accepted a position as Professor of Zoölogy in the University of Texas. There, with the aid

WILLIAM MORTON WHEELER

From a photograph taken in 1915 by Professor A. L. Melander at
Berkeley, California, during the summer meeting of the American
Association for the Advancement of Science.

of a single instructor and several laboratory assistants he gave all the zoölogical instruction in the University. This included general biology, comparative anatomy, embryology and histology and even special work in entomology to a group of several more advanced students. He was exceptionally well fitted to give all these courses, and in addition his tireless energy was still able to overflow into other channels. He now turned his attention to ants and almost immediately began to publish papers on the habits of these insects. Thus with studies on Texan ants began the long series of investigations that later molded his biological career. Each summer he went north, either to Woods Hole or to his summer home at Colebrook, Connecticut, rapidly extending his interest in myrmecology.

Wheeler remained in Texas for only four years, but during that time the zoölogical laboratory of the University quickly rose to a position where it commanded the respect and admiration of the biological fraternity throughout the World.

He left the University of Texas during the summer of 1903 to become Curator of Invertebrate Zoölogy in the American Museum of Natural History. I know that he regretted greatly having to give up his university teaching, but he knew that he would have more time to devote to his work on ants, and furthermore a greater opportunity to travel and to engage in field work than was possible for him as a University professor. Also he was supplied in his new position with the necessary clerical and scientific assistance that had previously been lacking. He enjoyed greatly also the association with several members of the staff, especially his friend Dr. H. C. Bumpus, at that time director of the American Museum. He remained in New York for five years, during which time he accomplished an enormous amount of scientific work, attested by the long series of extensive and important papers published during these years. The manuscript of his book on ants was nearly completed during this period, although not finally published until 1910.

In 1908 he deserted the museum to again become an active teacher, going to Harvard University as Professor of Economic Entomology. His laboratories were located in the Bussey Institution, organized as a graduate school for re-

search and for the training of students in the several
branches of applied biology. At first the Bussey Institution
formed a part of the Graduate School of Applied Sciences,
but a few years later the institution staff was made a separate faculty of the University and Professor Wheeler was appointed its dean. He served in this capacity from 1915 to
1929. He frequently spoke of this long stay at the Bussey
as including the best years of his life. During that time he
always had clustered about him some half a dozen graduate
students working in entomology toward the degree of Doctor
of Science, which was the applied science degree awarded by
the University to students in applied biology. Most of these
students now hold responsible positions in colleges, univer-
sities or similar institutions in America and abroad, and
their consistently high attainments show very clearly the
deep influence exercised by his remarkable intellect upon
their subsequent careers.

In 1929 he resigned from the deanship and moved his work
to Cambridge, pending the completion of the New Biological
Laboratories. No new dean was appointed, as the several
biological units of the University were soon to be consoli-
dated and made a part of the Faculty of Arts and Sciences,
with headquarters in the new building. There he spent his
last years, continuing to teach until his retirement in 1934.
After that he still retained his same quarters in the laboratory, where he worked continuously until the last day of his
life, even more actively than before, since the time previously
devoted to lectures and students could be spent upon his own
research. During this time his energy and enthusiasm never
lagged and, as he told me only a few days before his death,
he had already on hand collections of ants that would take
him many years to work up. This, of course, did not take
into account the many related biological problems that con-
tinually arose in his mind in connection with taxonomic
work. At that moment he was just finishing his last extensive manuscript dealing with mosaic anomalies in ants, an
investigation which had unexpectedly developed from the
study of some collections of ants recently received from the
American tropics.

Most persons conversant with Professor Wheeler's published contributions to biological science and to entomology

in particular, will regard these as his greatest achievements.
There are, however, a favored few who have had the good
fortune to derive from him, through personal contact, either
as students or colleagues, a vast amount of information and
inspiration which they will always treasure and some of
which they will be able to pass on to their own students and
younger associates. Wheeler always dealt with his students
as he would with colleagues. With his broad intellectual
viewpoint he could do this with ease, and without apparent
effort he would quickly stimulate these young men to accomplishments quite beyond their own expectations. He was
always enthusiastically interested in his own work and however deeply immersed in it, was always ready to welcome the
student who wandered into his laboratory at any time. Frequently, such conferences would turn to an account of what
he was doing at the moment or to a critical review of some
important book which he had just read. The immediate
effect of such contacts was frequently disheartening in the
extreme, as it emphasized the extent of any biological problem and the inadequate background of the young man who
was attempting to solve it. However, the final result of a
series of such meetings was highly salutary, and it gave to
most of his students the impetus needed to complete their
work well, and furthermore to prolong their studies after the
inevitable doctor's thesis had been finished. This ability to
instill his own ideals of research into the minds of younger
men was a salient characteristic of his personality and it has
done much to further the real advance of entomological investigation in many fields.

To see him casually in his laboratory, working over a box
of mounted specimens of ants and attaching to them labels
with their Latin names, one would have taken him for a
taxonomist pure and simple. Under such circumstances he
was, and the endless amount of material from all parts of
the world that passed through his hands during the thirty-
five years that he was an authority on the classification of
ants resulted in the description of an enormous number of
new species, sub-species and varieties. Such work requires
immense concentration, continuous study and perfect familiarity with a maze of literature. As a result most taxonomic
workers lose interest in all the problems of general biology.

Wheeler was a glaring exception to this rule as his encyclo-paedic familiarity with the structure and adaptations of ants not only served to increase his interest and curiosity in the many other phases of biology, but enabled him to approach them with a minute, systematic knowledge of detail utterly beyond the common range. This method of approach is especially notable in connection with his papers on gynan-dromorphs in ants, the behavior of ant-lions and worm-lions, and his contributions on the evolution of social and parasitic habits among insects.

Professor Wheeler's thirst for reading was insatiable and as he read the several common European languages with great facility, the literary field in which he could browse was very wide. His interest in literature was almost exclusively serious although it was by no means restricted to entomol-ogy, biology or even to the natural sciences. It was, however, primarily confined to biology, psychology and philosophy in the widest sense, although few of his friends or colleagues were ever able to bring to his attention any book of general interest with which he was unacquainted. Most frequently he had read it through (which meant literally that) for although he read with great rapidity, his very retentive memory allowed no details to be forgotten. In addition, a pencil in his hand was intermittently busy underlining sen-tences or marking paragraphs to which he might wish later to refer. Similarly, every bundle of reprints that came to his desk, and there were a great many of these, was care-fully examined, first, to cull out any in which he could see nothing of interest. The others were read almost in their entirety.

He had such a keen sense of humor that he derived a great deal of fun from many books and dissertations that were not intended to furnish amusement. This undoubtedly made up in great part for the lack of light reading on his book-shelves. In company, however, he was very fond of a good story, and no matter what the subject; his conversation was always enlivened with a humor uniformly appealing to his wide range of friends and colleagues. When it came to the point, Professor Wheeler was extremely outspoken and he did not mince words in voicing either approbation or disapproval no matter to whom his remarks might be directed. He always

spoke in good faith, however, and his opinions were almost
always accepted in the spirit they were given.

Much more could be said of Professor Wheeler's academic
career and scientific writings. A fine appreciation written
by several of his colleagues has appeared in Science.[1] He
received several honorary degrees and medals in recognition
of his entomological investigations. He enjoyed membership in numerous important societies; honorary membership
in three foreign and two American entomological societies.
During his long residence at Harvard he took a leading part
in the activities of the Cambridge Entomological Club and a
continued interest in its journal PSYCHE to which he contributed several short articles in almost every volume.

Wheeler was an unusually keen and enthusiastic collector.
After the first few years, his immediate interest was centered almost entirely on ants, but he never failed to bring
back from any excursion many other valuable specimens.
He traveled extensively through the United States, Mexico
and other parts of tropical America and twice visited
Australia; also his visits to Europe and North Africa offered
opportunities for collecting that were never neglected. He
had returned from an extensive and strenuous trip with his
wife into Mexico only a few weeks before his death.

The list of titles in the appended bibliography is believed
to be a practically complete list of Professor Wheeler's
biological books, memoirs and papers. It has been compiled
primarily from a catalogue which he himself maintained,
and I have one of his younger students, Professor F. M.
Carpenter to thank for preparing the preliminary draft
during my own protracted absence from America.

This bibliography speaks for itself as to the varied interests and accomplishments of Professor Wheeler. It cannot
of course give any indication of the great clarity of his
scientific statements and the fine literary style which per-
vades all of his writings. From the latter standpoint alone
several of his humorous and satirical addresses could lay
claim to rank as classics. In addition each contains several
cleverly concealed and well documented scientific pills which
represent the real thesis of the communication. By far the

[1]June 4, 1937; vol. 85, pp. 533-535.

greater number of papers deal with ants, many with other
social insects, a number with various types of parasitism and
with evolutionary phenomena. Although nearly all relate
to insects directly, only those concerned entirely with taxonomy can be classed as strictly entomological in that they
do not contain material of immediate interest to other
biologists.

Among those who knew him personally or through his
writings, he had a host of friends, almost no enemies, and
certainly all regarded his intellectual accomplishments with
an admiration that will never fade till they join him in the
great unknown.

HARVARD UNIVERSITY CHARLES T. BRUES

PUBLICATIONS OF WILLIAM MORTON WHEELER

1885

Catalogue of Specimens of Mollusca and Brachiopoda for
Sale at Ward's Natural Science Establishment. Rochester,
New York, 167 pp., 202 figs.

A List of Trees found in the City of Milwaukee. Proc.
Wisconsin Pharmaceut. Assoc., pp. 24-25.

1887

Distribution of Coleoptera along the Lake Michigan Beach
of Milwaukee County. Proc. Wisconsin Nat. Hist. Soc.,
April 1887, pp. 132-140.

1888

The Flora of Milwaukee Co., Wisconsin. Proc. Wisconsin
Nat. Hist. Soc., April 1888, pp. 154-190.

The Spiders of the Sub-family Lyssomanae. (With G. W.
and E. G. Peckham). Trans. Wisconsin Acad. Sci., Arts and
Lett., vol. 2, pp. 222-256, 1 plate.

1889

The Embryology of *Blatta germanica* and *Doryphora
decemlineata*. Journ. Morph., vol. 3, pp. 291-386, 7 plates,
16 figs.

Homologues in Embryo Hemiptera of the Appendages of

the First Abdominal Segment of other Insect Embryos. American Naturalist, vol. 23, pp. 644-645.

Ueber drüsenartige Gebilde im ersten Abdominalsegment der Hemipterenembryonen. Zool. Anzeig., Jahrg. 12, pp. 500-504, 2 figs.

On Two Species of Cecidomyid Flies Producing Galls on *Antennaria plantaginifolia*. Proc. Wisconsin Nat. Hist. Soc., April 1889, pp. 209-216.

Two Cases of Insect Mimicry. Proc. Wisconsin Nat. Hist. Soc., April 1889, pp. 217-221.

1890

Description of Some New North American Dolichopodidae. Psyche, vol. 5, pp. 337-343, 355-362, 373-379.

The Supposed Bot-fly Parasite of the Box-turtle. Psyche, vol. 5, p. 403.

Review of Poulton's "Colors of Animals". Science, vol. 16, p. 286.

Hydrocyanic Acid Secreted by *Polydesmus virginicus* Drury. Psyche, vol. 5, p. 442.

Review of R. H. Lamborn's "Dragon-Flies versus Mosquitoes". New York, Appleton. Science, vol. 16, p. 284.

On the Appendages of the first Abdominal Segment of Embryo Insects. Trans. Wisconsin Acad. Sci. Arts and Lett., vol. 4, pp. 87-140, 3 plates.

Note on the Oviposition and Embryonic Development of *Xiphidium ensiferum* Scud. Insect Life, vol. 2, pp. 222-225.

Ueber ein eigenthümliches Organ in Locustidenembryo. Zool. Anzeig., Jahrg. 13, pp. 475-480.

1891

The Embryology of a Common Fly. Psyche, vol. 6, pp. 97-99.

The Germ-band of Insects. Psyche, vol. 6, pp. 112-115.

Neuroblasts in the Arthropod Embryo. Journ. Morph., vol. 4, pp. 337-343, 1 fig.

Hemidiptera haeckelii. Psyche, vol. 6, pp. 66-67.

1892

Concerning the "Blood-tissues" of the Insects. Psyche, vol. 6, pp. 216-220, 233-236, 253-258.

A Dipterous Parasite of the Toad. Psyche, vol. 6, p. 249.

1893
A Contribution to Insect Embryology. Inaugural Dissertation. Journ. Morph., vol. 8, pp. 1-160, 6 plates, 7 figs.

The Primitive Number of Malpighian Vessels in Insects. Psyche, vol. 6, pp. 457-460, 485-486, 497-498, 509-510, 539-541, 545-547, 561-564, 2 figs.

1894
Syncœlidium pellucidum, a new Marine Triclad. Journ. Morph., vol. 9, pp. 167-194, 1 plate.

Planocera inquilina, a Polyclad inhabiting the Gill chamber of *Sycotypus canaliculatus*. Journ. Morph., vol. 9, pp. 195-201, 2 figs.

Protandric Hermaphroditism in Myzostoma. Zool. Anzieg., vol. 6, pp. 177-182.

1895
The Behavior of the Centrosome in the Fertilized Egg of *Myzostoma glabrum* Leuck. Journ. Morph., vol. 10, pp. 305-311, 10 text-figs.

Translation of Wilhelm Roux's "The Problems, Methods and Scope of Developmental Mechanics." Biological Lectures delivered at the Marine Biological Laboratory at Woods Hole, Summer Session of 1894. Boston, Ginn & Co., pp. 149-190.

1896
The Sexual Phases of Myzostoma. Mitth. a.d. Zool. Station zu Neapel, vol. 12, pp. 227-302, 3 plates.

The Genus Ochthera. Entom. News, vol. 7, pp. 121-123.

Two Dolichopodid Genera new to America. Entom. News, vol. 7, pp. 152-156.

A New Genus and Species of Dolichopodidae. Entom. News, vol. 7, pp. 185-189, 1 fig.

A New Empid with Remarkable Middle Tarsi. Entom. News, vol. 7, pp. 189-192, 3 figs.

An Antenniform Extra-appendage in *Dilophus tibialis* Loew. Arch. f. Entwickl.-Mech. d. Organism., vol. 3, pp. 261-268, 1 plate.

1897
A Genus of Maritime Dolichopodidae New to America. Proc. California Acad. Sci., vol. (3) 1, pp. 145-152, 1 pl.

The Maturation, Fecundation and Early Cleavage of

Myzostoma glabrum Leuckart.   Arch. Biol., vol. 15, pp. 1-77, 3 pls

Two Cases of Mimicry.   Chicago Univ. Record, vol. 2, p. 1.

[Marine Fauna of San Diego Bay, California].   Zoölogical Club, Univ. of Chicago, meeting of April 14, 1897.   Science, n.s., vol. 5, pp. 775-776.

1898

A New Genus of Dolichopodidae from Florida.   Zoöl. Bull., vol. 1, pp. 217-220, 1 text-fig.

Burger and Carrière on the Embryonic Development of the Wall-bee (Chalicodoma).   American Naturalist, vol. 32, pp. 794-798.

Review of A. S. Packard's "Text Book of Entomology".   Science, n.s., vol. 7, pp. 834-836.

A New Peripatus from Mexico.   Journ. Morph., vol. 15, pp. 1-8, 1 pl., 1 fig.

1899

George Baur's Life and Writings.   American Naturalist, vol. 33, pp. 15-30.

The Life History of Dicyema.   Zool. Anzeig., vol. 22, pp. 169-176.

Anemotropism and Other Tropisms in Insects.   Archiv. für Entwickl.-Mech. d. Organism., vol. 8, pp. 373-381.

The Prospects of Zoölogical Study in Texas.   Texas University Record, vol. 1, pp. 335-339.

New Species of Dolichopodidae from the United States.   Proc. California Acad. Sci., Zoöl., (3), vol. 2, pp. 1-84, 4 pls.

The Development of the Urinogenital Organs of the Lamprey.   Zool. Jahrb. Abth. f. Morph., vol. 13, pp. 1-88, 7 pls.

J. Beard on the Sexual Phases of Myzostoma.   Zool. Anzieg., vol. 22, pp. 281-288.

Kaspar Friedrich Wolff and the Theoria Generationis.   Biol. Lectures Marine Biol. Lab., Woods Hole, pp. 265-284.

1900

The Free-swimming Copepods of the Woods Hole Region.   Bull. U. S. Fish Commission for 1899, pp. 157-192, 30 figs.

On the Genus Hypocharassus Mik.   Entom. News, vol. 11, pp. 423-424.

The Study of Zoölogy.   Univ. of Texas Record, vol. 2, No. 2, pp. 125-135.

Review of Korschelt and Heider's "Text-book of Embryology". Science, n.s., vol. 11, pp. 148-149.

The Female of *Eciton sumichrasti* Norton, with some notes on the habits of Texan Ecitons. American Naturalist, vol. 34, pp. 563-574, 4 figs.

The Habits of *Myrmecophila nebrascensis* Bruner. Psyche, vol. 9, pp. 111-115, 1 fig.

A Singular Arachnid (*Koenenia mirabilis* Grassi) Occurring in Texas. American Naturalist, vol. 34, pp. 837-850, 3 figs.

A New Myrmecophile from the Mushroom Gardens of the Texan Leaf Cutting Ant. American Naturalist, vol. 34, pp. 851-862, 6 figs.

A Study of Some Texan Ponerinae. Biol. Bull., vol. 2, pp. 1-31, 10 figs.

The Habits of Ponera and Stigmatomma. Biol. Bull., vol. 2, pp. 43-69, 8 figs.

1901

The Males of Some Texan Ecitons. American Naturalist, vol. 35, pp. 157-173, 3 figs. (With W. H. Long).

Impostors Among Animals. Century Magazine, vol. 62, pp. 369-378.

The Compound and Mixed Nests of American Ants. American Naturalist, vol. 35, pp. 431-448, 513-539, 701-724, 791-818, 20 figs.

Microdon Larvae in Pseudomyrma Nests. Psyche, vol. 9, pp. 222-224, 1 fig.

The Parasitic Origin of Macroërgates among Ants. American Naturalist, vol. 35, pp. 877-886, 1 fig.

1901

An Extraordinary Ant-Guest. American Naturalist, vol. 35, pp. 1007-1016, 2 figs.

Notices biologique sur les fourmis Mexicaines. Ann. Soc. Entom. Belgique, vol. 45, pp. 199-205.

1902

A New Agricultural Ant from Texas, with Remarks on the North American Species. American Naturalist, vol. 36, pp. 85-100, 8 figs.

Review of G. N. Calkins "Biology of the Protozoa". American Naturalist, vol. 36, pp. 214-215.

A Consideration of S. B. Buckley's "North American Formicidae". Trans. Texas Acad. Sci. for 1901, vol. 4, pp. 17-31.

Empididae. Biol. Centrali-Americana. Diptera (Supplement) pp. 366-376. (With A. L. Melander).

A Neglected Factor in Evolution. Science, n.s., vol. 15, no. 385, pp. 766-774.

Natural History, Oecology or Ethology? Science, n.s., vol. 15, pp. 971-976.

Formica fusca Linn. subsp. *subpolita* Mayr. var. *perpilosa* n. var. Mem. y Rev. Soc. Cient. "Antonia Alzate", Mexico, vol. 17, pp. 141-142.

New Agricultural Ants from Texas. Psyche, vol. 9, pp. 387-393.

Translation of Carlo Emery's "An Analytical Key to the Genera of the Family Formicidae, for the Identification of the Workers". American Naturalist, vol. 36, pp. 707-725.

Review of "Temperaturverhältnisse bei Insekten" by P. Bachmetjew. American Naturalist, vol. 36, pp. 401-405.

Review of "The Elements of Insect Anatomy" by J. H. Comstock and V. L. Kellogg. Science, n.s., vol. 16, pp. 351-352.

An American Cerapachys, with Remarks on the Affinities of the Cerapachyinae. Biol. Bull., vol. 3, pp. 181-191, 5 figs.

The Occurrence of *Formica cinera* Mayr and *Formica rufibarbis* Fabricius in America. American Naturalist, vol. 36, pp. 947-952.

1903

Review of James Mark Baldwin's "Development and Evolution". Psyche, vol. 10, pp. 70-80.

Erebomyrma, A New Genus of Hypogaeic Ants from Texas. Biol. Bull., vol. 4, pp. 137-148, 5 figs.

Dimorphic Queens in an American Ant. (*Lasius latipes* Walsh). Biol. Bull., vol. 4, pp. 149-163, 3 figs. (with J. F. McClendon).

Ethological Observations on an American Ant. (*Leptothorax emersoni* Wheeler). Arch. f. Psychol. u. Neurol., vol. 2, pp. 1-31, 1 fig.

A Revision of the North American Ants of the Genus Leptothorax. Proc. Acad. Nat. Sci. Philadelphia, pp. 215-260, 1 pl.

Review of T. W. Headley's "Problems of Evolution".
Psychol. Rev., vol. 10, pp. 193-199.

A Decade of Texan Formicidae. Psyche, vol. 10, pp.
93-111, 10 figs.

The North American Ants of the Genus Stenamma (*sensu stricto*). Psyche, vol. 10, pp. 164-168.

How Can Endowments be Used Most Effectively for Scientific Research? Science, n.s., vol. 17, pp. 577-579.

The Origin of Female and Worker Ants from the Eggs of Parthenogenetic Workers. Science, n.s., vol. 18, pp. 830-833.

Review of "Report on the Collections of Natural History made in the Artarctic Regions during the Voyage of the "Southern Cross", London, 1902. Bull. American Geog. Soc., vol. 35, pp. 572-573.

Some Notes on the Habits of *Cerapachys augustæ*. Psyche, vol. 10, pp. 205-209, 1 fig.

Extraordinary Females in three Species of Formica, with Remarks on Mutation in the Formicidae. Bull. American Mus. Nat. Hist., vol. 19, pp. 639-651, 3 figs.

Some New Gynandromorphous Ants, with a Review of the Previously Recorded Cases. Bull. American Mus. Nat. Hist., vol. 19, pp. 653-683, 11 figs.

1904

Translation of August Forel's "Ants and Some Other Insects. An inquiry into the Psychic Powers of these Animals with an Appendix on the Peculiarities of their Olfactory Sense". The Monist, vol. 14, Nos. 1 & 2, Oct. & Jan. 1903-1904, pp. 33-36, Reprinted as No. 56 of the Religion of Science Library. Chicago, 1904, pp. 1-49.

Three New Genera of Inquiline Ants from Utah and Colorado. Bull. American Mus. Nat. Hist., vol. 20, pp. 1-17, 2 pls.

Review of C. W. Dodge's "General Zoology Practical, Systematic and Comparative". Science, n.s., vol. 18, pp. 824-825.

Review of E. E. Austen's "A Monograph of the Tsetse-flies (Genus Glossima, Westwood) based on the Collection in the British Museum". Bull. American Geog. Soc., vol. 35, pp. 573-575.

Woodcock Surgery. Science, n.s., vol. 19, No. 478, pp. 347-350.

The Obligations of the Student of Animal Behavior. The Auk, vol. 21, pp. 251-255.

A Crustacean-eating Ant (*Leptogenys* (*Lobopelta*) *elongata* Buckley). Biol. Bull., vol. 6, pp. 251-259, 1 fig.

The American Ants of the Subgenus Colobopsis. Bull. American Mus. Nat. Hist., vol. 20, pp. 139-158, 7 figs.

Dr. Castle and the Dzierzon Theary. Science, n.s., vol. 19, pp. 587-591.

The Ants of North Carolina. Bull. American Mus. Nat. Hist., vol. 20, pp. 299-306.

On the Pupation of Ants and the Feasibility of Establishing the Guatemalan Kelep, or Cotton-Weevil Ant in the United States. Science, n.s., vol. 20, pp. 437-440.

Social Parasitism Among Ants. American Mus. Journ., vol. 4, pp. 74-75.

A New Type of Social Parasitism Among Ants. Bull. American Mus. Nat. Hist., vol. 20, pp. 347- 375.

The Phylogeny of the Termites. Biol. Bull., vol. 8, pp. 29-37.

Some Further Comments on the Guatemalan Boll Weevil Ant. Science, n.s., vol. 20, pp. 766-768.

1905

An Interpretation of the Slave-making Instincts in Ants. Bull. American Mus. Nat. Hist., vol. 21, pp. 1-16.

Ethology and the Mutation Theory. Science, n.s., vol. 21, pp. 535-540.

The Ants of the Bahamas, with a List of the Known West Indian Species. Bull. American Mus. Nat. Hist., vol. 21, pp. 79-135, 1 pl., 23 figs.

Some Remarks on Temporary Social Parasitism and the Phylogeny of Slavery among Ants. Biol. Centralbl., vol. 25, pp. 637-644.

New Species of Formica. Bull. American Mus. Nat. Hist., vol. 21, pp. 267-274.

Ants from Catalina Island, California. Bull. American Mus. Nat. Hist., vol. 20, pp. 269-271. Same in Bull. Southern California Acad. Sci., vol. 4, 1905, pp. 60-63.

The Structure of Wings. Bird Lore, vol. 7, pp. 257-262.

A New Myzostoma, Parasitic in a Starfish. Biol. Bull., vol. 8, pp. 75-78, 1 fig.

How the Queens of the Parasitic and Slave-making Ants Establish their Colonies. American Mus. Journ., vol. 5, pp. 144-148.

The North American Ants of the Genus Dolichoderus. Bull. American Mus. Nat. Hist., vol. 21, pp. 305-319, 2 pls., 3 figs.

The North American Ants of the Genus Liometopum. Bull. American Mus. Nat. Hist., vol. 21, pp. 321-333, 3 figs.

An Annotated List of the Ants of New Jersey. Bull. American Mus. Nat. Hist., vol. 21, pp. 371-403, 4 figs.

Ants from the Summit of Mount Washington. Psyche, vol. 12, pp. 111-114.

Worker Ants with Vestiges of Wings. Bull. American Mus. Nat. Hist., vol. 21, pp. 405-408, 1 pl.

Dr. O. F. Cook's "Social Organization and Breeding Habits of the Cotton-Protecting Kelep of Guatemala". Science, n.s., vol. 21, pp. 706-710.

The Habits of the Tent-building Ant (*Crematogaster lineolata* Say). Bull. American Mus. Nat. Hist., vol. 22, pp. 1-18, 6 pls.

On the Founding of Colonies by Queen Ants, with Special Reference to the Parasitic and Slave-making Species. Bull. American Mus. Nat. Hist., vol. 22, pp. 33-105, 7 pls.

On Certain Tropical Ants Introduced into the United States. Entom. News, vol. 17, pp. 23-26.

The Ant Queen as a Psychological Study. Popular Science Monthly, vol. 68, pp. 291-299, 7 figs.

The Kelep Excused. Science, n.s., vol. 23, pp. 348-350.

Pelastoneurus nigrescens Wheeler, a synonym of *P. dissimilipes* Wheeler: a Correction. Entom. News, vol. 17, p. 69.

New Ants from New England. Psyche, vol. 13, pp. 38-41, 1 pl.

Fauna of New England. List of the Formicidae. Occas. Papers, Boston Soc. Nat. Hist., vol. 7, pp. 1-24.

A New Wingless Fly (*Puliciphora borinquenensis*) from Porto Rico. Bull. American Mus. Nat. Hist., vol. 22, pp. 267-271, 1 pl.

The Ants of Japan. Bull. American Mus. Nat. Hist., vol. 22, pp. 301-328, 1 pl., 2 figs.

The Ants of the Grand Canyon. Bull. American Mus. Nat. Hist., vol. 22, pp. 329-345.

The Ants of the Bermudas. Bull. American Mus. Nat. Hist., vol. 22, pp. 347-352, 1 fig.

Concerning *Monomorium destructor* Jerdon. Entom. News, vol. 17, p. 265.

An Ethological Study of Certain Maladjustments in the Relations of Ants to Plants. Bull. American Mus. Nat. Hist., vol. 22, pp. 403-418, 7 pls.

The Expedition to Colorado for Fossil Insects. The American Mus. Journ., vol. 6, pp. 199-203, 5 figs.

1907

A Collection of Ants from British Honduras. Bull. American Mus. Nat. Hist., vol. 23, pp. 271-277, 2 pls.

The Polymorphism of Ants, with an Account of Some Singular Abnormalities due to Parasitism. Bull. American Mus. Nat. Hist., vol. 23, pp. 1-93, 6 pls.

Notes on a New Guest Ant, *Leptothorax glacialis,* and the varieties of *Myrmica brevinodis* Emery. Bull. Wisconsin Nat. Hist. Soc., vol. 5, pp. 70-83.

On Certain Modified Hairs Peculiar to the Ants of Arid Regions. Biol. Bull., vol. 13, pp. 185-202, 14 figs.

The Fungus-growing Ants of North America. Bull. American Mus. Nat. Hist., vol. 23, pp. 669-807, 5 pls., 31 figs.

The Origin of Slavery Among Ants. Popular Science Monthly, vol. 71, pp. 550-559.

Pink Insect Mutants. American Naturalist, vol. 41, pp. 773-780.

1908

The Ants of Porto Rico and the Virgin Islands. Bull. American Mus. Nat. Hist., vol. 24, pp. 117-158, 2 pls., 4 figs.

Comparative ethology of the European and North American Ants. Journ. Psychol. u. Neurol., vol. 13, pp. 404-435, 2 pls., 5 figs.

The Ants of Jamaica. Bull. American Mus. Nat. Hist., vol. 24, pp. 159-163.

Ants from Moorea, Society Islands. Bull. American Mus. Nat. Hist., vol. 24, pp. 165-167.

Ants from the Azores. Bull. American Mus. Nat. Hist., vol. 24, pp. 169-170.

Vestigial Instincts in Insects and Other Animals. American Journ. Psychol., vol. 19, pp. 1-13.

Studies on Myrmecophiles. II. Hetaerius. Journ. New York Entom. Soc., vol. 16, pp. 135-143.

The Ants of Texas, New Mexico and Arizona. I. Bull. American Mus. Nat. Hist., vol. 24, pp. 399-485, 2 pls.

Honey Ants, with a Revision of the American Myrmecocysti. Bull. American Mus. Nat. Hist., vol. 24, pp. 345-397, 28 figs.

The Polymorphism of Ants. Ann. Ent. Soc. America, vol. 1, pp. 39-69, 1 pl.

Studies on Myrmecophiles. I. Cremastochilus. Journ. New York Entom. Soc., vol. 16, pp. 68-79, 3 figs.

The Ants of Casco Bay, Maine, with Observations on Two Races of *Formica sanguinea* Latreille. Bull. American Mus. Nat. Hist., vol. 24, pp. 619-645.

A European Ant (*Myrmica levinodis*) Introduced into Massachusetts. Journ. Econ. Entom, vol. 1, pp. 337-339.

Studies on Myrmecophiles. III. Microdon. Journ. New York Entom. Soc., vol. 16, pp. 202-213, 1 fig.

1909

A Small Collection of Ants from Victoria, Australia. Journ. New York Entom. Soc., vol. 17, pp. 25-29.

Ants collected by Professor Filippo Silvestri in Mexico. Bull. Lab. Zool. Gen. e. Agrar. R. Scuola Sup. Agric. Portici, vol. 3, pp. 228-238.

Review of P. Deegener's "Die Metamorphose der Insekten". Science, n.s., vol. 29, pp. 384-387.

Predarwinian and Postdarwinian Biology. Popular Science Monthly, vol. 74, pp. 381-385.

Ants Collected by Professor Filippo Silvestri in the Hawaiian Islands. Boll. Lab. Zool. Gen. e. Agrar. R. Scuola Sup. Agric. Portici, vol. 3, pp. 269-272.

Ants of Formosa and the Philippines. Bull. American Mus. Nat. Hist., vol. 26, pp. 333-345.

A Decade of North American Formicidae. Journ. New York Entom. Soc., vol. 17, pp. 77-90.

A New Honey Ant from California. Journ. New York Entom. Soc., vol. 17, pp. 98-99.

The Ants of Isle Royale, Michigan. Report Michigan Geol. Surv., 1908, pp. 325-328.

Review of A. D. Hopkins "The Genus Dendroctonus". Journ. Econ. Entom., vol. 2, pp. 471-472.

Observations on Some European Ants. Journ. New York Entom. Soc., vol. 17, pp. 172-187, 2 figs.

1910

Ants: Their Structure, Development and Behavior. (Columbia University Biological Series vol. 9) Columbia Univ. Press, New York, 1910, pp. xxv+663, 286 figs.

Two New Myrmecophilous Mites of the Genus Antennophorus. Psyche, vol. 17, pp. 1-6, 2 pls.

Review of W. Dwight Pierce's "A Monographic Revision of the Twisted Winged Insects Comprising the Order Strepsiptera Kirby". Journ. Econ. Entom., vol. 3, pp. 252-253.

Small Artificial Ant-Nests of Novel Patterns. Psyche, vol. 17, pp. 73-75, 1 fig.

Review of H. Friese's "Die Bienen Afrikas". Science, n.s., vol. 31, pp. 580-582.

The Effects of Parasitic and Other Kinds of Castration in Insects. Journ. Exper. Zoöl., vol. 8, pp. 377-438, 8 figs.

Colonies of Ants (*Lasius neoniger* Emery) Infested with *Laboulbenia formicarum* Thaxter. Psyche, vol. 17, pp. 83-86.

An Aberrant Lasius from Japan. Biol. Bull., vol. 19, pp. 130-137, 2 figs.

Three New Genera of Myrmicine Ants from Tropical America. Bull. American Mus. Nat. Hist., vol. 28, pp. 259-265, 3 figs.

A New Species of Aphomomyrmex from Borneo. Psyche, vol. 17, pp. 131-135, 1 fig.

A Gynandromorphous Mutillid. Psyche, vol. 17, pp. 186-190, 1 fig.

The North American Forms of *Lasius umbratus* Nylander. Psyche, vol. 17, pp. 235-243.

The North American Forms of *Camponotus fallax* Nylander. Journ. New York Entom. Soc., vol. 18, pp. 216-232.

The North American Ants of the Genus Camponotus Mayr. Ann. New York Acad. Sci., vol. 20, pp. 295-354.

A List of New Jersey Formicidae in J. B. Smith's Report of the Insects of New Jersey, 1910, pp. 655-663.

1911

The Ant-Colony as an Organism. Journ. Morph., vol. 22, pp. 307-325.

Additions to the Ant-fauna of Jamaica. Bull. American Mus. Nat. Hist., vol. 30, pp. 21-29.

Review of K. Escherich's "Termitenleben auf Ceylon". Science, n.s., vol. 33, pp. 530-534.

On *Melanetærius infernalis* Fall. Psyche, vol. 18, pp. 112-114, 1 fig.

Two Fungus-Growing Ants from Arizona. Psyche, vol. 18, pp. 93-101, 2 figs.

A New Camponotus from California. Journ. New York Entom. Soc., vol. 19, pp. 96-98.

Three Formicid Names which have been Overlooked. Science, n.s., vol. 33, pp. 858-860.

Ants Collected in Grenada, W.I., by Mr. C. T. Brues. Bull. Mus. Comp. Zoöl., vol. 54, pp. 167-172.

Review of v. Kirchner's "Blumen und Insekten". Science, n.s., vol. 34, pp. 57-58.

A List of the Type Species of the Genera and Subgenera of Formicidae. Ann. New York Acad. Sci., vol. 21, pp. 157-175.

Literature for 1910 on the Behavior of Ants, their Guests and Parasites. Journ. Anim. Behavior, vol. 1, pp. 413-429.

Notes on the Myrmecophilous Beetles of the Genus Xenodusa, with a description of the Larva of *X. cava* Leconte. Journ. New York Entom. Soc., vol. 19, pp. 163-169.

Pseudoscorpions in Ant Nests. Psyche, vol. 18, pp. 166-168.

Descriptions of Some New Fungus-growing Ants from Texas, with Mr. C. G. Hartman's Observations on their Habits. Journ. New York Entom. Soc., vol. 19, pp. 245-255, 1 pl.

An Ant-nest Coccinellid (*Brachyacantha 4-punctata* Mels.). Journ. New York Entom. Soc., vol. 19, pp. 169-174, 1 fig.

Miastor Larvae in Connecticut. Journ. New York Entom. Soc., vol. 19, p. 201.

Lasius (Acanthomyops) claviger in Tahiti. Journ. New York Entom. Soc., vol. 19, p. 262.

A Desert Cockroach. Journ. New York Entom. Soc., vol. 19, pp. 262-263.

Three New Ants from Mexico and Central America. Psyche, vol. 18, pp. 203-208.

Insect Parasitism and its Peculiarities. Popular Science Monthly, vol. 79, pp. 431-449.

1912

The Ants of Guam. Journ. New York Entom. Soc., vol. 20, pp. 44-48.

New Names for Some North American Ants of the Genus Formica. Psyche, vol. 19, p. 90.

Notes on a Mistletoe Ant. Journ. New York Entom. Soc., vol. 20, pp. 130-133.

Notes About Ants and Their Resemblance to Man. Nat. Geogr. Mag., vol. 23, pp. 731-766, 34 figs.

Additions to our Knowledge of the Ants of the Genus Myrmecocystus Wesmael. Psyche, vol. 19, pp. 172-181, 1 fig.

The Male of *Eciton vagans* Olivier. Psyche, vol. 19, pp. 206-207.

Review of J. H. Comstock's "Spider Book". Science, n.s., vol. 36, pp. 745-746.

1913

Notes on the Habits of Some Central American Stingless Bees. Psyche, vol. 20, pp. 1-9.

A Giant Coccid from Guatemala. Psyche, vol. 20, pp. 31-33, 1 fig.

Review of Sladen's "The Humble Bee, its Life History and How to Domesticate it". Science, n.s., vol. 37, pp. 180-182.

A Revision of the Ants of the Genus Formica (L.) Mayr. Bull. Mus. Comp. Zoöl., vol. 53, pp. 379-565, 10 figs.

Observations on the Central American Acacia Ants. Trans. 2nd Internat. Entom. Congress, Oxford, 1912, vol. 2, pp. 109-139.

Hymenoptera II; Ants (Formicidae). Rec. Indian Mus., vol. 8, pp. 233-237.

Corrections and Additions to the "List of the Type Species of Genera and Subgenera of Formicidae". Ann. New York Acad. Sci., vol. 23, pp. 77-83.

Ants Collected in Georgia by Mr. J. C. Bradley and Mr. W. T. Davis. Psyche, vol. 20, pp. 112-117.

The Ants of Cuba. Bull. Mus. Comp. Zoöl., vol. 54, pp. 477-505.

Ants Collected in the West Indies. Bull. American Mus. Nat. Hist., vol. 32, pp. 239-244.

A Solitary Wasp (*Aphilanthops frigidus* F. Smith) that Provisions its Nest with Queen Ants. Journ. Anim. Behavior, vol. 3, pp. 374-387.

1914

The Ants of the Baltic Amber. Schrift. Physik-ökonom. Gesellsch. Königsberg, vol. 55, pp. 1-142, 66 figs.

The Ants of Haiti. Bull. American Mus. Nat. Hist., vol. 33, pp. 1-61, 27 figs. (with W. M. Mann).

Gynandromorphous Ants Described During the Decade 1903-1913. American Naturalist, vol. 48, pp. 49-56.

Ants Collected by Mr. W. M. Mann in the State of Hidalgo, Mexico. Journ. New York Entom. Soc., vol. 22, pp. 37-61.

Review of O. M. Reuter's "Lebensgewohnheiten und Instinkte der Insekten bis zum Erwachen der sozialen Instinkte". Science, n.s., vol. 39, pp. 69-71.

Formica exsecta in Japan. Psyche, vol. 21, pp. 26-27.

Notes on the Habits of Liomyrmex. Psyche, vol. 21, pp. 76-77.

Ants and Bees as Carriers of Pathogenic Microörganisms. American Journ. Trop. Diseases and Prevent. Med., vol. 2, pp. 160-168.

The American Species of Myrmica Allied to *M. rubida* Latreille. Psyche, vol. 21, pp. 118-122, 1 fig.

New and Little Known Harvesting Ants of the Genus Pogonomyrmex. Psyche, vol. 21, pp. 149-157.

1915

The Luminous Organ of the New Zealand Glow-worm. Psyche, vol. 22, pp. 36-43, 1 pl. (with F. X. Williams).

A New Linguatulid from Ecuador. Rept. First Harvard Exped. to South America (1913), appendix, pp. 207-208, 1 pl.

Neomyrma *versus* Oreomyrma, a Correction. Psyche, vol. 22, p. 50.

Some Additions to the North American Ant-fauna. Bull. American Mus. Nat. Hist., vol. 34, pp. 389-421.

The Australian Honey-Ants of the Genus Leptomyrmex Mayr. Proc. American Acad. Arts and Sci., vol. 51, pp. 255-286, 12 figs.

Paranomopone, a New Genus of Ponerine Ants from

Queensland. Psyche, vol. 22, pp. 117-120, 1 pl.

Hymenoptera. In "Scientific Notes on an Expedition into the North-western Regions of South Australia". Trans. Roy. Soc. South Australia, vol. 39, pp. 805-823, 3 pls.

A New Bog-inhabiting Variety of *Formica fusca* L. Psyche, vol. 22, pp. 203-206.

Two New Genera of Myrmicine Ants from Brazil. Bull. Mus. Comp. Zoöl., vol. 59, pp. 45-54, 2 pls.

On the Presence and Absence of Cocoons among Ants, the Nest-spinning habits of the Larvae and the Significance of the Black Cocoons Among Certain Australian Species. Ann. Entom. Soc. America, vol. 8, pp. 323-342, 5 figs.

1916

The Marriage-flight of a Bull-dog Ant (*Myrmecia sanguinea* F. Smith). Journ. Anim. Behavior, vol. 6, pp. 70-73.

Formicoidea. In "The Hymenoptera of Connecticut". Connecticut State Geol. & Nat. Hist. Surv., Bull. 22, pp. 577-601.

Prodiscothyrea, a New Genus of Ponerine Ants from Queensland. Trans. Roy. Soc. South Australia, vol. 40, pp. 33-37, 1 pl.

The Australian Ants of the Genus Onychomyrmex Emery. Bull. Mus. Comp. Zoöl., vol. 60, pp. 45-54, 2 pls.

Ants Collected in British Guiana by the Expedition of the American Museum of Natural History during 1911. Bull. American Mus. Nat. Hist., vol. 35, pp. 1-14.

The Ants of the Phillips Expedition to Palestine during 1914. Bull. Mus. Comp. Zoöl., vol. 60, pp. 167-174, 1 fig. (with W. M. Mann).

Ants Collected in Trinidad by Professor Roland Thaxter, Mr. F. W. Urich and Others. Bull. Mus. Comp. Zoöl., vol. 60, pp. 323-330, 1 fig.

Jean-Henri Fabre. Journ. Anim. Behavior, vol. 6, pp. 74-80.

Four New and Interesting Ants from the Mountains of Borneo and Luzon. Proc. New England Zoöl. Club, vol. 6, pp. 9-18, 4 figs.

Review of H. St. J. K. Donisthorpe's "British Ants, Their Life-History and Classification". Science, n.s., vol. 43, pp. 316-318.

Some New Formicid Names. Psyche, vol. 23, p. 40.

Notes on Some Slave Raids of the Western Amazon Ant (*Polyergus breviceps* Emery). Journ. New York Entom. Soc., vol. 24, pp. 107-118.

The Australian Ants of the Genus Aphaenogaster Mayr. Trans. Roy. Soc. South Australia, vol. 40, pp. 213-223, 2 pls.

The Mountain Ants of Western North America. Proc. American Acad. Arts & Sci., vol. 52, pp. 457-569.

Note on the Brazilian Fire Ant, *Solenopsis sævissima* F. Smith. Psyche, vol. 23, pp. 142-143.

An Anomalous Blind Worker Ant. Psyche, vol. 23, pp. 143-145, 2 figs.

Questions of Nomenclature Connected with the Ant Genus Lasius and its Subgenera. Psyche, vol. 23, pp. 168-173.

Two New Ants from Texas and Arizona. Proc. New England Zoöl. Club, vol. 6, pp. 29-35, 2 figs.

A Phosphorescent Ant. Psyche, vol. 23, pp. 173-174.

An Indian Ant Introduced into the United States. Journ. Econ. Entom., vol. 9, pp. 566-569, 1 fig.

The Australian Ant-Genus Myrmecorhynchus Ern. André and its Position in the Subfamily Camponotinae. Trans. Roy. Soc. South Australia, vol. 41, pp. 14-19.

Ants Carried in a Floating Log from the Brazilian Mainland to San Sebastian Island. Psyche, vol. 23, pp. 180-183.

1917

A New Malayan Ant of the Genus Prodiscothyrea. Psyche, vol. 24, pp. 29-30.

A List of Indiana Ants. Proc. Indiana Acad. Sci., 1917, pp. 460-466.

The North American Ants Described by Asa Fitch. Psyche, vol. 24, pp. 26-29.

The Ants of Alaska. Bull. Mus. Comp. Zoöl., vol. 61, pp. 15-22.

The Phylogenetic Development of Apterous and Subapterous Castes in the Formicidae. Proc. Nat. Acad. Sci., vol. 3, pp. 109-117.

The Synchronic Behavior of Phalangidae. Science, n.s., vol. 45, pp. 189-190.

Jamaican Ants Collected by Prof. C. T. Brues. Bull. Mus. Comp. Zoöl., vol. 61, pp. 457-471, 2 pls., 3 figs.

The Temporary Social Parasitism of *Lasius subumbratus* Viereck. Psyche, vol. 24, pp. 167-176.

Notes on the Marriage Flights of Some Sonoran Ants. Psyche, vol. 24, pp. 177-180.

The Pleometrosis of Myrmecocystus. Psyche, vol. 24, pp. 180-182.

1918

The Ants of the Genus Opisthopsis Emery. Bull. Mus. Comp. Zoöl., vol. 62, pp. 343-362, 3 pls.

The Australian Ants of the Ponerine Tribe Cerapachyini. Proc. American Acad. Arts & Sci., vol. 53, pp. 215-265.

Ants Collected in British Guiana by Mr. C. William Beebe. Journ. New York Entom. Soc., vol. 26, pp. 23-28.

A Great Opportunity for Applied Science. Harvard Alumni Bulletin, vol. 20, pp. 264-266.

A Study of Some Ant Larvae, with a Consideration of the Origin and Meaning of the Social Habit among Insects. Proc. American Philos. Soc., vol. 57, pp. 293-343, 12 figs.

Vermileo comstocki sp. nov., an Interesting Leptid fly from California. Proc. New England Zoöl. Club, vol. 6, pp. 83-84.

Quick Key to a Knowledge of Common Insects: Review of F. E. Lutz's "Field Book of Insects". American Mus. Journ., vol. 18, pp. 381-382.

Introduction to Phil and Nellie Rau's "Wasp Studies Afield". Princeton Univ. Press, 1918, pp. 1-8.

1919

Two Gynandromorphous Ants. Psyche, vol. 26, pp. 1-8, 2 figs.

The Parasitic Aculeata, A Study in Evolution. Proc. American Philosoph. Soc., vol. 58, pp. 1-40.

The Ants of Borneo. Bull. Mus. Comp. Zoöl., vol. 63, pp. 43-157.

A New Subspecies of *Aphænogaster treatæ* Forel. Psyche, vol. 26, p. 50.

The Ant Genus Lordomyrma Emery. Psyche, vol. 26, pp. 97-106, 4 figs.

A New Paper-making Crematogaster from the Southeastern United States. Psyche, vol. 26, pp. 107-112.

The Ants of Tobago Island. Psyche, vol. 26, p. 113.

The Ant Genus Metapone Forel. Ann. Entom. Soc. America, vol. 12, pp. 173-191, 7 figs.

The Ants of the Galapagos Islands. Proc. California Acad. Sci., vol. 2, pp. 259-297.

The Ants of Cocos Island. Proc. California Acad. Sci., vol. 2, pp. 299-308.

A Singular Neotropical Ant (*Pseudomyrma filiformis* Fabricius). Psyche, vol. 26, pp. 124-131, 3 figs.

The Phoresy of Antherophagus. Psyche, vol. 26, pp. 145-152, 1 fig.

1920

The Termitodoxa, or Biology and Society. Scientific Monthly, vol. 10, pp. 113-124.

The Subfamilies of Formicidae, and Other Taxonomic Notes. Psyche, vol. 27, pp. 46-55, 3 figs.

Euponera gilva Roger, a Rare North American Ant. Psyche, vol. 27, pp. 69-72. (with F. M. Gaige).

Charles Gordon Hewitt. Journ. Econ. Entom., vol. 13, pp. 262-263.

The Feeding Habits of Pseudomyrmine and Other Ants. Trans. American Philos. Soc., vol. 22, pp. 235-279, 5 pls. (with I. W. Bailey).

Review of Bouvier "La Vie Psychique des Insectes". Science, n.s., vol. 52, pp. 443-446.

1921

A New Case of Parabiosis and the Ant Gardens of British Guiana. Ecology, vol. 2, pp. 89-103, 3 figs.

The Organization of Research. Science, n.s., vol. 53, pp. 53-67.

Chinese Ants. Bull. Mus. Comp. Zoöl., vol. 64, pp. 529-547.

Observations on Army Ants in British Guiana. Proc. American Acad. Arts & Sci., vol. 56, pp. 291-328, 10 figs.

Professor Emery's Subgenera of the Genus Camponotus Mayr. Psyche, vol. 28, pp. 16-19.

A Study of Some Social Beetles in British Guiana and of Their Relations to the Ant-plant, Tachigalia. Zoölogica, New York, vol. 3, pp. 35-126, 5 pls., 12 figs.

The Tachigalia Ants. Zoölogica, New York, vol. 3, pp. 137-168, 4 figs.

Notes on the Habits of European and North American

Cucujidae. Zoölogica, New York, vol. 3, pp. 173-183.
On Instincts. Journ. Abnorm. Psych., vol. 15, pp. 295-318.
Chinese Ants Collected by Prof. C. W. Howard. Psyche,
vol. 28, pp. 110-115, 2 figs.
Vespa arctica Rohwer, a Parasite of *Vespa diabolica* De
Saussure. Psyche, vol. 28, pp. 135-144, 3 figs. (with L. H.
Taylor).

1922
Ants of the Genus Formica in the Tropics. Psyche, vol.
19, pp. 174-177.
The Ants of Trinidad. American Mus. Novitates, No. 45,
pp. 1-16, 1 fig.
A New Genus and Subgenus of Myrmicinae from Tropical
America. American Mus. Novitates, No. 46, pp. 1-6, 2 figs.
Report on the Ants of the Belgian Congo. Bull. American
Mus. Nat. Hist., vol. 45, pp. 1-1139. (with the collaboration
of J. Bequaert, I. W. Bailey, F. Santschi, and W. M. Mann).

I.   On the Distribution of the Ants of the Ethiopian and
     Malagasy Regions, pp. 13-37.
II. The Ants Collected by the American Museum Congo
     Expedition, pp. 39-270.
VII. Keys to the Genera and Subgenera of Ants, pp.
     631-710.
VIII. A Synonymic List of the Ants of the Ethiopian
     Region, pp. 711-1004.
IX. A Synonymic List of the Ants of the Malagasy Region,
     pp. 1005-1055.

Observations on *Gigantiops destructor* Fabricius, and
Other Leaping Ants. Biol. Bull., vol. 42, pp. 185-201, 3 figs.
Neotropical Ants of the Genera Carebara, Tranopelta and
Tranopeltoides, New Genus. American Mus. Novitates, No.
48, pp. 1-14, 3 figs.
The Mating of Diacamma. Psyche, vol. 29, pp. 203-211,
4 figs. (with J. W. Chapman).

1923
The Dry-Rot of Our Academic Biology. Science, n.s., vol.
57, pp. 61-71.
A Singular Habit of Sawfly Larvae. Psyche, vol. 30, pp.
9-13, 1 fig. (with W. M. Mann).
Formicidae from Easter Island and Juan Fernandez. In

"The Natural History of Juan Fernandez and Easter Island". Ed. by Dr. Carl Skottsberg, vol. 3, pp. 317-319.

Report on the ants Collected by the Barbados-Antigua Expedition from the University of Iowa in 1918. Univ. of Iowa Studies Nat. Hist., vol. 10, pp. 3-9.

Social Life Among the Insects. Scientific Monthly, vol. 14, 15 and 16, June 1922—March 1923: 14, pp. 497-525; 15, pp. 67-88; 119-131; 235-256; 320-337; 385-404; 527-541; 16, pp. 5-33; 159-176; 312-329.

Chinese Ants Collected by Professor S. F. Light and Professor A. P. Jacot. American Mus. Novitates, No. 69, pp. 1-6.

Formicidae. Wissenschaftliche Ergebnisse der Schwedischen entomologischen Reise des Herrn Dr. A. Roman in Amazonas 1914-1915. Arkiv. f. Zool., vol. 15, No. 7, pp. 1-6.

Social Life Among the Insects, pp. 3+375. Harcourt, Brace & Co., New York.

Ants of the Genera Myopias and Acanthoponera. Psyche, vol. 30, pp. 175-192, 5 figs.

The Occurrence of Winged Females in the Ant Genus Leptogenys Roger, with Descriptions of New Species. American Mus. Novitates, No. 90, 16 pp., 5 figs.

1924

Two Extraordinary Larval Myrmecophiles from Panama. Proc. Nat. Acad. Sci., vol. 10, pp. 237-244, 3 figs.

A Gynandromorph of *Tetramorium guineënse* Fabr. Psyche, vol. 31, pp. 136-137, 1 fig.

Hymenoptera of the Siju Cave, Garo Hills, Assam. Records of the Indian Museum, vol. 26, Pt. 1, pp. 123-125.

On the Ant-genus Chrysapace Crawley. Psyche, vol. 31, pp. 224-225.

The Formicidae of the Harrison Williams Expedition to the Galapagos Islands. Zoölogica, New York, vol. 5, pp. 101-122, 8 figs.

Ants of Krakatau and Other Islands in the Sunda Strait. Treubia, vol. 5, pp. 1-20, 1 map.

1925

Courtship of the Calobates; The Kelep Ant and the Courtship of its Mimic *Cardiacephala myrmex*. Journ. Heredity, vol. 15, pp. 485-495, 8 figs.

A New Guest-Ant and other new Formicidae from Barro

Colorado Island, Panama. Biol. Bull., vol. 49, pp. 150-181, 8 figs.

The Ants of the Philippine Islands. Part I. Dorylinae and Ponerinae. Philippine Journ. Sci., vol. 28, pp. 47-73, 2 pls. (with J. W. Chapman).

Neotropical Ants in the Collections of the Royal Museum of Stockholm. Part. I. Ark. Zool., vol. 17A, No. 8, pp. 1-55.

Zoölogical Results of the Swedish Expedition to Central Africa 1921. Insecta 10, Formicidae. Ark. Zool., vol. 17A, No. 25, pp. 1-3.

The Finding of the Queen of the Army ant *Eciton hamatum* Fabricius. Biol. Bull., vol. 49, pp. 139-149, 8 figs.

L'Evolution des Insectes Sociaux. Rev. Scient., vol. 63, pp. 548-557, 6 figs.

Carlo Emery. Entom. News, vol. 36, pp. 318-320.

1926

Les Sociéteés d'Insectes: leur origine, leur évolution. Doin, Paris, 468 pp.

Translation of an unpublished manuscript of Réaumur, "The Natural History of Ants". 280 pp. New York, A. A. Knopf, 1926.

Social Habits of Some Canary Island Spiders. Psyche, vol. 33, pp. 29-31.

A New Word for an Old Thing. (Review of Watson's "Behaviorism"). Quarterly Rev. of Biol., vol. 1, pp. 439-443.

Emergent Evolution and the Social. Science, n.s., vol. 44, pp. 433-440.

Ants of the Balearic Islands. Folia Myrmecologica et Termitologica, vol. 1, pp. 1-6.

1927

The Occurrence of *Formica fusca* Linné in Sumatra. Psyche, vol. 34, pp. 40-41.

Burmese Ants Collected by Professor G. E. Gates. Psyche, vol. 34, pp. 42-46.

Chinese Ants Collected by Professor S. F. Light and Professor N. Gist Gee. American Mus. Novitates, No. 255, pp. 1-12.

The Physiognomy of Insects. Quarterly Rev. of Biol., vol. 2, pp. 1-36.

Ants Collected by Professor F. Silvestri in Indochina.

Boll. Lab. Zoöl. Gen. Agrar. Portici, vol. 20, pp. 83-106, 9 figs.

Ants of the Genus Amblyopone Erichson. Proc. American Acad. Arts & Sci., vol. 62, pp. 1-29, 8 figs.

A Few Ants from China and Formosa. American Mus. Novitates, No. 259, pp. 1-4.

The Ants of the Canary Islands. Proc. American Acad. Arts & Sci., vol. 62, pp. 93-120, 2 pls.

The Ants of Lord Howe and Norfolk Island. Proc. American Acad. Arts & Sci., vol. 62, pp. 121-153, 12 figs.

Carl Akeley's Early Work and Environment. Natural History, vol. 27, pp. 133-141, 5 figs.

The Occurrence of the Pavement Ant (*Tetramorium cæspitum*) in Boston. Psyche, vol. 34, pp. 164-165.

Conserving the Family, a Review of three books on Human Reproduction and the Family. Journ. Hered., vol. 18, pp. 119-120.

Emergent Evolution and the Social. Psyche Miniatures, Gen. Ser. No. 11, London. Kegan Paul etc.

1928

Foibles of Insects and Men. xxvi+217+xi pp. A. Knopf, New York.

The Social Insects, their Origin and Evolution. 378 pp. London. Kegan Paul etc.

Ants Collected by Prof. F. Silvestri in China. Boll. Lab. Zoöl. Gen. Agrar., Portici, vol. 22, pp. 3-38, 3 figs.

The Evolution of Ants. In Frances Mason's "Creation by Evolution", pp. 210-224, New York, MacMillan.

A New Species of Probolomyrmex from Java. Psyche, vol. 35, pp. 7-9, 1 fig.

Ants of Nantucket Island, Mass. Psyche, vol. 35, pp. 10-11.

Mermis Parasitism and Intercastes among Ants. Journ. Exper. Zoöl., vol. 50, pp. 165-237, 17 figs.

Ants Collected by Prof. F. Silvestri in Japan and Korea. Boll. Lab. Zool. Gen. Agrar. Portici, vol. 21, pp. 96-125.

Emergent Evolution and the Development of Societies. 80 pp. New York, W. W. Norton.

Zatapinoma, a new Genus of Ants from India. Proc. New England Zoöl. Club, vol. 10, pp. 19-23, 1 fig.

Societal Evolution in E. V. Coundry's "Human Biology and

Racial Welfare." Chapter VI, pp. 139-155. New York, Hoeber.

1929

Amazonian Myrmecophytes and their Ants. Zool. Anz. (Wasmann-Festband), vol. 82, pp. 10-39. (with J. C. Bequaert).

Two Interesting Neotropical Myrmecophytes (*Cordia nodosa* and *C. alliodora*). IV. Int. Congress of Entom., Ithaca, Aug. 1928, vol. 2, pp. 342-353.

Present Tendencies in Biological Theory. Scientific Monthly, vol. 28, pp. 97-109.

The Identity of the Ant-genera Gesomyrmex Mayr and Dimorphomyrmex Ernest André. Psyche, vol. 36, pp. 1-12, 1 fig.

Three New Genera of Ants from the Dutch East Indies. American Mus. Novitates, No. 349, pp. 1-8.

Ants Collected by Professor F. Silvestri in Formosa, The Malay Peninsula and the Philippines. Boll. Lab. Zool. Gen. Agrar., Portici, vol. 24, pp. 27-64.

Two Neotropical Ants Established in the United States. Psyche, vol. 36, pp. 89-90.

Note on Gesomyrmex. Psyche, vol. 36, pp. 91-92.

The Ant-Genus Rhopalomastix. Psyche, vol. 36, pp. 95-101.

A Camponotus Mermithergate from Argentina. Psyche, vol. 36, pp. 102-106.

Some Ants from China and Manchuria. American Mus. Novitates, No. 361, pp. 1-11.

Review of H. Friedmann's "The Cowbirds, A Study in the Biology of Social Parasitism". Science, n.s., vol. 70, pp. 70-73.

The Entomological Discoveries of John Hunter In "Exercises in Celebration of the Bicentenary of the Birth of John Hunter". New England Journ. Medicine, 1929, pp. 810-823.

Is *Necrophylus arenarius* Roux the larva of *Pterocroce storeyi* Withycombe? Psyche, vol. 36, pp. 313-320.

1930

History of the Bussey Institution In S. E. Morison's "Development of Harvard University since the Inauguration of

Pres. Elliot 1869-1929". Harvard Univ. Pres, 1930, pp. 508-517.

The Ant *Prenolepis imparis* Say. Ann. Entom. Soc. America, vol. 23, pp. 1-24, 3 figs.

A Second Note on Gesomyrmex. Psyche, vol. 37, pp. 35-40.

Two New Genera of Ants from Australia and the Philippines. Psyche, vol. 37, pp. 41-47.

Two Mermithergates of Ectatomma. Psyche, vol. 37, pp. 48-54.

Formosan Ants Collected by Dr. R. Takahashi. Proc. New England Zoöl. Club, vol. 11, pp. 93-106, 2 figs.

A New Emeryella from Panama. Proc. New England Zoöl. Club, vol. 12, pp. 9-13, 1 fig.

A New Parasitic Crematogaster from Indiana. Psyche, vol. 37, pp. 55-60.

Review of Auguste Forel's "Social World of the Ants". Journ. Soc. Psychol., vol. 1, pp. 170-177.

Philippine Ants of the Genus Aenictus with Descriptions of the Females of Two Species. Journ. New York Entom. Soc., vol. 38, pp. 193-212, 7 figs.

Ant-tree Notes from Rio Frio, Colombia. Psyche, vol. 37, pp. 107-117, 1 pl. (with P. J. Darlington, Jr.).

Demons of the Dust, A Study in Insect Behavior. xviii+378 pp. W. W. Norton, New York.

1931

New and Little-known Species of Macromischa, Croesomyrmex and Antillaemyrmex. Bull. Mus. Comp. Zoöl., vol. 72, pp. 3-34.

A List of the Known Chinese Ants. Peking Nat. Hist. Bull., 1930-31, vol. 5, pp. 53-81.

What is Natural History? Bull. Boston Soc. Nat. Hist., No. 59, pp. 3-12.

Concerning Some Ant Gynandromorphs. Psyche, vol. 38, pp. 80-85.

Neotropical Ants of the Genus Xenomyrmex Forel. Rev. Entom., vol. 1, pp. 129-139.

Hopes in the Biological Sciences. Proc. American Philos. Soc., vol. 70, pp. 231-239.

The Ant *Camponotus* (*Myrmepomis*) *sericeiventris* Guérin and its Mimic. Psyche, vol. 38, pp. 86-98.

1932

Ænictoteras chapmani gen. et sp. nov., an Extraordinary Ant-Guest from the Philippines. Liv. du Centenaire Soc. Entom. France, 1932, pp. 301-310.

Ants of the Marquesas Islands. Bull. 98, Bernice P. Bishop Mus., Honolulu, pp. 155-163.

Ants from the Society Islands. Pacific Ent. Survey Publ. 6, article 3, pp. 13-19.

A Cuban Vermileo. Psyche, vol. 38, pp. 166-169.

A List of the Ants of Florida. Journ. New York Entom. Soc., vol. 40, pp. 1-17.

How the Primitive Ants of Australia Start their Colonies. Science, n.s., vol. 76, pp. 532-533.

Some Attractions of the Field Study of Ants. Scientific Monthly, vol. 34, pp. 397-402.

An Australian Leptanilla. Psyche, vol. 39, pp. 53-58, 1 fig.

1933

Colony-founding among Ants, with an Account of Some Primitive Australian species. 179 pp. Harvard Univ. Press, Cambridge.

The Lamarck Manuscripts at Harvard. 202 pp. Harvard Univ. Press, Cambridge. (with T. Barbour).

Mermis Parasitism in Some Australian and Mexican Ants. Psyche, vol. 40, pp. 20-31.

Unusual Prey of Bembix. Psyche, vol. 40, pp. 57-59. (with R. Dow).

Formicidae of the Templeton Crocker Expedition 1933. Proc. California Acad. Sci., vol. (4), 21, pp. 57-64.

New Ants from China and Japan. Psyche, vol. 40, pp. 65-67.

A Second Parasitic Crematogaster. Psyche, vol. 40, pp. 83-86.

Translation of Maurice Bedel's "My Uncles, Louis Bedel and Henri d'Orbigny". Rev. Biol., vol. 8, pp. 325-330, 1 fig.

A New Species of Ponera and Other Records of Ants from the Marquesas Islands. Bernice P. Bishop Mus., Honolulu, Bull. 114, pp. 141-144.

An Ant New to the Fauna of the Hawaiian Islands. Proc. Hawaiian Entom. Soc., vol. 8, pp. 275-278, 1 fig.

A New Myrmoteras from Java. Proc. New England Zoöl. Club, vol. 13, pp. 72-75, 1 fig.

Three Obscure Genera of Ponerine Ants. American Mus. Novitates, No. 672, pp. 1-23.

1934

Some Aberrant Species of Camponotus (Colobopsis) from the Fiji Islands. Ann. Entom. Soc. America, vol. 27, pp. 415-424.

Ants from the Islands off the West Coast of Lower California and Mexico. Pan Pacific Entom., vol. 10, pp. 132-144.

A Second Revision of the Ants of the Genus Leptomyrmex Mayr. Bull. Mus. Comp. Zoöl., vol. 77, pp. 67-118.

A Revised List of the Ants of the Hawaiian Islands. Occasional Papers, Bernice P. Bishop Mus., Honolulu, vol. 10, No. 21, pp. 1-21.

A Study of the Ant Genera Novomessor and Veromessor. Proc. American Acad. Arts & Sci., vol. 69, pp. 341-387. (with W. S. Creighton).

Animal Societies (Biology & Society). Scientific Monthly, vol. 39, pp. 289-301.

Formicidae of the Templeton Crocker Expedition 1932. Proc. California Acad. Sci., vol. 21, pp. 173-181, 1 fig.

Contributions to the Fauna of Rottnest Island, West Australia. Journ. Roy. Soc. Western Australia, vol. 20, pp. 137-163.

An Australian Ant of the Genus Leptothorax Mayr. Psyche, vol. 41, pp. 60-62.

A Specimen of the Jamaican Vermileo. Psyche, vol. 41, pp. 236-237.

Introduction to O. E. Plath's "Bumblebees, their Life History, Habits and Economic Importance", pp. vii-x. MacMillan Co., New York.

Neotropical Ants Collected by Dr. Elisabeth Skwarra and Others. Bull. Mus. Comp. Zoöl., vol. 77, pp. 157-240.

Some Ants from the Bahama Islands. Psyche, vol. 41, pp. 230-232.

1935

Two New Genera of Myrmicine Ants from Papua and the Philippines. Proc. New England Zoöl. Club, vol. 15, pp. 1-9.

Observations on the Behavior of Animals during the Total

Solar Eclipse of August 31st, 1932 (Insects by Wheeler). Proc. American Acad. Arts & Sci., vol. 70, pp. 36-45.

The Ants of the Genera Belonopelta Mayr and Simopelta Mann. Rev. de Entomologia, vol. 5, pp. 8-19.

The Australian Ant-genus Mayriella Forel. Psyche, vol. 42, pp. 151-160.

A Checklist of the Ants of Oceania. Occasional Papers, Bernice P. Bishop Mus., Honolulu, vol. 11, pp. 1-56.

New Ants from the Philippines. Psyche, vol. 42, pp. 38-52.

Myrmecological Notes. Psyche, vol. 42, pp. 68-72.

Ants of the Genus Acropyga Roger with Description of a New Species. Journ. New York Entom. Soc., vol. 43, pp. 321-329.

1936

Binary Anterior Ocelli in Ants. Biol. Bull., vol. 70, pp. 185-192.

Entomology at Harvard University. From "Notes Concerning the History and Contents of the Museum of Comparative Zoölogy". Cambridge, 1936, pp. 22-32.

Ants from Hispaniola and Mona Island. Bull. Mus. Comp. Zoöl., vol. 80, pp. 196-211.

Notes on Some Aberrant Indonesian Ants of the Subfamily Formicinae. Tijdschr. Entom., vol. 79, pp. 217-221.

Review of Thomas Elliott Snyder's "Our Enemy the Termite". Psyche, vol. 43, pp. 27-29.

The Australian Ant-genus Froggattella Forel. American Mus. Novitates, No. 842, pp. 1-12.

A Singular Crematogaster from Guatemala. Psyche, vol. 43, pp. 40-48.

Ecological Relations of Ponerine and Other Ants to Termites. Proc. American Acad. Arts & Sci., vol. 71, pp. 159-243.

A Notable Contribution to Entomology. (Review of Tarlton Rayment's "A Cluster of Bees"). Quarterly Rev. Biol., vol. 11, pp. 337-341.

Ants from the Society, Austral, Tuamotu and Mangareva Islands. Occasional Papers, Bernice P. Bishop Mus., Honolulu, vol. 12, no. 18, pp. 1-17.

1937

Additions to the Ant-fauna of Krakatau Island and Verlaten Island. Treubia, vol. 16, pp. 21-24.

Ants mostly from the Mountains of Cuba. Bull. Mus.
Comp. Zoöl., vol. 81, pp. 439-465.

Mosaics and Other Anomalies Among Ants. 95 pp., 18
figs. Harvard University Press, Cambridge.

——— ——

In collaboration with his former student, Dr. Wm. S.
Creighton, Professor Wheeler had begun the preparation of
a Handbook of North American Ants. Much of the preliminary manuscript for this volume was already finished
and Dr. Creighton plans to carry the work to completion in
the near future.

PIN-LABELS IN MULTIPLES OF 1000, ALIKE

One Dollar Per Thousand

Smallest Type. Pure White Ledger Paper. Not over 4 Lines nor 30 Characters (13 to a line) Additional Characters, 3 cents each, in total and per line, per 1000. Trimmed so one cut makes a label.

C. V. BLACKBURN, 7 Emerson St., STONEHAM 80, MASS.

CAMBRIDGE ENTOMOLOGICAL CLUB

A regular meeting of the Club is held on the second Tuesday of each month (July, August and September excepted) at 7.45 p.m. in Room B-455, Biological Laboratories of Harvard University, Divinity Ave., Cambridge. Entomologists visiting Boston are cordially invited to attend.

WARD'S ENTOMOLOGICAL SERVICES

Entomological Supplies and Equipment
Carefully designed by professional entomologists. Material of high quality at low prices. **Send for Supply Catalog No. 348.**

Insect Preparations
Life Histories, Type Collections, Collections of Economic Insects and Biological Insect Collections. All specimens are accurately determined.

Insects for the Pest Collection
We have in stock over three hundred species of North American Insect Pests. **Send for Price List No. 349.**

Ward's Entomological Bulletin
A monthly publication sent free to all entomologists requesting it.

Information for the Beginner
Send for **"Directions for Collecting and Preserving Insects"** by Dr. A. B. Klots. A mine of useful information. Price 15 cents.

WARD'S NATURAL SCIENCE ESTABLISHMENT, Inc.
P. O. Box 24, Beechwood Station
Rochester, N. Y., U. S. A.
The Frank A. Ward Foundation of Natural Science of the University of Rochester

BACK VOLUMES OF PSYCHE

The Cambridge Entomological Club is able to offer for sale the following volumes of Psyche. Those not mentioned are entirely out of print.

Volumes 2, 3, 4, 5, 6, 7, 8, 9, 10; each covering a period of three years, $5.00 each.

Volumes 12, 14, 17, each covering a single year, $1.00 each.

Volumes 18, 19, 20, 21, 22, 23, 24, 25, 26, each covering a single year, $1.50 each.

Volumes 27, 28, 29, 30, 31, 32, 33, 34, 35, 36, 37, 38, 39, 40, 41, 42, 43, each covering a single year, $2.00.

Orders for 2 or more volumes subject to a discount of 10%.

Orders for 10 or more volumes subject to a discount of 20%.

A set of all the volumes available (39 in all) will be sold for $77.00.

All orders should be addressed to

F. M. CARPENTER, Associate Editor of Psyche,
Biological Laboratories,
Harvard University,
Cambridge, Mass.

PSYCHE

A JOURNAL OF ENTOMOLOGY

ESTABLISHED IN 1874

VOL. XLIV   DECEMBER, 1937   No. 4

TABLE OF CONTENTS.

CAMBRIDGE ENTOMOLOGICAL CLUB

OFFICERS FOR 1937-1938

President	. C. A. FROST
Vice-President	J. C. BEQUAERT
Secretary	V. G. DETHIER
Treasurer	RICHARD DOW
	THOMAS BARBOUR
Executive Committee	F. M. CARPENTER
	C. H. BLAKE

EDITORIAL BOARD OF PSYCHE

EDITOR-IN-CHIEF
C. T. BRUES, HARVARD UNIVERSITY

ASSOCIATE EDITOR
F. M. CARPENTER, HARVARD UNIVERSITY

CONSULTING EDITORS

NATHAN BANKS,
Harvard University.

A. E. EMERSON,
University of Chicago.

THOMAS BARBOUR,
Harvard University.

A. L. MELANDER,
College of the
City of New York.

RICHARD DOW,
New England Museum of
Natural History,
Boston, Mass.

J. G. NEEDHAM,
Cornell University.

PSYCHE is published quarterly, the issues appearing in March, June, September, and December. Subscription price, per year, payable in advance: $2.00 to Subscribers in the United States; foreign postage, 25 cents extra, Canada 15 cents. Single copies, 65 cents.

Cheques and remittances should be addressed to Treasurer, Cambridge Entomological Club, Biological Laboratories, Harvard University, Cambridge, Mass.

Orders for back volumes, missing numbers, notices of change of address, etc., should be sent to Professor F. M. Carpenter, Biological Laboratories, Harvard University, Cambridge, Mass.

IMPORTANT NOTICE TO CONTRIBUTORS
Manuscripts intended for publication, books intended for review, and other editorial matter, should be addressed to Professor C. T. Brues, Biological Laboratories, Harvard University, Cambridge, Mass.

Authors contributing articles over 8 printed pages in length will be required to bear a part of the extra expense, for additional pages. This expense will be that of typesetting only, which is about $2.00 per page. The actual cost of preparing cuts for all illustrations must be borne by contributors; the expense for full page plates from line drawings is approximately $5.00 each, and for full page half-tones, $7.50 each; smaller sizes in proportion.

AUTHOR'S SEPARATES
Reprints of articles may be secured by authors, if they are ordered before, or at the time proofs are received for corrections. The cost of these will be furnished by the Editor on application.

Printed by the Eliot Press Inc., Jamaica Plain, Mass., U. S. A.

PSYCHE

| VOL. XLIV | DECEMBER, 1937 | No. 4 |

NOTES ON THE HABITS OF STRUMIGENYS

By WILLIAM STEEL CREIGHTON

Dept. of Biology, College of the City of New York

The singular cephalic characteristics which mark the ants of the genus Strumigenys have given rise to a number of postulates concerning the habits of these strange insects. Such postulates have, for the most part, remained speculative. This result is not surprising if one considers the obscurity which surrounds these forms. Although widely distributed and not excessively rare in some areas Strumigenys is one of the least conspicuous genera in our ant fauna. This will not, however, entirely account for the dearth of ecological data concerning the group. Published records attest that nearly every American myrmecologist has taken specimens of Strumigenys in the field. The opportunity for habit studies has been allowed to pass and the specimens have given rise to little more than an additional locality record. If it were not for the abundant evidence to the contrary one might almost believe that myrmecologists suffer from a distressing sort of alcoholism which impells them to pop rare specimens into that fluid as soon as these are unearthed. This might have been the fate of the colony described in this paper had it not been accidentally divided into two groups on exposure. The first of these went into alcohol at once but the second was not noticed until the initial acquisitive frenzy had passed. It was thereupon placed in a live-bottle where it survived a three day trip home. The ensuing notes are based upon observations made on this fragment of the original colony.

I regard the specimens as identical with that form of *S. louisianae* described by Dr. M. R. Smith as the subspecies *laticephala*. It may be recalled that Dr. Smith in his monograph of the North American Strumigenys (1) expressed the belief that the range of the subspecies *laticephala* might be more extensive than his published records indicated. The locality of the colony described herein fully supports Dr. Smith's supposition and at the same time furnishes a new northeastern record not only for the subspecies but for the subgenus as well. The insects were secured on April 22 in a well-developed stand of pine a mile or two to the east of Rocky Mount, North Carolina. The previous records of this subspecies were limited to Mississippi and Alabama where its known range extended almost to the northern border of each state. In point of fact the North Carolina record is only about eighty miles further to the north but the wide swing to the east is very significant. It definitely places *laticephala* with that interesting group of southern species whose range begins in the Gulf States and extends northward through the tidewater area of the Atlantic seaboard. It is, perhaps, not too much to assume that the northern end of the range of *laticephala* may lie in the New Jersey pine barrens.

On reaching home the fifteen surviving workers were placed in a small plaster nest. In addition I placed in the nest chambers a quantity of the bark which had formed the walls of the original nest. Except for shredding this bark so that it would not interfere with the closing of the glass top of the nest it was in its original condition. This was done with a view to promoting fungal growth since Kennedy and Schramm, in a paper published in 1933 (2) had postulated that these insects might be fungus feeders. Their supposition was based upon an analysis of *S. (Cephaloxys) ohioensis*, a species which they described in the same paper. After boiling the insects in KOH the cleared specimens were examined for chitinous remains of other insects. The results were negative, no such fragments being found. Accordingly Kennedy and Schramm gave up the idea that Strumigenys is insectivorous because they believe that such fragments occur "in the bodies of other ants which feed on insects". I find this statement confusing. I presume that it must refer to the infra-buccal pocket which sometimes contains chitinous remains. I cannot believe that the authors imply that such fragments pass into the abdominal portion of the digestive tract. If the infrabuccal pocket is meant, however, it should be recalled that Wheeler and Bailey have clearly shown (3) that this structure may be entirely devoid of recognizable insect remains in the case of an ant known to be insectivorous. The absence of such remains is, therefore, no proof that insect tissues are not used as food. While I could not accept the above conclusion as offered I was anxious to test the hypothesis of the two authors that the ants might be fungus feeders. This seemed entirely amenable to investigation if living specimens were available for study. I determined, therefore, to give the colony every opportunity for cultivating a food fungus. With this in mind the nest was kept very moist and there soon developed on the surface of the bark two distinctly different fungi.

The first of these appeared during the initial twenty-four hours after the establishment of the artificial nest. It consisted of numerous, slender, twisted hyphae. These colorless strands strongly resembled the filaments of Rhizopus but they never formed a heavy mycelium nor, as far as I could tell, did they ever produce fruiting bodies. The second fungus appeared on the following day. It consisted of spherical tufts of short hyphae radially arranged around what seemed to be a central point of attachment. The diameter of the mature colony was about one millimeter and as they approached maturity the color changed from white to blue-grey. As each tuft seemed entirely isolated and as they showed a progressive development through the nest chambers it seems likely that this second fungus may have formed spores although I never saw any.

During the course of many hours of observation I saw the Strumigenys repeatedly crawl around and over each of the two fungi. When doing so they would touch the hyphæ with their antennæ but, as they constantly explore their surroundings with these organs while moving, there is no reason to attribute special significance to this fact. In no case did I see any evidence of the ants feeding on the fungus and it was only rarely that the palps came in contact with them. It may be argued that neither of the two fungi which developed on the bark was the hypothetical food fungus. I see no reason to suppose that such a view can be maintained. From what we know of the Attine ants there is abundant evidence to show that the fungus feeders permit only the food fungus to develop in the nest. Moreover, while the full development of the mycelia of such a fungus is usually restricted to the actual garden, fragments of the hyphæ are widely dispersed throughout the nest because they adhere to the bodies of insects which tend them. From what has been said above it is obvious that the conditions in the artificial nest were favorable to the growth of fungi. If the ants had been cultivating a food fungus it is scarcely thinkable that it should have failed to develop while two foreign fungi grew well.

It may further be objected that Kennedy and Schramm applied their postulate to a member of the subgenus Cephaloxys while my observations were made upon a species belonging to the subgenus Strumigenys. I am ready to agree that the habits of the two groups may differ but I would incline to the view that of the two Cephaloxys might be expected to show more nearly general feeding habits than Strumigenys. The mandibles of most species of Cephaloxys are far less aberrant than those of Strumigenys and, in addition, the workers of Cephaloxys forage outside the nest in a perfectly normal manner. I have been able to observe this forraging in the case of three species of Cephaloxys and do not doubt that the other members of the group behave in a similar fashion. On the other hand I have never seen a worker of the subgenus Strumigenys outside the nest although I have taken these insects in several localities. There is, perhaps, little need for such elaborate refutation when it can be stated that the members of the captive colony readily fed on the tissues of other insects or, when these were not available, on a mixture of egg yolk and sugar. They refused sugary foods containing little protein. Indeed they were the first ants which I have ever known to reject a diet of bananas. With these observations in mind it seems to me that one cannot escape the conclusion that under natural conditions Strumigenys is insectivorous.[1]

[1] After this article had gone to press the author received from Mr. L. G. Wesson, Jr., a most interesting paper describing his studies on the feeding habits of *Strumigenys pergandei*. (Entomological News,

We now come to another postulate concerning the habits of Strumigenys which was advanced by the author in a paper published in 1930 (4). This publication, primarily concerned with the genus Myrmoteras, carried introductory remarks on various genera possessing linear mandibles. The matter of retrosalience was necessarily discussed but I attempted to show that this phenomenon represented the fortuitous outcome of a type of mandibular organization which I styled "trap-jawed". I pointed out that such mandibular apparatus would be a very decided advantage to sluggish ants enabling them to capture other insects more agile than themselves. It is gratifying to be able to state that this supposition has proven correct in the case of Strumigenys. Because much of what is to follow presupposes a knowledge of the structure of the mandibles of Strumigenys I have prefaced the account of their activities with the needful morphological description.

Each mandible of *S. louisianae* subsp. *laticephala* (Fig. 1) is inserted close to the midline of the head and consists of a rather stout blade which is rounded on the outer face and flattened on the inner. This blade bears two prominent apical teeth and a third subapical tooth which is about half as long as the other two. All three teeth are sharp and slender and set at right angles to the long axis of the blade. As the tip of the blade is somewhat rounded at the rear of the two apical teeth the resulting structure is not unlike what would be produced if the tines of a fork were bent at right angles to the handle. There is, however, this difference, the "fork" has only two tines and these are separated by the thickness of the blade of the mandible. There is thus a considerable space between the apical teeth, a fact which will be later shown to be of importance. When in repose the mandibles can be brought close together so that their inner faces are almost in contact. This appears to be the usual

---

Vol. 47, No. 7, pp. 171-174, 1936.). Mr. Wesson showed that the normal food of this ant consists of various species of springtails. The Collembola are hunted down by the ants but not seized until they blunder into the open mandibles of their captors. Mr. Wesson considers that the presence of various species of Strumigenys in the nests of other ants constitutes what he calls a "loose form of symbiosis." The Strumigenys benefit because of the abundant supply of springtails and are tolerated by the other ant which may benefit by the removal of the springtails.

position of the mandibles. I am by no means certain that the inner faces ever actually come in contact with each other although it seems likely that such contact may follow the snapping together of the mandibles during an attack. When the mandibles are held in the position just described the apical teeth lie close together and parallel to each other with their tips extending beyond the inner border of the opposite mandible (Fig. 2). If one looks down the long axis of the closed mandibles the four apical teeth may be seen to enclose a diamond-shaped area whose size will depend upon the degree of closure of the mandibles (Fig. 3). The mandibles can be opened to an astonishing extent, their outer borders approaching the sides of the head under extreme conditions. As a rule, however, they are not opened so widely, their usual position during attack being approximately at right angles to the long axis of the head. Under such circumstances the trigger hairs may be readily seen (Fig. 4). These do not arise from the mandibles themselves, as is the case with other forms possessing similar gnathal apparatus, but are borne on two conical lobes which lie between the bases of the mandibles. The trigger hairs are about two-thirds as long as the mandibles, and, since they project forward, it may be readily seen that objects which they touch should lie within the arcs described by the closing jaws. Anyone familiar with the mandibular organization of Odontomachus or Anochetus will recognize the essential similarity of the structures just described in Strumigenys. Since we know that Odontomachus is able to dismember other insects with its pincer-like mandibles it seems reasonable to expect analogous reactions in the case of Strumigenys. My observations have supported this expectation but it must be borne in mind that the exceedingly deliberate actions of Strumigenys result in a type of attack which appears very different from the energetic activities of Odontomachus.

As soon as the colony had recovered from the shock of transplantation and seemed at home in its new surroundings I cast about for a suitable victim with which to test the idea just mentioned. The small size of the Strumigenys worker considerably limited the choice. I wished to have the victim a more active insect than the Strumigenys and prudence forbade the use of any form which might possibly damage the

Strumigenys during the attack. With these points in mind
I selected *Brachymyrmex heeri* var. *depilis* as most suitable
although under natural conditions it may be doubted if the
two species often come in contact. For my purposes the
choice was a most satisfactory one for each of the thirteen
Brachymyrmex workers introduced into the nest was killed
by the Strumigenys although some of them managed to
avoid death for a number of hours. The method of attack
employed by the Strumigenys was remarkably constant, so
much so that I feel it unnecessary to cite individual cases
unless there is some point of special interest.

The sequence of events was as follows:

On admitting the Brachymyrmex to the nest it began a
series of exploratory investigations during which it visited
the various nest chambers. As the Strumigenys preferred
to stay in one of the narrow passages connecting two of the
chambers it frequently happened that the Brachymyrmex
actually ran over the quiescent Strumigenys workers. The
latter roused at once and opened the mandibles but it seldom
happened that any of them struck at the Brachymyrmex at
that time. It may be added that, until it was attacked, the
Brachymyrmex showed little fear of the Strumigenys. After
becoming aware of the presence of the Brachymyrmex the
Strumigenys workers would begin to move slowly about
the nest. It is hard to depict the extreme deliberation of
their movements. They proceed literally a step at a time
and this gives to their actions an air of stealth which is probably spurious since they never move rapidly under any circumstances. Eventually one or more of the Strumigenys
workers would approach within striking distance of the
Brachymyrmex. If the latter were quiet the attacker would
locate its position by cautious explorations with the antenna
before it struck. Not infrequently, however, the Brachymyrmex blundered into the open jaws of the Strumigenys
which were promptly snapped shut as the trigger hairs were
touched. The closure of the mandibles is extremely rapid
and is followed by a distinct backward jerk of the body of
the attacker. These two movements seem to be the only
rapid motions of which the Strumigenys worker is capable.
The effect of the attack on the Brachymyrmex is very
marked. It would at once begin an elaborate series of clean-

ing reactions involving the antennal funiculi, the fore legs and sometimes the tip of the gaster. A single injury such as might have been received from the mandibles of the attacker would scarcely be expected to evoke such a general response. Moreover, as I shall presently show, injuries are rarely sustained by the Brachymyrmex during the initial attack. Yet this cleaning reaction after the attack is an exceedingly constant one. I observed it so often that I am led to suspect that some irritating substance is ejected by the Strumigenys at the moment of striking. I much regret that I cannot prove this point which is very interesting if true.

While the Brachymyrmex was busy cleaning itself other Strumigenys workers would arrive and encircle it. Although the advantage of a concerted attack would seem obvious I never saw this happen. Each Strumigenys attacks separately moving in with great deliberation and ascertaining the position of the Brachymyrmex with the antennae before striking. It is interesting to note that this particular reaction prevents the Strumigenys from striking each other. Quite frequently the positions of the attackers would be such that they would have struck one another had they relied solely upon the trigger hairs to release the mandibular mechanism. By bringing the antennae into play they were enabled to recognize their nest mates and would alter their position accordingly. In the hundreds of times which I witnessed the Strumigenys attack I never saw one strike a nest mate. During this phase of the attack the Brachymyrmex would, of course, be struck at repeatedly. Not infrequently it would break out of the circle of attackers and run to another part of the nest. This, however, merely delayed the final result for sooner or later it was again surrounded. After the Brachymyrmex had been struck at perhaps twelve or fifteen times it usually became much dejected. It ceased the cleaning movements which it had continued up to this time and made no further attempts to avoid attack. I wish to stress the fact that this dejection, if I may use that term, was not due to injuries. Except in rare cases the Brachymyrmex would reach this stage of the attack without any visible sign that it had sustained damage from the mandibles of its attackers. The change in its reactions was, nevertheless, most pronounced and this again leads me to the conclusion that its lethargic condition may have resulted from the cumulative effects of some substance ejected upon it by the Strumigenys.

With the decreasing activity of the Brachymyrmex the Strumigenys became, if possible, more methodical than ever. They would deliberately manoeuver the mandibles so that they would close on a leg or antenna of the victim and the better success of this attack was evidenced by the appearance of injuries in the parts just mentioned. The distress of the Brachymyrmex was now very apparent. It would undergo spasmodic shudderings or lift its body as high as possible with the legs stiff and straight beneath. As a rule it lost the power of muscular coordination a short time afterward and the attack would end with the Brachymyrmex lying on the floor of the nest with its legs drawn tightly beneath it.

In most cases the Strumigenys would later carry out the corpses of their victims and deposit them on the "kitchen midden", in this case one of the food chambers of the nest. I was thus enabled to relax the remains of the Brachymyrmex workers and study the extent and character of the injuries. As might have been expected these were remarkably uniform. The antennal funiculi suffered the most. One or both usually showed injuries involving the loss of several joints. Not infrequently the entire funiculus, except the basal joint, was missing. The fore and middle tarsi, while less frequently damaged than the funiculi, were often injured. The hind tarsi were usually intact. In one specimen the tip of the gaster was torn but this injury was so slight that I would probably not have noticed it had it not been for the actions of the ant while it was still alive. This was the sole injury involving the body of the victim. Although I made a most careful search for evidences of piercing on various parts of the body I never found the slightest indication that the teeth of the attackers had penetrated the integument of the Brachymyrmex. As it would be hard to find an ant in which the integument is softer or thinner than that of Brachymyrmex the lack of body wounds can scarcely be attributed to the inability of the Strumigenys to pierce the chitin. On the contrary it seems obvious that they make little effort to do so preferring rather to cripple the victim by removing the joints of the appendages. While this view checks with observed facts it is far from satisfactory as an explanation covering the death of the Brachymyrmex. We may admit that most ants are severely affected by injuries involving the antennae but it rarely happens that such injuries are immediately followed by death. The loss of a tarsal joint or two is usually a matter of slight consequence. Yet in thirteen cases injuries of the nature just described were accompanied by the rapid demise of the victim. Again I find myself led to the view that some substance is ejected by the Strumigenys as they strike at the victim. It would seem necessary to believe that this substance is not only

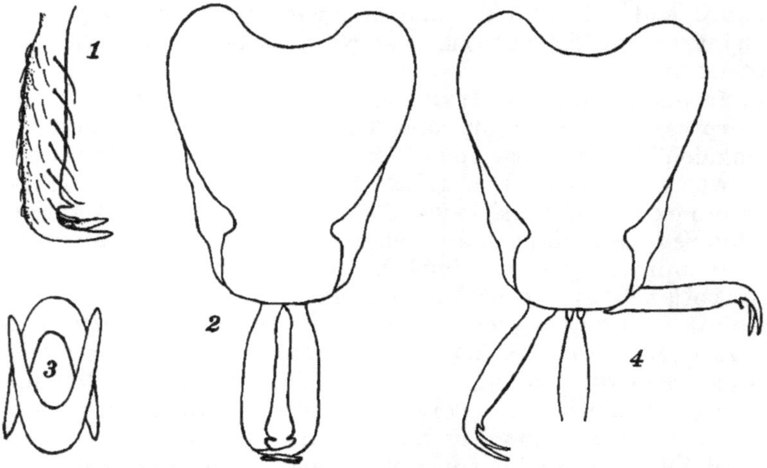

Fig. 1. Cephalic structures of *Strumigenys louisianae* subsp. *laticephala* Smith. For explanation of figures see text.

irritating but toxic. Again I must stress the fact that I cannot prove this assumption. It is, however, the only explanation which appears to cover the facts.

I wish to add a few more observations concerning the manner in which the Strumigenys workers use their mandibles. The first of these involves a detailed discussion of the role of the mandible during attack, a matter which is more complex than might be supposed. The extreme rapidity with which the mandibles are closed in striking makes this process very difficult to follow. Repeated observations have, however, convinced me that the mandibles of Strumigenys, unlike those of Odontomachus, do not act as shearing organs. I have already pointed out that each time a Strumigenys worker strikes at a victim the closure of the mandibles is immediately followed by a backward jerk of the insect. At first this used to annoy me considerably since it seemed to defeat the whole plan of attack by moving the Strumigenys out of range. I later learned to appreciate the vital part that this sudden backward motion plays in the amputation of appendages on which the mandibles close. It may be readily observed that when the Strumigenys workers close in for the final attack the damages to the antennal funiculi and tarsi of the victim involve mangled joints. The portion of the appendage beyond the injured joint will often bend in a fashion which plainly indicates that the joint has been badly crushed. As a rule the part of the appendage beyond the damaged joint is quickly removed as the result of further attacks. As its final removal is accomplished with the speed of a conjuring trick it was some time before I realized exactly how this is done. It is obvious that the initial damage to the appendage is caused by the flattened inner faces of the mandibles of Strumigenys which crush the joint on which they close but lack the power to completely sever it. I have already pointed out that in repose the mandibles of Strumigenys do not quite meet and this may account for their deficiency as pincers. It might be supposed that the backward jerk which follows this initial damage would sever the appendage but this is not usually the case. I believe that this can be explained if we consider that the crushed joint is free to move along the approximated inner faces of the mandibles which are smooth and without teeth except for the three at the apex. As I have already stated the final removal of the distal portion of a damaged appendage is a very speedy process and I am by no means certain that the method which I am about to describe is invariably employed. There has been ample opportunity, however, to observe that it is frequently used. It involves a relation between the appendage and the mandibles such that the four apical teeth close around the appendage. Because of the shape of the space included between these apical teeth (*vide supra*) they can lock against the appendage. This is particularly true if the latter happens to be an antennal funiculus which increases in diameter toward the tip. The backward jerk of the Strumigenys is then exerted in the direction of the long axis of the already injured appendage which may break in consequence at the damaged joint. It may be added that unless the appendage has been previously crushed it cannot be pulled off when caught by the apical teeth. Under such circumstances there ensues a sort of a tug-of-war with the Strumigenys holding grimly to the appendage and the victim struggling frantically to get free.

Aside from their vital role in attack the mandibles of Strumigenys are little used. They occasionally employ them in carrying nest mates about but this was seldom observed. I never saw any indications that the mandibles play a part in the trophic reactions of these insects. Feeding is entirely cared for by the palps and other mouthparts. When Strumigenys is feeding the mandibles are kept closed and thrust upward over the food until the stubby palps come in contact with its surface. The palps apparently act both as rasps and spoons for both liquids and semisolids are ingested by their help. The feeding reactions of Strumigenys are exceedingly difficult to follow because all the more delicate mouth parts are reduced in size and closely packed into the small buccal cavity. It is interesting to note that the mandibles are kept closed during regurgitation. This results in a rather awkward situation for both regurgitant and recipient. The closed mandibles prevent the usual approximation of the two heads and it is only after considerable preliminary fencing that the correct posture is assumed. Each ant turns its head sidewise so that ventral surfaces are parallel although not opposite. The closed mandibles are then crossed and slid over each other until the palps are close enough for the transfer. It seems a remarkably clumsy way of securing a result which could be easily reached by simply opening the mandibles.

There remains the matter of retrosalience. I saw this phenomenon only twice during the many hours that the captive colony was under observation. In one case it resulted when the mandibles of an attacking Strumigenys worker closed on the convex surface of a glass tube which led to one of the feeding chambers. The resulting leap threw the insect against the top of the nest whence it was deflected to the floor at a point not much more than three-quarters of an inch from its original position. Had the leap been unimpeded it would probably have been more extensive. The second case occurred under similar circumstances and with much the same result. As far as I am aware this is the third time in which retrosalience has been reported for a member of the genus Strumigenys. Hetschko (*teste* Mayr) observed it in the South American *S. saliens* about 1887 (5) and ten years later Biro (*teste* Emery) saw the same phenomenon in the case of *S. chyzeri* which he studied in New Guinea (6). Each of the above accounts is rather meager but it seems likely that both species frequently resorted to retrosalience. It is not impossible that it had come to play a protective role in their habits as is the case with Anochetus and Odontontomachus. I cannot believe that retrosalience plays any such part in the case of *S. louisianae*. The phenomenon is so rare and the conditions which would produce it so unusual that it must play little or no part in the ecology of this form.

LITERATURE CITED

1. Smith, M. R. Ann. Ent. Soc. America. Vol. XXIV, No. 4, p. 690, (1931).
2. Kennedy, C. H. & Schramm, M. M. Ibid. Vol. XXVI, No. 1, p. 104, (1933).
3. Wheeler, W. M. & Bailey, I. W. Trans. American Philos. Soc. N.S., Vol. XXII, No. 4, p. 247-248, (1920).
4. Creighton, W. S. Jour. New York Ent. Soc. Vol. XXXVIII, p. 177, (1930).
5. Mayr, G. Zool-bot. Ges. Wien Vol. XXXVII, p. 575, (1887).
6. Emery, C. Term. Füzetek, Vol. XX, p. 576, (1897).

CANNIBALISM AMONG LEPIDOPTEROUS LARVAE

V. G. DETHIER

Biological Laboratories, Harvard University

The occurrence of the carnivorous habit in lepidopterous larvæ is known in certain rather widely separated groups, one of which, the Lycænidæ, is outstanding (Brues, 1936). It is known also that some phytophagous larvæ will become carnivorous for a period of time either regularly or in the absence of a plentiful food supply (Brues, 1920). I have observed this and also cannibalism many times while breeding various species.[1] A few examples may be cited.

When larvæ of the Arctiid, *Apantesis arge* Drury, were confined to a limited area (three to four larvæ to eight square inches) with a moderate supply of food, the smallest, least healthy, or least active larva was usually attacked while still alive and almost entirely eaten by a more robust specimen. Fifty of these larvæ were divided into lots of two, three, and four, each lot being limited to an area of eight square inches. In nearly seventy-five percent of all cases cannibalism occurred. It was noted more frequently when four larvæ were confined together or when one larva was smaller or weaker than its neighbors, as stated above. Moore (1912) reported that *Phœbis eubule* L., when confined even in the presence of an ample food supply, ate smaller larvæ of its own species. The more aggressive individuals also devoured the more peaceful ones. Perkins (1928) found that *Nemoria viridata* L. in the presence of an abundance of food also showed cannibalistic tendencies. The larvæ from a large batch of eggs feasted upon one another till there was but one left. This animal pupated and a normal adult emerged. Subsequent breedings with other batches of eggs of the same species revealed no further cases of cannibalism.

I have observed that larvæ of *Estigmene acræa* Drury and *Diacrisia virginica* Fab. when confined with those of other

[1]For cases of oöphagy see Schultz (1928, 1935).

species, notably *Papilio polyxenes* Fab., *P. philenor* L., and
Danaus plexippus L., in ample space but with a limited
food supply, readily attacked and ate pupating larvae and
chrysalids of the butterflies.   They also ate pupæ of their
own species, devouring all the hair and silk of the cocoon as
well.   *Papilio philenor* L. speedily attacked chrysalids and
pupating larvæ of its own species as soon as the food supply
dried up or diminished.   This has also been reported by
Clark (1925) as occurring in *P. polyxenes* Fab. and *Danaus
plexippus* L.   Orfila (1927) reported that *Ecpantheria
indecisa* Walkr. in the presence of an abundance of food
devoured chrysalids of *Tatochila autodice* Hb. and also the
parasites (*Apanteles sp?*) with which the chrysalids were
infected.

The most striking example that I observed was the case of
a noctuid, *Autographa sp?*, which attacked other larvæ of its
own species although plenty of food was available.   It is
interesting to note that this noctuid also fiercely attacked
healthy and active larvæ of *Danaus plexippus* L. and
Malacosoma americanum Fab.   While the victim struggled
the noctuid stood upon it and chewed its way rapidly into
the flesh.

Bell is quoted (de Niceville 1901) as being of the opinion
that a larva will never eat another larva feeding on a food
plant different from its own.   He also advanced the idea that
"—cannibal larvæ are hardly conscious that they are eating
up each other, being only guided to their proper food by the
sense of taste, or possibly to a less extent by the sense of
smell".   The noctuid referred to above could not be induced
to feed either upon cherry (the food plant upon which *M.
americanum* was feeding) or upon milkweed (the food plant
of *D. plexippus*) although it would feed upon other plants.
The question had been raised by Bird (1925) as to whether
or not the food plant imparted a flavor to larvæ which was
repellent to internal parasites (the conditions would be the
same in the case of cannibals).   Whether or not this is the
case can not be definitely stated at the present time.   Undoubtedly the gut of the larva attacked would, if it contained
food, taste of the food plant which had been eaten.   It
appears unlikely that the cannibal larva would be able to
distinguish its prey before it had attacked it, and, therefore,

should, theoretically, *attack* any larva regardless of what it had eaten.

v. Roesel v. Rosenhof (1749) reported that *Chariclea delphinii* L. frequently ate larvæ of its own species. *Calyminia trapexzina* (L.) and *Agrotis ypsilon* (Rott.) have been reported to be cannibalistic by Berg (1875, 1892). Lederer (1932) reports the case of a noctuid, *Scopelosoma satellitia* L., attacking and eating the posterior end of its own body. It is known that some larvae when injured in this region of the body will devour themselves. Schultz (1935) reports that the following larvæ ate chrysalids of their own species: *Acidalia herbariata* F., *Eupithecia castigata* Hb., and *Dianthœcia capsincola* Hb. He further states that Arctiidæ commonly nibble at chrysalids and that *Caradrina exidua* is cannibalistic.

Mr. C. M. Williams (unpublished data) noticed that when *Hæmorrhagia thysbe* Fab. larvæ were crowded some would attempt to eat others. He also noticed when many *Telea polyphemus* Cramer larvæ were crowded in confinement with an ample supply of their food plant that certain individuals attacked others and succeeded in breaking through the integument. In neither case, however, was the attack carried beyond this point.

Another interesting case is that of a larva of *Epizeuxis lubricalis* Geyer which I observed devouring a considerable portion of the wings of a dried *Colias philodice* Godart contained in the same collecting box. The caterpillar then proceeded to build a cocoon with what remained of the butterfly.

While this last case should really be classed as saprophagy, it should be noted that the remaining cases of cannibalism occurred under laboratory conditions rather than in nature. The reversion to a meat diet in many cases seemed to follow conditions of crowding or of lack of sufficient food. The following cases, especially the first, are offered to show that similar conditions can and undoubtedly do prevail in nature.

From October eleventh to November third 1937 I observed (Dedham, Mass.) an immense swarm of the larvæ of *Isia isabella* Smith & Abbot which was estimated at not less than one hundred thousand. One could collect five hundred of these larvæ in three minutes without visibly decreasing the hordes covering the ground. The area thus overrun was

marsh land, approximately half a square mile in extent, cut
from north to south by a river, and bounded on all sides by
highways. The larvæ were found only on the east side of
the river. Of the thousands which were traveling back and
forth between the river and the highway many were killed
by passing vehicles and pedestrians. Practically every fifth
caterpillar that had been killed was being eaten by one or
more of the same species which were consuming all parts of
the dead ones, except the hairs. The green vegetation in the
vicinity was restricted to a narrow belt along each side of
the highway. The scarcity of low-lying vegetation was evident. Practically the only green plant was an aster, *Aster
lævis*, growing to a height of four feet. The larvæ which
were not feasting on the dead specimens were eating the
tops of the asters. Feeding on tall vegetation is unusual for
a characteristically ground-loving species like *Isia isabella*.
It is noteworthy that nearly all the larvæ showed signs of
hunger. It would seem that the summer of 1937 was for
some reason especially favorable to the development of this
species. With the approach of autumn the supply of food
plants in the area to which the caterpillars were confined
gave out in the presence of such overwhelming numbers.
The larvæ were prevented from traveling west by the river,
hence they swarmed upon the highway where they were
killed in large numbers. The hungry survivors either
feasted upon the dead or climbed the asters. No cannibalism
was observed in the few individuals of *D. virginica* and *E.
acræa* which were also present.

On the occasion of an exceedingly large swarm of
Ecpantheria, Orfila (1927) noticed three animals avidly
devouring the remains of a fourth which was still living.

The following are also said to be cannibalistic in nature:
Laphygma frugiperda Smith & Abbot (Moore 1912),
Vanessa caryæ Hb. (Berg 1875, 1892), and *Heliothis obsoleta*
Fab. (Berg 1875, 1892). Berg reported that *H. obsoleta* ate
from six to seven larvæ in twenty-four hours.

The question as to why larvæ show cannibalistic tendencies
is a difficult one to answer. Three alternative solutions have
been suggested by Orfila (1927) : 1) it is due to an internal
physiological cause, 2) an organic disarrangement produces
an alimentary upset, 3) cannibalistic manifestations herald

a return to a past carnivorous diet. Orfila believes that the original diet was vegetable, and while he points out that sporadic cannibalism may be the forerunner of a more widespread carnivorous diet in the future, he leans toward the belief that cannibalism is due to an upset in internal organic conditions. Berg (1892) maintained that climatic conditions (in Patagonia) caused the supply of food plants to diminish so that larvæ were driven to cannibalism by hunger. This is undoubtedly correct. He further maintained, however, that the cannibalistic character was inherited, and that many larvæ could not return to a vegetable diet after having eaten meat. It is not improbable that natural selection could be responsible for the high percentage of cannibalism found in many species. I have observed, however, that our native species will return to a vegetable diet if given the opportunity. Schultz (1935) is of the opinion that cannibalism may be due not only to hunger but also to a need for satisfying thirst. Without a doubt thirst is a contributing factor. This much may be said, that cannibalism may be induced experimentally by crowding and by an insufficient food supply, but that it appears to crop out under conditions of favorable population densities and food supply as well. It is not improbable that this phenomonon will be found to be more widespread in lepidopterous larvæ than is realized at the present time. Thus far cannibalism has been reported in Geometridæ, Noctuidæ, Arctiidæ, Saturniidæ, Bombycidæ, Sphingidæ, Danaidæ, Nymphalidæ, Papilionidæ, Pieridæ, and Lycænidæ. It does not appear, however, that larvæ are forced to adopt a meat diet under favorable conditions but simply do so accidentally when in close proximity to another individual. Or, they may attack when unduly disturbed, and having tasted meat, continue to eat more or less automatically as long as its taste is not repellent. Larvæ taken off a meat diet will survive with no apparent ill effects on a normal vegetable diet.

LITERATURE CITED

Berg, C., 1875. Patagonische Lepidopteren. Bul. Soc. Imp. Nat. Moscou, 49(2): 191-193.
———— 1892. Canibalismo entre insectos. Anal. Soc. Cient. Argentina, 34: 386-388.
Bird, H., 1925. New life histories in Papaipema No. 23 (Lepidoptera). Canadian Ent., 57(12): 305.

Brues, C. T., 1920. The selection of food plants by insects, with special reference to lepidopterous larvae. American Nat., 54: 313-332.
—————— 1936. Aberrant feeding behavior among insects and its bearing on the development of specialized food habits. Quart. Rev. Biol., 2(3): 305-316.

Lederer, G., 1932. Tiere, die versuchten, sich selbst aufzufressen. Int. Ent. Zeit., 26(2): 28.

Moore, H. W. B., 1912. Ways and habits of caterpillars. Timehri, 2(1): 197, 198.

de Niceville, L., 1901. Cannibalism among caterpillars. Canadian Ent., 33(5): 131, 132.

Orfila, R. N., 1927. Sobre canibalismo en insectos. Rev. Soc. Ent. Argentina, 2(4): 65, 66.

Perkins, R. C. L., 1928. Proc. Ent. Soc. London, 3(1): 20.

v. Roesel v. Rosenhof, B., 1749. Insektenbelustigung Zweyte Classe der Nachtvögel, p. 82.

Schultz, V. G. M., 1928. Taeniocampa populi Ström. (= populeti Fr.) Int. Ent. Zeit., 21(46): 439-442.

—————— 1935. Lepidopterologische Beiträge. Einige Fälle von oophagem und chrysalidophagem Kannibalismus bei Grossschmetterlingsraupen. Int. Ent. Zeit., 28(41): 501-504, 556.

A MEGAMORPHIC AND TWO CURIOUS MIMETIC FLIES

BY FRANK M. HULL

University of Mississippi

At a recent visit to the Carnegie Museum the writer was afforded the privilege of studying the unidentified Syrphid flies in the collections. Among this material were discovered certain curious types upon which it is desired to report at this time. The bulk of the material will be reported upon later. I wish to express my thanks to Dr. Hugo Kahl for the opportunity to study this material.

Chysidimyia, new genus

Eyes bare. Antennæ slender, third joint densely erect pubescent, the dorsal arista thickest in the middle. Whole face extended as a rounded lump anteriorly, a crease separating the lower face from the upper, and lying shortly above the oral margin. Antennæ inserted from ventral surface of an overhanging frontal shelf. Scutellum with two spines, moderately separated. Abdomen oval-elongate; the sides of the second segment greatly thickened and overlapping the corners of the succeeding segment making possible a downward deflection of the remainder of the abdomen. Whole lateral margins of the abdomen enormously thickened and inrolled; segments three, four and five entirely fused. Legs simple, an oblique groove on the basal part of hind femora.

Whole head, thorax, abdomen and legs everywhere brilliant metallic green and extraordinarily deeply punctate. The punctures are actual depressions, which on the posterior rim of the second abdominal segment, become grooves.

Wings with the posterior angles of the first posterior and discal cells rounded, that of the first posterior gives off a spur to wing margin. There is a spur cutting down towards the spurious vein from the third longitudinal vein.

Genotype: *Chysidimyia chrysidimima* new species.

Chysidimyia chrysidimima new species

Eyes nearly touching, approaching in an angular fashion which is but little over a right angle, perhaps 110 degrees. Eyes quite noticeably short, whitish pilose. Vertex swollen, the eyes gradually excavated behind so that the occiput and post vertex is for some distance rounded and enormously thickened. Ocelli inserted at highest point, some distance from post occipital margin and almost midway from antennae. Antennæ situated a little above midline of profile, to the lower surface of a slight shelving prominence. The face below antennæ slightly excavated for a short distance, then swelling to large rounded mammiform area and falling off just a short distance before the oral margin, not right at the margin. A marginal crease delimits the very small cheeks. Lower occiput very thin. There is a vertical crease down the midline of face. Antennæ elongate, black, the first joint as long as the third; the second one-fifth or one-sixth of the third. The third is thickest just before the rounded apex. The arista is basally thickened, shorter than third and black and bare. Pile of face, except for a few dark hairs on front, whitish. Whole face and head everywhere deeply and remarkably punctate.

Pile of thorax quite short, very appressed, black with a few pale hairs. Scutellum armed with two short spines set slightly closer than length of scutellum in midline.

Abdominal pile short, scanty, appressed, black with a few pale hairs and in the margins more pale hair. The greatly thickened tergites at the sides are inrolled and the apical margin of the second segment is greatly thickened and equipped at the corners to overlap the rest of the abdomen in down folding.

Legs black, the terminal tarsal joints dark brown; the tibiae and femora metallic green, with small punctures; the hind basitarsi not extraordinary, nor the hind femora greatly thickened. Wings grey, terminal section of fourth longitudinal vein straight, a spur dropped from third longitudinal vein into the first posterior cell. Spurious vein present.

Length 9 mm.

One male. Santarem, Brazil, June 1919. (S. M. Klages). Accession 6324. Type in the Carnegie Museum.

The whole insect is remarkably brilliant blue-green, metallic, vitreous, covered everywhere with deep punctures or pits, and on the abdomen small creases, in shape and appearance presenting an astonishing resemblance to a *Chrysidid* wasp, altogether the most remarkable case of mimicry I have ever beheld.

Tityusia new genus

Large flies, the males narrowly holoptic, the upper facets slightly enlarged, the antennal prominence well developed, the antennæ have the third joint suborbicular and the arista bare. First and second joints short. Face with a very low median tubercle, not greatly produced either anteriorly or ventrally. Post-occiput flared posteriorly backwards about central opening, and long pilose.

Thorax and scutellum normal, with very dense pile of median length, the rim of the latter simple. Metanotum with a horizontal depression or crease. Abdomen broadly oval, broad basally, tapering posteriorly, yellow maculate somewhat similar to species of *Helophilus* and *Mesembrius*.

Hind femora moderately thickened, but unarmed posteriorly with either spines or setae. The black basal patch of setulae present. Anterior femora greatly thickened, especially apically and from the apical third of the posterior margin a very thick brush of dense dark pile is sent backward, much as if the hairs of a brush had been wetted. Fore tibiæ still more extraordinary, enormously thickened, grooved, twisted and distorted, the median and lateral edges bare, dense fringes of dark pile extremely long, extremely matted, directed backward. Fore tarsi extravagantly flattened on the dorso-ventral axis, the lateral edges of the second, third and fourth segments prolonged into narrow down curving lobes. Median pair of legs simple, except that their tarsi are flattened somewhat. Posterior tibiae slightly flattened. Posterior basitarsi nearly as long as post tibiae, on its distal end bearing an enormous brush of dark matted hair, its basal end equipped with the characteristic globuliferous hairs of *Mesembrius*. Marginal cell of wings narrowly open. Halteres long stalked, the knob with a deep cup shaped depression. This may be due to drying.

Genotype: *Tityusia regulus* new species.

Tityusia **regulus** new species

Male. Eyes bare, touching narrowly. Vertical triangle quite narrow. Frontal (antennal) prominence well developed, shining brownish black. Face and cheeks similarly colored, the former light yellow on the sides and covered with pale yellow pubescence and similar longer pile, the pubescence being sparse on the weak low tubercle. Pile of front and vertex black, of occiput above and below, long and pale golden in color. Antennæ and arista dark brown.

Thoracic dorsum black, opaque or at best subshining, an obscure yellowish pollinose stripe on the middle of either side, and even more obscure and narrower vitta lying on the midline. Anterior three-fifths of dorsum clothed with dense moderately long, pale golden pile, the tips of the hairs crinkled and a few very fine black hairs intermixed. The posterior part of dorsum, short, thick, black pilose, the scutellum golden pilose. All the thoracic pile very erect. The brown humeri largely bare, what pile is present (including humeri) is long, tufted, crinkled, and pale golden.

Abdomen: first segment, the fore and hind borders of second and a narrow median connection widening quickly in either direction, dark brown to black. A brown subshining apical band on the third segment with its fore border raised into a low acute pyramid, and a similar apical band on the fourth segment with a rounded fore margin that nearly reaches the base of that segment, also dark brownish black but shining as well. This leaves two very large orange spots, shaped like the ends of a parabola on the second segment and a similarly colored band at the base of the third segment. The base of the fourth segment is densely greenish yellow pubescent. Pile on the surface of the segments and in the middle, black and appressed becoming more erect, longer and golden in color on the sides. Some straggled, curious, long, flat, appressed golden hairs on base of the second segment.

All the legs dark brownish to black, subshining, the very narrow bases of tibiae pale, and the tarsi varying shades of yellow brown. Pile of femora, except anterior pair, long, pale, crinkly. That of hind tarsi, fore tibiae and fore femora a most extraordinary mat of dense, excessively long hair. Fore tarsi pale, flattened and laterally produced in an extravagant way, reminding one of *Platychirus*. See the generic description for further details.

Length 18 mm.

One male. Efufup, Kamerun, W. Africa, August 30, 1919. Carnegie Museum. Accession No. 6552. Holotype male in Carnegie Museum.

This fly is to the Syrphidae what *Calotarsa* is to the *Platypezidae*, a curious convergent type of structural development.

Syrphipogon new genus

Very large flies related to *Microdon*.

Eyes bare, broadly dichoptic in male. Antennae slender, the first joint sub-equal to last two. Arista thick, its surface pubescent. Hair of upper front directed upward, of vertex directed forward and upward so that the two converge above ocelli. Lower face just above mid oral margin equipped with a beard of long thick shining black bristles.

Thorax normal, thick black bristly, greatly appressed. Scutellum with a pair of enormous spines, deeply sulcate between, directed upward and posteriorward at an angle of 45 degrees. Abdomen broad and thick, the lateral posterior margins of the third segment and adjoining base of the fourth deeply sunken, followed by a simple situation on the next segment so that a strong ridge lies between. Hind basitarsi longer than remaining joints, greatly widened and flattened. Remaining joints similarly widened and flattened, but less so.

Last section of fourth longitudinal vein (subapical cross vein) bluntly angulate outward, just before terminus the posterior angles of the first posterior and discal cells not angulate but evenly rounded. No spurs except for the posterior cell spur cutting down to terminys of spurious vein. Wings black basally, blackish on a narrow distal apex, and yellow with yellow veins between.

Genotype: *Syrphipogon fucatissimus* new species.

Syrphipogon fucatissimus new species

Male. Whole face and head shining black, the face with a faint purplish tinge. Arista pale yellow. Antennae black, elongate. Last two joints about as long as first, not set on a pedicel. Third joint one and three-fourths times length of second. Second about equal width of front at narrowest point. Pile of head and face everywhere black, vertical pile and that of upper front converging to come together just above ocelli. Pile of upper face exceedingly appressed, black, bristly, the face punctate, developed on the lower face into a black beard of long bristles above oral margin.

Dorsum of thorax shining black, covered thickly with very short appressed bristles, a few golden ones on the sutures. Pleurae similar but with longer bristly pile. Scutellum developed into a pair of enormous black spines, deeply sulcate in the middle, and black bristly or pilose to their apices. Spines held at a forty-five degree angle.

Abdomen shining black, a deep excavation on the apical lateral half of the third and again on the fourth segments. Apical half of second segment long, golden pilose, a similar annulus or transverse band across the middle of the fourth segment so that the first excavation lies between and is black. Remainder of abdomen, except for a little more black following the second golden band, is deep bright orange reddish pilose.

Legs everywhere dark shining black, black bristly, the hind metatarsi (and the following ones to a less extent) enormously flattened and broadened, but not markedly thick.

Wings with basal half or three-fifths black, (very dark brown) the remainder except for light brown tip, yellow with yellow veins.

Length 25 mm.

South America, without further data. Type in the Carnegie Museum.

Curiously, this fly forms part of a three-part mimetic complex, the others being an Asilid fly and a bee from the same region.

WEST INDIAN CARABIDÆ IV: THREE NEW COLPODES

BY P. J. DARLINGTON, JR.

Museum of Comparative Zoölogy, Cambridge, Mass.

Two of the following three new species were the chief prizes in a small but interesting lot of Carabidæ recently collected in the West Indies by Mr. Chester Roys. The third species was collected by myself in Haiti in 1934, but was only recently found to be distinct.

Colpodes sellensis n. sp.

Very Agonum-like (similar to *Colpodes agonellus* Darl., PSYCHE Vol. 42, 1935, p. 187); piceous brown, appendages not distinctly paler. *Head* slightly less than ⅔ width prothorax. *Prothorax* about ⅓ wider than long; base about ¼ or slightly less wider than apex; posterior angles rounded, although sometimes a little irregularly so. *Elytra* oval, with broadly rounded humeri. Inner wings vestigial, not reaching beyond middle of *second* ventral segment. Other characters as in *agonellus*. Length 7.5; width 3 mm. (slightly ±).

Haiti: holotype ♀ (M. C. Z. no. 23,013) and 1♂ 2♀ paratypes from La Visite and vicinity, Massif de la Selle, 5,000-7,000 ft. altitude, Sept. 16-23, 1934.

This new species differs from *agonellus* in having the prothorax narrower, with slightly narrower base and more rounded posterior angles; elytra more oval and with more rounded humeri; and wing vestiges shorter (in 70 *agonellus* with vestigal wings the tips of the vestiges reach to above, or rarely just beyond or just short of, the *third* ventral segment).

Colpodes bromeliarum n. sp.

Moderately elongate, somewhat flattened; shining blue, lower surface and appendages black, except legs bluish in some lights and antennae with segments 4-11 brown at sides.

Head elongate, about ¾ wide as prothorax; eyes prominent; genae long and oblique; 2 supraocular setae each side; antennae moderate, 4th segment 4 or more times long as greatest width; mentum tooth acutely triangular. *Prothorax* subquadrate, about 1/7 wider than long at middle (by measurement), very slightly narrowed at base, arcuately narrowed at apex; base truncate except slightly and broadly emarginate in median half, apex more distinctly emarginate; base about ½ wider than apex; sides arcuate in anterior half, very broadly and slightly sinuate in basal half, with margins moderately reflexed, each with seta at basal angle but without anterior lateral seta; basal and apical angles narrowly rounded; base and apex finely margined; disk slightly convex, with median line well impressed at middle, basal and apical transverse impressions less sharply defined; baso-lateral foveae moderate, extending forward supparallel to margins nearly to apex, finely punctate basally. *Elytra* about ½ wider than prothorax, slightly narrowed basally but with humeri about normally prominent; sides slightly sinuate before subindependently rounded apices; sutural angles subdenticulate; striae moderate, entire, punctulate; discal intervals slightly convex, 3rd tripunctate, anterior puncture attached to 3rd stria, others to 2nd stria. Metepisterna long, inner wings full. Lower surface impunctate except for traces of punctures at front of mesepisterna and 1st ventral segment. Tibiae not sulcate externally; posterior tarsi each with first 2 segments broadly and vaguely impressed or flattened each side, subcarinate at middle; front tarsi each with only basal segment thus modified; all tarsi of both sexes exceptionally wide and densely pubescent below; 4th segment posterior tarsus deeply emarginate, with outer lobe a little longer than inner; 5th segment without accessory setae. Male with 1, female with 2 setae each side apex last ventral. Length 10.5-13; width 3.7-4.4 mm.

Jamaica: holotype ♂ (M. C. Z. no. 23,014) and 7 paratypes from Swift River town, Portland, 1,000 ft. altitude, March 22, 1937; 2 paratypes from Bath, St. Thomas, Jamaica, 300 ft. altitude, April 3, 1937; all taken by Mr. Chester Roys. Some at least were in epiphytic bromeliads; the somewhat flattened body of the insect is probably an adaptation to life between the bromeliad leaf bases.

Related to *Colpodes punctus* Darl. and *bruesi Darl.*, both
of Jamaica, but differs from *punctus* in metallic color and
much less punctate lower surface, and from *bruesi* in punctulate elytral striae as well as in other details.

Colpodes roysi n. sp.

Moderately elongate, less flattened than *bromeliarum;*
moderately shining dark blue, lower surface and appendages
piceous except sides of antennal segments 4-11 brown. *Head*
about ⅔ wide as prothorax, somewhat shorter than in
bromeliarum, but similar in details of structure. *Prothorax*
about 1/7 wider than long, strongly narrowed anteriorly,
scarcely so basally; base nearly truncate, apex broadly
emarginate; base about 3/5 wider than apex; sides broadly
rounded in anterior ¾, faintly sinuate before approximately
right, scarcely blunted posterior angles; margins moderately
reflexed, each with seta at basal angle, without anterior
lateral seta; base and apex finely margined; disk slightly
more convex than *bromeliarum* but with similar impressions,
baso-lateral foveae similarly finely punctate. *Elytra* about
½ wider than prothorax, slightly stouter and more convex
than in average *bromeliarum* but similar in details of structure *except* apices each with a short spine opposite end of
3rd interval, and striae not distinctly punctulate. Metepisterna elongate, inner wings full. Lower surface without
distinct punctation. Tibiae not sulcate on outer edge; posterior tarsi each with first 3 segments sulcate each side above
and also vaguely sulcate at middle, so rather indefinitely
bicarinate; front tarsi with basal segment vaguely sulcate
each side and at middle; 4th segment posterior tarsi deeply
emarginate, outer lobe somewhat longer than inner. Length
11; width 4 mm.

Jamaica: holotype ♂ (M. C. Z. no. 23,015), unique, from
Bath, St. Thomas, Jamaica, 300 ft. altitude, April 3, 1937;
from bromeliads, collected by Mr. Chester Roys.

Related to the preceding (*bromeliarum*) and more distantly to *punctus* and *bruesi*, but at once distinguishable by
the spinose elytra, and differing in other less obvious details.
The difference in tarsal sulci between this species and
bromeliarum is surprising.

OBSERVATIONS AND EXPERIMENTS ON THE CASE-BUILDING INSTINCT OF TWO SPECIES OF TRICHOPTERA

By Manton Copeland and Sears Crowell

Searles Biological Laboratory, Bowdoin College, Brunswick, Maine

The observations recorded here concern the case-building activities of two species of caddis fly larvæ. The first of these belongs to the Limnephilidæ, the other is a species of *Molanna*. Our interest in studying the case-building of these animals has centered around the experimental modification of the process, and we have endeavored to determine the extent to which this instinctive activity may be altered or adapted to changed conditions. Dembowski (1933) has made a very careful study of the case-building of *Molanna*, regarding this process as significant in indicating the plasticity of an animal's actions. Many papers on the case-building of caddis flies are to be found, but no others with this viewpoint. (See bibliography of Betten, Lloyd, or Greene and Milne.) Although our experimental work awaits completion, it has seemed proper to publish those observations which are believed to be new and which may be of assistance to others who are studying animal behavior or the natural history of the Trichoptera.[1] The various materials which these animals are able to use in the construction of the cases are described, as well as a few experiments in which there was an opportunity for the animals to use more than one kind of material, or to select the more appropriate one. The early steps in the formation of the cases are described in some detail. We believe no complete account of these has been published for any caddis fly larva except *Molanna*. This is unfortunate since this part of the process is the most difficult, and we have observed a greater differ-

[1]Since 1933 several authors have published comprehensive papers on Trichoptera as shown in the bibliography. In fact it was largely through the interest of one of these, Mr. Milne, that we undertook the publication of these observations made by us in 1930.

ence in the method of procedure of different species at this
stage than at any other.

The limnephilid which we studied builds a case of the "log
cabin" type, that is of small pieces of plant material placed
transversely with respect to the long axis of the case. In
studying the animals it was customary to push them out of
their cases with a blunt needle and place them in a small dish
with water and materials with which they might build a case.
All of the materials mentioned in the accounts which follow
which would not usually sink in water (e.g. paper and pine
needles) were kept in it until they became waterlogged
before being used.

The typical case-building procedure as observed in the
laboratory is as follows. A larva, pushed from its case, is
placed in a dish containing plant debris similar to that ordi-
narily used in its case. It crawls about for a time, then
commences to gather bits of plant material beneath itself,
holding them partly with its legs and partly by curling its
abdomen downward. Soon, by employing a salivary secretion, it joins to one another the plant fragments that have
been collected. In this way an irregular chain is formed
composed of the pieces of building material. When the
chain is of sufficient length the larva holds one end of it with
the legs of one side and with a leg of the other side reaches
around in back of itself for the free end of the chain. This
is then drawn around to the ventral side and the two ends
joined. The procedure is similar to that followed by a person
in putting on a belt: he holds one end in front of himself and
with his other hand reaches around in back for the free
end which is then brought forward and fastened. In his
account of the case-building of a caddis-worm, *Limnephilus
flavicornis*, Gorter refers to this wrapping of the girdle
around the larva in forming a "provisional case". He does
not, however, describe the procedure.

The girdle formed of the chain of loosely-joined pieces
constitutes the foundation on which the first part of the case
proper is built. This girdle is held by the larva at the level
of the metathorax and pieces of plant material are added,
one at a time, to the forward edge.

The method of building the case from this point on has
been described by others (See Lloyd 1921, Gorter 1929), and

we have no new observations on this part of the process. Each piece of plant material is taken by the larva, smeared with the salivary secretion and set in place. As the case is extended, the original girdle and the completed part of the case are moved backward so that they cover the abdomen. The end to which new material is being added stays in the same position where it is easily reached by mouth-parts and legs. By the addition of material at the forward end the case is eventually completed.

Observations were also made on case-building in *Molanna*. Using sand grains these larvae build cases consisting of a central cylindrical tube, having at the anterior end a broad extension or overhanging hood that protects the animal from above even when its head and thorax are projected from the tube proper. This broad hood extends backward on either side of the main part of the case and forms lateral flanges possibly useful in preventing the case from rolling on its side.

The typical case-building procedure of a *Molanna* larva when pushed from its case and supplied with sand to the depth of about a centimeter is as follows. For about a minute the larva crawls about over the sand. It then curls its abdomen downward so that it no longer moves forward even though it continues to move its legs. This results in the digging of a slight pit in front of the larva and in the formation of a pile of sand beneath the body. Presently the head is forced down into the pit and turned underneath the pile of sand and underneath the body of the larva. Thus the animal is curled and lies on the back of its head as in the first step of a somersault. It then digs farther into the sand, joining the sand grains together loosely with the salivary secretion. Its head finally emerges at the surface on the side of the small pile of sand where the abdomen was located when the process began. The larva at this point has nearly completed a somersault and lies on its back in a sort of tunnel beneath the pile of sand. It next joins together the sand grains around the opening of the tunnel. When the sand grains which line the entrance to the tunnel have been firmly cemented together the animal is encircled by a firm girdle. As in the limnephilid, this is the foundation to which further building material is added to effect the completion of the case. In *Molanna* the girdle may be completed within fifteen minutes. It is clear that the formation of the girdle, the initial and most difficult step in case-building, is accomplished here by a quite different method than in the limnephilid.

The larva remains partly buried in the sand and by adding sand grains to the anterior edge of the girdle extends it to form a tube. This is similar to the method employed by the limnephilid in completing its case.

The hood which overhangs the anterior opening of the tube is constructed as soon as the latter is finished, but its backward extensions (flanges) on either side of the tube may not be completed for one or two days.

On several occasions a larva of *Molanna* was put into a dish with only a small amount of sand, that is with an amount insufficient to permit the burrowing and tunnel formation as described above. Under these circumstances the larva forms the girdle in a somewhat different manner, as follows: The larva collects sand grains into a small pile beneath itself. These are then joined loosely together by the salivary secretion. The larva then thrusts its head into this loosely aggregated mass of sand. If the sand holds together on all sides the larva thus surrounds itself with a girdle. Often the mass of sand breaks apart as the larva burrows into it. When this occurs the procedure is repeated.[1]

From this it appears that a *Molanna* larva, when there is only a small amount of sand, forms the girdle by burrowing, even though this is difficult and often unsuccessful. Since no attempt is made to form a girdle by wrapping the aggregated sand grains around itself, the method is not like that employed by the limnephilid, a procedure which might be more effective than the one actually used. It seemed to us that this method of girdle formation very closely resembled that employed by *Molanna* in deep sand, the only difference consisting in the cementing together of some sand grains before burrowing commenced.

It is well known that caddis-fly larvae are able to employ unusual materials in the construction of cases. We found that the limnephilid larvae were able to build cases of small

[1]Dembowski (1933) reports one case in which a larva of *Molanna*, receiving an insufficient supply of building material, burrowed between the pile of material and the glass bottom of the dish, ultimately using the dish as the under side of its case.

bits of pine needle (*Pinus Strobus*), or in part of paper. The *Molanna* larvæ built cases of assorted debris when no sand was present; they built cases of both sand and plant bits when both were present; and were also able to make a case composed only of small pieces of broken glass.

The method of construction and the form of the case in all observed instances depends on the species rather than on the type or scarcity of material employed. Our observations lead us to regard the modification in the behavior of a larva when supplied with insufficient or unusual material as rather slight. The animal adheres as closely as possible to its usual method of case-building.

Dembowski, who studied only one species (*Molanna*, though probably not the same species as that used by us), emphasizes the variability and plasticity of the animals' activities under varied circumstances. Comparison of the behavior of various species, especially during the early steps of case-building when the larvæ work rapidly, leads us to regard the variations within each species as slight and of little significance.

A few tests were made with limnephilid larvæ to determine whether they would select short pieces of pine needles rather than longer ones which would require cutting by the larvae if they were to be used at all. In one test a larva with a case partly completed was given 50 bits of pine needle 3.5 mm. in length (about the length normally used) and 30 bits 11 mm. in length (a length greater than that of any of the pieces in any observed case built by larvae of this species). A few days later there were only 19 short bits left in the dish though 25 of the longer ones remained. The larva had certainly discarded the long pieces except in a very few instances. Since there were no long pieces in the case it is clear that the animal must have cut up the missing 5 long pieces. In a similar experiment performed later on the same animal 3 out of 25 short pieces were unused and 14 out of 15 long pieces were unused, that is, with but one exception, only the short pieces were accepted.

If a larva which has no case at all is given 11 mm. bits of pine needle it joins the pieces and forms a girdle but the structure is too cumbersome and inflexible to permit its being wrapped around the animal. The larva will again and again make the motions of wrapping the chain about itself, and failing will make another chain, or add to the same one and then again "endeavor" to complete a girdle. It does not, however, cut the pieces to a length which would permit their effective use. With 3.5 mm. bits a girdle may be completed. Larvae supplied with a mixture of long and short pieces use both to make the chain of material that precedes the formation of the girdle, but because this contains some long ones they are unable to wrap it around themselves to complete it. We found no evidence of a selection of material during the early steps in case formation when the length of the pine needle fragments was the only varying factor. Gorter (1929, p. 92) in the limnephilid that he studied observed that: "In the construction of the provisional tube all kinds of material were employed by the larvae, but the pieces could not be too large, for the larva did not bite the material into smaller pieces during the provisional building-process. Biting takes time and during the provisional building-process the larva makes the impression of being in a great hurry. Speed is the chief thing, not firmness, as with the final structure. . . ."

These observations clearly indicate that during girdle formation there is little or no selection and no cutting of materials, but that later when the case is partly completed there is both selection and cutting. However, if the choice during the early steps lay between flexible and stiff material the animals might have shown some selection, for Gorter (p. 92) observes: "In the provisional building-process one thing was very remarkable: there was a great preference for algae, a flexible and soft material, which can be quickly wrapped around the larva without being bitten off." We have not tested this point.

No thorough tests were made to determine whether *Molanna* would show selection of building materials during the early stages when it works rapidly. However, as the case nears completion and the animal works more slowly there is evidence of selection.

Examination of cases of *Molanna* shows that the sand grains of the tube are more varied in size than those of the flange and hood. The latter are nearly all relatively large grains. In one instance in which a larva had been supplied with a mixture of glass and sand the result was a completed case almost all of sand but with some glass in the older part

ALBERT PITTS MORSE, 1863–1936

of it. In another instance a larva was supplied with plant
bits only. Using these it formed a case, complete except for
the flanges on the sides. The animal remained in the dish
with plant bits for two days. No pieces of material were
added during the second day. On the third the larva in its
case was put into a dish containing sand. It at once began
to add sand grains at the anterior end, at first on the hood,
then at the edge of the tube proper. By the next day quite a
good deal of sand had been added at the anterior end though
the main part of the case was of the plant bits. Further
investigation, however, is needed to indicate clearly the
extent to which *Molanna* selects appropriate materials at
different stages in the process of case-building.

SUMMARY

1. The first steps in case-building, *i.e.*, the formation of a
girdle, are described both for a limnephilid and for *Molanna*.
The method is quite different in the two species.

2. Both the limnephilid and *Molanna* are able to employ
a variety of unusual materials in the construction of their
cases.

3. Even when supplied with insufficient or unusual materials, these caddis fly larvae build cases in close accordance
with the method characteristic of the species.

4. In the limnephilid there is little evidence that the
animals select the more appropriate lengths of materials
during early steps of case construction. As the case
nears completion, however, considerable selection does occur.
Incomplete evidence is presented of a similar situation in
Molanna.

BIBLIOGRAPHY

Betten, C. 1934. The Caddis Flies or Trichoptera of New York State.
    New York State Museum Bulletin. No. 292, pp. 1-576.

Dembowski, Jan. 1933. Über die Plastizität der tierischen Handlungen.
    Beobachtungen und Versuche an Molanna-Larven. Zool. Jahrb.
    Abt. allg. Zool. u. Physiol., vol. 53, pp. 261-311.

Gorter, F. 1929. Experiments on the case-building of a caddis-worm
    (*Limnophilus flavicornis* Fabr.) Tydschrift der Nederlandsche
    Dierkun dige Vereeniging. (3) vol. 1, pp. 90-93.

Greene, M. J. and L. J. Milne, in press. Immature North American
    Caddis Flies (Trichoptera). 1. A summary and extension of
    our knowledge of these forms.

Lloyd, L. T. 1921. The biology of North American caddis fly larvæ.
    Bulletin of the Lloyd Library of Botany, Pharmacy and Materia
    Medica. No. 21, pp. 1-124.

SYNONYMY OF THE GENUS PSEUDOXENOS SAUNDERS (STREPSIPTERA, XENIDÆ) AND RECORDS OF STYLOPIZED HYMENOPTERA FROM NORTH CAROLINA

By Richard M. Bohart

University of California, Berkeley

The genus *Pseudoxenos* was erected in 1872 by S. S. Saunders for parasites of the eumenid genus *Odynerus*. Further taxonomic work on members of the genus was done by Pierce, 1908, 1909, 1911, 1918; A. Ogloblin, 1924; Monod, 1925; and Esaki, 1932. Altho considerable information is available as a result of the efforts of these men, certain important characters of the female and first larva have been inadequately described.

Males, females, and first stage larvae of several undescribed species of *Pseudoxenos* are in the author's collection. From this material the following has been observed. In the male the anterior edges of the scutellum may be convergent or may be nearly parallel, thus invalidating the character used by Pierce, 1918, to separate the tribe Pseudoxenini from parasites of the Sphecoidea; the female has three genital tubes as do the parasites of Sphecinæ; and the first stage larva has five ocelli as in all the known strepsipterous parasites on wasps.

A careful comparison in all stages of these typical *Pseudoxenos* with specimens in the author's collection of the genera erected by Pierce, 1908, 1909, on the basis of host relationships and insufficient data; that is, *Leionotoxenos* from *Odynerus* and *Eupathocera, Ophthalmochlus, Homilops,* and *Sceliphronecthrus* from Sphecinæ, has failed to show any generic differences whatsoever. The characters used by Pierce, such as the shape of the scutellum and "consistency" of the postlumbium in the male, and shape of the cephalothorax and position of the spiracles in the female, vary widely and hence are useless.

Therefore, the author has come to the inescapable conclusion that the aforementioned genera are synonymous with *Pseudoxenos*. Altho no specimens have been examined of *Macroxenos* Schultze, 1925, from *Odynerus*, according to the description and figures this genus should also be referred to *Pseudoxenos*.

The following is a synopsis of the genus as herein redefined.

Genus **Pseudoxenos** Saunders, 1872

Eupathocera Pierce, 1908a; *Ophthalmochlus* Pierce, 1908b; *Homilops* Pierce, 1908c; *Leionotoxenos* Pierce, 1909a; *Sceliphronecthrus* Pierce, 1909b; *Macroxenos* Schultze, 1925.

Male. Radius of the hind wing with the detached apical portion distinct and originating posterior to the main vein; otherwise similar to *Xenos*. Metathoracic scutellum strongly narrowed anteriorly and with its anterior edges usually convergent but sometimes almost parallel. Metathoracic postlumbium not strongly spindle-shaped but frequently somewhat constricted at the middle. Ædeagus extremely variable according to species and apparently without generic significance.

Female. Cephalothorax darker on the anterior one-half than on the posterior one-half. Abdomen with three genital tubes entering the brood canal, as contrasted with four in *Xenos*.

First Stage Larva. Each eye composed of five ocelli, three dorsal, one lateral, and one ventral. Hind femur with one apical bristle, hind tibia with one outer bristle and three inner bristles, hind tarsus with a small subterminal pulvillus giving it a forked appearance in profile. Abdomen with six rows of stout bristles on sternites two to seven. Sternite nine bearing a pair of short stout tubercles furnished with long apical bristles and very short subapical ones. Tenth abdominal segment with a pair of latero-dorsal spines which are approximately half as long as the terminal stylets.

STYLOPIZED HYMENOPTERA FROM NORTH CAROLINA

It is interesting to note that only very rarely has the State of North Carolina been included as a locality in lists of

Hymenoptera parasitized by Strepsiptera. The only previous record with which the author is familiar was made by George Salt, 1927, who recorded a parasitized specimen of *Chlorion pennsylvanicum* (Linn.) from Southern Pines.

Additional records are now available thru the efforts of Mr. C. S. Brimley of the North Carolina Department of Agriculture who has sent the author a number of stylopized specimens and furnished additional records by letter.

Whenever possible the identity of the parasite has been determined and included in the following list. The portion of each reference before the colon refers in every case to the host and that after the colon to the parasite.

Sphecidae

Chlorion (Ammobia) flavitarsus (Fernald). Swannanoa, Sept. 3, 1924, one specimen, T. B. Mitchell coll.: mature male, *Pseudoxenos*[1] sp. near *smithii* (Von Heyden).

Chlorion (Ammobia) habenum (Say). Raleigh, Aug. 24, 1921, two specimens, C. S. Brimley coll.: male puparium and female, *Pseudoxenos* sp. near *smithii* (Von Heyden).

Chlorion (Ammobia) ichneumoneum (Linn.). Raleigh, June 16, 1933, three specimens, D. L. Wray coll.: male puparium, exuvia, and two females, *Pseudoxenos smithii* (Von Heyden).

Chlorion (Ammobia) pennsylvanicum (Linn.). Raleigh, Sept. 2, 1927, two specimens; Aug. 6, 1924, one specimen; Aug. 6, 1904, one specimen; C. S. Brimley coll.: male puparium, exuvia, and three females, *Pseudoxenos* sp. near *smithii* (Von Heyden).

Sphex aureonotatus (Cam.) (det. by H. T. Fernald). Raleigh, mid June, 1914, one specimen, C. L. Metcalf coll. Raleigh, mid July (no year), three specimens; Sept. 8, 1921, one specimen; Sept. 9, 1904, one specimen; Sept. 13, 1921, one specimen; C. S. Brimley coll. Raleigh, mid Sept., 1921, T. B. Mitchell coll. Willard,

---

[1]Refer to *Homilops* Pierce and *Ophthalmochlus* Pierce in the synopsis of this paper.

July 15, 1925, one specimen, C. S. Brimley coll.
Charlotte, July 6, 1921, one specimen, T. B. Mitchell
coll. Elizabeth City, early Aug., 1919, one specimen,
F. Sherman coll.: two mature males, two male
puparia, two exuviae, and thirteen females, *Pseudoxenos* sp.'

Sphex urnarius (Dahlb.) (det. by H. T. Fernald). Raleigh,
June 30, 1921, one specimen; Sept. 13, 1921, one
specimen; early Nov. (no year), one specimen; C. S.
Brimley coll. Southern Pines, June 11, 1911, A. H.
Manee coll.: four exuviae and three females, *Pseu-
doxenos* sp. (apparently the same species as that on
S. aureonotatus).

Vespidæ

Ancistrocerus fulvipes (Sauss.). Raleigh, Aug. 13, 1925,
one specimen, C. S. Brimley coll.: female, *Pseudoxenos* sp.

Odynerus pedestris Sauss. Raleigh, mid April, 1921, one
specimen, C. S. Brimley coll.: male puparium and
female, *Pseudoxenos* sp. (probably *pedestridis*
Pierce).

Zethus spinipes Say var. *variegatus* Sauss. Beaufort,
Aug. 11, 1902, one specimen, F. Sherman coll.: female, probably *Pseudoxenos* sp.

Polistes canadensis (Linn.) var *annularis* (Linn.) Biltmore, July 29, 1933, one specimen, D. L. Wray coll.:
female, *Xenos pallidus* Brues.

Polistes fuscatus (Fabr.) var. *pallipes* (Lepel). Raleigh,
Apr. 10, 1905, one specimen, G. M. Bentley coll.; mid
Oct., 1917, one specimen, J. E. Eckert coll. Currituck,
June 5, 1935, one specimen, D. L. Wray coll. Fayette-
ville, June 25, 1933, one specimen, D. L. Wray coll.
Elizabeth City, mid Aug., 1919, one specimen, F.
Sherman coll.: one mature male, three male puparia,
exuviae, four females, *Xenos peckii* Kirby.

Polistes fuscatus (Fabr.) var *variatus* (Cresson). Raleigh,
June 7, 1933, one specimen, D. L. Wray coll. Ashe-

'Refer to *Eupathocera* Pierce in the synopsis of this paper.

ville, Sept. 6, 1932, one specimen, D. L. Wray coll.: eight male puparia and one female, *Xenos peckii* Kirby.

Andrenidæ

Andrena sp. Raleigh, Mar. 24, 1925, one specimen on willow, T. B. Mitchell coll.: female, *Stylops* sp.

Halictidæ

Halictus (Chloralictus) sp. Late May, 1921, one specimen on *Penstemon*, T. B. Mitchell coll.: female *Halictoxenos crawfordi* Pierce.

Halictus (Chloralictus) sparsus Robt. Bryson City, no date: *Halictoxenos sparsi* Pierce. (Host and parasite determined by J. C. Crawford).

Halictus (Chloralictus) versatus Robt. Bryson City, July 8, 1923: *Halictoxenos versati* Pierce. (Host and parasite determined by J. C. Crawford).

Halictus (Chloralictus) zephyrus Smith. Bryson City, Aug. 23, 1923: *Halictoxenos zephyri* Pierce. (Host and parasite determined by J. C. Crawford).

Panurgidæ

Panurginus sp. Bryson City, no date: *Crawfordia* sp. (Recorded by J. C. Crawford).

The last four references above were taken from correspondence with Mr. C. S. Brimley.

With records from Bryson City, Biltmore, Asheville, and Swannanoa in the west; Charlotte, Southern Pines, Fayetteville, and Raleigh in the central portion; and Beaufort, Elizabeth City, and Currituck in the east; Strepsiptera are now well represented in records from North Carolina.

REFERENCES

Esaki, T. 1932. Strepsiptera, in Iconographia Insectorum Japanicorum. Nippon Konchu Zukan, Hokuryukan, Tokyo.

Monod, T. 1925. Sur un Pseudoxenos parasite d'Odynerus crenatus Lepeletier. Bull. Soc. Zool. Paris, vol. 50, pp. 230-244, 3 figs.

Ogloblin, A. A. 1924. New and little known Strepsiptera from Poland. Polskie Pismo Entomologiczne, vol. 3, pp. 113-122, illus.

Pierce, W. D. 1908. A preliminary review of the classification of the order Strepsiptera. Proc. Ent. Soc. Wash., vol. 9, pp. 75-85.

———— 1909. A monographic revision of the twisted winged insects comprising the order Strepsiptera Kirby. Bull. U. S. Nat. Mus., No. 66, pp. 1-232, 15 Pls.

———— 1911. Notes on insects of the order Strepsiptera with descriptions of new species. Proc. U. S. Nat. Mus., vol. 40, pp. 487-511.

———— 1918. The comparative morphology of the order Strepsiptera together with records and descriptions of insects. Proc. U. S. Nat. Mus., vol. 54, pp. 391-501, 15 Pls.

Salt, G. 1927. Notes on the Strepsiptera and their hymenopterous hosts. Psyche, vol. 34, pp. 182-192.

Saunders, S. S. 1872. Stylopidarum, ordinem Strepsipterorum Kirbii constituentium, mihi tamen potius Coleopterorum familiae, Rhipiphoridis Meloidisque propinquae, monographia. Trans. Ent. Soc. Lond. Part I, (April) pp. 1-48, 1 Pl.

Schultze, W. 1925. Macroxenos pierci, a new genus and species of wasp parasites from the Philipine Islands. Phil. Jour. Sci., vol. 27, pp. 238, illus.

BIOLOGY OF THE TACHINID *WINTHEMIA DATANÆ* TNS.

By Frank L. Marsh

Union College, Lincoln, Nebraska

In a recent study of the parasites of Cecropia in the Chicago area based on the examination of over three thousand Cecropian cocoons collected in that region[1] some interesting facts were discovered in the life-history of the tachina fly *Winthemia datanae* Tns. For the identification of this insect the writer is indebted to Mr. J. M. Aldrich of the U. S. National Museum. In this instance every case of tachinid parasitization appeared to be the work of this single species. Over the entire area at least three percent of the mature Cecropian larvæ were destroyed by this insect.

Emergence, Breeding Habits, and Oviposition

During a normal season the first adults emerge the second week in July. This appearance happens to be well timed because at that juncture the earliest of the Cecropian larvae have molted the last time before spinning their cocoons. When considered over the whole area the parasitization is rather light but it is the habit of this tachinid to work in limited spots probably including a half dozen trees. In these sporadic areas the infestation is heavy often amounting to the total destruction of the host larvae. Where taller trees were infested by Cecropia six times as many of its cocoons were parasitized by this tachinid when spun below the fifteen-foot level as when spun above that level.

Copulation and egg-laying occur rather intermittently. The males rest on the leaves of the infected trees, at times engaging the females during temporary cessation of their

[1]Marsh, F. L. 1934. "A Regional Study of *Samia cecropia* and Nine Associated Parasites and Hyperparasites." An unpublished Master's Thesis in the Northwestern University Library, Evanston, Illinois.

egg-laying activities. During oviposition the female hovers over the back of the larva, clinging to its tubercles while the eggs are securely attached by their adhesive coating to the skin of the host along the dorsal line. The largest number observed on one larva was 76 while the average was 21. In every case observed larvæ in the earlier stages were passed by, eggs being placed only on those which had molted the last time before spinning. Because of this adaptive behavior the eggs are not shed with the larval skin at molting time. The host larvæ give little heed to the egg-laying, only temporarily stopping their feeding. Oviposition occured more commonly in the latter part of the afternoon on the shaded side of trees and bushes.

Egg and Larva

The eggs are white and measure about 0.8 mm. x 0.3 mm. In about thirty-six hours the endophagous larva gnaws an opening near one end on the adhering side of the egg and tunnels down directly into the cœlomic fluid of its host. Bacterial action causes a blackening of the area of the cuticle where the tunneling occurs and a characteristic dried patch appears around the egg shells in a few hours.

The larvae develop rapidly but due to the eggs having been laid on mature larvæ the host almost invariably completes at least the outer shell of its cocoon before being killed. Such cocoons are usually white in color. If few tachinid larvæ are present the cocoon may be fully completed before the host larva is killed. In every case observed the infected larva always died although it may have been parasitized by but a single tachinid larva. In instances of heavy infestation death of the host occurs in three or four days after the parasites emerge from the eggs.

The dead host turns brown in color and usually presents a distended appearance. Oxygen seems very essential to adult tachinid larvæ, evidenced by an opening which is invariably made in the skin of the host, usually on the ventral surface. This same hole is later used as an exit from the tough, dried skin of the host. The larvæ mature in from six to eight days and may crawl out immediately or may rest for a time in the dried host skin. If a cocoon containing adult maggots is agitated even slightly the parasites appear much disturbed and usually crawl out immediately.

Once outside the dead host's skin, the larva finds itself still a prisoner in the Cecropian cocoon. It never punctures this cocoon and not uncommonly dies from dehydration before it can escape. The only way out is through the valve of the cocoon. The larva has no fear of dropping and its tough skin insulates it effectively from the shock of landing. In an experiment a handful of these larvae were tossed from a third-story window to cement below. Though bounding several feet with the force of the impact still they began to wriggle away immediately and in each case pupated later, apparently uninjured by the experience.

Upon reaching the ground the maggot at once begins to push into the soil. The depth to which it penetrates depends on how far it must go to find reasonably damp soil, usually from three to eight inches. At the proper depth the soil is pushed out till a cell is formed in which the larva will either pupate after a few days and emerge as an adult in about a week or the larva will hibernate through the winter and pupate the following July. In the region studied the second brood of this tachinid in a summer was the exception rather than the rule. Proper moisture appears to be very necessary for the survival of the larva or puparium. For that reason puparia formed in the host cocoon where the larvæ have failed to escape must immediately develop into adults or perish. If adults chanced to emerge in such situations, they could not escape from the host cocoon. In this study the only successful individuals were those which pupated in the ground.

Three reasons why *W. datanae* is not a more effective parasite of Cecropia in the Chicago area are its habit of ovipositing only on mature larvae, the failure of many of the maggots to escape from the host cocoon, and the great sensitiveness to dehydration on the part of both hibernating larvæ and the puparia.

NOTES ON THE COURTSHIP AND MATING OF THE FLY, *PTECTICUS TRIVITTATUS* SAY[1]

By Phil Rau

Kirkwood, Missouri

During several summers before these notes were made in 1930 and also several summers afterwards, large numbers of these attractive greenish-colored flies were seen hovering in courtship dances above garbage heaps on the rear of a lot. They were first observed on the 20th day of May of that year and they continued their activities over this restricted area until the middle of July; to be exact, they appeared in much reduced numbers on July 19th and had completely disappeared by July 25th. There are probably two generations a year, for they again appeared on August 22nd and were seen thereafter until September 11th.

They spend much of their time flying slowly and noiselessly over this "island" of color and odor commencing sometimes as early as 5:30 in the morning when only a few may be seen; they increase in numbers with the passing of the hours and the rising of the temperature. They dance almost incessantly throughout the long day, and even into the dusk may the motion of their frail forms be seen. To say that they dance incessantly is not wholly true for individuals often leave the throng to rest on a tin-can or bottle or cantaloupe skin. The temperature readings when these dances occur varies from 65 to 75 degrees F.; one can, however, hardly refer to the phenomenon as a "sun dance" because the flies are equally active in sunshine or shade, as well as in shadowy stretches splashed with spots of sunlight. Both males and females are present in the dance, and the sexes are about equal.

It is, indeed, a pretty sight to see a flock of these flies moving in a horizontal plane in more-or-less irregular circles

[1]Specimens were kindly identified by Mr. C. T. Greens of U. S. Dept. of Agriculture.

and in figure eights just an inch or two above the mass of multi-colored refuse. As one singles out certain individuals, however, one soon realizes that frequently they describe circles within still larger circles. Each fly circles about horizontally in an area of ten or twelve inches with occasional breaks by an insect into another's circle; all this gives the assemblage a placid and slow-moving appearance. Often a fly will leave the dance to rest on a tin-can or on a glass bottle, many of which stud the heap. Sometimes one will go in pursuit of another and quarreling occurs. When the quarrel culminates mating usually takes place. Mating is consummated while they are on the wing but the pair soon settle down amid the garbage to rest, remaining in copulo for 10 or 15 minutes. So intent are they in this affair that the object upon which they repose may be carried for a long distance without arousing them.

When one examines a mated pair closely one finds that the larger insect, the female, is invariably on top of the smaller one, the male. Both heads are close together and during the process the female caresses the face and eyes of the male with her front legs. This behavior is very much like that of a fond mother petting her child. It is quite evident that the male enjoys this procedure, for he responds by licking her leg with his proboscis. Often his mouth parts will actually reach out to meet her leg, but sometimes he holds them alert in attentive readiness. One pair behaved this way for 15 minutes while I held the bottle upon which they rested in my hand.

The flies, singly or *in copula*, never rest on the moist portions of the garbage but always upon some hard dry object in the mass. Sometimes they rest on the grass-stems near their stamping grounds. They have never been seen to feed on garbage and I have never seen them lay eggs there, although I have watched carefully to detect both activities. However, oviposition must occur on objects nearby and also very soon after mating, for on one occasion when a mated pair separated in my hand, the female deposited about a hundred eggs in less than ten minutes.

Psyche Dec.1937
    Information
    Missing pp 143-44
    TP Removed placed
    in front of v.

            Binding Unit..

PSYCHE

INDEX TO VOL. XLIV, 1937

INDEX TO AUTHORS

INDEX TO SUBJECTS

All new genera, new species and new names are printed in SMALL CAPITAL LETTERS.

PIN-LABELS IN MULTIPLES OF 1000, ALIKE

One Dollar Per Thousand

Smallest Type. Pure White Ledger Paper. Not over 4 Lines nor 30 Characters (13 to a line) Additional Characters, 3 cents each, in total and per line, per 1000. Trimmed so one cut makes a label.

C. V. BLACKBURN, 7 Emerson St., STONEHAM 80, MASS.

CAMBRIDGE ENTOMOLOGICAL CLUB

A regular meeting of the Club is held on the second Tuesday of each month (July, August and September excepted) at 7.45 p.m. in Room B-455, Biological Laboratories of Harvard University, Divinity Ave., Cambridge. Entomologists visiting Boston are cordially invited to attend.

WARD'S ENTOMOLOGICAL SERVICES

Entomological Supplies and Equipment
Carefully designed by professional entomologists. Material of high quality at low prices. **Send for Supply Catalog No. 348.**

Insect Preparations
Life Histories, Type Collections, Collections of Economic Insects and Biological Insect Collections. All specimens are accurately determined.

Insects for the Pest Collection
We have in stock over three hundred species of North American Insect Pests. **Send for Price List No. 349.**

Ward's Entomological Bulletin
A monthly publication sent free to all entomologists requesting it.

Information for the Beginner
Send for **"Directions for Collecting and Preserving Insects"** by Dr. A. B. Klots. A mine of useful information. Price 15 cents.

WARD'S NATURAL SCIENCE ESTABLISHMENT, Inc.
P. O. Box 24, Beechwood Station
Rochester, N. Y., U. S. A.
The Frank A. Ward Foundation of Natural Science of the University of Rochester

BACK VOLUMES OF PSYCHE

The Cambridge Entomological Club is able to offer for sale the following volumes of Psyche. Those not mentioned are entirely out of print.

Volumes 2, 3, 4, 5, 6, 7, 8, 9, 10; each covering a period of three years, $5.00 each.

Volumes 12, 14, 17, each covering a single year, $1.00 each.

Volumes 18, 19, 20, 21, 22, 23, 24, 25, 26, each covering a single year, $1.50 each.

Volumes 27, 28, 29, 30, 31, 32, 33, 34, 35, 36, 37, 38, 39, 40, 41, 42, 43, 44, each covering a single year, $2.00.

Orders for 2 or more volumes subject to a discount of 10%.

Orders for 10 or more volumes subject to a discount of 20%.

A set of all the volumes available (40 in all) will be sold for $79.00.

All orders should be addressed to

F. M. CARPENTER, Associate Editor of Psyche,
Biological Laboratories,
Harvard University,
Cambridge, Mass.

PSYCHE

A Journal of Entomology

Volume XLV

1938

EDITED BY CHARLES T. BRUES

Published by the Cambridge Entomological Club
Biological Laboratories
Harvard University
Cambridge, Mass., U.S.A.

PSYCHE

A JOURNAL OF ENTOMOLOGY

ESTABLISHED IN 1874

VOL. XLV   MARCH, 1938   No. 1

TABLE OF CONTENTS

CAMBRIDGE ENTOMOLOGICAL CLUB

OFFICERS FOR 1937-1938

President . .	. C. A. Frost
Vice-President .	J. C. Bequaert
Secretary	V. G. Dethier
Treasurer	Richard Dow
	Thomas Barbour
Executive Committee {	F. M. Carpenter
	C. H. Blake

EDITORIAL BOARD OF PSYCHE

EDITOR-IN-CHIEF
C. T. Brues, Harvard University

ASSOCIATE EDITOR
F. M. Carpenter, Harvard University

CONSULTING EDITORS

Nathan Banks,
Harvard University.

A. E. Emerson,
University of Chicago.

Thomas Barbour,
Harvard University.

A. L. Melander,
College of the
City of New York.

Richard Dow,
New England Museum of
Natural History,
Boston, Mass.

J. G. Needham,
Cornell University.

PSYCHE is published quarterly, the issues appearing in March, June, September, and December. Subscription price, per year, payable in advance: $2.00 to Subscribers in the United States; foreign postage, 25 cents extra, Canada 15 cents. Single copies, 65 cents.

Cheques and remittances should be addressed to Treasurer, Cambridge Entomological Club, Biological Laboratories, Harvard University, Cambridge, Mass.

Orders for back volumes, missing numbers, notices of change of address, etc., should be sent to Professor F. M. Carpenter, Biological Laboratories, Harvard University, Cambridge, Mass.

IMPORTANT NOTICE TO CONTRIBUTORS
Manuscripts intended for publication, books intended for review, and other editorial matter, should be addressed to Professor C. T. Brues, Biological Laboratories, Harvard University, Cambridge, Mass.

Authors contributing articles over 8 printed pages in length will be required to bear a part of the extra expense, for additional pages. This expense will be that of typesetting only, which is about $2.00 per page. The actual cost of preparing cuts for all illustrations must be borne by contributors; the expense for full page plates from line drawings is approximately $5.00 each, and for full page half-tones, $7.50 each; smaller sizes in proportion.

AUTHOR'S SEPARATES
Reprints of articles may be secured by authors, if they are ordered before, or at the time proofs are received for corrections. The cost of these will be furnished by the Editor on application.

Printed by the Eliot Press Inc., Jamaica Plain, Mass., U. S. A.

PSYCHE

| VOL. XLV | MARCH, 1938 | No. 1 |

LECTOTYPES OF NORTH AMERICAN CADDIS FLIES IN THE MUSEUM OF COMPARATIVE ZOOLOGY[1]

By Herbert H. Ross

Illinois State Natural History Survey,
Urbana, Illinois

Few species of caddis flies described by Hagen and Banks have had lectotypes designated for them. In a few cases the type series of one species contains representatives of more than one species, a condition which has led to confusion of names due to different interpretations made by different authors. The only way to obviate further repetition of this is to place on a single type basis (by lectotype designations) all those species described from a series of cotypes. This paper sets lectotypes for 229 species, all the lectotypes being in the collection of the Museum of Comparative Zoology.

The method followed in selecting the single type specimens has taken into account very little work done by other authors, since a large number of the species represent segregations seldom recognized by others. Furthermore both Hagen and Banks used a labelling system which left no doubt as to which specimen they considered the real type. Hagen placed his label on only one specimen and marked it with an asterisk if it were a type or plesiotype in the sense of present usage. Other specimens in the series were simply placed in

[1]A grant from the travel fund of the Illinois State Natural History Survey, Urbana, Illinois, made it possible for me to visit the Museum of Comparative Zoology and make these studies. I wish to acknowledge my gratitude and appreciation to the Survey for this grant.

a row after the first labelled specimen; undoubtedly some specimens which are not actually types were put in these series at the same time or subsequently, either by Hagen himself or inadvertantly by others. In selecting lectotypes of Hagen's species the specimen labelled by Hagen has been taken in each case. Lectotypes have been designated for all the species from North America described by Hagen unless they have been previously set in literature, even if only represented in the collection by a single individual. This is done because of the possibility of specimens appearing in other collections which might erroneously be considered as types.

There is a possibility that some specimens designated as lectoallotypes have not been correctly associated with the lectotypes, that is, do not represent the opposite sex of the same species as the lectotypes. In a very high proportion of the North American caddis fly species it is impossible, with our present studies, to separate the females of closely related forms, so that we have to rely to an inordinate extent on collection data as a basis for association.

All the specimens mentioned as "allotype" represent designations made for the first time in this paper.

In the Banks collection the specimens listed without definite collector from the eastern states were taken by Banks himself, except in a few cases.

Banks' species have his own label on the first specimen and simply a "TYPE" label on the others. The first specimen with the label has been taken as the lectotype, a procedure which Mr. Banks has requested and which seems perfectly logical.

In rare cases when these first specimens have been females and the cotype series contained males, an exception to the foregoing procedure has been instituted and a male selected as the lectotype.

No attempt has been made to analyze any of the cotype series except the lectotypes, the remainder automatically becoming paratypes. Such a study would have little significance since the paratypes will have only historic and minor taxonomic interest. Furthermore so many of the specimens have been sent in exchanges, etc., to institutions in widely scattered countries that it has been impossible for me to gather the necessary information.

The species treated are listed within each family alphabetically according first to genus and then to species. Many of the species have been transferred from genus to genus several times. In attempting to find some method which would be easy to follow and at the same time show the generic placement, I am using the following double entry when a change has been made. If a species is placed in a genus other than the one in which it was described, it is listed both under the genus in which it was originally described and under the genus in which I am placing it. For example, *Hydropsyche sordida* Hagen is now placed in the genus *Cheumatopsyche*. Therefore, it is listed under both *Hydropsyche sordida* in the h's and under *Cheumatopsyche sordida*. Under the former, note is made of the genus in which it is placed.

Professor Nathan Banks, Curator of insects at the Museum of Comparative Zoölogy, and Professor F. M. Carpenter of the Division of Biology, Harvard University, have been of inestimable help during the course of this work in giving information and advice, in placing at my disposal study facilities and equipment, and in the many courtesies accorded me during my visit to the Museum of Comparative Zoology.

Dr. C. O. Mohr, of the Illinois State Natural History Survey, has made most of the drawings for this paper, and I wish to express my gratitude for this.

Family RHYACOPHILIDÆ

Agapetus malleatus Banks, 1914, p. 202, fig. 57.

Lectotype, male.—Los Angeles County, California, San Gabriel Mts., 3000 ft., June 17, 1907, F. Grinnell, Jr. No. 11723. *Lectoallotype, female.*—Same data.

The genitalia of the lectotype are shown in fig. 1.

Baerea? maculata Hagen.—see *Protoptila maculata* (Hagen)

Glossosoma nigrior Banks.—see *Mystrophora nigrior* (Banks)

Glossosoma parvulum Banks, 1904a, p. 108, fig. 13.

Lectotype, male.—Pecos, New Mexico, August 10, at

light. No. 11748. *Lectoallotype, female.*—Same data, but August 13.

The genitalia of a homotype are shown in fig. 2.

Mystrophora lividum (Hagen), 1861, p. 295 (*Tinodes*).

Lectotype, female.—St. Lawrence River, Canada, Osten Sacken. No. 11081.

Milne has determined the male of this species as that illustrated by Betten as *Mystrophora sp.* (1934, pl. 9, figs. 15-17).

Mystrophora nigrior (Banks), 1911, p. 355, fig. 23. (*Glossosoma*)

Lectotype, male.—Black Mountain, North Carolina, north fork Swannanoa River, May. No. 11745. *Lectoallotype, female.*—Same data.

At present there appear to be two valid species in this genus, the two illustrated by Betten (1934) as *americana* and *Mystrophora sp.* No good characters have been discovered as yet which separate the females of the two species, so that the exact status of the names *americana* Banks and *lividum* Hagen is problematic. It seems best at present to consider as *nigrior* the species treated as *americana* by most authors and illustrated by Betten (1934, pl. 8, figs. 4-6 and pl. 9, figs. 1-14), and to consider *americana* as an unidentified species.

Protoptila maculata (Hagen), 1861, p. 296. (*Baerea?*)

Lectotype, male.—St. Lawrence River, Canada, 1859, Sacken. No. 11093. *Lectoallotype, female.*—Same data.

This species has been illustrated by both Banks and Betten (1934).

Rhyacophila acropedes Banks, 1914, p. 201, fig. 39.

Lectotype, male.—Deer creek, Provo Canon, Utah, August 21, Spalding. No. 11741.

This species is closely allied to *coloradensis* Banks, but differs in details of the male genitalia, fig. 6.

Rhyacophila atrata Banks, 1911, p. 351.

Lectotype, male.—Black Mountain, North Carolina, north fork Swannanoa River, May. No. 11739. *Lectoallotype, female.*—Same data.

The genitalia of the type are shown in fig. 3.

Rhyacophila brunnea Banks, 1911, p. 252.

Lectotype, female.—Beulah, New Mexico, July 16. No. 11735.

There is a series of males and females in the M. C. Z. from Cultus Lake, B. C., the females of which appear exactly like the lectotype of *brunnea* in color and external genitalia. A male of this series has been selected as the allotype. It belongs to the *acropedes* group, fig. 4, but is readily distinguished by details of the genitalia.

Allotype, male.—Cultus Lake, British Columbia: May 18, 1933, W. E. Ricker.

Rhyacophila carolina Banks, 1911, p. 353, fig. 31.

Lectotype, male.—Black Mountain, North Carolina, north fork Swannanoa River, May. No. 11727. *Lectoallotype, female.*—Same data.

In addition to those in the original description, illustrations of the genitalia have been given by Betten (1934, pl. 5, figs. 4-7).

Rhyacophila coloradensis Banks, 1905b, p. 10.

Lectotype, male.—Fort Collins, Colorado. No. 11728.

This species is close to *bifila* Banks, but is readily distinguished by details of the genitalia, fig. 5.

Rhyacophila fairchildi Banks, 1930a, p. 130, figs. 4, 7.

Lectotype, male.—Baddeck, Cape Breton Island, Nova Scotia, September 4, 1928. No. 16237. *Lectoallotype, female.*—Same data.

The genitalia of the lectotype agree perfectly with the illustrations of *glaberrima* Ulmer and with the genitalia of the type of *andrea* Betten. There seems little doubt, therefore, that both *fairchildi* and *andrea* are synonyms of Ulmer's species, originally described from Georgia.

Rhyacophila formosa Banks, 1911, p. 353.

Lectotype, female.—Delaware Water Gap, New Jersey. No. 11078.

To date no male has been associated with this form, drawings of which are given by Milne (1936).

Rhyacophila grandis Banks, 1911, p. 350, fig. 27.

Lectotype, male.—Bon Accord, British Columbia, June 14. No. 11737. *Lectoallotype, female.*—Same data, but June 19.

The genitalia of the lectotype are well exposed without clearing, including the apex of the side tubes on the ædeagus. They are identical with those of the homotype illustrated in fig. 8.

Rhyacophila hyalinata Banks, 1905b, p. 10.

Lectotype, male.—South West Colorado, July 23, 1899. No. 11738.

The genitalia of the lectotype have been cleared and compared critically with those of the specimen illustrated in fig. 7.

Rhyacophila luctuosa Banks, 1911, p. 351, fig. 24.

Lectotype, male.—Woodworth Lake, Fulton County, New York, June 23, 1910, Alexander. No. 11740. *Lectoallotype, female.*—Same data.

The male genitalia are shown in fig. 9. The species is listed as a synonym of *invaria* Walker by Banks (1930b).

Rhyacophila minora Banks, 1924, p. 444, fig. 37.

Lectotype, male.—White Mountains, New Hampshire, Morrison. No. 14857. *Lectoallotype, female.*—Same data.

This species was described and illustrated by Betten (1934, p. 134, pl. 7, figs. 10, 11) as *Rhyacophila* sp. 1.

Rhyacophila nevadensis Banks, 1924, p. 443, fig. 53.

Lectotype, male.—Reno, Nevada, Morrison, 1878. No. 14855. *Lectoallotype, female.*—Same data.

Rhyacophila nigrita Banks, 1907a, p. 132, fig. 16.

Lectotype, female.—Black Mountain, North Carolina, June. No. 11742.

The male of this species has been figured in considerable detail by Betten (1934, pl. 7, figs. 1-5). The allotype will have to be designated from one of his specimens.

Rhyacophila rotunda Banks, 1924, p. 443, fig. 33.

Lectotype, male.—Reno, Nevada, 1878, Morrison. No. 14856. *Lectoallotype, female.*—Same data.

Rhyacophila torva Hagen, 1861, p. 296.

Lectotype, male.—Washington, D. C., Sacken. No. 11078.

The genitalia of this species have been illustrated by Banks (1907a, p. 132, fig. 7) and Betten (1934, pl. 7, figs. 6-9).

Tinodes lividum Hagen.—see *Mystrophora lividum* (Hagen)

Family PHILOPOTAMIDÆ

Chimarrha aterrima Hagen, 1861, p. 297.
Lectotype, male.—Mus. Berol. Penn. No. 11098.
The male genitalia have been illustrated by Betten (1934, pl. 16, figs. 6-9).

Chimarrha femoralis (Banks), 1911, p. 358. (*Wormaldia*).
Lectotype, male.—Sacandaga River, Sport Island, New York, June 27, 1910. No. 11520.
This species is a synonym of *socia* Hagen. Betten has figured the genitalia under the latter name (1934, pl. 16, fig. 13).

Chimarrha plutonis (Banks), 1911, p. 358, fig. 34. (*Wormaldia*).
Lectotype, male.—Delaware Water Gap. No. 11519.
The male genitalia of this species have been illustrated by Betten under the name *lucia* Betten (1934, pl. 16, figs. 10-12).

Chimarrha texana Banks, 1920, p. 360.
Lectotype, female.—San Antonio, Texas, August, Snow. No. 10914.
To date no reliable characters have been found for separating the females of this genus, so that for the present this species must be considered of doubtful identity.

Dolophiliella gabriella Banks.—see *Dolophilus gabriella* (Banks).

Dolophilus breviatus Banks, 1914, p. 254, fig. 61.
Lectotype, male.—Ithaca, New York, in Coy Glen, August. No. 11518.
The male genitalia of this type are broader than those of *moestus*, but the study of additional specimens indicates that this difference may be only individual variation.

Dolophilus gabriella (Banks), 1930b, p. 230, fig. 14. (*Dolophiliella*).
Lectotype, male.—San Gabriel Mountains, California, June 29. No. 16326.
The most distinctive feature of this species is the more or

less spatulate process of the eighth sternite.

Dolophilus major Banks, 1914, p. 254, fig. 66.
Lectotype, male.—Black Mountain, North Carolina, May.
No. 11517.
This is the largest eastern species in the family.

Philopotamus aequalis Banks, 1924, p. 450, fig. 48.
Lectotype, male.—Tolland, Colorado, Dodds. No. 14853.
Lectoallotype, female.—Same data.
This western species is readily distinguished by its dark color and the male genitalia.

Philopotamus americanus Banks, 1895, p. 316.
Lectotype, male.—New York. No. 11512.
Both Banks and Betten have given illustrations showing a difference between this species and *distinctus* Walker. While these differences do occur, I have found all intergradations between them in a study of specimens from Michigan, New York, North Carolina and Maryland. All collections which I have seen containing specimens of both sexes are alike in having the females with minute, vestigial wings. This evidence indicates that only one species is involved in this material.

Wormaldia femoralis Banks.—see *Chimarrha femoralis* (Banks).

Wormaldia plutonis Banks.—see *Chimarrha plutonis* (Banks).

Family HYDROPTILIDÆ

Agraylea fraterna Banks, 1907b, p. 164.
Lectotype, male.—Falls Church, Virginia, May 1. No. 11591.
This species is a synonym of *multipunctata* Curtis.

Allotrichia flavida Banks, 1907b, p. 164.
Lectotype, female.—Fort Collins, Colorado, June 9. No. 11593.
No males have yet been associated with this form, so that its exact placement cannot be given.

Allotrichia maculata Banks.—see *Hydroptila maculata* (Banks).

Hydroptila albicornis Hagen, 1861, p. 275.

Lectotype, male.—St. Lawrence River, Canada, Osten Sacken. No. 11105.

This species is easily identified by the ædeagus and claspers, fig. 10. Hagen says the type is a female, but he was evidently misled by the retracted condition of the genitalia.

Hydroptila maculata (Banks), 1904b, p. 116, 3 figs. (*Allotrichia*).

Lectotype, male.—Falls Church, Virginia. No. 11595.

The unique male genitalia, fig. 11, are approached only by *waubesiana* Betten, but many differences separate the two.

Hydroptila tarsalis Hagen.—see *Polytrichia tarsalis* (Hagen).

Hydroptila transversa Banks, 1907b, p. 163.

Lectotype, male.—Washington, D. C., September, at light. No. 11592.

This is a synonym of *maculatus* (Banks).

Orthotrichia americana Banks, 1904b, p. 116, 1 fig.

Lectotype, male.—Washington, D. C., August 13. No. 11598. *Lectoallotype, female.*—Same data.

Illustrations of the cleared male genitalia have been given by Morton, 1905, under the name *brachiata*, which falls as a synonym of *americana* Banks. The species *americana* of authors will take the name *cristata* Morton.

Orthotrichia nigritta Banks, 1907b, p. 163, figs. 1-3.

Lectotype, male.—Austen, Texas, March 3, 1901. No. 11596.

This striking, black species from the southwest is different in many respects from the usual definition of *Orthotrichia* and should be placed in a new genus.

Metrichia new genus

Characteristics.—Ocelli present, close to eye. Tibial spur count, 1-3-4; spur on front tibia apical and small. Wings, fig. 14, narrowing to a pointed apex. Front wings with Sc very stocky, and all the other veins well developed; M1-2 almost fused with Rs; Cu & Cu2 running close to the hind margin of the wing. Hind wing with R1 apparently reduced to a short "cross-vein", and M1-2 fused for a short distance with Rs.

Genotype.—*Orthotrichia nigritta* Banks (by original designation).

This genus keys out with *Stactobia* but differs from it in the position of Cu & Cu2, the shortening of R1, and in other characters.

Orthotrichia pallida Banks.—see *Oxyethira pallida* (Banks)

Orthotrichia pictipes Banks.—see *Stactobia pictipes* (Banks)

Oxyethira dorsalis Banks, 1904d, p. 216, pl. 2, fig. 5.

Lectotype, female.—Falls Church, Virginia, June 26, No. 11600.

That portion of the type series which corresponds to the original description, especially in having the characteristic white line down the dorsum, contains only female specimens. Until the females and males of more species in the genus have been associated nothing can be done to settle the specific identity of this species.

Oxyethira pallida (Banks), 1904d, p. 215, pl. 2, figs. 2, 7.

Lectotype, male.—Washington, D. C. No. 11599. *Lectoallotype, female.*—Same data.

This species is the same as *viminalis* Morton, which now becomes a synonym of *pallida*.

Polytrichia tarsalis (Hagen), 1861, p. 275. (*Hydroptila*)

Lectotype, male.—St. Lawrence River, Canada, Osten Sacken. No. 11104.

This species has been illustrated by Betten (1934, pl. 12, figs. 11-14) under the name *confusa* Morton. Morton's species is not this one, but according to original figures belongs to another section of the genus.

Stactobia pictipes (Banks), 1911, p. 359.

Lectotype, male.—Johnstown, New York, June 28, Hale's Creek. No. 11597. *Lectoallotype, female.*—Same data.

The spur of the front tibiae put this species in the heterogeneous *Stactobia*. The male genitalia are illustrated in fig. 12. They are strikingly different from any other Nearctic species.

Family POLYCENTROPODIDÆ

Cernotina pallida (Banks), 1904d, p. 214.   (*Cyrnus*)
Lectotype, male.—High Island, Maryland, June 17.   No. 11539.

This interesting species belongs in the subfamily Psychomyiinæ.   The male genitalia are very distinctive, fig. 18. The only females in the M. C. Z. under this name do not belong to this species, so that as yet an allotype cannot be designated.

Cyrnus fraternus Banks.—see *Nyctiophylax fraternus* (Banks)

Cyrnus pallidus Banks.—see *Cernotina pallida* (Banks)

Plectrocnemia albipuncta Banks.—see *Polycentropus albipunctus* (Banks)

Plectrocnemia aureola Banks, 1930a, p. 130, figs. 2, 3, 5.
Lectotype, male.—Baddeck, Cape Breton Island, Nova Scotia, July 20, 1928.   No. 16323.   *Lectoallotype, female.*— Same data.

Illustrations of the male genitalia are given in fig. 13.

Plectocnemia cinerea (Hagen), 1861, p. 293.   (*Polycentropus*)
Lectotype, male.—St. Lawrence River, Canada, 1859, Osten Sacken.   No. 11039.   *Lectoallotype, female.*—Same data.

The genitalia of this species have been illustrated by Betten (1934, pl. 24, figs. 1-8) under the specific name *canadensis* Banks.

Plectrocnemia flavicornis (Banks), 1907b, p. 162, fig. 1. (*Holocentropus*)
Lectotype, male.—Washington, D. C.   No. 11526.

This is a synonym of *cinerea* (Hagen).

Plectrocnemia pallescens Banks, 1930b, p. 231, fig. 3.
Lectotype, male.—Put-in-Bay, Ohio, July 3, 1924, on Middle Bass Island, G. Townsend.   No. 16322.   *Lectoallotype, female.*—Same data, but July 6, 1926.

The genitalia of this specimen appear identical with those of *cinerea* (Hagen), but the color is lighter.   It is my belief that the specimen is slightly teneral.   In several species of caddis flies I have taken large collections every specimen of which was uniformly teneral.

Holocentropus flavicornis Banks.—see *Plectrocnemia flavicornis* (Banks)

Holocentropus interruptus Banks, 1914, p. 257, fig. 71.

Lectotype, male.—Hampton, New Hampshire, June 15, 1908. No. 11543.

This species was illustrated by Betten (1934, pl. 24, fig. 9). It has line priority over *orotus* Banks.

Holocentropus longus Banks, 1914, p. 258, figs. 65, 68.

Lectotype, female.—Framingham, Massachusetts, June 4, 1904, C. A. Frost. No. 11542.

The size and color of this specimen leaves little doubt but that it is the same as *interruptus*, although sure diagnostic characters have not yet been discovered for the females of this genus.

Holocentropus orotus Banks, 1914, p. 257, fig. 69.

Lectotype, male.—Clear Creek, Colorado. No. 11541. *Lectoallotype, female.*—Chimney Gulch, Boulder, Colorado, Oslar.

This species is a synonym of *interruptus* Banks, which has line priority.

Holocentropus placidus Banks.—see *Phylocentropus placidus* (Banks)

Neureclipsis parvulus Banks, 1907b, p. 163, figs. 2, 3.

Lectotype, male.—High Island, Maryland, June 17. No. 11509.

In addition to the original description, the genitalia have been illustrated by Betten (1934, pl. 22, fig. 8, and pl. 23, fig. 1).

Nyctiophylax fraternus (Banks), 1905b, p. 17. (*Cyrnus*)

Lectotype, female.—Plummer's Island, Maryland, August 28. No. 11538.

A species of doubtful standing, placed as a synonym of *vestitus* by Milne (1935).

Nyctiophylax marginalis Banks, 1930b, p. 231, fig. 15.

Lectotype, male.—Put-in-Bay, Ohio, August 5, 1926, G. Townsend. No. 16325.

The male genitalia of this species are very distinctive, especially the sclerotized point on the mesal side of the clasper. They have been illustrated by Mosely under the name *Cyrnellus zernii* Mosely (1934, p. 142), which becomes a synonym of *marginalis*.

Nyctiophylax mœstus Banks, 1911, p. 359.
    Lectotype, male.—Peachland, British Columbia, August 19, 1909, J. B. Wallis. No. 11536.
    A synonym of *vestitus* Hagen.

Nyctiophylax vestitus (Hagen), 1861, p. 293.   (*Polycentropus*)
    Lectotype, female.—Washington, D. C., Osten Sacken. No. 11036.
    The color and venation of this specimen associates it indubitably with the concept of this species as used by Banks, Betten and others.

Phylocentropus lucidus (Hagen), 1861, p. 294.   (*Polycentropus*)
    Lectotype, male.—Trenton Falls, New York, 1858, Osten Sacken. No. 11037.
    The genitalia of this species also have been figured by Betten (1934, pl. 23, figs. 9-14).

Phylocentropus placidus (Banks), 1905b, p. 15.   (*Holocentropus*)
    Lectotype, male.—Washington, D. C., August 25. No. 11540.
    The essential features of the genitalia of this species have been illustrated by Betten (1934, pl. 23, figs. 2-18). The species *carolinus* Carpenter has been placed as a synonym erroneously by Milne.

Polycentropus albipunctus (Banks), 1930a, p. 131, figs. 6, 9.   (*Plectrocnemia*)
    Lectotype, male.—Point Brevis, Cape Breton Island, Nova Scotia, July 10, 1928. No. 16324. *Lectoallotype, female.*— Same data.
    The genitalia of the male of this species are shown in fig. 17.

Polycentropus arizonensis Banks, 1905b, p. 16.
    Lectotype, male.—Huachua Mts., Arizona, June 21. No.

11546. *Lectoallotype, female.*—Same but July 20, 1903.
The genitalia of this distinctive species are shown in fig. 15.

Polycentropus cinereus Hagen.—see *Plectrocnemia cinerea* (Hagen)

Polycentropus lucidus Hagen.—see *Phylocentropus lucidus* (Hagen)

Polycentropus remotus Banks, 1911, p. 359.
Lectotype, male.—Peachland, British Columbia, August 23, 1909, J. B. Wallis. No. 11549.
The male genitalia are shown in fig. 16.

Polycentropus vestitus Hagen.—see *Nyctiophylax vestitus* (Hagen)

Psychomyia diversa (Banks), 1914, p. 253, fig. 64.
Lectotype, male.—Black Mountain, North Carolina, May, along north fork Swannanoa River. No. 11533. This is close but distinct from *griselda* (Betten).

Psychomyia flavida Hagen.—see *Psychomyiella flavida* (Hagen)

Psychomyia pulchella Banks.—see *Psychomyiella pulchella* (Banks)

Psychomyiella flavida (Hagen), 1861, p. 294. (*Psychomyia*)
Lectotype, female.—St. Lawrence River, Canada, 1859, Osten Sacken. No. 11055.
The structure of the male genitalia, fig. 19, indicates that this species belongs to *Psychomyiella* Martynov, and that *Quissa* Milne, with *flavida* as its genotype, is a synonym of it. The female genitalia are distinctive, allowing certain determination of this type. The species is widely distributed.

Psychomyiella pulchella (Banks), 1899, p. 217.
Lectotype, male.—Colorado, accession no. 2022. No. 11534. A synonym of *flavida* (Hagen).

Family HYDROPSYCHIDÆ

Arctopsyche grandis (Banks), 1900a, p. 258. (*Hydropsyche*)
Lectotype, male.—South West Colorado, July 20, 1899. No. 11514.

The mottled wings and male genitalia, fig. 36, will serve to distinguish this species from other nearctic members of the genus.

Cheumatopsyche analis (Banks), 1903b, p. 243.   (*Hydropsyche*)

Lectotype, male.—Riverton, New Jersey, July 16.   No. 11532.

The elongate apical segment of the clasper, the V-shaped ridge on the dorsum of the tenth tergite, and the inconspicuous apical lobes on the tenth tergite, fig. 20, distinguish the species from others in the genus.   To date I have seen no specimens of this species except the type.

The much used name "*Hydropsychodes analis*" has been applied to at least six different species in the past, and records under this name can not be accepted.

Cheumatopsyche gracilis (Banks), 1899, p. 216.   (*Hydropsyche*)

Lectotype, male.—Colorado, accession no. 2022. No. 11497.

The elongate apical segment of the clasper combined with the elongate-trapezoidal apical lobes of the tenth tergite will serve to distinguish this species, fig. 23.

Cheumatopsyche minuscula (Banks), 1907a, p. 130, pl. 8, fig. 5.   (*Hydropsyche*)

Lectotype, male.—Plummers Island, Maryland, August 29. No. 11530.   *Lectoallotype, female.*—Same data.

The pointed and approximate apical lobes of the tenth tergite, fig. 21, set this species off at once from *sordida* (Hagen), with which it was incorrectly synonymized by Milne.

Cheumatopsyche sordida (Hagen), 1860, p. 285.   (*Hydropsyche*)

Lectotype, male.—St. Lawrence River, Canada, 1859, Sacken.   No. 11015.

This black species is distinguished by the widely separated apical lobes of the tenth tergite; these lobes have a dorsal, truncate apex, fig. 24.

Cheumatopsyche speciosa (Banks), 1904d, p. 214, pl. 2, fig. 6.   (*Hydropsyche*)

Lectotype, male.—Plummers Island, Maryland, August 28. No. 11502. *Lectoallotype, female.*—Same data.

In addition to the three large yellow spots of the front wings, the genitalia are distinctive of the species (Betten, 1934, pl. 20, fig. 14).

Diplectrona modesta Banks, 1908b, p. 266, pl. 19, fig. 13.
Lectotype, male.—Riverside, Massachusetts, June 4, C. W. Johnson. No. 11523. *Lectoallotype, female.*—Same data.

The details of the male genitalia have been illustrated by Betten (1934, pl. 17, figs. 3-7).

Hydropsyche analis Banks.—see *Cheumatopsyche analis* (Banks)

Hydropsyche bifida Banks, 1905b, p. 15, fig. 14.
Lectotype, male.—Colorado, accession no. 2175. No. 11503. *Lectoallotype, female.*—Colorado, accession no. 2135, Fort Collins, June.

The male genitalia of this species, fig. 32, are distinguished by the short, widely separated apical processes of the tenth tergite and the small spur at the end of the lateral processes of the aedeagus. The species is widely distributed across the continent.

Hydropsyche californica Banks, 1898, p. 217.
Lectotype, male.—Tahoma, California, August 28, 1897. No. 11304.

The somewhat moniliform apex of the aedeagus distinguishes this species from others in the *scalaris* group, fig. 26.

Hydropsyche chlorotica Hagen, 1861, p. 290.
Lectotype, male.—St. Lawrence River, Canada, 1859, Sacken. No. 11016.

This specimen is identical in genitalia with the lectotype of *morosa* Hagen recently erected by Banks (1938). Diagnostic features include the flattened spur at the end of the lateral arm of the aedeagus, and the relatively simple apex of the aedeagus, fig. 33.

Hydropsyche cockerelli Banks, 1905b, p. 14.
Lectotype, male.—Pecos, New Mexico, June 26, M. Grabham. No. 11506. *Lectoallotype, female.*—Same, August 14, at light, Cockerell.

The long, curved spur at the end of the lateral process of the ædeagus, combined with the short, upright and notched apical processes of the tenth tergite, set off this species from its close relatives, fig. 34.

Hydropsyche depravata Hagen, 1861, p. 290.

Allotype, male.—Georgia, 1860, Gerhard.

This specimen agrees perfectly in color, habitus and labels with the female type of the species. There is no doubt that it is the same species. The genitalia are quite distinct, fig. 31, and in a large number of points suggest that this species and its close allies form the most primitive stock in the genus.

Hydropsyche divisa Banks.—see *Smicridea divisa* (Banks)

Hydropsyche gracilis Banks.—see *Cheumatopsyche gracilis* (Banks)

Hydropsyche grandis Banks.—see *Arctopsyche grandis* (Banks)

Hydropsyche hageni Banks, 1905b, p. 14, figs. 6, 10, 12.

Lectotype, male.—Travilah, Maryland, July. No. 11996.

The greatly lengthened and flattened apico-lateral plates of the ædeagus set the species off from others of the *scalaris* group easily, fig. 22.

Hydropsyche incommoda Hagen, 1861, p. 290.

Lectotype, male.—Georgia, Winthem. No. 11028.

This species is a member of the *scalaris* group. The structures at the apex of the ædeagus are shown in fig. 29.

Hydropsyche kansensis Banks.—see *Potomyia kansensis* (Banks)

Hydropsyche minuscula Banks.—see *Cheumatopsyche minuscula* (Banks)

Hydropsyche novamexicana Banks, 1904a, p. 110, fig. 12.

Lectotype, male.—Roswell, New Mexico, August 22, Cockerell. No. 11505.

This species is a synonym of *occidentalis* Banks.

Hydropsyche occidentalis Banks, 1900a, p. 258.

Lectotype, male.—Pullman, Washington, August 7, 1898. No. 11500.

This species is closest to *scalaris* and *venularis*, but differs from both in details of the genitalia, fig. 27.

Hydropsyche oslari Banks, 1905b, p. 13, fig. 2.

Lectotype, male.—South West Colorado, July 23, 1899. No. 11501. *Lectoallotype, female.*—Same, but July 17.

The long, apical segment of the claspers and the short, approximate apical processes of the tenth tergite are diagnostic for this species, fig. 35.

Hydropsyche partita Banks, 1914, p. 252, figs. 58, 59.

Lectotype, male.—Switzers Camp, San Gabriel Mts., California, June. No. 11498.

This is a synonym of *oslari*.

Hydropsyche phalerata Hagen, 1861, p. 287.

Allotype, male.—Great Falls, Virginia, July 27.

The great similarity between the pinned lectotype and this allotype leaves no doubt of the correct association of the two. The upturned apex of the tenth tergite and the slightly enlarged apex of the aedeagus are diagnostic, fig. 25.

Hydropsyche recurvata Banks, 1914, p. 253, fig. 73. (*H. slossonæ* var.)

Lectotype, male.—Go Home Bay, Ontario, Split Rock, June 9, E. M. Walker. No. 11507.

This species is distinguished by the combination of a long, curved spur at the end of the lateral process of the aedeagus and the apex of the aedeagus being developed into a pair of large, lateral lobes. The species *codona* Betten (1934, pl. 18, figs. 10-12) is a synonym of *recurvata*.

Hydropsyche slossonæ Banks, 1905b, p. 14, figs. 4, 7.

Lectotype, male.—Franconia, New Hampshire. No. 11495. *Lectoallotype, female.*—Same data.

In general appearance this species resembles other members of the *"alternans"* group, but is distinguished from all others by the male genitalia, fig. 30. Diagnostic characters include: simple, spine-like spur on end of lateral process of aedeagus, three large pockets of spines within apex of aedeagus, and long, excavated processes of tenth tergite which form an apical horseshoe.

Hydropsyche sordida Hagen.—see *Cheumatopsyche sordida* (Hagen)

Hydropsyche speciosa Banks.—see *Cheumatopsyche speciosa* (Banks)

Hydropsyche venularis Banks, 1914, p. 252, fig. 62.
Lectotype, male.—Washington, D. C., June 22. No. 11508.
A member of the *scalaris* group, characterized by the greatly enlarged head at the apex of the ædeagus, which is half again as deep as the stalk, fig. 28.

Macronema carolina Banks, 1909, p. 342.
Lectotype, male.—Southern Pines, North Carolina, June, 1924, A. H. Manee. No. 11529.
This species, although widely distributed, always occurs south of the range of *zebratum* Hagen.

Macronema flavum Hagen.—see *Potomyia flava* (Hagen)

Macronema zebratum Hagen, 1861, p. 285.
Lectotype, male.—St. Lawrence River, Canada, 1859, O. Sacken. No. 11027. *Lectoallotype, female.*—Same data.
This northern species is larger than *carolina* Banks and has the basal antennal segment more bulbous.

Potomyia flava (Hagen), 1861, p. 285. (*Macronema*)
Lectotype, male.—St. Louis, Missouri, 1859, Sacken. No. 11026.
This species has been illustrated by Betten (1934, pl. 21, figs. 1-3).

Potomyia kansensis (Banks), 1905b, p. 15. (*Hydropsyche*)
Lectotype, female.—Douglas County, Kansas, July, electric light. No. 11499.
This represents the female of *flava* (Hagen), and is a synonym of this name.

Smicridea divisa (Banks), 1903a, p. 244, pl. 4, fig. 12. (*Hydropsyche*)
Lectotype, male.—Salt River, Arizona, April, Oslar. No. 11528. *Lectoallotype, female.*—Same data, but April 10.
This species is a synonym of McLachlan's *fasciatella*. The male genitalia show more relationship to *Potomyia* than to any other genus in the family.

Family ODONTOCERIDÆ

Heteroplectron dissimilis Banks, 1897, p. 30.

Lectotype, female.—Sea Cliff, Long Island, New York, June. No. 11718.

A synonym of *indecisum* (Walker).

Heteroplectron rufa (Hagen), 1861, p. 276. (*Molanna*)
Lectotype, male.—Trenton Falls, New York, 1858, Osten Sacken. No. 10956. *Lectoallotype, female.*—Same data.
This species also is a synonym of *indecisum* (Wlk.)

Molanna rufa Hagen.—see *Heteroplectron rufa* (Hagen)

Nerophilus californicus (Hagen), 1861, p. 272. (*Silo*)
Lectotype, female.—California. No. 10994. *Allotype, male.*—Same data.
The allotype may have been of the original type series. It displays the same distinctive color pattern as the female.

Silo californicus Hagen.—see *Nerophilus californicus* (Hagen)

Family MOLANNIDÆ

Molanna cinerea Hagen, 1861, p. 276.
Lectotype, female.—St. Lawrence River, Canada, 1859, O. Sacken. No. 10957.
Only fragments of head and legs, and a fairly complete set of wings are left.

Molanna flavicornis Banks, 1914, p. 261, fig. 46.
Lectotype, male.—Husavick, Manitoba, July 2, 1916, J. B. Wallis. No. 11590. *Lectoallotype, female.*—Winnepeg, Manitoba, May 31, 1911, J. B. Wallis.
The diagnostic features separating this species from others in the genus have been given by Betten (1934).

Family LEPTOCERIDÆ

Athripsodes albostictus (Hagen), 1861, p. 276. (*Leptocerus*)
Lectotype, female.—America, September, Winthem. No. 10963.
At the present time no satisfactory characters have been found to separate the females of this group of species. For the present, therefore, it will be necessary to consider this species of doubtful identity.

Athripsodes dilutus (Hagen), 1861, p. 277. (*Leptocerus*)

Lectotype, male.—Chicago, Illinois, Osten Sacken. No. 10965.

This species is a very close relative of *annulicornis* (Stephens), but may be readily separated from it on the basis of the ædeagus having two internal, large spines, and the clasper having a pedunculate sclerotized process, fig. 42. *Dilutus* has been incorrectly synonymized with *annulicornis;* it is really distinct and seems to be the only name available for the species.

Athripsodes flavus (Banks), 1904d, p. 212, pl. 2, fig. 4.
   (*Leptocerus*)
   Lectotype, male.—Falls Church, Virginia. No. 11572.
Lectoallotype, female.—Same data.

The angulate basal process of the claspers illustrated in the original description serves to differentiate this species from its only close ally, *ancylus* (Vorhies).

Athripsodes futilis (Banks), 1914, p. 264, figs. 44, 49.
   (*Leptocerus*)
   Lectotype, male.—Go Home Bay, Ontario, July 11, E. M. Walker. No. 11574. *Lectoallotype, female.*—Same data, but August 12.

The male genitalia of this type agree with those of a male from Europe determined by Hagen as *annulicornis* (Stephens) and answer in detail the illustrations of Mc-Lachlan.   There seems no doubt but that *futilis* must be considered a synonym of *annulicornis*.   The chief diagnostic characters are in the ædeagus, which has only a single, large, internal spine, and the clasper, which has a short, digitate, sclerotized process, fig. 41.

Athripsodes lugens (Hagen), 1861, p. 276. (*Leptocerus*)
   Lectotype, male.—St. Lawrence River, Canada, 1859, O. Sacken. No. 10966. *Lectoallotype, female.*—Same data.

This species, also, is a synonym of *annulicornis*.

Athripsodes maculatus (Banks), 1898, p. 214. (*Leptocerus*)
   Lectotype, female.—Washington, D. C. No. 11576.

The type matches that of *transversus* (Hagen) so perfectly that there is no doubt that the two are the same species. Both type series were collected at Washington.

Athripsodes transversus (Hagen), 1861, p. 279. (*Leptocerus*)
Lectotype, female.—Washington, D. C., Osten Sacken.
No. 10967. *Allotype, male.*—Washington, D. C., June 22.
A large series of this species in the M. C. Z. shows that it
is the common one in the vicinity of the type locality, and
that the designated allotype is correctly associated with
Hagen's type. The male genitalia of the allotype are shown
in fig. 40.

Athripsodes variegatus (Hagen), 1861, p. 278. (*Leptocerus*)
Lectotype, male.—Chicago, Illinois, Osten Sacken. No.
10964.
The genitalia of this species have been illustrated by
Betten under the name *aspinosus* Betten (1934, pl. 31, figs.
5-10). Both *variegatus* and *aspinosus* are synonyms of
resurgens (Walker), according to the identification of Banks
and Milne.

Leptocella candida (Hagen), 1861, p. 280. (*Setodes*)
Lectotype, male.—Florida, May, 1858, Sacken. No.
10972.
No attempt is made here to determine the status of any
species in this genus.

Leptocella coloradensis Banks, 1899, p. 215.
Lectotype, male.—Colorado, accession no. 2059. No.
11582. *Lectoallotype, female.*—Colorado, accession no. 2022.

Leptocella minuta Banks, 1900a, p. 257.
Lectotype, female.—Pullman, Washington, August 9,
1898. No. 11581. *Allotype, male.*—Same data, but
August 19.
The allotype bears no type label but is undoubtedly of the
type lot.

Leptocella nivea (Hagen), 1861, p. 281. (*Setodes*)
Lectotype, male.—St. Lawrence River, Canada, 1859,
Sacken. No. 10969.

Leptocella pavida (Hagen), 1861, p. 282. (*Setodes*)
Lectotype, female.—Washington, [D. C.], O. Sacken. No.
10970.

Leptocella stigmatica Banks, 1914, p. 262, fig. 48.

Lectotype, male.—Jemey Mts., New Mexico, July 20. No. 11583.

Leptocella texana Banks, 1905b, p. 19.
Lectotype, male.—Zavalla County, Nueces River, Texas, April 27, 1910, Hunter & Pratt. No. 11578.

Leptocerus albostictus Hagen.—see *Athripsodes albostictus* (Hagen)

Leptocerus americana (Banks), 1899, p. 215. (*Setodes*)
Lectotype, female.—Washington, D. C. No. 11567. *Lectoallotype, male.*—Same data.
This species was made the basis for a new genus *Ymyia* by Milne. All characters except the genitalia, however, group it with the genotype of *Leptocerus*.

Leptocerus dilutus Hagen.—see *Athripsodes dilutus* (Hagen)

Leptocerus flavus Banks.—see *Athripsodes flavus* (Banks)

Leptocerus futilis Banks.—see *Athripsodes futilis* (Banks)

Leptocerus grandis (Banks), 1907a, p. 128, pl. 8, fig. 4. (*Setodes*)
Lectotype, male.—New Haven, Connecticut, June 23, 1904, H. L. Viereck. No. 11564. *Lectoallotype, female.*—Falls Church, Virginia, June 21.
This species is a synonym of *americana*.

Leptocerus lugens Hagen.—see *Athripsodes lugens* (Hagen)

Leptocerus maculatus Banks.—see *Athripsodes maculatus* (Banks)

Leptocerus transversus Hagen.—see *Athripsodes transversus* (Hagen)

Leptocerus variegatus Hagen.—see *Athripsodes variegatus* (Hagen)

Mystacides canadensis Banks, 1924, p. 448, fig. 47.
Lectotype, male.—Sherbrooke, Canada. No. 14852.
This represents the banded form of *longicornis* (L.). Field observations indicate that the unbanded specimens are simply rubbed, since the bands are formed only by hairs.

Mystacides interjecta Banks, 1914, p. 262, figs. 2, 5.
(*Œcetina*)
Lectotype, female.—Go Home Bay, Ontario, August 22,
E. M. Walker. No. 11551.
This species is a synonym of *longicornis* (L.).

Œcetina disjuncta Banks.—see *Œcetis disjuncta* (Banks)

Œcetina flavida Banks.—see *Œcetis flavida* (Banks)

Œcetina floridana Banks.—see *Œcetis floridana* (Banks)

Œcetina fumosa Banks.—see *Œcetis fumosa* (Banks)

Œcetina interjecta Banks.—see *Mystacides interjecta*
(Banks)

Œcetina parvula Banks.—see *Œcetis parvula* (Banks)

Œcetina persimilis Banks.—see *Œcetis persimilis* (Banks)

Œcetis cinerascens (Hagen), 1861, p. 282. (*Setodes*)
Lectotype, male.—Washington, [D. C.] No. 10971.
This species is illustrated by Betten (1934, pl. 35, figs.
2-7) under the name *resurgens* (Walker).

Œcetis disjuncta (Banks), 1920, p. 351, fig. 100. (*Œcetina*)
Lectotype, male.—Arroyo Seco Canyon, San Gabriel Mts.,
California, June 17, 1913, F. Grinnell, Jr. No. 10915.
The male genitalia resemble those of *avara* (Banks) very
closely.

Œcetis flaveolata (Hagen), 1861, p. 282. (*Setodes*)
Lectotype, female.—Washington, [D. C.,] Osten Sacken.
No. 10978.
This is the same species as *inconspicua* (Walker) as
determined by Milne.

Œcetis flavida (Banks), 1899, p. 216. (*Œcetina*)
Lectotype, male.—Kissimmee, Florida. No. 11557.
Lectoallotype, female.—Same data.
This is the same species as *inconspicua* (Walker) as
determined by Milne.

Œcetis floridana (Banks), 1899, p. 216. (*Œcetina*)
Lectotype, male.—Biscayne Bay, Florida. No. 11555.
This is the same species as *inconspicua* (Walker) as
determined by Milne.

Œcetis fumosa (Banks), 1899, p. 216.   (*Œcetina*)
Lectotype, female.—Washington, D. C.   No. 11556.
This species is a synonym of *cinerascens* (Hagen).

Œcetis immobilis (Hagen), 1861, p. 283.   (*Setodes*)
Lectotype, male.—St. Lawrence River, Canada, 1859.   No.
10977.
The peculiar claspers, illustrated by Betten (1934, pl. 34,
figs. 4, 5) readily distinguish this species.

Œcetis micans (Hagen), 1861, p. 283.   (*Setodes*)
Lectotype, male.—Washington, [D. C.,] O. Sacken.   No.
10973. *Lectoallotype, female.*—Same data.
This is a synonym of *inconspicua* (Walker) as determined
by Milne.

Œcetis parva (Banks), 1907a, p. 130, pl. 9, figs. 24, 26.
(*Setodina*)
Lectotype, male.—Kissimmee, Florida.   No. 11562.
The genitalia of this minute leptocerid are illustrated in
fig. 39.   They are extremely similar to those of *avara* except
for the claspers, which shows that *Setodina* must be considered at most a subgenus of *Œcetis*.

Œcetis parvula (Banks), 1899, p. 215.   (*Œcetina*)
Lectotype, female.—Washington, D. C.   No. 11554.
This is the same as *inconspicua* (Walker) as determined
by Milne.

Œcetis persimilis (Banks), 1907a, p. 129.   (*Œcetina*)
Lectotype, male.—High Island, Maryland.   No. 11552.
Lectoallotype, female.—Same data, in coitu with lectotype.
The distinctive male genitalia are illustrated by Betten
(1934, pl. 34, fig. 12).

Œcetis sagitta (Hagen), 1861c, p. 284.   (*Setodes*)
Lectotype, female.—Florida, March, 1858, O. Sacken.
No. 10975.
This is the same as *inconspicua* (Walker) as determined
by Milne.

Setodes americana Banks.—see *Leptocerus americana*
(Banks)

Setodes candida Hagen.—see *Leptocella candida* (Hagen)

Setodes cinerascens Hagen.—see *Œcetis cinerascens* (Hagen)

Setodes flaveolata Hagen.—see *Œcetis flaveolata* (Hagen)

Setodes grandis Banks.—see *Leptocerus grandis* (Banks)

Setodes immobilis Hagen.—see *Œcetis immobilis* (Hagen)

Setodes injusta Hagen.—see *Triænodes injusta* (Hagen)

Setodes micans Hagen.—see *Œcetis micans* (Hagen)

Setodes nivea Hagen.—see *Leptocella nivea* (Hagen)

Setodes pavida Hagen.—see *Leptocella pavida* (Hagen)

Setodes sagitta Hagen.—see *Œcetis sagitta* (Hagen)

Setodina parva Banks.—see *Œcetis parva* (Banks)

Triænodes borealis Banks, 1900a, p. 257.

Lectotype, female.—St. Anthony Park, Minnesota. No. 11586.

Until definite characters are discovered for the lucid separation of the females of this genus, it will be necessary to consider this species of unknown status. Sufficient color antigeny exists in this genus to prevent the matching of males and females of each species on conventional characters alone.

Triænodes dentata Banks, 1914, p. 261, fig. 45.

Lectotype, male.—Johnstown, New York, June 28. No. 11589.

The male genitalia, fig. 38, are distinct in having the tenth tergite divided into a pair of long filaments, and having the lateral arm of the clasper of only medium length.

Triænodes flavescens Banks, 1900a, p. 257.

Lectotype, male.—New Brunswick, New Jersey, October. No. 11588.

The details of the male genitalia have been illustrated under the name *ignita* (Walker) by Betten (1934, pl. 39, figs. 1-3).

Triænodes frontalis Banks, 1907a, p. 127, pl. 9, fig. 11.

Allotype, male.—Ft. Collins, Colorado, June 26, accession no. 2154.

This specimen was probably a part of the type series but did not bear a type label. The male genitalia differ from those of *grisea* Banks chiefly in the long and whip-like mesal process of the clasper, fig. 37A.

Triænodes grisea Banks, 1899, p. 214.

Lectotype, female.—Colorado, accession no. 2184. No. 11585. *Allotype, male.*—Denver, Colorado, June 27.

This specimen was probably a part of the type series but did not bear a type label. The genitalia resemble those of *frontalis*, but differ in the short mesal processes of the claspers, fig. 37.

Triænodes injusta (Hagen), 1861, p. 283. (*Setodes*)

Lectotype, male.—St. Lawrence River, Canada, 1859, Osten Sacken. No. 10976.

The genitalia of this species have been illustrated by Betten (1934, pl. 39, figs. 4-6).

Family PHRYGANEIDÆ

Agrypnia colorata Hagen, 1873, p. 424.

Lectotype, male.—Saskatchewan, 1860, Kennicott. No. 10734.

The male genitalia were illustrated by Milne (1931, figs. 10-11) under the name *bradorata* Milne.

Agrypnia straminea Hagen, 1873, p. 425.

Lectotype, male.—Saskatchewan, 1860, Kennicott. No. 10735.

The genitalia have been illustrated by Betten (1934, pl. 42, figs. 10-12) under the name *curvata* Banks, which is a synonym of *straminea*.

Neuronia angustipennis Hagen, 1873, p. 400.

Lectotype, male.—House, C[ambridge, Massachusetts?], July 9, 1863. No. 10739.

Neuronia stygipes Hagen, 1873, p. 388.

Lectotype, male.—West Roxbury, Massachusetts, April 26, 1868. No. 10741.

The male genitalia have been illustrated by Betten (1934, pl. 42, figs. 8, 9.

Family LIMNEPHILIDÆ

Acronopsyche pilosa Banks.—see *Neophylax pilosus* (Banks)

Anabolia assimilis Banks.—see *Limnephilus assimilis* (Banks)

Anabolia curta Banks.—see *Limnephilus curtus* (Banks)

Anabolia modesta Hagen.—see *Limnephilus modestus* (Hagen)

Anabolia montana Banks.—see *Limnephilus montanus* (Banks)

Anabolia nigricula Banks.—see *Limnephilus nigricula* (Banks)

Anisogamus costalis (Banks), 1901, p. 286. (*Asynarchus*)
Lectotype, male.—Las Vegas Range, New Mexico, June 28. No. 11676.
The generic placement of this species seems to me somewhat doubtful. The male genitalia, fig. 44, show this species to belong to a residue of forms whose relationships are obscure.

Anisogamus disjunctus Banks, 1914, p. 156, fig. 22.
Lectotype, male.—Bon Accord, British Columbia, May 22. Russell. No. 11673. *Lectoallotype, female.*—Same data, but May 18.
The male genitalia, fig. 43, lead to the same remarks as applied to the preceding.

Anisogamus edwardsi Banks.—see *Drusinus edwardsi* (Banks)

Apatania canadensis Banks.—see *Glyphopsyche canadensis* (Banks)

Apatania pallida Hagen.—see *Apatelia pallida* (Hagen)

Apatania shoshone Banks.—see *Apatelia shoshone* (Banks)

Apatelia incerta (Banks), 1897, p. 28. (*Enoicycla*)
Lectotype, male.—Sea Cliff, New York. No. 11681. *Lectoallotype, female.*—Franconia, New Hampshire.
The male genitalia are illustrated in fig. 47. Milne (1935) considered this the same as *nigra* (Wlk.). There are, however, two different species of *Apatelia* with long, needle-like claspers, and it is very likely *nigra* applies to one and *incerta* to the other.

Apatelia pallida (Hagen), 1861, p. 270. (*Apatania*)
 Lectotype, male.—St. Lawrence River, Canada, 1859, O.
Sacken. No. 14715.
 This is a synonym of *stigmatella* (Zett.).

Apatelia shoshone (Banks), 1924, p. 442, figs. 35, 42.
 (*Apatania*)
 Lectotype, male.—Yellowstone Park, Wyoming, H. S.
Smith. No. 14850. *Lectoallotype, female.*—Same data.
 The genitalic characters mentioned in the original description will separate this species from its closest ally, *stigmatella*
(Zett.).

Apolopsyche pallida Banks.—see *Limnephilus pallidus*
 (Banks)

Asynarchus centralis Banks, 1900a, p. 253.
 Lectotype, male.—Clear Cr., Colorado, September 10, 1899,
Oslar. No. 11670.
 The male genitalia, fig. 45, are suggestive of some species
of *Limnephilus*, but other characters, such as the unusually
long maxillary palpi, are quite distinctive. For the present
it seems better to regard the generic assignment as open to
question.

Asynarchus costalis Banks.—see *Anisogamus costalis*
 (Banks)

Asynarchus pallidus Banks, 1903b, p. 242.
 Lectotype, female.—South Park, Colorado, August 23,
1899, Oslar. No. 11671.
 The species represents the opposite sex of *centralis* Bks.
and is a synonym of it.

Asynarchus tristis Banks.—see *Dicosmœcus tristis* (Banks)

Chilostigma subborealis Banks.—see *Glyphopsyche subboreale* (Banks)

Clistoronia maculata (Banks), 1904a, p. 107, pl. 1, figs. 2, 4.
 (*Dicosmoecus*)
 Lectotype, male.—Pecos, New Mexico, August 24, at light,
Cockerell.   No.   11653.   *Lectoallotype, female.*—South
Arizona, August, 1902, F. B. Snow.
 This species is the same as *formosus* (Banks). The male
genitalia, fig. 46, show that the genus *Clistoronia* Banks is

closely allied to the *Limnephilus* section of the family, rather than to the *Stenophylax* section.

Colpotaulius medialis Banks.—see *Limnephilus medialis* (Banks)

Colpotaulius minusculus Banks.—see *Limnephilus minusculus* (Banks)

Colpotaulius tarsalis Banks.—see *Limnephilus tarsalis* (Banks)

Dicosmœcus atripes (Hagen), 1875, p. 600. (*Platyphylax*)
Lectotype, male.—Colorado Mts., August 1873, Comporte. No. 10701.
The male genitalia are illustrated in fig. 49. The color of legs is variable (see *D. gilvipes*).

Dicosmœcus gilvipes (Hagen), 1875, p. 601. (*Stenophylax*)
Lectotype, male.—Quesnel Lake, British Columbia, August 27, Crotch. No. 10716.
The genitalia of this type are identical with those of *atripes* (Hagen). The color of the legs, previously used to separate the two, was found to vary over a large series of specimens. *Gilvipes*, therefore, becomes a synonym of *atripes*.

Dicosmœcus maculatus Banks.—see *Clistoronia maculata* (Banks)

Dicosmœcus tristis (Banks), 1900a, p. 254. (*Asynarchus*)
Lectotype, male.—South Park, Colorado, August 17, 1899, Oslar. No. 11634. *Lectoallotype, female.*—Same data, but August 20.
This is a synonym of *unicolor* (Banks). The male genitalia differ considerably from those of *atripes*, fig. 48.

Drusinus calypso (Banks), 1911, p. 350, pl. 13, fig. 25. (*Stenophylax*)
Lectotype, male.—Catskills, New York, June. No. 11672.
This species is identical with *sparsus* (Bks).

Drusinus edwardsi (Banks), 1920, p. 345. (*Anisogamus*)
Lectotype, male.—Marin County, California, H. Edwards. No. 10881. *Lectoallotype, female.*—California.
The genitalia, illustrated in the original description, and general structure place this species in *Drusinus* Betten.

Ecclisomyia maculosa Banks, 1907a, p. 123, pl. 9, fig. 18.
Lectotype, female.—Boulder, Colorado, July 31, 1904, Oslar. No. 11680. *Allotype, male.*—Slate Cr., Summit County, Colorado, August 2, 8, 211 ft. elevation, S. C. Clagg. The male genitalia, fig. 50, are quite distinctive.

Enoicycla incerta Banks.—see *Apatelia incerta* (Banks)

Enoicycla lepida Hagen.—see *Stenophylax lepidus* (Hagen)

Glyphopsyche bellus (Banks), 1903b, p. 241. (*Glyphotaelius*)
A male in the M. C. Z. identical in external characters with the female type is here designated the allotype. The male genitalia, fig. 51, are quite distinctive.
Allotype, male.—March 23, 1903.

Glyphopsyche bryanti Banks, 1904c, p. 141.
Lectotype, male.—Wellington, British Columbia, Bryant. No. 11640. *Lectoallotype, female.*—Same data.
This lectotype is identical with paratypes of *intercisus* (Wlk.) in the M. C. Z., which species in turn has been synonymized with *irroratus* (Fabricius), fig. 53.

Glyphopsyche canadensis (Banks), 1924, p. 442, fig. 5. (*Apatania*)
Lectotype, male.—Winnipeg, Manitoba, October 1, 1909, J. B. Wallis. No. 14851.
The genitalia, fig. 52, are similar in general conformation to those of other nearctic members of the genus.

Glyphopsyche subboreale (Banks), 1924, p. 441, fig. 32. (*Chilostigma*)
Lectotype, male.—Alaska. No. 14847. *Lectoallotype, female.*—Beaver Mts., Alaska, May 15, 1917, A. B. Twitchell.
The male genitalia are illustrated in fig. 54.

Glyphopsyche taylori (Banks), 1904c, p. 140. (*Halesus*)
Lectotype, female.—Wellington, British Columbia, Bryant. No. 11666.
The extremely striking appearance of this species, the genotype of *Halesochila* Banks, is the chief character separating it from *Glyphopsyche*. Since it agrees so well with this latter genus in structural characters, it seems advisable to reduce *Halesochila* to subgeneric rank.

Glyphotælius bellus Banks.—see *Glyphopsyche bellus* (Banks)

Glyphotælius hostilis Hagen, 1864, p. 814.
Lectotype, male.—Saskatchewan, 1860, Kennicott. No. 10730. *Lectoallotype, female.*—Fort Resolution, Great Slave Lake, Canada, 1862, Kennicott.
This large, distinctive species with the incised wing apex needs no comment.

Goniotaulius coloradensis Banks.—see *Limnephilus coloradensis* (Banks)

Grammataulius praecox Hagen, 1873, p. 451.
Lectotype, male.—Fort Resolution, Great Slave Lake, Canada, 1862, Kennicott. No. 10732.
The species has been synonymized with *interrogationis* Zett.

Halesus amicus Hagen.—see *Platycentropus amicus* (Hagen)

Halesus hostis Hagen.—see *Platycentropus hostis* (Hagen)

Halesus taylori Banks.—see *Glyphopsyche taylori* (Banks)

Halesus mutatus Hagen.—see *Limnephilus mutatus* (Hagen)

Hesperophylax alascensis (Banks), 1908b, p. 265, pl. 19, fig. 14. (*Platyphylax*)
Lectotype, male.—Sitka, Alaska. No. 11647.
This species is very close to and may be the same as *designatus* (Walker).

Hesperophylax consimilis Banks, 1900a, p. 253. (*Limnephilus*)
Lectotype, male.—South Park, Colorado, August 25, 1899, Oslar. No. 11612. *Lectoallotype, female.*—Same data but July 20.
Differentiated by the sharp tenth tergite, fig. 55, this species is close to *magnus* Banks.

Hesperophylax magnus Banks, 1918, p. 20, fig. 9.
Lectotype, male.—Palmerlee, Cochise County, Arizona, Biedermann. No. 10075. *Lectoallotype, female.*—Stockton, Utah, July 22, Spaulding.

This species is quite distinct from the other nearctic species of the genus on the basis of the cercus (see original description). It has been considered a subspecies of *designatus* Wlk. erroneously by Milne (1935).

Hesperophylax occidentalis Banks, 1908b, p. 265, pl. 19, fig. 16. (*Platyphylax*)

Lectotype, male.—Florrisant, Colorado, August 3, 1907, S. A. Rohwer. No. 11646. *Lectoallotype, female.*—Ft. Wingate, New Mexico, August, Wingate.

A close ally but not a synonym of *designatus* (Wlk.).

Homophylax crotchi Banks, 1920, p. 345.

Lectotype, female.—Victoria, British Columbia, July, Crotch. No. 10877.

The striking wing pattern of yellow and dark brown will serve to identify this species.

Homophylax flavipennis Banks, 1900a, p. 255.

Lectotype, male.—South Park, Colorado, August 23, 1899, Oslar. No. 11635. *Lectoallotype, female.*—Same data.

The male genitalia show many points of similarity to those of *Glyphopsyche*.

Leptophylax gracilis Banks, 1900a, p. 252.

Lectotype, female.—St. Anthony's Park, Minnesota. No. 11637.

The male was described by Betten (1934, pl. 44, figs. 2-5). This seems to be one genus of the *Limnephilus* group sufficiently distinct to be recognized. At least, it can be keyed out in both sexes without difficulty.

Limnephilus Leach

Inability to find satisfactory characters for segregating the females into the same groups as the males has led me to consider as only of subgeneric rank such groups as *Anabolia*, *Anabolina*, *Colpotaulius*, *Goniotaulius* and some others.

Limnephilus abbreviatus Banks, 1908b, p. 263, pl. 18, fig. 8.

Lectotype, male.—Tabernash, Colorado, August, E. S. Tucker. No. 11625. *Lectoallotype, female.*—Same data.

The male genitalia are quite distinctive, fig. 71.

Limnephilus aequalis Banks, 1914, p. 150, figs. 14, 31.

Lectotype, male.—Bon Accord, British Columbia, June 7, Russell. No. 11624.

This species is a synonym of *harrimani* Bks., fig. 82.

Limnephilus americanus Banks, 1900a, p. 253.
Lectotype, female.—Idaho, C. V. Piper. No. 11631.
This is considered a synonym of *sublunatus* Prov., fig. 73.

Limnephilus argenteus Banks, 1914, p. 152, fig. 13.
Allotype, male.—Hardisty Island, Great Slave Lake, Canada, June 5, 1924, J. Russell.
The male genitalia, fig. 56, are very different from any described Nearctic species in the genus.

Limnephilus assimilis (Banks), 1908b, p. 262, pl. 19, figs. 9, 10. (*Anabolia*)
Lectotype, male.—Prescott, Arizona. No. 11648. *Lectoallotype, female.*—Same data, June 15, 1902, Oslar.
The slender and branched lateral arms of the ædeagus, fig. 58, distinguish this species from its closest allies.

Limnephilus bifidus Banks, 1908b, p. 263, figs. 11, 13-15.
Lectotype, female.—Pullman, Washington, C. V. Piper. No. 11627.
The type series contains only females.

Limnephilus brevipennis (Banks), 1899, p. 209. (*Stenophylax*)
Lectotype, male.—Colorado, Gillette. No. 11612.
In this species the male genitalia, fig. 77, appear to have the claspers much reduced and the lobes of the tenth tergite again divided.

Limnephilus canadensis Banks, 1908b, p. 264, pl. 18, fig. 4.
Lectotype, female.—Laval County, Canada, June 29. No. 11619.
Until more female characters are worked out for this genus, the identity of this species cannot be determined.

Limnephilus clausus Banks, 1924, p. 440, fig. 56.
Lectotype, male.—Long Lake, Colorado, Cockerell. No. 14844. *Lectoallotype, female.*—Same data.
This species is closely related to *kincaidi* Bks., the chief difference being in the lateral arms at the base of the apical portion of the ædeagus, fig. 64.

Limnephilus cockerelli Banks, 1900b, p. 124.
Lectotype, female.—Top of Range between Sapello and

Pecos Rivers, New Mexico, August 2, 1900, 11,000' elev.,
T. D. A. & W. P. Cockerell. No. 11613. *Allotype, male.*—
Top Las Vegas Range, New Mexico.

The male genitalia show this species to be a close relative
of *moestus* Bks. The chief differences are found in the proportions of the tenth tergite and cerci, and details of the
ædeagus, fig. 84.

Limnephilus coloradensis (Banks), 1899, p. 208.   (*Gonio-
    taulius*)

Lectotype, male.—Colorado. No. 11621.

The curious ædeagus, fig. 76, and flattened claspers group
this species with *kennicotti* Banks, although the two are by
no means the same.

Limnephilus concolor Banks, 1899, p. 207.

Lectotype, male.—Tacoma, Washington, September 5,
1897. No. 11611. *Lectoallotype, female.*—Same data.

The abdomen of the lectotype is missing, hence it is impossible at present to give the diagnostic characters for the
species.

Limnephilus consimilis Banks.—see *Hesperophylax con-
    similis* (Banks)

Limnephilus curtus Banks, 1920, p. 345, fig. 57.   (*Anabolia*)

Lectotype, male.—Massachusetts. No. 10874. *Lectoallotype, female.*—White Mts., New Hampshire.

This species has been synonymized with *planifrons*
Kolenati.

Limnephilus diversus (Banks), 1903a, p. 244, pl. 4, fig. 5.
    (*Anabolina*)

Lectotype, male.—Prescott, Arizona, Oslar. No. 11649.
Lectoallotype, female.—Same data.

The cerci, fig. 79, distinguish this species from its closest
relative, *productus* Bks.

Limnephilus elongatus Banks, 1920, p. 344, figs. 92, 94, 98,
    99.

Lectotype, male.—Fort Resolution, Great Slave Lake,
Canada, 1862, Kennicott. No. 10870.

This species is a close relative of *sublunatus* Prov., but is
readily distinguished by characters of the male genitalia,
fig. 72.

Limnephilus externus Hagen, 1861, p. 257.

Lectotype, female.—North Red River, Canada, 1854, Uhler. No. 10727.

The wing pattern is distinctive for the species. The male genitalia are illustrated in fig. 80.

Limnephilus flavastellus Banks, 1918, p. 20, pl. 1, figs. 16, 17.

Lectotype, male.—Jones Collection. No. 10072. *Lecto-allotype, female.*—Wellington, British Columbia, September 23, 1903.

This species is a synonym of *externus* Hagen.

Limnephilus gravidus Hagen, 1861, p. 257.

Lectotype, female.—California. No. 10723. *Allotype, male.*—Santa Cruz, California, May 20, 1905.

The abdomen of the type is partly gone. A male agreeing well with the type and designated allotype has male genitalia, fig. 75, differing from those of *vastus* Hagen chiefly in details of the tenth tergite.

Limnephilus hageni Banks, 1930b, p. 226, figs. 7-9.

Lectotype, male.—Fort Resolution, Great Slave Lake, Canada, 1862, Kennicott, No. 16316. *Lectoallotpe, female.*—Same data.

Belongs to the *sublunata* group, differing from other members as follows, fig. 69 : appendages of the genitalia abbreviated, the preanal appendages with a small sclerotization near the apex on the dorsal margin, and the sclerotized part of the lateral arms of the ædeagus stockier.

Limnephilus hyalinus Hagen, 1861, p. 258.

Lectotype, male.—North Red River, Canada, 1858, Uhler. No. 10722.

The male genitalia have been illustrated by Betten under the designation *"Limnephilus sp. 1"* (1934, pl. 46, fig. 5 and pl. 47, fig. 7).

Limnephilus medialis (Banks), 1905b, p. 8, pl. 1, fig. 3.
(*Colpotaulius*)

Lectotype, male.—Muskoka, Ontario, July, 1888, E. P. Van Duzee. No. 11656. *Lectoallotype, female.*—Ithaca, New York, electric light.

This species has been synonymized with *consocia* Wlk.

Limnephilus janus new name for

Limnephilus minusculus (Banks), 1924, p. 439, fig. 52.
(*Colpotaulius*). Preoccupied by *Limnephilus minus-culus* (Banks), 1906, p. 120. (*Stenophylax*).
Lectotype, male.—Tolland, Colorado, Dodds. No. 14842.
Lectoallotype, female.—Same data.
The male genitalia, fig. 59, are distinctive. I do not believe
that this Colorado species is the same as *perpusillus* Walker,
as stated by Milne.

Limnephilus modestus (Hagen), 1861, p. 265. (*Anabolia*)
Lectotype, male.—Labrador, 1858, Hugo Christoph. No.
10711.
The differences between the genitalia of this species and
mutatus (Hagen) are found chiefly in the cerci, fig. 65.

Limnephilus moestus Banks, 1908a, p. 62, pl. 2, figs. 4, 8, 10,
11.
Lectotype, male.—Grand Lake, Newfoundland, July 28,
1906, O. Bryant. No. 11629. *Lectoallotype, female.*—Same
data.
A close relative of *harrimani* Bks., this species is distinguished by the shorter cerci and less ornamented lateral
arms of the aedeagus, fig. 83.

Limnephilus montanus Banks, 1907a, p. 119. (*Anabolia*)
Lectotype, female.—Mt. Katahdin, Maine. No. 11661.
This species has been synonymized with *planifrons* Kol.
and *curtus* Banks. Better characters in the female sex of
this genus will have to be discovered to determine this with
certainty.

Limnephilus morrisoni Banks, 1920, p. 343, figs. 5, 32 and 96.
Lectotype, male.—Reno, Nevada, 1878, Morrison. No.
10873. *Lectoallotype, female.*—Sierra Nevada, 1876,
Crotch.
The male genitalia are illustrated in fig. 81. The generic
assignment of this species is unsettled.

Limnephilus mutatus (Hagen), 1861, p. 267. (*Hallesus*)
Lectotype, female.—Labrador, Winthem. No. 10688.
Allotype, male.—Labrador, 1865, Moeschler.
The allotype matches the lectotype so perfectly in general

characteristics and color that there seems no doubt of the correctness of the association. The male genitalia, fig. 66, are distinctive.

Limnephilus nigriculus (Banks), 1908b, p. 262, pl. 19, fig. 11. (*Anabolia*)

Lectotype, male.—Clear Cr., Colorado, September 10, 1889, Oslar. No. 11664.

The male genitalia are illustrated in fig. 68. They form an intermediate step between *modesta*, fig. 65, and *mutatus*, fig. 66.

Limnephilus occidentalis Banks, 1908b, p. 264, pl. 18, figs. 1, 3.

Lectotype, male.—Tacoma, Washington, September 5, 1897. No. 11620. *Lectoallotype, female.*—Wellington, British Columbia, Bryant.

The male genitalia, fig. 60, have small cerci and broad claspers. The lateral arms of the ædeagus are a primitive type.

Limnephilus oslari Banks, 1907a, p. 121, pl. 9, fig. 19.

Lectotype, female.—South Park, Colorado, August 25, 1899. No. 11632.

The color pattern shows this to be the same as *externus* Hagen.

Limnephilus pacificus Banks, 1899, p. 207.

Lectotype, male.—Olympia, Washington, Kincaid. No. 11610. *Lectoallotype, female.*—Tacoma, Washington, September 5, 1897.

This species has been synonymized with *sitkensis* (Kolenati).

Limnephilus nepus new name for

Limnephilus pacificus (Banks), 1900a, p. 254. (*Stenophylax*). Preoccupied by the preceding species.

Lectotype, male.—Pullman, Washington. No. 11663. *Lectoallotype, female.*—Same data, May 4, 1898.

The male genitalia, fig. 67, have a curious ædeagus which is a simple derivative of the *modesta* type (see figs. 65, 66).

Limnephilus pallidus (Banks), 1924, p. 442, fig. 54. (*Apolopsyche*)

Lectotype, male.—Winnipeg Lake, Canada, 1860, Kennicott. No. 14849.

This is a synonym of *parvulus* (Banks).

Limnephilus perjurus Hagen, 1861, p. 258.

Lectotype, female.—Ins. Kenae. No. 10721.

The type lacks the abdomen.

Limnephilus pudicus Hagen, 1861, p. 262.

Lectotype, female.—Washington, D. C., Osten Sacken. No. 10720.

This is a synonym of *submonilifer* Wlk.

Limnephilus pulchellus Banks, 1908a, p. 63, pl. 2, figs. 5, 9.

Lectotype, male.—Grand Lake, Newfoundland, July 28, 1906, O. Bryant. No. 11626. *Lectoallotype, female.*—Same data.

This small species has male genitalia, fig. 78, which bear a marked resemblance to the *vastus* group.

Limnephilus roberti Banks, 1930b, p. 226, figs. 10-12.

Lectotype, male.—Winnipeg Lake, 1860, Kennicott. No. 16318. *Lectoallotype, female.*—Same data.

This species is a synonym of *parvulus* (Banks), fig. 61. The type of this latter species lacks the abdomen, but a topotype specimen which probably belonged to the type series but did not bear a type label agrees perfectly with the lectotype of *roberti*.

Limnephilus sansoni Banks, 1918, p. 19, fig. 8.

Lectotype, male.—Banff, Alberta, Spray Lake, August 25, Sanson. No. 10089. *Lectoallotype, female.*—Banff, August 31.

Belongs to the *sublunatus* group, set off from other members of the group by the following characters, fig. 70: Preanal appendages very wide, with an inner band of heavily sclerotized points; sclerotized portion of the side arms of the ædeagus subdivided at their apex into small projections, otherwise the ædeagus is like *sublunatus*.

Limnephilus secludens (Banks), 1914, p. 152, figs. 17, 27.

Lectotype, male.—Saskatchewan, July. No. 11623.

Close to *tarsalis* Banks, but separated on details of the male genitalia, fig. 63.

Limnephilus sordidus Hagen, 1861, p. 264.
Lectotype, male.—North Red River, Canada, 1858, Uhler. No. 10710.
This species has been considered a synonym of *bimaculatus* Wlk.

Limnephilus spinatus Banks, 1914, p. 149, fig. 8, 9.
Lectotype, male.—Vineyard, Utah, August 22. No. 11617.
Lectoallotype, female.—Same data, but August 28.
The slender and undivided lateral arms of the ædeagus distinguish this species, fig. 57.

Limnephilus tarsalis (Banks), 1920, p. 342, fig. 104. (*Colpotaulius*)
Lectotype, male.—Ward, Colorado, Oslar. No. 10880.
The male genitalia, fig. 62, resemble most closely those of *secludens* (Banks).

Limnephilus vastus Hagen, 1861, p. 257.
Lectotype, male.—Ins. Kenae. No. 10724.
The abdomen of the type is missing.

Neophylax fuscus Banks, 1903b, p. 242.
Lectotype, male.—Agricultural College, Michigan, Pettit. No. 11643. *Lectoallotype, female.*—Franconia, New Hampshire, Mrs. Slosson.
The male genitalia of this species are illustrated in fig. 86. The species considered and illustrated as this by Betten is quite different.

Neophylax occidentis Banks, 1924, p. 441, figs. 51, 58.
Lectotype, male.—Reno, Nevada, 1878, Morrison. No. 14848.
The male genitalia of this western species are illustrated in fig. 85. The similarity of the fundamental pattern of genitalia with the eastern species, and having the distinctive wart behind the lateral ocellus, indicate that this species forms a primitive subgenus of *Neophylax*.

Neophylax pilosus (Banks), 1930b, p. 228, fig. 13. (*Acronopsyche*)
Lectotype, male.—Modoc Co., California, July 20, 1922, Lindsey. No. 16319. *Lectoallotype, female.*—Same data.
This species, the genotype of *Acronopsyche* Banks, is a synonym of *occidentis* Banks.

Platycentropus amicus (Hagen), 1861, p. 265.   (*Halesus*)
   Lectotype, female.—New Orleans. No. 10690.
No definite placement of this species can be made until
well associated males are found, or good structural characters for separating the females.

Platycentropus hostis (Hagen), 1861, p. 266.   (*Halesus*)
   Lectotype, male.—North Red River, Canada, 1858, Uhler.
No. 10689.   *Lectoallotype, female.*—Data illegible.
This species has recently been synonymized with *indicans*
(Walker) by Milne (1936).

Platyphylax alascensis Banks.—see *Hesperophylax alascensis* (Banks)

Platyphylax atripes Hagen.—see *Dicosmoecus atripes*
   (Hagen)

Platyphylax occidentalis Banks.—see *Hesperophylax occidentalis* (Banks)

Pycnopsyche similis Banks.—see *Stenophylax similis*
   (Banks)

Stenophylax brevipennis Banks.—see *Limnephilus brevipennis* (Banks)

Stenophylax calypso Banks.—see *Drusinus calypso* (Banks)

Stenophylax gilvipes Hagen.—see *Dicosmoecus gilvipes*
   (Hagen)

Stenophylax lepidus (Hagen), 1861, p. 269.   (*Enoicycla*)
   Lectotype, male.—Pennsylvania. No. 10697.
The male genitalia have been figured by Betten (1934,
pl. 50, figs. 4-6).   *Lepida* was sunk by Milne as a synonym
of *subfasciata* (Say) but is distinct from that species.

Stenophylax pacificus Banks.—see *Limnephilus pacificus*
   (Banks)

Stenophylax similis (Banks), 1907a, p. 122, pl. 9, fig. 22.
   (*Pycnopsyche*)
   Lectotype, male.—Chatham, Michigan, August 23, 1900.
No. 11659.
The male genitalia show this to be a synonym of *guttifer*
Walker.

Family SERICOSTOMATIDÆ

Alepomyia bryanti Banks.—see *Lepidostoma bryanti* (Banks)

Arcadopsyche prominens Banks.—see *Lepidostoma prominens* (Banks)

Atomyia modesta Banks.—see *Lepidostoma modesta* (Banks)

Brachycentrus incanus Hagen, 1861, p. 272.
Lectotype, female.—Washington, D. C., April, 1859, O. Sacken. No. 10455.
This is probably *numerosus* (Say) or *lateralis* (Say). To date, however, diagnostic characters have not been found for the females of this genus.

Brachycentrus occidentalis Banks, 1911, p. 355, pl. 13, fig. 32.
Lectotype, male.—Bon Accord, British Columbia, May 14. No. 11685.
The long, separate cerci and slender, angled claspers, fig. 88, are diagnostic for this western species.

Brachycentrus similis Banks, 1907a, p. 124, pl. 9, fig. 21.
Lectotype, male.—Tabernash, Colorado, August, E. S. Tucker. No. 11684. *Lectoallotype, female.*—Boulder, Colorado, August 9, at light, T. D. A. Cockerell.
This species is a synonym of *americanus* Bks. The short, fused cerci and bilobate claspers, fig. 87, are diagnostic for this widespread species.

Dasystoma rusticum Hagen.—see *Micrasema rusticum* (Hagen)

Helicopsyche arizonensis Banks, 1907a, p. 125.
Lectotype, female.—Nogales, Arizona, July, 1903, Oslar. No. 11694.

Helicopsyche californicus Banks, 1899, p. 210.
Lectotype, male.—Colton, California. No. 11696.
The genitalia are remarkably similar to those of *borealis* (Hagen).

Helicopsyche borealis (Hagen), 1861, p. 271. (*Notidobia*)
Lectotype, male.—St. Lawrence River, Canada, 1859, O. Sacken. No. 10939.

This widespread species has been illustrated by Betten (1934, pl. 66).

Lepidostoma Rambur

Many of the species here placed in *Lepidostoma* have been considered previously as belonging to genera separated from *Lepidostoma* on the basis of male characters such as venation, folds in the wing, structure of antennae, etc. The male genitalia show that in many cases these definitions cut across phylogenetic lines, grouping together species which are at most distantly related and separating species which are really extremely closely related. The male genitalia show further that many of the most distinct of these groups are, at the most, an offshoot of a group of species placed in another genus. I feel, therefore, that many of these genera are only artificial segregates of species without any consideration to relationships. For this reason, I am defining the genus *Lepidostoma* very broadly. I agree with Mr. Banks that a thorough revision of the entire world fauna of this group will be necessary to correctly evaluate the genera.

Lepidostoma bryanti (Banks), 1908a, p. 65, figs. 1, 2, 13.
   (*Alepomyia*)
   Lectotype, male.—Grand Lake, Newfoundland, July 28, 1906, O. Bryant. No. 11709.
   This species is a synonym of *wisconsinensis* Vorhies.

Lepidostoma carolina (Banks), 1911, p. 356, pl. 13, fig. 28.
   (*Notiopsyche*)
   Lectotype, male.—Southern Pines, North Carolina, April 28, A. H. Manee. No. 11704.
   This species belongs to the *togatum* group as evidenced by the genitalia, fig. 92.

Lepidostoma costalis (Banks), 1914, p. 265, pl. 10, fig. 34.
   (*Olemira*)
   Lectotype, male.—Woodworth's Lake, Fulton Co., New York, August 19, 1909. No. 11701. *Allotype, female.*—Same data.
   The allotype is evidently of the type series but did not bear a type label. The species has been illustrated by Betten (1934, pl. 64, figs. 1-5).

Lepidostoma grisea (Banks), 1911, p. 357, pl. 12, figs. 17, 19, 22. (*Phanopsyche*)
Lectotype, male.—Woodworth's Lake, Fulton Co., New York, August 22. No. 11693.

Characteristics of this species have been illustrated by Betten (1934, pl. 64, fig. 6-12). It is a member of the *wisconsinensis* group.

Lepidostoma modesta (Banks), 1905a, p. 217. (*Atomyia*)
Lectotype, male.—Black Mts., North Carolina, May. No. 11702.

The elongate processes of the male tenth tergite, fig. 93, will identify this species.

Lepidostoma prominens Banks, 1930a, p. 129, figs. 1, 8, 10. (*Arcadopsyche*)
Lectotype, male.—Cape North, Cape Breton Island, Nova Scotia, August 7, 1928. No. 16321. *Lectoallotype, female.* —Same data.

The female bears the same label as the lectotype but did not have a type label. The tenth tergite of the male, fig. 91, is diagnostic.

Lepidostoma stigma Banks, 1907a, p. 125, pl. 8, fig. 10.
Lectotype, female.—Boulder, Colorado, August 9, at light, T. D. A. Cockerell. No. 11692.

The placement of this species requires first identification of its corresponding male.

Lepidostoma togatum (Hagen), 1861, p. 273. (*Mormonia*)
Lectotype, female.—St. Lawrence River, Canada, 1859, Osten Sacken. No. 10942.

The traditional interpretation of this species is very likely correct, but until better diagnostic characters are found for the females of this genus, there is no guarantee of it.

Lepidostoma vernalis (Banks), 1897, p. 29. (*Mormonia*)
Lectotype, male.—Sea Cliff, Long Island, New York, March 28. No. 11687. *Lectoallotype, female.*—Same data.

The male genitalia, fig. 90, are characterized by the tooth-beset claspers, hooked processes of the tenth tergite and a pair of setal brushes on the ninth tergite.

Micrasema charonis Banks, 1914, p. 266, figs. 3, 47, 51.

Lectotype, male.—Black Mts., North Carolina, May. No. 11698.

This species differs from *rustica* (Hagen) in the curved apex of the claspers and more elliptic ædeagus, fig. 95.

Micrasema falcatum Banks, 1914, p. 265, fig. 52.

Lectotype, male.—Great Falls, Virginia, May 12. No. 11697.

This is a new synonym of *rusticum* (Hagen).

Micrasema rusticum (Hagen), 1868, p. 272. (*Dasystoma*)

Lectotype, male.—Saskatchewan, Canada, 1860, Kennicott. No. 10938. *Lectoallotype, female.*—Same data.

The details of the genitalia are illustrated in fig. 96.

Mormonia togatum Hagen.—see *Lepidostoma togatum* (Hagen)

Mormonia vernalis Banks.—see *Lepidostoma vernalis* (Banks)

Neothremma alicea Banks, 1930b, p. 229, figs. 4, 5.

Lectotype, male.—Colorado, G. S. Dodds. No. 16320. *Lectoallotype, female.*—Same data.

The male genitalia are illustrated in fig. 89.

Notidobia americana Banks, 1900a, p. 256.

Lectotype, male.—Falls Church, Virginia, June. No. 11714.

This species appears to be the same as *grisea* (Bks.), described from the female.

Notidobia assimilis Banks, 1907a, p. 124, pl. 8, fig. 8.

Lectotype, male.—San Diego, California, G. H. Fields. No. 11715.

This species has been considered the same as *griseola* McL. but is distinct from it on the basis of the claspers, fig. 94.

Notidobia borealis Hagen.—see *Helicopsyche borealis* (Hagen)

Notidobia lobata Banks, 1911, p. 356, pl. 12, figs. 18, 20. (*Schizopelex*)

Lectotype, male.—Woodworth's Lake, Fulton Co., New York, June 22, 1910. No. 11712.

This is a synonym of *distincta* (Ulmer).

Notidobia moesta Banks, 1914, p. 264, fig. 12. (*Psiloneura*)
Lectotype, female.—Cambridge, Massachusetts, September. No. 11717.
This represents the female of the above, and is a synonym of it.

Notiopsyche carolina Banks.—see *Lepidostoma carolina* (Banks)

Olemira costalis Banks.—see *Lepidostoma costalis* (Banks)

Phanopsyche grisea Banks.—see *Lepidostoma grisea* (Banks)

Psiloneura moesta Banks.—see *Notidobia mœsta* (Banks)

Schizopelex lobata Banks.—see *Notidobia lobata* (Banks)

BIBLIOGRAPHY

Banks, Nathan
1895 New Neuropteroid Insects. Transactions American Entomological Society, 22: 313-16.
1897 New North American Neuropteroid Insects. Transactions American Entomological Society, 24: 21-31.
1899 Descriptions of New North American Neuropteroid Insects. Transactions American Entomological Society, 25: 199-218.
1900a New Genera and Species of Nearctic Neuropteroid Insects. Transactions American Entomological Society, 26: 239-59.
 b Some Insects of the Hudsonian Zone in New Mexico. Psyche, 9: 123-26.
1901 Some Insects of the Hudsonian Zone in New Mexico. Neuropteroid Insects. Psyche, 9: 286-87.
1903a Neuropteroid Insects from Arizona. Proceedings Entomological Society Washington, 5: 237-45, 1 pl.
 b Some New Neuropteroid Insects. Journal New York Entomological Society, 11: 236-43.
1904a Neuropteroid Insects from New Mexico. Transactions American Entomological Society, 30: 97-110, 1 pl.
 b Two Species of Hydroptilidae. Entomological News, 15: 116-17.
 c Two New Species of Caddice-Flies. Proceedings Entomological Society Washington, 6: 140-42.
 d A List of Neuropteroid Insects, Exclusive of Odonata, from the Vicinity of Washington, D. C. Proceedings Entomological Society Washington, 6 no. 4: 211-17, 1 pl. Trichoptera, p. 211-17.
1905a Descriptions of New Species of Neuropteroid Insects from the Black Mountains, N. C. Bulletin American Museum Natural History, 21: 215-18.
 b Descriptions of New Nearctic Neuropteroid Insects. Transactions American Entomological Society, 32: 1-20, pls. 1-2.

1907a   Descriptions of New Trichoptera. Proceedings Entomological
        Society Washington, 8 nos. 3, 4: 117-32, pls. 8-9.
    b   New Trichoptera and Psocidae. Journal New York Entomo-
        logical Society 15: 162-66. Trichoptera, p. 162-64, figs. 1-5.
1908a   Some Trichoptera and Allied Insects from Newfoundland.
        Psyche, 15, no. 4: 61-67, pl. 2.
    b   Neuropteroid Insects—Notes and Descriptions. Transactions
        American Entomological Society, 34: 255-67, pls. 17-19.
1909   Two New Caddis Flies. Entomological News, 20: 342.
1911   Descriptions of New Species of North American Neuropteroid
        Insects. Transactions American Entomological Society, 37
        no. 4. Trichoptera, p. 350-60, pls. 12-13.
1914   American Trichoptera—Notes and Descriptions. Canadian En-
        tomologist, 46: 149-56, 201-5, 252-58, 261-68, pls. 9, 10, 15, 20.
1918   New Neuropteroid Insects. Bulletin Museum Comparative
        Zoology Harvard, 62. Trichoptera p. 19-22, pl. 1.
1920   New Neuropteroid Insects. Bulletin Museum Comparative
        Zoology Harvard, 64: 299-362, 7 pls. Trichoptera, p. 342-62.
1924   Descriptions of New Neuropteroid Insects. Bulletin Museum
        Comparative Zoology Harvard, 65. Trichoptera, p. 439-55,
        pl. 1, 3, 4.
1930a   Trichoptera from Cape Breton, Nova Scotia. Bulletin Brooklyn
        Entomological Society, 25: 127-32, 10 figs.
    b   New Neuropteroid Insects from the United States. Psyche, 37:
        223-33, 15 figs.
1936   Notes on some Hydropsychidae. Psyche, 38: 126-130, 10 figs.

Betten, Cornelius
1934   The Caddis Flies or Trichoptera of New York State. New
        York State Museum Bulletin, no. 292: 576 pp., 61 text figs.,
        67 pls.

Hagen, Herman A.
1860   Die Phryganiden Pictet's nach Typen Bearbeitet. Stettiner
        Entomologische Zeitung, 21: 274-90.
1861   Synopsis of the Neuroptera of North America, with a list of
        the South American Species. Smithsonian Miscellaneous
        Collections. 347 p. Trichoptera, p. 249-98, 328-29.
1864   Phryganidarum Synopsis Synonymica. Verhandlung Zoolo-
        gische Botanische Gesellschaft Wein, 14: 799-890.
1868   Monographie der Gattung Dasystoma Rambur. Stettiner En-
        tomologische Zeitung, 29: 267-73.
1873   Beitrage zur Kenntnis der Phryganiden. Verhandlung Zoolo-
        gische Botanische Gesellschaft Wien, 23: 377-452.
1875   Report on the Pseudo-Neuroptera Collected by Lieut. W. L.
        Carpenter in 1873 in Colorado. Report United States Geo-
        logical Survey of the Territories for 1873, p. 571-606.

Milne, Lorus J.
1934-36 Studies in North American Trichoptera. Cambridge, Mass.,
        128 pp., 2 pls.

Morton, Kenneth J.
1905   North American Hydroptilidae. New York State Museum
        Bulletin 86: 63-75, fig. 15 and pls. 13-15.

Mosely, Martin E.
1934   Some new exotic Trichoptera. Stylops, 3: 139-142, 13 figs.

PLATE IV

Fig. 25. *Hydropsyche phalerata* Hagen, male genitalia; A, apex of
æedeagus, ventral view.
Fig. 26. *Hydropsyche californica* Banks, apex of æedeagus, ventral
and lateral views.
Fig. 27. *Hydropsyche occidentalis* Banks, apex of æedeagus, ventral
and lateral views.
Fig. 28. *Hydropsyche venularis* Banks, æedeagus, lateral and ventral
views.
Fig. 29. *Hydropsyche incommoda* Hagen, apex of æedeagus, ventral
and lateral views.
Fig. 30. *Hydropsyche slossonæ* Banks, tenth tergite, lateral view; A,
same, dorsal view; B, æedeagus.
Fig. 31. *Hydropsyche depravata* Hagen, male genitalia; A, apex of
æedeagus, ventral view.
Fig. 32. *Hydropsyche bifida* Banks, æedeagus; A, tenth tergite, dorsal
view; B, æedeagus, dorsal view.
Fig. 33. *Hydropsyche morosa* Hagen, æedeagus.
Fig. 34. *Hydropsyche cockerelli* Banks, male genitalia.
Fig. 35. *Hydropsyche oslari* Banks, æedeagus; A, male genitalia.

PLATE V

Fig. 36. *Arctopsyche grandis* (Banks), male genitalia.
Fig. 37. *Triænodes grisea* Banks, male genitalia; A, *Triænodes
frontalis*, clasper, lateral aspect.
Fig. 38. *Triænodes dentata* Banks, male genitalia; A, clasper,
ventral view.
Fig. 39. *Œcetis parva* (Banks), male genitalia.
Fig. 40. *Athripsodes transversus* (Hagen), male genitalia.
Fig. 41. *Athripsodes annulicornis* (Stephens), clasper, caudal view.
Fig. 42. *Athripsodes dilutus* (Hagen), male genitalia; A, clasper,
caudal view.
Fig. 43. *Anisogamus disjunctus* Banks, male genitalia; A, æedeagus.
Fig. 44. *Anisogamus costalis* (Banks), male genitalia; A, æedeagus.
Fig. 45. *Asynarchus centralis* Banks, male genitalia; A, æedeagus.
Fig. 46. *Clistoronia formosa* (Banks), male genitalia; A, æedeagus.
Fig. 47. *Apatelia incerta* (Banks), male genitalia.

PLATE VI

Fig. 48. *Dicosmœcus unicolor* (Banks), male genitalia.
Fig. 49. *Dicosmœcus atripes* (Hagen), male genitalia.
Fig. 50. *Ecclisomyia maculosa* Banks, male genitalia; A, clasper.
Fig. 51. *Glyphopsyche bellus* (Banks), male genitalia; A, æedeagus;
B, male genitalia, dorsal view.
Fig. 52. *Glyphopsyche canadensis* (Banks), male genitalia; A, same,
dorsal view; B, æedeagus.

Fig. 53. *Glyphopsyche irroratus* (Fabricius), male genitalia; A, ædeagus.
Fig. 54. *Glyphopsyche subborealis* (Banks), male genitalia; A, ædeagus; B, same, dorsal view of apex.
Fig. 55. *Hesperophylax consimilis* Banks, male genitalia.
Fig. 56. *Limnephilus argenteus* Banks, male genitalia; A, ædeagus.

PLATE VII

Fig. 57. *Limnephilus spinatus* Banks, male genitalia; A, ædeagus.
Fig. 58. *Limnephilus assimilis* (Banks), male genitalia; A, ædeagus.
Fig. 59. *Limnephilus janus* Ross, male genitalia; A, ædeagus.
Fig. 60. *Limnephilus occidentalis* Banks, male genitalia; A, ædeagus.
Fig. 61. *Limnephilus parvulus* (Banks), male genitalia; A, ædeagus.
Fig. 62. *Limnephilus tarsalis* (Banks), male genitalia; A, ædeagus.
Fig. 63. *Limnephilus secludens* (Banks), male genitalia; A, ædeagus.
Fig. 64. *Limnephilus clausus* Banks, lateral arm of ædeagus.
Fig. 65. *Limnephilus modestus* (Hagen), male genitalia; A, ædeagus.
Fig. 66. *Limnephilus mutatus* (Hagen), male genitalia; A, ædeagus.
Fig. 67. *Limnephilus nepus* Ross, male genitalia; A, ædeagus.

PLATE VIII

Fig. 68. *Limnephilus nigriculus* (Banks), male genitalia; A, ædeagus.
Fig. 69. *Limnephilus hageni* Banks, male genitalia; A, ædeagus.
Fig. 70. *Limnephilus sansoni* Banks, male genitalia; A, ædeagus.
Fig. 71. *Limnephilus abbreviatus* (Banks), male genitalia; A, ædeagus.
Fig. 72. *Limnephilus elongatus* Banks, male genitalia; A, ædeagus.
Fig. 73. *Limnephilus sublunatus* Provancher, male genitalia; A, ædeagus.
Fig. 74. *Limnephilus vastus* Hagen, male genitalia; A, same, dorsal view; B, lateral arm of ædeagus.
Fig. 75. *Limnephilus gravidus* Hagen, male genitalia; A, same, dorsal view; B, lateral arm of ædeagus.
Fig. 76. *Limnephilus coloradensis* (Banks), male genitalia; A, B, ædeagus.

PLATE IX

Fig. 77. *Limnephilus brevipennis* (Banks), male genitalia; A, ædeagus.
Fig. 78. *Limnephilus pulchellus* Banks, male genitalia; A, same, dorsal view; B, ædeagus.
Fig. 79. *Limnephilus diversus* (Banks), male genitalia; A, ædeagus.
Fig. 80. *Limnephilus externus* Hagen, male genitalia; A, ædeagus.
Fig. 81. *Limnephilus morrisoni* Banks, male genitalia; A, ædeagus.

Fig. 82.   *Limnephilus harrimani* Banks, male genitalia; A, ædeagus.
Fig. 83.   *Limnephilus mæstus* Banks, male genitalia; A, ædeagus.
Fig. 84.   *Limnephilus cockerelli* Banks, male genitalia; A, ædeagus.
Fig. 85.   *Neophylax occidentis* Banks, male genitalia.
Fig. 86.   *Neophylax fuscus* Banks, male genitalia, caudal view; same, ventral view.

PLATE X

Fig. 87.   *Brachycentrus americanus* Banks, male genitalia.
Fig. 88.   *Brachycentrus occidentalis* Banks, male genitalia.
Fig. 89.   *Neothremma alicea* Banks, male genitalia.
Fig. 90.   *Lepidostoma vernalis* (Banks), male genitalia; A, same, dorsal view.
Fig. 91.   *Lepidostoma prominens* Banks, male genitalia.
Fig. 92.   *Lepidostoma carolina* (Banks), male genitalia; A, tenth tergite, dorsal view.
Fig. 93.   *Lepidostoma modesta* (Banks), tenth tergite, lateral view.
Fig. 94.   *Notidobia assimilis* Banks, clasper.
Fig. 95.   *Micrasema charonis* Banks, male genitalia; A, ædeagus and tenth tergite, dorsal view.
Fig. 96.   *Micrasema rusticum* (Hagen), ædeagus and tenth tergite, dorsal view; A, tenth tergite, lateral view; B, clasper, lateral view; C, style of tenth tergite.

Psyche, 1938 VOL. 45, PLATE I.

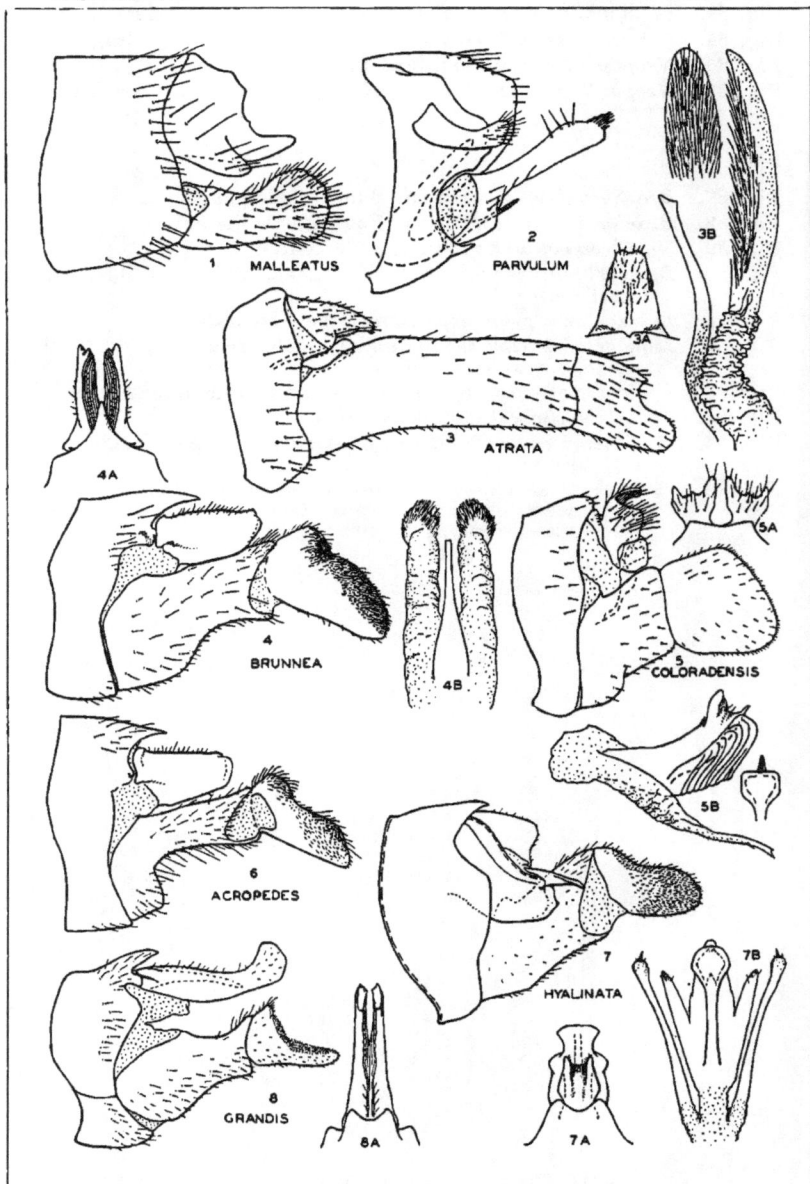

Ross — North American Caddis Flies

Psyche, 1938   VOL. 45, PLATE II.

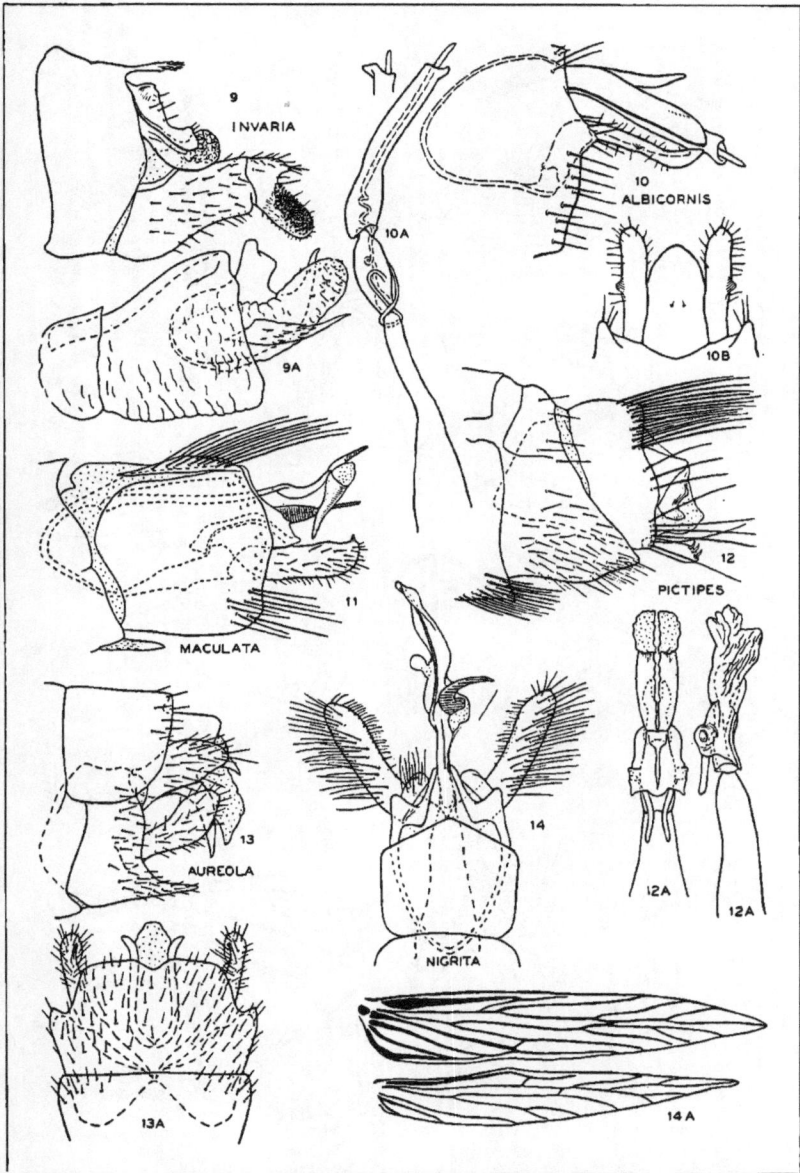

Psyche, 1938 VOL. 45, PLATE III.

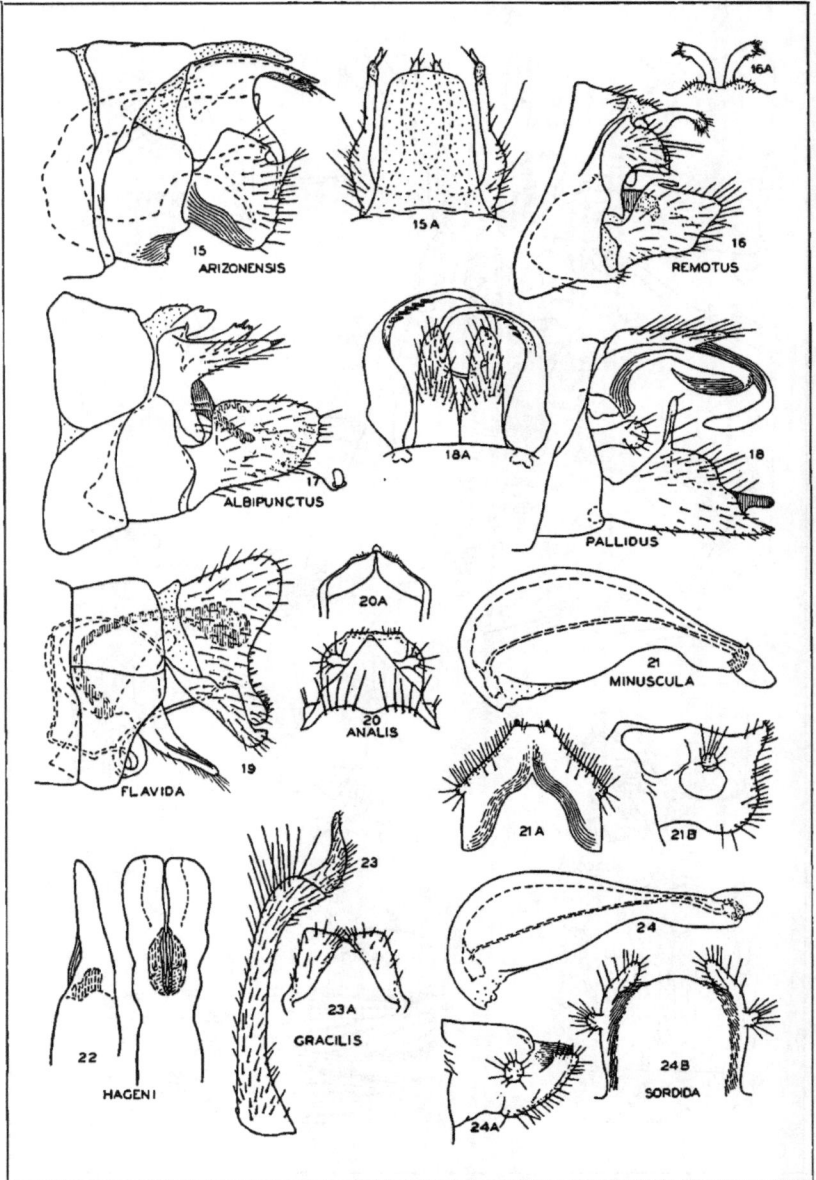

Ross — North American Caddis Flies

Psyche, 1938 VOL. 45, PLATE IV.

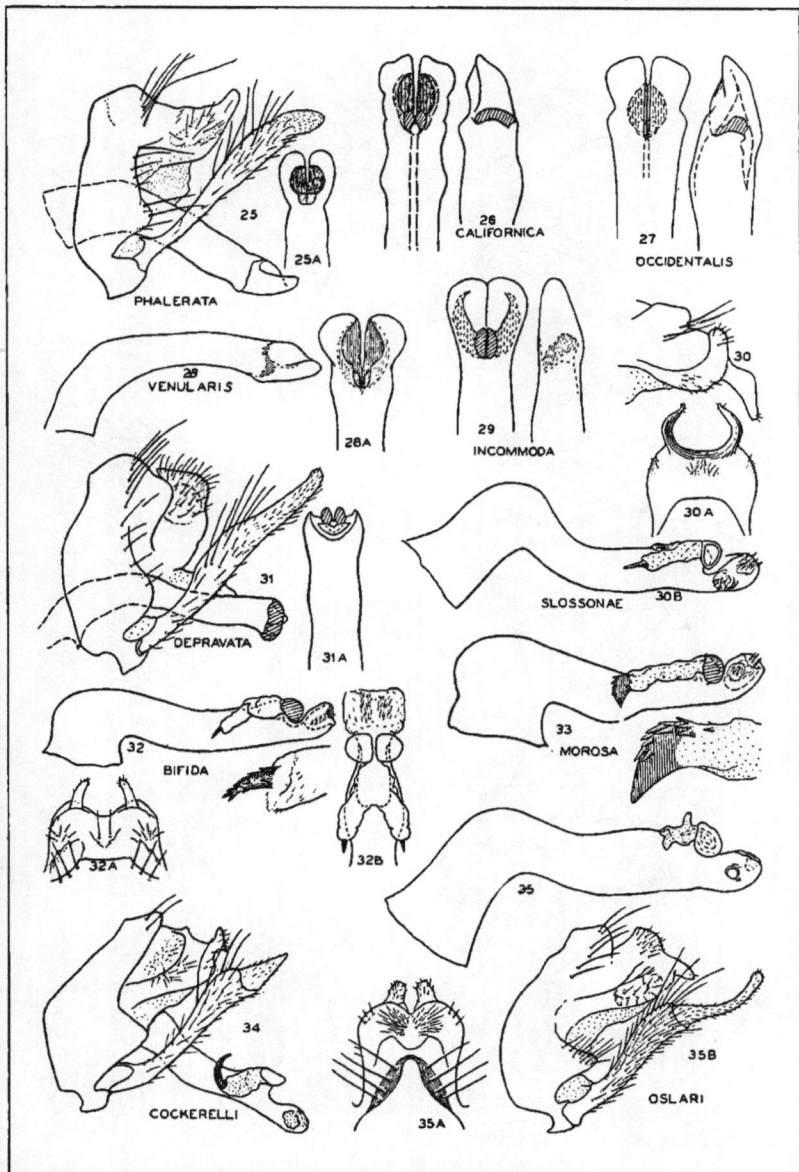

Psyche, 1938 VOL. 45, PLATE V.

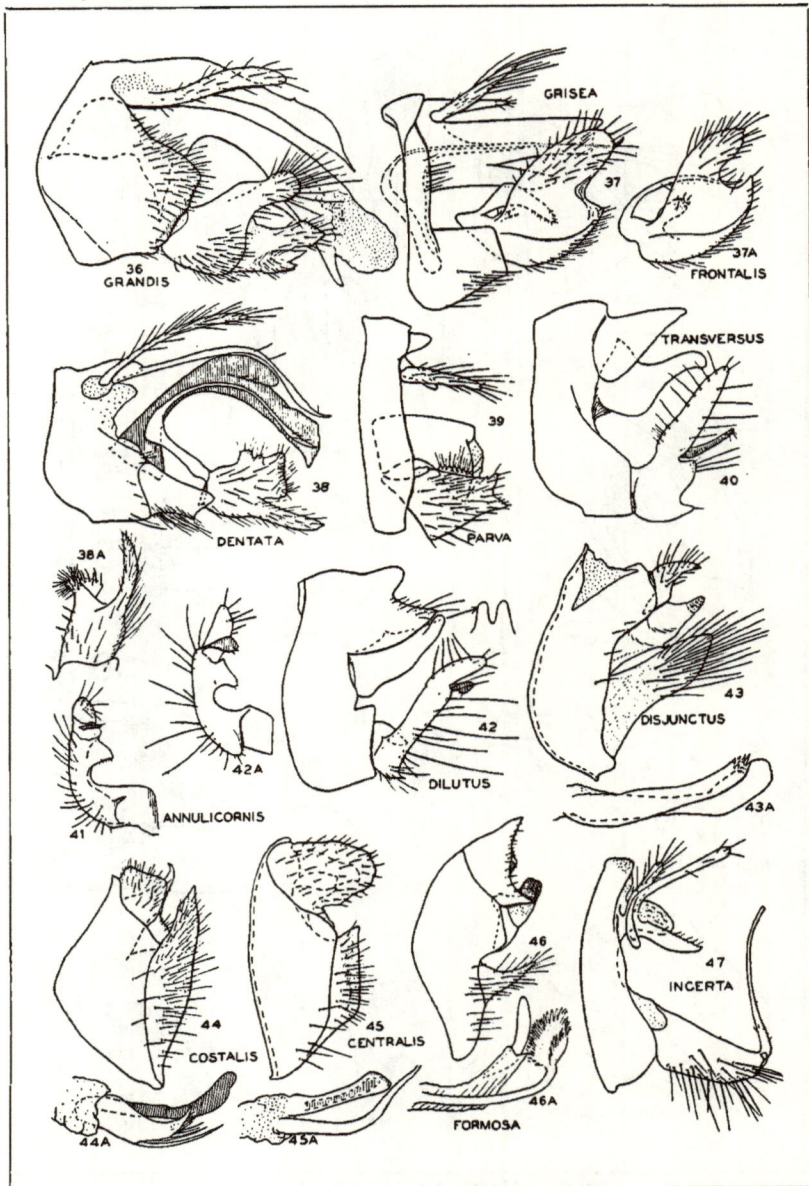

Ross — North American Caddis Flies

Psyche, 1938   VOL. 45, PLATE VI.

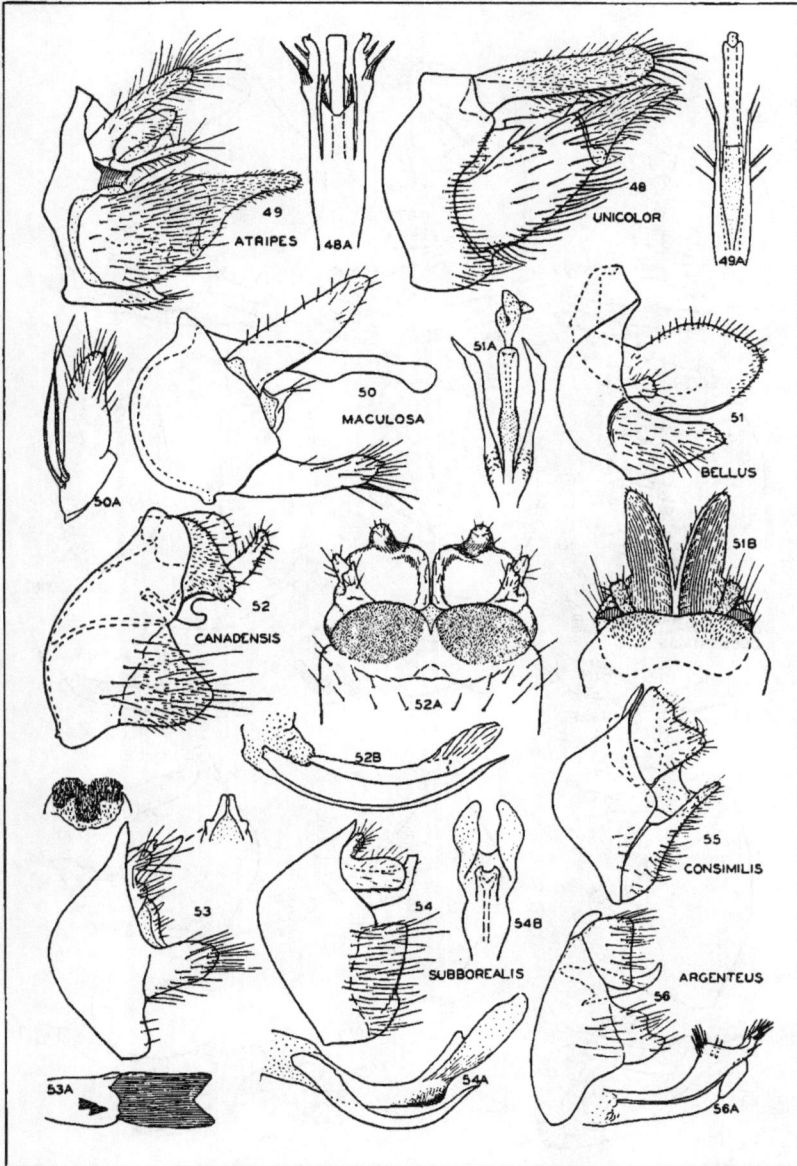

Ross — North American Caddis Flies

Psyche, 1938 VOL. 45, PLATE VII.

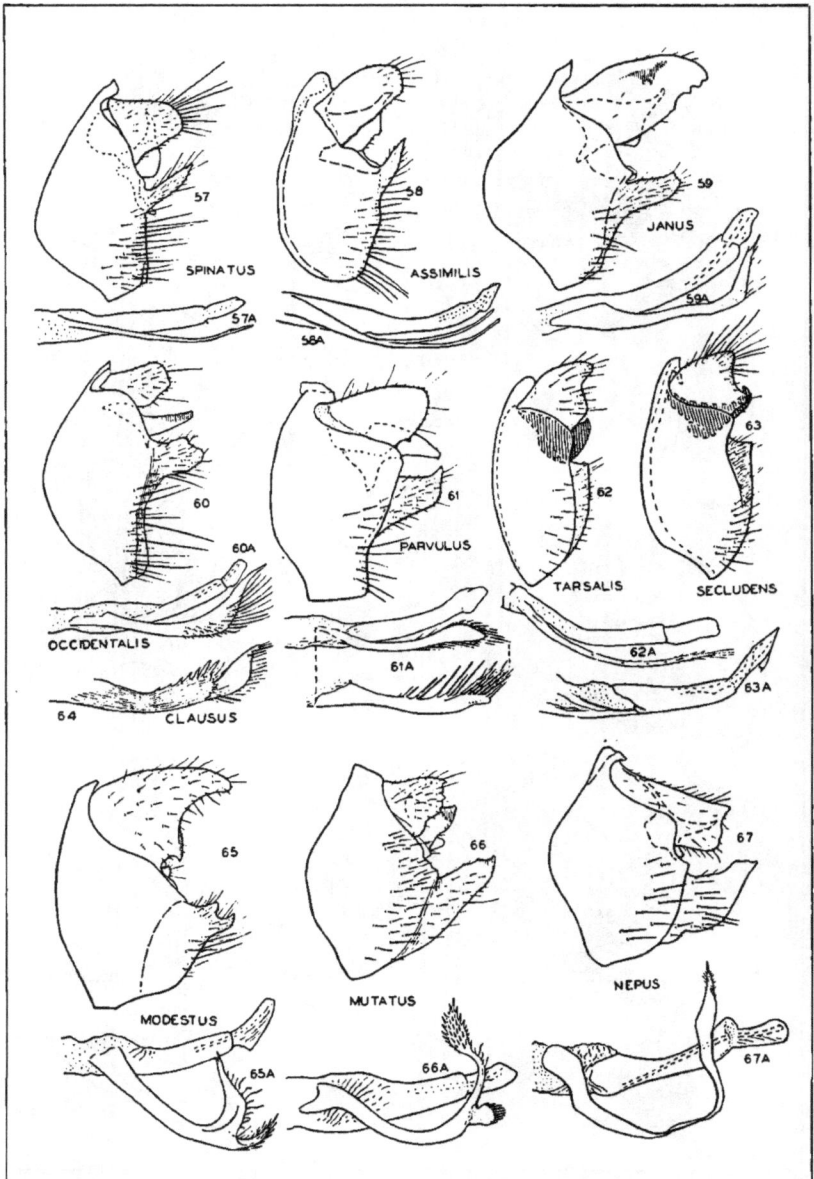

Ross — North American Caddis Flies

Psyche, 1938   VOL. 45, PLATE VIII.

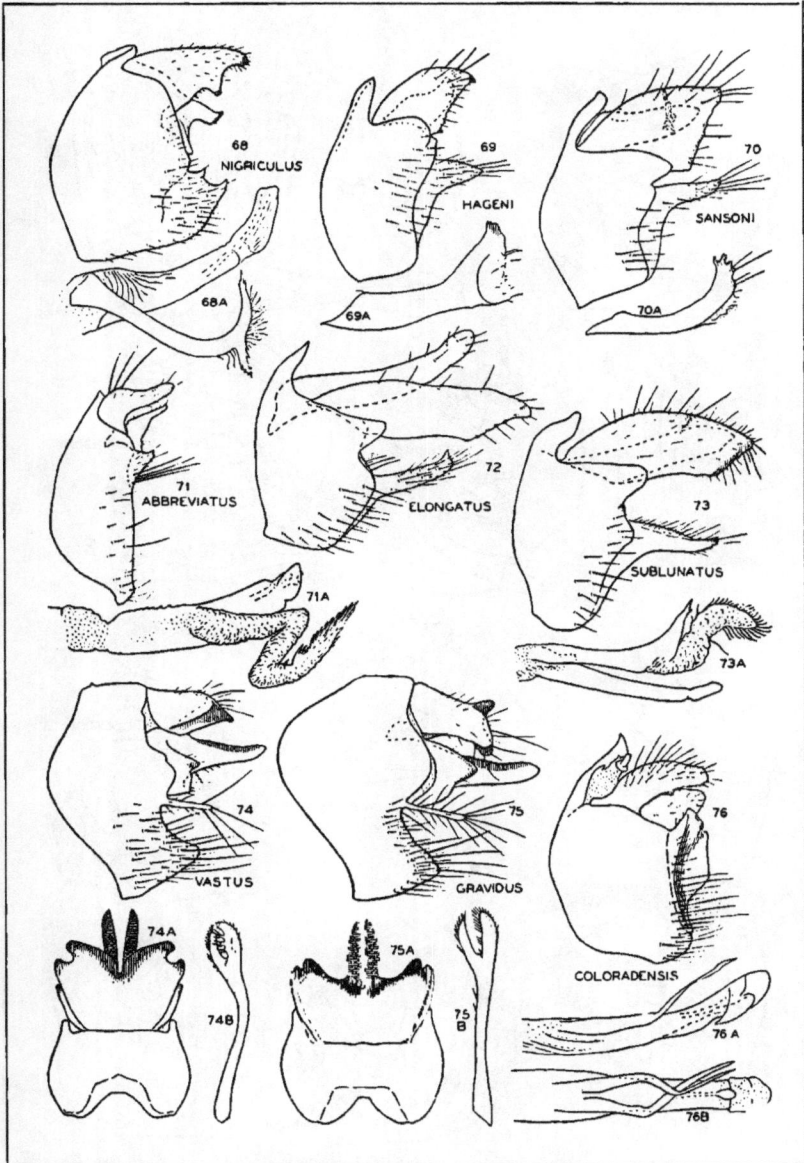

Ross — North American Caddis Flies

Psyche, 1938 VOL. 45, PLATE IX.

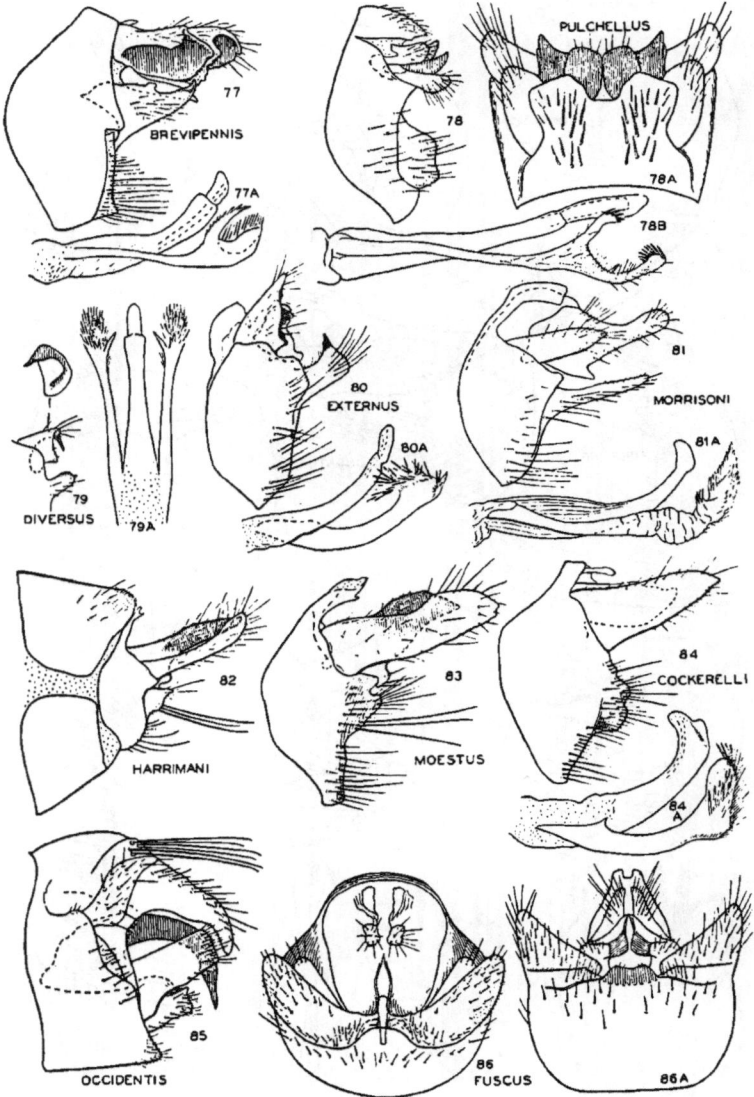

Ross — North American Caddis Flies

Psyche, 1938 VOL. 45, PLATE X.

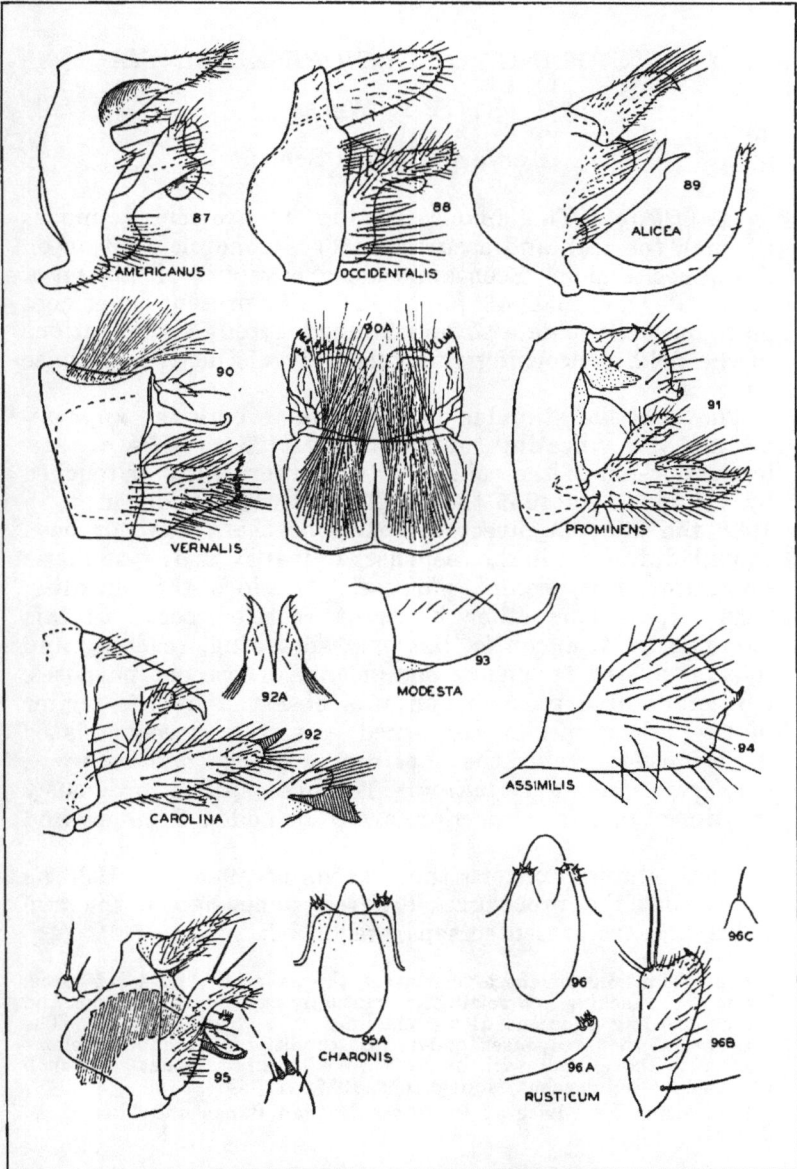

Ross — North American Caddis Flies

"SHUTTLING" IN *ARGIOPE AURANTIA*

By F. L. Wells

Harvard Medical School

"Shuttling: The spider, resting at orb-centre, moves through the web and assumes a corresponding position on the opposite side. Seen almost exclusively in *A. aurantia.* ..." (Psyche, 1936, 43, pp. 11-12). The present paper goes on to discuss the data so far obtained, through observations in the field, concerning this relatively distinctive response pattern.

The effective stimulus to shuttling is here the approximating of a vibrating tuning fork, of 128 or 256 v.d. rate, to the dorsum of the spider, no web intervening or touched by the fork. In 1935 the 128 fork was generally used, in 1936 the 256; in direct comparisons there has not been enough difference in the responses to justify their systematic separation for present purposes. Besides the shuttling behavior, various other kinds of reaction occur to this stimulus in *A. aurantia,* but only spreading, reaching and seizing[1] are of frequency significant for present purposes. No comparable phenomenon was observed by the writer in the other species concerned, *viz.* the closely related *A. trifasciata,* and the *Epeiras cavatica, domiciliorum, insularis, stellata, trifolium.* To these species previously mentioned in this connection, are to be added *C. conica* and *E. strix.*[2]

These studies concern the seasons of 1935 and 1936 as above, but the procedures differed somewhat in the two years, and are presented separately.

[1]For definitions of these terms, see the paper of above reference. Spreading, reaching and seizing are mutually continuous patterns, and their recording proceeds along the lines of a "rating scale." The notation of such responses under field conditions presents problems similar to those dealt with by R. W. Washburn, J. Genet. Psychol. 1932, 40, 84-89; Psychol. Monographs, 1936, 47, 74-82.

[2]Taxonomy by advice of Professor Nathan Banks and Miss E. B. Bryant.

1935 Data

The 1935 observations concern 55 individuals, with 167 fork-to-dorsum responses, on 129 occasions.[3] The points to be dealt with concern maturation effects, repetitions of stimulus, accessory responses and shuttlings to other than the normal stimulus.

Maturation. It appears that the shuttling pattern is to no little extent a function of the degree of maturation. *A. aurantia* changes in appearance so characteristically in the course of its growth, that statement in these terms should not be too difficult, but the present observations are recorded by date only. The following figures represent the situation with the fork-to-dorsum stimuli where the response involved shuttling, and if shuttling did not occur, the nature of the principal response that was made.

Dates	to 7-31-35	8-1-35 to 8-17-35	9-1-35 to 9-15-35	9-16-35 to 9-30-35	10-1-35 on
No. of responses	31	75	30	21	10
per cent shuttle	58	17	23	10	0
per cent spread	19	40	3	10	40
per cent reach	6	16	23	24	10
per cent seize	0	18	23	28	0
per cent others	13	7	23	14	10
per cent imperceptible	3	1	3	14	40

[3]An "occasion" is here a period during which an individual is observed uninterruptedly. Notes of observations on one individual, then on a second individual, then on the first again, would embody three "occasions."

The figures in this report share in the limitations that beset quantitations of behavior generally, "intelligence quotients" for example. Their function is to depict in specially condensed form, the trend of a mass of detail. Even numbers of individuals are approximations. One may perhaps take for granted that an identical appearing individual occupying the same nest, is the same spider; but less so that an *A. aurantia* appearing in a new location has not been previously observed in another one. One night in early September, 1934, a high wind blew from a southerly direction across the area under study. On next visit (9-10-34) nearly all the *aurantias* had disappeared from a certain portion, and newcomers were plentifully distributed along a stone wall bounding this portion on the north.

The location is some old pasture land in Hopkinton, Mass., 20-25 miles from the writer's domicile and work, which accounts for the irregular periods of observation. In each year, the writer was absent during the latter half of August.

The meaning of these data is believed to be, essentially, that the response pattern increased in aggressiveness as the summer advanced, and subsequently regressed with the coming of autumn. This is directly represented in the progressive decrease of shuttlings, with increase of seizings until the autumn. The reachings show similar increases followed by decrease. In the spreadings, the first increase represents a stage in the maturing of the attack pattern; the second increase was similarly a phase of regression in the attack pattern. The large proportion of "imperceptibles" during the final period will be noted.

Repetition of stimulus. If the spider has once shuttled, she normally, if undisturbed, returns of herself to the original position after an interval of seconds or minutes (see below, 1936 data). If the fork-to-dorsum stimulus be applied to the spider in the changed position, she normally shuttles back, and this process can be repeated to various extents. Only quite limited trials of this nature were made in 1935, but numbers of shuttling repetitions actually observed were,

times shuttled   2-3-4-5-6-*-20

times observed   9-3-0-1-1-4- 1

(*denotes designation in field notes as "repeatedly".)

The extreme case (8-17-35) was otherwise distinguished. A mature individual, she had been remarked on several previous occasions for an exceptional tendency to drop to the ground when approached, which had made tuning fork observation difficult. In this respect and in the shuttling, she was presenting an immature, regressive type of behavior, at a somatic age when more aggressive patterns were characteristic of her neighbors. When various individuals are observed repeatedly, as in these studies, one comes to recognize distinctive "personalities" in certain of them, sometimes regressive as here, sometimes peculiarly aggressive (cf. 1936 data, below).

Accessory responses. The above individual in the last five trials preceded the shuttling with a slight spreading. In only two instances, in other individuals, was extinction of the shuttling responses observed, after 3 and 5 shuttlings respectively; it was then replaced by spreading. The shuttling response appeared to mask the spreading in the less behaviorally matured individuals, but the shuttling being on its way to extinction, the spreading became overt.

A word as to the significance of the spreading pattern. As seen in *A. aurantia*, it commonly involved the first pair of legs only; inviting the anthropopsychic analogy of "stick 'em up" (to a threatening stimulus, as an attacking wasp). A lay observer indeed interpreted this and the reaching movements as "fending off" the fork. Actually, it is here

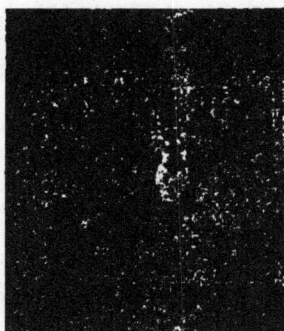

Fig. 1. A. *aurantia* no. 10 (7-18-36); an individual of specially aggressive response pattern. Note relative size of cephalothorax. The posture, and web stabilimentum are also relatively close to the adult type.

looked on as a frustrated pattern of aggression; of which it is the necessary initial phase, the spider extending the legs preliminary to grasping the prey in them. The reaching pattern represents a transition stage to the fully developed seizing pattern common in the maturer individuals.

One has then, to do with a mixture of the clearly regressive shuttling pattern, and the undeveloped aggression of spreading. In 18 of the above 129 occasions of 1935, the shuttling occurred in combination with one or more of the other response types. In most cases the response in question preceded the shuttling, and naturally, since shuttling removes the spider from the characteristic stimulus. After shuttling, the venter is towards the fork, a quite different stimulus situation, having its own patterns of response. On these 18 occasions, shuttling was preceded by spreading in 9 instances; by reaching in 5 instances, by seizing in one instance. In two instances the spider after shuttling, retreated, and in another instance withdrew the abdomen (common response in the young *trifasciata*). The spreading, reaching and seizing here combine with the shuttling in reverse order of their aggressiveness, but this was not the case in 1936.

Shuttling to other stimulus. In the 129 occasions of present reference, the stimulus is given by the fork approximated to the spider's dorsum, at orb-centre. Other analogous stimuli, to perhaps six times this number, were also applied, including fork vibrating in other positions, and silent but oscillated. Shuttling was observed to stimuli other than vibrating fork-to-dorsum on 9 of these occasions. One of these shuttlings was to a vibrating fork touched to the periphery of the orb; two were on fork-to-dorsum but spider not at orb-centre; two were on the approach of a fork silent but rapidly oscillated. One individual shuttled upon vibrating fork stimuli applied to dorsum, venter and orb periphery. When to venter, it is *towards* the fork; there was one other instance of this anomalous response. In one instance the shuttling occurred when the fork touched a leg; in another, upon the examiner's mere approach. Fork-to-dorsum with *aurantia* not at orb-centre is a situation little observable, but the response to it is probably similar to that at orb-centre.

1936 Data

During 1933, 1934 and 1935, *A. aurantia* was abundant in the area concerned. At the close of the 1935 season, eggsacs were found with exceptional readiness. In 1936, the earliest individuals were observed at a date comparable to 1935 (about 3 weeks later than 1934), and in numbers compared well with the young of the two previous years; but although search was carried on with similar care, a scant dozen individuals were observed during this year, that were past the adolescent stage. (The *Argiopes* seemed more affected than other species; *trifasciata* especially so.) The total occasions

involving fork-to-dorsum stimuli is but 50 against 129 of
1935. The amount of observation in the 1936 studies is comparable, being more intensive and controlled than previously.

The following figures are with reference to time of year,
tabulated in the same general manner as the 1935 data, by
occasion, only one response reckoned per occasion; shuttling
if it occurred, otherwise the principal response that was
made:

Dates	7-11-36 to 7-31-36	8-1-36 to 8-15-36	9-5-36 to 9-20-36
Occasions with fork- to-dorsum stimulus	28	11	11
per cent shuttle	57	36	9
per cent spread	7	27	45
per cent reach	11	9	18
per cent seize	14	27	18
per cent others	0	0	0
per cent imperceptible	11	0	9

The psychology indicated differs somewhat from that of
1935. More in detail; on 7-11-36 four young *aurantias* were
observed for the first time of any that year. In these individuals and one other, the apparent order of somatic maturation was one day later, from least to most, nos. (3), (1), (5),
(4), (2). To initial fork-to-dorsum stimulus, (1) and (4)
shuttled at once; (2) reached and then shuttled; (3) reached
slightly, then dropped to substratum. Response to subsequent (not necessarily in succession) fork-to-dorsum
stimuli were:

1 After spontaneous return in 2 minutes, reaching reactions, diminishing to imperceptible (fork 128); spread to fork 256.

2 Four shuttlings with spontaneous returns, in about 10″, 45″, 4′ and
   5′ respectively; succeeding four shuttlings preceded by reaches,
   but no extinction.

3 After return to orb-centre in 5′, seven shuttlings from original
   position, with time of spontaneous return as follows: 30″, 2′, 1′,
   15″, 7″, 10″, 40″.

4 Four alternate shuttlings and back, all to stimulation; on next
   stimulus, drop to substratum.

On next observation, 7-12-36, 4 was unavailable, others reacted as
follows:

Spider No.	Fork-to-dorsum-stimulus No.			
1	2	3	4	5
drop 8 in., back in 10"	drop 6 in., back in 3"	shuttle	shuttle back[1]	shuttle
2 reach, then shuttle, back in 5"	reach, then shuttle, back in 5"	reach, then shuttle, back in 1'	shuttle	shuttle back
3 shake	shake, then shuttle	shuttle back	shuttle	shuttle back
5 shuttle, back in 1'	shuttle	shuttle back	shuttle	shuttle back

Subsequent

1 Changes to reaching, continuing for three successive stimuli by fork 128.

2 Alternate shuttle and back for eight further stimuli, with accompanying spread or reach; later stimuli no shuttle, spread or reaching only, including final stimuli by fork 128.

3 With one intercurrent exception (shift and shake) seven each alternate shuttle and shuttle back, no reach or spread, no diminution of reactivity.

5 Uncomplicated shuttle and shuttle back for 22 more stimulations, last four to fork 128. Later occasion, this date, 34 responses: shuttling changing to reaching, to fork 256; then repeated shuttling to fork 128; then again shuttling changing to spread to fork 256; then further shuttling and back to fork 128.

In 1935, and in the earlier observations of 1936, the fork was regularly approximated tip to spider's dorsum, long axis of fork about 45° to vertical axis of orb, moved through a plane at right angles to the plane of the orb. It was noted that in minor asymmetries of stimulation therein arising, the spider uniformly shuttled in a direction away from that of the fork's approach, though the movement might not begin till the fork seemed quite opposite the dorsum. In later observations, principally those of 7-18-36, effort was made at more control of this factor. The fork was held vertical, and moved in a plane parallel to the plane of the orb. The tip of the fork then approached the dorsum either by a lateral movement from right or left (designated L) or downward from above (designated A; location of nests made it impracticable to approach upward from below). In such observations it is vital that no strand of the web be touched by the vibrating fork; often no easy matter, as it is

[1]"Shuttle" denotes movement from normal station; "shuttle back" denotes return to normal station.

the frequent practise of these creatures to put a screen of
irregular threads on the side of the orb where they normally
rest.

If the shuttling were due essentially to asymmetry of fork
stimulation, it should be relatively inhibited in the case óf
stimulation given as symmetrically as possible. In the
7-18-36 observations, each of the young *aurantias* available
had its first fork-to-dorsum stimulus downward from
above. Responses to this and subsequent stimulations were
essentially as follows:

Spider No.	Stimulus No., Direction and response			Subsequent
	1	2	3	
4	A reach	L reach spread	A reach, spread	L reach, spread
5	A spread	A spread, shuttle	L shuttle back	L shuttle and back, then imperceptible; after 1' one shuttle and back, then refractory to both forks.
9	A seize	L seize	L spread	To 6 subsequent L stimuli: 4 reaches, 2 seizes, no shuttle.
10	A seize	L shuttle	L shuttle back	L, to 7 stimuli shuttle and back, then spread, then imperceptible. Same pattern on two subsequent series this date.
11	A seize	A reach	A imperceptible	To 15 subsequent L stimuli, all spread or reach except 1 shuttle, 1 seize.

In these and an added number of other observations prior
to August 1, the indication is, that shuttling is somewhat
less likely to occur if the stimulus is symmetrical or nearly
so. In only one of the 7-18-36 trials of stimulus from above
did shuttling occur, and the failure of shuttling in the case
of lateral stimulus appears in general a phase of negative
adaptation. The uniformity of shuttling in a direction opposite to the fork's approach, is confirmed. The seizings are
puzzling. It is hard to exaggerate the violence with which
the diminutive creature would literally hurl itself upon the
fork, wholly abandoning the nest, and needing to be scraped
off the fork for return to the nest. Nothing resembling it

was seen in the adolescent *aurantias* of 1935. Stimulus
from above (often the only way to give a bilaterally symmetrical stimulus, owing to the "screen") is apparently
among the factors, but individual difference at least as
much so. The aggressive patterns of **10** were especially
conspicuous (fig. 1).

The following indicates the distribution of responses to
all fork-to-dorsum stimuli recorded 7-18-36 to 7-31-36 (9
individuals):

per cent	shuttle	spread	reach	seize	other	imperceptible
Stimulus from above (18)	11	11	17	33	17	11
Stimulus lateral (102)	38	13	20	11	12	5

These figures compare as follows for responses of 7-12-36
and for those subsequent to 7-31-36 (10 individuals):

per cent	shuttle	spread	reach	seize	other	imperceptible
7-12-36 (114)	82	8	8	0	3	0
after 7-31-36 (52)	17	33	11	23	4	11

With regard to accessory responses, the situation is similar to that of 1935. Reaching, spreading or seizing may
precede the shuttling, but in the 1936 series, the response
most frequently combined is reaching rather than spreading.
Reaching and spreading again appear, as in 1935, as the
shuttling response becomes extinguished. Dropping, a response prominent in the literature of such-like stimulation,
is nearly absent from these observations, but from its
rare instances, and experience with it in other species,
it is surmised to be a response more characteristic than
shuttling among individuals younger than have here come to
observation.

Only one instance is recorded of shuttling to a stimulus
other than fork-to-dorsum; this was on the touching of a leg
by an electric vibrator (not the "buzzer" mentioned in the
previous report; 11, 8-8-36). This vibrator, made from an
electric bell, was little applied as a "to dorsum" stimulus, but
gave evidence of being a weaker stimulus than either of the
forks.

In conclusion, the evidence for shuttling as a pattern distinctive of *A. aurantia* among the species of present study,

is briefly reviewed. So far as the other species were available, they were studied in the same manner as *A. aurantia;* but relative scarcity of individuals (*e.g., E. stellata*) and/or differences of habit (*e.g., E. strix*) interfere with close comparisons. The following gives the writer's view of the evidence from these observations for the *absence* of shuttling as a comparable response pattern in the species concerned (there is at hand no evidence of its presence) :

	adolescent	adult	day	night
A. trifasciata	good	good	only	none
C. conica	fair	good	only	none
E. cavatica	fair	good	good	good
E. domiciliorum	meagre	fair	fair	fair
E. insularis	meagre	good	X	only
E. stellata	meagre	fair	only	none
E. strix	good	good	X	only
E. trifolium	meagre	good	X	only

The apparent absence of the pattern in *trifasciata, aurantia's* near biological relative, will be noted. *C. conica* and the *Argiopes* are normally at orb-centre by daylight; *E. cavatica, E. domiciliorum* and *E. stellata* may be either at orb-centre or in retreat. *E. insularis, strix* and *trifolium* are normally in retreat during daylight. The effect of night on the shuttling behavior of *A. aurantia* also awaits further study; the general tendency of the observations is however, that the behavior of the various species concerned is more aggressive at night.

NEW NATIVE NEUROPTEROID INSECTS

By Nathan Banks

The following few descriptions are based on materials gradually accumulating in the Museum of Comparative Zoology. A generic synopsis of our Capniinae, including two new genera, is based on characters that, I believe, are better than those previously used in this group.

ORDER CORRODENTIA

Family Psocidae

Polypsocus corruptus Hag.

In the South there are two varieties which should be named:

P. corruptus var. pictilis n. var.

Females differing from typical *corruptus* in having a large pale area in middle of fore wing, similar to that of the normal male of *corruptus*, but more distinct; the preapical pale band is as in normal females. In male this middle pale area is more extended so as to meet the pale apical spot beyond the stigma, thus isolating the dark stigma. In none of these specimens is the stigma reddish as is common, but not constant, in typical *corruptus*. Size same as typical form. This form was very common in the Smoky Mountains of Tennessee, near Newfound Gap, at about 5000 feet, in September. In the valleys the typical form was common. Type M.C.Z. no. 22659.

P. corruptus var. omissus n. var.

The male differs from the typical form in lacking all pale marks in the fore wing, neither the median area nor the triangular area beyond stigma, only the minute pale dot at base of stigma, and at base of areola postica. The two males have slightly shorter wings than usual. From Great Falls, Va., 21 July, and Clarksville, Ga., 10 Aug. Type M.C.Z. no. 22660.

ORDER PLECOPTERA

FAMILY PERLIDAE

Capniinae

The genera occurring in the United States can be tabulated as follows:

1. The radius at origin of radial sector plainly bends forward a little 2

   Radius at origin of radial sector straight 4

2. Several cross-veins in the subapical area ..... *Capnoura*

   No such cross-veins 3

3. First anal vein bends around a large triangular scar
   Capnia

   First anal, although slightly curved, not bent around a large scar .... subgen. *Arsapnia*

4. Anal area of hind wing reaches to the tip of wing
   Allocapnia

   Anal area not reaching more than three-fourths of way to wing tip 5

5. No oblique cross-vein beyond end of the subcosta, very slender species .... *Nemocapnia*

   An oblique cross-vein beyond end of the subcosta 6

6. Large, heavy species; setae very long, usually five or six costal cross-veins .... *Isocapnia*

   Slender, small species, setae very short, of only a few joints, but one or two costal cross-veins . *Eucapnopsis*

Isocapnia gen. nov.

Rather large, heavy species; radius not bent at origin of radial sector, an oblique vein beyond end of subcosta, several (five or more) costal cross-veins; setae long, twenty or more joints, four or five or more near base very short; anal area of hind wing not reaching to tip of wing. Much larger species than others of the subfamily.

Genotype, *Arsapnia grandis* Bks.

There are at least four species, *Capnia crinita* Claassen,

I. fumosa, herewith described, and a clear winged species in which the radial sector is forked beyond the cross-veins; all are from the northwestern parts of United States and western Canada.

Isocapnia fumosa sp. nov.

Figure 3

Body black, posterior parts of meso and metanotum polished, legs, antennae, and setae also uniformly black. Both wings fumose, almost black on front part, the cells behind are paler in the middle, veins black. Body with only minute hairs, those on legs not half as long as in *I. crinita.*

Pronotum a little broader than long, scarcely at all narrowed behind.

In fore wings six to nine costal cross-veins, oblique vein arising about its length beyond the subcosta; all apical veins unforked; in hind wings several (four to five) costal cross-veins, lower branch of medius forked; anal area reaches about two thirds way to tip.

The last dorsal segment of the abdomen projects at a slight angle in the middle. The ventral plate is broad and broadly rounded, each side of its median tip a ridge runs obliquely over the next segment.

Length of fore wing 16 mm.

From Oregon National Forest, Herman, Oregon, 18 April, 1920, and Junction City, Oregon, 7 April, 1919 (both A. C. Burrill). Type M.C.Z. no. 22661.

Nemocapnia gen. nov.

Body and wings slender, radius not bent at origin of radial sector, no oblique cross-vein beyond end of subcosta, rest similar to *Arsapnia;* in hind wings the anal area reaches only a little beyond middle of wing; setae probably short, the joints beyond the first two three much elongate; in type species apparently but seven joints.

Nemocapnia carolina sp. nov.

Figures 1, 2, and 6

Body black, antennae and legs slightly paler, all densely

clothed with long hair, especially long on the legs; fore wings nearly hyaline, slightly gray, veins brown, veins and margin with short hair, membrane with very minute hairs; hind wings similar. Fore wings slender, radius not bent at origin of radial sector, only one or two costal cross-veins and these near tip; no cross-vein beyond end of subcosta, none of apical veins forked, and all subparallel. Hind wings with subcosta ending before middle of wing, lower branch of medius with a long fork.

Pronotum a little broader than long, sides parallel. Setae with seven joints (possibly have been more), all but the basal two elongate, longer than in related forms.

The male has the long median piece (in the only male) projecting behind, but probably normally recurved.

Fore wing 6 mm. long.

From Morgantown, N. Car. (Morrison), mixed in with specimens returned from a loan as "Leuctra spp.". Type M.C.Z. No. 22662.

ORDER NEUROPTERA

FAMILY CHRYSOPIDAE

Abachrysa gen. nov.

Body broad and heavy; antennae close together at base, not as long as wings; pronotum about twice as broad as long; fore wings with divisory cell much as in *Nodita,* six cubital cross-veins beyond it; costal area only moderately broad; the branches from cubitus to hind margin are in pairs, the two from each cell close together at base, or often united in one stem; the cross-vein from subcosta to radius is nearly as far out as base of divisory cell; the second cubital cell no longer than the first.

In the hind wing there is no trace of the triangle between base of radial sector and the medius, the radial sector, apparently, is here united to the upper median vein.

Genotype, *Chrysopa eureka* Bks.

It differs from *Chrysopa* and many other genera in the broad pronotum, in the short second cubital cell, in the paired branches of cubitus to margin, etc. Besides the type specimen from Arkansas, I have one collected by Prof. Frank Hull at Agricultural College, Miss.

Chrysopa crotchi sp. nov.

Pale green. Face with two black spots each side, one under eye near to clypeus and one at outer side of clypeus; palpi pale, unmarked; antennae wholly pale, the basal joints rather short, antennae much shorter than fore wings; pronotum much broader than long, hardly narrowed in front, unspotted.

Wings moderately long, almost acute at tips. Fore wing with costal area rather narrow, divisory veinlet ends beyond the cross-vein, eight cubital cross-veins beyond it; radial sector but slightly curved, fifteen radial cross-veins; the gradate veinlets in even and nearly parallel series and parallel to outer margin, about ten in each row, post-cubital area nearly twice as wide as cubital; veins greenish, most of the costals marked with black toward base, some radials with short dark mark, basal vein from cubitus to anal black, and the gradates dark; hairs on veins short, on costals hardly one-half a cell's width; stigma pale green, not prominent.

In hind wings the costals, radials, and gradates also partly dark, eight cubital cross-veins, fifteen radials.

Length of fore wing 16 mm., width 5.5 mm.

From Victoria, Vancouver Island, July (Crotch). Type, M.C.Z. No. 22975.

ORDER TRICHOPTERA

Family Limnephilidae

Dicosmoecus obscuripennis sp. nov.

Figures 4 and 5

Face yellowish, vertex black, both with black hair; antennæ brown, black on basal joint; palpi brown, paler on base; thorax black, pro- and mesonotum with yellowish hair; abdomen dark brown; legs brown, rather paler toward tips, spurs brown, spines black. Fore wings uniform brown (darker than in *D. tristis*), dot in base of fork two only distinct darker mark, veins yellowish, hairs mostly erect and black; hind wings paler brown, almost yellowish toward base.

Fore wings a little broader than in *D. tristis;* venation of both pairs practically the same as in *D. tristis.*

The male genitalia have the lower appendages widely outspread, the apical part about as slender as in *D. tristis* and with a sharp point; the superior appendages are much smaller than in *D. tristis*, slender, cylindric, scarcely clavate, while in *D. tristis* they are fully twice as broad and flattened and near tip roundedly widened.

Fore wing 19 mm. long, 7 mm. wide.

From Alaska. Type M.C.Z. No. 22658.

FAMILY LEPTOCERIDAE

Arthripsodes slossonae sp. nov.

Figure 7

Body yellowish brown; antennae dark, each joint pale on base; hair on head mostly pale, but a large tuft of dark hair each side in front of eye and below antenna, and some dark on posterior warts, thoracic notum mostly with pale hair, some dark near sides; legs pale; front legs of male with the tibiae dark on inner sides, and also the tips of tarsal joints dark. Fore wings a nearly uniform yellowish brown; a snow white mark at the end of anal vein, one at base of the stigma, and faintly over end of discal cell; hind wings gray, unmarked.

In fore wings the median cell does not reach nearly as far basally as the discal cell (more subequal in *transversus*).

The male genitalia has the clasper much as in *A. transversus*, the apical segment a little shorter, but the curved appendage is here very much shorter and stouter toward base; in length but little, if any, more than one half of the apical segment; each side of the base of the penis is a lobe fringed with stout bristles (not in *A. transversus*).

Length of fore wing 10 mm.

From Bellaire, Florida (Slosson) and Harrisburg, Pa., 13 July (Champlain). Type M.C.Z. No. 22655.

FAMILY HYDROPHYCHIDAE

Hydropsyche carolina sp. nov.

Figure 8, 9

A small species with the penis of the *depravata* type. Head and thorax dark, head with white hair, thorax in front with pale yellowish hair; antennae pale, obliquely dark on joints as usual; palpi a little brownish; legs very pale, rather brown on tarsi, hind tibiae with long white hair, spurs pale; abdomen dark brown above, paler beneath, a white lateral stripe where dorsum and venter meet.

Fore wings mostly clothed with brown hair, dark at stigma and toward tip, a curved row of white spots, often united in a band, across the apical cells, a whitish spot before the stigma, an elongate white spot somewhat before outer angle, not extending upward beyond median vein, and a little before it is another white spot, sometimes the two nearly connected.

The male genitalia have an angular incision in the superior plate, the apical part of clasper is slender and curved; the penis, seen from side, is enlarged at tip, mostly on lower side.

Fore wings 7 mm. long.

From North Carolina (no further locality). Type M.C.Z. No. 22657.

Of the size of *H. phalerata*, it is readily separated by the differently marked wings, and by the very different genitalia.

EXPLANATION OF PLATE XI

1, *Nemocapnia carolina*, ventral plate; 2, *Nemocapnia carolina*, fore wing; 3, *Isocapnia fumosa*, ventral plate; 4, *Dicosmœcus obsuripennis*, genitalia, side; 5, *Dicosmœcus obsuripennis*, genitalia, below; 6, *Nemocapnia carolina*, male venter, below; 7, *Arthripsodes slossonæ*, genitalia, below; 8, *Hydropsyche carolina*, clasper and penis; 9, *Hydropsyche carolina*, superior plate, above.

Psyche, 1938   VOL. 45, PLATE XI.

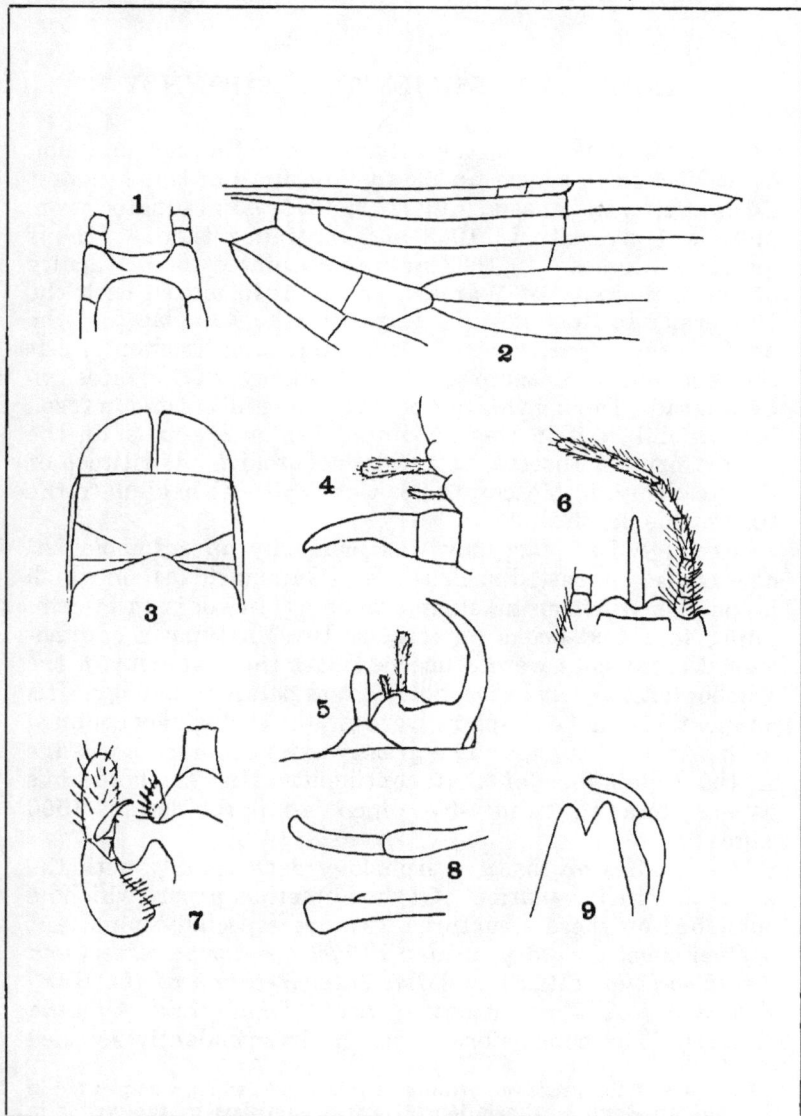

Banks — New Neuropteroid Insects

ANDREAS VASSILIEVITCH MARTYNOV

Dr. A. V. Martynov, the distinguished Russian entomologist, died from cancer on the twenty-ninth of last January.
Born at Riazan, Russia, August 9, 1879, he graduated from
Moscow University in 1902 and continued there with his
graduate studies. In 1908 he was appointed to the faculty
of the University of Warsaw, and in 1915 moved with the
University to Rostoff. Six years later he was placed at the
head of the department of Neuroptera and Trichoptera at
the Zoological Museum of the Academy of Sciences, in
Leningrad. During this period he became interested in fossil
insects and in 1936 was appointed Senior Specialist in the
Department of Insecta, at the Palaeontological Institute of
the Academy, in Moscow, a position which he held up to the
time of his death.

Although Dr. Martynov was primarily an entomologist,
he was also interested in Crustacea (Gammaridae), on which
he published fifteen taxonomic papers. In addition to com-
piling four text-books on insects, Dr. Martynov's entomological researches were concerned with the taxonomy of the
Trichoptera, general morphology, and paleoentomology. His
publications on Trichoptera were almost exclusively confined
to the Asiatic fauna, and he greatly extended our knowledge
of the caddis-flies of that continent. His Trichopterous
papers, totaling twenty-five, include approximately 1500
pages.

The studies on insect morphology dealt mainly with the
wings and their venation. Of the numerous papers which he
published on these structures, two are especially important
—*Uber zwei Grundtypen der Flügel bei den Insekten und
ihre Evolution* (1925) and *The Interpretation of the Wing
Venation and Tracheation of the Odonata and Agnatha*
(1924)[1]. The conclusions which he independently reached

[1]Because of the great importance of this paper, which was printed in
Russian, an English translation of it was published by the writer in
Psyche, vol. 37, pp. 245-280.

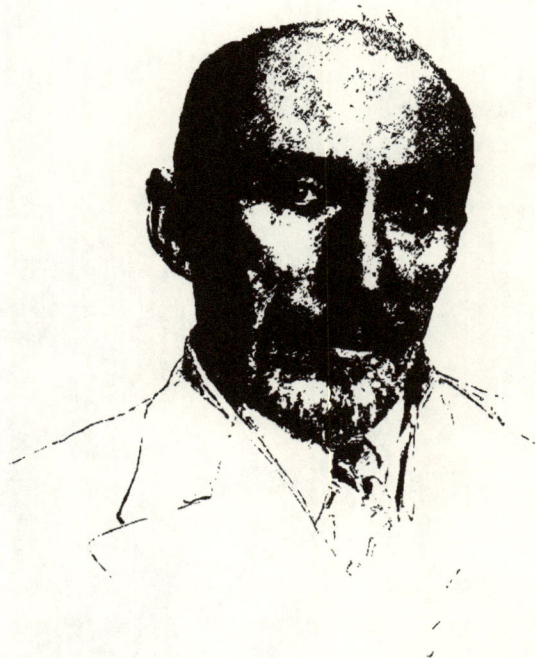

Andreas Vassilievitch Martynov

in the latter paper paralleled those just previously arrived at by Lameere (1922).

It was by the researches on fossil insects, however, that Dr. Martynov made his greatest contributions to entomology. The forty papers which he published on paleoentomology contain very nearly a thousand pages. His early work on fossil insects (1925-1927) dealt with a very remarkable series of Jurassic fossils from Turkestan. In 1928, however, before he had completed his studies on these, he became interested in Permian insects and devoted most of the next ten years to them. When he began these investigations only thirteen species were known from the Permian of Russia; at the present time, almost entirely as a result of Dr. Martynov's studies and field work, the number of such species has exceeded three hundred. Their significance is apparent when we consider that they are almost the only Permian insects known, apart from those described from Kansas and Australia. The Russian Permian fauna thus fills in what would otherwise be a very disconcerting gap in our record of the Permian insects.

Although I have had a regular correspondence with Dr. Martynov for the past twelve years, since he started work on fossil insects, I did not have the opportunity to meet him, and I am consequently unable to add to this account any intimately personal details of his life. Mrs. Martynov kindly sent me the accompanying picture, which was made in 1929, while Dr. Martynov was at the Zoological Museum in Leningrad.

F. M. CARPENTER.

DYTISCUS HABILIS SAY IN TEXAS

In the Schaeffer collection of Dytiscus, which was recently presented to the Museum of Comparative Zoölogy through the kindness of Mr. Kenneth W. Cooper, were two male specimens of *Dytiscus habilis* Say from Alpine, Texas, dated June 2. This Mexican species seems not to have been recorded before north of the border. It is close to *C. marginicollis* Lec. but is smaller (24 to 26 mm. long), more evenly oval, with prothorax even more broadly margined with yellow in front and behind. These two Texan specimens have been compared with four from Mexico in the M.C.Z.

P. J. DARLINGTON, JR.

LOXANDRUS INFIMUS BATES IN TEXAS

Of *Loxandrus infimus* Bates, previously known only from Mexico and Central America, I took a series at Brownsville, Texas, June 11-16, 1933, at light and in cracks in dried mud on the edge of a pond. Dr. Fritz van Emden has kindly compared two of my specimens with Bates' types in the British Museum. This species differs from all other Loxandrus found north of Mexico in being dull and not iridescent, with distinct alutaceous microsculpture on the elytra.

P. J. DARLINGTON, JR.

PIN-LABELS IN MULTIPLES OF 1000, ALIKE

One Dollar Per Thousand

Smallest Type. Pure White Ledger Paper. Not over 4 Lines nor 30 Characters (13 to a line) Additional Characters, 3 cents each, in total and per line, per 1000. Trimmed so one cut makes a label.

C. V. BLACKBURN, 7 Emerson St., STONEHAM 80, MASS.

CAMBRIDGE ENTOMOLOGICAL CLUB

A regular meeting of the Club is held on the second Tuesday of each month (July, August and September excepted) at 7.45 p.m. in Room B-455, Biological Laboratories of Harvard University, Divinity Ave., Cambridge. Entomologists visiting Boston are cordially invited to attend.

WARD'S ENTOMOLOGICAL SERVICES

Entomological Supplies and Equipment
Carefully designed by professional entomologists. Material of high quality at low prices. **Send for Supply Catalog No. 348.**

Insect Preparations
Life Histories, Type Collections, Collections of Economic Insects and Biological Insect Collections. All specimens are accurately determined.

Insects for the Pest Collection
We have in stock over three hundred species of North American Insect Pests. **Send for Price List No. 349.**

Ward's Entomological Bulletin
A monthly publication sent free to all entomologists requesting it.

Information for the Beginner
Send for **"Directions for Collecting and Preserving Insects"** by Dr. A. B. Klots. A mine of useful information. Price 15 cents.

WARD'S NATURAL SCIENCE ESTABLISHMENT, Inc.
P. O. Box 24, Beechwood Station
Rochester, N. Y., U. S. A.
The Frank A. Ward Foundation of Natural Science of the University of Rochester

BACK VOLUMES OF PSYCHE

The Cambridge Entomological Club is able to offer for sale the following volumes of Psyche. Those not mentioned are entirely out of print.

Volumes 2, 3, 4, 5, 6, 7, 8, 9, 10; each covering a period of three years, $5.00 each.

Volumes 12, 14, 17, each covering a single year, $1.00 each.

Volumes 18, 19, 20, 21, 22, 23, 24, 25, 26, each covering a single year, $1.50 each.

Volumes 27, 28, 29, 30, 31, 32, 33, 34, 35, 36, 37, 38, 39, 40, 41, 42, 43, 44, each covering a single year, $2.00.

Orders for 2 or more volumes subject to a discount of 10%.

Orders for 10 or more volumes subject to a discount of 20%.

A set of all the volumes available (40 in all) will be sold for $79.00.

All orders should be addressed to

F. M. CARPENTER, Associate Editor of Psyche,
Biological Laboratories,
Harvard University,
Cambridge, Mass.

PSYCHE

A JOURNAL OF ENTOMOLOGY

ESTABLISHED IN 1874

VOL. XLV   JUNE-SEPTEMBER, 1938   Nos. 2-3

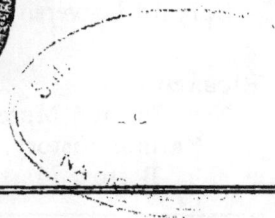

TABLE OF CONTENTS.

CAMBRIDGE ENTOMOLOGICAL CLUB

OFFICERS FOR 1937-1938

President .	. C. A. Frost
Vice-President	J. C. Bequaert
Secretary	V. G. Dethier
Treasurer	Richard Dow
	Thomas Barbour
Executive Committee	F. M. Carpenter
	C. H. Blake

EDITORIAL BOARD OF PSYCHE

EDITOR-IN-CHIEF
C. T. Brues, Harvard University

ASSOCIATE EDITOR
F. M. Carpenter, Harvard University

CONSULTING EDITORS

Nathan Banks,
Harvard University.

A. E. Emerson,
University of Chicago.

Thomas Barbour,
Harvard University.

A. L. Melander,
College of the
City of New York.

Richard Dow,
New England Museum of
Natural History,
Boston, Mass.

J. G. Needham,
Cornell University.

PSYCHE is published quarterly, the issues appearing in March, June, September, and December. Subscription price, per year, payable in advance: $2.00 to Subscribers in the United States; foreign postage, 25 cents extra, Canada 15 cents. Single copies, 65 cents.

Cheques and remittances should be addressed to Treasurer, Cambridge Entomological Club, Biological Laboratories, Harvard University, Cambridge, Mass.

Orders for back volumes, missing numbers, notices of change of address, etc., should be sent to Professor F. M. Carpenter, Biological Laboratories, Harvard University, Cambridge, Mass.

IMPORTANT NOTICE TO CONTRIBUTORS

Manuscripts intended for publication, books intended for review, and other editorial matter, should be addressed to Professor C. T. Brues, Biological Laboratories, Harvard University, Cambridge, Mass.

Authors contributing articles over 8 printed pages in length will be required to bear a part of the extra expense, for additional pages. This expense will be that of typesetting only, which is about $2.00 per page. The actual cost of preparing cuts for all illustrations must be borne by contributors; the expense for full page plates from line drawings is approximately $5.00 each, and for full page half-tones, $7.50 each; smaller sizes in proportion.

AUTHOR'S SEPARATES

Reprints of articles may be secured by authors, if they are ordered before, or at the time proofs are received for corrections. The cost of these will be furnished by the Editor on application.

Printed by the Eliot Press Inc., Jamaica Plain, Mass., U. S. A.

PSYCHE

VOL. XLV   JUNE—SEPTEMBER, 1938   Nos. 2-3

ADDITIONAL REMARKS ON WEST INDIAN GYRINIDÆ

By Georg Ochs

Frankfurt a. Main, Germany

In 1924 (American Museum Novitates, No. 125) I published a paper on West Indian Gyrinidæ and at that time believed that our knowledge of the family in that area was pretty complete. Recently, however, through the kindness of Dr. P. J. Darlington, Jr., I have studied a large collection of these beetles from the Antilles and Bahamas in the Museum of Comparative Zoölogy at Harvard College, Cambridge, Mass., and to my great surprise have found four new forms (two species, one variety and one form) from Cuba and Haiti. Moreover, several new records can be added for different species on the different islands.

I take this opportunity of offering my sincere thanks to Dr. Darlington for his kindness in enabling me to work on this interesting material.

Gyrinus rugifer Rég.

Hitherto known from Guadeloupe, Dominica, Puerto Rico and Haiti. Dr. Darlington has found the species in Cuba and Jamaica and added further records from Haiti.

Haiti: La Selle Range, La Visite and vicinity, 5000-7000 feet, Sept. 16-23, 1934; Mt. La Hotte, N. E. foothills, 2000-4000 feet, Oct. 10-24, 1934; Mt. Trou d'Eau, Nov. 19, 1934.

Jamaica: Blue Mts., Whitfield Hall, near 4500 feet, Aug. 13-20, 1934; Cinchona ca. 5000 feet, Aug. 16, 1934; Ocho Rios, Aug. 20-24, 1934; Moneague, Aug. 26, 1934.

Cuba: Santa Clara Prov., Matagua, 2000 feet, Oct. 14, 1927 (Wilson); Cienfuegos, Soledad, June, 1929; Trinidad Mts., Buenos Aires, 2500-3500 feet, May 8-14, 1936; Trinidad Mts., San Blas and vicinity, 1000-3000 feet, May 9, 1936.

Comparison with specimens from Guadeloupe, where the types came from, shows no essential differences in the series from the different localities. Generally male specimens are much smaller in size than the females, but in the series from La Hotte there are single females not surpassing the size of the males, and exceptionally (series from La Visite) males attain the maximum size of females. The punctuation of the elytra mentioned by Regimbart is generally visible only at the tip of the elytra (even under high power); the reticulate area on the elytra of the female varies in extent. The 11th interval (between the 10th and 11th series of punctures) is always smooth, as are also the basal and the apical portions of elytra to a greater or less extent; towards the suture the reticulation usually reaches the third series of punctures, and sometimes passes it.

Dineutus (*Cyclinus*) americanus L.

In the Cambridge collection are good series from:

CUBA: Soledad, Feb. 22, 1925 (Geo. Salt); Cienfuegos, Soledad, Oct. 27-28, 1926, Nov. 2, 1926, June, 1929, Aug. 2-12, 1934 (Darlington); Trinidad Mts., Hanabanillo Falls, Apr. 30, 1936, and Buenos Aires, 2500-3500 ft., May 8-14, 1936 (Darlington); Rangel Mts., P. de R. Prov., about 1500 ft., Aug. 24, 1936 (id.); eastern Oriente Prov., upper Ovando River, 1000-2000 ft., July 17-20, 1936 (id.); Oriente Prov., Maisi, July 17, 1936 (id.).

JAMAICA: Mandeville (Thomas Barbour); Blue Mts., near 4500 ft., Aug. 13-20, 1934 (Darlington); Ocho Rios, Aug. 20-24, 1934 (id.).

HAITI: Grande Anse (P. R. Uhler); Jérémie (Dr. Weinland); La Hotte, N. E. foothills, 2000-4000 ft., Oct. 10-24, 1934 (Darlington); S. W. Peninsula, Etang Lachaux, under 1000 ft., Oct. 26-27, 1934 (id.).

BAHAMAS: Andros Isl., Apr., 1905, 1 ♀, somewhat doubtful, perhaps not correctly labelled?

From earlier determination work the following records

are to be added: Cuba: Prov. Pinar del Rio, Sierra del Rosario, Rio Las Pozas near la Mulatta (Bierig don., in coll. Ochs). Jamaica: Rio Gohre Canal, 1895 (Carnegie Museum); Castleton Gardens, 500 ft., Jan. 4, 1913 (W. Harris coll., U. S. Nat. Mus.). Puerto Rico: Desengano, Apr., 1924 (Cornell Univ. Coll.); Aguadilla, Jan., 1899 (Aug. Busck coll., U. S. Nat. Museum). Haiti: Suzanne, 1925 (Hofmann coll., U. S. Nat. Museum).

I cannot find essential differences in the specimens of the different series. The species seems to be constant over its range from Guadeloupe to Cuba and Jamaica.

Dineutus (*Cyclinus*) **carolinus** Lec. subsp. **mutchleri** Ochs.

Hitherto recorded only from Nassau (Bahamas). The Cambridge collection contains the following series: New. Providence Is. (-Nassau) July, 1904 (Barber); Andros Is., Apr., 1905; and a single female from Cat. I., Arthurs Town, July 5, 1935 (W. J. Clench).

Dineutus (*s. str.*) longimanus Oliv.

In the Cambridge collection from:

HAITI: Furcy (W. M. Mann); Mt. Basil, to 4700 ft., Sept. 9, 1934 (Darlington); Trou Caiman, Sept. 15-20, 1934 (id.); Mt. La Hotte, N. E. foothills, 2000-4000 ft., Oct. 10-24, 1934 (id.); Mt. La Hotte, Desbarrière, near 4000 ft., Oct. 12-14, 1934 (id.); Miragoane, Oct. 30-Nov. 2, 1934 (id.).

Dineutus longimanus, subsp. cubensis Ochs 1926

CUBA: Upper Yara Valley, taken on a shallow river, Oct. 18-28 (L. C. Scaramuzza); Cienfuegos, Soledad, June, 1929 (Darlington); Trinidad Mts., June, 1929 (id.); Trinidad Mts., Hanabanillo Falls, April 30, 1936 (id.); Trinidad Mts., Buenos Aires, 2500-3500 ft., May 8-14, 1936 (id.); Rangel Mts., P. de R. Prov., about 1500 ft., Aug. 24, 1936 (id.); Pico Turquino, S. side, 1500 ft., June 25, 1936 (id.); Oriente Prov., Cobre Range, Loma del Gato, about 3000 ft., July 3-7, 1936 (id.); eastern Oriente Prov., upper Ovando River, 1000-2000 ft., July 17-20, 1936 (id.); eastern Oriente Prov., Mts. N. of Imias, 3000-4000 ft., July 25-28, 1936 (id.). In my collection through the kindness of Mr. Bierig, Habana, from the

Province of Pinar del Rio: Sitio de Inferno and San Vicente, in mountain streams; Sierra del Rosario, Rio las Pozas near la Mulatta.

Dineutus longimanus subsp. jamaicensis subsp. nov.

Good series in the Cambridge collection show that specimens from Jamaica are somewhat different from those of Haiti, Puerto Rico and Cuba. They are characterized by rufous anterior legs, testaceous undersurface, upper surface with silky lustre, anterior tibiae of the male with double incurvation.

Type ♂ and numerous paratypes in the Cambridge collection (Type No. 23,058) from Jamaica, Blue Mts., near 4500 ft., Aug. 13-20, 1934 (Darlington), further specimens from Ocho Rios, Aug. 20-24, 1934 (id.); Kingston, Feb. 14, 1928 (id.); Mandeville (A. E. Wight); Castleton, Botanical Garden (Petrunkevitch).

In the males of the Jamaican series the oedeagus is subparallel, about ⅔ as wide as the lateral lobes in their basal part, apical fifth finely acuminate; sometimes (immature or shrivelled), narrower and slightly attenuated in the middle of the length. In the Haitian specimens the oedeagus is slightly attenuated from the base in basal third, thence subparallel, slender, about ⅓ as wide as the lateral lobes, apical fourth acuminate. In the Cuban and Puerto Rican specimens the male genitalia are still somewhat different, as described by me (1924, l.c.); in several individuals, however, we meet with abnormal features approaching those of the other races. Also the other racial characters are not constant in every case, but generally the different subspecies are to be distinguished as follows:

	anterior legs	under surface	upper surface	incurvation of anterior tibiae ♂
Haiti	dark rufous	testaceous	metallic	simple
Puerto Rico	rufous	testaceous	metallic	simple
Jamaica	rufous	testaceous	silky	double
Cuba	brownish	infuscated	silky	double

Hatch (1930, Publ. Univ. Oklahoma Biol. Surv. 2, pp. 18-21) placed this species in the subgenus Cyclinus. I should, however, prefer to put it with Dineutus s. str., as the large size and the highly developed anterior legs of the males show more affinity with the representatives of the latter subgenus. Hatch, among many other erroneous suppositions, in his publications on the Gyrinidæ, adds in the same paper the statement that spinous elytral apexes are a character entirely lacking in Dineutus *s. str.* He overlooks the fact that in several species from the Madagascar and the Ethiopian region we meet with such a condition, so the spinose elytral apex does not exclude *D. longimanus* from the subgenus Dineutus *s. str.* Moreover, in *D. truncatus* Sharp from Central America, we can recognize the truncature of *D. longimanus* in a moderate form. A profemoral tooth, the presence of which is denied by Hatch for the species, is weakly intimated in large males of *D. longimanus*.

Gyretes vulneratus Aubé

Of this species, which hitherto was represented only by a few specimens in old collections (i.a. Mus. Berlin, Bremen, Senckenberg; types in coll. Dejean), the Cambridge Museum possesses a considerable series, all from Haiti. The specimens in a series from Furcy (W. M. Mann) agree rather well with the ancient ones seen by me, which are perhaps from the same region as Aubé's types. All females are very strongly reticulate on the disc of pronotum and elytra, and on the sides of the latter there are two abbreviate ridges with a short longitudinal depression between them.

Gyretes vulneratus, forma ♀ laevicollis forma nov.

In several series taken in Haiti by Mr. Darlington, most of the females have the disc of pronotum and elytra smooth (reticulation very fine) as in the males, and on the sides of elytra there is no noticeable ridge or depression; only the tips of elytra show a strong reticulation.

Type and several paratypes (type no. M. C. Z. 23,059) from Mt. La Hotte, N. E. foothills, 2000-4000 ft., Oct. 10-24, 1934; further specimens from Mt. La Hotte, Desbarrières, near 4000 ft., Oct. 12-14, 1934 and Tardieu, 3000 ft., Oct. 14, 1934; Camp Perrin, near 1000 ft., Oct. 8-27, 1934; Ennery, near 1000 ft., Sept. 6-11, 1934.

In the last mentioned series there are, besides smooth females, also reticulate female specimens approaching the typical female form with ridges and lateral depression on the elytra. In all these series the size is on the average a little less than in the specimens from Furcy, a yellowish longitudinal spot is more evident on the pygidium, and in the males the anterior tibiae and tarsi are less strongly developed.

The male genitalia in *G. vulneratus* are of a very singular form: the oedeagus is very short and broad, the apical part bent upwards, bottonlike, and joined to the base by a keeled longitudinal ridge.

Chevrolat (1863, Ann. Soc. Ent. France (4) 3, p. 203) mentions *G. vulneratus* from Cuba; perhaps he confused it with the following species.

Gyretes darlingtoni sp. nov.

Length 5-5.5 mm. Oval, hardly elongate, posteriorly attenuate, very convex. Surface shining, black, slightly brassy; lateral margin brownish, very narrow on prothorax and at base of elytra, much wider and more yellowish towards apex of latter; pygidium yellowish, with two short black longitudinal stripes at the base; body beneath rufous, anal segment and epipleurae yellowish. Labrum rufous or yellowish, transverse, anteriorly rounded and brightly ciliated, surface slightly reticulated, posteriorly at the sides deeply punctured and bristly. Clypeus well defined, with dispersed punctures, a narrow anterior margin smooth, posteriorly strongly reticulate, with short transverse meshes. Reticulation less strongly impressed on the head anteriorly and becoming still more superficial towards the vertex, nearly invisible on the prothorax and very fine and most transverse on the elytra; in the ♀ there is a longitudinal area of strongly impressed nearly round meshes on the last ⅔ of each elytron, on which longitudinal striae are sometimes indistinctly marked. Tomentous border of the prothorax reaching opposite middle of eye anteriorly, obliquely narrowed and hardly half as wide posteriorly; still narrower on the base of elytra, regularly and moderately broadened from the humeral part for about ⅔ of the length of elytra, thence more strongly bent inwards and reaching the truncature obliquely at about its inner third; in the ♀ tomentous border of elytra regularly broadened to about ¾ of the length of elytra, the last part of the border therefore a little narrower than in the ♂, reaching the truncature less obliquely and slightly convexly curved. Truncature of elytra moderately oblique in the ♂, more oblique and slightly concave in the ♀, exterior angle a little projecting, briefly denticulate, sutural angle broadly rounded, more produced in the ♀. Anterior tibiæ of the ♂ dilated towards the apex, exterior apical angle rounded; anterior tarsi moderately dilated, narrower than the tibiæ, slightly attenuate towards the apex. In the ♀ the anterior tibiæ are less dilated, the tarsi narrower, subparallel. Ædeagus pale yellow, long and slender, about as wide as the lateral lobes, subparallel basally, attenuate in about apical third, apex finely acuminate.

Habitat: Cuba, eastern Oriente, Mts. N. of Imias, 3000-4000 ft., July 25-28, 1936 (Darlington).

Type ♂ and Allotype ♀ (Type no. M. C. Z. 23,060) in the Museum of Comparative Zoölogy at Harvard College, Cambridge, Mass.); paratypes 9 ♂ ♂, 8 ♀ ♀. Further specimens, 1 ♂ 1 ♀, from eastern Oriente, upper Ovando river, 1000-2000 ft., July 17-20, 1936 (Darlington) agree with the typical specimens.

A small series however (4 ♂ ♂, 1 ♀) from the Cobre Range, Oriente Prov., about 3000 ft., July 3-7, 1936 (Darlington) differ by the pygidium being nearly totally black, only the tip yellow (=a. *pygidialis* nov., type no. M. C. Z. 23,061). Also these specimens are a little larger in size, and in the ♀ longitudinal striae are more distinctly marked on the reticulate portion of the elytra.

The new species differs from *Gyretes cubensis* Rég., the only species of Gyretes hitherto known from Cuba, by its larger size, broader, less elongate and less vaulted body, yellowish labrum and tip of pygidium, brighter coloured undersurface, sutural angle of elytra and apical exterior angle of anterior tibiae rounded.

Somewhat resembles *G. vulneratus* Aubé from Haiti, but a little smaller in size and differing by the somewhat narrower tomentous border of elytra, the yellow tip of pygidium, rounded exterior apical angle of anterior tibiae, the latter less broadened in the ♂, with narrower anterior tarsi. The

♀ of the new species is easily distinguished from the typical female form of *G. vulneratus* by the lack of strong reticulation on the disc of pronotum and the anterior part of elytra, longitudinal striae are less distinctly marked on the latter and the lateral impression is wanting. The smooth female form of *G. vulneratus* differs from the ♀ of the new species by the lack of any strong reticulation on the elytra except at the tip, darker pygidium, and broader tomentous border of the elytra. Male genitalia are quite different in the two species.

Gyretes nigrilabris sp. nov.

Length 6.25 mm. Broadly oval, posteriorly attenuated, moderately convex. Surface shining, black, slightly brassy; lateral margin brownish and very narrow on the prothorax and at base of elytra, moderately enlarged and more yellowish toward apex of latter; pygidium black; body beneath ferruginous, epipleura yellowish. Labrum black, transverse, anterior margin flatly rounded and with yellow cilia, surface reticulated, base at the sides with some deep punctures bearing bristles. Clypeus well separated, anterior margin dark rufous, reticulated, with dispersed punctures. Reticulation on labrum and clypeus only slightly impressed, with short transverse meshes; strongly impressed on the head anteriorly, meshes becoming rounded and less impressed towards vertex and on disc of prothorax; head and prothorax with dispersed punctures; elytra not punctured, reticulation fine and very transverse in the ♂, much more strongly impressed in the ♀, with short meshes. Tomentous border of prothorax reaching opposite middle of eye anteriorly, diminishing to about ⅔ of the anterior width towards the base and continued on the elytra, on the latter slightly and regularly enlarged (a little more in the ♀) towards the apex, shortly before the latter the inner outline, which is flatly concave, is curved convexly, thus reaching the truncature nearly perpendicularly. Truncature of elytra oblique and concave in both sexes, outer angle sharp, sutural angle dehiscent, obtusely rounded, more produced in the ♀. Anterior tibiae of the ♂ dilated towards apex, exterior apical angle nearly rectangular, briefly rounded; anterior tarsi moderately dilated, narrower than the tibiae, strongly attenuated towards apex. In the ♀ the anterior tibiae are less dilated, the front tarsi narrow, subparallel. Ædeagus dark yellow, lateral lobes infuscated apically, median lobe a little broader than the lateral ones, subparallel, slightly enlarged at the beginning of the short triangular acumination of the apex, tip obtusely rounded.

Habitat: Haiti, Furcy (W. M. Mann).

Type ♂ and Allotype ♀ (type No. 23,062) in the Museum of Comparative Zoölogy at Harvard College, Cambridge, (Mass.).

A little larger than *G. vulneratus* Aubé, with which it was associated and which it resembles very much. Easily distinguished, however, by the black labrum, darker undersurface, and body more attenuated posteriorly. Anterior tibiae in the ♂ less triangularly dilated, exterior apical angle less pronounced, front tarsi narrower and more attenuated, genitalia quite different. In the ♀ the prothorax is not strongly reticulate, elytra without lateral depression.

ON THE SYNONYMY OF *ORUSSUS SAYII* WESTWOOD[1]

BY HARRY D. PRATT

Specimens of the genus *Orussus* Latr. are comparatively rare in most insect collections. Therefore it was with some surprise that the author discovered on June 25, 1935, near his summer home in Jacksonville, Vermont, a dead sugar maple (*Acer saccharum*) with at least twenty specimens of *Orussus* on it. *Orussus* has the habit of jumping, almost like a *Haltica*, before flying and then returns often almost to exactly the same spot from which it flew. Collection is most easily made by covering them with a wide-mouth cyanide jar, since they frequently fly out under the side of a net if it is snapped against the side of the tree. Subsequent collecting in 1936 and 1937 has shown that *O. sayii* Westwood emerges as early as May 31 in 1936, while *O. terminalis* Newman persists at least until mid-July.

If Mr. H. E. Burke's article (Proc. Ent. Soc. Wash., 1917, vol. 19: pages 87-88) is correct, and "Oryssus is Parasitic" on Buprestidae, then the host is likely to be a species of *Dicerca*, probably *divaricata* Say, since what appears to be this species occurs commonly in the same tree.

Careful examination and dissection of *O. sayii* showed that this species occurred only in the male sex, while *O. terminalis* occurred only in the female. This fact in itself would make one suspicious as to the synonymy of the two, and becomes all the more interesting from a biological viewpoint, since it is a well-known fact that in parasitic Hymenoptera the males usually emerge before the females, the reason apparently being that they can mate with the larger females as the latter emerge, while they are still somewhat teneral and unable to resist the advances of the male. As mentioned earlier, *O. sayii* emerges before *O. terminalis*, usually a week

[1]Contribution from the Entomological Laboratory of Massachusetts State College, Amherst, Mass.

earlier.   This fact should be significant in declaring the two synonymous.

S. A. Rohwer (Proc. Ent. Soc. Wash., 1917, vol. 19: p. 95) wrote, "We have not yet been able to locate a male to go with this female (*O. terminalis*), and it is possible that the male of the species will have the abdomen entirely black and that it is at present confused under the name *sayii.*"

In view of Mr. Rohwer's statement, and judging from some hundred and more specimens collected from a single tree over a period of three years, it seems quite probable that *O. sayii* and *O. terminalis* are the sexes of the same species, which, according to priority, should be called *Orussus sayii* Westwood, since it was described in 1835, while Newman's species was not described until 1838.

It may be of interest here to note that the figure of *Orussus terminalis* in H. H. Ross' "Generic Classification of the Nearctic Sawflies" on plate IX, fig. 169 belongs to *sayii*. According to a letter from Dr. Ross, the specimen does have the abdomen black and would key out to *sayii*.

The synonymy of the species then is as follows:

Oryssus sayii Westwood, Zool. Journ., 1835, vol. 5: p. 440.

Oryssus terminalis Newman, Ent. Mag., 1838, vol. 5: p. 486 (New Synonymy).

Oryssus haemorrhoidalis Harris, Rept. Ins. Mass., 1841: p. 394 (Synonymy by Rohwer, Proc. Ent. Soc. Wash., 1917, vol. 19: p. 95).

NOTES ON NORTH AMERICAN NITIDULIDAE, II: CRYPTARCHA SHUCKARD

By C. T. Parsons

Biological Laboratories, Harvard University

The genus Cryptarcha embraces many species which are found in all parts of the world. The six species occuring in the United States have apparently two origins. *Cryptarcha ampla, grandicollis, glabra* and *strigatula* n. sp. are closely related to the numerous Neotropical forms, whereas the smaller *concinna* and *gila* n. sp. are more closely related to the Palaearctic *imperialis* Fabr. and its allies. The apparently two origins are reflected in the two subgenera, which are keyed below.

1. Prosternum broad between the coxæ and extending beyond the middle of the mesosternum; anterior margin of the metasternum transverse or broadly rounded anteriorly; species usually longer than 4 mm.
.... *Cryptarcha* s. str.

2. Prosternum more or less narrow between the coxæ and not extending beyond the middle of the mesosternum; anterior margin of the metasternum acutely rounded anteriorly; species usually shorter than 4 mm.
.... *Lepiarcha* Sharp

Subg. **Cryptarcha** *s. str.*

This subgenus comprises at least the Palaearctic *strigata*, the North American *strigatula* n. sp., *ample, glabra*, and the Neotropical species.

1. Unicolorous above ....2.
   Elytra with irregular pale fasciæ ....3.

2. Apex of prosternal process rounded .... *ampla* Er.
   Apex of prosternal process truncate .... *glabra* Schaef.

3. Apex of prosternal process emarginate ..... *strigata* Fabr.
Apex of prosternal process rounded .... *strigatula* n. sp.

Cryptarcha ampla Erichson

Cryptarcha ampla Erichson, 1843, in Germar, Zeitschr. Ent. 4: 356.

The color varies from nigro-piceous to testaceous and the size from 4.5 mm. to 7.8 mm. The upper surface may be almost glabrous.

It has been collected at sap of maple and willow, and extends from Quebec to Florida, west to California and Oregon.

Cryptarcha grandicollis Reitter

Cryptarcha grandicollis Reitter, 1875, Verh. Nat. Ver. Brünn, 13: 118.

This species was described from Venezuela but is recorded from North America by Grouvelle, 1913, Coleopt. Cat., pars 56, p. 179. Dr. R. Jeannel has written that there is no specimen of this species in the Grouvelle collection in Paris; so, until confirmed, its inclusion in the North American list must remain doubtful.

Cryptarcha glabra Schaeffer

Cryptarcha glabra Schaeffer, 1909, Bull. Brooklyn Mus. 1: 375.

This rare species is remarkable for being glabrous above, and in having parallel sides. Since only six specimens are known, their data are given. Huach. Mts., Ariz. VIII. 9 in U. S. N. M. (type) : Carr Canyon, Huachuca Mts., Ariz. VII, 7-30 in Cal. Acad. Sci.; 4050 ft., Kits Peak, Rincon, Baboquivari Mts., Ariz. in A.M.N.H.; two from Baboquivari Mts., Ariz., April and August in H. C. Fall collection; San Bernardino Ranch, 3750 ft., Cochise Co., Ariz., August in the writer's collection.

Cryptarcha strigata Fabr.

Cryptarcha strigata Fabr., 1787, Mant. Ins. 1: 51.

This species is here restricted to the Palaearctic fauna. The North American individuals that have previously had this name are separated below and the differences between the two species are given in the description of *strigatula*.

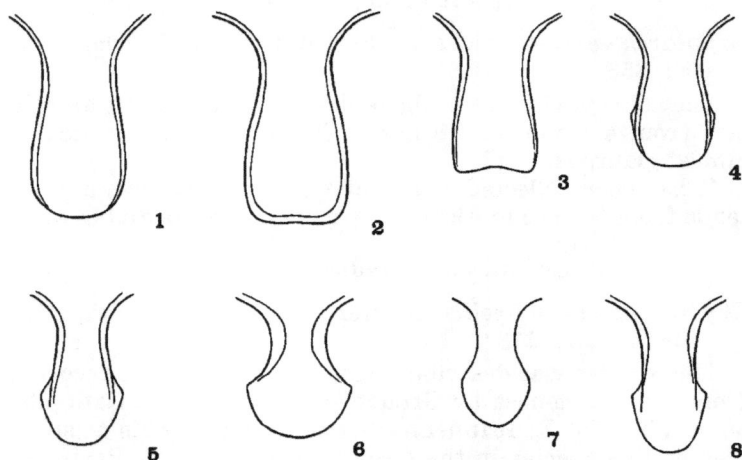

Fig. 1. Ventral views of the prosternal processes in *Cryptarcha*. 1, *C. ampla;* 2, *C. glabra;* 3, *C. strigata;* 4, *C. strigatula* n. sp.; 5, *C. imperialis;* 6, *C. gila* n. sp.; 7, *C. omositoides* (after sketch of B. M. specimen by Dr. H. Scott) ; 8, *C. concinna*.

Cryptarcha strigatula n. sp.

Cryptarcha strigata auctt. (*partim*).

Cryptarcha concinna Melsh., Reitter, 1873, *nec* Melsh., 1853, Syst. Eintheil. Nitid.: p. 150.

As the name implies this species is a diminuitive relative of *strigata*. It is very similar to *strigata*, egg-shaped, piceous, alutaeous, sparsely pubescent, with pale setae irregularly arranged on the pronotum but in seven indistinct rows on each elytron. The two transverse sinuous fasciae are much as in *strigata*, except that the anterior may reach the sutural margin of the elytra. The prosternal process is broadened and emarginate at the tip in *strigata*, but only slightly broadened and rounded at the tip in *strigatula* (figs. 3, 4). The length is 2.7-3.2 mm., whereas the length of *strigata* is 3.2-4.2 mm. The minimum length of *strigata* is from the literature and must be unusual, since the smallest specimen in the collections of the British Museum and the writer measures 4.0 mm.

Holotype, male, from the Bronx, New York, Aug. 15, 1896, in the writer's collection. Paratypes from Massachusetts, Pennsylvania, New Jersey, Georgia, Illinois in the collections of the Museum of Comparative Zoology, American Museum of Natural History, C. A. Frost, and the writer. Specimens have been seen from as far west as Texas and north to Michigan.

Subg. **Lepiarcha** Sharp

Lepiarcha Sharp, 1891, Biol. Centr. Amer. Col. II, pt. 1: 385
  (type *Cryptarcha omositoides* Reitter).
Cryptarchula Ganglbauer, 1899, Käf. Mitteleur. 3: 551
  (type *Cryptarcha* (*Cryptarchula*) *imperialis* Fabr.)

This subgenus contains at least the European *imperialis* and its allies, the Central American *omositoides* Reitter, and the following species.

Prosternal process greatly expanded at tip (fig. 6) *gila* n. sp.
Prosternal process only slightly expanded at tip (fig. 8) ......
                                          concinna Melsh.

Cryptarcha gila n. sp.

Elongate, piceous above, testaceous beneath. The anterior half of head, lateral fourths of the pronotum, epipleurae, and elytral fasciae testaceous. The upper surface closely punctate, finely pubescent, with numerous pale setae. The setae are arranged in eight rows on each elytron. The under surface obsoletely punctate and more sparsely pubescent. The prosternal process expanded, as shown in fig. 6. Anterior and middle coxae pale testaceous. The mandibles are of equal length and notched at tip. Length 2.5-3.3 mm.

Holotype male, allotype, and paratypes from Wheatfields near Globe, Arizona, May 4, 1934, D. K. Duncan, in the collection of the author. Paratypes with similar data in the collection of H. C. Fall. Also paratypes from Bakersfield, Calif. in the E. C. Van Dyke collection of the California Academy of Sciences.

This species is more elongate and a little longer than *concinna*. The apices of the elytra are more pointed than in *omositoides* and *concinna,* agreeing in this respect with *imperialis.* The margins of the thorax and the epipleurae are more narrowly reflexed than in *concinna* and more broadly reflexed than in *imperialis.*

Cryptarcha concinna Melsheimer

Cryptarcha concinna Melsheimer, 1853, Cat. of the desc. Col. of U. S., p. 41.

Cryptarcha liturata Leconte, 1863, List Col. of N. Amer. 1: 30.

Cryptarcha picta Melsheimer, 1866, Proc. Acad. Sci. Philadelphia 2: 107.

Cryptarcha bella Reitter, 1873, Syst. Eintheil. Nitid. p. 150.

This is an extremely variable species, but is distinctive in its oval outline, explanate pronotal margins, and shape of the prosternal process as shown in fig. 8. The range of *concinna* is from Massachusetts to Florida, west to southern California and Oregon.

A REVISION OF THE GENUS ZILORA

BY EDITH W. MANK
Lawrence, Mass.

The genus Zilora belongs among those Melandryidæ which are characterized by (1) a thorax narrower at the base than the base of the elytra, (2) depressions at the base of the thorax, (3) an abdomen where the first two segments are decidedly longer than the last three.

As represented in the United States, the genus includes beetles with the head short, the antennæ slender, the last segment of the maxillary palpi securiform, at least the posterior part of the lateral edge of the thorax sharp, parallel sided elytra. On the under side, the episternal sutures are present, the anterior coxal cavities have a lateral fissure, the trochantin is visible, the middle coxæ are separated by the mesosternum. The pubescence, except in *Zilora nuda* where all types of erect pubescence are wanting, consists of two kinds. The general pubescence is suberect and plentiful but there are also fine erect hairs in rows, only seen when the specimen is viewed in profile. The erect hairs either form complete rows or are confined to the rear half of the elytra.

Of the American Ziloras previously described, the type of *Zilora hispida* Lec. has been examined. The type of *Zilora nuda* Prov. is known to me personally only from description, but specimens of *nuda* in my possession have been compared for me by Mr. N. M. Comeau with the type which is in the Museum at Quebec and they were found to be identical with the type. A specimen labeled as the type of *Zilora canadensis* Hausen is in the Winn collection which is now in the collection at McGill University. Through the kind offices of Mr. G. Chagnon, it has been possible to examine this specimen. The specimen bearing the type label was found to be a Scotochroa and not a Zilora. It seems probable that the type is lost for this beetle does not have the securiform terminal segment of the palpi, nor the erect hairs mentioned by Hausen himself as present in Zilora, nor is the punctuation of the head and thorax more dense and fine than on the wing covers as he describes it. Moreover, his specimen as he says "seems to be a male, the penis is protruded and bilobed at the extremity." The specimen at McGill is a female.

From the table given below, *Zilora canadensis* Hausen has, therefore, been omitted.

Thanks are due to Mr. Ralph Hopping who placed at my disposal his Ziloras, including long series of *Zilora nuda* Prov. and the new western species, *Zilora occidentalis;* to Mr. P. J. Darlington Jr. of the Museum of Comparative Zoology at Harvard University for access to all the Ziloras in that collection; and to Mr. H. C. Fall for the use of all his material in this genus and for his unfailing advice in the revision of this genus. The types of *Zilora alabamensis* and *occidentalis* are in Mr. Fall's collection.

TABLE OF AMERICAN SPECIES OF ZILORA

A. Erect pubescence, smooth area margining the eye posteriorly, lateral edge of abdominal segments margined the entire length of the body, male with denser patch of pubescence on the inferior edge of middle and hind femora.

   B. Hind angle of thorax very nearly rectangular, color fusco-castaneous, species of Eastern North America.

      C. Surface of scutellum rough but without well defined round punctures, hind angles of thorax slightly reflexed, narrower compared with length than in *Z. hispida* Lec. The type is from Saraland, Alabama.   *alabamensis* n. sp.

      CC. Surface of scutellum showing definite punctures, not rough, hind angles of thorax not reflexed, posterior angles of scutellum, also, not reflexed, body slightly wider compared with the length than in *Z. alabamensis*. The type is from N. H.   *hispida* Lec.

   BB. Hind angle of the thorax perceptibly obtuse, color darker than in the above species, from Western coast of North America. The type is from Kern Co., Cal.   *occidentalis* n. sp.

AA. No erect pubescence, no smooth area margining the eye posteriorly, lateral edge of abdominal segments not margined beyond the anterior part of the second segment, area at middle of thorax quite smooth with only a few punctures, terminal segment of maxillary palpi not as large as in the other species of Zilora, male without denser patch of pubescence on the inferior edge of middle and hind femora. The type is from Cape Rouge, Quebec.

      nuda Prov.

Zilora alabamensis n. sp.

More slender than *hispida*. Punctures on head coarser

and deeper than in *hispida*. Eyes bulging, with smooth rim posterior to the eye. Forehead above front flattened.

Thorax finely margined at base; sides sharp clear to front edge although anterior quarter of margin is much less distinct; posterior angles of thorax very nearly rectangular, slightly reflexed. Thorax coarsely punctured, sometimes with cross ridges between punctures over middle part of thorax; two basal impressions not as deep as in *hispida*. Elytra and thorax with erect and suberect pubescence. Erect pubescence in complete rows. Sides of elytra fairly parallel, rows of punctures poorly defined. Scutellum broad with posterior angles slightly reflexed; punctures on the scutellum not well defined, surface rough, however. On under surface large fissure on the anterior coxal cavity with trochantin plainly visible. Abdomen margined laterally clear to the tip.

Length 6-7 mm.; width 2-2.5 mm.

The type and two other specimens examined were from Saraland, Ala. and were collected by Mr. H. P. Loding of Mobile.

Zilora hispida Lec.

Head short from antennæ down; membranous piece joining labrum to front; head fairly hairy; punctuation close on front, less so posteriorly; eyes bulging with smooth rim bordering them on the posterior edge. Thorax finely margined at base and laterally more than half way to anterior edge; depressions on basal part of thorax deep and sharply defined; posterior angles of thorax very nearly rectangular, not reflexed; punctuation of thorax fairly close; at base decidedly narrower than the width of the elytra.

On under surface, suture between prosternum and episternum present but flat; lateral fissure present on anterior coxal cavity; trochantin visible. Middle coxae separated by process of the mesosternum. Rows of erect hairs running the length of the elytra. The pubescence both erect and suberect. The pubescence is longer than in the other species, making the specimens look more hairy.

Abdomen margined laterally to the tip.

Length 5-5.1 mm.; width 1.5-2 mm.

The type is marked N. H. Other specimens have been examined marked Mt. Washington.

Zilora occidentalis n. sp.

Punctuation, in general, more sparse than in the eastern forms. Front of head above eyes not as bulging as in *hispida*. Smooth area present posterior to eye. Lateral margin of thorax sharp at least ¾ of distance to anterior margin. Hind margin of thorax perceptibly obtuse. Scutellum very finely and profusely punctured. The rows of erect hairs on the elytra confined to apical half. Color darker than in the preceding species. Abdomen margined laterally to the tip.

Length 7.1 mm.; width 2-2.5 mm.

The type is from Kern Co., Cal. Other specimens were examined from Fresno Co., Cal., Seattle, Wash., Trinity Valley, B.C., Merritt, B.C., Pender Harbor, B.C., and Aspen Grove, B.C.

Zilora nuda Prov.

No erect pubescence. No traces of punctures on the elytra. Depression at middle of thorax at base quite smooth with only a few punctures. Terminal segment of maxillary palpi not as large as in other species of the genus. Slightly hairy front but pubescence not erect. No smooth rim bordering the eye posteriorly. Much coarser punctures on scutellum than in Zilora occidentalis.

Lateral edge of the abdominal segments not margined beyond the beginning of the second segment, while in the other Ziloras the abdominal margin is continuous to the tip of the abdomen.

Length 7 mm.; width 2 mm.

The type is from Cape Rouge, Quebec. Specimens have been examined from Duparquet, Quebec, Can.

FOSSIL INSECTS FROM THE CREEDE FORMATION, COLORADO

PART 1. INTRODUCTION, NEUROPTERA, ISOPTERA AND DIPTERA

BY F. M. CARPENTER, T. E. SNYDER, C. P. ALEXANDER, M. T. JAMES
AND F. M. HULL

INTRODUCTION

BY F. M. CARPENTER

Harvard University

During the past twenty-five years, intensive geologic work in the Rocky Mountain region has revealed several Tertiary lake-bed deposits, the presence of which had not previously been suspected. One of these beds, termed the Creede formation by Emmons and Larson (1923), is extensively exposed on the slopes of Willow Creek, near the town of Creede, Colorado. The formation is highly fossiliferous with plants, and a preliminary account of its flora has been published by Knowlton (1923). In 1932, Mr. Allan Caplan, then a senior in the Creede High School, found that insects also were not uncommon in the formation, and an examination of some of his specimens convinced me that a collecting trip to this formation would be a practicable and profitable undertaking. With the aid of a grant from the Milton Fund of Harvard University, the collecting trip was made during the summer of 1934. In addition to the writer and his wife, the party consisted of Mr. C. T. Parsons, a student in Harvard College, and Mr. Caplan, who joined us at Creede. In the course of the summer about two thousand insects were secured; most of these were actually found by Mr. Caplan, while the rest of the party collected in the Green River shales of Utah.

The present series of papers is based mainly upon the specimens obtained on this trip, but it also covers a collection of about two hundred other Creede insects, sent to me for determination by Professor Case of the University of Michigan, who had previously secured them from Mr. Caplan. All of the fossils have been sorted into orders and most of them into families or superfamilies. As in the case of the insects of the Latah formation and of the Manitoban amber, I have referred these Creede fossils to specialists on various groups of living insects. Although this procedure tends to delay in large measure the publication of the results, it is the only way capable of yielding authentic determinations and conclusions. Since several more years may elapse before all the specimens of the Creede collection have passed through the hands of specialists, it has seemed advisable to publish the results in several parts, all under the same general title, whenever a sufficient number of manuscripts have been completed. The descriptive part of the present paper deals with the fossils belonging to the following orders and families: Neuroptera (F. M. Carpenter), Isoptera (T. E. Snyder), Diptera, Tipulidae (C. P. Alexander), Bibionidae (M. J. James), and Syrphidae (F. M. Hull). To these specialists and those who are working upon other families I am grateful for their indispensable cooperation.

Since this is the first extensive account of the Creede insects, it is pertinent to include a brief discussion of their geologic occurrence and environment. The geology of Creede district has been thoroughly investigated by Emmons and Larsen (1923). According to them, the Creede formation was deposited in a lake that occupied a valley carved out of the rocks of the Potosi volcanic series. The lower part of the formation consists chiefly of fine-textured, thin-bedded, rhyolite tuffs, usually light grey or light brown. Thicker beds of sandy material, lenses of conglomerate, and numerous bodies of travertine are also present. It is this lower part of the formation that contains the insects and the best plant material. The upper part is of coarser texture and consists of well bedded breccia and conglomerate, with some fine tuff. The origin of the formation seems to have been much like that of the Florissant shales, which lie more than a hundred miles to the north-east. Some of the ash thrown out by local volcanoes fell into the lake and together with sand and mud was deposited at the bottom. Insects flying over the water were of course caught and entombed by the ash.

Knowlton's study of the Creede plants led him to conclude that the Creede formation was about the same age as the Florissant deposit, i.e., upper Miocene. At the same time, however, he noticed an obvious difference in the composition of the two floras, the most abundant element in the Creede flora being Coniferae, which, although very rare at Florissant, comprised about a third of the species and nearly a half of the individual specimens. The general content of the Creede flora strongly indicates that the lake-bed was deposited at a considerable higher elevation than the Florissant shales.[1] As Cockerell has stated of the Creede flora, very few, if any, high altitude insect faunas have been preserved. The chief importance of the Creede specimens, therefore, depends not so much on their geologic age as on the environment in which they existed. It is of course far too soon to say anything definite about the biotic indications of the Creede insects, but even a cursory survey of the collection at hand, made during the sorting of the specimens into families, indicates that the fauna is an exceedingly small one, there being an extraordinary duplication of a few species. This is of course typical of existing faunas at high altitudes.

ORDER NEUROPTERA

FAMILY CHRYSOPIDÆ

BY F. M. CARPENTER

Eleven specimens of this family are contained in the collection from Creede. This is proportionally a much greater number than has been found in the Florissant shales, which have produced only about the same number in a total of approximately 40,000 specimens. Two species are represented in the Creede series, one apparently being identical with a Florissant species, and the other, already described, being peculiar to the Creede formation. The phylogenetic significance of the Tertiary Chrysopidae has already been discussed in an earlier paper (1935).

[1] At the present time, however, both lake deposits have an elevation of about 8200 ft.

Palaeochrysa creedei Carp.

Palæochrysa creedei Carpenter, 1935, Journ. Paleont., **9**:
265, fig. 3.

This species, although similar to the following, is characterized by the extraordinary length of the basal Banksian cell of the fore and hind wings.[2] The holotype is No. 4316 ab, Museum of Comparative Zoology.

Palaeochrysa stricta Scudd. (Fig. 1)

Palæochrysa stricta Scudder, 1850, U. S. Geol. Survey Terr.
Rept., **13**: 166; pl. 14, fig. 13, 14.

There are ten Chrysopids (4462-4471) in the Creede collection which seem to be identical in every way with this

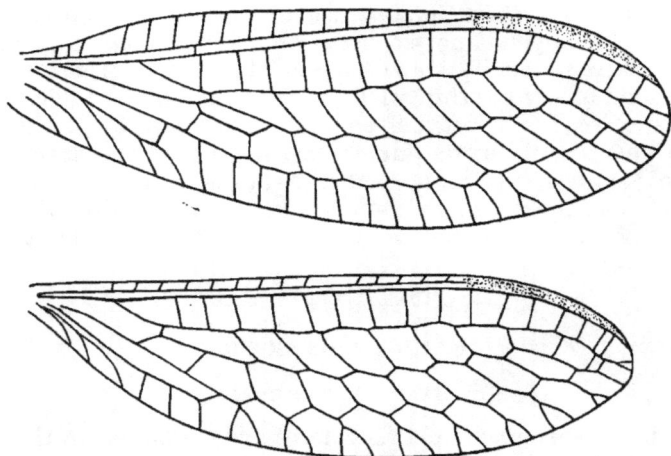

Fig. 1. *Palæochrysa stricta* Scudd. A. Fore wing (No. 4462, M. C. Z.), length, 12 mm. B. Hind wing (No. 4464, M. C. Z.), length, 9.8 mm. Miocene of Creede, Colorado.

species, previously known solely from the Florissant shales. Since this is the only Creede species of those so far determined which appears to be common to the two beds, I have included drawings of its venation. It should, however, be borne in mind that among the Recent Chrysopidae the venation of closely related species usually shows no differences.

[2]In my account of the fossil Chrysopidae (Journ. Paleont., **9**: 259-271, 1935) the captions for figures 2 and 7 should be interchanged.

FAMILY RAPHIDIIDAE

Raphidia creedei Carp.

Raphidia creedei Carpenter, 1936, Proc. Amer. Acad. Arts Sci., 71 : 150, fig. 12.

This species differs from those of Florissant by the more slender wings and narrower costal area. The holotype, No. 3639 ab in the Museum of Comparative Zoology, is the best preserved fossil snake-fly which has been found, apart from those in amber. The members of the Raphidiodea are exceedingly rare in the Florissant shales, and the presence of even one in the relatively small Creede collection at hand is another indication of the biotic differences represented. Like the Florissant Raphidiodea, this Creede species belongs to a genus now restricted to the Old World.[3]

ORDER ISOPTERA

FAMILY RHINOTERMITIDÆ

BY THOS. E. SNYDER

Senior Entomologist, Division of Forest Insects, Bureau of Entomology and Plant Quarantine, United States Department of Agriculture

The single fossil wing sent to me for identification proves to represent a species of *Reticulitermes* new to science. Five fossil species of this genus are already known—four from Baltic amber and one from the Miocene shale of Florissant, Colorado. *Reticulitermes* is confined to the temperate regions of the world. A living species (*R. tibialis* Banks) occurs in localities in Colorado, but nowhere in the state at an elevation of over 7,000 feet. The wing of *tibialis* is larger than in this fossil.

Reticulitermes creedei Snyder, n. sp. (Plate 13, fig. 3)

Wing (hind wing (?)) : Costal area indistinct. Median vein *not* free from stump or wing scale; closer to subcosta than to cubitus; branches to tip of wing. Cubitus running

---

[3]An account of the geographic distribution of the fossil and Recent Raphidiodea is contained in my revision of the Nearctic species (Proc. Amer. Acad. Arts Sci., 70: 89-157, 1936).

in about the middle of wing area, with numerous branches, to posterior margin of wing.

Length of wing—6.5 mm.
Width of wing —1.7 mm.

Wing smaller than in *Reticulitermes fossarum* Scudder from Florissant, Colorado, in Miocene shale.

Holotype: Museum of Comparative Zoology, No. 4472 ab; collected in the Miocene shales at Creede, Colorado.

ORDER DIPTERA

FAMILY TIPULIDAE

BY CHARLES P. ALEXANDER
Massachusetts State College

I am greatly indebted to Dr. F. M. Carpenter for the privilege of studying the series of Tipulidae collected by him at the fossil beds located near Creede, Colorado. As indicated elsewhere by Dr. Carpenter, the Creede formation is of approximately the same age as the Florissant shales (Miocene), about a hundred miles to the northeast, near Pikes Peak, Colorado.

All of the specimens pertain to the single genus *Tipula* Linnaeus and virtually all seem to belong to a single species that I am herewith describing as new under the name *Tipula carpenteri.* In almost all of these individuals, the wings are the only parts that are well preserved. Throughout the vast complex of forms now included within the limits of the genus *Tipula* (approximately 1000 species, Recent and fossil), the wing venation is singularly uniform and offers but slight aid in the subdivision of the genus into smaller groups. In the recent fauna, the definition of species in this genus is based in great part upon the structure of the male hypogygium, characters that are quite unavailable in the present fossil series. A careful analysis of wing-pattern and venation has been made since any determination of the present series must depend chiefly or solely upon such characters.

More than a score of fossil *Tipula* and closely allied groups have been described from the early Tertiary of western

North America by Scudder and Cockerell, the majority from the Florissant shales. Scudder (1894) proposed four supposedly new generic groups centering about *Tipula* that must be analyzed and evaluated in relation to the great increase in our knowledge of the Tipulidae in the past thirty years.

Manapsis Scudder (l.c., pp. 222, 223) with cell *M1* lacking or imperfectly developed. Affinities with other Tipulinae uncertain, due to the difference in venation in the two wings of the type. Several Recent Tipuline groups are now known in which cell *M1* is lacking (as *Idiotipula* Alexander, *Xenotipula* Alexander, and others).

Rhadinobrochus Scudder (l.c., pp. 223, 224) based on the character of an unusually narrow cell *1st M2*, which, in one wing of the unique type, shows an extra vein issuing therefrom, lying between veins *M1+2* and *M3* of the normal Tipuline venation. The value of this character is questionable, especially in the present instance where the venation appears to be abnormal (see Alexander, 1919).

Tipulidea Scudder (l.c., pp. 238, 239) was separated from *Tipula* s.s. only on the basis of small physical size (wing, 9.5-13.5 mm.) and the relative shortness of *Rs* which is approximately equal to *m-cu*. Both of these characters are duplicated in the recent subgenus *Schummelia* Edwards of the genus *Tipula*. The status of *Tipulidea* must remain in question until more evidence becomes available but it seems possible that the group may be maintained as a valid subgenus of *Tipula*.

Micrapsis Scudder (l.c., pp. 242-243) is based on a single imperfect specimen. The characters upon which the group is founded are very weak, consisting of the shortness of *Rs* and of an unusually small *1st M2*, with vein *M4* forking at base of this cell, with *m-cu* placed some distance beyond the origin of *M4*. The latter combination of characters is much as in *Nephrotoma* and some *Tipula* and the status of the group is very much in question.

In my opinion, none of the four Tipuline groups discussed above is well founded and all should wait upon the discovery of further material to substantiate or disprove their claims. It appears to me that all except *Tipulidea* may well be found to be based on teratological specimens, while all are based on uniques in an indifferent state of preservation. The figures supplied by Blake do not always conform to the descriptions of Scudder (as in *Manapsis*, where in the left wing vein $R1+2$ is shown as being distinctly preserved, whereas on the right wing it is not indicated and is either atrophied or poorly evident. In *Rhadinobrochus*, the venation of the two wings of the unique type is so dissimilar that the veins of the two sides cannot be homologized).

Tipula carpenteri Alexander, n. sp. (Plate 13, figs. 1, 2)

Male.—Length about 16-17 mm.; wing 17-18 mm.

Female.—Length about 21-22 mm.; wing 20-24 mm.

General coloration dark. Praescutal pattern apparently consisting of three entire dark stripes on a somewhat paler ground. Abdomen dark, the tergites with a still darker median longitudinal stripe that is narrowly interrupted at posterior border of each segment; lateral tergal stripes narrower and less distinct; sternites with a similar but much narrower median vitta.

Antennae of male longer than in female, subequal to the combined head and thorax; flagellar segments bicolorous, the basal enlargement darker than the apex; verticils short. In female, antennae about twice the length of head. In both sexes, flagellar segments with poorly developed basal enlargements to appear subcylindrical.

Wings subhyaline, with a conspicuous brown and white pattern; brown areas include a medium-sized marking at origin of *Rs;* stigma and a confluent seam on anterior cord; *m-cu* and adjoining portions of vein *Cu;* a dark cloud in cells *M* and *Cu* at near midlength of vein *Cu*, with another similar dark area near outer end of *Cu*, chiefly in cell *M*, the two dark markings separated by a whitish or ground area at near two thirds the length of cell *M*; distal portions of cells *R2* and *R3* slightly darkened but outer half of cell *R5* somewhat paler; the white areas appear chiefly as a broad poststigmal fascia involving cell *Sc2*, basal third of cell *R2*, subbasal third of cell *R3* and the subproximal end of cell *R5;* additional obliterative areas involving base of cell *1st M2* and the adjoining basal portions of cells *M3* and *M4*. Wings relatively broad, the length about 3.6 times the greatest width.   Venation: Rs relatively long, about one half longer than m-cu, or subequal to the width of cells R and M opposite its origin; vein $R1+2$ preserved; petiole of cell $M1$ variable in length, from one third as long to subequal to m; m-cu at fork of $M3+4$; cell $2nd\ A$ of moderate width.

Hypopygium moderately enlarged, the outer end truncated. Ovipositor with relatively stout valves.

Holotype: No. 4536, Museum of Comparative Zoology, collected by Allan Caplan; this consists of a nearly complete insect.

Paratypes (both sexes) : twenty-three in the Museum of Comparative Zoology (Nos. 4473-4495), and one in the University of Michigan Museum (No. 15383).   The specimens figured are the holotype and paratype no. 4489.

I take unusual pleasure in naming this interesting Miocene *Tipula* in honor of Dr. F. M. Carpenter. As shown by the figures, there is a somewhat marked variation in the wing-pattern and venation in different individuals.   The possibility exists that more than a single species is included in the present series but this does not seem to be the case.   In some specimens the radial cells beyond the post-stigmatic white fascia are more uniformly darkened than in others, as shown by the figures, which represent extremes within the series.   In No. 4489, figured, cell $M4$ is more strongly narrowed at wing-margin than in the holotype, while vein $R3$ is slightly less extended.   This individual, while represented chiefly by the wings, is evidently a female and is the largest specimen whose measurements are given above.

The species that is most similar to the present fly would appear to be *Tipula limi* Scudder, which is somewhat smaller, with narrower wings.   Scudder describes the species as having a darkened cloud at origin of Rs but in neither of his figures (l.c., Pl. 8, fig. 4, ♀ ; Pl. 9, fig. 1, ♂) is this distinctly shown.   This Florissant species has distinct lateral stripes on the abdominal tergites in addition to the subequal median vitta.

The various allied Miocene species having patterned wings may be separated by the accompanying key:

1. Wings with vein Sc relatively short, $Sc2$ ending at near midlength of cell $R1$ and about opposite two thirds the length of Rs.   2

Wings with *Sc* longer, *Sc2* ending beyond midlength of
cell *R1* and nearly opposite three fourths the length
of *Rs*.   *carpenteri* sp. n.

2. A conspicuous darkened cloud at origin of *Rs*.   3
   No darkened cloud at origin of *Rs*.   4

3. *Rs* unusually long, approximately twice *m-cu;* wings
   broad, about 3.5 times as long as wide. *tartari* Scudder
   Rs of moderate length, approximately one and one half
   times as long as *m-cu;* wings narrower, approximately
   four times as long as wide.   *limi* Scudder

4. A conspicuous dark cloud at near midlength of vein *Cu*,
   extending caudad into cell *Cu;* abdominal pattern of
   individual tergites transverse; size large (wing, female,
   23 mm.).   *maclurei* Scudder
   No dark cloud at midlength of vein *Cu;* abdominal
   pattern of the individual tergites longitudinal; size
   medium (wing, female, to 17.5 mm.).
                                          carolinæ Scudder

Tipula spp.

In addition to the material previously discussed, the
Creede collections included seven specimens that appear to
represent one or more additional species. These belong to
the group with wings immaculate or virtually so and no
attempt can be made to make a more detailed identification.
The specimens included bear the numbers 4496.

FAMILY BIBIONIDAE

BY MAURICE T. JAMES
Colorado State College

Plecia creedensis James, n. sp. (Fig. 2)

This species differs from the Florissant species and from
those described by Handlirsch from the Canadian Tertiary
in that vein *R2+3* arises from the radial sector a considerable distance before the apex of *R1*, is strongly and distinctly
elbowed at its origin, and runs almost parallel to *R1* for a
considerable distance.

♀. A yellowish species, the thorax, head, palpi, and base of the proboscis brown; the abdomen is very light yellow along the narrow posterior margins and on the venter; the antennae are slightly darkened basally. Pile concolorous

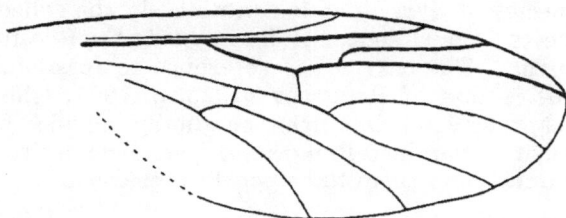

Fig. 2. *Plecia creedensis* James, n. sp., drawing of wing of holotype, No. 4523, M. C. Z.

with the background. Halteres evenly light yellow. Each tibia with a short, black preapical bristle. Wings slightly yellow-fumose, the veins yellow; those of the posterior part of the wing evident, though definitely lighter than the heavy anterior veins.

Length, 12 mm.; of abdoment, 8 mm.; of wing, 9 mm. The following measurements are in millimeters. Anterior femur, 2, tibia, 2.3, tarsus, 2.6; middle femur, 1.8, tibia, 1.8, tarsus, 1.9; posterior femur, 2.7, tibia, 2.8, tarsus, 2.4; length of head, .8, of antennae, .8, of thorax, 2.7; length of vein Rs to cross-vein r-m, 1.5, of Rs from r-m to origin of $R2+3$, .7, of cross-vein r-m, .4, of M from r-m to the furcation, .4; distance of apex of $R1$ from base of wing, 6.4, of origin of $R2+3$ from base of wing, 5.1.

Holotype (female): No. 4523, Museum of Comparative Zoology. This specimen is well preserved and is in lateral position, so that practically all characters of taxonomic importance are visible.

Paratypes: twelve females; eleven (Nos. 4524-4532) in the Museum of Comparative Zoology, and one in the Museum of the University of Colorado. Eight other specimens are present in the collection at the Museum of Comparative Zoology, but they are not designated as paratypes because of poor preservation.

FAMILY SYRPHIDAE

BY F. M. HULL
University of Mississippi

One species of Syrphidae is contained in the collection of fossil insects from Creede. This belongs to the Recent genus Platycheirus. The only other reference to fossil forms of this genus is that of Pongracz (1928, p. 190), who places here two species from Oeningen, originally included by Heer in Syrphus. I examined Pongracz's specimens in the British Museum and found them to be poorly preserved.

Platycheirus persistens n. sp. (Fig. 3)

Male. Length 10.0 mm.; of abdomen and scutellum 6.0 mm.; of wing 7.2 mm.; second specimen, length 10.0 mm.; thorax and abdomen 6.2 mm.; of wing 8.8 mm.

Head: hemispherical, obviously narrower than thorax. Eyes narrowly dichoptic. Face dark in color. No details of antennae visible. *Thorax:* dark, though very little pigment is preserved, and no details of pile can be seen. Scutellum semicircular, the margin evenly convex, the width about one and three fourths greater than the length. *Abdomen:* slender, the sides not quite parallel, but slightly convex, leaving the middle segments barely wider. The first segment juts beyond the rim of the scutellum by a fifth the latter's length. Second and third segments of nearly equal length, the former the longer. Fourth segment slightly shorter than third. Fifth segment two fifths as long as the preceding one. Hypopygium prominent and smoothly rounded. The segments are marked with brown. The posterior two-fifths of the second segment with a median wedge, pointing to and reaching the anterior border, and similar pattern on the two succeeding segments, the brown of the posterior border on the fourth segment occupying nearly the whole of the posterior half. The fifth segment is clear. *Legs: slender.* For the most part, they are not well preserved, but one set of tarsi, apparently the left hind tarsi, is well preserved and shows decided expansion and thickening of the joints. *Wings:* poorly preserved.

Female.   Specimen Nos. 3950 and 3951 is without head, obverse and reverse.   These wings are a little better preserved and show the third longitudinal vein and costa ending quite beyond the tip of wing, though not nearly as much as in *Rhingia*.   The abdominal pattern is quite similar; beyond the fact that the segments are slightly wider, I am unable to detect differences of importance.   One whole hind leg

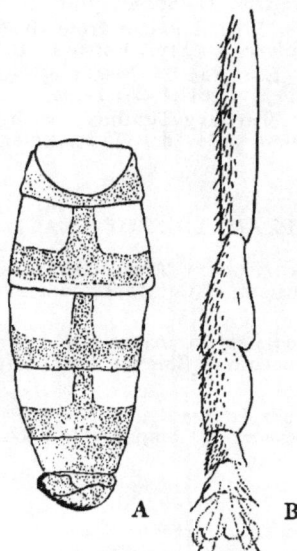

Fig. 3.   *Platycheirus persistens* Hull, n. sp.   A, abdomen; B, tibia and tarsus of holotype, No. 3949, M. C. Z.

(right) is preserved.   The femora were slightly thickened one and two-fifths the width of tibiae and the tarsi were not dilated.   The obverse is fragmentary and poor.   Perhaps a trace of antennae appears upon it.   The opposite hind tarsus is shown, the maculation is deceptive and the abdomen also appears disproportionately short and wide.

Holotype: 1 male, No. 3949; in the Museum of Comparative Zoology.

Paratype: 1 female, No. 3950; in the Museum of Comparative Zoology.

REFERENCES

Alexander, C. P.   1919.   The crane-flies of New York.   Part 1.   Cornell
    Univ. Agr. Exp. Sta. Memoir 25: 767-993.
Carpenter, F. M.   1935.   Tertiary Insects of the Family Chrysopidæ.
    Journ. Paleon., 9: 259-272.
Cockerell, T. D. A.   1933.   A Fossil Sawfly from the Miocene Shales
    near Creede, Colorado. Bull. Brook. Ent. Soc., 28: 186-187.
    1934. An Ancient Foxtail Pine. Nature, 133: 573.
Emmons, W. H., and Larsen, E. S.   1923.   Geology and the Deposits
    of the Creede District, Colorado. Bull. U. S. Geol. Surv., 718.
Knowlton, F. H.   1923.   Fossil Plants from the Tertiary lake-beds of
    south-central Colorado. Prof. Paper U. S. Geol. Surv., 131G.
Pongracz, A.   1928.   Die Fossile Insekten von Ungarn.   Annales
    Musei Nationalis Hungarici, 25: 1-194.
Scudder, S. H.   1894.   Tertiary Tipulidae, with Special Reference to
    those of Florissant, Colorado. Proc. Amer. Phil. Soc., 32 (143):
    1-83.

EXPLANATION OF PLATE 13

Fig. 1. *Tipula carpenteri* Alexander, n. sp.   Photograph of
holotype, No. 4536, Museum of Comparative Zoology. Length of wing,
18 mm.

Fig. 2. *Tipula carpenteri* Alexander, n. sp.   Photograph of
paratype, No. 4489, Museum of Comparative Zoology. Length of wing,
17 mm.

Fig. 3. *Reticulitermes creedei* Snyder, n. sp.   Photograph of
holotype, No. 4472, Museum of Comparative Zoology. Length of wing,
6.5 mm.

Psyche, 1938   VOL. 45, PLATE XIII.

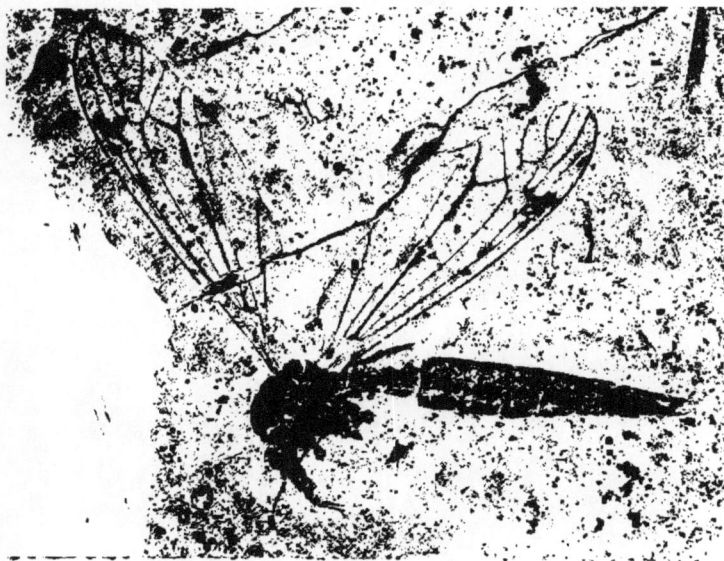

1

2

3

Fossil Insects from Creede

THOMAS SAY'S FREE-LIVING MITES REDISCOVERED[1]

By ARTHUR PAUL JACOT

U. S. Forest Service, New Haven, Conn.

Thomas Say, the earliest American to record mites from the United States, described a possible six species of free living mites from eastern Georgia and Florida. They were obtained from the late fall to the early spring. Say mentions as places visited by him (9) Fernandina (on Amelia Island), St. Mary's, Darien, Cumberland Island, and Savannah which he reached (homeward bound) on April 11th 1818.

Although I was able to collect at these localities during April, I found the soil and litter so dry that there were very few mites about. I was informed by the Weather Bureau that it had not rained for two months, a very unusual condition. The Islands east of Savannah were much burned over and I obtained no mites from them. The only type of collecting done was to look under the bark of trees and under stones—these being the only niches mentioned by Say. I found no stones, but a few tiles at one place. They yielded nothing.

Say described two species of Trombidium. I found three species of mites resembling Trombidiids, securing nineteen specimens of a Smaris, fourteen specimens of a Trombicula, and four specimens of a Microtrombidium. All these were taken from under the bark of prone trunks. A careful study of Say's *T. sericeum* reveals a body shape typical of Smaris. The only character that does not fit Smaris is the short, silken hair.

Now turning to Say's *T. scabrum*. If one divides a Trom-

[1]Aided by a grant of the Elizabeth Thompson Science Fund.

bicula at the constriction, calling the portion behind the
constriction the abdomen and the part anterior to it the
thorax, then Say's description: "ovate body, broadest and
very obtusely rounded before, with thorax *ob*triangular,"
accords with that genus, at least far more so than with any
other Trombidioid. Moreover the surface of this Trombicula is "unequal, with numerous indentations." The dis-
crepancies are, "minutely scabrous." "With hardly perceptible hairs" may be true enough but these two statements
seem contradictory. The description of the hairs of
T. sericeum fits *T. scabrum* and vice versa! Eyes white is
difficult to explain unless Say took for eyes what I take to be
eyes in this otherwise eyeless genus. If he saw these eyes
he must have seen the hairs correctly in both species
(genera) but must have gotten his two descriptions mixed.

At any rate he secured two Trombidioid looking mites
from trees in April. I secured two species from the same
localities and niche in April. My most common species is
unquestionably the same as his most common (Smaris). On
the whole his descriptions fit my two commonest Trom-
bidioids. Therefore, until someone can duplicate our collecting and get quite different results, I will have to accept
these two species as described below.

Trombiculoides gen. nov.

Resembling Trombiculus but with area sensiligera much
more highly developed, triangular, with one of the angles
directed posteriad, the others laterad (figures 1 and 2);
immediately posteriad of the lateral angles are rounded
bosses which appear to be eyes. This area sensiligera is
situated in a hollow or recess formed by the highly developed
lateral lobes of the thorax, which extend far anteriad and
tower above the sensiligerous area. The anterior edge of
the abdomen (s.s.) also encroaches on the area and
also towers high above it, thus very much secluding this
sensitized area.

Type: *Trombiculoides scaber* comb. nov.

The presence of eyes (for the structures in question have
every appearance of eyes) in this area and in this group,
makes this species quite distinct from all other Trombidiids.

Trombiculoides scaber (Say) 1821, p. 69

(Figures 1 and 2)

Diagnostic characters: Superficially resembling a Trombicula, but with the characters of this genus. Pseudostigmatic organs long, fine, simple; palps with simple bristles on dorsal face, and unilaterally ciliate bristles on sides, especially the lateral sides, the three spines of palptibia closely approximated (figure 2); palptarsus nearly three times as long as broad.

Description: Size fairly large, ovigerous females 1.36 mm. long; tarsi I oval, 0.246 mm. long and 0.09 mm. high; color rose red; abdomen broadly oval, constriction strong, lateral lobes of "thorax" large, bulby (figure 1); prothorax low, extending considerably beyond lobes of metathorax, anterior edge notched (figure 1), covered with bristles (only the anterior three of one side are figured); all bristles of abdomen and thorax typical of Trombicula, with about sixteen cilia along the bristle but irregularly disposed, so that the bristle is ciliate all about; base of sensiligerous area with a few bristles (insertions only indicated in figure 2), anterior edge with a median crest or ridge, another such ridge at lateral angles; pseudostigmata widely separated, close to lateral angles, sides of area ribbed; the "eyes" much larger than pseudostigmata; legs rather short (figure 1); legs I as long as body; tarsi I not much larger than tibiae I, but longer, with small hooks; tarsi II to IV with distal end tapering conspicuously.

Material obtained: Nine specimens from under the bark of a large prone oak; outskirts south of Savannah, slides 36S3, 36S5. Five specimens from under bark of prone pine trees, outskirts north of Darien; slide 36S6-1.

In the same niche with these mites were many mollusks, some pseudoscorpions, and the blue-tailed skink [*Eumeces fasciatus* (L.)]. Would this lizard be the host of the larvae of this Trombiculoid?

Smaris sericea (Say) 1821, p. 70

(Figures 3 to 6)

Diagnostic characters: Body elongate, ovate, with rather

short "rostrum" (figure 3) ; eyes one on each side, colorless ; pseudostigmatic organs present at both ends of crista, setaceous ; bristles of dorsum short blunt, forming a boat-shaped crest backed by an oval shield ; thumb of palptibia with five bristles (figure 5).

Description: Size of ovigerous females : length 1.36 mm., breadth 0.68 mm. ; color of body vermillion, legs paler ; shape of body (figure 3) ovate, rather elongate, rounded behind, anterior end broad, with rounded "shoulders," cephaloprothorax much narrower, capable of considerable lateral retraction so that in most alcoholic specimens the posterior half is much broader than anterior half (figure 3), in nature the upper part of the cephaloprothorax is slender so that the lower half flares out on each side (figure 4) ; crista metopica extends as a slender almost undifferentiated area from broadest area of abdomen nearly to tip of "rostrum" where it divides to straddle this region (figure 4) ; both pairs of pseudostigmatic organs setaceous, gradually tapering but lined with four rows of short, crowded, black cilia ; anterior pair one-and-a-half times length of body bristles, posterior pair two to three times length of body bristles ; eyes on transverse plane passing through center or slightly posteriad of center of crista, colorless, diameter equal to length of body bristles.

Bristles of dorsum of body formed of an ovate, membranous plate or shield strengthened by fine radiating ribs the ends of which barely project beyond edge of shield. From the longitudinal center of this shield there springs the keel of a canoe-shaped crest, the edges or gunwales of which are studded by the protruding ribs of the boat (figures 6). Bristles of venter more slender, crest more slender, both crest and shield barbs lengthened into long spines which are fewer in number. These spines give the bristle the appearance of a bearded wheat head.

Legs I a little longer than body (figure 3), other legs shorter ; legs I with distal trochanters as long as femora ; legs II to IV with distal trochanters shorter than femora and somewhat fused to femora to form a semianchylosed, nonfunctional joint. Leg bristles as body bristles but more elongate, crest more slender, parallel sided, points of barbs much produced as minute spines. Tarsal bristles with five longitudinal rows of such spinules springing from outer face of bristles, giving them the appearance of well combed hedge-hogs.

Bristles of palps simple to slightly burred at base, fairly long (figure 5).

Material obtained: One specimen from under bark of a large prone oak, outskirts south of Savannah; slide 36S3. One specimen from under bark of felled pine trees, outskirts north of Darien, slide 36S8-1. These mites and *Trombiculoides scaber* occurred to the extent of one in about every twenty linear feet. Thirteen specimens from under bark of old log, St. Simon Island; slides 36S8-2 and 36S8-3. Four specimens from under bark of old log, Amelia Island, between Fernandina and the sea beach; slide 36S10.

The nearest European species is *S. ampulligera* (2, fasc. 39:10) but the bristles are entirely different. I am, at present, unaware of synonyms.

I have this species from the woodlands of western North Carolina. *Smaris longilinealis* (3, p. 61, pl. 9, fig. 14; 4, p. 88, pl. 4, figs. 22, 23) from Marion and Urbana, Illinois, judging from the armature of the palps, seems to be this species. I have not seen the types. In the original description Ewing reports a single pair of eyes; in his later description he records a double pair. The size given in this second description corresponds to the Georgia specimens.

Smaris sp. (Figure 7)

Similar to the European species in that there are foliose bristles on palps. Bristles of abdomen broad cuneiform, distal end truncate to emarginate, the crest barely standing out from the shield, usually bearing three longitudinal rows of barbs (figure 7, right upper) or two divaricating rows (figure 7, left upper). Figure 7, right lower, is distofrontal aspect, while the left lower are distal aspects.

From under bark at base of hickory trees, Coscob headland, Conn.

Erythraeus mamillatus Say 1821, p. 70

The description calls to mind Labidostoma; the marginal impressed line being the juncture of notogaster and ventral plate which might give this effect. The description fits no Erythraeus.

I found no Labidostoma.

Gamasus spinipes Say 1821, p. 71

This may be a Holostaspis (s.l.) or a Cyrtolaelaps (s.l.). I know of no free living species which fits the description which is rather detailed as to leg characters. As all of Say's other Parasitids were parasitic, this one also may have been. He gives neither locality, habitat nor host.

Oribata glabrata Say 1821, p. 73

I have already referred to this species (5, p. 260). None were found. It is the commonest Oribotritia of the south.

Bdella oblonga Say 1821, p. 74
(Figure 8)

Say describes the distal segment of the palp (the palptarsus) as "attenuated towards the base and truncated at tip." This places the species in Bdella sensu strictu. The size, "rather more than one-twentieth of an inch" that is one-sixteenth, makes it the common species of Bdella of that region. This species differs from the European *Bdella longicornis* in that: of the two lateral bristles of palptarsus (figure 8), the distal is much shorter and finer than the proximal (the reverse is true in specimens from northern Europe) ; the pseudostigmatic organs are quite persistent while they seem quite deciduous in the European species.

Bdella decipiens (7 and 8) seems to be closely related, but palptarsus has only six bristles.

Bdella oblonga seems to be common throughout the eastern United States. I find no geographical races. *Bdella cardinalis* (1, p. 219) is therefore a synonym. *Bdella lata* (4, p. 69, pl. 2, fig. 9) is also a synonym and Ewing's figure 9 a very good toto figure of *Bdella oblonga* except that one bristle of palptarsus has been omitted. The toto figure of *Bdella cardinalis* (4, pl. 1, fig. 6) is inaccurate and should be discarded. Figure 5 is good as far as it goes, but figure 7 lacks two bristles on palptarsus and has two extra bristles on the genual.

Florida specimens of *Bdella oblonga* are without dark pigment, but dark material sometimes occurring inside the body gives the abdomen a mottled appearance. One specimen from Florida (lot 90) has "black" pigmented eyes. One specimen from among several from Mt. Logan, Chillicothe, Ohio (slide 32M108a1) and one from Bent Creek, Buncombe Co., N. Car., each have the two lateral bristles of palptarsus subequal. In identifying this species one must bear in mind that the bristles of palptarsus have a varied appearance depending on orientation of the segment. In what I would call the optimum orientation four of the bristles are on one face of the segment (though near the edge) while a fifth (seventh) is on the opposite face (figure 8).

Material examined: Four specimens from well decayed fallen trunks, and moss thereon, top of slope, Calhoun Pines, Cornwall, *Conn.;* taken August 26th 1932, slides 3255a1 and -a2. Three specimens from leaf mould, Shawnee State Forest, Otway, *Ohio;* taken September 23rd 1926 by August E. Miller, slide 34M22a2. One specimen from ant's nest under bark of dead stumps, Eselgroth's woods, (four miles east of) Chillicothe, Ohio; taken April 26th 1925 by Miller, slide 32M57a2. Of eighty-six square-foot blue-grass sod samples taken weekly by A. E. Miller at Mt. Logan, Chillicothe, the following were obtained: one specimen May 5th 1924, slide 32M94a; two on August 10th 1924, slide 32M108a1; one on October 6th 1924, slide 32M81a2; three on March 9th 1925, slide 32M139a; two on March 16, slide 32M140a; one on March 30th, 32M137a2; one on April 13, 32M63a; one on April 20, 32M9a; one on April 27, 32M7a; one on May 4, 32M21a1; one in October 19, 32M35a; one on December 7, 32M58a (thus, in grassland, commonest in the early spring). The following were taken by Vera G. Smith: one specimen from ground, forest edge (flood plain), lower striplands, Vermillion Co., *Ill.;* taken June 29th 1926, slide 2390; from University woods, Urbana: three from leaves, March 29th 1926, slide 1085; one from leaves, August 2nd, lot 5815; one from leaves, August 16th, lot 3548; one from herbs, August 21st, lot 4370. Two specimens from bark chips, Dodson's woods, Urbana; taken August 21st 1926 by Miller, slide 32M1a. One under loose bark of untoped, fallen white oak, same woods; taken June 6th 1927 by Miller, slide 32M125a1. One under loose bark, Brownfield's woods, Urbana; taken June 9th 1926 by Miller, slide 32M13. Four from exposed logs and stumps in open woods near Muncie, Ill.; taken June 22nd 1927 by Miller, slide 32M147. One from under loose bark of fallen log, open woods meadow, Sidney, Ill.; taken June 21st 1926 by Miller, slide 32M8a. Four from moist, loose bark of fallen log in woods along Salt Fork Creek, south of Oakwood, Ill.; taken May 11th 1926 by Miller, slide 32M124a. One specimen from beneath bark of fallen tree, a few miles south of Savannah, *Ga.;* taken April 1936, slide 36S5. Two specimens from litter, horticultural grounds Gainesville, *Fla.;* taken February 13th 1928 by Edgar F. Grossman, lot 13. One (with pigmented eyes) from same place, taken February 29th, lot 30. One from near insectary, horticultural grounds, Gainesville; no date, taken by H. E. Bratley, lot 90. One from hickory litter, Pinkoson Springs; taken March 4th 1928 by Grossman, lot 33. One from long leaf pine litter, south shore of Newman's Lake, Gainesville; taken March 25th 1928 by Grossman, lot 55. Two from *Tamola littoralis* litter, shore bay, north beach, St. Augustine, Fla.; taken March 7th 1928 by Grossman, lot 34. Two from same locality; taken April 1st 1928 by Grossman, lot 63. One from live oak litter, Crescent City, Fla.; taken May 1st 1928 by Grossman, lot 82. One from litter, Bradenton, Fla.; taken May 2nd 1928 by George F. Weber, lot 87. Two from live oak and pine litter, Perry, Fla.; taken February 2nd 1928 by Grossman, lot 10. One from pine litter, between Perry and Mayo, Fla.; taken April 28th 1928 by Grossman, lot 78. Nine from deciduous litter, Villa Tasso, Choctawhatchee Bay, Fla.; taken May 18th 1928 by R. W. Blacklock, lot 101.

The following species are undescribed:

Bdella trisetosa *sp. nov.*

(Figure 9)

Small, total length of largest specimen 0.82 mm.; with dark pigment generally distributed but abdomen paler; rostrum with only two pairs of bristles (in addition to the distal) ; mandibles with attenuate chelae; lateral bristles (of cephaloprothorax) subequal to interpseudostigmatic, nearly as long as dorsal bristles of abdomen; eyes with pigmented ground; posterior eyes at widest part of cephaloprothorax, anterior eyes twice their diameter from posterior eyes; pseudostigmata on transverse plane slightly anterior to posterior eyes; the usual nine bristles of dorsum of abdomen fairly long but the three anterior mesal pairs not as long as their interspaces; lateral face of palptarsus with three subequally long bristles (figure 9), the posterior of the three is most ventrally inserted; distal end of palptarsus tapering markedly, hyaline collar of lateral bristle quite long and prominent (figure 9).

Cotypes: Two specimens from leaf litter about base of trees in an abandoned orange grove, five miles beyond Micanope, Fla.; taken February 26th 1928 by Edgar F. Grossman, slide G28Bd1 and -Bd2.

Spinibdella wilsoni *sp. nov.*
(Figures 10 and 11)

Fairly large, total length of gravid female 1.3 mm.; with dark pigment restricted to prothorax and cephalon in immatures, slightly more extensive in adults; rostrum with two pairs of bristles (in addition to the distal); mandibles with attenuate chelae, the only bristle inserted near base of chelae (figure 11); lateral bristles of cephaloprothorax much shorter than interpseudostigmatic which are about half length of dorsal bristles of abdomen; eyes with pigment, distant their own diameter; anterior bristles of dorsum of abdomen nearly as long as interspaces; dorsal face of palptarsus with one long (longer than the segment) straight bristle; lateral edge with two bristles (figure 10): the distal one subequal to length of segment, the proximal one much shorter, mesal face with two bristles, both rather short, distal end with both major bristle cups highly developed (figure 10).

Material examined: One specimen from leaf litter, sunny, rather dry, live oak and pine, Perry, Fla.; taken February 2nd 1928 by E. F. Grossman, slide G10Bd1. One specimen from leaf litter, high, dry, under hickory tree, Pinkoson Springs, Gainesville, Fla.; taken March 4th 1928 by Grossman, slide G33Bd1. Six specimens from leaf litter of *Tamola littoralis*, shore bay, seven miles from south point of North Beach, St. Augustine, Fla.; taken March 7th 1928 by Grossman, slides G34Bd1 to -Bd4 (*cotypes*). One specimen from leaf litter and grass, old laboratory, Bradenton, Fla.; taken March 14th 1928 by George F. Weber, slide G44Bd1 (more pigmented). One specimen from Cortez, Fla.; taken March 15th 1928 by Weber, slide G45Bd1.

Material collected under the Elizabeth Thompson Science Fund is to be deposited at the Museum of Comparative Zoölogy. Material from the Grossman collection is being returned to Dr. J. W. Wilson of the Agricultural Experiment Station of Florida.

LITERATURE CITED

1. Banks, Nathan, 1894 (June), Some New Acarina, Trans. Am. Ent. Soc., vol. 21, pp. 209-222.
2. Berlese, Antonio, 1882-1900, Acari, Myriapoda et Scorpiones hucusque in Italia reperta. Padova, 101 fasc. (10 vols.).
3. Ewing, H. E., 1909 (Aug. 16), New North American Acarina, Trans. Acad. Sci. St. Louis, vol. 18, pp. 53-77, pls. 8-11.
4. Ewing, H. E., 1910 (Mar. 1), A Systematic and Biological Study of the Acarina of Illinois, The University Studies, vol. 3 as part of Univ. Ill. Bull., vol. 7, no. 14, 120 pp., 8 pls., 6 txt. figs.
5. Jacot, A. P., 1933 (April), Phthiracarid Mites of Florida, Jour. Elisha Mitchell Sci. Soc., vol. 48, pp. 232-267, pls. 19-22, 2 txt. figs.
6. Say, Thomas, 1821, An Account of the Arachnides of the United States, Jour. Acad. Nat. Sci. Phil., vol. 2, pp. 59-82.
7. Thorell, T., 1871, Om Arachnider fr. Spetsbergen och Beeren-Eiland, Oefv. Kongl. Vet.-Akad. Förhandl., vol. 28, no. 6, p. 699.
8. Trägardh, Ivar, 1902, Zur Kenntnis der Litoralen Arten der Gattung Bdella Latr., Bihang till K. Sven. Vet.-Akada. Handl., vol. 27, Afd. 4, no. 9, 24 pp., 2 pls.
9. Weiss, H. B., and Ziegler, 1931, Thomas Say, Early American Naturalist.

DESCRIPTION OF PLATE XIV

Trombiculoides scaber (Say)

Fig. 1. Dorsal aspect, appendages of one side and bristles omitted; ratio x24.

Fig. 2. Dorsal aspect of cephaloprothorax and a palp, most of the bristles omitted; ratio x200.

Smaris sericea (Say)

Fig. 3. Dorsal aspect, three legs and bristles omitted; ratio x24.

Psyche, 1938   VOL. 45, PLATE XIV.

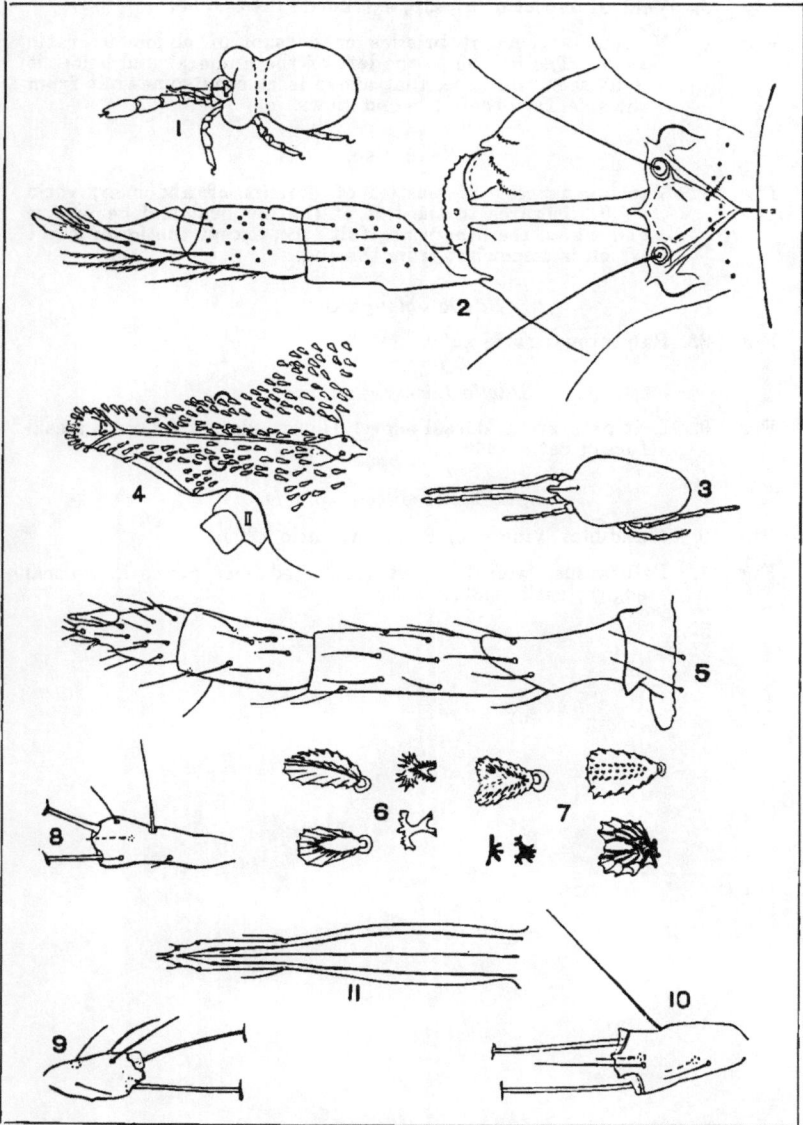

Fig. 4. Dorsal aspect of cephaloprothorax; ratio x75.

Fig. 5. Ventral aspect of a palp, extruded; ratio x330.

Fig. 6. Various aspects of bristles of dorsum of abdomen; ratio x440. The bristle to the left of the numeral and below it is as seen full face, that above is as seen somewhat from the side, the others are end views.

Smaris sp.

Fig. 7. Various aspects of bristles of dorsum of abdomen; ratio x440. Figures to the left of the numeral and below are end views, the others are full face, except the lower right which is somewhat from the end.

Bdella oblonga Say

Fig. 8. Palptarsus; ratio x200.

Bdella trisetosa sp. nov.

Fig. 9. Left palptarsus, dorsal aspect (lower edge of figure is mesal face) ; ratio x440.

Spinibdella wilsoni sp. nov.

Fig. 10. Mandibles lying over rostrum; ratio x200.

Fig. 11. Palptarsus, lateral aspect (lower edge of figure is ventral edge) ; ratio x330.

A REVIEW OF THE AMERICAN BEES OF THE GENUS MACROPIS (HYMEN., APOIDEA)

By CHARLES D. MICHENER

University of California, Berkeley, Calif.

Since the genus *Macropis* has not previously been recorded in America west of eastern Colorado, it is of interest to find *M. morcei*, the most widely distributed of our species, in Montana, and a new form of *M. steironematis* in Washington State, an extension of the known range of the genus by well over one thousand miles.

A comparison of our species with the descriptions and figures of Old World forms shows that the North American species belong to *Macropis* s.str., not to the subgenus *Paramacropis*[1]. Indeed the genitalia and sternites of our species agree in all essential points with the figures of *M. labiata* given by Saunders[2]. There are, however, certain differences, both in the genitalia and in the sternites. In *M. morcei* and *ciliata* the lateral projections of the eighth sternite, slender in *labiata*, are mere angles, while in *M. steironematis opaca*, described below, they are broad, rather truncated anteriorly, and about as long as in *labiata*. In *M. morcei* the genitalia are very similar to those of *M. ciliata* but differ in the somewhat shorter outer ramus of the stylus. I have not been able to study the genitalia of *M. patellata* or typical *M. steironematis*.

If *M. longilinguis* Provancher[3], described from the female, proves to be true *Macropis*, it is probably a synonym of *ciliata* or *patellata*. *Scrapter andrenoides* Smith[4], which was referred to *Macropis* by Dalle Torre is placed in *Pseudopanurgus* by Cockerell[5].

[1]Popov and Guiglia, 1936, Ann. Mus. Civ. Storia Nat. Genova, 59:287.
    Popov, 1936, Proc. Royal Ent. Soc. London (B) 5:78.
[2]Saunders, 1882, Trans. Ent. Soc. London, pl. 10.
[3]Provancher, 1888, Add. Faun. Ent. Can. Hym., p. 424.
[4]Smith, 1853, Cat. Hym. Brit. Mus., 1:121.
[5]Cockerell, 1904, Can. Ent., 36:303.

Macropis steironematis opaca Michener n. subsp.

Male: Similar to *M. steironematis* but hind metatarsus dull, very minutely roughened on outer side; punctures of hind tibiæ smaller than in *M. steironematis*, the surface between them minutely roughened; punctures of vertex more numerous, leaving only very small impunctate regions; surface between punctures of vertex slightly roughened. Length 9 mm.

Holotype: Morgan's Ferry, Yakima River, Washington, July 1, 1882, in the collection of the Museum of Comparative Zoölogy at Cambridge, Massachusetts.

Differs from the typical form of this species by the much duller surface of the legs and vertex.

Macropis morcei Robertson

Two specimens from Montana (no further data) are from the collection of the Academy of Natural Sciences of Philadelphia.

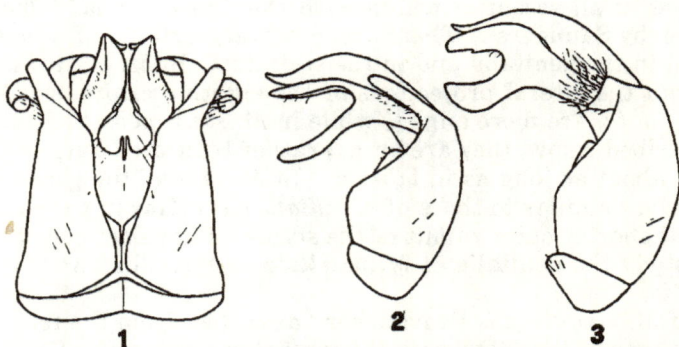

Fig. 1. 1, Dorsal view of genitalia of *Macropis ciliata* Patton; 2, Lateral view of genitalia of *Macropis ciliata* Patton; 3, Lateral view of genitalia of *Macropis steironematis opaca* Michener.

The following key will separate the American species of the genus:

1. Entire body closely punctured; length about 9 mm. *Male:* Middle metatarsus broad, wider near base, and tapering apically; supraclypeal area yellow, and lateral face

marks extending above antennal sockets; hind tibial spurs
not inserted beneath teeth. 2

—.Body much more sparsely punctate, punctures of abdomen
separated by five or more times their diameters; length
about 7 mm. *Male:* Middle metatarsus slender, parallel
sided; lateral face marks not extending above antennal
sockets. 3

2. *Male:* Outer surface of hind metatarsus polished between the hairs; punctures of hind tibiae larger, the surface
between them smooth; vertex shiny, with some fairly large,
almost impunctate, smooth, areas. (East of Rocky Mountains) .... *steironematis*[6]

—.*Male:* Outer surface of hind metatarsus dull, minutely
roughened; vertex less shiny, with more punctures, the surface between them slightly roughened. *Female:* Unknown.
(Washington State). .... *steironematis opaca*

3. *Male:* Hind tibial spurs not arising from beneath teeth;
supraclypeal area black or with little yellow; lateral face
marks reduced to short lines near sides of clypeus. *Female:*
Pubescence of hind metatarsus largely black on outer side.
                                                    morcei[7]

—.*Male:* One or both hind tibial spurs arising beneath a
tooth; supraclypeal area yellow; lateral face marks occupying entire space between clypeus and eye margin to a point
above upper margin of clypeus. *Female:* Pubescence of
hind metatarsus white. 4

4. *Male:* Outer hind tibial spur only arising beneath a
tooth; lateral face marks ending about opposite middle of
antennal sockets. *Female:* "Punctation, especially of
scutel, sparse."[8] .... *ciliata*[9]

—.*Male:* Each hind tibial spur arising beneath a tooth;
lateral face marks truncated and ending below the level of
antennal sockets. *Female:* "Punctation, especially of
scutel, dense."[8] .... *patellata*[10]

[6]Robertson, 1891, Trans. Am. Ent. Soc., 18:63.
[7]Robertson, 1897, Trans. Acad. Sci. St. Louis, 7:338.
[8]Viereck, 1916, Hym. Connecticut, p. 720.
[9]Patton, 1880, Ent. Mon. Mag., 17:31.
[10]Patton, 1880, Ent. Mon. Mag., 17:33.

A NEW GENUS OF PERLIDAE

By Nathan Banks
Museum of Comparative Zoology, Cambridge, Mass.

The sternal structures of Perlidæ have not been investigated as fully as some other parts of their structure. In examining Acroneuria for some structure to distinguish the females from other Perlidæ, I noticed that in two of our species the grooves on the meso- and metasterna were different from other species of Acroneuria. In the figures I have shown the differences. In the typical Acroneuria the anterior grooves are widely devergent, in *A. pacifica* they are short and nearly parallel. This sternal difference is correlated with the broader ocellar triangle, and the position of the lateral bosses, as well as in the last segment of the male. I shall, therefore, make *A. pacifica* the type of a new genus.

Hesperoperla gen. nov.

Anterior meso- and metasternal grooves short and nearly parallel; the ocellar triangle plainly broader than long; the lateral bosses on a level with the anterior ocellus; in the male the last ventral segment has a nearly quadrangular boss instead of the usual elliptic or rounded one; in the fore wing the second anal vein is frequently forked (rarely in Acroneuria). In Acroneuria the ocellar triangle is as long as broad, and the lateral bosses are higher. In Beloneuria the anterior sternal grooves are somewhat as in Hesperoperla, but curve outward more, but not nearly as much as in Acroneuria; the lateral bosses are higher, although the ocellar triangle is broader than long; the peculiar structure of the last ventral segment of the male in Beloneuria, somewhat like that of some Pteronarcys, will readily distinguish this genus, as well as the irregular apical venation.

Genotype: *Acroneuria pacifica* Bks.

Hesperoperla obscura sp. nov.

In general structure much as in *H. pacifica*. Body brown to almost black, venter pale through the middle, some yellowish on head, anterior margin of head a little more projecting than in *H. pacifica;* sculpture of pronotum as in *H. pacifica;* last dorsal segment gently, evenly rounded; the ventral plate of female with a distinct median emargination.

Fig. 1. a—Hesperoperla, mesosternal grooves; b—*Hesperoperla obscura*, ventral plate; c—Acroneuria, mesosternal grooves.

Wings less distinctly yellowish than *H. pacifica*, venation similar.

Expanse 48 to 50 mm.

From Laggan, Alberta 22 July (Osburn coll.).

In *H. pacifica* Bks. the ventral plate of the female is rounded and entire; the head and pronotum more yellowish. Type, M. C. Z., no. 23223.

I believe that these grooves from the inner ends of the slits of the meso- and metanotum have an important bearing on the classification of the Perlidæ. They are present mostly in the old genus Perla, now much divided. In our fauna they are in Perla, Acroneuria, Togoperla, and Banksiella; in Asia they occur in Tylopyge, Oyamia, Kaminuria, Mesoperla, Niponiella, Kalidasia, and Schistoperla.

They are not present in Isogenus, Clioperla, Hydroperla, Perlesta, Isoperla, Perlinella, nor in Paraperla which I propose to put in a separate tribe, the Isogenini. They are not present in the Cloroperlini (Alloperla and Chloroperla), nor in the Peltoperlini, but are evident, though sometimes fainter, in the Neoperlini. The Peltoperlini have the middle part of the metasternum very much broader than in the other groups.

PIN-LABELS IN MULTIPLES OF 1000, ALIKE

One Dollar Per Thousand

Smallest Type. Pure White Ledger Paper. Not over 4 Lines nor 30 Characters
(13 to a line) Additional Characters, 3 cents each, in total and per line, per
1000. Trimmed so one cut makes a label.

C. V. BLACKBURN, 7 Emerson St., STONEHAM 80, MASS.

CAMBRIDGE ENTOMOLOGICAL CLUB

A regular meeting of the Club is held on the second Tuesday
of each month (July, August and September excepted) at 7.45
p.m. in Room B-455, Biological Laboratories of Harvard University, Divinity Ave., Cambridge. Entomologists visiting Boston
are cordially invited to attend.

WARD'S ENTOMOLOGICAL SERVICES

Entomological Supplies and Equipment
Carefully designed by professional entomologists. Material of high quality at
low prices. **Send for Supply Catalog No. 348.**

Insect Preparations
Life Histories, Type Collections, Collections of Economic Insects and Biological Insect Collections. All specimens are accurately determined.

Insects for the Pest Collection
We have in stock over three hundred species of North American Insect Pests.
Send for Price List No. 349.

Ward's Entomological Bulletin
A monthly publication sent free to all entomologists requesting it.

Information for the Beginner
Send for **"Directions for Collecting and Preserving Insects"** by Dr.
A. B. Klots. A mine of useful information. Price 15 cents.

WARD'S NATURAL SCIENCE ESTABLISHMENT, Inc.
P. O. Box 24, Beechwood Station
Rochester, N. Y., U. S. A.
The Frank A. Ward Foundation of Natural Science of the University of Rochester

BACK VOLUMES OF PSYCHE

The Cambridge Entomological Club is able to offer for sale the following volumes of Psyche. Those not mentioned are entirely out of print.

Volumes 2, 3, 4, 5, 6, 7, 8, 9, 10; each covering a period of three years, $5.00 each.

Volumes 12, 14, 17, each covering a single year, $1.00 each.

Volumes 18, 19, 20, 21, 22, 23, 24, 25, 26, each covering a single year, $1.50 each.

Volumes 27, 28, 29, 30, 31, 32, 33, 34, 35, 36, 37, 38, 39, 40, 41, 42, 43, 44, each covering a single year, $2.00.

Orders for 2 or more volumes subject to a discount of 10%.

Orders for 10 or more volumes subject to a discount of 20%.

A set of all the volumes available (40 in all) will be sold for $79.00.

All orders should be addressed to

F. M. CARPENTER, Associate Editor of Psyche,
Biological Laboratories,
Harvard University,
Cambridge, Mass.

PSYCHE

A JOURNAL OF ENTOMOLOGY

Established in 1874

VOL. XLV   DECEMBER, 1938   No. 4

TABLE OF CONTENTS

CAMBRIDGE ENTOMOLOGICAL CLUB

OFFICERS FOR 1938-1939

President .	. W. S. CREIGHTON
Vice-President	. C. H. BLAKE
Secretary .	. V. G. DETHIER
Treasurer . .	RICHARD DOW

	. F. M. CARPENTER
Executive Committee {	C. H. BLAKE
	. C. A. FROST

EDITORIAL BOARD OF PSYCHE

EDITOR-IN-CHIEF
C. T. BRUES, HARVARD UNIVERSITY

ASSOCIATE EDITOR
F. M. CARPENTER, HARVARD UNIVERSITY

CONSULTING EDITORS

NATHAN BANKS,
Harvard University.

A. E. EMERSON,
University of Chicago.

THOMAS BARBOUR,
Harvard University.

A. L. MELANDER,
College of the
City of New York.

RICHARD DOW,
New England Museum of
Natural History,
Boston, Mass.

J. G. NEEDHAM,
Cornell University.

PSYCHE is published quarterly, the issues appearing in March, June, September, and December. Subscription price, per year, payable in advance: $2.00 to Subscribers in the United States; foreign postage, 25 cents extra, Canada 15 cents. Single copies, 65 cents.

Cheques and remittances should be addressed to Treasurer, Cambridge Entomological Club, Biological Laboratories, Harvard University, Cambridge, Mass.

Orders for back volumes, missing numbers, notices of change of address, etc., should be sent to Professor F. M. Carpenter, Biological Laboratories, Harvard University, Cambridge, Mass.

IMPORTANT NOTICE TO CONTRIBUTORS

Manuscripts intended for publication, books intended for review, and other editorial matter, should be addressed to Professor C. T. Brues, Biological Laboratories, Harvard University, Cambridge, Mass.

Authors contributing articles over 8 printed pages in length will be required to bear a part of the extra expense, for additional pages. This expense will be that of typesetting only, which is about $2.00 per page. The actual cost of preparing cuts for all illustrations must be borne by contributors; the expense for full page plates from line drawings is approximately $5.00 each, and for full page half-tones, $7.50 each; smaller sizes in proportion.

AUTHOR'S SEPARATES

Reprints of articles may be secured by authors, if they are ordered before, or at the time proofs are received for corrections. The cost of these will be furnished by the Editor on application.

Printed by the Eliot Press Inc., Jamaica Plain, Mass., U. S. A.

PSYCHE

| VOL. XLV | DECEMBER, 1938 | No. 4 |

ARE ANT LARVÆ APODOUS?

By George C. Wheeler

University of North Dakota

Imms[1] states that "in all the higher Hymenoptera the prevalent larval type is apodous." Practically, of course, this is true of ant larvæ. But what is one to say of the pairs of small structures found near the posterior border of the ventral surface of each thoracic segment?

A study of the larvæ of some four hundred species of ants in 130 genera representing all of the subfamilies has convinced me such structures are of general occurrence throughout the Family Formicidæ. They are to be found in the subfamilies Dorylinæ, Cerapachyinæ, Ponerinæ, Myrmicinæ, Dolichoderinæ, and Formicinæ. I have not found them in the Pseudomyrminæ, but this may be due to the fact that the ventral surface of the thorax is so complicated by exudatoria and by the trophothylax that a small linear structure might easily be concealed or confused with a wrinkle in preserved material. The solution of the problem requires living specimens. I have not searched for the structures in the Leptanillinæ, partly because the larvæ are so minute and partly because my material is so scarce that I dare not risk any of it at this stage of my study of ant larvæ.

In the literature on ant larvæ I have found no mention of these structures. Imms[1] says that "vestiges, in the form of papillæ, of what appear to be the remains of thoracic appendages have been detected in Polysphincta and certain other

[1] Imms, A. D. 1937. Recent advances in entomology (2 ed.). Philadelphia: P. Blakiston's Son and Company, Inc., p. 60.

of the Ichneumonoidea." Keilin[2] has found comparable structures on the apterous larvæ of many families of Diptera. He calls them *organes sensoriels vestigiaux des pattes*. They are always in the same position on the thoracic segments and they always consist of three or four sensory hairs, which are sometimes mounted on small protuberances. Keilin concludes that they are vestigial legs because of their general occurrence throughout the Diptera; because of the constancy of their form and constitution; because they are found exclusively on the ventral surface of the thoracic segments; and finally because of their relations to the imaginal buds. This conclusion is in accord with that of Pérez.[3]

Among the ant larvæ these leg vestiges attain their maximum size in the army ants (Dorylinæ). In the genera Dorylus, Eciton, and Cheliomyrmex they are relatively large, subcircular, convex, slightly elevated papillæ. In the mature larvæ of *Eciton hamatum* (Fabr.) (Fig. 1) and *Dorylus* (*Anomma*) *wilverthi* Emery the diameter of the papilla is 0.05 mm. This is also the size in both young (?) larva (2.8 mm. long) and a mature larva (5 mm. long) of *Cheliomyrmex megalonyx* Wheeler. I can find nothing to suggest a sensory function. In *E. hamatum* the surface of the papilla is roughened, but in the other two species it is apparently quite smooth. The close relationship between vestigal legs and imaginal buds is shown in Figs. 2, 3, and 5. In some genera of other subfamilies the vestiges are small transversely elliptical papillæ, but more commonly they appear merely as short transverse lines (grooves or ridges?) which are often difficult to find (Fig. 11). In some genera I have found no trace of the vestiges (*e.g., Eusphinctus steinheili* Forel and *Lioponera luzuriagae* Wheeler & Chapman).

It is not surprising that these vestigial legs have been overlooked in ant larvæ, for in addition to being minute and inconspicuous (except in the Dorylinæ), it is very difficult to distinguish them except in exoskeletons cleaned with a solution of potassium hydroxide and stained with acid fuchsin.

In addition to the vestigial legs I have found some other puzzling structures in ant larvæ. On the mesothorax and

[2]Keilin, D. 1915. Bull. Soc. France Belgique. 49: 166-173.
[3]Pérez, C. 1911. C. R. Soc. Biol., Paris. 71: 498-501.

metathorax there are small paired structures—probably
grooves—located one on each side approximately midway
between the leg vestige and the spiracle, *i.e.*, ventrolateral
and therefore in close proximity to the imaginal buds of the
wings. These can hardly be termed wing vestiges since
there is no reason for assuming that the ancestral larva had
functional wings. They may, however, be the vestiges of
wing pads of the nymph of a heterometabolous ancestor.
Finally, they may be prothetelous, *i.e.*, adult structures
appearing prematurely in the larva. I shall call them
provisionally "wing rudiments."

In the male larva of the army ant, *Eciton* (*Acamatus*)
schmitti Emery (Fig. 4), these wing rudiments appear as
short transverse lines (grooves?). They are not present in
the worker larva of the same species nor are they to be
found in the worker larva of *E. hamatum*. A larva of the
Australian bulldog ant, *Myrmecia gulosa* Fabr. has short
(0.045 mm.) transverse lines (slits?). Similar structures
occur in both worker and male larvæ of *Cephalotes atratus*
(L.) and also in the larvæ of *Dorymyrmex pyramicus*
var. *flavus* McCook. In the sexual larva of *Dolichoderus*
(*Hypoclinea*) *taschenbergi* Mayr the wing rudiments have
a complicated internal cuticular structure. I can find no
evidence of such structures in *Cerapachys* sp., *Paraponera*
clavata Fabr., or *Melophorus bagoti* Lubbock.

There is also to be found among ant larvæ a third type of
related structure, namely vestigial gonopods. I have so
designated them because typically they are paired and
located on the ventral surface of the seventh, eighth, and
ninth abdominal segments and only on those segments.
Gonopods are generally asserted to be the modified appendages of the eighth, ninth, and tenth abdominal segments,
but in the larva of *Eciton hamatum* (Fig. 1) the gonopodal
imaginal discs are to be found on the seventh, eighth, and
ninth.

As a rule these vestigial larval gonopods are short transverse lines (slits?). Frequently the members of a pair are
fused to form a single median line. In *Pseudomyrma*
arboris-sanctæ symbiotica var. *lœwensohni* Forel, however,
they are subelliptical papillæ. In some species one or more
pairs are apparently lacking, *e.g.*, that of the seventh in

Melophorus bagoti and that of the ninth in *Pseudomyrma læwensohni;* in the male larva of *Eciton* (*A.*) *schmitti* there is none on the seventh and eighth and only a very faint trace on the ninth; in *Eusphinctus steinheili* there is none at all.

It is interesting to note here that these same structures also occur in other aculeate Hymenoptera. Three pairs of vestigial legs, two pairs of wing rudiments, and three pairs of vestigial gonopods (on the seventh, eighth, and ninth abdominal segments) are present in the larvae of the hornet, *Vespula* (*Dolichovespula*) *maculata* (L.) ; of the yellow jackets, *Vespula* (*V.*) *maculifrons* (R. du Buysson) and *V.* (*V.*) *arenaria* (Fabr.) ; of the wasp, *Polistes pallipes* LePeletier (Fig. 8) ; and of an undetermined mud dauber (Sphecidæ). I have, however, been unable to find any such structures in the worker honeybee, in the drone honeybee, nor in an undetermined bumblebee.   ·

The leg vestiges in *Vespula arenaria* (Fig. 7) are open transverse grooves, which fact of itself suggests a possible sensory function. Furthermore one of my sections shows a structure (Fig. 9), which might be nervous, extending from the bottom of this groove to the hypodermis. A section of a gonopodal imaginal disc reveals in the overlying integument a small sensilliform structure (Fig. 6).

Four possible interpretations of these structures have occurred to me. (1) All three types are vestiges : vestigial legs on the three thoracic segments; vestigial abdominal legs (gonopods) on the seventh, eighth, and ninth abdominal segments; and vestigial wing pads on mesothorax and metathorax. (2) All three types are rudiments of adult structures appearing prematurely in these holometabolous larvæ. (3) The six pairs of ventral structures are vestiges, while the two pairs limited to the mesothorax and metathorax are prothetelous rudiments. (4) All are the results of purely developmental processes and limited to the cuticula at the points where the hypodermis first invaginates to form the imaginal buds. Personally I am inclined to prefer the third interpretation.

EXPLANATION OF PLATES

PLATE 15

Fig. 1. Larva of *Eciton hamatum* (Fabr.), ventral view, hairs omitted, X 11. Fig. 2. Ventral view of thorax of same showing relation of vestigial legs to the underlying imaginal buds, X 42. Fig. 3. Parasagittal optical section of same to show relation of vestigial leg to imaginal bud, X 135. Fig. 4. Male larva of *Eciton* (*Acamatus*) *schmitti* Emery, ventral view of thorax, hairs omitted, X 11. Fig. 5. Larva of *Eciton vagans* (Olivier), parasagittal section through imaginal bud and vestigial leg, X 95. T_1, T_2, T_3, thoracic segments; L_1, L_2, L_3, vestigial legs; C, cuticula; H, hypodermis; W_1, W_2, wing rudiments; G_1, G_2, G_3, vestigial gonopods.

PLATE 16

Fig. 6. Larva of *Vespula* (*V.*) *arenaria*, parasagittal section through imaginal bud of gonopod, showing sensilla (S), X 138. Fig. 7. Parasagittal section through thorax of same, showing imaginal buds of legs and vestigial legs, X 34. Fig. 8. Larva of *Polistes pallipes* LePeletier, ventral view, X 6. Fig. 9. Enlargement of mesothoracic portion of Fig. 7, showing nerve (?) to vestigial leg, X 138. Fig. 10. Larva of *Pseudomyrma gracilis* (Fabr.), ventral view of posterior end, X 34; A_7, A_8, A_9, seventh, eighth, and ninth abdominal segments. Fig. 11. Larva of *Dilobocondyla* sp., ventral view of anterior end, X 27.

PSYCHE, VOL. XLV　　　　　　　　　　　　　　　　PLATE 15

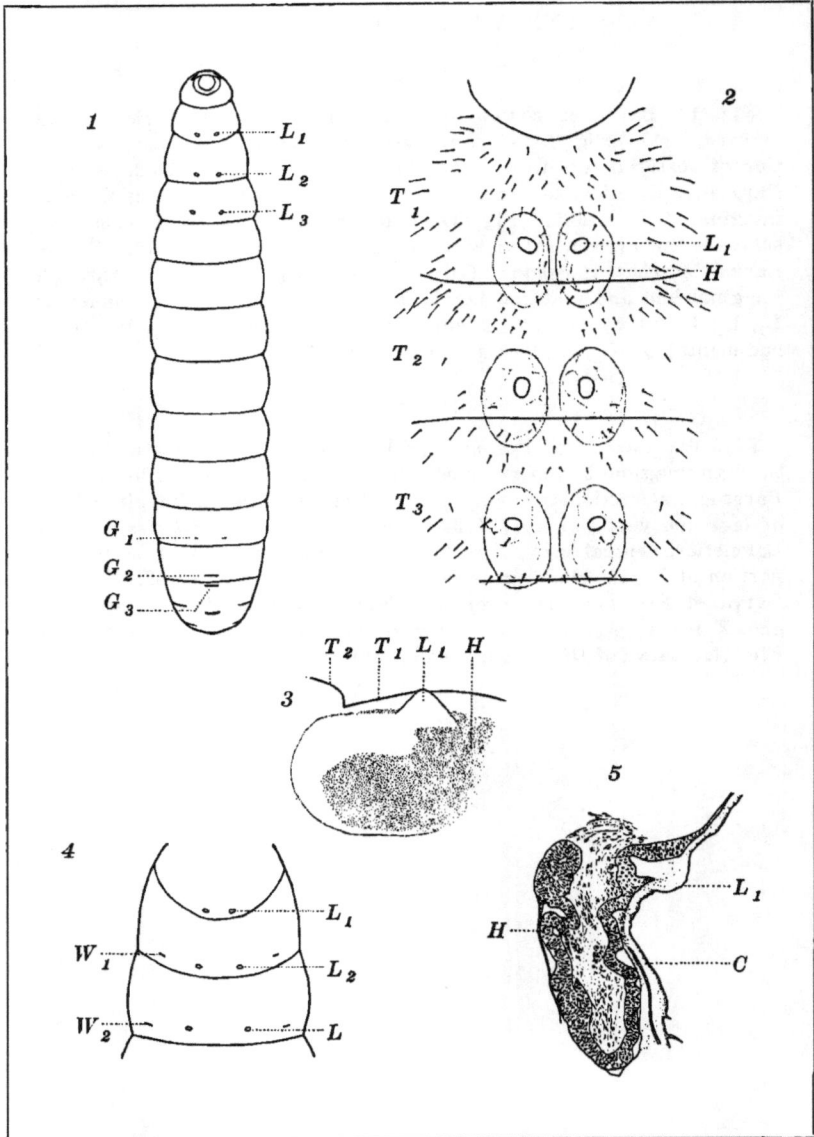

WHEELER — ANT LARVÆ

PSYCHE, VOL. XLV PLATE 16

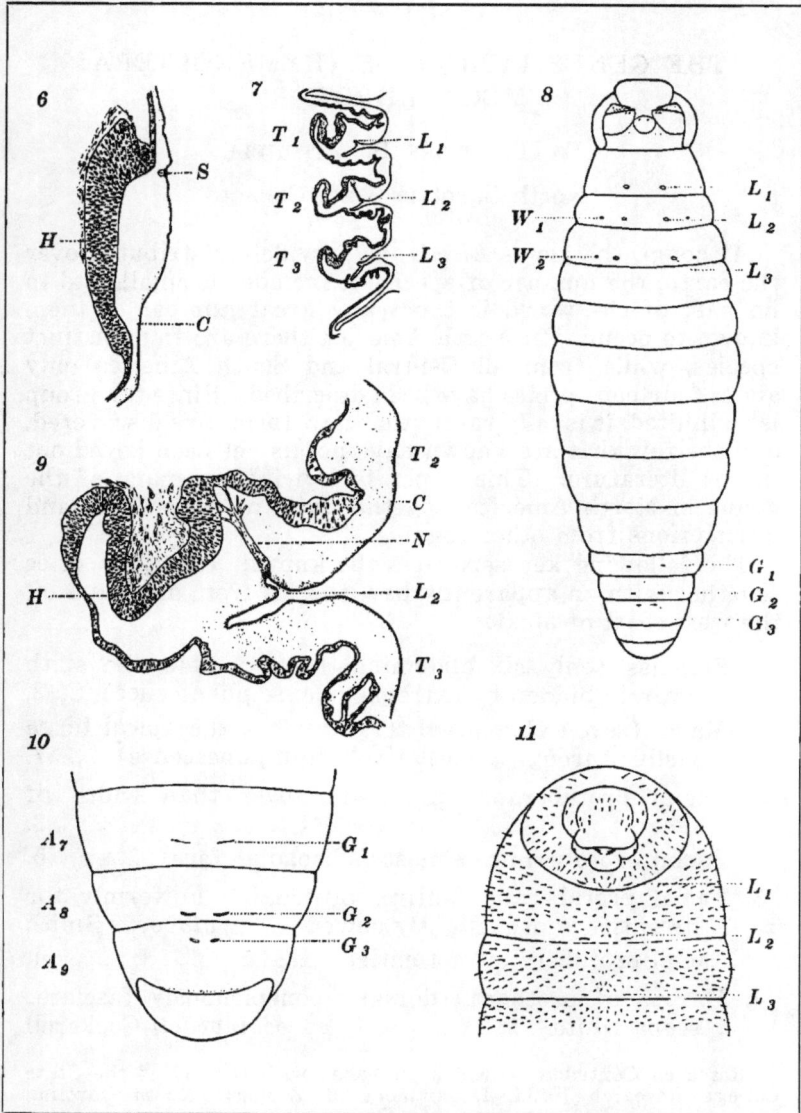

WHEELER — ANT LARVÆ

THE GENUS LITHURGUS (HYMENOPTERA: MEGACHILIDÆ)[1]

By Theodore B. Mitchell

North Carolina State College

Although the genus *Lithurgus* is widely distributed over the earth, the number of species it includes is small, and in no part of the world is there any great number of them known to occur. In North America there are four distinct species, while from all Central and South America only about fourteen species have been described. Since the group is so limited, it is only rarely that new forms are discovered, and the few that are known have not as yet been keyed out in the literature. This paper is a brief summary of the genus in North America, together with a few records and descriptions from other regions.

The following key separates the known Nearctic species together with an apparently new species from an island off the west coast of Mexico

1. Females (only six abdominal terga visible, the sixth entirely hidden by extremely dense pubescence) ......2.

   Males (seven abdominal terga visible, the apical terga visible through the relatively thin pubescence) ....7.

2. Facial protuberance much narrower than width of face ....3.

   Facial protuberance almost as broad as face ....5.

3. Facial protuberance entire, protruding uniformly for its entire width, slightly bowed .... *gibbosus* Smith

   Facial protuberance not entire ....4.

4. Margin of prothorax dorsally conspicuously fasciate; scopa white .... *echinocacti* Cockerell

[1]Research Contribution No. 2 published with the aid of the State College Research Fund, Department of Zoology, North Carolina State College of Agriculture and Engineering of the University of North Carolina.

Margin of prothorax only very thinly fasciate; scopa
yellowish-orange .... *socorroensis* new species

5. Pubescence at tip of abdomen bright ferruginous ....
    .... *apicalis* Cresson

    Pubescence at tip of abdomen black ....6.

6. Apical margin of clypeus with a single median emargi-
    nation; scopa without black hairs ....
    .... *apicalis* var. *opuntiae* Cockerell[2]

    Apical margin of clypeus with a small median emargi-
    nation and a slightly deeper one on each side; scopa
    on sixth sternum black, with a few black hairs usually
    on the fifth also .... *bruesi* Mitchell

7. Clypeus and supraclypeal area quite densely rugose or
    punctate ....8.

    At least the supraclypeal area shining and very sparsely
    punctate ....9.

8. Labrum with a prominent basal tubercle visible just
    above mandibles .... *gibbosus* Smith

    Labrum not tuberculate .... *echinocacti* Cockerell

9. Labrum with a pair of conspicuous parallel spines
    toward the base .... *bruesi* Mitchell

    Labrum with a single median tubercle or none ....10.

10. Labrum with a basal median spine-like acute tubercle;
    supraclypeal area almost impunctate, the clypeus
    quite closely punctate .... *socorroensis* new species

    Labrum not tuberculate; supraclypeal area with sparse
    scattered punctures, the clypeus also sparsely punc-
    tate medially ....11.

----

[2]*L. arizonensis* ♀ Cockerell has been described recently (Bull. So.
Calif. Ac. Sc. 36, p. 108, 1938), but I was unaware of it at the time
this manuscript was prepared. According to its description, it would
run in this key to *opuntiae*, and is apparently very closely allied to it.
Cockerell separates it from *opuntiae* ♀ by its more flattened clypeus,
having larger punctures, and the facial punctures deeper and more
widely separated. It seems probable that it is another variant of
apicalis, but I am not warranted in forming any positive opinion until
I have had the opportunity of examining it, and of examining a longer
series of var. *opuntiae* than has hitherto been possible.

11. Pubescence at tip of abdomen rather dark ferruginous
or fuscous .... *apicalis* var. *opuntiae* Cockerell
Pubescence at tip of abdomen light ferruginous ....
.... *apicalis* Cresson

Lithurgus apicalis Cresson

Lithurgus apicalis Cresson, Wheeler's Rep. Geogr. Expl. W.
100th Merid., p. 724, 1876. Cresson, Proc. Dav. Ac. 1,
p. 209, 1876. Cockerell, Bull. Univ. N. Mex. 1, p. 64,
1898. Cockerell, Am. Nat. 34, p. 488, 1900. Cockerell,
Ann. Mag. Nat. Hist. (7) 14, p. 24, 1904. Cockerell,
Ann. Mag. Nat. Hist. (7) 17, p. 306, 1926. Cockerell,
Am. Mus. Nov. 697, p. 13, 1934.

Lithurgopsis apicalis Fox, Ent. News 13, p. 139, 1902.

This species may be quickly recognized among the Nearctic
species, by the conspicuous bright ferruginous pubescence
at the tip of the abdomen.

ARIZONA: 1 ♂, no locality record. Recorded from Santa
Rita Mts. (July) and Temez Mts.

CALIFORNIA: 1 ♀, Laguna, San Diego County, June 21,
1926 (W. S. Wright). 1 ♀, Mammoth, July 8 (or Aug. 7?),
1933.

COLORADO: 4 ♂, 3 ♀, no locality record. 1 ♂, Boulder,
June 13, 1933 (M. T. James). 1 ♀, Buena Vista, July 6,
1937, (L. Lanham). 1 ♀, Las Animas, June 21, 1931. 1 ♂,
Paonia, Delta County, June 14, 1926 (E. C. Van Dyke.)
1 ♀, Trinidad, June 13, 1899. 1 ♂, 1 ♀, White Rocks,
Valmont, July 2 and 4, 1933 and May 30, 1934 (M. & H.
James). Recorded also from Chimney Gulch, Fort Garland,
Glenwood Springs, Mesa Verde, Ridgeway and Ute Creek.

NEVADA: 1 ♀, Mt. Charleston, 7500 ft., Aug. 13, 1931,
(E. E. Tinkham).

NEW MEXICO: 2 ♀, Alamogordo, May 5 and June 9, 1902.
1 ♂, Highrolls, June 2, 1902. 1 ♂, E. Las Vegas, June 24,
1902. 5 ♂, 7 ♀, San Antonio, June 1921. 1 ♀, San Jose,
Apr. 13, 1934, (M. & H. James). 1 ♂, Santa Fe, July 24,
1926 (E. C. Van Dyke).

TEXAS: 1 ♂, no locality record.

WYOMING: 1 ♀, Lake Bamforth, June 24, 1934 (R. O. &
V. D. Christenson). Recorded also from Green River
(July), Laramie River and Sheridan (Aug., on *Carduus*).

Specimens of *apicalis* have also been recorded from
Kansas—Hamilton County; Nebraska—War Bonnet Canyon (June) ; and South Dakota—Custer.

Lithurgus apicalis var. opuntiæ Cockerell

Lithurgus apicalis opuntiæ Cockerell, Ent. News 13, p. 182,
    1902.   Cockerell, Proc. U.S.N.M. 40, p. 251, 1911.
    Cockerell, Ann. Mag. Nat. Hist. (8) 13, p. 433, 1914.

There is no evident structural difference between this
form and typical *apicalis*, the chief difference being one of
color. It bears a close resemblance to *L. bruesi*, the females
especially of the two being very similar. The presence of a
single median emargination on the apical margin of the
clypeus seems to be a constant character which will distinguish it from the female of *bruesi* in which there are
three emarginations. The simple labrum of the male will
easily distinguish it from *bruesi* in which that part is
bispinose basally.

ARIZONA: 1 ♀, no locality record. 1 ♂, Kits Peak, Rincon,
Baboquivari Mts., Aug. 1-4, 1916. 1 ♂, 1 ♀, S. Rita Mts.,
5-7 and 12-6. Recorded also from Fort Grant.

CALIFORNIA: 1 ♂, Andrews Canyon, Apr. 5, 1925, (Tim-
berlake, on *Opuntia*) [Timberlake].

COLORADO: 2 ♂, White Rocks, Valmont, May 30, 1934.

MEXICO: 1 ♂, 1 ♀, N. Sonora (Morrison) [Brit. Mus.].

TEXAS: Recorded from Valentine.

Lithurgus apicalis var. littoralis W. P. Cockerell

Lithurgus apicalis littoralis W. P. Cockerell, Journ. N. Y.
    Ent. Soc. 25, p. 191, 1917.

I have had no opportunity to examine this form. It was
briefly described from material collected at Point Isabel,
near Brownsville, Texas. The size (10 mm.) and the presence of distinct black hair on the discs of the abdominal
terga suggest that it is distinct from *apicalis*. I have one
small male of *bruesi* which fits the description of *littoralis*

fairly well, but as no structural details are mentioned in the
description it can only be suggested as possible that the two
are the same.

Lithurgus bruesi Mitchell

Lithurgus bruesi Mitchell, Psyche 34, No. 2, p. 104, 1927.
Parks, Bull. Brooklyn Ent. Soc. 25, p. 265-7, 1930.

The female of this species was not known at the time that
the male was described. Mr. H. B. Parks of San Antonio,
Texas, has since collected it in numbers and the following
description is based on that material.

Female: — Size: Length, 13-15 mm.; breadth of abdomen, 4.5-5 mm.; anterior wing, 10-11 mm.

Structure: Facial quadrangle about as broad as long;
eyes subparallel; facial protuberance broad, evenly incurved, the lateral angles conspicuous; clypeus with shining
impunctate apical margin which has a small median emargination and a slightly deeper emargination on each side of
the middle; a shining malar space evident, this separated
below from cheeks by a quite deep concavity; mandibles
obtusely 3-dentate, with a triangular punctate basal area
delimited by deep sutures; all the tibiæ with prominent
spine-like tubercles, largely confined to a single row on the
front pair, but covering the posterior center surfaces of the
others.

Puncturation: Punctures sparse and scattered on the
relatively dull clypeus, close and rather fine at sides of face,
on vertex back of ocelli, and most of cheeks, more coarse
and scattered on cheeks below, more widely separated just
above eyes; mesonotum and scutellum rather finely rugosopunctate, the pleura finely and closely punctate above,
becoming more coarse and sparse below, the propodeum
tessellate, but hardly punctate, the tegulæ impunctate and
dull; abdomen impunctate basally, becoming distinctly
punctate laterally and apically, the punctures of segment 5
quite deep and conspicuous, quite widely separated medially
but close laterally.

Color: Black; antennæ and tegulæ very slightly reddened;
wings faintly smoky, the nervures piceous to blackish; spurs
brownish-yellow.

Pubescence: Thin and greyish but rather long on vertex, whiter and more dense around antennæ, at sides of face, and on cheeks behind and below, clypeus with an apical fringe which is white laterally but brownish medially; dorsum of thorax almost bare, pubescence laterally and beneath rather long, thin and greyish-white, whitish on legs basally, becoming more brownish apically, blackish on hind tarsi; abdomen basally largely bare above, with very short dark pubescence evident laterally, segment 5 with relatively long conspicuous fuscous pubescence, that on segment 6 fuscous and extremely dense; segments 2-5 with white apical fasciæ, interrupted medially on segments 2-4; scopa yellowish, fuscous to black on segment 6 and with some of the same color on segment 5 across apical margin; sterna 2-5 with entire white apical fasciæ beneath scopa.

9 ♂, 44 ♀, Bexar County (San Antonio), Texas. 1 ♂, Austin, Texas, Apr. 16, 1933 (both H. B. Parks). 1 ♀, Big Bend Park, Brewster Co., Texas, June 17, 1937, (R. H. Baker).

Lithurgus echinocacti Cockerell

Lithurgus echinocacti Cockerell, Ann. Mag. Nat. Hist. (7) 2, p. 453, 1898. Cockerell, Am. Nat. 34, p. 487, 1900. Cockerell, Ann. Mag. Nat. Hist. (9) 8, p. 368, 1921.

Lithurgopsis echinocacti Fox, Ent. News 13, p. 139, 1902.

This species bears some resemblance to *socorroensis* but differs from it in the following characters:

♀ — Prothorax with a distinct and conspicuous white fascia along its posterior margin; polished concavity of facial protuberance with scattered punctures; transverse process of labrum broader and less deeply emarginate.

♂ — Prothorax fasciate as in ♀; supraclypeal area more closely and coarsely punctate; labrum without a basal tubercle.

ARIZONA: 1 ♂, Coyote Mts., Aug. 3-7, 1916, about 3500 ft. [Am. Mus. Nat. Hist.]. Recorded from Palmerlee and Tempe (July and Aug.).

Lithurgus gibbosus Smith

Lithurgus gibbosus Smith, Cat. Hym. Brit. Mus. 1, p. 147, 1853. Cockerell, Am. Nat. 34, p. 487, 1900. Cockerell,

Entomologist 33, p. 244, 1900. Cockerell, Ann. Mag.
Nat. Hist. (8) 13, p. 433, 1914.

Lithurgus compressus Smith, Cat. Hym. Brit. Mus. 1, p. 147,
1853.

Lithurgopsis gibbosus Fox, Ent. News 13, p. 140, 1902.

This species is the single representative of the genus
occurring east of the Mississippi River.

FLORIDA: 1 ♀, Capron, Apr. 18. 2 ♂, Enterprise, Apr. 18,
1902 (Dr. Castle) and Apr. 24, 1903. 2 ♂, 1 ♀, Flamingo,
Apr. 13, 1923.

GEORGIA: 1 ♀, St. Simons, June 2, 1922 (Mitchell, on
Opuntia).

NORTH CAROLINA: 2 ♀, Carolina Beach, June 12, 1930.
1 ♂, Raleigh, June 7, 1922 (on *Opuntia*). 1 ♀, Tarheel,
July 22, 1928 (on *Helianthus*). 4 ♀, White Lake, May 20,
1934 (on *Opuntia*) ; (all Mitchell).

TEXAS: 2 ♂, no locality record, 12 ♂, 20 ♀, Bexar County
(San Antonio), May 12 to June 1, 1930 (H. B. Parks). 1 ♂,
Fedor, May 1, 1897. Recorded also from Austin and Lee
County.

Lithurgus socorroensis new species

Female. — Size: Length 11 mm.; breadth of abdomen
3.7 mm.; anterior wing 7.5 mm.

Structure: Facial quadrangle slightly narrower above
than long; eyes convergent below; clypeal margin straight
and entire; labrum with a basal transverse process which
is abruptly emarginate medially; facial protuberance low,
concave, highly polished, somewhat conical on each side;
lateral ocelli subequally distant from eyes and edge of vertex; vertex rounded; cheeks subequal in width to eyes; basal
joint of flagellum equal to pedicel, the second joint broader
but slightly shorter; mandibles 3-dentate, the middle tooth
prominent; all the metatarsi slender, the hind pair equalling
their tibiæ in length, the others shorter than their respective
tibiae; pulvilli inevident; outer posterior faces of all the
tibiæ conspicuously tuberculate, the tubercles short and
acute, those on the front tibia more robust apically, forming
a quite distinct posterior comb apically, those on the middle

tibia in two distinct rows, the surface between polished, those on the hind tibia scattered, the surface polished between them; apical margins of abdominal segments slightly depressed, more so toward sides.

Puncturation: Close and fine on face, vertex and on pleura above; coarse and rather sparse on pleura below and on the shining clypeus; cheeks finely and quite closely punctate above, rather coarsely so below; mesonotum rather coarsely striately rugose, especially medially, becoming finely rugose or subpunctate toward prothorax; scutellum rather finely rugose; basal segments of abdomen impunctate medially, becoming rather finely and closely punctate laterally, and the more apical segments quite distinctly punctate, the fifth with moderately coarse and distinctly separated punctures.

Color: Black; tegulæ and wing nervures piceous; antennæ beyond the basal joint of the flagellum ferruginous; wings subhyaline, faintly clouded apically; spurs yellow.

Pubescence: White at sides of face, around antennæ, on cheeks, pleura, propodeum, dorsum of thorax anteriorly, and on legs; white, but thin and inconspicuous on vertex; mesonotum, scutellum and basal abdominal terga almost bare, fifth tergum with scattered erect dark hairs, the apical one with dense fuscous pubescence; second to fifth terga with entire and conspicuous white apical fasciæ; sterna also with narrower but entire white apical fasciæ beneath the reddish or orange scopa.

Male. — Size: Length 10 mm.; breadth of abdomen 3 mm.; anterior wing 7 mm.

Structure: Face with breadth above about equal to length; eyes convergent below; lateral ocelli slightly nearer edge of vertex than to eyes; cheeks subequal in width to eyes; clypeal margin nearly straight, entire; labrum with a basal median conical robust tubercle; supraclypeal area flattened, impunctate medially, polished; basal joint of flagellum subequal to pedicel and to the second joint; mandibles 3-dentate; tibiæ finely tuberculate or rugose on outer faces, the metatarsi slender, shorter than their tibiæ; claws deeply cleft, a small but distinct pulvillus between them; apical margins of abdominal terga slightly depressed, especially toward sides.

Puncturation: Close and fine on vertex and pleura, becoming coarser but close on face and on clypeus; fine and close, but shallow and obscure on cheeks; mesonotum and scutellum finely rugose; punctures minute and rather sparse on fifth tergum, close and more coarse on sixth.

Color: Black; tegulæ and wing nervures reddish-piceous; flagellum ferruginous; wings subhyaline, faintly clouded apically; spurs pale yellow.

Pubescence: White on face, cheeks, pleura, propodeum, legs and basal segment of abdomen; intermixed light and dark on vertex, mesonotum and scutellum; very short and blackish on the second and following segments of abdomen, becoming rather long on the more apical segments, especially on the sixth and seventh, the second to the sixth terga with entire white apical fasciae, the corresponding sterna with very narrow apical fasciae, the discs covered with long thin yellowish scopa-like hairs.

Type. — Female; Braithwaite Bay, Socorro Island, Revillagigedo Group (Mexico), May 7, 1925, (H. H. Keifer) [Calif. Ac. Sc. no. 4602].

Allotype. — Male; topotypical.

Paratypes. — 1 ♀, 21 ♂, topotypical.

Lithurgus corumbæ Cockerell

Lithurgus corumbæ Cockerell, Proc. Ac. Sc. Phil. 53, p. 216, 1901.

The specimen described below bears the same data as the female described by Cockerell under this name and agrees with his description as to size and quite well also as to pattern of pubescence, allowing for sexual differences. There seems little doubt therefore that this specimen represents the other sex of the species.

Male. — Size: Length 7 mm.; breadth of abdomen 2 mm.; anterior wing 5 mm.

Structure: Face narrow, eyes slightly converging below, clypeus flat, the apical margin straight, labrum simple, without spines or tubercles, mandibles short, of the usual 3-dentate type, supraclypeal area with a pair of obscure low tubercles, one below each antenna, lateral ocelli slightly nearer edge of vertex than to eyes, cheeks narrower than eyes, all the tarsi very slender, hind femora short and rather robust, about equalling the combined coxa and trochanter in length, pulvillae absent on all the legs, the claws deeply cleft, seventh tergum forming a nearly equilateral triangle, the apex sharply pointed.

Puncturation: Fine and densely crowded over face, clypeus, and median portion of vertex, more distinctly separated on vertex laterally, very fine and close, but not crowded, on cheeks; deep, close and distinct over most of thorax, but with evident shining spaces between, moderately coarse, becoming quite fine and crowded on sternum; very minute and crowded on median abdominal terga, becoming yet more fine and obscure toward the base, but quite coarse and distinct toward the apex.

Color: Black; mandibular teeth reddened; apical tarsal joints pale ferruginous; spurs pale yellow; tegulae ferruginous; wings subhyaline, the nervures fuscous.

Pubescence: White on head and thorax, but vertex and mesonotum with some very short and inconspicuous reddish pubescence, hind margin of prothorax above with a narrow but distinct white fascia and tubercles fringed with white; second to fourth abdominal terga with white apical fasciæ broadly interrupted medially, the fifth and sixth terga with entire white fasciae, pubescence of the discs black, sterna with longer thin, white pubescence, black on the sixth and on the fifth laterally, no ventral fasciæ evident.

1 ♂, Corumba, Brazil, April. (H. H. Smith) [A. N. S. P.]

Lithurgus albofimbriatus Sichel

6 ♀, Nukahiva, Marquessas Islands, Aug. 1923 (Simeon Delmar).

Lithurgus rubricatus Smith

1 ♀, Bilode, Queensland, Australia, 9. V. 25 (F. G. Holliday). [Univ. Minn.]. 1 ♂, Queensland (Smith coll. pres. by Mrs. Farren White, 99-303) [Brit. Mus.].

NOTES ON NORTH AMERICAN NITIDULIDAE, III: PHENOLIA, SORONIA, LOBIOPA, AMPHOTIS

BY C. T. PARSONS

Biological Laboratories, Harvard University

Erichson, who erected the genera *Phenolia, Soronia, Lobiopa,* and *Amphotis,* in 1843, had a clearer idea of their relationships than subsequent workers. For instance, Reitter placed *Phenolia,* and *Lobiopa* in *Soronia;* whereas Horn suppressed *Amphotis* as well as *Lobiopa* but resurrected *Phenolia.* Later Sharp and then Grouvelle, without giving reasons, raised them all to the good standing they have had subsequently. Since all of the writers have made mistakes in their diagnoses and since their descriptions have been incomplete, the genera are here redescribed.

1. Front lobed over the insertion of the antennæ .... 2.
   Front not lobed over the insertion of the antennæ .... ..
   .... *Phenolia* Er.
2. Antennal grooves parallel .... 3.
   Antennal grooves strongly convergent posteriorly ....
   .... *Soronia* Er.
3. Mentum not emarginate anteriorly   *Lobiopa* Er.
   Mentum emarginate anteriorly ....*Amphotis* Er.

Phenolia Erichson

Phenolia Erichson, 1843, in Germar, Zeitschr. Ent., 4: 299.
Soronia (pars) Reitter, 1873, Syst. Eintheil, Nitid., p. 47.

The front not lobed over the insertion of the antennæ; eye facets about as in *Lobiopa,* coarser than in *Soronia* and *Amphotis;* mandibles bidentate at tip; antennal grooves parallel; labrum feebly bilobed; labial palpi incrassate; mentum distinctly pentagonal; prosternum behind the coxæ expanded and deflexed; elytra feebly costate; epipleuræ extending to apex of elytra but not to the suture; anterior tarsi feebly, middle more feebly, and posterior very feebly dilated.

Phenolia is Nearctic in distribution and contains only one variable species.

Phenolia grossa (Fabricius)

Nitidula grossa Fabricius, 1801, Syst. Eleuth., 1: 347.

This species is found beneath bark and in fungi from Canada and Maine to Wyoming and Texas.

Soronia Erichson

Soronia Erichson, 1843, in Germar, Zeitschr. Ent., 4: 277.

The front lobed over the insertion of the antennæ; eye facets about as in *Amphotis,* finer than in *Lobiopa;* mandibles bifid at tip, the inner cusp slightly proximal to the outer and smaller; antennal grooves strongly convergent posteriorly; labrum feebly bilobed or emarginate, labial palpi filiform, mentum rectangular with small process in center of anterior margin; elytra very feebly costate; epipleurae may extent to the suture; tarsi very feebly dilated; outline more oblong and less oval than in *Lobiopa.*

Although *Soronia* is widely distributed in the Old World, only three species are known from the New World, one each from North America, Brazil, and Mexico to Brazil. Blatchley and Hamilton each described a species from eastern United States. Both species, however, belong in *Lobiopa.*

Soronia guttulata (Leconte)

Lobiopa guttulata Leconte, 1863, Smiths. Misc. Coll., 6: 64.

Leconte described this species from a specimen collected by Ulke in Illinois. In the Leconte collection there is no specimen from Illinois, but there is one from Canada labelled "type" and one each from Marquette, Michigan and Arizona. It has been taken in New York, and specimens from Iowa, Oregon, and California (McCloud, Carrville, and Facht) have been seen. The dates of capture are from April to June 26.

Lobiopa Erichson

Lobiopa Erichson, 1843, in Germar, Zeitschr. Ent., 4: 291.
Cerophorus (pars) Castelnau, 1840, Hist. Nat. Col., 2: 10.
Soronia (pars) Reitter, 1873, Syst. Eintheil. Nitid., p. 46.
 Horn, 1879, Trans. Am. Ent. Soc., 7: 306.

Front lobed over the insertion of the antennæ; mandibles bifid at tip, the inner cusp may be smaller than the outer; eye facets about as in *Phenolia*, coarser than in *Soronia;* labrum feebly bilobed; labial palpi more or less incrassate; antennal grooves parallel; mentum rectangular with a small process at center of anterior margin; elytra not costate; epipleurae not extending around apex of elytra; tarsi very feebly dilated.

Lobiopa contains a number of species confined to the New World. In addition to the three species already in the North American list, one is transferred from *Soronia*, three are described as new, and one described as a *Soronia* is synonymized.

1. Six or seven distinct rows of setae on the disc of each
  elytron .... 2.

  About nine distinct rows of setæ on the disc of each
  elytron .... *setosa* Harold.

2. From above, eyes not as long as pronotal emargination
  is deep .... 3.

  From above, eyes as long or longer than pronotal emargination is deep .... 5.

3. Distinctly less than twice as long as wide .... 4.
  Twice as long as wide .... *oblonga* n. sp.

4. Submentum finely punctate, length 3.6-5.3 mm. ..
  .... *undulata* (Say).

  Submentum coarsely punctate, length 5.3-6.7 mm. ....
  .... *falli* n. sp.

5. Above with pubescence, setæ, and coarsely punctate,
  length more than 4.4 mm. .... 6.

  Above nearly glabrous, finely punctate, length 3.5-4.5
  mm. .... *brunnescens* Blatch.

6. Lateral margins narrowly explanate ....*punctata* n. sp.
  Lateral margins broadly explanate ...... *insularis* (Cast.).

Lobiopa setosa Harold

Fig. 5.

Lobiopa setulosa Leconte (non Erichson), 1863, Smiths. Misc. Coll., 4: 63.

Lobiopa setosa Harold, 1868, Col. Hefte, 4: 104.

Soronia undulata (pars) Horn, 1879, Trans. Am. Ent. Soc., 7: 307.

Soronia substriata Hamilton, 1893, Can. Ent., 25: 306.

Dr. Hugo Kahl kindly sent me the type of *substriata* Hamilton. After comparison with the type in the Leconte collection, *substriata* turns out to be a synonym of *setosa*. The type of *substriata* is one millimeter longer than Leconte's type, darker above, with slightly more pointed elytra. Since individuals in this genus are very variable, these differences are unimportant. This rare species tends to be broader, more depressed, duller, and darker than its closest relative *undulata*. Specimens have been seen ranging from Massachusetts to Utah, north to Kamloops, B. C., March 21. In Pennsylvania it has been found in May under the bark of maple (*Acer rubrum*).

Lobiopa oblonga new species

Fig. 6.

Length twice the width, oblong oval, feebly convex. Above dull rufo-piceous with faint, irregular, pale maculæ. Margins of thorax and elytra rufo-testaceous. Beneath, including antennæ and legs, dark rufo-testaceous. Head pubescent; closely, finely punctate; very broadly, shallowly impressed between the eyes. The lobes over the insertion of the antennæ more prominent than in all the other North American species except *falli* n. sp. Labial palpi incrassate. Prothorax more emarginate anteriorly than *brunnescens* but less so than the other North American species; with broadly explanate, flatly arcuate lateral margins; hind angles rather broadly rounded; hind margin feebly bisinuate; surface closely finely punctate, finely pubescent, sparsely covered with short pale setæ. Prosternal process relatively more narrow between the coxæ than in the other

species.   Visible part of scutellum forming an equilateral
triangle.   Elytra with broadly explanate, feebly arcuate
margins; closely, finely punctate; finely pubescent; each
elytron with six or seven rows of pale setæ. Beneath closely
finely punctate, rather sparsely pubescent. Length of holotype 5.0 mm., width 2.5 mm.; allotype 4.2 mm., width 2.2 mm.

Described from the female holotype, Marble Fork Bridge,
3000-5000 ft., Sequoia National Park, California, June 12,
1929; and male allotype, Upper Soda Spring, Siskiyou

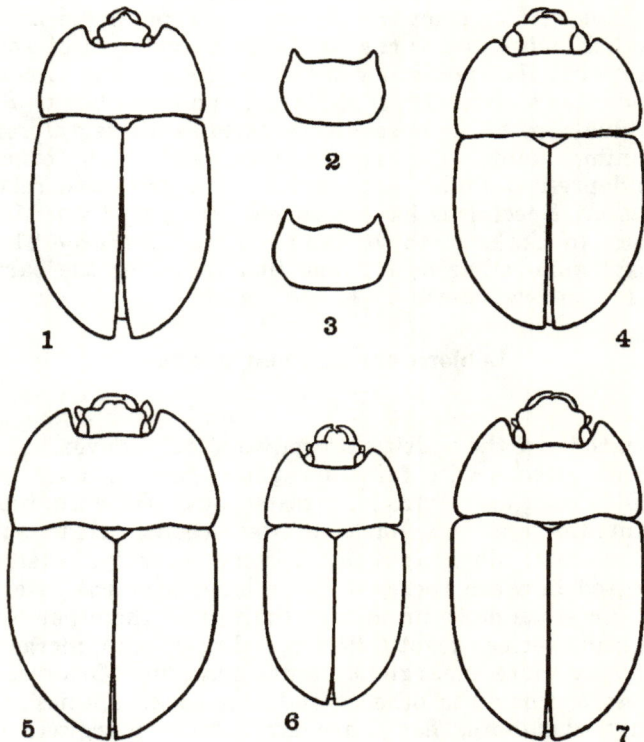

Figs. 1—7. 1, *Amphotis schwarzi* (cotype); 2, mentum of same; 3,
mentum of *A. ulkei* (topotype); 4, *Lobiopa punctata* n. sp. (holotype);
5, *L. setosa* (holotype of *substriata*); 6, *L. oblonga* n. sp. (holotype);
7, *L. falli* n. sp. (holotype).

County, California, Aug. 6, 1906, E. N Erhrkom collector;
both in the Van Dyke collection of the California Academy
of Sciences.

This species, apparently closest to *falli* n. sp., is distinctive in its oblong form. It is less convex than *brunnescens*,
punctata n. sp., and *falli* n. sp. but more convex than the
other species.

Lobiopa undulata (Say)

Nitidula undulata Say, 1825, Journ. Acad. N. S. Philad.,
    5: 179.

Soronia undulata Horn, 1879, Trans. Am. Ent. Soc., 7: 307.

Lobiopa undulata Sharp, 1890, Biol. Centr.-Amer. Col., vol.
    2, pt. 1, p. 321.

This species varies considerably in color, shape, and size
(3.6-5.3 mm.). It is found at sap in the spring and autumn
and hibernates beneath logs. The range is Maine and Michigan to Florida, Texas, and "northern Sonora" (Sharp).
Sharp's record may refer to the following new species.

Lobiopa falli new species

Fig. 7.

More oval than oblong; feebly convex. Above dull rufo-
piceous with the margins of the prothorax and elytra rufo-
testaceous. Also there is on the upper surface faint, irregular, pale maculæ, in particular usually a transverse pale
band at the posterior third extending half way across each
elytron. This band is more evident in *insularis* and *undulata*. Beneath rufo-piceous with the legs paler. Head with
a few, thick, erect setæ; pubescent; rather coarsely com-
pactly punctate; alutaceous; with a broad, transverse impression between the eyes; lobes over the insertion of the
antennæ very prominent, more so than in the other North
American species. Eyes of ordinary size. Labial palpi
incrassate. Prothorax as emarginate anteriorly as in *setosa*
and *undulata*, more so than in *insularis*, in which the prothorax is more emarginate than in *oblonga* n. sp. Prothorax
with lateral margins broadly explanate, evenly and flatly
arcuate, narrowing shortly before the acute hind angles;

hind margin distinctly bisinuate; surface closely and rather coarsely punctate, alutaceous, pubescent, sparsely covered with thick setæ. Visible part of the scutellum forming a strongly transverse triangle. Elytra with broadly explanate margins; rather close, coarse, obsolete punctures; alutaceous; finely pubescent; each elytron with about seven rows of thick setæ. Beneath coarsely punctate, sparsely and finely pubescent. Length 5.3-6.7 mm., width 3.1-4.1 mm.

Holotype female, allotype male, and 2 paratypes from Arizona in the Leconte collection, Museum Comp. Zool.; 14 paratypes from 6-7000 ft., Strattòn, S. Catalina Mts., July 27, 1917, W. M. Wheeler collector; 1 paratype, Patagonia Mts., Arizona, July 20-Aug. 6, 1930 in the Mus. Comp. Zool. In the U.S.N.M. 25 paratypes from Oracle, Arizona, October 7; 4 paratypes from Palmerlee, Arizona; 7 paratypes from the Santa Rita Mts. and Fort Grant, Arizona. In the University of Kansas collection 4 paratypes from the Chiricahua and Huachuca Mts., July-Aug. One paratype each from Prescott, Arizona, Chisos Mts. and Alpine, Texas, July, in the collection of H. C. Fall. Also 2 paratypes from the Huachuca Mts., 2 paratypes from Oracle, June 7, and 3 paratypes from Globe, Arizona in the collection of the author.

This species varies in outline and in color. In the pale specimens the maculation is most evident, whereas in those that are piceous the maculation is not discernible. The species is distinctive in the prominent lobes over the insertion of the antennae, transverse scutellum, and the unusual covering of thick setæ. It is apparently related to *undulata;* in fact Mr. Fall has specimens of *undulata* from Texas which approach *falli* in the maculation, setæ and lobes over the insertion of the antennæ. But in *falli* the scutellum is more transverse, punctures beneath more coarse, and shape usually more oval.

Lobiopa brunnescens (Blatchley)

Soronia brunnescens Blatchley, 1917, Can. Ent., 49: 238.

This species is definitely a *Lobiopa* and related to *insularis.* The types are from Dunedin, Florida, June 10. In addition there are specimens in the U.S.N.M. from Coving-

ton, La., June 13 which differ from the types in showing
faint maculation similar to that in *insularis* and slightly
coarser punctation of the prothorax.   It is remarkable that
F. M. Jones collected a specimen Aug. 21, 1931 on Martha's
Vineyard, Mass.   This specimen, which is in the Boston
Soc. Nat. Hist., has no maculation as in the types.   Apparently this record cannot be accounted for by hurricanes,
since the last one passed over Martha's Vineyard in 1928.

Lobiopa punctata new species

Fig. 4.

Oblong oval, rather strongly convex, shining, rufo-testaceous above and beneath.   Head sparsely pubescent, closely,
coarsely punctate; broadly impressed between the eyes;
lobes over the insertion of the antennæ more transversely
produced than in the other North American species; labial
palpi incrassate.   Prothorax as emarginate in front as
brunnescens, therefore less emarginate than in the other
North American species; lateral margins narrowly explanate
and evenly arcuate; hind angles broadly rounded and obtusely angled; hind margin feebly bisinuate; surface closely,
coarsely punctate, with sparse pubescence and with sparser
small setæ.   Prosternal process only slightly reflexed behind the coxæ.   Elytra with narrowly explanate, feebly
arcuate lateral margins; eight rows of small setæ; finely
pubescent; each elytron with two pale spots extending
across anterior median agle, a transverse pale band across
inner half at posterior third, and center somewhat darker.
Beneath closely, coarsely punctate, finely pubescent.   Length
5.2-4.5 mm., width 3.1-2.5 mm.

Described from four males; holotype and paratype from
Miami, Florida, March 11, 1924 in the collection of H. C.
Fall; one paratype from Miami, Florida, March 31 in the
Van Dyke collection in the Calif. Acad. of Sciences; and a
paratype from Balaclava, Jamaica, A. E. Wright, in the
Mus. Comp. Zoology.

This species is apparently closest to *brunnescens*, particularly in the convexity of the body and degree of emargination of the pronotum.   It differs from *brunnescens* in its
larger size, much coarser punctation and pubescence, nar-

rower lateral margins, and in the prosternal process being
only slightly arched longitudinally between the coxæ; whereas in *brunnescens* the prosternal process is strongly arched
between the coxæ and reflexed posteriorly.

Amphotis Erichson

Amphotis, Erichson, 1843, in Germar, Zeitschr. Ent., 4: 290.
Soronia (pars) Horn, 1879, Trans. Amer. Ent. Soc., 7: 287.

Front lobed over the insertion of the antennæ; labrum
feebly bilobed; mandibles bifid at tip; labial palpi filiform;
eye facets about as in *Soronia*, finer than in *Lobiopa*; antennal grooves parallel; mentum emarginate; elytra distinctly costate; epipleurae extend to suture; tarsi feebly
dilated.

Amphotis contains two North American and three European species.

Amphotis ulkei Leconte

Fig. 3.

Amphotis ulkei Leconte, 1866, Proc. Ac. N. S. Philad., p. 376.
Soronia ulkei Horn, 1879, Trans. Amer. Ent. Soc., 7: 307.

This species extends from Massachusetts to the District
of Columbia in the nests of *Crematogaster lineolata*, *Formica
schaufussi*, and *Formica integra*. It is strictly myrmecophilous in the early spring but in the fall of the year is
found in decaying fungi.

Amphotis schwarzi Ulke

Fig. 1, 2.

Amphotis schwarzi Ulke, 1887, Ent. Amer., 3: 77.

Dr. Hugo Kahl of the Carnegie Museum has kindly loaned
me the types (collected by Schwarz June 17 at Ft. Monroe,
Virginia), all of which are testaceous. Two specimens in
the U.S.N.M. from Mobile, Alabama, December 6 are dark
testaceous, and a specimen from Southern Pines, N. C.,
March 3 in the collection of C. A. Frost is rufo-piceous. This
species differs from *ulkei* in the additional two costæ on each
elytron and in the narrower and less emarginate mentum.

THE INTERRELATIONSHIPS AND LINES OF DESCENT OF LIVING INSECTS

By G. C. CRAMPTON,

Massachusetts State College, Amherst, Mass.

The lines of descent shown in the accompanying phylogenetic tree should be interpreted as though the figure were a three dimensional one (as is indicated by the basal attachments of the branches of the tree), since the usual method of portraying the lines of descent in the form of a dichotomously branching tree, drawn in one plane, does not bring out the fact that several lines of descent may converge upon a common ancestry, and does not indicate the complicated interrelationships of these lines of descent at all accurately. In fact, sections of cones made up of converging lines would better illustrate the fact that some lines of descent intergrade "horizontally" as well as "vertically," but the method of illustrating the interrelationships of the lines of descent shown in the accompanying figure will serve well enough for all practical purposes, if the figure is interpreted as a three dimensional one.

The hypothetical "Protomalacostraca" shown at the base of the phylogenetic tree, represent the extinct common ancestors of the higher Crustacea (such as the Tanaidacea, Mysidacea, Anaspidacea, etc.) insects and "myriopods". The character of the head, with its sessile eyes, the monocondylar mandibles, with their differentiated incisor and projecting molar regions, the large paragnaths, the slender multiarticulate, cerci-like uropods, and other feature of the Tanaidacea (such as *Tanais*, *Apseudes*, *Leptochelia*, etc.) are strikingly suggestive of the precursors of similar structures in the Machiloid insects, and the ancestors of the Tanaidacea (represented by the hypothetical "Prototanaidacea in the diagram) must have been extremely closely related to the more direct ancestors of the Hexapoda (represented in the diagram by the hypothetical "Protohexapoda") and those of the "'Myriopoda" (represented in the diagram by the hypothetical "Protosymphyla" — which would include the direct ancestors of the Chilopoda, Pauropoda, etc., as well as those of the Symphyla themselves).

The hypothetical "Protapterygota," or common ancestors of the Apterygota (and consequently the ultimate ancestors of the Pterygota also), are best represented by the *Machilis*-like Apterygota, although some investigators insist that the Dicellura (such as *Campodea, Anajapyx, Japyx*, etc.), or the Protura, are the most primitive or most "ancestral" insects, despite the fact that the *Machilis*-like Apterygota are morphologically the most primitive (and hence the most "ancestral") of all insects. Some of the features which indicate that *Machilis* (or the family Machilidæ), rather than the Dicellura or other forms, represents the ancestral type better than any other living insect, is indicated by the following facts. (1) *Machilis* has more abdominal limbs (represented by eight pairs of distinct, styli-bearing coxites) than any other insect, including *Campodea* and other Dicellura. (2) The abdominal limbs, or coxites, of *Machilis* project free and distinct from the sternites (and the coxites of the ninth segment are hugely developed), while the abdominal limbs of the Dicellura, for example, are reduced to mere styli-bearing areas scarcely distinguishable from the abdominal sternites with which they have merged — and no other Apterygota have more than three pairs of abdominal limbs. (3) The cerci, or limbs of the eleventh abdominal segment, are larger and better developed than those of any other insect. (4) The terminal abdominal segments of *Machilis* are more distinct, or less fused, than those of the Dicellura, for example. (5) The thoracic terga are better developed and overlap the lateral regions in a more primitive, or Crustaceoid fashion, in *Machilis* (and *Lepisma*), while in other Apterygota the thoracic terga are not of this type. (6) The thoracic limbs are best developed in *Machilis*, and bear styli (epipodites?) in the Machilidae alone. (7) *Machilis* has primitive compound eyes structurally similar to those of Crustacea, and also has well developed ocelli (which likewise occur in certain trilobites, Anaspidacea, etc.), while the Dicellura are eyeless — as is also the case in the Protura (which likewise lack antennae). (8) *Machi-*

lis has preserved the primitive archicephalic or supramandibular suture, characteristic of such Crustacea as *Branchippus, Anaspides*, etc. (9) The huge flagelliform antennæ of *Machilis* are the most like those of trilobites and other primitive arthropods. (10) The huge monocondylar mandibles of *Machilis* are better developed and are more Crustaceoid (with separate incisor and elongated molar regions) than the reduced and highly specialized mandibles of the Dicellura and Protura. (11) The well developed paragnaths (superlinguæ) of *Machilis* are larger and more Crustaceoid than those of other Apterygota. (12) The well developed maxillæ of *Machilis*, with their huge limb-like palpi, are far more primitive than those of any other insects. (13) The lacinial fringes of *Machilis* are more primitively Crustaceoid than those of other insects. (14) The labial palpi etc., of *Machilis* are better developed, and are of a more primitive character than those of other Apterygotan insects. (15) The traces of the second maxillæ forming the under lip are more distinct in *Machilis* than in other Apterygota. (16) The head of *Machilis* is of the ectognathous type, and is much more primitive than the entognathous type (with overgrown mouthparts) found in the Dicellura and Protura, etc.

There are many more features which might be cited to prove that *Machilis* is more primitive or "ancestral" than any other insect, but the facts cited above should be sufficient to convince any impartial investigator that *Machilis* is the most ancestral of all insects. Furthermore, its numerous unmistakably Crustaceoid features clearly prove that *Machilis*, and the other primitive insects descended from similar ancestors, were derived from Crustacea resembling the "Prototanaidacea" in many respects. The well known fact that many Apterygota exhibit striking similarities to various types of "myriopods," merely indicates that both insects and "myriopods" were ultimately descended from the same (Crustacean) ancestry — and the Crustacea are the only intermediate forms serving to connect the insects and "myriopods" with the trilobites and other primitive forms at the base of the common arthropodan stem.

If the Machilidæ are the most primitive or "ancestral" insects, it is obviously misleading to insist that the Dicellura (such as *Campodea, Anajapyx,* etc.) are the most ancestral insects, since they are much more specialized than the Machilidæ. In fact, the Dicellura could readily be derived from a slender blind *Nicoletia* type of Lepismatid Tysanuroid insect (descended from Machilis like forebears) but by no stretch of the imagination could the primitive *Machilis* type of insect be derived from any Dicelluran type — which should be the case if the Dicellura represent the ancestral insects (leading back to some type of "myriopod").

Because they have mouthparts of the concealed type, the Dicellura are sometimes grouped with the Collembola (and Protura) in the division Endognatha, in contradistinction to the Ectognatha, or Thysanuroid forms with mouthparts of the exposed type. The modifications of the mouthparts of the Dicellura, however, are not very similar to the modifications exhibited by the Collembola and Protura; and the Dicellura are only very distantly related to the other "endognathous" Apterygota, while the occurrence of cerci, and styli-bearing coxites, in the Dicellura, allies them more closely with the Thysanuroid Apterygota. It is therefore preferable to unite the Dicellura with the Lepismatidæ (Thysanura) and Machilidae (Protothysanura) in the section *Styligera,* characterized by the occurrence of styli-bearing coxites, and cerci, as opposed to the *Astyligera* (Collembola and Protura), in which these structures are lacking. The Dicellura were possibly derived from some *Niceletia*-like Lepismatid insect, and the Lepismatidæ themselves were apparently derived from ancestors closely allied to the Machilidæ. The Lepismatidæ, in turn, serve to connect the *Machilis*-like ancestors of the Apterygota with the ancestors of the Pterygota, which are best represented by "larval" Ephemerida (which have three caudal filaments like those of Thysanuroid Apterygota), so that the Lepismatid line of development is an extremely important one for the study of the evolution of the higher insects.

The Protura are the most primitive representatives of the section Astyligera, although they have lost the eyes and antennæ, and their mouthparts are rather highly specialized. They differ from the rest of insects by the fact that they exhibit a postembryonic increase in the number of segments (they have nine abdominal segments as "larvae", and eleven as adults) and are sometimes called Anamerentoma, in contradistinction to the rest of insects (called Holomerentoma) which exhibit no such postembryonic increase in segmentation. Their line of development evidently branched off at the base of the Apterygotan stem, and ends blindly, unless it leads to the Collembola.

The line of development of the Collembola is a rather isolated one, but the Collembola resemble the Protura in that they have a ventral head-groove, a postantennal organ, and similarly modified endognathous mouthparts, etc. The Collembolan line of development may have branched off from that of the Protura, although it is also possible that the Collembola represent degenerate offshoots of the primitive Machiloid ancestors of the Apterygota, since the lacinial fringes of such Collembola as *Tetrodontophora* are very like those of certain Machilids. In any case, the line of development of the Collembola is a very isolated one, and has no significance for tracing the lines of descent of other insects.

As was mentioned before, the "larvæ" (naiads) of the Ephemerida, with their *Lepisma*-like terminal filaments (a pair of cerci and an unpaired median terminal filament), and their large paragnaths (superlinguæ), and primitive type of mandibles, provided with a lacinia mobilis like the mandibles of higher Crustacea, etc., are the most archaic representatives of the Pterygota, and suggest that winged insects arose from *Lepisma*-like forebears, which lead back to the Crustaceoid Apterygota such as *Machilis*. "Larval" Ephemerida and Odonata agree in having the lacinia and galea united to form a single lobe in the maxilla, and "larval" Ephemerida and Zygoptera agree in having an unpaired median terminal structure, represented by a gill plate in the Zygopteran naiad, and by a terminal filament in the Ephemerid naiad.

The Ephemerida, Odonata, Megasecoptera and Palæodictyoptera, etc., comprise the division of Pterygota called the *Palæopterygota*, characterized by their inability to lay the wings back along the body in repose. They consequently do not develop a basal fold of the wing, and do not have more than two or three axillary sclerites. Their wings are primitively homonomous, and a neala is not developed in them. The rest of the Fterygota comprise the division *Neopterygota,* characterized by their ability to lay the wings back along the body in repose. They consequently develop a basal fold in the wing, and have more than two or three axillary sclerites. Their wings were originally heteronomous, with an anal fan in the hind wing (though this is lost in many of their descendents), and a neala is developed in the postero-basal region of the wings. This division of the Pterygota is a much more fundamental one than the usual division into Exopterygota and Endopterygota (on the basis of the external or internal development of the wings) which makes an unnatural separation of closely related forms, and lumps together others which are not at all closely related.

The common ancestors of all of these forms are represented in the diagram by the hypothetical "Protopalæodictyoptera". The Palæodictyoptera are the nearest known representatives of these common ancestors, and represent their direct descendents. The Ephemerida were probably derived from the common ancestors of the group by way of the Protephemerida, while the Odonata were derived from them by way of some unknown, extinct forms, to which the Protodonata are very closely related; and the line of descent of the Megasecoptera apparently branched off from the common Palæodictyopteriod stock near the origin of the ancestors of the Odonata. The Odonata are the most "Orthopteroid" of the above-mentioned insects, while the Ephemerida are the most primitive living representatives of the group. The Ephemerida and Protephemerida might be grouped into a superorder called the Panephemeroptera (or Ephemeropteria), characterized by the occurrence of three caudal filaments in many members of the superorder, while the Odonata and Protodonata might be grouped in a second superorder, the Pantyloptera (or Tylopteria) characterized by the skewness of the thorax etc., but too little is known of the morphological details of the fossil forms to enable us to group them correctly at this time.

The Neopterygota may be grouped into three divisions called the Orthopteroid insects (Paurometabola or Orthopteradelphia), the Hemipteroid insects (Parametabola or Hemipteradelphia), and the Neuropteroid insects (Holometabola or Neuropteradelphia) ; and the Orthopteroid insects represent the ancestral types of the group as nearly as any known forms. The Orthopteriod insects were apparently not derived directly from the Palæodictyoptera, but were probably derived from the Palæodictyopteran stock by way of *Synarmoge* (or *Synarmogoge* as it is sometimes spelled). Since only a fragment of one wing of *Synarmogoge* is known, however, all that can be said concerning it is that it exhibits certain characters intermediate between the Palæodictyoptera and the Protorthoptera.

The Protorthoptera, shown at the base of the lines of descent of the higher insects in the accompanying phylogenetic tree, include the Protoblattids (which have a demarked claval region in the fore wings) as well as the Protorthoptera in the narrower sense (which have no demarked claval area), since the Protoblattids and Protorthoptera merge so indistinguishably that they may be combined into a single ancestral group from which all of the higher insects were ultimately derived. The Protoblattids are the most primitive representatives of the group, and are more like the direct ancestors of the Blattids, Mantids and Isoptera, while the other members of the Protorthoptera are somewhat closer to the direct ancestors of the Orthoptera.

The Orthopteroid insects are characterized by the fact that the cerci are well developed and the parapodial plates (paraprocts) are distinct in all of the members of the group. An anal fan is developed in the hind wings of most of the Orthopteroid insects, but in some of them, such as the Embiida and Isoptera (excepting *Mastotermes*) the wings are secondarily homonomous. The Orthopteroid insects have been grouped into three superorders called the Panorthoptera (or Orthopteria), the Panplecoptera (or Plecopteria), and the Panisoptera (or Isopteria).

The superorder Panisoptera (Isopteria) includes the Palæoptera (Blattids and Mantids) and the Isoptera, and is characterized by the fact that the lateral cervical sclerites are contiguous in the midventral line, the mesothoracic trochantins do not unite basally with the episternum ; a claval area is usually demarked in the fore wings, and the seventh abdominal sternite projects below the ovipositor in the members of this superorder. The Blattids have preserved the most primitive venation of any living members of the superorder, while the Isoptera have preserved the various features of the body in as primitive a condition as any members of the superorder. These insects are the most primitive of the Orthopteroid insects, and are practically the direct descendents of the Protoblattid type of Protorthoptera.

The Embiids and Plecoptera are included in a superorder called the Panplecoptera (or Plecopteria), characterized by the fact that the postscutellum of the mesothorax is well developed, and the trochantin of the mesothorax unites basally with the episternum above it, in the members of this superorder. The mesothoracic coxæ tend to become ring-like rather than conical, and the tarsi are trimerous. The eighth and ninth abdominal segments are not greatly narrowed in the females of these insects, which are ovipositor-less. The Plecoptera are usually grouped with the Odonata and Ephemerida (rather than with the Embiids among the Orthopteroid insects) but the character of their thoracic sclerites is so strikingly similar, and the venation of the fossil forms intergrades so markedly, that there can be no doubt that the Embiids and Plecoptera are extremely closely related, and were descended from a common Protorthopteran ancestry. The fossil Protoperlaria are rather specialized Plecopteroid insects which branched off at the base of the Plecopteran stem, and the fossil Protembiids apparently branched off at the base of the Embiid stem, but the actual Protorthopteran ancestors from which all of these insects were ultimately derived have not as yet been discovered.

The Orthoptera (including the Grylloblattidæ) and the Cheleutoptera, or Phasmida, and possibly the Dermaptera also (although the closest affinities of the Dermaptera may be with the Blattoid insects comprising the superorder Panisoptera), are included in the superorder Panorthoptera (or Orthopteria), characterized by the huge development of the anal fan, and the consequent reduction of the preanal region of the hind wings. The ovipositor is well developed in most of them, and is overlapped basally by the eighth abdominal sternite (excepting the Dermaptera, which may not belong in this superorder). The male genitalia are usually rather symmetrically developed and the cerci frequently bear mesal prongs, etc., in the members of this superorder.

These insects are the more or less direct descendents of the Protorthoptera in the restricted sense (*i.e.*, the Protorthopteran forms other than the Protoblattids), and their most primitive representatives are the Grylloblattids, which are practically living Protorthoptera, closely related to the Stenopelmatoid Orthoptera (including the *Gryllacris*-types). The latter are connected with the Grylloid Orthoptera by the Prophalangopsidæ (and Tridactyloid types), and are connected with the Acridoidea by the Tettigoniidæ (unless the Tridactyloidea furnish the intermediate forms leading to the Acridoidea).

The Hemipteroid or Psocoid insects comprise the division Hemipteradelphia, or Parametabola, characterized by the development of a mesal detached lacinial structure forming a setiform, or a chisel-like portion of the maxilla (excepting the Zoraptera, which have a normal type of maxilla). The insects belonging to this division may be grouped into two superorders, namely the Panpsocoptera (Psocopteria) including the Psocoptera, Mallophaga and Anoplura, and the Panhemiptera (Hemipteria) including the Hemiptera and Thysanoptera. The lacinial structures are usually chisel-like in the members of the superorder Panpsocoptera, and are setiform in the members of the superorder Panhemiptera.

The Zoraptera are the most primitive representatives of the Hemipteroid insects, and exhibit so many characters suggestive of a close relationship to the Isoptera, that this might be taken to indicate that they and the Hemipteroid insects in general were derived from the same Protorthopteroid ancestry as the Isoptera were. On the other hand, the venation of the Zoraptera shows that they are members of the order Psocoptera, closely related to such Psocids as *Archipsocus* and *Embidopsocus* which exhibit some characters suggestive of a derivation from Embiid-like ancestors; and the Psocoptera in general were probably derived from the common Protorthopteroid ancestors of the Isoptera and Embioptera. The Mallophaga are undoubtedly descended from ancestors extremely closely related to the Psocoptera, and may represent merely degenerate wingless

Psocoptera. The Anoplura were probably derived from ancestors closely allied to the Mallophaga; and all of these insects are sometimes grouped together as Corrodentia, although they are apparently worthy of ordinal rank.

The mouthparts of the Thysanoptera (which have distinct maxillary and labial palpi) are much more primitive than those of the Hemiptera, and it is possible that the Thysanoptera were descended from a slightly more primitive type than the Hemiptera were. At any rate, the Thysanoptera were apparently descended from Protorthopteroid ancestors very closely related to those from which the Hemiptera were derived, and these ancestors evidently resembled the Psocoptera very closely. The Hemiptera were evidently descended from the same Protorthopteroid ancestors from which the Psocoptera were derived, and the Psocoptera have departed the least of any living insects from the types ancestral to the Hemiptera. Not only does the venation of living Psocoptera parallel that of certain Hemiptera-Homoptera strikingly closely, but the venation of certain fossil Hemiptera merges with that of certain fossil Psocoptera so intimately that there can be no doubt that the two groups had a common Protorthopteroid ancestry; and the fact that many Hemiptera have a claval area demarked in their fore wings may possibly indicate that their Protorthopteroid ancestors resembled Protoblattids (in which the claval area is also demarked) in some respects. At any rate, the Hemiptera could not possibly have been derived from such Palæodictyopteroid insects as *Eugereon* (mistakenly called "Protohemiptera"), since *Eugereon* belongs in the section Palæopterygota, whose members are incapable of laying the wings along the body in repose, while the Hemiptera were evidently descended from ancestors capable of laying the wings back along the body in repose, and the venation of primitive Hemiptera does not bear the slightest resemblance to that of *Eugereon*.

Some Parametabola (Hemipteroid insects) parallel the Holometabola remarkably closely in their method of development, and indicate very clearly that complete metamorphosis arose through an increasing divergence between the immature and mature forms (rather than through the precocious emergence of "free-living embryos", as certain investigators insist is the case) as the result of mutational changes in the genetic or hereditary material of these insects. Thus in larval Aleurodidæ, for example, the wings arise internally from wing buds, and become external in a quiescent pupal stage,[1] as they do in the Holometabola; and the development of certain Thysanoptera and other Hemipteroid insects clearly suggests the beginning of Holometabolism.

In this connection, it may be noted that the internal development of the wings in the Aleurodidæ, and the external development of the wings in the closely related Psyllidæ and other Hemiptera-Homoptera, clearly indicates that the usual division of winged insects into Exopterygota and Endopterygota, on the basis of the external or internal development of the wings, is utterly meaningless from the standpoint of phylogeny. Such a division would group together the remotely related Palæodictyopteroid, Orthopteroid and Hemipteroid insects, and would separate the Holometabola from their Orthopteroid relatives, etc.; and this division of winged insects should be abandoned in favor of the more natural and fundamental grouping of winged insects into Palæopterygota and Neopterygota (on the basis of the method of folding the wings in repose), since this grouping does not separate the Holometabola from their Hemipteroid and Orthopteroid relatives.

The section Holometabola (or Neuropteradelphia) includes all insects with complete metamorphosis, and the group is evidently a monophyletic one since their larvæ intergrade so intimately that all of the Holometabola must have had a common ancestry. The fact that some Holometabola are somewhat Psocid-like, and the fact that some Psocoid (or Hemipteroid) insects, such as the Aleurodidæ, etc., clearly foreshadow Holometabolism, would seem to indicate that both Parametabola (Hemipteroids) and Holometabola were descended from closely allied Protorthoptera —which may have resembled the Protoblattids venationally, although their bodies probably exhibited features occurring in the ancestral Isoptera, Embiids and Grylloblattids.

The most primitive representatives of the Holometabola are the Neuroptera, Hymenoptera and Coleoptera, and their

[1] A quiescent pupal stage is also foreshadowed in the Isoptera.

complicated interrelationships (both "vertical" and "horizontal" in the phylogenetic groupings) make it very difficult to decide how to distribute them in the superorders of the Holometabola. There are at least two superorders of Holometabola, in one of which, the Pancoleoptera or Coleopteria (including the Coleoptera and Strepsiptera), the mesothoracic coxae are not divided into eucoxa and meron, the mesothoracic postscutellum is not well developed, and the cerci are usually not developed, while in the other superorder called the Panneuroptera or Neuropteria (including the Neuroptera, Mecoptera, Diptera, Trichoptera, Lepidoptera and Siphonaptera) the mesothoracic coxae are divided into a eucoxa and meron, the mesothoracic postscutellum is usually well developed, and cerci are frequently present.

The Coleoptera are the most Orthopteroid representatives of the Holometabola, and are strikingly similar to the Dermaptera in numerous features of the body. It is possible that the Coleoptera and Dermaptera were derived from Protorthopteroid ancestors which had bodies somewhat like those of the primitive Isoptera, while the wings of their ancestors may have been like those of certain Protoblattid Protorthoptera. At any rate, the wings of the so-called Protocoleoptera (such as *Protocoleus*) are very Orthopteroid, and may have been derived from a Protorthopteroid type related to the Protoblattids.

The most primitive Coleoptera are the Cantharoid (Lampyroid) beetles, and the Strepsiptera may have been derived from ancestors resembling Cantharoid beetles in some respects. The larvæ of the Strepsiptera are very Meloid in appearance, while the adult Strepsiptera resemble Rhipiphorid beetles in some respects, so that it is very probable that the Strepsiptera were derived from a Coleopteroid stock, although the exact character of their ancestors has not been determined.

The Neuroptera have retained the most primitive type of venation occurring in any Holometabola (with the possible exception of the Mecoptera), and the structures of the body of the primitive Sialid Neuroptera suggest that their ancestors had bodies resembling those of primitive Isoptera and Embiids in many respects, while the venation of the

Corydalid Neuroptera is rather suggestive of that of certain Protoblattid Protorthoptera. The venation of the Protorthopteroid insect *Metropator* (which is regarded as a "Palæodictyopteroid" insect by Handlirsch) exhibits certain features suggestive of the precursors of the Sialid type of venation, but *Metropator* is an oligoneurous form (with few veins) and it is hardly probable that the more richly veined (polyneurous) types of Neuroptera, especially the fossil forms, were derived from the oligoneurous *Metropator* type of Protorthopteroid insect. In fact, it is very probable that the Protorthopteroid ancestors of the Neuroptera were both oligoneurous and polyneurous, and both tendencies would naturally reappear in their Neuropterous descendents if both tendencies occurred in the ancestral stock. Some investigators consider that the venation of the Neuroptera indicates that they were derived from Palæodictyoptera, but the Neuroptera are clearly Neopterygota capable of laying the wings back along the body in repose, and their larvae intergrade extremely closely with those of the Coleoptera, clearly indicating that the Neuroptera were derived from the same Protorthopteroid ancestors as the Coleoptera, and the venation of the primitive Neuroptera might readily be derived from the type exhibited by certain Protoblattid Protorthoptera.

The Mecoptera are extremely closely related to the Neuroptera, and were evidently derived from the same Protorthopteroid ancestors from which the Neuroptera were descended. The venation of the primitive Mecoptera suggests that their ancestors were similar to the Protoblattid Protorthoptera in certain respects, although Tillyard considers that the Mecoptera were derived from ancestors of the *Metropator* type, and Tillyard likewise considers that the Mecoptera are more primitive than the Neuroptera. The head and mouthparts of the Mecoptera are more specialized than those of the Sialid Neuroptera, however, and the thoracic sclerites of the Neuroptera are of a much more primitive type than those of the Mecoptera, while some Neuroptera such as *Raphidia* have retained an Orthopteroid ovipositor which is lost in typical Mecoptera, so that the Neuroptera are more primitive, in general, than the Mecoptera are, and have departed less than the Mecoptera have, from the ancestral Holometabolous stock, which was probably a Protorthopteran type with body structures like those of primitive Isoptera and Embiids, and with a venation resembling that of certain Protoblattids. Handlirsch would derive the Mecoptera from Megasecoptera, but the Megasecoptera belong in the section Palæopterygota, whose members are incapable of laying the wings back along the body in repose, while the Mecoptera are clearly Neopterygota capable of laying the wings back along the body in repose, and the resemblance between the venation of certain Mecoptera and Megasecoptera is apparently the result of convergence.

The Diptera were undoubtedly descended from Mecoptera-like forebears, as is evidenced by all of their structural features; and fossils such as *Aristopsyche* (called Paratrichoptera or Protodiptera), which have a venation strikingly suggestive of the ancestors of the Diptera, merge so indistinguishably with the Mecoptera, that it is very doubtful that they are worthy of ordinal rank, and it is preferable to group them with the Mecoptera as a suborder of Mecoptera. Among the living Mecoptera, such forms as *Nannochorista* have preserved numerous features suggestive of the ancestors of the Diptera,[2] and clearly indicate that the labella of Diptera, for example, are merely modified segments of the labial palpi.

The Trichoptera have likewise preserved a great number of characters strikingly suggestive of the precursors of the Diptera, but the Trichoptera are more closely allied to the Lepidoptera than any other insects. In fact, the Rhyacophilid Trichoptera merge so indistinguishably with the Micropterygid Lepidoptera that it is very doubtful if the two groups are worthy of ordinal rank, although it is preferable to treat them as distinct orders for the sake of convenience. Fossils such as *Belmontia* (usually placed in a distinct order the Paramecoptera or Prototrichoptera) are strikingly suggestive of the common ancestors of the Trichoptera and Lepidoptera and lead back to ancestors

[2]The Tanyderidae and Trichoceridae are the most primitive living Diptera, and the Anisopodidae are very like the ancestors of the Brachycera, whose most primitive representatives are the Therevidae and Rhagionidae (Leptidae), while the Syrphidae have departed but little from the ancestors of the Cyclorrhapha.

resembling the fossil Mecoptera. The venation of *Belmontia* is so like that of certain Rhyacophilid Trichoptera that the differences hardly seem to be of ordinal value. At any rate, the Trichoptera have departed the least of any living insects from the ancestors of the Lepidoptera, and the Mecoptera are the nearest living representatives of the forms ancestral to the Trichoptera.

The origin and closest affinities of the Siphonaptera, or fleas, is still a subject of much dispute, and it is impossible to decide the question in the present state of our knowledge of the group. It is quite evident, however, that the Siphonaptera resemble both Diptera and Trichoptera in numerous features of their larval and adult anatomy, and this probably indicates that the fleas were descended from the common ancestors of the Diptera and Trichoptera. Since the Mecoptera are the nearest living representatives of the common ancestors of the Diptera and Trichoptera, the fleas were doubtless derived from Mecopteroid ancestors as yet unknown.

The Hymenoptera combine in themselves so many characters occurring in both the Coleopteroid and the Mecopteroid insects that it is very difficult to determine their closest affinities, although they have a greater number of characters in common with the Mecopteroid insects than with any other group, and their larvae (particularly those of the sawflies) are strikingly similar to larval Mecoptera, Lepidoptera, etc. These facts may be interpreted as indicating that the Hymenoptera should be grouped with the Mecopteroid insects in the superorder Panneuroptera (Neuropteria), but since the Hymenoptera are in many respects intermediate between the Coleopteroid and Mecopteroid insects their annectant character may be better indicated by placing them in a distinct superorder, the Panhymenoptera (or Hymenopteria), occupying a position intermediate between the Mecopteroid insects (Panneuroptera) and Coleopteroid insects (Pancoleoptera), and characterized by the occurrence of an ovipositor (represented by a saw or a sting), forcipate male genitalia, cerci, an Orthopteroid head, etc., and by the absence of the meron in the mesothoracic coxæ.

Tillyard considers that the Hymenoptera were derived

from the so-called "Protohymenoptera", which have been shown by Carpenter to be merely modified Megasecoptera, having nothing to do with the true ancestors of the Hymenoptera. The Megasecoptera belong in the division Palæopterygota, whose members are incapable of laying the wings back along the body in repose, while the Hymenoptera were evidently descended from ancestors which were capable of laying the wings back along the abdomen in repose. Their ancestors apparently were Protorthoptera with bodies like those of primitive Isoptera and Embiids, while the venation was probably like that of certain Protoblattids. In other words, the Hymenoptera were descended from a common ancestry with the Sialid Neuroptera (and the Lampyroid Coleoptera), and their line of descent also merges with that of the Mecoptera and Trichoptera, or branches off from the common stem near the point of origin of the lines of descent of the Mecopteroid insects. The most primitive living representatives of the Hymenoptera are the Xyelidæ, and the Cephidæ are the nearest representatives of the ancestors of the higher Hymenoptera (or Clistogastra), whose most primitive representatives are the Trigonalidæ.

The views briefly summarized above, have already been presented in a series of papers dealing with the comparative morphology of recent insects in the light of what is known of the fossil forms, but since these views differ very radically from those commonly accepted by recent writers, or by those who have reviewed the recent progress in insect phylogeny, they have not been taken into consideration by recent writers. When a more extensive study of the available evidence is made, however, it becomes readily apparent that many of the currently accepted views are quite untenable; and the foregoing brief summary of certain alternative views on the subject has been made in order to call attention to the fact that the currently accepted views concerning the origin and interrelationships of the insectan orders are not the only possible ones, or necessarily the correct ones, and some consideration should also be given to these alternative views if they are evidently more nearly in accord with the available evidence on the subject.

PSYCHE, VOL. XLV PLATE 17

TP:pp183-84
removed placed in front
of Vol..

Binding Unit..

PSYCHE

INDEX TO VOL. XLV, 1938

INDEX TO AUTHORS

INDEX TO SUBJECTS

All new genera, new species and new names are printed in SMALL CAPITAL LETTERS.

PIN-LABELS IN MULTIPLES OF 1000, ALIKE

One Dollar Per Thousand

Smallest Type. Pure White Ledger Paper. Not over 4 Lines nor 30 Characters (13 to a line) Additional Characters, 3 cents each, in total and per line, per 1000. Trimmed so one cut makes a label.

C. V. BLACKBURN, 7 Emerson St., STONEHAM 80, MASS.

CAMBRIDGE ENTOMOLOGICAL CLUB

A regular meeting of the Club is held on the second Tuesday of each month (July, August and September excepted) at 7.45 p.m. in Room B-455, Biological Laboratories of Harvard University, Divinity Ave., Cambridge. Entomologists visiting Boston are cordially invited to attend.

WARD'S ENTOMOLOGICAL SERVICES

Entomological Supplies and Equipment
Carefully designed by professional entomologists. Material of high quality at low prices. **Send for Supply Catalog No. 348.**

Insect Preparations
Life Histories, Type Collections, Collections of Economic Insects and Biological Insect Collections. All specimens are accurately determined.

Insects for the Pest Collection
We have in stock over three hundred species of North American Insect Pests. **Send for Price List No. 349.**

Ward's Entomological Bulletin
A monthly publication sent free to all entomologists requesting it.

Information for the Beginner
Send for **"Directions for Collecting and Preserving Insects"** by Dr. A. B. Klots. A mine of useful information. Price 15 cents.

WARD'S NATURAL SCIENCE ESTABLISHMENT, Inc.
P. O. Box 24, Beechwood Station
Rochester, N. Y., U. S. A.
The Frank A. Ward Foundation of Natural Science of the University of Rochester

BACK VOLUMES OF PSYCHE

The Cambridge Entomological Club is able to offer for sale the following volumes of Psyche. Those not mentioned are entirely out of print.

Volumes 2, 3, 4, 5, 6, 7, 8, 9, 10, each covering a period of three years, $5.00 each.

Volumes 12, 14, 17, each covering a single year, $1.00 each.

Volumes 18, 19, 20, 21, 22, 23, 24, 25, 26, each covering a single year, $1.50 each.

Volumes 27, 28, 29, 30, 31, 32, 33, 34, 35, 36, 37, 38, 39, 40, 41, 42, 43, 44, 45, each covering a single year, $2.00.

Orders for 2 or more volumes subject to a discount of 10%.

Orders for 10 or more volumes subject to a discount of 20%.

A set of all the volumes available (40 in all) will be sold for $81.00.

All orders should be addressed to

F. M. CARPENTER, Associate Editor of Psyche,
Biological Laboratories,
Harvard University,
Cambridge, Mass.

PSYCHE

A Journal of Entomology

Volume XLVI

1939

EDITED BY CHARLES T. BRUES

Published by the Cambridge Entomological Club
Biological Laboratories
Harvard University
Cambridge, Mass., U.S.A.

PSYCHE

A JOURNAL OF ENTOMOLOGY

ESTABLISHED IN 1874

VOL. XLVI   MARCH, 1939   No. 1

TABLE OF CONTENTS

CAMBRIDGE ENTOMOLOGICAL CLUB

OFFICERS FOR 1938-1939

President .	W. S. Creighton
Vice-President	C. H. Blake
Secretary	V. G. Dethier
Treasurer	Richard Dow
	F. M. Carpenter
Executive Committee {	C. H. Blake
	. C. A. Frost

EDITORIAL BOARD OF PSYCHE

EDITOR-IN-CHIEF
C. T. Brues, Harvard University

ASSOCIATE EDITOR
F. M. Carpenter, Harvard University

CONSULTING EDITORS

Nathan Banks,
Harvard University.

A. E. Emerson,
University of Chicago.

Thomas Barbour,
Harvard University.

A. L. Melander,
College of the
City of New York.

Richard Dow,
New England Museum of
Natural History,
Boston, Mass.

J. G. Needham,
Cornell University.

PSYCHE is published quarterly, the issues appearing in March, June, September, and December. Subscription price, per year, payable in advance: $2.00 to Subscribers in the United States; foreign postage, 25 cents extra, Canada 15 cents. Single copies, 65 cents.

Cheques and remittances should be addressed to Treasurer, Cambridge Entomological Club, Biological Laboratories, Harvard University, Cambridge, Mass.

Orders for back volumes, missing numbers, notices of change of address, etc., should be sent to Professor F. M. Carpenter, Biological Laboratories, Harvard University, Cambridge, Mass.

IMPORTANT NOTICE TO CONTRIBUTORS

Manuscripts intended for publication, books intended for review, and other editorial matter, should be addressed to Professor C. T. Brues, Biological Laboratories, Harvard University, Cambridge, Mass.

Authors contributing articles over 8 printed pages in length will be required to bear a part of the extra expense, for additional pages. This expense will be that of typesetting only, which is about $2.00 per page. The actual cost of preparing cuts for all illustrations must be borne by contributors; the expense for full page plates from line drawings is approximately $5.00 each, and for full page half-tones, $7.50 each; smaller sizes in proportion.

AUTHOR'S SEPARATES

Reprints of articles may be secured by authors, if they are ordered before, or at the time proofs are received for corrections. The cost of these will be furnished by the Editor on application.

Printed by the Eliot Press Inc., Jamaica Plain, Mass., U. S. A.

PSYCHE

| VOL. XLVI | MARCH, 1939 | No. 1 |

A SIMPLE STROBOSCOPIC METHOD FOR THE STUDY
OF INSECT FLIGHT

BY LEIGH E. CHADWICK

Biological Laboratories, Harvard University

The methods which have been used for the study of insect wing motion may be reduced for purposes of comparison to six types. Briefly these are (1) the deductive method, (2) the acoustic method, (3) the visual or optical method, (4) the graphic method, (5) the photographic method, and (6) the stroboscopic method. A short discussion of them and of the sort of information they have yielded will be useful in judging the possibilities of the new application of the stroboscopic method outlined below. Further details and references may be found in the works of Prochnow (1924), Weber (1933), Magnan (1934) and Snodgrass (1935).

The deductive method is essentially that of the earlier anatomists. Supplemented by manipulation of dead or anæsthetized specimens it is still useful in studying the more intimate mechanism of the thorax. It cannot be expected to give exact information as to the actual motions of the wings in flight, nor *a fortiori* as to their rate.

The principle employed in the acoustic method is to match the insect's *Flugton* with the tone of a tuning fork or other instrument of known frequency. This method was applied extensively by Landois (1867) for rate determinations, but his results have not agreed too well with those obtained more directly with kymograph or camera. The relation between the pitch of an insect's tone and the frequency of its wing motion is still not completely understood, and in many cases it appears likely that harmonics may be mistaken for the fundamental. For this reason, and because of difficulties thought to be introduced by the Doppler effect, not much attention has been given to this method by later workers.

The optical method of Wheatstone (1827) was applied by Marey (1868) to the study of wing motion. By gilding areas of the wing he was able to observe its trajectory in living insects held with forceps, and confirmed Pettigrew's (1868) deduction that the wing stroke follows the outline of a figure-8. The type of problem for which this method is suitable is illustrated further by the work of Stellwaag (1916), who was able thus to observe the differential action of the wings in steering. The method cannot be called on, however, for the sort of detail available so abundantly in a photograph, and has the further disadvantage that information gained from it must often pass through a stage of subjective interpretation before it reaches the record. It permits some degree of measurement of the various amplitudes of the wing motion, but affords no data as to rate.

Marey (1868) also introduced the use of the kymograph in the study of wing motion. This instrument gives a permanent non-subjective record, from which it is easy to calculate frequencies, but is limited in other directions. The wing of the insect, used as the recording lever, is of fixed radius, and its motion is complex. If undue friction is to be avoided, only a small fraction of the arc described by the wing tip may be recorded at one time. Insofar as frequency measurements are concerned, the results obtained by Marey and other students who have used the graphic method agree, on the whole, within the limits of normal variation with data derived from other techniques. The distortions bulk larger, however, where it is desired to achieve a true picture of the unhampered motion of the wing. Naturally the kymograph may be used only with fastened and not with freely flying insects.

A third technique introduced by Marey and in the development of which his followers have had a large share is that of high-speed photography. Theoretically this is the most advantageous method for the study of insect flight, but its application is difficult. The high rate at which the wings are moved, 150–250 beats per second being not uncommon among the Diptera and Hymenoptera, fixes the length of exposure, and the duration between successive exposures for motion pictures, at exceedingly low limits. To obtain adequate illumination at such frequencies becomes a very real problem, which is intensified by the small size of many species. Added to the photographic difficulties are those of posing the often unwilling specimens. Under these conditions, the method proves expensive in time, film and apparatus,—yet the results which it promises serve amply to justify continued efforts toward its perfection. The extent to which the obstacles mentioned have been overcome at present may be gauged by reference to the fine reproductions in Magnan (1934).

With the more evident merits and disadvantages of these several methods in mind, we may proceed to discuss the stroboscopic technique. The stroboscopic principle has been the basis of most of the attempts at high-speed photography, but Oehmichen (1920) appears to have been the only worker who has previously made much use of the stroboscope for the visual study of insect flight. With the stroboscope, cyclic motions may be made to seem to stand still (and to proceed slowly forward or in reverse) no matter what the actual frequency may be. All that is necessary is an intermittent source of light tuned to synchrony (or near synchrony) with the motion to be observed. In Oehmichen's apparatus light was provided by electric discharge across a spark gap or through a Geissler tube. Frequency could be synchronized automatically with that of the wings by an ingenious arrangement which allowed air currents produced by the wing to open a very light key in the primary circuit at a given phase in each beat. If a variable control of frequency was desired, this key was replaced by a rotary interruptor, the speed of which was regulated by a potentiometer. With this apparatus Oehmichen made visual and photographic observations of much interest, but neither his results nor his method have received much attention since their publication.

The recent development of the Edgerton stroboscope (Germeshausen and Edgerton, 1937) should give a new impetus to studies along this line. Earlier stroboscopes have suffered from shortcomings, either in regard to the source of light, which was not dependable, or in regard to control of the frequency, which was unwieldy because of rotational inertia, etc. No difficulties of this sort are met with in the instrument under discussion, in which the flash-frequency of a neon or other low-pressure-filled bulb is controllable instantly by an adjustable electric oscillator. The instrument as supplied operates on 110 V 60-cycle AC, and gives direct scale readings in RPM over a range of 600–14,400 cycles per minute (10–240 per second). Values above and below these limits may be calculated easily from harmonic relationships. The accuracy is within ±1.0% over the full range.

The motion of an insect's wings is fundamentally a cyclic phenomenon, and may therefore be studied by this means. In theory one may place any flying insect before the instrument and by suitable tuning either "stop" the wings completely at any phase in the cycle or permit the cycle to proceed slowly through its several phases while observations are made. How fully these desired conditions may be attained in practise varies considerably with different insects, but, given appropriate treatment of the specimens, the theoretical expectations may be realized very satisfactorily.

Rates may be determined quickly and easily.

Study of the complex motions of the wings is more exacting. Here results depend partly on the operator's patience, since the problem is largely one of inducing the specimens to fly steadily and for longer intervals. Favorable responses can be had in the majority of cases, and are well worth the effort, for the details of the wing motion are displayed with a clarity that is far beyond that of any photographs so far published.

The most evident disadvantage of the method is that, like other visual techniques, it gives no permanent record beyond the notes of the observer. In respect of rate determinations, this objection is less forceful, since one simply tunes to synchrony with the wing frequency, thus obtaining a single standing image, and reads the figures from the dial. Reference to adjacent harmonics quickly settles any doubt as to whether one has been observing the true fundamental or one of its submultiples.

Because of the natural variation in rate, it is often difficult to retain a standing image over any extended period, though

constant frequency over an interval as long as one minute
has been observed not infrequently in *Drosophila*. In deter-
mining rates, this is again of no particular disadvantage in
most cases, for here the limits of variation are the significant
feature and may be measured quite accurately. Where observations of wing motion as such are to be made, however,
it is of importance to know whether or not the apparent
motion has the same sign as the true motion. For example,
the wings of a noctuid moth during the downstroke show a
marked upward curvature of the flexible tips. If the stroboscope be tuned to a frequency slightly above that of the
wings, there will be a slow apparent motion in reverse of the
true motion, and the wing tip will then *seem* to be bent
upward during the upstroke. Such incongruities may be
less patent in the motions of a smaller or more stiff-winged
insect, so that caution is necessary. This is particularly so
of insects with a very variable rate, whose true frequency
may be now to one side and now to the other of the setting
on the dial.

Transient motions, for example those involved in starting
or in stopping flight, are beyond the scope of such a method.
Here, as in many other instances, the ultimate recourse must
be the motion-picture camera.

A further weakness of the instruments obtainable at
present is that the intensity of the neon bulb is rather low.
This means that specimens must be placed close to the
source, and outside illumination cut off or reduced to a
minimum. In theory it should be quite possible to observe
with stroboscopic light the motions of an insect flying freely
in a room; practically this ideal is difficult to attain. Even
with completely adequate lighting such methods could not be
satisfactory with the smaller species. With larger forms, of
the size of *Leucania unipuncta* Haw., for instance, they may
be useful, once the essential improvements have been made.

With the cooperation of Professor Edgerton, of the
Massachusetts Institute of Technology, the writer has been
supplied with additional equipment, including tubes of
higher intensity. These give a bluish-white light which is
suitable for certain types of photographic work. Photography with the neon tubes is out of the question. Unfortunately the bluish-white light seems to have an inhibitory

effect upon many insects, so that these tubes have not been as useful in the study of free flight as had been hoped. Whether this is due to some peculiarity of the spectrum, or to an effect of flicker at the higher intensities, which is lacking with the neon bulb, has not been determined. Certain moths are sensitive to noise, and respond adversely to the high-voltage crackle from these tubes as well as to the quality of the light. Still it has been possible to take readings on the wing rate of these and other insects flying freely in a room 12′ x 15′, and observations on specimens confined in jars and other containers are often productive. The brighter bulbs have also been used to advantage in studying specimens held in fixed position. At present it is not possible to obtain tubes of this sort which will operate at frequencies much above 100 per second. In connection with the problem of lighting, it may be remarked that, no matter how perfect it may be made, there will always be the natural variation in wing frequency to deal with, as well as the limitation set by what the human eye can observe in a small object traveling rapidly through space.

Where specimens held in fixed position are to be studied, the technique of fastening them is important. A discussion of the problems this introduces would lead beyond the limits of this article, and must be deferred to another occasion.

Finally, one additional limitation of the stroboscopic method should be noted. At rates well below the fusion frequency for the human eye, there is, as might be expected, a disagreeable flicker. This is especially objectionable when one is observing through the binoculars. Fortunately the wing rate of most insects is high enough so that this drawback is of minor consequence. The writer finds observation not uncomfortable at frequencies as low as 20 or 25 per second, where detail, such as motions of parts of the thorax, is to be studied. Direct rate readings are possible down to the limit of 10 per second, or may be taken in higher multiples if this seems preferable.

In concluding this criticism of the stroboscopic method, one may point again to the great advantage of being able to make direct visual observation of the motions of flight, at a rate determined by the observer, and also to the large number of observations that can be made within a limited time.

It is quite practicable to take a series of rate readings on one individual at 10-second intervals. With a series of specimens, where one observer has done all the handling and recording, the interval between readings has been about 40 or 50 seconds; if the recording is done by a second person, rates may be read on several specimens within a minute.

It is felt that a great deal can be added to our knowledge of insect flight by the more extended use of this type of stroboscope. Much that is now conjectural in regard to the motions of the wings can be replaced by fact, easily and at relatively small expense. Even after high-speed photography has reached the state of perfection desired, and the day is not yet, the stroboscope will still have its own field of usefulness. There is need for extensive observation of living specimens under experimental conditions where photography may be neither necessary nor possible. For the photographer himself the stroboscope is a valuable adjunct which permits him to study in advance the rate and type of motion which he is about to attempt to photograph. The various shortcomings and difficulties to which attention has been called above are those which have presented themselves during six months work with this instrument on the problems of insect flight and should serve to indicate the natural limitations of the method.

The application of the stroboscope in the study of wing motion has been simplified by the generous cooperation of Professor H. E. Edgerton of the Massachusetts Institute of Technology. The writer wishes to take this opportunity of acknowledging his assistance and of thanking Professors C. T. Brues and A. C. Redfield, of the Department of Biology, Harvard University, for their encouragement in this work.

LIST OF REFERENCES CITED.

Germeshausen, K. J. & Edgerton, H. E. 1937. The Strobotron. Electronics 10 No. 2: 12, Feb. 1937.

Landois, H. 1867. Die Ton- und Stimmapparate der Insekten in anatomisch-physiologischer und akustischer Beziehung. Z. wiss. Zool. 17: 105-184, 187.

Magnan, A. 1934. La locomotion chez les animaux I. Le vol des insectes. Paris, Hermann & Cie., 1934.

Marey, E.-J. 1868. Déterminations expérimentales du mouvement des ailes des insectes pendant le vol. C. R. Acad. Sci. Paris, 67: 1341.

Oehmichen, E.   1920.   Nos maîtres les oiseaux.   Étude sur le vol
     animal.   Paris, Dunod, 1920.
Pettigrew, J. B.   1868.   On the mechanical appliances by which flight
     is attained in the animal kingdom.   Trans. Linn. Soc. London,
     26: 197.
Prochnow, O.   1924.   Mechanik des Insektenfluges.   *In* Schröder, Chr.,
     Handbuch der Entomologie Bd. I, Jena, 1928.
Snodgrass, R. E.   1935.   Principles of Insect Morphology.   New York,
     1935.
Stellwaag, F.   1916.   Wie steuern die Insekten während des Fluges?
     Biol. Zbl. 36: 30.
Weber, H.   1933.   Lehrbuch der Entomologie.   Jena, 1933.
Wheatstone, Sir Charles.   1827.   Description of the Kaleidophone, etc.
     Quart. J. Sci. Lit. Art. 1: 21.

IMMATURE NORTH AMERICAN TRICHOPTERA

BY MARGERY J. MILNE

Randolph-Macon Woman's College,
Lynchburg, Va.

Several keys to the larvæ and two to the pupæ of North American Trichoptera are already available[1] but none of them summarizes recent study of adequate material, and all but one are based either directly or indirectly on tables presented by European workers.

A search for family and subfamily characters in North American caddis larvæ and pupæ has yielded the two keys below. Since the pupal stage is much less completely known than the larval, the key to the former is more artificial than that to the latter, especially with respect to members of the families Odontoceridæ and Sericostomatidæ. To somewhat offset this disadvantage, a very useful list of spur formulæ is appended, summarizing the known information on this character.

[1]1901. Betten, C. in Bull. 47, N. Y. State Mus. pp. 563-564. A larval key compiled from European papers by Klapalek and Struck.
1915. Krafka, J. Jr. in Can. Ent. 46: 217-225. Original keys to larvae, guided by Ulmer's 1909 European work.
1921. Lloyd, J. T. in Bull. 21, Lloyd Lib. (Ent. Ser. 1) p. 15. A slightly modified translation of Ulmer's 1909 key, larvae only.
1921. Lutz, F. E. in Field Book of Insects (Putnam) pp. 58-60. A modification of Betten's 1901 key to larvae.
1925. Comstock, J. H. in Introduction to Entomology (Comstock) p. 560. A modification of Lloyd's 1921 key to larvae.
1926. Essig, E. O. in Insects of Western North America (Macmillan) p. 175. A modification of the key to larvae in Lloyd 1921 and Comstock 1925.
1926. Sibley, C. K. in Bull. 27, Lloyd Lib. (Ent. Ser. 5). An apparently original key to the pupae of species found on the Lloyd-Cornell Reservation, N. Y.
1933. Brues, C. T. & A. L. Melander in Bull. 73, Mus. Comp. Zool. Harvard, pp. 195-197. A modification of Krafka's 1915 key to larvae.
1934. Betten, C. in Bull. 292, N. Y. State Mus. pp. 117-123, the larval key a copy of Krafka's 1915 work, the pupal key from Ulmer's 1909 key.

Caddis larvæ inhabiting movable cases have the head bent downward so that the mandibles are ventral (hypognathous) in position, the long axis of the head at an obtuse or even a right angle with the long axis of the body. Those with a right-angled attachment are said to be *eruciform* larvæ, those with an obtuse angle to be *suberuciform*. Caseless larvæ have the long axis of the head in line with the long axis of the body and the jaws hence at the anterior end of the animal (prognathous). Such larvæ are said to be thysanuriform or *campodeiform*.

Case-bearing larvæ frequently have fleshy tubercles on the sides and notum of the first abdominal segment. These are called *spacing humps,* and serve to keep a passage for respiratory water between the larva and its case. Such larvæ also often have a prominent projection from the prosternum, extending between the front coxæ. This is the *prosternal horn* or prosternal spine.

The head capsule or *epicranium* splits at ecdysis into right and left halves. It bears the articulating surfaces for the mandibles antero-laterally and may or may not meet on the mid-line ventrally, anterior to the neck opening *(occipital foramen)*. In some forms a submentum or *gula* is well developed, the gula being sometimes quadrate, at other times triangular or crescentic. It may keep the epicranial halves entirely apart, extending from the labium to the occipital foramen, or it may separate them only anteriorly, so that the foramen is entirely surrounded by epicranium. A U- or V-shaped emargination in the anterior margin of the epicranium on the mid-dorsal line accommodates the *frons* to which the *labrum* is attached by a flexible membrane. There is no clypeus. The antennae are usually very small.

Many larvæ have a fringe of hairs along the abdominal lateral line, the so-called *"lateral fringe."* The abdomen frequently bears along the dorsal, lateral and ventral surfaces filamentous or branched structures called *gills*, although their respiratory function is doubtful. Around the anus filamentous or sac-like structures are often seen. These are the *rectal gills*, which are seemingly retractible into the rectum. Also apical on the abdomen are the *prolegs*, fleshy structures with claws, used in locomotion. The thoracic appendages are true *legs*, and consist of five segments, a large *coxa* articulating with the pleurite, a small trochanter (always indistinctly divided), a large *femur*, a *tibia*, and a one-segmented *tarsus* bearing a movable *claw*. Usually the tibia ends in a spur. In Leptoceridæ and some Odontoceridæ, the middle and hind legs have the *femora divided* into two, the proximal half shorter than, or equalling the distal half.

In the pupæ imaginal structures such as antennæ, maxillary and labial palpi, ocelli, tibial spurs, sternal ligulæ and genitalia may be studied, in addition to the labral bristles, gills and anal processes of the pupal skin itself. All females have the *maxillary palpi* 5-segmented, but the males of some families show a reduction in this number. In some families in which both sexes have 5-segmented maxillary palpi, the terminal segment is secondarily annulated. *Labial palpi* are always 3-segmented. There are 3 *ocelli* present or none are found. The fore tibiæ may have as many as 3 spurs, the middle and hind tibiæ as many as 4 spurs. When no more than 2 spurs are present, they are terminal. A third or fourth spur is added part way up the tibia. The number of spurs is indicated by a *spur formula*. Thus 1-3-4 indicates that the fore tibia bears one (terminal) spur, the middle tibia a pair of terminal and a subapical spur(s), the hind tibia a pair of terminal and a pair of subapical spurs. The *labral bristles* are used to clean the gratings which allow entrance of water into the pupal case. The *gills* are much like those of the larva but often differ in number and arrangement. The *anal* processes are extensions of the pupal skin which cover the cerci and genitalia and often bear bristles for cleaning the grating which allows exit of water from the pupal case.

KEY TO NORTH AMERICAN CADDIS LARVAE

1. Abdomen very much wider than thorax; very minute species with all three thoracic segments heavily sclerotized above, living in portable silken cases which are much larger than the larvæ: *Hydroptilidæ*

    Abdomen not much wider than thorax; much larger species, never with all three thoracic nota heavily sclerotized above in any case-bearing species, the cases when present not much larger than the larvæ 2

2. Last abdominal segment never with a sclerotized shield
above; body campodeiform, the head held straight
forward, forming a continuation of the long axis of
the body; abdomen of nine segments, the prolegs distinct from one another; no tubercle on first abdominal segment; no prosternal horn; no lateral line
fringe; abdomen depressed, the sutures between the
segments deeply impressed; gills usually absent;
rectal gill structures generally present but not
always everted; larvæ not constructing a movable
case 3

Last abdominal segment usually with a sclerotized
shield above—if lacking it, the body eruciform
(hypognathous) and the larva living in a movable
case (Leptoceridæ) ; gills usually present 10

3. Labrum soft, whitish, retractile under edge of frons 4
Labrum wholly sclerotized 5

4. Mandible with a prominent tooth at middle of medial
margin; frons with a deep asymmetric emargination : .... *Philopotamidæ*, subfamily *Chimarrhinæ*
Mandible with no such prominent tooth; frons scarcely
emarginate : ....
.... *Philopotamidæ*, subfamily *Philopotaminæ*

5. Claws of legs long and slender, nearly straight, with
only one basal spur; penultimate segment of maxil-
lary palpus very long : ....
.... *Psychomyiidæ*, subfamily *Polycentropodinæ*
Claws of legs short, stout, curved; penultimate segment
of maxillary palpi not especially long 6

6. Gills absent; only two bristles on convex side of man-
dibles 7

Gills present; numerous bristles on convex outer side
of mandibles; all three thoracic nota sclerotized 8

7. Only prothorax sclerotized dorsally : ....
.... *Psychomyiidæ*, subfamily *Psychomyiinæ*
All three thoracic nota sclerotized : ....
.... *Psychomyiidæ*, subfamily *Ecnominæ*

8. Gula an elongate, rectangular plate separating epicranial halves completely; all gill filaments in clus-

ters arising from the ends of stalks, somewhat like
the tentacles of Hydra; large forms: ....
.... *Hydropsychidæ*, subfamily *Arctopsychinæ*
Gula triangular, never reaching hind margin of head,
the epicranial halves contiguous for some distance;
gill filaments arising from the side as well as the end
of the stalk, more comb-like 9

9. Dorsal surface of head flattened, forming a broad disc,
enclosed by a strong carina which crosses the frons
near its apex, setting off a small triangle; mandibles
with broad, blunt teeth on whole inner margin, the
interspaces broad and deep: ....
.... *Hydropsychidæ*, subfamily *Macronematinæ*
Dorsal surface of the head flattened, but with no carina
defining its limits; mandibles with sharp teeth apically: .... *Hydropsychidæ*, subfamily *Hydropsychinæ*

10. Body campodeiform, the abdomen depressed; larvæ
never constructing a movable case though sometimes
building a fixed shelter 11
Body eruciform or suberuciform, the head bent down-
wards at an angle to the rest of the body; abdomen
cylindrical, the sutures between the segments usually
feebly impressed; gills usually present; larvæ always
living in a movable, tubular shelter 12

11. Prolegs very well developed, entirely separate from
each other; proleg claws long and slender, without
teeth on convex surface; accessory claws sometimes
present at sides of main proleg claws; maxillary
lobes long and slender: ....
.... *Rhyacophilidæ*, subfamily *Rhyacophilinæ*
Prolegs short, the basal segments wholly sclerotized
and fused to the ninth abdominal segment in a nearly
vertical position; proleg claws very short, with small
teeth on the convex side; maxillary lobes short and
broad; construction of a fixed shelter in late larval
life is usual: . . ..
.... *Rhyacophilidæ*, subfamily *Glossosomatinæ*

12. Prosternum with a horn or spine projecting down-
wards between the front coxæ 13

No such prosternal horn 15

13. Body suberuciform; lateral gills on segments 2 to 7
     usually pubescent with black hairs; mesonotum gen-
     erally soft like metanotum, rarely with two small
     sclerotized plates; abdominal constrictions well
     marked: .... *Phryganeidæ*

     Body eruciform; lateral gills on segments 2 to 7 never
     pubescent with black hairs; mesonotum generally
     entirely sclerotized, sometimes only with small
     plates, rarely completely soft 14

14. Mesonotum entirely sclerotized; metanotum with three
     pairs of plates; mesothoracic legs stouter and longer
     than hind legs: .... *Limnephilidæ*

     Mesonotum not entirely sclerotized; metanotum usually
     entirely soft; middle legs not longer than hind legs:
     A few *Sericostomatidæ* (Goerinæ & Lepidostomatinæ)

15. Femora of middle and hind legs divided into a shorter
     basal and a longer apical piece; right mandibles
     without inner bristles; no accessory bristles on back
     of mandibles: 16

     Femora not divided 17

16. Lateral line well developed 17

     Lateral line little developed or absent: ...... *Leptoceridæ*

17. Lateral line well developed, the 8th segment never with
     only sclerotized points representing the line; labrum
     with a transverse row of many stout bristles before
     the middle, or if lacking these, then much longer
     than broad: .... *Odontoceridæ*

     Lateral line very faint, incomplete or absent, its place
     sometimes occupied on some segments by sclerotized
     points; labrum neither with a transverse row of
     bristles nor longer than broad 18

18. Antennæ rudimentary; pronotum sclerotized, meso-
     notum never more than partially sclerotized: ....
     .... *Sericostomatidæ*

     Antennæ large, the basal segment broad, 2nd more
     slender and tipped with a fine bristle; pro- and meso-
     notum both sclerotized 19

19. Distal spurs of fore and middle tibiæ not on promi-
    nences; hind legs with normal claws; cases curved
    tubes, never broad: .... *Beræidæ*

    Distal spurs of fore and middle tibiæ on prominences;
    claws of hind legs abnormal; cases of sand, broadly
    shield-shaped like a turtle shell, except those of very
    young larvæ which have straight sand tubes, often
    with bits of mollusk shells: .... *Molannidæ*

KEY TO NORTH AMERICAN CADDIS PUPAE

1. Pupæ very small (not more than 5 mm. long, usually
    less than 3.5 mm.), with very short thick antennæ;
    maxillary palpi 5-segmented in both sexes; cases
    mostly of silk only or of silk covered with very fine
    sand, the cases flat or thickest in the middle, usually
    attached at each end by circular discs of silk: ....
    .... *Hydroptilidæ*

    Pupæ usually larger, the antennæ nearly as long as the
    body, not especially thickened; maxillary palpi some-
    times 3- or 4-segmented in the male; cases never as
    above 2

2. Lacking both ocelli and a complete tubular case 3

    Either ocelli or a complete tubular case or both present
    5

3. Gills absent: ....
    .... *Psychomyiidæ*, subfamily *Psychomyiinæ*

    Gills present 4

4. Spurs 3-4-4; anal processes large, blunt, not long; cases
    made of pieces of leaves or small sand grains, the
    ventral side of silk only (in Phylocentropus the case
    is a long, branched tube of sand with only a turret
    projecting; in Neureclipsis the case is a trumpet-
    shaped net) ; ....
    .... *Psychomyiidæ*, subfamily *Polycentropodinæ*

    Spurs 2-4-4 or fore tibiæ with one or no spur; anal
    processes long and heavily sclerotized, with many
    bristles: .... *Hydropsychidæ*

5. Case complete, the pupa never in an inner silken
    cocoon; gills often present; anal processes often long,

rod-like and strongly sclerotized; legs with or without claws 9

Case incomplete, the pupa in an inner silken cocoon; gills absent; no long or rod-like or strongly sclerotized anal processes; legs with good claws 6

6. Inner silken cocoon spindle-shaped like a zeppelin or a fly puparium, attached to the case only at its posterior end; case barn-shaped, usually of pebbles; 5th segment of maxillary palpi not annulated   7

Inner silken cocoon either not complete or fused to case wall near its equator; when incomplete, the anterior end lacking, the posterior end much as in Rhyacophilinæ; 5th segment of maxillary palpi long, curved and distinctly annulated 8

7. Spurs 2-4-4:   *Rhyacophilidæ*, subfamilies *Glossosomatinæ* & *Hydrobiosinæ*

Spurs 3-4-4: *Rhyacophilidæ*, subfamily *Rhyacophilinæ*

8. Spurs 2-4-4: *Philopotamidæ*, subfamily *Philopotaminæ*

Spurs 1-4-4: *Philopotamidæ*, subfamily *Chimarrhinæ*

9. Ocelli present 10

Ocelli absent 12

10. Posterior margin of 1st abdominal tergite produced caudad in a distinct median process extending over base of 2nd segment; mandibles with a prominence from which the bristles arise; anal processes flat, somewhat rhombic, with 4 long bristles at the end; spurs 2-4-4; male maxillary palpi 4-segmented:
.... *Phryganeidæ*

Posterior margin of 1st abdominal tergite not produced caudad but with a saddle-shaped prominence, laterally with short spines or with only two lateral tubercles set with numerous hairs or denticles; mandibles with no such prominence; never more than one protibial spur; male maxillary palpi 3-segmented; anal processes long, more slender 11

11. Labrum semicircular, anteriorly emarginate, the dorsal surface elevated, with a transverse furrow back of its mid line; spurs 1-1-1, 1-2-2, 1-2-3, 1-2-4, 1-3-3 or in most, 1-3-4: .... *Limnephilidæ*

Labrum roughly rectangular, the anterior margin formed of 3 curves, in each of the two emarginations of which is a fine bristle; 5 longer bristles with curved tips vertically on either side of labrum; spurs 1-2-4 (Pharula) or 1-3-4 (Neothremma) : ....

.... *Sericostomatidæ*, subfamily *Georinæ* in part

12. Antennæ very long, the outer part wound around the abdominal apex 13

Antennæ scarcely longer than body, the ends never wound as above 14

13. Two mesotibial spurs; mouthparts so placed that the pupal mandibles point upwards: .... *Leptoceridæ*

Four mesotibial spurs; mouthparts normal or as above: .... some *Odontoceridæ*

14. Spurs 2-2-2 (Micrasema) or 2-3-2 or 2-3-3 (Brachycentrus) ; labrum obtusely triangular to semicircular; maxillary palpi shorter than or but little longer than labial palpi, never stouter : ....

.... *Sericostomatidæ*, subfamily *Brachycentrinæ*

Spurs not as above 15

15. Case shaped like a snail shell, coiled in a flat spiral, made of sand grains of small size: ....

.... *Sericostomatidæ*, subfamily *Helicopsychinæ*

Case never of this form 16

16. Less than four mesotibial spurs 17

Four mesotibial spurs 18

17. Body length not less than 5 mm.; robust species: ....

.... *Sericostomatidæ*, subfamily *Sericostomatinæ*

Body length not over 4 mm.; slender, small species: ....

.... *Beræidæ*

18. Less than 4 metatibial spurs: .... some *Odontoceridæ*

Four metatibial spurs, the formula 2-4-4 19

19. Anal processes lobate: ....

.... *Sericostomatidæ*, subfamily *Lepidostomatinæ*

Anal processes rod-like 20

20. Case of sand, flattened dorso-ventrally and with lateral flanges, closed by discs of silk at the ends, that at the posterior end having a vertical slit, that at the anterior end a horizontal slit: .... *Molannidæ*

Case not as above, and differently closed 21
21. Case of stones with ballast rocks at the side, straight,
never curved : ....
.... *Sericostomatidæ,* subfamily *Goerinæ* in part
Not as above; case with a definite curvature : ....
.... some *Odontoceridæ*

In families Hydropsychidæ (with subfamilies Hydropsychinæ, Arctopsychinæ and Macronematinæ), Psychomyiidæ (with subfamilies Psychomyiinæ, Polycentropodinæ
and Ecnominæ) and Philopotamidæ (with subfamilies
Philopotaminæ and Chimarrhinæ), the 5th segment of the
maxillary palpi is secondarily segmented in the pupa and
adult. In Leptoceridæ it is long and slender and often
curved but never segmented. In males of Phryganeidæ, the
fifth segment is lacking, so that the maxillary palpi are
4-segmented; in males of Limnephilidæ (with subfamilies
Apataniinæ and Limnephilinæ) and Sericostomatidæ (with
subfamilies Brachycentrinæ, Helicopsychinæ, Lepidostomatinæ, Goerinæ and Sericostomatinæ) the 4th and 5th segments are lacking so that the palpi are 3-segmented. The
females of these families and both sexes of families Hydroptilidæ, Rhyacophilidæ (with subfamilies Rhyacophilinæ,
Hydrobiosinæ, Glossosomatinæ), Beræidæ, Molannidæ and
Odontoceridæ (with subfamilies Odontocerinæ and Cala-
moceratinæ) have five segments to the maxillary palpi. In
all Limnephilidæ, Philopotamidæ, Phryganeidæ, Rhyacophilidæ, two genera of Sericostomatidæ (Thremma and Neothremma of Goerinæ), and in six genera of Hydroptilidæ
(Agraylea, Allotrichia, Ithytrichia, Neotrichia, Oxyethira,
and Polytrichia) there are ocelli, but elsewhere they are
lacking.

SPUR FORMULAE OF NORTH AMERICAN TRICHOPTERA

Formula	*Family*	*Genera Concerned*
0-2-2	Leptoceridæ	Leptocella, Leptocerus, Setodina, Ymymia
0-2-3	Hydroptilidæ	Neotrichia
0-2-4	Hydroptilidæ	Hydroptila
0-3-4	Hydroptilidæ	Agraylea, Allotrichia, Ithytrichia, Ortho-trichia and Polytrichia

Formula	Family	Genera Concerned
0-4-4	Hydropsychidæ	sometimes Hydropsyche
	Rhyacophilidæ	Protoptila
1-1-1	Limnephilidæ	Glyphopsyche (areolatus)
1-2-2	Leptoceridæ	Œcetis, Triaenodes, Ylodes
	Limnephilidæ	Apatidea (nigra), Chilostigma, Glyphopsyche (bellus, canadensis, irroratus, pritus), Homophylax (nevadensis), Ironoquia, Neophylax (fuscus), Stenophylax (subfasciatus), Zaporota
1-2-3	Limnephilidæ	Anabolina (litha, assimilis), Neophylax (ornatus)
1-2-4	Limnephilidæ	Anisogamus (antennatus), Apatidea (all but nigra), Ecclisomyia (all but simulata)
1-3-3	Limnephilidæ	Acronopsyche, Drusinus, Glyphopsyche (ullus), Halesochila, Oligophlebodes, Platycentropus, Stenophylax (circularis, dan, guttifer)
1-3-4	Limnephilidæ	all genera and species not indicated above
	Sericostomatidæ	Neothremma
1-4-4	Hydropsychidæ	sometimes Hydropsyche
	Philopotamidæ	Chimarrhinæ
	Sericostomatidæ	Pharula
2-2-2	Leptoceridæ	Athripsodes, Mystacides
	Sericostomatidæ	Micrasema
2-2-4	Beræidæ	all
	Sericostomatidæ	Helicopsyche, Sericostomatinæ
2-3-2	Sericostomatidæ	some Brachycentrus
2-3-3	Sericostomatidæ	some Brachycentrus
2-4-2	Odontoceridæ	some Marilia, some Heteroplectron
2-4-3	Odontoceridæ	some Ganonema, some Notiomyia
2-4-4	Hydropsychidæ	Arctopsychinæ, Hydropsychinæ except some Hydropsyche
	Molannidæ	all
	Odontoceridæ	some Ganonema, some Notiomyia, some Marilia, some Heteroplectron, all Namamyia, all Nerophilus
	Philopotamidæ	Philopotaminæ
	Phryganeidæ	all
	Psychomyiidæ	Psychomyiinæ
	Rhyacophilidæ	Glossosomatinæ, Hydrobiosinæ
	Sericostomatidæ	Goera, Pseudogoera, Lepidostomatinæ
3-4-4	Psychomyiidæ	Polycentropodinæ
	Rhyacophilidæ	Rhyacophilinæ

THE MIMETIC RESEMBLANCE OF FLIES OF THE GENUS SYSTROPUS TO WASPS

By Charles T. Brues

Biological Laboratories, Harvard University

Together with a few relatives the genus Systropus is of very different appearance from the other members of the family Bombyliidæ to which it belongs. The body is extremely elongated and the dense pile that generally covers the body in the other, more or less thick-set bombyliids is so greatly reduced that the flies appear almost bare.

During a recent visit to the Dutch East Indies, I was fortunate in taking with the net two species of this genus on the island of Sumatra. Having previously observed and collected one of our common North American species, *Systropus macer* Loew, I was at once struck by the very different color pattern of its Sumatran relatives. Also the latter appear to mimic entirely different types of wasps, suggesting that two independent lines of evolution have been active in developing widely divergent, but equally fine cases of mimetic resemblance in the two hemispheres. This situation appeared so remarkable, that I attempted to follow it further by an inquiry into the color patterns of the other numerous members of the genus which is known to be almost world-wide in distribution. On account of their striking appearance and easy recognition a great many species have been described by a considerable number of entomologists.

Bezzi, in his taxonomic review of Systropus has already commented on the general color pattern which prevails among the species inhabiting two of the great zoological regions. He refers to the Oriental forms as having the aspect of vespids and the Nearctic ones as ammophiloid, *i.e.*, like the sphecoid genus "Ammophila" now called Sphex by taxonomists. The comparison is particularly apt in the case of the North American species as the resemblance to these digger-wasps is very great. Indeed, when in flight our com-

mon *Systropus macer* Loew may be readily mistaken for a
species of "Ammophila", but it has the habit, frequently
seen in dipterous mimics of wasps and bees, of resting on
the leaves of plants even during the brightest hours of
sunshine.

Among the Oriental and Indomalayan species the resemblance to vespid wasps is not nearly so close, but nevertheless
very striking.   In the case of *Systropus numeratus* de
Meijere of which I collected a male at Bangkinan, Sumatra,
during May 1937, it would appear that the model is *Stenogaster micans* Sauss.[1] as this wasp was flying very abundantly in the vicinity at the time the Systropus was taken.
The two are of approximately the same size, but the gaster
of the wasp is much stouter and the yellow markings on the
thorax are larger, darker and do not coincide in size or position; likewise the wasp is brilliantly spotted on the sides of
the gaster which is not the case in the fly.   Nevertheless
when alive the close resemblance is unmistakable although it
is not borne out by a too critical comparison of the pinned
specimens.

Another species, *Systropus varipes* Edwards, collected
near Pematangsiantar, Sumatra is much smaller with
darker legs and abdomen, and although quite wasp-like, is
less conspicuously so and no vespids that resemble it at all
closely were observed flying at the same time.   Several of
the small social species which are there common were present; all of these are much stouter and could not under any
circumstances be confused with the Systropus.

In general, the species of Systropus in this part of the
world are "vespoid" mainly by reason of a conspicuous
spotting of the thorax which is marked with light yellow.
Although the pattern varies, the basic arrangement of markings is of one type with permutations in shape and size.   The
coloration of the abdomen is black, varied with reddish
brown or dull yellow, the reddish usually at the base and the
yellow on the apical segments or venter.

In the Nearctic "ammophiloid" species the pale spotting
of the thorax disappears and the reddish color is restricted
to the petiolar basal segments of the abdomen while the

[1]Kindly identified for me by Dr. Jos. Bequaert.

yellowish abdominal markings are lost. This coloration, in combination with the shape of the body produces the really astonishing resemblance between the fly and wasp, since most of our common "Ammophilas" have the conspicuous red basal abdominal marking.

The African species are in general colored like the Nearctic ones with the ferruginous color sometimes extending conspicuously on to the thorax, although pale spotted ones are known also from this continent.

Among the species known from the Neotropical region the thorax may be conspicuously marked with whitish or yellowish or this pale pattern may be almost entirely suppressed. They are thus intermediate between the "vespoid" and "ammophiloid" series.

A Tasmanian species, *S. clavifemoratus* Hardy is of the unspotted type and also one from Madagascar while *S. studyi* Enderlein from South China is said by its describer to resemble *Ammophila atripes*.

If then we consider the species from the several zoological regions together the development of two such divergent mimetic types is not so surprising for each appears to represent a modification of not such very great extent from a somewhat intermediate pattern. As the "ammophiloid" type is more widely distributed, extending even into the Australian region, we may consider the development of conspicuous yellowish spotting as the more recent pattern.

SOME EXTRACTS FROM THE HISTORY OF ENTOMOLOGY IN CHINA

By Gaines Liu

Biological Laboratories, Harvard University

The following extracts are of historical interest only. They are published here, not in the spirit of questioning the scholarship of those whose work I shall mention, but to render available some of the historical facts to those who might care to have them but who are handicapped by language difficulties. My point can be better explained by a very good instance. In a book, called Chow Li, one of the 13 Classics published long before the Christian era, we find a detailed account of a "Bureau of Entomology" which would be considered well organized even under our modern standard. Yet China is not even mentioned by Dr. L. O. Howard, one of the best known and the most respected entomologists of the world today, in his "History of Applied Entomology". It is very plain in this case that the whole trouble is due to an inability to consult Chinese literature. Later on I shall publish a note on this ancient "Bureau of Entomology". For the present I should like to add some information to supplement the following books, namely:

1. The Biological Control of Insects, by H. L. Sweetman, 1936.
2. The Insect Singers, by J. G. Myers, 1929.
3. Entomology, by J. A. Folsom and R. A. Wardle, 1934.

1. *The Biological Control of Insects — Earliest Record ca. 889-903.*

This book appeared in 1936. I ordered it last year when I was in China but the war came earlier than the book, and it was only lately that I had the pleasure of making the acquaintance of this excellent work. On the first page, Dr. Sweetman writes as follows:

"The first written record we have of the movement of beneficial insects is that of Forskål (1775). He states that the date palms in Arabia were attacked by ants, which often destroyed the trees. The growers introduced colonies of predatory ants annually from the mountains and these controlled the pest species."

Dr. Sweetman is well aware of the practice of using ants in pest control in that part of the world, for immediately he writes that "the use of ants for the protection of orchards from insect pests is a practice of long standing in various Asiatic countries, and is still employed today". To this, based upon my personal field data, I quite agree and I can add a few more uses of the ants and some other forms of biological control of insects as practiced in my country. But what concerns us now is the "first written record". The following is a translation of a Chinese record.

"There are many kinds of ants in Lingnan (South China). Sometimes one finds that the ants are carried in a bag and sold on the market. The ants are yellow with long legs, larger than ordinary ants and live in a nest made from leaves and twigs. They are bought for the protection of the orange for it is said that without these ants most of these fruits would be wormy."

This record is contained in a book called Ling Pio Lu Yi or Wonders from South China by Liu Shun. There is no way to tell when this book was published. We know, however, that the author served as an army officer in Kwangtung during the reign of Tsao Chung of Tang (889-903) and the time must have been near the end of the 9th or the beginning of the 10th century. The same fact was mentioned in "Book on Tree Planting" by Yu Tsung Ben, a writer from the Yuan Dynasty (1280-1368). Thus Dr. Sweetman will be glad to know that the written records of insect control really go back much earlier. The ants in question were determined, according to the correspondence I have had with Prof. W. E. Hoffmann of Lingnan University, Canton, as *Œcophylla smaragdina* Fab. and were determined probably by the late Professor Wheeler. Today in Canton nests of these ants may be bought for about one silver dollar each.

2.   The Insect Singers — *"Chu Ki" is Lycorma not Huechys.*

Although this book was published in 1929, I had not seen it until recently when I came to work on the cicadas I brought from China. Dr. Myers, the author, has given us a handy and readable book on the natural history of these insects. What interests me particularly are those occasions where he speaks on cicadas in China. Here it gives me the impression that, being unable to get at the original sources and consequently relying on what others have to say, Dr. Myers, in some cases, unfortunately subscribed as an innocent victim to those mistakes committed by others.

For instance on page 3 he states, "the mention of cicadas apparently does not occur until the authoritative edition, the Pen Ts'ao Kang Mu, of A.D. 1578." The author gives one the impression that the cicadas were not mentioned until 1578 while what he really means, if I interpret correctly, is that they were not mentioned in the Pen Ts'ao. In either case, however, if one is able to read Chinese he will find that this is not correct. He will discover, for instance, many references to these insects both in the Li Chi or Book of Rites and the Shih Ching or Book of Odes as these two Classics are respectively known in English. This would mean that the earliest mention occurs at least not later than 500 B.C. because these two Classics were connected in one way or another with Confucius (551-479 B.C.). In short, Dr. Myers has been entirely deceived by the Japanese version.

On page 23, Dr. Myers writes: "the cicada itself was labelled Tchen, while the nymph—the tettiometra or cicada mother, of the Greek—Tchen touy, i.e. the cicada with a skin which falls like that of a serpent." Here we have another mistake that can easily be rectified if one knows Chinese. Tchen touy is the shed skin. How it came to be interpreted as "nymph" is abstruse because "touy" means shed and the shed skin of cicada is the form generally mentioned as a drug in the Chinese pharmacopoeia.

That Chu ki is a Lycorma (*L. delicatula* White), a fulgorid common in north China, not *Huechys sanguinea* De Geer, has never been suspected ever since the day when Amyot created the genus Huechys in 1836. It was fully accepted

by Distant in his Monograph of Oriental Cicadidae (1892)
and Dr. Myers of course could not avoid the pitfall. I know
that chu ki is Lycorma but I had not associated chu ki with
Huechys until I read Myers' book (p. 22), although I have
always tried to identify Huechys in Chinese ever since I
learned from Distant that this insect is employed by the
Chinese as a drug. Now it is clear that Huechys is a direct
romanization of the Chinese term chu ki.

There are several ways to prove that chu ki is *L. delicatula*
and not *Huechys sanguinea*. "Ki" means a "fowl" and the
general form of a Lycorma resembles a fowl while the form
of a Huechys does not. On the other hand, Huechys is a
southern species, and becomes rare as we approach the
Yangtze valley. Among the large number of specimens collected, I have only a single specimen from Wuchang and another one from Ichang (two new records for this species)
while all the old specimens in the Harvard collection came
from south China. The case with Lycorma seems to be just
reverse. Although *delicatula* is known as far south as India,
it is not so common in the south as in the north, although
the south has its own species. Now all the writers of the
Chinese Pen Ts'ao were people from the north. It seems to
be more reasonable to assume that the insect in question is
a northern species instead of a southern one. But the best
proof is found in the description of chu ki as it was given by
various medical men and for this I submit the following
translation.

"These insects are very common in Honan. They look
like a moth but with the abdomen larger and the head and
the legs blackish. There are two pairs of wings, the outer
pair (tegmina) is grey while the inner pair (wings) is deep
red, decorated with all five colors"—from Pen Ts'ao Yen Yi
by Kio Chung Pi (1111–1116).[1]

"The chu are the ill-smelling Ailanthus trees. The outer
wings of the insects (chu ki) are greyish yellow while the
inner ones are decorated with all five colors. They generally
line up on the tree and by the late fall, deposit their eggs on
the bark. The nymph has six legs, with wings (?) doubled
and black and the head depressed and truncated in front."—
From Pen Ts'ao Kang Mu by Li Shih Chen (1578).

[1]This is the period with which the name of the author is connected.

The "greyish yellow" is very accurate for those specimens I have from Peiping. From these descriptions, it is evident that chu ki is Lycorma and not Huechys.[2] Huechys, the black cicada with a red head, is called "Er", according to Fang Yen, another Chinese Classic appearing long before the Christian era.

In closing I have one other statement to make for those who are interested in biological problems in ancient China. Based upon my personal experience, obtained in preparing a "History of Entomology in China", a work encouraged by Professor C. T. Brues and Dr. G. Sarton, I have found that the earlier Chinese as a whole were quite vague in their expression. Exactly the same term may mean entirely different things to different authors and sometimes it is very difficult to distinguish them unless one has as a general background some knowledge of the fauna and flora of the region whence the author came. Thus it is not even safe to trust the translation of those who know Chinese unless they are duly qualified from a biological standpoint.

3. *Entomology — Fireflies as Imperial Entertainment in China.*

The following paragraph from Folsom and Wardle, page 521, is very interesting to me.

"Annually the people of Gifu collect many thousands of fireflies which are sent to Tokio and on a certain night are liberated for the enjoyment of the emperor."

This paragraph is interesting to me because it reminds me of the following story about one of the romantic emperors of China.

"In the 12th year of Da Yeh (616), emperor Yang visited the Ching Hua Palace. Bushels of fireflies were collected by imperial order. In the evening, the Emperor and his courtiers went up the mountain. The fireflies were then released and the whole valley became immediately enlivened with the sparklings of these insects."—Sui Shu or Annals of the Dynasty of Sui.

---

[2]For detailed description of these two insects, see page 157 (*Huechys sanguinea* De Geer) and page 207 (*Lycorma delicatula* White) in Distant, Fauna British India, Rhynchota, Vol. 3, 1906.

Whether the Japanese custom was introduced from China, we do not know. Japan did send a large number of students to China during the Tang Dynasty (618-907). The fireflies are still one of the best evening entertainments the Chinese children have today. Mothers are generally requested by their children to save their empty egg-shells in which the youngsters house their catch and watch the flashing in the dark when they go to bed.

FURTHER NOTES ON CANNIBALISM AMONG LARVÆ

By V. G. Dethier

Biological Laboratories, Harvard University

In a previous communication (Dethier, 1937) most of the reported cases of cannibalism among lepidopterous larvæ were discussed. Hunger and crowding, with thirst as a contributing cause were found to be the prime factors inducing this anomalous diet. This confirms the conclusions of Hering (1926) whose book was previously unavailable to the writer. The present notes offer further explanatory data pertaining to hunger and crowding as causes of a meat diet. The effects of such a diet and the ability of a phytophagous larva to survive on one are considered. Additional cases are also cited.

I

In an effort to understand more fully the various causes initiating cannibalism and the carnivorous habit in general among lepidopterous larvæ the following experiments were designed.

Two final instar larvæ of *Estigmene acrea* Drury and one last instar larva of *Isia isabella* A. & S. were placed in a dry jar approximately twenty inches in volume. Also placed in the jar were one pupating *E. acrea* larva from which the cocoon had been removed, a smaller arctiid in similar condition, and one freshly killed *I. isabella* larva which had been slit open longitudinally. The experimental animals had neither eaten nor drunk for four days. It was observed that they crawled ceaselessly around the bottom of the container exploring the surface with their antennæ and mouthparts. Some dry fæces when encountered were nibbled at slightly. No unusual behavior occurred until the slit carcass was encountered. Here the live animals immediately sucked up the body fluids. After a period of five minutes all three experimentals were eating the tissues of the exposed larva. Next a decapitated *Encoptolophus sordidus* Burm. was placed in the jar. Its metathoracic legs were removed to prevent kicking. The grasshopper was investigated by the larvæ but no attack made upon it; however, when the carcass was slit open, the larvæ that chanced upon it started feeding almost immediately. The flesh, the eggs contained within the abdomen, and as much of the cuticle as was not too heavily sclerotized were eaten. At this stage the small pupating arctiid was also eaten by the *I. isabella.*

It can be seen from these observations that larvæ are more readily attacked and eaten when their tissues are exposed. It is to be expected that caterpillars would be more attracted to exposed tissues because there is a more concentrated odor arising from them than from an insect completely sheathed in cuticle. Also, there is no stimulation of the mouthparts by an unmutilated carcass. On the other hand, body juices exposed to the air may stimulate the mouthparts directly. Further there is the possibility that larvæ partaking of body juices are prompted to do so by thirst. An unmutilated carcass is attacked only when the larvæ reach such a degree of starvation that they bite frequently at near-by objects.

In order to ascertain the exact series of events occurring when an animal with cannibalistic or carnivorous tendencies approaches another larva, a single live naked noctuid larva was placed in the jar with one *E. acrea.* In the limited area the two frequently encountered each other. The *E. acrea* had reached the stage in which it bit at all objects encountered. When it endeavored to take several bites of the noctuid, however, the latter thrashed about vigorously. Although the arctiid stabbed viciously at its intended victim several times, it finally withdrew. The noctuid's cuticle had not been pierced. On numerous occasions the same process was repeated. Finally the noctuid was rendered more or less quiescent by the buffeting of the more active and aggressive arctiid. In this quiescent state, more or less bathed in its own regurgitated juices and those of its attacker, the noctuid was eaten. Undoubtedly this procedure takes place in most instances when one live insect is eaten by another. The higher percentage of cannibalism noted under crowded conditions (Dethier, 1937) may be explained by the fact that chance meetings are more frequent. When similar conditions were reproduced in a cage twelve by sixteen inches, both animals eventually died of starvation.

While experiments with mutilated animals indicate that thirst may be one factor in inducing cannibalism, the following experiments demonstrate that hunger by itself is an important factor.

One *E. acrea* was kept in a moist atmosphere, given its fill of water, and presented with every opportunity to continue drinking. When given a mutilated larva of the same species the experimental animal began feeding almost immediately. Repetitions of this experiment prove that hunger as distinct from thirst is one factor in inducing a carnivorous diet.

The experimental animals never chose a diet of meat in preference to plants. Plant food was always accepted even after the larvæ had gorged themselves with meat. In three hours a single *E. acrea* consumed one *E. sordidus*, another consumed one entire *Gryllus assimilis* Fab., and an *I. isabella* consumed one full-grown larva of *Vanessa virginiensis* Drury. These three arctiids pupated and produced normal adults.

With regard, therefore, to the rôle played by hunger and crowding in causing cannibalism the following conclusions seem justified: First, the degree of hunger is of considerable importance. Larvæ in the initial stages of hunger are not readily induced to eat flesh unless stimulated probably by the odor of the body fluids and more certainly by direct contact with them. Larvæ in the final stages of starvation yet still active enough to crawl about do not require such an intense stimulation. Since animals in this condition habitually nibble at near-by objects, they eventually bite through the integument of an intact carcass or a quiescent animal. At this juncture they too are stimulated by the flesh within. An exceedingly active victim is not actually eaten till it has been rendered more or less quiescent although it may still be capable of considerable movement. Second, crowding facilitates the initiation of the events already mentioned as caused by hunger. In addition crowding induces attacks not prompted by hunger (Balduf, 1931; Dethier, 1937).

II

It was observed that relatively large blocks of tissue were present in the fæces of these carnivorous larvæ. In order to facilitate the examination of these tissues to determine what benefit the larvæ were deriving from their diet the fæces were preserved in alcohol, sectioned in paraffin, and stained with Delafield's hematoxylin and eosin.

Examination revealed that the tracheae as well as all other chitinous structures had passed through the alimentary canal completely untouched. This was to be expected since the occurrence of an enzyme acting upon chitin is very limited (Uvarov, 1928). Epithelium had been completely broken down. Relatively large blocks of muscle tissue were present in the fæces. These were recognizable as such; but digestion had been more or less complete, nothing remaining but a faint indication of the muscle fibers. No conclusion could be drawn concerning the fate of fat due to the histological procedure employed. Plant material from the gut of the victim was also present in the fæces. Serial sections revealed that cell walls in the majority of cases were intact although the entire contents had been removed. This is in accord with Biedermann's (1919) contention that all the active components of the digestive juice can diffuse through cell membranes.

In order to throw further light upon the situation, larvæ were tested for the presence of various digestive enzymes. Tests were adapted from Swingle's (1925), Wigglesworth's (1928), Cole's (1928), and Feigl's (1937) techniques. No attempt was made to conduct a differential analysis. Invertase and maltase were present. Neither lipase, lactase, nor amylase were detected. Amylase had been found occurring quite commonly, however (Dirks, 1922; Straus, 1909; Biedermann, 1911 and 1919). Lactase had been reported from some species. Proteases and glycogenase also occur (Uvarov, 1928). It is apparent from the standpoint of the enzymes found present by various workers that phytophagous larvæ are capable of digesting a meat diet. That both proteases and diastases occur in carnivorous insects and phytophagous insects alike is well known.

As seen by the examination of fæces most of the constituents of a meat diet were utilized. Furthermore, all the

dietary requirements for complete development are met by
a meat diet. The above considerations coupled with the fact
that phytophagous larvæ have been successfully raised to
maturity on a meat diet refute the belief that a plant diet is
necessary for the well-being of these larvæ.

III

The following additional reports of cannibalism and the
carnivorous habit have been gleaned from the literature.[1]
Most of them may be explained on the basis of the principles
set forth above and in a previous paper.

Riley, Packard, and Thomas (1883) stated that *Laphygma
frugiperda* A. & S. and *Cirphis unipuncta* Haw. resort to
cannibalism to satisfy their hunger when migrating. Many
individuals are killed in this manner. Aitken and Davidson
(1890) reported *Ornithoptera minos* Cram. as eating its
own pupæ when normal food was wanting. Witfield (1889)
regarded *Papilio ajax* L. as showing more highly developed
cannibalistic propensities than any other Papilionid larva
of his acquaintance. Floersheim (1909) found, on the contrary, that this species exhibits such behavior only during a
shortage of food and then not very readily, since of twenty
individuals but two were lost by cannibalism although the
food shortage was extreme. Sorhagen (1899) listed all the
cases (about eighty) of cannibalism known to him at the
time. Forbes (1905) also reported *L. frugiperda* as being
cannibalistic in nature when migrating. *Thecla w-album*
according to Tutt (1905-1906) is commonly supposed to
leave its food in order to feast upon the newly-formed pupæ
of its own species. Hering (1926) designated eighty-one
species as "Mordraupen" of which nine cases had been reported as occurring in nature. This list is based on that
of Sorhagen. Lommatzoch (1926) reported *Spilosoma
lubricipeda* Esp. as eating a dead noctuid when its food
supply had been exhausted. The report of Junglung (1930)
that *Scopelosoma satellitia* L. resorted to coprophagy in
captivity when food was lacking is interesting. Small larvæ

---

[1]Berg's paper quoted in Psyche 44(4): 114, 1937 was also reviewed
in Kosmos, Zeit. f. einheitliche Weltanschauung auf Grund der
Entwicklungslehre, 3: 362-363, 1878.

of *Carpocapsa pomonella* L. when crowded exhibit cannibalism (Balduf, 1931). Buckstone (1938) recorded an instance in which the larvæ of *Pieris rapae* L. and ova of
P. brassicae were confined in the same box. When the latter
emerged, they ate the former although the enclosed cabbage
leaves were still fresh.

With further regard to cannibalism under natural conditions I am grateful to Dr. H. G. Crawford of the Department of Agriculture, Canada for permission to quote from
correspondence with departmental officers in the field.

During the summer of 1938 outbreaks of *Cirphis unipuncta* Haw. occurred but no cannibalism was observed.
However, Mr. R. P. Gorham reported that larvæ under
laboratory conditions fed on pupæ although they showed no
interest in larvæ even when massed together in great numbers. The same officer noticed no cannibalism in *Nephelodes
emmedonia* Cram. *Agrotis fennica* Tausch repeatedly attack one another in captivity. Mr. Gorham is of the opinion
that most of our common garden cutworms are cannibalistic
on pupæ in the laboratory. No cannibalism was observed in
Euxoa ochrogaster Guen. or *Loxostege sticticalis* L. Mr.
K. M. King and Mr. H. L. Seamans report that larger larvæ
of *Agrotis orthogonia* Morr. attack smaller and weaker ones
especially in the laboratory. *Chizagrotis auxiliaris* Grote
according to Mr. Seamans is markedly cannibalistic under
conditions of migration. When the advance of the larvæ is
checked by some obstacle such as a furrow, the weaker
larvæ are quickly attacked. Curiously enough larvæ which
have been killed by poisoned bait are frequently eaten.

LITERATURE CITED

Aitken, E. H. and Davidson, J., 1890. Notes on the larvæ and pupæ
    of some of the butterflies of the Bombay Presidency. J. Bombay
    Nat. Hist. Soc., 5:362.
Balduf, W. V., 1931. Carnivorous moths and butterflies. Trans.
    Illinois State Acad. Sci., 24(2): 156-164.
————1938. The rise of entomophagy among Lepidoptera. American
    Nat., 72: 358-379.
Biedermann. W., 1911. Die Aufnahme, Verarbeitung und Assimilation
    der Nahrung. Pt. 9. Die Ernährung der Insekten. Winter-
    stein, Handb. vergl. Physiol. 2(1): 726-902.
————1919. Beiträge zur vergleichenden Physiologie VII and VIII.
    Pflügers Archiv f. die ges. Physiologie, 174: 358-425.

Buckstone, A. A. W., 1938. *Pieris rapæ* a cannibal. Entomologist, 71(897) : 34.
Cole, S. W., 1928. Practical Physiological Chemistry. 8th ed., Baltimore.
Dethier, V. G., 1937. Cannibalism among lepidopterous larvæ. Psyche, 44(4): 110-115.
Dirks, E., 1922. Liefern die Malpighischen Gefässe Verdauungsekrete? Arch. f. Naturgesch., 4: 161-220.
Feigl, F., 1937. Qualitative Analysis by Spot Tests, 314-316, N. Y.
Floersheim, C., 1909. Larval habits of *Iphiclides ajax*. Ent. Rec., 21(5): 113-115.
Forbes, S. A., 1905. 23d Report State Ent. Illinois, 82.
Hering, M., 1926. Biologie der Schmetterlinge, 71-75, Berlin.
Junglung, G., 1930. Ein Fall von Koprophagie (Kotfressen) bei *Scopelosoma satellitia* L. (Lep.). Ent. Zeit. Frankfurt a. M., 43: 57.
Lommatzoch, W., 1926. Sonderbare Mordegelüste einer Raupe. Int. Ent. Zeit., 20: 232.
Riley, C. V., Packard, A. S., and Thomas, C., 1883. Third Report of the U. S. Ent. Commission, 117.
Sorhagen, L., 1899. Mordraupen. Illustr. Zeit. f. Ent., 4(4): 49-51, 4(6): 82-85, 4(9): 135-137.
Straus, J., 1909. Über das Vorkommen einiger Kohlenhydratfermente bei Lepidopteren und Dipteren in verschiedenen Entwicklungs-stadien. Zeit. f. Biol., 52(1-3): 95-106.
Swingle, H. S., 1925. Digestive enzymes of an insect. Ohio J. Sci., 25(5): 209-218.
Tutt, J. W., 1905-1906. British Lepidoptera, 8: 37, London.
Uvarov, B. P., 1928. Insect nutrition and metabolism. A summary of the literature. Trans. London Ent. Soc., 76(2): 255-343.
Wigglesworth, V. B., 1928. Digestion in the cockroach. III The digestion of proteins and fats. Biochem. J., 22(1): 150-161.
Witfield, 1889. Scudder's Butterflies of the Eastern United States and Canada, 2: 1273.

ADDITIONAL RECORDS OF ONYCHOPHORA FROM THE ISLAND OF HAITI

By Charles T. Brues

Biological Laboratories, Harvard University

When he visited Haiti several years ago Dr. P. J. Darlington, of the Museum of Comparative Zoology, obtained specimens of Onychophora from a number of localities in the Republic of Haiti. These proved to represent five distinguishable forms of the genus Peripatus *s. str.* Two of these, *P. manni* Brues and *P. dominicæ* Pollard, var. *haitiensis* Brues had been previously described by the writer from material collected by Dr. Wm. M. Mann.[1]

The other three are additional forms of *P. dominicæ* and were described as varieties by the writer from Dr. Darlington's material.[2]

Quite recently Dr. Austin H. Clark[3] described another species belonging to the related genus Macroperipatus from Haiti as *M. insularis*. This augments the list of Haitian Onychophora to six, including two genera and three species, one of the latter with four named varieties.

Last autumn Dr. Darlington again visited Haiti, this time extending his investigations eastward into the north and central portions of the Dominican Republic. There he secured series of Peripatus at five additional localities.

An examination of these series shows them all to be referable to *P. dominicæ* Pollard, var. *basilensis* Brues previously known from Mount Basil in the northwestern part of the island.

The distribution of *basilensis* is thus greatly extended by this material as indicated below.

(1) Mt. Diego de Ocampo, Northern Range, Dominican Republic. 3500-4000 feet (July 1938). One specimen, quite typical, but with 30 pairs of legs instead of 28 as in the type.

(2) North slope of Loma Rucilla, Central Range, Domin-

[1]Bull. Mus. Comp. Zool., vol. 54, pp. 519-521 (1913).
[2]Psyche, vol. 42, pp. 58-62 (1935).
[3]Proc. U. S. National Mus., vol. 85, No. 3027, p. 3 (1937).

ican Republic, about 8000 feet (June 1928). Six specimens
with 27 pairs (four individuals) or 28 pairs of legs (two
individuals).

(3) North of Loma Rucilla, Central Range, Dominican
Republic, 6000-7000 feet (June 1938). Two large females,
each with only 26 pairs of legs.

(4) Constanza, Central Range, Dominican Republic,
3000-4000 feet (August 1938). Eight specimens with 27-31
pairs of legs; one ♂ with 27 pairs, one with 29 pairs, four
with 30 pairs and two with 31 pairs.

(5) Vic Valle Neuvo, southeast of Constanza, Central
Range, about 7000 feet (August 1938). Two specimens,
each with 28 pairs of legs.

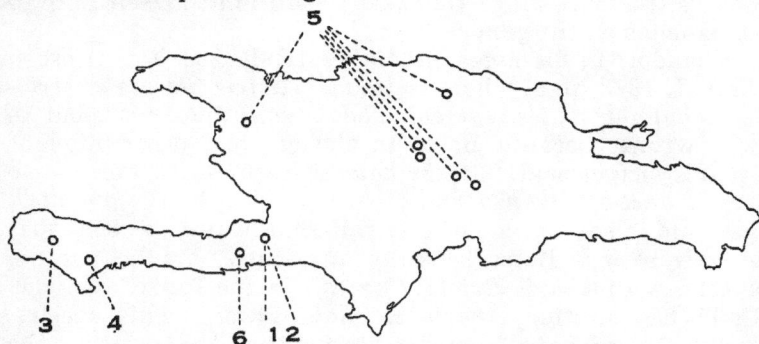

Fig. 1. Outline map of Haiti showing the known distribution of
Onychophora. 1, *Peripatus manni;* 2, *Peripatus dominicæ,* var.
haitiensis; 3, *Peripatus dominicæ,* var. *darlingtoni;* 4, *Peripatus
dominicæ,* var. *lachauxensis;* 5, *Peripatus dominicæ,* var. *basilensis;*
6, *Macroperipatus insularis.*

It thus appears that *Peripatus dominicæ* var. *basilensis*
extends eastward from Mt. Basil into the Northern Range
of Mountains and also into the Central Range. All of the
specimens listed above are very similar to the types although many of them have more pairs of legs. However,
the number apparently never reaches that present in what I
have considered to be the nearest relative, var. *darlingtoni*
Brues which is so far known only from well out on the south-
western peninsula on the Massif de la Hotte.

The accompanying outline map, kindly drawn for me by
Mrs. A. S. O'Connor summarizes our present knowledge of
the distribution of Onychophora on the island of Haiti.

ON THE GENUS ABARIS DEJ.
(COLEOPTERA; CARABIDÆ)

By S. L. Straneo
Parma, Italy

I have been trying for many months to secure typical examples of all of the known species of the genus *Abaris* Dej., for a revision of the genus. However, I have been unable to secure all of them, so I shall limit myself here to some notes on the genus.

Chaudoir in his notes on *Abaris* (Bull. Soc. Nat. Moscou XLVII, 1873, p. 97) has written: *"Abaris picipes et striolatus qui ont . . . les segments abdominaux sillonnés"*; but he was wrong, because Bates in the original description of *Abaris picipes* said, *"ventre haud sulcato"* and, *"there is no appearance of a transversal groove on the ventral segments"*. He said also (Biologia Centrali-Americana, p. 85) that *Abaris picipes* Bates is really an *Abaris*, but he put the species with *Abaris striolata* Bates. In the Junk Catalogue, Csiki has omitted *Abaris striolata* Bates. This species, known to me only from description, has the claws of the tarsi pectinated (Bates, *l. c.*, p. 85) and the ventral segments grooved; owing to these characters, it should be inserted in the genus *Abaridius* Chaud. or in a new genus near *Abaris* and *Abaridius*.

Here follows the description of a new species found in the material sent to me by P. J. Darlington Jr. of the Museum of Comparative Zoölogy of Cambridge, Massachusetts.

Abaris darlingtoni n. sp. (fig. 1)

Aeneous, lightly virescent, head and pronotum very shiny, elytra a little less nitid; antennae, legs, and mouth ferrugineous, joints 1-3 of antennae a little darker in the middle, femora and apex of mandibles darker, lateral margin of pronotum ferrugineous, last ventral segment at apex broadly flavous. Length: 5.5 mm.; max. lat. 2.1 mm.

Head very similar to that of *Abaris aenea* Dej.; large, smooth, neck evidently constricted, eyes large and convex, frontal foveæ moderately deep, short, rather united by a vague frontal impression behind clypeal suture.

Prothorax wide, sides gently rounded, lateral margin slightly explanate and moderately reflexed in basal half, median line very fine, interior basal foveæ rather deep, the exterior ones more superficial, with a few large punctures, and rugosities, not extended to lateral margin; anterior margin a little less wide than the head with the eyes; base distinctly wider than the anterior margin.

Fig. 1.   *Abaris darlingtoni* n. sp.

Elytra oblongo-ovate, a little wider than the prothorax, one half longer than wide, with the greatest width before the middle; striæ strongly impressed, the scutellary one vestigial; third interstice a little less wide than the first and second together, with a single puncture behind the middle.

Underside smooth, metapisterna long, ventral segments not sulcate.

Claws of the tarsi finely pectinated; onychium with some fine setæ on the underside.

The microsculpture, invisible on the prothorax, on the elytra is rather faint and transversal.

Locality: Panama Canal Zone: Barro Colorado Island (Van Tyne and Darlington), 2 examples. Holotype in the

Museum of Comparative Zoölogy at Cambridge, Massachusetts (type no. 23,393) ; allotype in coll. Straneo.

This new species is closely allied to *Abaris aenea* Dej. and *notiophiloides* Bates by the lack of a scutellary stria and by the lateral margin of the pronotum distinctly reflexed near the basal angles. Compared with *A. aenea* Dej. the 3rd interstice of elytra is wider (nearly as wide as in *notiophiloides*) and the lateral margin is a little less reflexed near the base: compared with *A. notiophiloides* Bates, the legs are ferrugineous and the femora darker (in *notiophiloides*, flavo-testaceous) and the base of the pronotum is punctured only near the basal foveæ (in *notiophiloides*, also in the basal part of lateral margin).

KEY TO THE SPECIES OF THE GENUS ABARIS DEJ.

(1)	(8)	No scutellary stria.
(2)	(7)	Lateral margin of pronotum in the basal part wide and distinctly reflexed.
(3)	(4)	Third interstice of elytra subequal to or only a little wider than second. .... *aenea* Dej.
(4)	(3)	Third interstice of elytra distinctly wider than 2nd, about as wide as first and second together.
(5)	(6)	Legs flavous; base of pronotum punctured, including the basal part of lateral margin. .... *notiophiloides* Bates
(6)	(5)	Legs ferrugineous red, femora darker; base of pronotum punctured only near basal foveae. .... *darlingtoni* n. sp.
(7)	(2)	Lateral margin of pronotum even near base narrow and not reflexed. .... *aequinoctialis* Chaud.
(8)	(1)	Scutellary stria present and rather elongate.
(9)	(10)	Size smaller (5-5.5 mm.). *basistriatus* Chaud.
(10)	(9)	Size larger (6.5-8 mm.).
(11)	(12)	External basal foveae of pronotum not distinct, because lateral margin is widely reflexed. .... *robustulus* Tschit.

(12) (11)   External basal foveae of pronotum very dis-
             tinct, lateral margin of the pronotum not re-
             flexed (from description). ....
             .... *bigenera* Bates & *picipes* Bates

I do not know these last species, and in the original de-
scription there are no useful differential characters, for
A. bigenera is compared with *Pseudobaris substriatus*
Chaud. which belongs to another genus.

I have to thank Mr. H. E. Andrewes and Dr. P. J. Darlington Jr. for the specimens kindly sent to me for examination,
and my friend Dr. F. Capra for his help in connection with
old descriptions.

PIN-LABELS IN MULTIPLES OF 1000, ALIKE

One Dollar Per Thousand

Smallest Type. Pure White Ledger Paper. Not over 4 Lines nor 30 Characters (13 to a line) Additional Characters, 3 cents each, in total and per line, per 1000. Trimmed so one cut makes a label.

C. V. BLACKBURN, 7 Emerson St., STONEHAM 80, MASS.

CAMBRIDGE ENTOMOLOGICAL CLUB

A regular meeting of the Club is held on the second Tuesday of each month (July, August and September excepted) at 7.45 p.m. in Room B-455, Biological Laboratories of Harvard University, Divinity Ave., Cambridge. Entomologists visiting Boston are cordially invited to attend.

WARD'S ENTOMOLOGICAL SERVICES

Entomological Supplies and Equipment
Carefully designed by professional entomologists. Material of high quality at low prices. **Send for Supply Catalog No. 348.**

Insect Preparations
Life Histories, Type Collections, Collections of Economic Insects and Biological Insect Collections. All specimens are accurately determined.

Insects for the Pest Collection
We have in stock over three hundred species of North American Insect Pests. Send for Price List No. 349.

Ward's Entomological Bulletin
A monthly publication sent free to all entomologists requesting it.

Information for the Beginner
Send for **"Directions for Collecting and Preserving Insects"** by Dr. A. B. Klots. A mine of useful information. Price 15 cents.

WARD'S NATURAL SCIENCE ESTABLISHMENT, Inc.
P. O. Box 24, Beechwood Station
Rochester, N. Y., U. S. A.
The Frank A. Ward Foundation of Natural Science of the University of Rochester

BACK VOLUMES OF PSYCHE

The Cambridge Entomological Club is able to offer for sale the following volumes of Psyche. Those not mentioned are entirely out of print.

Volumes 2, 3, 4, 5, 6, 7, 8, 9, 10, each covering a period of three years, $5.00 each.

Volumes 12, 14, 17, each covering a single year, $1.00 each.

Volumes 18, 19, 20, 21, 22, 23, 24, 25, 26, each covering a single year, $1.50 each.

Volumes 27, 28, 29, 30, 31, 32, 33, 34, 35, 36, 37, 38, 39, 40, 41, 42, 43, 44, 45, each covering a single year, $2.00.

Orders for 2 or more volumes subject to a discount of 10%.

Orders for 10 or more volumes subject to a discount of 20%.

A set of all the volumes available (40 in all) will be sold for $81.00.

All orders should be addressed to

F. M. CARPENTER, Associate Editor of Psyche,
Biological Laboratories,
Harvard University,
Cambridge, Mass.

PSYCHE

A JOURNAL OF ENTOMOLOGY

ESTABLISHED IN 1874

VOL. XLVI   JUNE-SEPTEMBER, 1939   Nos. 2-3

TABLE OF CONTENTS

CAMBRIDGE ENTOMOLOGICAL CLUB

OFFICERS FOR 1939-1940

President .	C. H. BLAKE
Vice-President	. F. M. CARPENTER
Secretary	C. T. PARSONS
Treasurer	RICHARD DOW
	T. BARBOUR
Executive Committee {	C. H. BLAKE
	R. T. HOLWAY

EDITORIAL BOARD OF PSYCHE

EDITOR-IN-CHIEF
C. T. BRUES, HARVARD UNIVERSITY

ASSOCIATE EDITOR
F. M. CARPENTER, HARVARD UNIVERSITY

CONSULTING EDITORS

NATHAN BANKS,
Harvard University.

A. E. EMERSON,
University of Chicago.

THOMAS BARBOUR,
Harvard University.

A. L. MELANDER,
College of the
City of New York.

RICHARD DOW,
New England Museum of
Natural History,
Boston, Mass.

J. G. NEEDHAM,
Cornell University.

PSYCHE is published quarterly, the issues appearing in March, June, September, and December. Subscription price, per year, payable in advance: $2.00 to Subscribers in the United States; foreign postage, 25 cents extra, Canada 15 cents. Single copies, 65 cents.

Cheques and remittances should be addressed to Treasurer, Cambridge Entomological Club, Biological Laboratories, Harvard University, Cambridge, Mass.

Orders for back volumes, missing numbers, notices of change of address, etc., should be sent to Professor F. M. Carpenter, Biological Laboratories, Harvard University, Cambridge, Mass.

IMPORTANT NOTICE TO CONTRIBUTORS

Manuscripts intended for publication, books intended for review, and other editorial matter, should be addressed to Professor C. T. Brues, Biological Laboratories, Harvard University, Cambridge, Mass.

Authors contributing articles over 8 printed pages in length will be required to bear a part of the extra expense, for additional pages. This expense will be that of typesetting only, which is about $2.00 per page. The actual cost of preparing cuts for all illustrations must be borne by contributors; the expense for full page plates from line drawings is approximately $5.00 each, and for full page half-tones, $7.50 each; smaller sizes in proportion.

AUTHOR'S SEPARATES

Reprints of articles may be secured by authors, if they are ordered before, or at the time proofs are received for corrections. The cost of these will be furnished by the Editor on application.

Printed by the Eliot Press Inc., Jamaica Plain, Mass., U. S. A.

PSYCHE

VOL. XLVI   JUNE-SEPTEMBER, 1939   Nos. 2-3

NOTES ON BUTTERFLIES FROM HISPANIOLA

By Marston Bates

Museum of Comparative Zoology, Cambridge, Mass.

The island of Hispaniola, broken into many life zones and habitats by its lofty mountain ranges, presents the most interesting—and least known—fauna of any island in the West Indies. Sharpe (1898) and Hall (1925) have given lists of butterflies from the island, the latter enumerating 139 species. The Hispaniolan butterfly fauna is surely as large as that of Cuba and perhaps larger (159 species are now known from Cuba: Bates, 1935; 1936) and almost any collection from the island includes species not previously known from there. The Museum of Comparative Zoology and the American Museum of Natural History now have fairly extensive collections from Hispaniola, and a worthwhile study of the butterfly fauna could be made on the basis of this material. Since, however, there is little likelihood that any such study will be made in the near future, it seems best to publish the following notes on certain particularly interesting species.

The best account of the zoogeography of the island seems to be that of Wetmore and Swales (1931) and most of the localities mentioned in the present paper can be found on their map.

The nomenclature and sequence used in the present paper conforms with that of my "Butterflies of Cuba" (Bates, 1935).

Eurema dina (Poey)

There seem to be two species of *Eurema* in Hispaniola belonging to the *dina* complex: one related to the Cuban

dina and the other to the Bahaman *helios*. Klots, in his
revision of the genus Eurema (1929, p. 139) has considered
that *dina* presents a peculiarly complicated taxonomic problem; but this may be due to the frequency with which morphologically distinct local populations are encountered.
Individuals from a given population seem to have a quite
uniform facies, as is shown by the long series in the M. C. Z.
from Cuba *(dina)*, New Providence *(helios)* and Honduras
(westwoodi). There is considerable variation in the genital
structures as Klots (1928, p. 66) has pointed out; but this
variation seems in part at least to be geographical.

The Bahaman populations that I have called *"Eurema
chamberlaini* Butler" (Bates, 1934, p. 134) seem to belong
to the *dina* complex, and the Cuban *Eurema laræ* (Bates,
1936, p. 226) may also belong there, although as our only
specimen lacks the abdomen it is impossible to place it with
any certainty. The Puerto Rican *Eurema sanjuanensis*
(Watson, 1938) is unknown to me.

The known West Indian *dina* populations might, then, be
arranged as follows:

> *Eurema dina dina* (Poey)   Cuba
> *dina memulus* (Butler)   Hispaniola
> *dina parvumbra* (Kaye)   Jamaica
> *laræ* (Herrich-Schäffer)   Cuba
> *helios helios* Bates   New Providence, Andros
> *helios mayobanex* subsp. nov.   Hispaniola
> *chamberlaini chamberlaini* (Butler)   Great Inagua
> *chamberlaini mariguanæ* Bates   Mariguana
> *chamberlaini* subsp. indescr.   Cat Is.

Eurema dina memulus (Butler)

Terias memulus Butler, 1871, p. 251, pl. 19, f. 6.

♂. Wings above light orange, somewhat deeper in color
toward the margins; apex of forewing black, the inner edge
of this black patch evenly rounded or slightly dentate,
extending from a point about two thirds of the way out on
the costa to the inner angle. Under side yellow: immaculate or with scattered brownish spots on the hindwing.
Length of forewing, 16–17 mm.

2 ♂ ♂ in the M. C. Z. from Haiti: Ennery (2500 ft.,
Aug., Bates) and "San Domingo" (Weeks Coll.).

This differs from the Cuban form *(E. dina dina)* in the complete absence of a black border on the hindwing, and in the greater extent of the apical black patch of the forewing. Our specimens agree very well with Butler's description and figure.

Eurema helios mayobanex subsp. nov.

♂. Wings above uniform orange, with a fine black border on the hindwing and a conspicuous border on the forewing, about the same as in the Cuban *dina*. Under side immaculate orange except for a minute double cell spot on the hindwing.

♀. Deeper orange toward the edge of the wings; no black margin to hindwing; apical border of forewing brown rather than black. Under side with a reddish patch at apex of forewing, and another on the margin of hindwing between veins Rs and M_1; some scattered purplish spots on disc of hindwing. Length of forewing, 20–22 mm.

Type (♂) and paratypes (2 ♂ ♂, 1 ♀) from Haiti: Ennery (2500 ft., Aug., Bates).

This form may be distinguished from *dina (s. s.), parvumbra* or *memulus* by the dark orange ground color of both sexes, and from *helios* by the comparatively broad apical border of the forewing.

The "distal process" of the male genitalia of *mayobanex* (Klots, 1928 for terminology) is about twice as wide as in *memulus,* and the various lobes are much more strongly developed in the former species. The genitalia of two specimens of *mayobanex* and of one of *memulus* were examined.

The four specimens of *mayobanex* and the Ennery specimen of *memulus* were all caught on the same day, as were specimens of *Eurema lisa* and *E. proterpia*.

Kricogonia castalia (Fabricius)

In the M. C. Z. there are 21 ♂ ♂, 7 ♀ ♀ from: Haiti: Cabaret (Aug.) ; Mont Rouis (Aug.) ; Mt. Bourette, La Selle Range (5000 ft., Sept.) ; Cap Haitien; Rep. Dom.: Bonao (Aug.) ; Saona Is. (Jan.).

The pattern variation of this species seems to show no

geographical correlation, except insofar as certain populations seem to be more uniform than others (*e.g.*, the Bahamas). Very dissimilar specimens from the same region show identical structure in the male genitalia, but there seems to be some, though slight, geographically correlated variation in these organs. The genitalia of the Cuban *K. cabrerai* have not been examined, but the form seems to be distinct. With this exception it seems to me that, pending adequate material from all regions for comparative study, the best course is to treat the entire complex under the oldest name *(Papilio castalia* Fabricius, 1793, Entom. Syst., 3, 1, p. 188, presumably from Jamaica), and to describe the variation shown by different populations in terms as general as possible.

In the Hispaniolan series there are two types of males:

A, with the wings immaculate whitish above, except for the orange area at the base of the forewing, and a light longitudinal streak on the under side of the hindwing;

B, similar above except for a black postmedian bar on the costa of the hindwing, but with the underside of the hindwing uniform light yellow except for a shadow of the black bar of the upper side.

These two types show no intergrades; three specimens belong to type A, the remaining eighteen to type B. We have specimens like type A from Arizona, Nicaragua and Jamaica; like type B from Arizona. These might be considered as "incipient species" but the genitalia of A and B from Hispaniola seem to be identical and slightly different from the genitalia of A and B from Arizona!

Three types of females occur on Hispaniola:

C, above entirely lemon yellow, slightly darker at the base of the forewing; similar below, but with a prominent light longitudinal streak (really a fold) on the hindwing, and a faint silvery reticulation on this wing (1 specimen, Saona Is.);

D, chalky white above, darker on the base of the forewing; similar below, but bright yellow on the base of the forewing, the ground color of the hindwing and the apex of the forewing slightly yellowish, the fold of the hindwing prominent but not marked with contrasting scales (5 specimens);

E, similar but with an indication of a postmedian row of dark spots on the underside of the hindwing (1 specimen, Cabaret).

We have specimens of type C from Texas, Honduras and Nicaragua (the last somewhat intermediate between C and D) ; of type D from Texas; of type E from Texas. A sixth type with the apex of the forewing rather broadly marked with brown, and with the hindwing somewhat darker than the forewing above, occurs in Guatemala, Honduras and Arizona.

Dismorphia spio (Godart)

Pieris spio Godart, 1819, p. 167 (Antilles).

In the M. C. Z. there are 10 ♂ ♂, 9 ♀ ♀ from Haiti: Cap Haitien; La Hotte Peninsula, Camp Perrin, 1000 ft., Oct.; Etang Lachaux, Oct.; Rep. Dom.: San José de las Matas, 1000-2000 ft., June.

The variation in this series is very interesting. The two males from the La Hotte peninsula (Camp Perrin) may represent a distinct population, as they are smaller than any of the other specimens and have the yellow area of the costal margin of the upper side of the hindwing broadly connected with the orange postdiscal area, instead of separated by a black bar as in specimens from Cap Haitien. One yellow male from San José de las Matas, however, has the black bar only partially developed.

Both sexes of this species seem to be dimorphic: of the males in the series, six have orange markings and four have yellow markings; of the females, three are orange and six are yellow. Avinoff (1926, p. 363, pl. 33, f. 1) has described a yellow form from Puerto Rico as "ab. *virago*". The yellow females are strikingly similar to the normal females of the Cuban *Dismorphia cubana*.

Genus **Calisto** Hübner

In my review of the genus *Calisto* (Bates, 1935) I described five new species from Hispaniola, bringing the total known from the island up to nine. This seemed like a very large number of species, and I was greatly surprised to find two more very distinct new species in material collected by Dr. P. J. Darlington in the Dominican Republic in 1938.

One of these is the largest and most striking species of *Calisto* yet to be described. When the island is thoroughly explored, it will probably be found that the various mountain ranges are inhabited by distinct local populations of many of these *Calisto* species, and there is evidence of such geographical variation in some of the series in the collection of the M. C. Z.; there seems, however, to be no point in giving names to such subspecific populations at the present time.

Calisto arcas sp. nov.

♂ ♀. Sexes similar. Upper side: forewing: dark fuscous with a row of large more or less confluent submarginal fulvous spots extending from the inner margin to vein M_2; hindwing with the basal half fuscous, the distal half fulvous, except for a narrow, sharply defined, burnt orange submarginal line and a fuscous margin at the outer angle extending to vein M_1. Under side: forewing: dark reddish brown from base to just beyond cell, except for a black area along the inner margin; postmedian area fulvous, marked off by narrow brown lines; margin somewhat darker; ocellus in the fulvous area: black surrounded by a yellow ring; two bluish white central dots. Hindwing a rich brown, the basal half slightly yellowish, the distal half reddish; distinct antemedian, postmedian and submarginal dark lines; two ocelli of about equal size, both marked with yellow rings, the center black enclosing small, central, bluish-white dots; one ocellus in the M_1—M_2 area, the other in the Cu_1—Cu_2 area; an isolated white dot in the M_2—M_3 area; Length of forewing, 24—27mm.

♂. The androconia are limited to the Cu_1-Cu_2 and Cu_2-2A areas; they do not form a sharply defined patch. The genitalia of this species are quite distinctive: the uncus being asymmetrical, and the valves elongate, squared at the end.

Type (♂) and 3 ♂ ♂ 2 ♀ ♀ paratypes from Valle Nuevo, S. E. Constanza, Rep. Dom., Aug. 1938, c. 7000 ft., P. J. Darlington; 3 ♂ ♂ and 3 ♀ ♀ from Loma Vieja, S. Constanza, Aug. 1938, c. 6000 ft., P. J. Darlington.

The position of vein R_1 of the forewing, which arises at the end of the cell, and the symmetrical ocelli of the hind-

wing, indicate that this species should be put in the Arche-
bates Group. It differs strikingly, however, from the other
members of this group and from all other species of the
genus both in genital structure and in pattern. It is the
only known species with fulvous markings on the upper
side of the forewing, and the only species, except the new
one described below as *grannus*, with two symmetrical
ocelli on the under side of the hindwing.

Calisto chrysaoros Bates

Dr. Darlington captured four specimens of this species
in the "foothills of the Cordillera Central S. of Santiago"
and one "between Constanza and Valle Nuevo, 6000 ft." in
the Dominican Republic. These differ from the typical
specimens from the La Hotte and La Selle mountains of
Haiti in having the under side of the hindwing fuscous
rather than brown, and in having the white median band
of this wing somewhat nearer the similar band over the
ocellus. This species, then, seems to occur at high eleva-
tions in several parts of the island.

Calisto grannus sp. nov.

Upper side: dark fuscous, the disc of the forewing
(androconia patch) very dark. Under side: forewing:
fuscous, with a fine dark postmedian line extending from
the costal to the inner margin, and with two wavy submarginal lines along the outer margin; ocellus of the usual
design: black, ringed with yellow, with two minute white
pupils. Hindwing: fuscous, with fine reddish-brown antemedian and postmedian lines and with two very irregular
submarginal lines; two symmetrical ocelli (black ringed
with yellow or orange, with a single central white dot) :
one, slightly smaller, in the M_1-M_2 area, the other in the
Cu_1-Cu_2 area; a prominent white spot in the M_2-M_3 area and
another in the M_3-Cu_1 area. Length of forewing, 16–18 mm.

♂. Androconia patch like that of *C. hysius*. Genitalia
strikingly similar to those of *C. hysius*, differing only in
details of proportion and chitinization.

Type (♂) and one paratype ♂ from Valle Nuevo, S. E.
Constanza, Rep. Dom., Aug. 1938, c. 7000 ft., P. J. Darling-

ton; 3 paratypes ♂ ♂ from Loma Rucilla, June 1938, 8000 ft., P. J. Darlington.

The three specimens from Loma Rucilla differ from the others in that the lines of the under side are more obscure, the ocellus of the forewing smaller.

This species, structurally, seems to be close to *C. hysius*, but it differs from all other species of the *hysius* group in having two symmetrical ocelli on the under side of the hindwing—instead of one asymmetrical ocellus—and in the absence of a distinct red patch in the cell of the forewing.

Calisto pulchella Lathy

Dr. Darlington caught four males of this species in the Constanza region (3000–4000 ft.) which differ rather strikingly from the common Haitian form in having the under side of the hindwing marked with orange rather than reddish-orange, and in having the antemedian and postmedian lines more widely separated.

Hypolimnas misippus (Linnaeus)

There is one male in the M. C. Z. collection from Haiti: Cul-de-Sac Plain, Jan., A. Audant. This is the first record of the species from Hispaniola.

REFERENCES

Avinoff, A.
  1926. Descriptions of some new species and varieties of Rhopalocera in the Carnegie Museum. Ann. Carnegie Mus., vol. 16, pp. 355–374, pl. 30–33.

Bates, M.
  1934. New Lepidoptera from the Bahamas. Occ. Papers Boston Soc. Nat. Hist., vol. 8, pp. 133–138.
  1935. The butterflies of Cuba. Bull. Mus. Comp. Zool., vol. 78, pp. 63–258, 24 figs.
  1935b. The Satyrid genus *Calisto*. Occ. Papers Boston Soc. Nat. Hist., vol. 8, pp. 229–248, 10 figs.
  1936. Notes on Cuban butterflies. Mem. Soc. Cubana Hist. Nat., vol. 9, pp. 225–228, 1 fig.

Butler, A. G.
  1871. Descriptions of some new species and a new genus of Pierinae, with a monographic list of the species of *Ixias*. Proc. Zool. Soc. London, pp. 250–254, pl. 19.

Godart, J. B.
    1819. Papillon. *in* Encycl. Meth., Hist. nat., Entomologie. Tome
           IX. Paris, 828 pp.
Hall, A. H.
    1925. List of the butterflies of Hispaniola. The Entomologist,
           vol. 58, pp. 161–165; 186–190.
Klots, A. B.
    1928. A revision of the genus *Eurema*. Part. I. New World
           species, morphology and phylogeny. Journ. N. Y. Ent.
           Soc., vol. 36, pp. 61–72, pl. 2–4.
    1929. A revision of the genus *Eurema*. Part II. New World
           species, taxonomy and synonymy. Entom. Amer., vol. 9,
           pp. 99–163, pl. 1–4.
Sharpe, E. M. B.
    1898. On a collection of Lepidopterous insects from San Domingo.
           With field notes by the collector, Dr. Cuthbert Christy.
           Proc. Zool. Soc. London, pp. 362–369.
Watson, F. E.
    1938. A new *Eurema* from Puerto Rico. Am. Mus. Nov., No.
           971. 2 pp.
Wetmore, A and Swales, B. H.
    1931. The birds of Haiti and the Dominican Republic. U. S.
           Nat. Mus., Bull. 155. 483 pp., 26 pls., map.

NOTES AND DESCRIPTIONS OF ORIENTAL ŒSTROPSYCHINÆ (TRICHOPTERA)

By Nathan Banks

Museum of Comparative Zoology

There are a number of species in this group in the Orient, although for many years it was the custom to call every specimen of Polymorphanisus, *P. nigricornis*, and every Œstropsyche as *Œ. vitrina*.

Having a considerable number of specimens from India, it is seen that each is fairly constant in structural characters, both of body and wings.

Polymorphanisus

The species of this genus fall into two sections; one with the fourth fork sharply acute at base and extending well back on the median cell and with the fore wing not especially broad; to this belongs *nigricornis* and some allied forms; the other section has broad, rather short wings, and the fork four is broad at base and goes back but little, if at all, on the median cell; to this group belong *indicus, ocularis, astictus*. The females of the first group from Asia known to me can be separated as follows:

1. Head swollen in front in a rounded lobe, mesoscutellum with two black stripes, discal cell very short .*tumidus*

   Head not prominently swollen in front 2

2. Fringe of mid tarsi blackish, antennæ black 3

   Fringe of mid tarsi paler 4

3. A dark spot on mesoscutellum, discal cell short, front legs pale .... *unipunctus*

   No spot on mesoscutellum, discal cell about one half as long as median cell, front tibiæ and often femora blackish .... *nigricornis*

4. Legs yellowish, fringe of mid tarsi yellowish; antennæ
   dark only at joints; front tibiæ with only a dark dot
   at tips .... *flavipes*

   Legs pale, not distinctly yellowish, fringe of mid legs
   silvery, outer half of front tibiæ black; fore wings
   rather broader than usual .... *hainanensis*

P. taonicus Navas from South China I do not know.

Polymorphanisus nigricornis Walk.

Walker says the antennæ and the fringe on legs black.
This form has the front tibiæ more or less dark, and often
the femora also.   The discal cell is about one-half as long
as the median cell, fork one longer than its pedicel, fork
four well back on median cell, but not halfway to the cross-
vein, latter before middle of cell, cross-vein from median
fork to cubitus is straight and about twice its length before
base of median cell.   There are no distinct marks on the
mesonotum, nor does Walker mention any.

Many specimens from Shimoga, Mysore, India.

Polymorphanisus unipunctus Bks.   Fig. 4

From Suifu (Graham) and Chin Chi Shan (Gaines Liu),
both Szechuan; fork one is very short as well as the discal
cell.

Polymorphanisus flavipes sp. nov.

Pale greenish, rarely a trace of dark each side on the
mesonotum, abdomen dark, ventral segments more or less
tipped with pale; antennæ pale, sometimes somewhat darkened toward tips, the joints narrowly black at tips, basal
joint behind with a black streak; legs yellowish, front and
mid tibiæ with dark dot at tips, fringe of mid legs plainly
yellowish.

Wings greenish, with green veins; discal cell rather
short, not one-half of median cell; fork one longer than
pedicel, fork four back on median cell about width of
median, not halfway to the cross-vein which is much before
the middle of cell; cross-vein from median fork to cubitus

about two and one-half times its length before median cell; venation of hind wings much as in *nigricornis*.

Length of fore wing 20 to 23 mm.

From Shimoga, and Bhadravati, Mysore, India, in May, June, August, September, and October (Susai Nathan). Two specimens with rather more yellowish wings have a very distinct black spot each side on the mesonotum, and the fourth apical cell is more narrow than in the other specimens. Type M. C. Z. no. 23467.

Polymorphanisus tumidus sp. nov.   Figs. 11, 12

Pale greenish, abdomen dull black, mesoscutellum with two short black stripes, antennæ greenish, black mark at the joinings, legs pale greenish, front pair unmarked, mid legs with the tibiæ and tarsi yellowish, a black spot at tips of tibiæ and tarsal joints, the fringe brownish yellow; front of head with a great, smooth, rounded swelling in front.

Fore wings greenish, veins green; discal cell very small, only about one-fourth as long as median cell, and fully as high as long; fork one about three times as long as the pedicel, fork four well back on median cell, but not halfway to the cross-vein, which is much before the middle of cell; cross-vein from median fork to cubitus fully three times its length before median cell; venation of hind wing much as usual.

Length of fore wing 19 to 20 mm.

From Shimoga, Mysore, India, 15 to 28 April (Susai Nathan coll.). Remarkable for the peculiar head. Type M. C. Z. no. 23468.

From the larger Malayan islands there are at least three species, and doubtless more.

Polymorphanisus semperi Brauer

In some specimens there are two faint dark marks on the mesoscutellum, and also present more plainly in all three males I have seen. All of my specimens are from Luzon.

Polymorphanisus fuscus Ulmer

Two females from Telang, Borneo (Grabowsky) have the black spots near base of fore wings; the mesoscutellum is almost wholly black, and two narrowly separated black spots in front on the margin of the mesonotum.

Polymorphanisus scutellatus sp. nov.   Fig. 9

Pale yellowish to greenish; no marks on head nor legs; antennæ pale, narrowly dark at tips of joints; mesoscutellum with two black spots; abdomen dull black. Wings greenish, veins green, the veins about discal cell and several apical veins in upper part are bordered with yellowish, much as in *P. semperi.*

Fore wings moderately slender, about as *nigricornis*, not at all sinuate on outer margin; discal cell is four-sided, fork two rather deeply indenting the anastomosis, the discal cell not nearly one-half as long as the median cell, cross-vein from lower side of discal to the median is obliquely backward; median cell very long, not nearly as wide as discal, fork four extending back on the median cell about one-half the width of cell; cross-vein from median cell to cubitus before middle of cell; fork one not nearly as long as its pedicel.

Venation of hind wing much as in *semperi*, except that fork five is only one half as long, shorter than in any other species noted.

Length of fore wing 15 to 18 mm.

From Baram River district, Sarawak, Borneo (H. W. Smith 1912) ; others marked Sarawak, and one from Hagen collection, Duson Tinoc, Borneo (Grabowsky). Type M.C.Z. no. 23472.

Differs from *semperi* by shape of fore wing and many points of venation.

A specimen from Buitenzorg, Java (T. Barbour) and one from Medan, Sumatra (G. Fairchild) have the same venation but the mesoscutellum is almost wholly black, and quite possibly represent another species.

Œstropsyche vitrina Hagen   Figs. 5, 14

Both of Hagen's males have the median cell longer than figured by Ulmer (Selys Monog. Trich. (2) fig. 21) for his Celebes or Sumatra specimen. Fork four is also more geniculate at base than he figures; in the hind wing the venation is much as he figures but forks two and three are well separated at base.

Œ. palingenia Brauer from the Philippines is distinct, and probably also some other island forms. In the female of *palingenia*, the discal cell is not so wide as in the male, and is nearly as far from the radius as its own width, and fork two is not short-pedicellate, but only much narrowed at base. I figure (Fig. 2,) the appendages of a male from Mt. Makeling, Luzon (U.S.N.M. coll.).

I have from India another species, possibly the one referred to *vitrina* by Martynov (Rec. Ind. Mus. XXXVII, p. 93). I give a figure of the fore wing of the type of *Œ. vitrina*.

Œstropsyche hageni sp. nov. Fig. 6

This has the same general appearance as Hagen's species, but is smaller; fore wing 12 mm., Hagen's type 15 mm. The median cell is about a fourth shorter than *vitrina*, with a very short margin on the cubitus, the inner side less sinuate, the fork four fully as much curved at base. In the hind wing fork one is very short, otherwise like *vitrina*. In the mid legs the second tarsal joint is nearly one-half of the first, in *vitrina* scarcely more than one-third, and the membranous margin is of a more even width.

The genitalia have the claspers of about the same proportions as in *vitrina*, but the tip of the penis in *vitrina* has a projection below, which is lacking in *hageni;* from above the superior plate is slightly projecting in the middle.

From Shimoga, Mysore, India, 21 July (Susai Nathan). Type M.C.Z. no. 23469.

Amphipsyche apicalis sp. nov. Figs. 1, 3, 8, 15

♂ Pale yellowish, face silvery on the sides, thorax and apical part of the abdomen rather darker yellow; legs pale whitish, unmarked; antennæ pale, joints narrowly dark at tips; palpi long, apical part rather dark.

Fore wing sparsely clothed with yellowish hair, more yellowish along anal margin, a brighter yellowish cloud before anastomosis, another one transversely beyond anastomosis, and the apical part broadly yellow, in the apical part of fork one is a rounded black spot; hind wings pale whitish. Fore wings rather long, tip broadly rounded. Venation much as in *A. nirvana* (*indica*), the radius strongly sinuate, radial sector nearly straight, median cell more slender than usual, a minute cell at base of fork two which is pedicellate; hind wings much as in other species, the cubital fork slender, as in *A. tricalcarata.* Spurs 1, 4, 4, the subapical pair of hind legs rather small and close together, but plainly two. Male genitalia above much as in *A. distincta*, but from beneath the claspers have the basal part very slender, not at all enlarged as in *distincta;* the penis has a large hump beyond middle, further from the tip than in *A. nirvana,* and the tip of penis, seen from below (or above) is slender and bifid.

Fore wings 13 mm. long.

From Shimoga, Mysore, India, 10 April (Susai Nathan). Type M.C.Z. no. 22677.

Two females from Coimbatore, have fork two pedicellate, but no cell at base, a small dark cloud near upper end of anastomosis, hind tibia with but one preapical spur, may be the female of this species.

Amphipsyche distincta Mart.

A species agreeing in genitalia, head and thorax markings and in venation is common in Mysore, India. Martynov does not mention the front femora which in these specimens are plainly blackish, and show very prominently from in front. The wings of fresh specimens are very plainly greenish. The female also has these black front femora, is smaller, the wings scarcely at all green, but the abdomen is green (at least when fresh). The mesonotum usually has a dark stripe each side, and scutellum largely dark; the brown on head as in male. The mid tibia are broadened as usual, there is a distinct, but sometimes minute, subbasal spur, and the apical spurs are simple, but inner much shorter than outer; hind legs with only the apical spurs. The venation is similar to that of the male, except that the radius, of course, is but little curved near tip, and the cross-vein from median cell to lower median vein is usually much nearer to the middle of cell, radial sector straight. The fore wing is

but 6.5 mm. long, male 9 mm. Many from Shimoga, Mysore
(Susai Nathan).

Amphipsyche magna sp. nov.   Figs. 13, 16, 17

Head and thorax pale yellowish, with more pale hair than
usual; abdomen brown; antennæ pale, tips of joints dark;
mesonotum with a brown stripe on each side toward wing-
base, and a spot each side on the posterior part of mesoscutellum; metanotum with a brown spot each side in front; legs
pale yellowish, unmarked; fore wings pale yellowish with
yellowish veins (green alive?), the subcosta and radius
faintly bordered with yellowish; hind wings very pale.

In fore wings the venation is typical; about seven faint
costal cross-veins; the subcosta before tip bends down and
then up, and the radius close by follows it, beyond which the
radius makes a deep bend; fork one about equal to its pedicel; the median cell broad and rather short, upper side in an
even curve.

Legs slender, femora fringed, spurs 1, 4, 2, one of the subbasal pair of mid leg is curved. From above the genitalia
show a broad, deeply divided superior plate, the long arms
slightly divergent, and almost swollen before tip; the claspers are long and very slender, the apical part straight, tapering, and hardly one-half of the basal part; the tip of the
penis from behind appears round, the two dark, pointed
processes standing upright, some distance apart.

Fore wing 19 mm. long.

One from Del Carmen, Philippine Islands (Uichanco),
15 Nov. Type M.C.Z. no. 23471.

Amphipsyche delicata sp. nov.   Figs. 7, 10

A small, pale yellowish gray species with unmarked
wings. Head pale yellowish; antennæ pale, faintly, narrowly annulate with dark; palpi pale, fully as long as usual;
legs pale, front tibia with a minute dark spot at tip; fore
wings pale yellowish gray, unmarked, the stigmal area
rather more yellowish than elsewhere. Venation much as
usual, but the median cell extends much beyond the anastomosis, rather more so than in *A. minima*, the median
cell is not so much widened in the middle as in *A. minima*,

and its upper border is plainly thickened; fork one is scarcely longer than pedicel; one costal cross-vein fairly distinct and sometimes a second shows, fork two sessile.

Mid leg of female with tibia less swollen than in most of the larger species; spurs 0, 4, 4, the preapical pair of hind legs very small, and one of the apical pair is much longer than the other.

Length of fore wing 7 to 7.5 mm.

From Chung Kon, 18 July; Dome Mt. 13 July, both on Hainan Island, and Kit Tau, South Kiangsi, China, 20 June (Gressitt). Type M.C.Z. no. 23470.

It differs from *A. minima* in not having fork two pedicellate, in lacking the faint brown band over anastomosis, and in shape of the median cell; from the equally small *A. distincta* it differs in not having front femora and tibiæ darkened, in shape of the median cell, etc.

EXPLANATION OF PLATES I AND II.

Fig. 1. *Amphipsyche apicalis*, fore wing.
    2. *Œstropsyche palingenia*, genitalia below.
    3. *Amphipsyche apicalis*, genitalia above, and penis from side and above.
    4. *Polymorphanisus unipunctus*, part of fore wing.
    5. *Œstropsyche vitrina*, tip of penis.
    6. *Œstropsyche hageni*, tip of penis.
    7. *Amphipsyche delicata*, part of fore wing and hind leg.
    8. *Amphipsyche apicalis*, genitalia below.
    9. *Polymorphanisus scutellatus*, part of fore wing.
  10. *Amphipsyche delicata*, part of hind wing.
  11. *Polymorphanisus tumidus*, part of fore wing.
  12. *Polymorphanisus tumidus*, head from side.
  13. *Amphipsyche magna*, tip of penis and clasper.
  14. *Œstropsyche vitrina*, median cell of fore wing of male.
  15. *Amphipsyche apicalis*, genitalia, side.
  16. *Amphipsyche magna*, superior plate, above.
  17. *Amphipsyche magna*, fore wing of male.

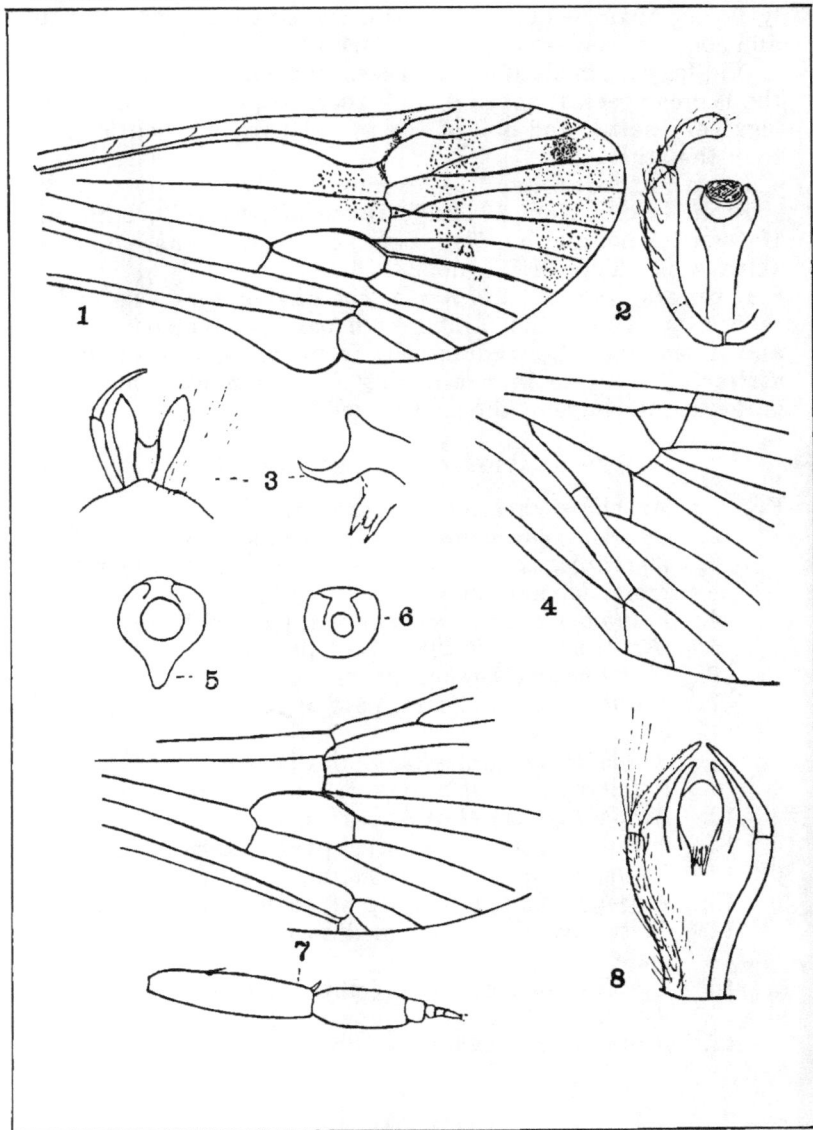

Banks — Oriental Œstropsychinæ

PSYCHE VOL. XLVI   PLATE 2

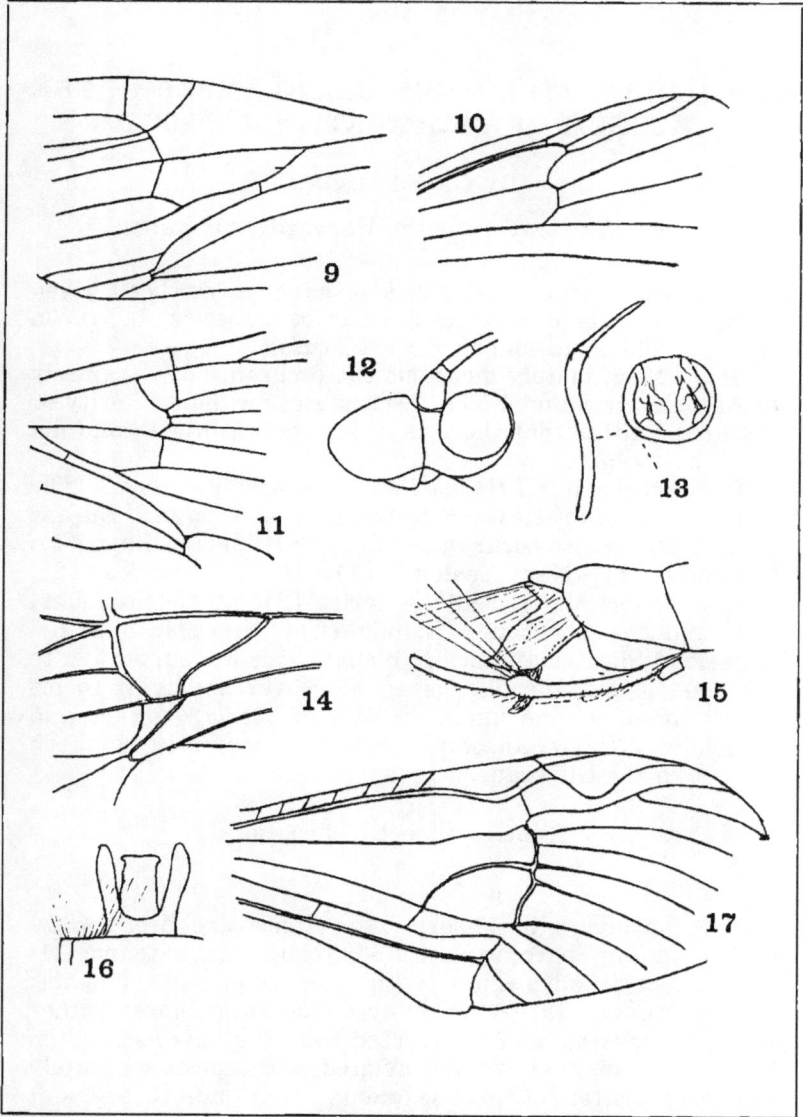

Banks — Oriental Œstropsychinæ

A PTILIID BEETLE FROM BALTIC AMBER IN THE MUSEUM OF COMPARATIVE ZOOLOGY

By C. T. Parsons

Biological Laboratories, Harvard University

In so far as no fossil *Ptiliidae* have as yet been given names, it may be of interest to describe a species of *Ptinella* from the Oligocene amber of East Prussia.

Helm, 1896, merely mentions the occurence of the family in Baltic amber, and Klebs, 1911, states on the authority of Edmund Reitter that there is in his collection a *Ptenidium* and a new genus.

Today the genus *Ptinella* has a remarkable range. The twenty known species are distributed as follows: Europe (7, 2 of which also occur in the Canary Islands), Japan (1), Honolulu (1), New Zealand (1), North America (2), Central America (3), South America (2), St. Helena Island (1), and the Seychelles Islands (2). Since such a distribution indicates an ancient history, it is not surprising to find the genus in the Oligocene. Moreover, the living forms most commonly occur under the bark of *Betula*, *Quercus*, and particularly *Pinus*, all of which were common in northern Europe in the Oligocene.

Ptinella oligocœnica n. sp.

Fig. 1, a-e

The characters of generic importance are brought together in one paragraph. Body elongate; antennæ 11-jointed, long and slender, with long setæ, club elongate; head prominent, rather large; eyes moderate; thorax rather small, transverse, and constricted near the base; scutellum large, triangular; elytra abbreviated, with apices separately rounded; venter of six segments, with apical segment simple; legs rather long and robust, posterior coxæ remote and apparently laminate, tarsi 3-jointed, with the apical joint very long and slender, claws long.

The body apparently corneous, somewhat depressed; head and antennæ as figured; outline of pronotum as figured, disc flat, surface sparsely punctate and transversely alutaceous, scutellum coarsely, closely punctate; elytra with discs flattened, humeral angles dentate, coarsely and closely punctate; metasternum sparsely punctate; first ventral segment punctate and as long as the following two combined; ventral segments 2-6 apparently smooth, apical segment with a fringe of hairs; femora and tibiæ covered with setæ; length .8 mm.

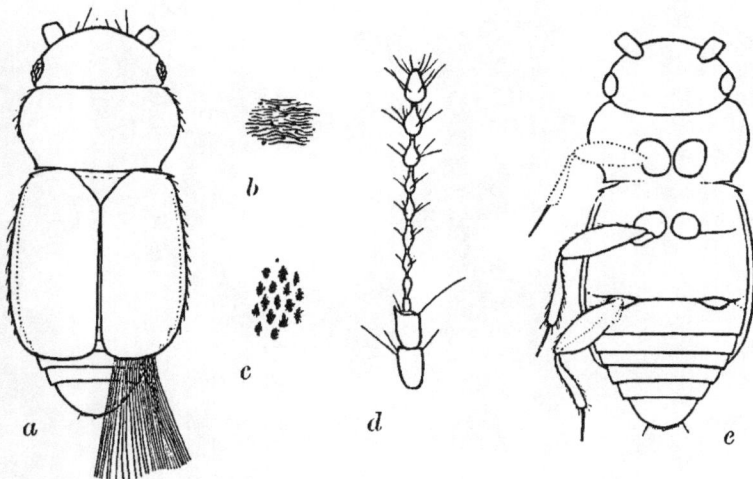

Fig. 1. Holotype of *Ptinella oligocænica* n. sp. *a*, dorsal aspect; *b*, surface of pronotum enlarged; *c*, surface of elytron enlarged; *d*, antenna; *e*, ventral aspect.

The above description is from the holotype no. 6839 in the Museum of Comparative Zoology. There is also in the same museum a less satisfactory specimen which is designated paratype no. 6629. Both specimens are part of the W. A. Haren collection.

Because of cloudiness, many important characters of the underside cannot be seen. The one anomalous character that can be made out is that the first ventral segment is unusually long. It is interesting that the muscles of the femur, as shown in the drawing of the hind leg, can be clearly seen.

This species differs from the types of *P. quercus* (Lec) and *P. fungi* (Lec.) in being more depressed, corneous, elytra longer, pronotum more transverse. The antennæ are identical with those of *P. quercus*.

PROTEPIPTERA, A NEW GENUS OF ACHILIDÆ FROM BALTIC AMBER (HEMIPTERA, FULGOROIDEA)

By ROBERT L. USINGER

California Academy of Sciences

Through the kindness of Mr. Walter W. Kawecki, a former resident of the free city of Danzig but now in San Francisco, I have been able to examine a collection of insects preserved in Baltic Amber. The material was collected along the shores of the Baltic Sea between Danzig and Königsberg and the pieces of amber were polished by an amber worker in Danzig.

The collection contains a single specimen of a moderate-sized Fulgorid immediately suggestive of our familiar forest-dwelling genus *Epiptera* Metcalf (1922) (= *Elidiptera* Auct. part., nec Spinola, = *Helicoptera* Am. & Serv.). The specimen is beautifully preserved with the wings of the left side conveniently spread. Every detail of the under surface can be seen as readily as on a living specimen. The upper surface, however, is completely covered by a white cloud, as in many amber specimens. The apex of the front wing has been sharply broken off as if cut with a knife.

Evidently the family Achilidae has not previously been recorded from Baltic Amber. Scudder (1890) has doubtfully referred a single specimen (*Elidiptera regularis* Scudder) to this group from his Florissant material of Miocene age. However, the nine species of *Cixius* described from Baltic Amber by Germar and Berendt (1856) need to be reëxamined with a view to their possible inclusion in the Achilidæ. This family, or subfamily as it was then called, was not proposed until ten years later when Stål (1866) monographed the group in his usual masterly way. Stål's classification has been confirmed and expanded by Muir's detailed genitalic studies which indicate that the extension of the claval vein to the apex of the clavus is a really significant character in separating the Achilids from their nearest allies (Muir, 1930). The specimen before me may be placed with certainty in the Achilidæ as distinguished from the Cixiidæ in which the claval vein enters the commissure before the apex. Unfortunately details of claval venation are not sufficiently clear in the figures of Germar and Berendt although it would appear that *C. vitreus* is a Cixiid while *testudinarius* is an Achilid. In size the present specimen is closest to *C. sieboldii* but, as the under side is invisible in that species, while the upper surface of the specimen before me is obscured, a direct comparison is impossible. Under the circumstances it seems best to propose a new specific name in order to avoid any possible confusion as to the identity of the genotype.

Protepiptera n. gen.

Similar to *Epiptera* Metcalf but with the vertex located distinctly in front of the eyes, its margins carinate and a longitudinal carina at middle; posterior margin of vertex concavely arcuate, subangulately so at middle, strongly, acutely produced postero-laterally and thus reaching or slightly surpassing level of anterior margins of eyes. Frons with its sides evenly arcuate, not abruptly narrowed between the eyes. Pronotum roundly projecting anteriorly between the compound eyes, the raised, carinate portion scarcely more than twice as broad as long.

Genotype: *Protepiptera kaweckii*, n. sp.

Protepiptera kaweckii n. sp.

A large, unicolorous species with very broad head, long pronotum, unicolorous frons, and very long rostrum.

Head three-fourths as wide, eyes included, as pronotum; vertex just twice as broad behind as long on median line; frons and clypeus together subelliptical, broadest a little before middle and attenuated posteriorly, about two and one-half times as long as greatest width, with a distinct longitudinaĺ carina at middle. Rostrum reaching almost to tip of abdomen or, more precisely, to middle of subgenital plate. Antennæ rather prominent, over half as long as greatest width of frons; second segment over twice as long as first, the flagellum quite short, scarcely longer than main portion of antennæ. Ocelli conspicuous as in *Epiptera*. Posterior margin of pronotum moderately, subangulately emarginate, the anterior and posterior margins laterally subparallel. Mesonotum one-fifth longer than width of head including eyes; disk obscured but with suggestions of three longitudinal carinæ. Legs more or less as in typical *Epiptera*, the front tibiæ one-sixth longer than femora. Posterior tibiæ two and one-half times as long as femora, each with a strong lateral tooth just beyond middle. Apices of hind tibiæ and first two tarsal segments beneath, each with a row of stout spines which are longest at the sides. First tarsal segment distinctly longer than second and third together. Venation on basal two-thirds of front wings precisely as in *Epiptera*, the wing broken off obliquely from beyond the apex of clavus to last of accessory subcostal branches.

Color rather uniformly dark brown, at least on the under side, with the under sides of the wings lighter and the ventral surface of the abdomen almost black.

Length 9.5 mm., greatest width approximately 3.5 mm.

This species will not fit in any of Kirkaldy's Australian genera (1906). It might fit the old definition of *Elidiptera* but certainly does not belong with the genotype, *callosa* Spinola, of that genus (see Muir, 1922). As noted elsewhere, it approaches Metcalf's recent genus *Epiptera* (1922) but differs in its anteriorly located vertex with a median longitudinal carina, non-constricted basal portion of frons between the eyes, very long pronotum, and somewhat longer tibiae.

LITERATURE CITED

Germar, E. F. and G. C. Berendt. 1856. Die im Bernstein befindlichen Organischen Reste der Vorwelt by G. C. Berendt, 1845-1856. Zweiter Band, I Abtheilung, Hemipteren und Orthopteren, pp. 12-16, Tab. I, figs. 18-25.
Kirkaldy, G. W. 1906. Leaf-hoppers and their natural enemies (Pt. IX. Leaf-hoppers. Hemiptera). Rep. H. S. P. A. Exp. Sta., Div. Ent., 1:417-418.
Metcalf, Z. P. 1922. On the genus Elidiptera. Can. Ent., 54: 263-264.
Muir, F. 1922. On the genus Elidiptera Spin. Can Ent., 54: 61.
        1930. On the classification of the Fulgoroidea. Ann. Mag. Nat. Hist., (10) 6: 461-478.
Scudder, S. H. 1890. The tertiary insects of North America. Rept. U. S. Geological Survey, 13: 297.
Stål, C. 1866. Hemiptera Africana. Holmiae. 4: 181-186.

TWO NEW TINGITIDS (HEMIPTERA) FROM PANAMA

By Carl J. Drake

Ames, Iowa

The present paper contains the description of two new species of lace-bugs collected in the Canal Zone, Panama, by the author. The types are in the Drake Collection.

Gargaphia paula sp. nov.

Moderately short, broad, testaceous, the elytra with an oblique fuscous band near the apex. Head black, with five, pale, testaceous spines, the median and hind pair longer. Antennæ slender, moderately long; segments I and II black, the former stouter and three times as long as the latter; III long, testaceous, two and one-half times as long as IV; IV long, the distal three-fourths black. Pronotum black, the triangular portion testaceous. Carinæ foliaceous, testaceous, uniseriate; lateral carinæ not quite extending as far forward as the base of the hood, slightly converging behind; median carina slightly more elevated. Hood moderately large, roof-shaped above, highest in front, projecting slightly forward in front. Paranota moderately broad, testaceous, biseriate, the outer margin rounded.

Rostrum extending to the interrupted channel. Elytra very similar in appearance and markings to *L. lineata* (Champ.); costal are mostly biseriate, triseriate in widest part, the areolæ hyaline; subcostal area broad, triseriate in widest part. Body beneath black.

Length, 2.40 mm.; width, 1.10 mm.

Holotype, male, Barro Colorado Island, Canal Zone, Panama, Feb. 8, 1939, C. J. Drake.

The oblique fascia of the elytra and the small size separate this species from other members of the genus. The interrupted rostral channel separates it from *Leptopharsa lineata* Champion.

Leptopharsa zeteki sp. nov.

Small, narrow. Head black, the frontal spines short and black. Antennæ moderately long, slender; segments I and II both short, black, the former about twice as long as the latter; III a little more than twice as long as IV, testaceous; IV slightly enlarged, embrowned towards the tip. Rostrum brown, black at apex, extending beyond middle of mesosternum. Rostral channel wide, wider and chordate on metasternum. Legs slender, testaceous, the tarsi brownish. Body beneath black.

Pronotum convex, finely pitted, black, testaceous behind; carinæ foliaceous, uniseriate, testaceous, some of the veinlets dark, the areolæ small; lateral carinæ slightly concave within in front, not so widely separated and subparallel behind. Paranota rather narrow, biseriate, testaceous, slightly wider in front, moderately reflexed. Hood small, testaceous, faintly produced forward in front. Elytra moderately constricted beyond the middle, strongly overlapping and jointly rounded behind; costal area moderately wide, testaceous, biseriate, the inner row of areolæ along the basal half of costal area smaller, the areolæ hyaline; subcostal area broad, triseriate, the veinlets opposite discoidal area black; sutural area elongate, impressed, the nervelets somewhat embrowned, three areolæ deep in widest part; sutural area becoming dark fuscous posteriorly, with three large, hyaline areolae near the apex.

Length, 2.00 mm.; width, .80 mm.

Holotype (male), allotype (female) and one paratype, Barro Colorado Island, Canal Zone, Panama, Feb. 1939. Three paratypes, near Colon, Canal Zone.

The short basal segment of antennæ and color separate this insect from other small species of the genus. This species (also *G. paula* n. sp.) was collected near the Barro Colorado Island Biological Laboratory, Gatun Lake, Institute for Research in Tropical America, Panama Canal, and is named in honor of the Director, Mr. James Zetek, who has taken a very active interest in the insect fauna of tropical America.

NOTES ON HIPPOBOSCIDÆ
13. A SECOND REVISION OF THE HIPPOBOSCINAE

By J. Bequaert

Harvard Medical School and School of Public Health,
Boston, Mass.

Since the publication of my synopsis of the Hippoboscinæ
(1931, Psyche, XXXVII, (1930), pp. 303-326), much additional information has come to light. One new species was
described recently by the late G. A. H. Bedford and I was
able to study several types, including those of *H. fulva*
Austen.

In the alphabetical list of names (p. 306), *martinaglia*
Bedford should be inserted as the ninth valid species; *longipennis* Fabricius is the valid name of *capensis* v. Olfers,
which becomes a synonym; and *variegata* Megerlé (not to
be credited to Wiedemann) is the valid name of *maculata*
Leach, which passes in the synonymy.

As pointed out before, the Hippoboscinæ differ from
other members of the family in several important characters. To those listed before may be added the presence of a
pair of deep, more or less pit-like depressions, placed laterally on the suture between mesonotum and scutellum; also
the well-defined pale yellow or white spots of head and
thorax, which are not duplicated elsewhere in the family.
While in other Hippoboscidæ color differences are of little
or no specific value, in *Hippobosca* the shape and arrangement of the pale spots produces a pattern to a large degree
diagnostic for each species. In this respect, there is an obvious analogy to the characteristic pattern of pale spots
found in many species of ticks (*Amblyomma* and *Derma-
centor*).

I have been at pains to discover additional specific characters, particularly in the case of closely allied forms. The
chetotaxy has been neglected thus far, yet offers reliable differences which should be investigated by the accepted bio-

metrical methods. My material is not extensive enough for the purpose. Considering only the chetotaxy of the scutellum, this sclerite in *Hippobosca* bears at the extreme apical margin and somewhat ventrally a dense fringe of short, soft hairs. Anterior to the fringe one finds groups or rows of long, stiff bristles, either black or pale-colored, which I shall call the *preapical bristles*. The groups may be either far apart and restricted to the extreme sides or more or less connected medially. In some species the bristles are placed in one row, in others they form two irregular rows or are merely bunched together. When there are many bristles, these are often mixed with a few soft, short hairs, sometimes forming a second row behind the stiff bristles. In most cases the number and arrangement of the preapical bristles is the same in both sexes. There are two exceptions. In *H. struthionis* the males have more bristles on the average than the females. In the males of *H. camelina* the preapical bristles occupy the same position as in the other species of the genus; but in the females, the bristles are placed nearer the middle, being rather discal or medio-scutellar, and are also fewer in number than in the males. Except for this case of the female *H. camelina*, there are no discal nor basal bristles, setæ or hairs on the scutellum in *Hippobosca*.

The variation of the preapical bristles of the scutellum is discussed under each species, but the following summary compares the species for diagnostic purposes. The number of specimens examined is given in parenthesis.

equina (106) : 5 to 11 bristles ♀ ♂ (average, 7).
longipennis (143) : 3 to 7 bristles ♀ ♂ (average, 5).
fulva (3) : 8 bristles ♀ ♂.
variegata (95) : 13 to 27 bristles ♀ ♂ (average, 18).
rufipes (95) : 12 to 23 bristles ♀ ♂ (average, 17).
hirsuta (6) : 14 to 18 bristles ♀ ♂.
martinaglia (not seen).
struthionis (23) : 4 to 12 b. ♀ (average, 6) ; 8 to 15 b. ♂ (average, 10).
camelina (31) : 3 to 8 b. ♀ (average, 5) ; 11 to 22 b. ♂ (average, 14).

In *Hippobosca*, the integument of the abdomen, behind the usual large tergal and small sternal sclerotized basal plates, is mostly soft and extensible. All species I have seen have

two pairs of sclerotized subapical (lateral) plates in both
sexes. In the males of *equina* and *longipennis,* the anterior
pair is small and fused with the median tergal plate, yet
recognized by the very long setæ it bears. In addition,
these two species have in both sexes three median tergal
sclerotized plates, which are much smaller in the female
than in the male. Median tergal plates are lacking in both
sexes of *variegata, rufipes, struthionis,* and *hirsuta,* and in
the female of *camelina.* The male of *camelina,* however, has
an extensive anterior sclerotized median plate, immediately
behind the basal tergal sclerite of the abdomen, and posteriorly a pair of small, median tergal plates. In the female
of *longipennis* and *equina* the anterior pair of subapical
(lateral) plates is slightly smaller than the posterior pair;
it is larger than the posterior pair in the female of *variegata,
hirsuta, camelina* and *struthionis;* and both pairs are about
the same size in the female of *rufipes.* In the males of
variegata, rufipes, hirsuta, camelina and *struthionis,* the
anterior pair of subapical plates is very large, the posterior
pair very small and readily overlooked. I have not examined the structure of the abdomen of *fulva* and *martinaglia.*

In the male genitalia, the claspers (or parameres) are very
similar in *equina, longipennis, fulva, variegata, rufipes* and
struthionis, being more or less slender, straight and rod-like,
ending in a point. In *camelina* they are of much the same
rod-like type, but thicker, curved in profile and ending in a
blunt, somewhat knobbed point. They are quite aberrant
in *hirsuta,* being thick and beam-like, with a broadly truncate and slightly emarginate tip. The genitalia of *martinaglia* are unknown.

To sum up, the nine species of *Hippobosca* now recognized
may be divided into four groups, expressing relationship
based on structural characters: (1) *equina, longipennis* and
fulva; (2) *variegata, rufipes, hirsuta* and possibly *martinaglia;* (3) *struthionis;* (4) *camelina.*

The following key supersedes that of my earlier paper
(pp. 308-309). *H. martinaglia* is inserted from the description only.

1. Second longitudinal vein ($R_{2 + 3}$) long, about as long
       as or longer than last section of third longitudinal,
       reaching costa much beyond tip of first longitudinal

(R_1) and usually apicad of anterior cross-vein (r-m) ;
last section of costa about three times the length of
penultimate section or shorter. Base of third longitudinal vein ($R_4 + _5$) bare. One pair of vertical
bristles. Preapical bristles of scutellum few (3 to
11). Abdomen with three median tergal sclerotized
plates in both sexes (in *equina* and *longipennis;* not
known in *fulva*). Two pad-like pulvilli at sides of
bristle-like empodium, one much larger than the
other. Parameres of male genitalia slender, rod-like,
ending in a point 2

Second longitudinal vein short, shorter than last section
of third longitudinal, reaching costa together with or
close to tip of first longitudinal; last section of costa
at least five times the length of penultimate section.... 4

2.   Larger species, the wing 6 to 8.5 mm. long. Apical
lobes of fronto-clypeus irregularly and broadly triangular, their inner margins curved. Scutellum
fuscous to ferruginous laterally, yellowish-white
medially, rarely more extensively yellowish; with a
regular row of 5 to 11 preapical bristles (usually
6 to 8), divided into two groups. Wing veins as a
rule rufous to dark brown .... *H. equina*

Smaller, the wing at most 6 mm. long. Scutellum as a
rule entirely or nearly entirely yellowish or ivory-
white 3

3.   Wing 5 to 6 mm. long. Apical lobes of fronto-clypeus
regularly and sharply triangular, separated by a
broad notch, their inner margins nearly straight.
Scutellum with 3 to 7 preapical bristles (usually 5
or 6). Wing veins mostly pale testaceous, usually
with some darker stretches .... *H. longipennis.*

Wing 4.2 to 4.5 mm. long. Apical lobes of fronto-clypeus
irregularly and broadly lobular, separated by a narrow slit, their inner margins curved. Scutellum with
about 8 preapical bristles .... *H. fulva*

4.   Base of third longitudinal vein (R_4+_5) setulose over
some length on the upper side. One pair of vertical
bristles. No median tergal plates in both sexes (in
variegata, rufipes and *hirsuta;* probably also in *mar-*

tinaglia). Only one pulvillus well-developed, the
other rudimentary 5

Base of third longitudinal vein bare 8

5. Second longitudinal vein very short, forming an oblique
cross-vein which ends in the first longitudinal and
runs from opposite or apicad of upper tip of anterior
basal crossvein (M₃) to basad of anterior cross-vein
(r-m). Frons distinctly narrower at occiput than at
fronto-clypeus, the postvertex much longer than wide.
Scutellum as a rule with three ivory-white spots, the
largest in the center; with 13 to 27 preapical bristles
(usually 16 to 20), in one or two irregular and fairly
continuous rows. Parameres of male genitalia slender, rod-like, ending in a sharp point. Wing 7 to 8
mm. long .... *H. variegata.*

Second longitudinal vein longer and more slanting, ending in costa at or beyond tip of first longitudinal and
running from basad of upper tip of anterior basal
cross-vein to opposite or basad of anterior cross-vein
.... 6

6. Smaller, the wing 4.5 mm. long. Frons wide, not ap-
preciably narrower at occiput than at fronto-clypeus,
the postvertex much wider than long. Mesonotum
reddish-brown, with an anterior median dark band
extending posteriorly to near the transverse suture
where it is more or less forked. Scutellum entirely
yellowish-white; with relatively few (probably eight
to ten) preapical bristles. Mesonotum moderately
bristly, bare in the center .... *H. martinaglia*

Larger, the wing 6.5 to 9 mm. long. Frons narrower,
the postvertex nearly as long as wide or slightly
longer. Color pattern of mesonotum different. Preapical bristles of scutellum more numerous (12 to
23) 7

7. Frons distinctly narrower at occiput than at fronto-
clypeus. Scutellum very wide and nearly rectangular,
with a median, rufous and two lateral, ivory-white
spots; with 12 to 23 heavy preapical bristles (usually
14 to 20), placed in one regular, almost continuous
row. Mesonotum moderately bristly, bare in the cen-

ter. Legs bright reddish-brown. Parameres of male
genitalia slender, rod-like, ending in a blunt point.
Wing 7 to 9 mm. long .... *H. rufipes*
Frons very slightly or not narrower at occiput than at
fronto-clypeus. Scutellum narrower and less rectangular, with a median ivory-white spot; with 14
to 18 soft and pale preapical bristles, placed in two
irregular, more or less connected groups. Mesonotum
very bristly, also in the center. Legs rufous-yellow.
Parameres of male genitalia thick, beam-like, truncate and slightly emarginate at tip. Wing 6.5 to 8
mm. long .... *H. hirsuta*

8. Two or three pairs of vertical bristles. Fronto-clypeus
shorter than its distance from the occipital margin.
Postvertex shorter than mediovertex, the latter much
narrowed medially by the broad inner orbits. Anterior basal cross-vein (M_3) very oblique and nearly its
own length from anterior cross-vein (r-m). Scutellum semi-elliptical, the hind margin distinctly convex
and slightly projecting medially; in the female with
3 to 8 discal bristles (usually 4 to 6), placed in two
linear groups; in the male with 11 to 22 preapical
bristles (usually 12 to 15), placed in two irregular
groups. No median tergal plates in the female; the
male with one large median plate behind the basal
tergal sclerite and a pair of small median tergal plates
posteriorly. No pad-like pulvilli; bristle-like empodium bare, except at base. Parameres of male
genitalia rod-like, but curved upward, the apex slightly swollen and knob-like. Wing 9 to 10 mm. long
.... *H. camelina*
One pair of vertical bristles. Fronto-clypeus nearly as
long as its distance from occipital margin. Postvertex as long as or longer than mediovertex, the latter moderately narrowed by the inner orbits. Anterior basal cross-vein short, almost vertical upon the
fourth longitudinal and more than twice its length
from anterior cross-vein. Scutellum nearly rectangular, the hind margin more straightly truncate; in
both sexes with preapical bristles placed in two widely
separated lateral groups, more numerous in the male

(8 to 15, usually 9 to 12) than in the female (4 to 12, usually 5 to 7). Abdomen in both sexes without median tergal plates. Two pad-like pulvilli; empodium feathered. Parameres of male genitalia slender, rod-like, ending in a sharp point. Wing 7 to 7.5 mm. long .... *H. struthionis*

1. *Hippobosca equina* Linnæus. — The locality "Reshadie" is near Smyrna.

Additional Specimens Examined. — Norway: Smaalenene. — Esthonia, one female off a duck, *Mergus* (or *Merganser*) *serrator* Linnaeus (sent by G. B. Thompson), an accidental host. — Finland: Kustö (C. Lundström). — Denmark: Seelland (Univ. Zool. Mus., Copenhagen). — Austria: Grünbach, Schneeberg region (Handlirsch). — Hungary. — Roumania: Bihar Mts. (K. Jordan); Herkulesbad (W. Rothschild and E. Hartert). — Bulgaria: Aladza near Varna; Bela Cerkva, Rhodope (Zerny). — Jugo-Slavia: Zljeb, New Montenegro; Stolac, Herzegovina (Penther); Bosnia. — France: Argentat, Auvergne, off a cow. — Italy: Triest; Taranto; Pola. — Corsica: Vizzavona (M. E. Mosely); Corte (M. E. Mosely); La Poce de Vizzavona (Yerbury); Ajaccio (F. Gugliemi). — Spain: Murcia (G. L. Boag); Sierra de Guadarrama, 6,000 to 8,000 ft. (B. Uvarov); Algeciras (Zerny); Noguera near Albarracin, Aragon (Zerny). — Canary Islands: La Caldera, Las Palmas Id. (W. M. Wheeler); Sa Cruz, Teneriffe; Puerto Cabias, Buenaventura. — Madeira (Lowe). — Albania: Kula Ljums; Hodzha near Prizren; Pashtrik; Korab; Durazzo. — Greece: Stavros, Macedonia (J. Waterston); Saloniki (J. Waterston); Helmas (Fonberg); Taygetos; Koystallopyghi (A. H. G. Alstoni); Attica; Poros; Vrissula; Mt. Pangaion; Struma; Carvalli (R. C. Shannon). — Asia Minor (Anatolia): Namerun; Cilician Taurus (Prince Abersperg); Sabandscha to Eskischebir; Ephesus. — Transcaucasia: Sagalu on Lake Göktschai (Zugmayer). — Turkestan. — Persia (Iran): Nissa, Elburs Mts. (Brandt); Tsiang-Kanspe, E. Persia (A. Teufigi); Enzeli, N. W. Persia (P. A. Buxton). — Arabia: Akaba, Hejaz (W. M. Mann). — Palestine: Haifa (P. J. Barraud); Beisan, Jordan Valley (P. A. Buxton). — Cyprus: Limasol (G. A. Mavromoustakis). — Egypt: Tisfa (Zool. Dept. Univ. Egypt). —

Libya: Dernah (Klaptocz). — Tunis: Gabes (Mik). — Algeria: Hamman Rirha; Hamman Meskoutine; El Kantara; Biskra (W. Rothschild and E. Hartert). — Morocco: Aguelman Sidi Ali bu Mohammed, Middle Atlas, 6,500 ft. (K. Chapman and J. W. S. Pringle) ; Ijoukak, Great Atlas, 3,900 ft. (K. H. Chapman and G. A. Bisset) ; Arround, Atlas, 1,950 m. (Ebner). — Australia: Sydney, on a horse imported from New Caledonia. — New Hebrides: Tanna Id. (E. Robertson) ; Vila, Efate (or Sandwich) Id., very common on horses (P. A. Buxton). — Philippines: Alabang, Rizal (M. B. Mitzmain). — Amboyna, off cattle (F. Muir). — Singapore (F. Muir).

The preapical bristles of the scutellum vary from 5 to 11 in 106 specimens examined (58 ♀ and 48 ♂), from 22 localities, 85 specimens having from 6 to 8 bristles. The specimens fall in the following groups: with 5 bristles: 3 (1 ♀ , 2 ♂) ; 6b.: 28 (17 ♀ , 11 ♂) ; 7b.: 22 (9 ♀ , 13 ♂) ; 8b.: 35 (24 ♀ , 11 ♂) ; 9b.: 10 (4 ♀ , 6 ♂) ; 10b.: 7 (3 ♀ , 4 ♂) ; 11b.: 1 (♂). There is no evidence of any sexual difference in this character. No locality is represented by enough specimens to make a further analysis of any significance. The bristles are evenly divided between both sides in 69 specimens, unevenly in 37, the uneven groupings observed being 2 + 3, 3 + 4, 3 + 5, 4 + 5, and 5 + 6.

The frons, in the male, is nearly parallel-sided and about as wide as an eye; in the female it is slightly widened medially, where it measures a little over the width of an eye.

In addition to the average larger number of preapical bristles of the scutellum, *H. equina* differs also from *H. longipennis* in the shape of the tergal plates of the abdomen. In the female of *H. equina*, the three median, setulose tergal plates are larger than in the female of *longipennis*, more transverse and ribbon-shaped, the median plate only slightly smaller than the hindmost plate, which is nearly as large as the anterior pair of subapical (lateral) plates. The median plates bear many more setae than in *longipennis*. In the male of *equina*, the three median tergal plates are large and ribbon-like, the hindmost (or third) plate fused with the anterior pair of ovate, widened subapical (lateral) plates (bearing longer bristles than the median plate proper). The shape and arrangement of the tergal plates are shown correctly by Ferris (1930, Philippine Jl. Sci., XLIII, p. 540, fig. 1 ♀, and p. 543, fig. 4*a* ♂).

The claspers (or parameres) of the male genitalia are slender, rod-like and regularly pointed at apex. They are figured in side view by J. I. Roberts (1927, Ann. Trop. Med. Paras., XXI, Pl. III, fig. 8) ; seen from above they are much narrower.

   2.   *Hippobosca longipennis* Fabricius, 1805. — A study of Fabricius' two types, marked "ex Tranquebar (Mus. Dom. Lund)", at the University Zoological Museum, Copenhagen, shows that they are the species commonly known as *H. capensis* v. Olfers (1816), *H. francilloni* Leach (1817), or *H. canina* Rondani (1878). Why Fabricius wrote "Caput et thorax ferruginea immaculata" is a mystery, as both his types show the characteristic *capensis* pattern. A specimen from Kalewa, Upper Burma, named *"longipennis"* by Major Austen, was studied at the British Museum and showed no structural characters differentiating it from the usual *H. capensis*. Fabricius' name antedates all other designations for the species, which is extremely variable in color. I have also seen, at the British Museum, a specimen of *H. francilloni*, apparently labelled by Leach and which may be the type, although it is not marked as such.

   Additional Specimens Examined. — Bulgaria: Sredne near Russe. — Greece: Struma (R. C. Shannon). — Transcaucasia: Sagalu on Lake Göktschai (Zugmayer). — Transcaspia: Imam-Baba, Merv District (L. Mistschenko). — Persia (Iran): Keredj, 40 Kilom. from Teheran (Brandt) ; Dschulfa, N. W. Persia. — Mesopotamia (Iraq) : Djerabis; Assur; Daurah (A. D. Fraser) ; Bagdad (T. C. Connor) ; Amara (T. C. Connor). — Syria: Beirut (E. S. Sewell). — Palestine: Amman, E. of Jordan (P. A. Buxton). — Arabia: Ras Fartak, Hadramaut (Simony). — Cyprus: Larnaca, off cow. — Egypt: Tisfa (Zool. Dept. Univ. Egypt). — Libya: Bengasi. — Tunis: Gabès. — Morocco: Marrakesh (G. B. Fairchild). — Anglo-Egyptian Sudan: Lugud, Darfur Province (H. Lynes) ; Khor Arbaat, Port Sudan. — Kenya Colony: Lake Jipe; Marsabit, Rendili Nyoro (C. A. Neave) ; Turkana District; Merifano (McArthur) ; Voi (Tate) ; Lemek, Masai Reserve (A. O. Luckman). — Tanganyika Territory: Valley of Ruaha River, N. Uhehe; Morogoro, Uluguru (A. G. Wilkins) ; W. shore of

Lake Manyara (B. Cooper) ; Mt. Meru, off lion (B. Cooper) ;
Ngare Nairobi, W. Kilimanjaro, 4,500 ft. (B. Cooper) ;
Shinyanga (N. C. E. Millar). — British Bechuanaland:
Ngamiland (G. D. H. Carpenter) ; Ghanzi, Monfalatseka,
Ngamiland, off dog (J. Maurice). — India: Quetta, Baluchi-
stan (D. Harrison) ; Nedungadu (P. S. Nathan) ; Arbham,
Vizagapatam (R. Senior-White) ; Chipurupalle, Vizaga-
patam (R. S. Patuck) ; Kangra Valley, Punjab (Dudgeon) ;
Dehra Dun; Bangalore; Bhowali, Kumaon, 5,700 ft. (Imms) ;
Allahabad; Bandra (Javakar). — Ceylon: Madulsima; Ban-
har (R. Senior-White) ; Trincomali. — Assam: Mungpoo,
Reang River (R. Senior-White). — Indo-China: Than-Moi,
Tonkin (H. Fruhstorfer). — China: Macao (F. Muir) ;
Tshusiung, Yunnan, 1,900 m. (Handel-Mazzetti) ; Tsinan,
S'hantung (E. Hindle) ; Hanchow, off dogs (Rose) ; Kachek,
Hainan Id. (L. Gressitt) ; Peiping; Yen-Ping. — Manchuoko
(Manchuria) : Harbin (Jettmar).

The preapical bristles of the scutellum vary from 3 to 7
in 143 specimens examined (79 ♀ and 64 ♂), from 23 localities, 126 specimens having 5 or 6 bristles. The several
numbers are represented as follows: with 3 bristles: 1
(♂) ; 4b.: 3 (1 ♀ , 2 ♂) ; 5b.: 19 (11 ♀ , 8 ♂) ; 6b.: 107
(60 ♀ , 47 ♂) ; 7b. 13 (7 ♀ , 6 ♂). There is apparently no
sexual difference in this character. The number from any
one locality is too small for further analysis. The bristles
are evenly divided in 110 specimens, unevenly in 33, the
uneven groups observed being $1 + 2, 2 + 3$, and $3 + 4$.

H. longipennis differs from *H. equina* in the shape of the
tergal plates of the abdomen, the difference being more
striking in the male than in the female. In the female of
H. longipennis the three median, setulose sclerotized plates
are very small, ovate or reniform, the second smaller than
either the first or the third, the third much smaller than
the anterior pair of subapical (lateral) plates. In the male,
the three median plates are large and ribbon-like, much of
the same shape as in the male of *H. equina;* but the hindmost (or third) plate is connected laterally with a pair of
small, attenuated lateral subapical plates (recognizable by
their bearing longer setae than the median plate proper).
No adequate figures of this species have been published.

The claspers (or parameres) of the male genitalia are
very similar to those of *H. equina.*

Historical Note. — There is every reason to believe that *Hippobosca longipennis*, the dog-fly of the Near and Far East, was well known by the ancient Greeks and Romans, as it is particularly abundant in the countries bordering the eastern Mediterranean.   Many are the references to *"kunamuya"* (in Greek) or *Cynomya* in the classic literature and early scientific writings.   Thus, in the Iliad, Ares, the god of war, upbraids Athene: "You dog-fly, why do you sow strife among the Gods? . . ." (Bk. 21, 394).   Elsewhere (Bk. 21, 421) Athene exclaims: "Now watch that dog-fly [meaning Aphrodite] leading Ares through the free-for-all. . . ."[1]   I am also inclined to think that the Greek word *"kunoraistai"* or dog-destroyers, used in the Odyssea (XVII, 300) and later by Aristoteles, covered the ectoparasites of dogs in general, hippoboscid flies as well as ticks.   Oudemans (1926, Tijdschr. v. Entom., LXIX, Suppl., pp. 49-59) claims that both *"kunoraistai"* and *"kunamuya"* were used by the Greeks for dog ticks only (*Ixodes reduvius* Linnaeus).   He is evidently unaware of the abundance cf *Hippobosca longipennis* on dogs in the Orient.   It seems most improbable that the Greeks would have called a tick a fly, since they had a special word for ticks (*"krotones"*) and must have been well acquainted with both types of parasites.   Moreover, the hippoboscid attracts more readily the attention and is more loathsome to the layman than the tick, owing to its habit of scurrying about in the fur and of flying from one dog to another or even onto people.   Hence the use of the word "dog-fly" as a reviling or scurrilous epithet.[2]

[1]The exact dating of the collection of epic poems now called the Iliad and credited to Homer is a matter of speculation.   Probably they had more or less crystallized into their present form by the eighth century B. C.

[2]Oudemans also claims that the *"muscæ"* or flies mentioned by Varro, Columella, Plinius and others as causing sores in dogs, were ticks.   But in warm countries certain biting flies, such as *Stomoxys* and *Phlebotomus*, may cause true sores on the ears of dogs.   Oudemans is apparently also mistaken in criticizing Albertus Magnus' use of the expression "muscæ bestiarum, quae dicuntur *cynomiæ sive muscæ caninæ*" (De Animalibus Libri XXVI, 1260).   Albertus, in my opinion, alluded correctly to the winged hippoboscids which in southern Europe infest horses and cattle, as well as dogs; the two species being so much alike that laymen would naturally call them by the same name.   In his second volume, Oudemans (1929, pp. 150-151) is quite elated over

Dr. Gaines Kan-chih Liu has called my attention to references to dog-flies in the early Chinese medical literature and has kindly translated some of these for my paper. In the *"Chi Tung Yeh Yu,"* by Chow Mi (who lived 1232 to 1308), one reads: "A colleague of mine, Chen P'o, of Quo Chang, is an old scholar. His grandson, when three years old, was seriously ill with fever for a week, after which *"to"* (or small-pox) broke out, the whole body turning black and the lips being icy cold. After all remedies had failed, the grandfather went to the temple to pray God for help. There he met a stranger, who, upon learning of the case, told the grandfather how to cure it. The prescription consisted of seven dog-flies, ground into a powder and taken with wine. The medicine was very effective and the child soon was in good health, the black color disappearing." In the later *"Pen Tsao Kang Mu"* (1578), by Li Shih-chen, one finds: "Dog-flies live on the body of the dog. They can fly, are yellow and fly-like and have a hard skin. They have a sharp beak and suck the blood of the dog. Formerly they were not known to be used in Medicine; but recently they have been recommended by the *Chi Tung Yeh Yu* for curing small-pox and by the *Yi Fang Da Chien* for malaria. It seems to me that they must act like the cattle-lice and the *chufoo* (or sawbugs). For malaria, the flies, after removal of the appendages, are made into pills with dough. They should be taken the morning of the day an attack of fever is due and the cure will be successful if vomiting is provoked. Another method is to make the flies into pills with wax and take the pills with wine. For small-pox and skin troubles, soak the fly in wine and then take both the fly and the wine." Finally the *"Chien Wu"* (1582), by Li Su, says: "The dog-flies deposit among the hairs of the dog their nits (puparia), which after molting become flies. They always live on the back of the neck, where they bite frequently and where the dog cannot reach them with its mouth or paws."

3. *Hippobosca fulva* Austen. — Through the courtesy of

his discovery that the Archbishop Eustace of Saloniki, in his Commentary of the Iliad, suggests that the Greek word *"kunamuya"* (which he proposes to emend to *"kunomuya"*) evidently meant the tick. But this statement proves only that the Archbishop was more proficient in philology than in natural history.

the late Major Austen, I was able to examine the holotype
and paratype at the British Museum. This species, which
has not been figured, is close to *H. longipennis,* the most important differences being given in the key. In addition, the
vertex is somewhat narrower than in *longipennis,* with the
inner margins slightly converging toward the occiput; the
postvertex is shorter; the inner orbits (or parafrontalia)
are narrower and of more uniform width throughout; the
fronto-clypeus also narrower. The insect is mostly reddish-
yellow; but scutellum, postvertex and fronto-clypeus are almost wholly pale ivory-yellow. I have seen also a male from
Tanganyika Territory (West shore of Lake Manyara).
This sex is almost exactly like the female. It has eight
strong pale-colored preapical bristles on the scutellum (also
present in both types), placed in a single row and widely
divided into two groups of four each. The structure of the
abdomen is not known, but is probably similar to that of
equina and *longipennis,* with minor differences in the relative size of the median tergal plates.

In the male of *fulva* examined, the parameres of the
genitalia are similar to those of *equina* and *longipennis,* but
the terminal point is blunter. *H. fulva* and *H. martinaglia*
are the smallest members of the genus.

4. *Hippobosca variegata* Megerlé von Mühlfeld, 1803,
(actual date of publication!), Appendix ad Catal. Insect.
Nov. 1802 Viennae Austriae Vendita, p.[14] (unnumbered)
(Bengal).

Synonyms: *H. maculata* Leach, 1817; *H. bipartita* Macquart, 1843; *H. aegyptiaca* Macquart, 1843; *H. fossulata*
Macquart, 1843;[1] *H. sudanica* Bigot, 1884; *H. sivae* Bigot,
1885; *H. calopsis* Bigot, 1885; *H. aegyptiaca* var. *benga-
lensis* Ormerod, 1895.

H. variegata appears to be the oldest valid name for this
species, the date 1823 given by Wiedemann being erroneous
(see Schenkling 1935, Arch. Morph. Taxon. Entom., Ber-
lin-Dahlem, II, p. 156). The original description is of the
briefest: "ex Beng. Aff. equin. sed maj. magisque varieg.
(1 Exemplar)." Yet it is sufficient to validate the name,
especially in view of the fact that Wiedemann (1830,

[1]Macquart's three names should be dated 1843, when the Mém. Soc.
Sci. Lille for 1842 were actually published.

Aussereurop. Zweifl. Ins., II, p. 603) based the more detailed and fully recognizable description of his *Hippobosca variegata* in part upon Megerlé's specimen.

I have seen, at the University Zoological Museum in Copenhagen, the fly from Tranquebar mentioned by Fabricius (1805, Syst. Antliat., p. 338) as a variety of *H. equina*. It is *H. variegata* and may well have been the specimen which Wiedemann mentioned from Tranquebar. I have also seen Leach's type of *H. maculata* at the British Museum. According to the label it came from Bengal.

Additional Specimens Examined. — French West Africa: Zinder, Niger River, off cattle and horses (A. Buchanan). — Gold Coast: Salaga, N. Terr., off cattle (F. J. A. Beringer) ; Yegi, N. Terr.; Accra (J. W. S. Macfie) ; Obuasi, Ashanti (W. M. Graham). — Northern Nigeria: Kaduna (J. J. Simpson) ; Azare (L. Lloyd) ; Zungeru, off horses. — Southern Nigeria: Lagos (C. B. Philip) ; Olokemeji, Ibadan. — Cameroon: Bamum. — Belgian Congo: Sankuru District, 5° S., 26° E. (A. Yale Massey). — Anglo-Egyptian Sudan: Khor Hanoieit, Port Sudan; Khartoum (S. Hirst) ; Erkowit, Red Sea Hills, biting man (J. G. Myers) ; near Meshra, Equatoria biting man (J. G. Myers). — Egypt: Luxor (Reimoser.) — Ethiopia: Hawash River, W. of Mt. Zaquala, 6,000 ft. (J. O. Couper) ; Maraquo (O. Kovacs). — Uganda: Mt. Debasien, 5,000 ft. (A. Loveridge). — Kenya Colony: Nakuru (van Someren). — Tanganyika Territory: Kigonsera (J. N. Erth). — Natal: Durban. — Madagascar: Betsiriry District, west of S. Central Plateau, off mules (F. P. Porter) ; Tsaratanana, N. Central District (W. C. Holden) ; Ampoza (E. I. White) ; Tanovana, Oriental Forest District (between Tamatave and Tananarive. — C. Lamberton). — Mesopotamia (Iraq): Daurah (A. D. Fraser). — India: Calcutta (Brunetti) ; Bhowali, Kumaon, 5,700 ft. (Imms) ; Deccan (Fischer) ; Mukteswar, United Prov. (J. D. R. Holmes) ; Pusa, Bihar, off cattle (R. Senior-White) ; Tranquebar. — Ceylon: Banhar (R. Senior-White) ; Matale, off horse (R. Senior-White) ; Luduganga, off cattle (R. Senior-White) ; Habarane, off cattle (R. Senior-White) ; Peradenyia, off cattle (A. Rutherford) ; Dambula, off cattle (L. G. Saunders) ; Hamsantota; Madulsima; Diyawa, 4,000 ft. — Assam: Coonoor, off cattle (R. Senior-White) ;

Baranri (R. Senior-White). — Timor. — Celebes: Manado, off horse (F. C. Kraneveld).

The preapical bristles of the scutellum are pale-colored and unevenly developed, usually placed on two irregular rows, the two lateral groups more or less connected in the middle. Counting only the heavy bristles and neglecting the small, hair-like ones, their number varies from 13 to 27 in 95 specimens examined (49 ♀ and 46 ♂), from 12 localities, 68 specimens having from 16 to 20 bristles. The specimens show the following grouping: with 13 bristles: 2 (all ♀); 14b.: 1 (♀); 15b.: 5 (2 ♀ , 3 ♂); 16b.: 7 (6 ♀ , 1 ♂); 17b.: 15 (7 ♀ , 8 ♂); 18b.: 15 (4 ♀ , 11 ♂); 19b.: 22 (13 ♀ , 9 ♂); 20b.: 9 (6 ♀ , 3 ♂); 21b.: 7 (4 ♀ , 3 ♂) ; 22b.: 2 (1 ♀ , 1 ♂); 23b.: 3 (2 ♀ , 1 ♂) ; 24b.: 4 (1 ♀ , 3 ♂); 25b.: 2 (all ♂) ; 27b.: 1 (♂). There is seemingly no sexual difference in this character. In one lot of 30 specimens (10 ♀ , 20 ♂) from Aden, off cattle, the bristles vary from 13 to 22, but 25 specimens have from 16 to 20 bristles. The bristles are evenly divided between both sides in 37 specimens, unevenly in 58, the uneven groupings observed being $6 + 7, 6 + 8, 7 + 8, 8 + 9, 9 + 10, 10 + 11, 11 + 12, 12 + 13,$ and $13 + 14$.

In *H. variegata*, the dorsum of the abdomen bears no median tergal sclerotized plates in either sex. In the female, the anterior pair of subapical (lateral) plates is somewhat larger than the posterior pair. In the male, the anterior pair is very large, so that the two plates nearly touch medially; the posterior pair is very small and hidden in a dorsal view. The abdomen of the female is shown correctly by Ferris (1930, Philippine Jl. Sci., XLIII, p. 545, fig. 5). There is no good figure of the male.

The claspers (or parameres) of the male genitalia are straight and rod-like, rather abruptly narrowed about mid-length and then very slender to the pointed tip.

5. *Hippobosca rufipes* v. Olfers.

Additional Specimens Examined. — Natal: Durban, off cattle (W. C. C. Pakes). — Cape Province: Van Rhyn's Pass (T.D.A. Cockerell) ; Milnertown near Cape Town (R. E. Turner) ; Waku (J. Bruce-Bays) ; Matjesfontein (R. E. Turner) ; Erraha (E. Gough). — South West Africa: Tsau, Great Namaqualand (Pöch) ; Otyivarongo, Damaraland (de

Schauensee); Windhoek to Gobabis (de Schauensee); Okahandja (R. E. Turner; J. Ogilvie); Otavifontein (K. Jordan); Usakos (J. Ogilvie); Hoffnung (K. Jordan). — Orange Free State: North Bank Halt, Norvals Poort (J. Ogilvie); Cotzies' Farm (W. L. Distant). — Bechuanaland Protectorate: Mongalatsela, Ghanzi, Ngamiland, off horse and off steinbok (J. Maurice). — Southern Rhodesia: Victoria Falls (R. Lowe Thompson). — Northern Rhodesia: Lunda, near Congo border (H. S. Evans). — Portuguese West Africa: Benguela, off cattle (W. C. C. Pakes). — Tanganyika Territory: Mt. Meru, 4,500 to 5,000 ft., off eland (B Cooper); Ngare Nairobi, W. Kilimanjaro, 5,000 ft. (B. Cooper); Ngaserai, W. Kilimanjaro, 3,000 ft. (B. Cooper).

The number of heavy, black preapical bristles of the scutellum is quite variable in this species and apparently shows no sexual difference. In 95 specimens examined (69 ♀ and 26 ♂), from 14 localities, the total number varies from 12 to 23, but 82 specimens have from 14 to 20 bristles. The specimens are distributed as follows: with 12 bristles: 2 (1 ♀ , 1 ♂); 13b.: 5 (4 ♀ , 1 ♂); 14b.: 10 (8 ♀ , 2 ♂); 15b.: 10 (all ♀); 16b.: 7 (6 ♀ , 1 ♂); 17b.: 17 (13 ♀ , 4 ♂); 18b.: 18 (11 ♀ , 7 ♂); 19b.: 12 (8 ♀ , 4 ♂); 20b.: 8 (4 ♀ , 4 ♂); 21b.: 5 (4 ♀ , 1 ♂); 23b.: 1 (♂).

Most localities are represented by one or a few specimens. In a series of 67 specimens taken off cattle at Windsorton, Cape Province, the proportion is as follows: with 13b.: 3 (all ♀); 14b.: 4 (3 ♀ , 1 ♂); 15b.: 9 (all ♀); 16b.: 5 (all ♀); 17b.: 12 (9 ♀ , 3 ♂); 18b.: 15 (10 ♀ , 5 ♂) ; 19b.: 8 (5 ♀ , 3 ♂); 20b.: 5 (2 ♀ , 3 ♂); 21b.: 5 (4 ♀ , 1 ♂); 22b.: 1 (♂). The bristles are more often unevenly divided between both sides (unevenly in 58 specimens, evenly in 37), the two groups only narrowly divided, so that the row is fairly continuous. The uneven groupings observed were 6 + 7, 7 + 8, 8 + 9, 6 + 8, 7 + 9, 8 + 10, 9 + 10, 9 + 11, 10 + 11, 9 + 12, and 11 + 12.

The structure of the abdomen of *H. rufipes* is similar to that of *H. variegata*. It is correctly shown for the female by Austen (1909, Illustr. African Blood-Suck. Flies, Pl. XIII, fig. 100).

The parameres of the male genitalia are straight and

rod-like, abruptly narrowed at basal third, beyond which they are thicker than in *H. variegata* and blunter at the pointed apex.

6. *Hippobosca hirsuta* Austen. — I have seen the types of the typical form and the var. *neavei* Austen at the British Museum.

Additional Specimens Examined. — Uganda: near Lake Albert (H. Hargreaves). — Nyasaland: Akamanga, Runyinya River, N. Nyasa, off waterbuck (J. B. Davey).

The preapical bristles of the scutellum are much weaker in this species than in most other members of the genus, and pale-colored. In the few specimens seen their total number varies from 14 to 18 (1 with 14, 1 with 15, 1 with 16, and 1 with 18, for the males; 1 with 14 and 1 with 16, for the females).

The structure of the abdomen is similar to that of *H. variegata* in both sexes.

The parameres of the male genitalia differ from those of all other species of the genus. They are broad and thick, beam-like, slightly wider basally and apically in side-view. The apex is straightly truncate, shallowly and evenly emarginate, so as to produce two blunt edges, one dorsal and one ventral.

7. *Hippobosca martinaglia* Bedford, 1936, Onderstepoort Jl. Vet. Sci. An. Ind., VII, pt. 1, p. 67, fig. (on p. 68) (♀ ♂ ; off Impalla, *Aepyceros melampus* (Lichtenstein) ; Bar R. Ranch, Swaziland, South Africa).

In the absence of specimens, I have inserted this species in my key on the assumption that there are setæ on the basal section of the third longitudinal vein and that only one of the pulvilli is well-developed, neither character being mentioned by the author. From the figure and description, it appears to be closest to *H. hirsuta*, likewise found on antelopes. It differs in the smaller size, the few short black setae of the mesonotum, the few preapical bristles of the scutellum, the wider frons, the narrower inner orbits or parafrontalia (less than half the width of the mediovertex or frontalia), and the short, semi-elliptical postvertex. The second longitudinal vein is described as "long", but the figure shows it to be "short", reaching the costa a short distance beyond the

tip of the first longitudinal vein, so that the last section of
the costa is about six times the length of the penultimate
section. No median tergal plates are shown in the figure of
the female. The coloration seems to fit some of my specimens of *H. longipennis (capensis)*, but the second longitudinal vein is much shorter than in that species. The
venation also separates *H. martinaglia* from *H. fulva*, a fly
of about the same size, likewise found on antelopes.

The original description is reproduced, as it appeared in a
periodical inaccessible to most entomologists: "A small
species; length of wing 4.5 mm. Head about as wide at the
occiput as at the fronto-clypeus, reddish-brown, the frontal
stripe slightly darker; posterior margin of head fringed
with minute, thick-set setæ, and a long seta at the base of
each eye; palpi dark brown, clothed with short setae of the
same colour. Thorax reddish-brown, with a median dark
band extending backwards almost to the transverse suture;
this band is forked posteriorly, usually more so than in the
figure, and in one specimen is completely divided down the
middle by a narrow line; on each side of the posterior portion of the median band there is a dark transverse band.
On each side beneath the transverse suture there is a narrow transverse dark band, and beneath this a small triangular spot, which is usually indistinct and may be absent.
At each latero-anterior angle there are two short setæ, one
on each side slightly distad and nearer the meson; on each
side above the base of the wing there are three very short,
thick-set black setæ, two more similar setæ slightly above
them and near the meson, and two larger setæ slightly above
them and near the meson, and two larger setæ below them;
on each side on the posterior margin there are five setæ.
Scutellum yellowish-white, fringed with short and a few
long setæ. On the venter there is a vertical dark band on
each side between the fore and mid coxæ. Legs pale reddish-brown, sparsely clothed with setæ; those on the tibiæ
and tarsi darker. Ungues black. Abdomen reddish-brown
with numerous pale setæ. Wings hyaline with pale reddish-
brown veins and short dark setæ on the costa. Second longitudinal vein (R_{2+3}) long, reaching beyond the apex of the
first longitudinal vein (R_1), but not extending to the anterior cross-vein. This new species can be easily recognised

by its pale colour and dark markings on the thorax and venter between the fore and mid coxae; also by the short thick-set setæ on the thorax and pale scutellum."

8. *Hippobosca struthionis* Janson. — I have seen the type from Mt. Stewart, Cape Province, at the British Museum.

Additional Specimens Examined. — Kenya Colony: Simba, 3,350 ft.; Makumbu; Ukamba; Machakos; Athi Plains, off horse; Merifano (McArthur); Taveta, off dog (C. W. Woodhouse). — Tanganyika Territory: Tabora, off ostrich (J. Rodhain); north of Tarengere River (W. A. Lamborn); Sanga River, Muruangani. — Transvaal: Pretoria; Deelfontein; near Limpopo River, N. Transvaal, off ostrich (R. A. Cooley). — Cape Province: Philipsdale, Worcester; Hopetown; Campbell; Cradock (Miss J. Brincker); Erreha (E. Gough). — Bechuanaland: Ghanzi, Ngamiland (J. Maurice). — South West Africa: Otavi (J. Ogilvie); Aus (R. E. Turner); Greater Spitzkopje near Usakos, Damaraland (de Schauensee).

This species is unusual in that the preapical bristles of the scutellum are crowded together in two widely separated groups, placed at the extreme sides; also in that the bristles are more numerous in the male than in the female. In 23 specimens (13 ♀ and 10 ♂) examined, from 4 localities, the bristles varied in the females from 4 to 12, 9 of the 13 ♀ having from 5 to 7; in the males, from 8 to 15, 7 of the 10 ♂ having from 9 to 12. The grouping was as follows: with 4 bristles: 2 (♀); 5b.: 3(♀); 6b.: 3 (♀); 7b.: 3 (♀); 8b.: 1 (♂); 9b.: 4 (1 ♀ , 3 ♂); 11b.: 2 (♂); 12b.: 3 (1 ♀ , 2 ♂); 13b.: 1 (♂); 14b.: 1 (♂) ; 15b.: 1 (♂). The bristles were divided into even groups in 8 specimens, unevenly in 15, the uneven groupings observed being 2 + 3, 3 + 4, 4 + 5, 5 + 6, 5 + 7, 6 + 7, and 7 + 8.

The structure of the abdomen of *H. struthionis* is similar to that of *H. variegata* in both sexes. The species has not been figured adequately.

The parameres of the male genitalia are slender, rod-like, gradually narrowed from the base to the pointed, sharp apex, and very similar to those of *H. equina*.

9. *Hippobosca camelina* Leach. — I have seen Leach's type, at the British Museum.

Additional Specimens Examined. — Morocco: Debdou-Taourirt (Ebner) ; Tendrara (Ebner). — Mauretania: Between Kiffa and Tidjidja, off camels (Mrs. Mary Steele). — Algeria: Biskra (Rothschild and Hartert); Ain Sefra (Rothschild ‚and Hartert) ; Touggourt (Rothschild and Hartert) ; Oued Nça, Mzab country (Hartert) ; Zahrez Gharbi (Zerny). — Tunis: Gabes (Mik) ; Tozeur (G. F. de Witte). — Libya: Tripoli (Klaptocz) ; Dernah (Klaptocz) ; Bengasi (Klaptocz). — Egypt: Old Cairo, off horse (Efflatoun Bey) ; Gebel Elba, S. E. Desert (Tewfik) ; near Pyramids (Reimoser). — Palestine: Jericho (P. A. Buxton) ; Jerusalem (P. Barraud). — Arabia: Djedda (H. W. Whyte) ; Tuwaiq, Riyadh (H. St. J. B. Philby) ; Keshin (Hein). — British Somaliland: without more definite locality (C. L. Collenette). — Kenya Colony: Lodwar, Turkana; Marsabit, Rendili Nyoro, N. Frontier District (C. A. Neave) ; near mouth of Kallilokwelli River, Lake Rudolf (E. B. Worthington). — Anglo-Egyptian Sudan: Khor Hanoieit, Port Sudan; Erkowit, Red Sea Hills, biting man (J. G. Myers).

H. camelina is in many respects the most aberrant member of the genus, particularly in the arrangement of the scutellar bristles and in the structure of the abdomen, both features showing remarkable sexual differences. If few specimens were examined, one might be led to think that two species are confused under the name *camelina*. Fortunately I was able to study a series of 20 specimens (10 ♀ and 10 ♂), collected in one locality of British Somaliland, removing all doubt in the matter.

In the male the scutellar bristles are preapical, placed as in the other species of the genus. In 14 males examined, from 4 localities, their number varies from 11 to 22, with the following groupings: 11 bristles: 1; 12b.: 4; 14b.: 2; 15b.: 4; 16b.: 1; 17b.: 1; 22b.: 1. They are divided into two even groups in 6 males, unevenly in 8. In the female the bristles are discal, placed near the middle of the scutellum and much more spaced. In 17 females, from 6 localities, their number varies from 3 to 8, as follows: 3 bristles: 1; 4b.: 6; 5b.: 4; 6b.: 3; 7b.: 2; 8b.: 1. They are evenly divided in 10 females, unevenly in 7.

In the female the dorsum of the abdomen is entirely soft

and extensible behind the usual basal tergal sclerite; posteriorly one finds on the extreme sides two pairs of subapical strongly sclerotized plates, bearing long bristles, the anterior pair being much larger than the posterior pair. In the male there is immediately behind the basal tergal sclerite a large ribbon-like median plate, somewhat triangular medially; much farther back, also a pair of very small median plates, rather far apart; two pairs of subapical plates are present, but the posterior pair are very small and hidden from view in a dorsal aspect. The abdomen is fairly correctly drawn for both sexes by Massonnat (1909, Ann. Univ. Lyon, N.S., CXXVIII, Pl. III, figs. 24 and 25).

The parameres of the male genitalia are peculiar. They are rod-like seen from above, but in side view more or less boat-shaped; the basal two-thirds are wide, with an evenly convex lower margin; the slender apical third is curved upward and ends in a blunt, somewhat knob-like point. The outer surface is raised into a median, curved, blunt ridge, running the whole length.

NOTES ON STRUMIGENYS FROM SOUTHERN OHIO, WITH DESCRIPTIONS OF SIX NEW SPECIES

By Laurence G. Wesson, Jr., and Robert G. Wesson

Baltimore, Md.

The following paper is a list, with biological notes, of 14 species of the peculiar and little known genus, *Strumigenys*, six of which are new and are here described.[1] All the material was collected within 45 miles of Jackson, which is located centrally in southern Ohio.

Strumigenys (Cephaloxys) pergandei Emery

In a previous paper[2] it was shown that *S. pergandei* lives, in southern Ohio at least, near the colonies of various other species of ants, hunting the Collembola which often abound in the nests of these other species. Since the publication of that paper, we have found *S. pergandei* on more than 30 occasions in this region, and only once was it not obviously associated with another ant. Stray workers have been found in nest galleries of *Camponotus herculeanus* subsp. *pennsylvanicus* (Degeer), *Formica fusca* (L.), and *F. truncicola* subsp. *integra* Nyl. Three workers were found in an outlying gallery of a *F. fusca* mound. The gallery led from the mound to a small kitchen midden to which the *pergandei* seemed to be going, not, as experiments have

[1] We wish to express our deep appreciation to Dr. M. R. Smith, U. S. National Museum, for his suggestions as to the relationship of several of the new forms, as well as for his loan of much cotype material for comparison.

The types of the new species are to be deposited in the collection of the Museum of Comparative Zoology, Cambridge, Mass. Paratypes, when present, will be deposited in the collections of Dr. C. H. Kennedy, Ohio State University, Columbus, Ohio, Dr. W. S. Creighton, College of the City of New York, the U. S. National Museum, Washington, D. C., the American Museum of Natural History, New York, and the authors.

[2] Wesson, L. G., Jr., Contributions to the Biology of *Strumigenys pergandei* Em., Ent. News, vol. 47, pp. 171-174 (1936).

indicated, for the debris there, but for the Collembola which lived about the refuse. Under a large, flat stone in maple woods was found a fine colony of *S. pergandei* in the center of a large *F. fusca* var. *subserica* Say colony the galleries of which surrounded the *pergandei* nest on all sides and below. Workers were observed in the galleries of about 28 additional nests of *Aphænogaster fulva* Roger under stones. Four or 5 *pergandei* workers could often be seen creeping away from the superficial galleries when a stone covering one of these nests was overturned. One such *fulva-pergandei* association was of special interest because of its similarity to the colony in the midst of the *F. subserica* nest described above. The *pergandei* were nesting in a shallow, nearly circular, earthen chamber about 3 cm. in diameter, immediately under a large, flat stone covering a colony of *A. fulva*. Large, flattened chambers and galleries of the *fulva* surrounded the *pergandei* nest for at least 8 cm. on all sides. The walls of the chamber separating the *Strumigenys* from the *Aphænogaster* were about ½ cm. thick. With one exception we have always found *S. pergandei* in the soil, that one exception being in the log mentioned below under *S. dietrichi* M. R. Smith.

Some further notes from observations of this species are recorded here. The developmental periods are approximately: egg, 15 to 16 days; larval stage, about 42 days; pupal stage, about 18 days. On 3 occasions workers were seen to bring alternately left and right forelegs to the vertex of the head, rubbing the tarsi forward and placing them on the ground. Whether this was a cleaning operation or a means of transfering some substance to the substratum, or has some other significance is not known. The ant did not clean the tarsus after rubbing the head, nor did it rub any other part of its body. Workers of different colonies fight viciously when brought together. On the other hand, a colony will adopt the brood of another colony, even of a different species of the subgenus.

Strumigenys (Cephaloxys) ornato Mayr

Two workers were found near the kitchen midden of a colony of *Aphænogaster fulva* subsp. *aquia* (Buckley) which was nesting under a large stone in a rather moist

hillside woods.   Another colony was found in an almost
identical situation in dense, oak woods.   In the latter case
a worker was first seen in a frequented gallery of *A. fulva
aquia* under a large stone.   The nest was located about 3 cm.
to one side of the stone, and consisted of an irregular cavity,
perhaps just a crack in the soil, barely beneath the humus.
It contained not more than 20 workers.   Both localities
were in Pike County.

Strumigenys (Cephaloxys) deitrichi M. R. Smith

We have taken this ant in Pike, Lawrence, and Adams
Counties.   On 4 occasions workers were found under the
bark of somewhat decayed logs in open, dryish woods.   In all
of these logs have been colonies of other species of ants, such
as *Formica truncicola* subsp. *integra* Nyl., *Aphænogaster
tennesseensis* Mayr, *A. lamellidens* var. *nigripes* M. R.
Smith, *A. fulva* Roger, *Proceratium crassicorne* var. *vestita*
Emery, *Ponera coarctata* subsp. *pennsylvanica* Buckley.
One long, decayed, hickory log, covered with a tough layer
of bark, was remarkable in containing colonies of at least
11 species of ants, including 5 species of *Strumigenys*.   The
log, lying on the edge of some woods, extended from deep
shade through a clump of bushes into broken sunlight.   The
ant species, in approximate order from shade to sun, were:
Strumigenys deitrichi M. R. Smith, *Ponera coarctata* subsp.
pennsylvanica Buckley, *Aphænogaster fulva* subsp. *aquia*,
Buckley, *Strumigenys pulchella* Emery, *Solenopsis molesta*
(Say), *Strumigenys medialis* new species, *Strumigenys rostrata* Emery, *Proceratium crassicorne* var. *vestitum* Emery,
Lasius niger var. *neoniger* Emery, *Strumigenys pergandei*
Emery, and *Crematogaster lineolata* (Say).   Several workers of *S. deitrichi* were found in the loose humus in the cedar
grove described below under *S. missouriensis* M. R. Smith.

In none of these cases did we observe definite indications
of an association between *S. deitrichi* and the other species
of ants living near them, such as the presence of *deitrichi*
workers in frequented galleries of the other.

Strumigenys (Cephaloxys) clypeata Roger

A nest of *clypeata* was found in the duff at the base of a
small pine tree a few inches from a colony of *Myrmica*

punctiventris Roger.   The location was on a dry sandstone
bluff in Jackson County on which many colonies of *S. pergandei* had been found.[3]

Strumigenys (Cephaloxys) medialis, sp.n.

Worker: (Pl. 3, fig. 1) : Length, 2.00 mm.

Sides of head converging anteriorly, the occipital lobes
posterior to the antennal insertions somewhat but not suddenly or strongly expanded; clypeus at greatest width $\frac{1}{3}$
the length of the head exclusive of the mandibles, evenly
and broadly rounded, but narrower than in *S. clypeata;*
mandibles when closed $\frac{1}{4}$ to $\frac{1}{5}$ the length of the remainder
of the head, with the stout basal teeth hidden beneath the
clypeus, the succeeding toothless space very short, the apical
teeth comprising 5 pair of long, acute teeth decreasing
somewhat in length anteriorly, and merging without a gap
into the apical series of numerous smaller teeth; posterior
border of head deeply excised; antennal scapes broadly
curved on the basal third; first joint of the funiculus distinctly shorter than the fourth, the terminal joint slightly
longer than the remainder of the funiculus.   Thorax as in
S. clypeata; the dorsum of the mesonotum somewhat flattened, not marginate laterally; mesoepinotal suture distinct
but not constricted; epinotal spines acute, slightly divergent, directed backwards; infraspinal lamellæ narrow, uniform in width.   Petiole, postpetiole and gaster as in *S.
clypeata* and related species.

Head, thorax and petiole coarsely and densely reticulate-
punctate, opaque; meso- and metapleura, dorsal surface of
postpetiole and gaster smooth and shining; first gastric
segment with numerous coarse longitudinal striae on the
basal $\frac{1}{3}$; sculpture of the clypeus much finer than the rest of
the head, densely and finely crenulate-punctate, subopaque.
Hairs on the clypeus numerous, erect, anteriorly curved,
narrowly squamose at their tips, those on the sides $\frac{1}{5}$ the
width of the clypeus, those in the middle somewhat shorter;
hairs on the rest of the head sparse, longer, thin, clavate,
1 or 2 on each side of the head very long and not clavate.
Hairs on antennal scapes numerous, similar to those on the
vertex of the head, curved toward the tip of the scapes;

[3]Wesson. L. G., Jr., Contributions to the Biology of Strumigenys
pergandei Em., Ent. News, vol. 47, pp. 171-174 (1936).

hairs on thorax irregular, long, thin, not clavate, the majority subappressed; gaster bearing 2 or 3 long hairs, usually near the base, a number of shorter hairs at the tip. Spongiform processes as in *S. clypeata* and related species.

Color dark ferruginous, the appendages slightly lighter, the gaster darker.

S. medialis possesses the general characteristics of *S. clypeata* and the species related to it. It may readily be separated from other forms, however, by (1) the longer mandibles, which are $\frac{1}{4}$ to $\frac{1}{5}$ the length of the head; (2) the more narrowly rounded clypeus, the surface of which is subopaque; (3) the pilosity of the clypeus, the hairs of which are longer, erect, feebly squamose and sharply curved apically, and (4) generally by the pilosity of the rest of the head and antennal scapes.

Type locality: Beaver, Pike County, Ohio.

Described from a colony of about 30 workers and several dealate females taken from the hickory log described above under *S. deitrichi*. The nest consisted of irregular cavities in the outer rotten portion of the log which appeared to be old galleries of beetle larvae. The colony was transferred to an artificial nest where, as did other species of *Strumigenys* we have had under observation, they fed on living springtails. In their hunting they were quite inactive, even more so than *S. pulchella;* the workers would remain in a crouching position, head close to the substratum, mandibles closed, antennae partially folded, for a great deal of the time. Occasionally some of the dealate females were observed hunting like the workers. Otherwise the hunting methods of this species resembled those of *S. pergandei.*

Strumigenys (Cephaloxys) bimarginata, sp. n.

Worker: (Pl. 3, fig. 2) : Length, 1.7 mm.

Head, exclusive of mandibles, 3.3 times the greatest width of the clypeus, 5.7 times the length of the exposed portion of the closed mandibles. Viewed anteriorly, the sides of the head anterior to the antennal insertions are straight, converging, their projections lying along the exterior border of the closed mandibles; clypeus rather narrow but evenly rounded, not acute, flattened dorsally; clypeus viewed from

the side with its edge broadly and deeply grooved along the
entire lateral and anterior borders, thus giving the clypeus
the appearance of having 2 margins, a thin but narrow
upper margin and a thicker broader lower margin which
projects beyond the upper margin and is visible when the
clypeus is viewed anteriorly. Mandibles rather slender and
elongate, the exterior border straight basally, feebly convex
apically; basal tooth stout, partially concealed by the clypeus
when the mandibles are closed; succeeding toothless space
very short; apical teeth comprising 7 or 8 large irregular
teeth which decrease in size anteriorly to merge into the
apical series of numerous small teeth. Antennal scapes
broadly curved basally, not angulate, fourth funicular joint
slightly longer than the first; terminal joint slightly longer
than the remainder of the funiculus. Sides of head posterior to the antennal insertions suddenly expanding to a
broadly circular border so that that portion of the head
appears subglobose when viewed anteriorly. Posterior
border narrowly and rather deeply excised. Thorax essentially as in *S. clypeata;* mesoepinotal suture distinct but not
constricted; median longitudinal carina prominent, especially on the basal surface of the epinotum. Petiole, postpetiole and gaster as in *S. clypeata.*

Head, thorax and petiole densely reticulate-punctate, subopaque; vertex of head with 8 or 10 broken irregular longitudinal rugae. Mandibles, clypeus, sides of mesonotum,
meso- and metapleura, dorsum of the postpetiole and gaster
smooth and shining; basal $\frac{1}{4}$ of the first gastric segment
with numerous coarse longitudinal striae.

Hairs on clypeus sparse, long, erect, more numerous on
the edges, each hair being fairly straight at the base, curved
and slightly enlarged on the apical $\frac{1}{3}$, $\frac{1}{4}$ to $\frac{1}{2}$ the width of
the clypeus; hairs on vertex numerous, shorter, erect,
clavate, curved anteriorly; antennal scapes with numerous
hairs similar to those on the vertex but less clavate, curved
toward the tips of the scapes; hairs on the thorax, petiole
and postpetiole numerous, variable, those on the thoracic
dorsum being rather long, slightly clavate, appressed, those
on the petiole and postpetiole averaging longer, more erect
and not clavate; gaster with sparse, long, slender, erect
hairs. Spongiform processes as in *S. clypeata* and related
species.

Color ferruginous; mandibles, antennae and legs slightly lighter; gaster darker.

This very distinctive species is readily recognized by (1) the doubly margined character of the clypeal border; (2) the smooth and shining surface of the clypeus, and the more extensive shining areas on the thorax; (3) the shape of the head (4) the pilosity of the head.

Type locality: Cedar Mills, Adams County, Ohio.

Described from a single worker found under a piece of bark lying on the ground in a somewhat open, grassy spot in rather brushy cut-over woods. A deälated female belonging to this species was found about 15 cm. distant in some thin, vegetable debris. Further search failed to reveal any more specimens.

Strumigenys (Cephaloxys) manni, sp. n.[4]

Worker: (Pl. 3, fig. 3) : Length, 1.8-2.0 mm.

Head 2.5 times as long as the greatest width of the clypeus, 1.3 times the greatest width across the occipital lobes; viewed anteriorly, the sides of the head anterior to the antennal insertions are gently convergent, slightly convex, in outline merging without definite change of slope with the exterior borders of the mandibles; clypeus with lateral borders gently convergent, nearly straight, the anterior border truncate at, or a little anterior to, the point of intersection of the lateral and external mandibular borders; in some specimens, the anterior border is slightly emarginate, in others it is somewhat angularly convex in the middle, but the truncate appearance is not lost. Occipital lobes expanding suddenly but not strongly from the anterior portion of the head, at first broadly convex, then more strongly convex as the posterior border is approached; posterior border rather broadly and moderately excised. Mandibles $\frac{1}{4}$ the length of the rest of the head, rather robust, the external border broadly and evenly convex; basal teeth very broad and short, partially concealed by the clypeus when the mandibles are closed, followed without an intervening toothless space by 5 pairs of moderately long acute teeth, the third

[4]It gives us pleasure to name this distinctive species after Dr. W. M. Mann, from whom we have received many kind favors.

pair somewhat longer than the others, these acute teeth followed by the apical series of several much smaller teeth. Eyes small, comprising 10 or 12 facets. Antennal scapes $\frac{3}{5}$ the length of the funiculi, rounded but not angulate on the basal third; fourth joint of the funiculus very slightly shorter than the first, terminal joint as long as the remainder of the funiculus. Thorax as in *S. clypeata*, humeri and lateral margins smoothly rounded, somewhat flattened on the dorsum of the mesonotum, mesoepinotal suture distinct, slightly constricted; epinotal spines acute, thin; infraspinal lamellae narrow, not expanded ventrally. Node of petiole in profile rather prominent, broadly convex, the anterior slope rising suddenly but gently from the peduncle, the posterior slope declining very distinctly to the junction with the postpetiole.

Head, thorax and petiole reticulate-punctate, subopaque; mandibles, meso- and metapleura, dorsum of the postpetiole and gaster smooth and shining; first gastric segment with numerous, coarse, longitudinal striae on the basal $\frac{1}{5}$.

Hairs on head and thoracic dorsum numerous, moderately long, thin, curved and somewhat clavate at their tips; those on the clypeus shorter, curved laterally and anteriorly, a few on the borders of the clypeus slightly longer, curved posteriorly; hairs on antennal scapes erect, clavate on the anterior edge, more numerous and thinner dorsally, deflected toward the tips of the scapes; hairs on the thorax more irregular in length and distribution, and less clavate; hairs on the petiole, postpetiole and gaster very long, thin, very few on the gaster.

Color, light to dark ferruginous; tarsi and antennal funiculi slightly paler; gaster darker.

Type locality: Pike County, near Sinking Spring, Ohio.

Described from 32 workers obtained by sifting dirt and humus in the small cedar grove described below under *S. missouriensis*. The spot was situated at the base of a hill where the soil above the underlying limestone was only 5 to 8 cm. deep. The ground was shaded by cedar and small oak trees and was covered with a rather thick, loose humus abounding with springtails.

In shape of the head, *S. manni* bears a superficial resemblance to *S. margaritæ* Forel, but differs from that form in characters too numerous to mention. It is distinguished generally by (1) the decidedly truncate appearance of the clypeus; (2) the long and robust mandibles; (3) the mandibular dentition; (4) the relative prominence of the node of the petiole; (5) the character of the pilosity of the head and thorax; (6) the shorter terminal joints of the antennae.

Strumigenys (Cephaloxys) rostrata Emery

Jackson, Pike, Ross and Scioto counties.

We have taken this species in both soil and wood, sometimes in decidedly dry situations. Three colonies were found respectively in the hickory log mentioned under *S. deitrichi*, the decaying portion of a large elm tree in which also lived a colony of *Aphaenogaster tennesseensis* Mayr, and in a crevice in a stump in a wooded pasture, a few centimeters from another colony of *A. tennesseensis*. 3 colonies were taken on the edge of some dry oak woods, all in or on the humus just under the dry oak leaves, which, with some grass and herbs, covered the ground. The nesting site of one was a rotten hickory nut; the second was in some cavities in a small decayed stick; the third was living in a crevice of a partly buried board. Workers were found under the leaves in the vicinity of the nests, presumably foraging. They were not apparently associated with any other ants. A few dead springtails were found in one of the nests. On one occasion a colony of *rostrata* was found living in a chamber in dry soil under a stone. Under the stone there also ran a few galleries of *Lasius umbratus mixtus* var. *aphidicola* (Walsh).

A *rostrata* colony was transferred to an artificial nest for observation. While employing the same general methods of hunting springtails as the other species studied, the *rostrata* workers differ in being more active. Instead of crouching in one spot awaiting the advent of a springtail, they spend most of their foraging time moving over the debris in the nest. When a worker scents a springtail 2 or 3 mm. away, she crouches, and, without touching it, tries various avenues of approach until she is so close that her mandibles almost touch the springtail. Then, head lowered,

mandibles closed, antennae partially folded, she waits until
the springtail, unaware of her presence, walks against her
head.   Then, seizing it with a quick snap of her mandibles,
she quickly dispatches it with her sting.   If, on the other
hand, the springtail moves away from the ant, the latter
repeats her approach.   If the springtail shows no inclina-
tion to move within a few minutes, the ant often acts as
though impatient, and tries to examine it with her antennae,
or to take it in her mandibles.

Strumigenys (Cephaloxys) pulchella Emery

We have found this species on about 15 occasions, each
time in dead wood.   A typical habitat seems to be a log or
stump or dead portion of a tree trunk, well-decayed for 3 or
4 cm. beneath the bark, moist but not wet, warm but not in
full sun.   Such desirable situations are almost always inhabited by species of *Aphænogaster, Lasius niger* var.
americanus Emery, or *Camponotus herculeanus pennsylvanicus* var. *ferrugineus* (F.).   Whether *S. pulchella* is
definitely associated with the other species, as is *S. pergandei,* or whether it is simply a matter of such a situation
being a very favorable one for other reasons, we have not
determined.   Although we have seldom taken *pulchella*
workers in the frequented galleries of other ants, the colonies have seemed to be much more definitely associated with
a larger species than chance alone would account for.

Several times when logs and stumps were broken open
pulchella workers were seen carrying dead springtails in
their mandibles, and when kept in an artificial nest they
readily captured and killed these insects.   They would,
however, accept bits of dead flies after having been starved
for a few days.   Their hunting methods are similar to those
of *S. pergandei,* but the workers are less active.   They walk
less around the galleries and amid the woody debris provided them and often crouch for hours at a cranny.   When
a springtail approaches, the worker merely lowers its head,
turns in the direction of the quarry and waits.   Only when
the springtail touches the fore part of its head and mandibles does the *pulchella* snap and seize it.   Once a dead
springtail was gently pushed close to a waiting *pulchella*
worker.   The latter crept up to about the length of its head
away, then crouched, holding its antennae partially folded.

After waiting in this position for a considerable time, it rose, extended its antennae and vibrated them rapidly, then crouched again. This was repeated two more times before the ant, as if impatient after ¾ of an hour, walked up to the springtail and seized it.

Winged phases were taken from nests in mid August.

Strumigenys (Cephaloxys) missouriensis M. R. Smith

Four colonies and numerous stray workers were found in a cedar thicket in western Pike County. The first workers were seen in and around some little-used galleries of *Aphænogaster fulva aquia* var. *picea* Emery under a small stone, and the colony was located about 30 cm. away just beneath the humus. Two other colonies were likewise in the soil, not more than 4 cm. below the surface. The latter, however, were not visibly associated with any other ants. Scattered, stray workers were found just under the top layer of the humus. The cedar grove was located on the gently sloping base of a hill. Mingled with the cedars were a few small oaks and an occasional maple sapling. The soil was a black clay from 5 to 15 cm. deep above the limestone bed rock. Above the clay was a thick, springy layer of loose decaying cedar needles, leaves and grass. Abounding in this debris were *Ponera coarctata* subsp. *pennsylvanica* Emery, *Myrmecina graminicola* (Latr.) subsp. and hordes of Collembola, as well as *Strumigenys*. Here, in an area of 3 by 9 meters, were found *S. missouriensis* M. R. Smith, *S. manni* new species, *S. deitrichi* M. R. Smith, and *S. venatrix* new species.

On careful comparison of our specimens with 2 worker cotypes loaned by Dr. M. R. Smith, we find that, although some of the workers agree closely with the cotypes, there is quite a perceptible amount of variation both among workers from the same colony and among the 4 colonies found. This variation lies almost entirely in the direction of forms which differ from the cotypes in the following details: (1) the head is slightly more robust; (2) the clypeus is slightly depressed in the middle; (3) the antennal scapes are somewhat more angulate; (4) the sculpture is distinctly coarser; (5) the hairs on the head are larger, especially on the clypeus, and are fewer in number.

Strumigenys (Cephaloxys) reflexa, sp. n.

Worker: (Pl. 3, fig. 4) : Length, 1.75-1.85 mm.

Head robust; exclusive of mandibles, 2 to 2.2 times as long as the greatest width of the clypeus, 1.3 times the greatest width across the occipital lobes; clypeus broadly rounded laterally, more narrowly rounded in the middle of the anterior border, the sides strongly scalloped; anterior portion of the head with a very broad distinct depression extending from the anterior portion of the clypeus to between the frontal carinae; occipital lobes broadly and rather evenly rounded; posterior border shallowly excised. Mandibles ⅙ the length of the rest of the head, moderately robust, the external borders gently convex; the pair of basal teeth stout, just hidden when the mandibles are closed, succeeded by a toothless space which is equal to ⅓ the length of the mandibles anterior to them, the toothless space followed by 4 or 5 pairs of rather short acute teeth which meet the apical series of numerous fine denticles. Antennal scapes rather sharply but not strongly angulate basally, ⅔ as long as the funiculi; fourth funicular joint decidedly shorter than the first, the terminal joint almost half again as long as the remainder of the funiculus.

Thorax as in *S. puchella;* mesoepinotal suture distinct, slightly constricted. Epinotal spines broad and thin; infraspinal lamellæ wide, broadly expanded ventrally.

Head, thorax and petiole reticulate-punctate, subopaque; head, especially on the dorsal posterior half coarsely tuberculate. Meso- and meta pleura, dorsum of the postpetiole and gaster, smooth and shining; first gastric segment with numerous coarse longitudinal striae on the basal ¼.

Clypeus with a few, short, irregular squamose hairs on the border; projecting from the edge of the clypeus on each side are 3, occasionally 4, long coarse squamose hairs which are strongly curved posteriorly; the rest of the dorsal surface of the head with more numerous erect, curved, narrow squamose hairs, curved predominately posteriorly; antennal scapes with 6 or 8 erect, clavate hairs on the outer border, most of which are slightly curved toward the bases of the scapes. Hairs on thorax sparse, irregular in length, erect, slightly enlarged apically. Petiole, postpetiole and gaster

with long thin erect hairs, slightly enlarged apically. Legs
and antennal funiculi with thin reclinate hairs. Spongiform processes as in *S. pulchella.*

Color ferrugineus; the gaster, darker.

Type locality: Jackson, Ohio.

We have compared *S. reflexa* with cotypes of *S. missouriensis* M. R. Smith and *S. sculpturata* M. R. Smith to both of
which it is very similar. From *S. missouriensis* it may be
distinguished by (1) the broad depression on the anterior
portion of the head; (2) the much more strongly scalloped
and sculptured head; (3) the less convex mandibles; (4)
character of the pilosity. From *S. sculpturata* it differs in
(1) the more robust head; (2) the rounded, non-truncate
clypeus; (3) the slightly less abundant pilosity, particularly
on the clypeus and gaster; (4) the appearance of the 6 large
fringing clypeal hairs which are curved strongly backward
—a feature by which this form may be easily recognized.

A colony of this species was found in a small, punky,
partly-buried board in moderate shade in a backyard in
Jackson. The colony was within a meter of a large log pile,
and workers were found foraging among the woody debris
at the base. Stray workers were discovered at 2 other places
in the yard. An early attempt to find the above colony gives
a check on the feeding habits of the species. A dead springtail was placed in front of a worker which had been discovered beneath a piece of bark. Apparently not greatly
disturbed, the ant continued to stalk among the debris
until she came within about 1 mm. of the springtail. She
then crouched and waited. After several minutes, the
springtail was gently pushed toward the ant until it was
partly on top of her head. The next instant the ant was to
be seen holding the already dead springtail tightly in her
mandibles and stinging it viciously. In a few seconds she
started off at a rapid pace with the springtail. In the artificial nest the hunting methods of the workers were similar
to those of *S. pulchella,* but even more sluggish.

Strumigenys (Cephaloxys) venatrix, sp. n.

Worker: (Pl. 3, fig. 5) : Length, 1.8-2.0 mm.

Head relatively slender, exclusive of the mandibles, 2.7
times the width of the clypeus, 1.4 times the greatest width

across the occipital lobes; anterior portion of the head as viewed from the front slightly but perceptibly converging; clypeus with sides converging gently on the basal $2/3$, the anterior border very broadly rounded, somewhat flattened in appearance, but definitely not truncate; the dorsal surface evenly convex, the edges with very small, inconspicuous scalloping; the occipital lobes very broadly convex anteriorly, more strongly convex as the posterior border is approached; posterior border broadly and rather deeply excised. Mandibles somewhat less than $1/5$ the length of the head alone, rather slender, the external borders gently convex; basal teeth stout, partially concealed by the clypeus when the mandibles are closed, followed by a toothless space $1/3$ the length of the mandibles anterior to the basal teeth, the toothless space terminated by 4 or 5 pair of acute teeth somewhat irregular in length, but longer basally, which meet the apical series of smaller irregular denticles. Antennal scapes moderately curved, not angulate basally, about $3/5$ the length of the funiculi; fourth funicular joint slightly longer than the first, terminal joint slightly longer than the remainder of the funiculus. Thorax similar to that of *S. pulchella;* with a distinct and somewhat constricted mesoepinotal suture. Epinotal spines moderately broad and thin; infraspinal lamellae moderately broad, not or very slightly expanded ventrally. Petiole in lateral profile with node rather low but broad, the anterior slope rather short.

Head, thorax and petiole reticulate-punctate, subopaque, the reticulations, especially on the mesonotum, tending to form faint longitudinal rugae. Meso- and metapleura, dorsum of the postpetiole and gaster smooth and shining. First gastric segment with numerous coarse longitudinal striae on the basal $1/3$.

Hairs on the clypeus short, subappressed, moderately squamose; the sides of the clypeus bearing a fringe of 10 or 12 anteriorly curved hairs on each side, the hairs occurring as pairs, one hair in each pair long, very narrowly squamose, the others, arising medially to the first, shorter and more squamose; hairs on antennal scapes comprising 5 or 6 moderately long, narrowly squamose hairs on the external border curved toward the tips of the scapes, and in addition numerous thin, straighter, subappressed hairs. Thorax with sparse, moderately long, thin, reclinate hairs. Petiole, postpetiole and gaster with sparse, long, thin, curved, erect hairs. Legs with thin, moderately long, reclinate hairs. Spongiform processes approximately as in *S. pulchella.*

Color ferrugineus; gaster darker.

Type locality: Kitts Hill, southern Lawrence County, Ohio.

Similar to *S. pulchella* Emery and *S. creightoni* M. R. Smith. From *S. pulchella, S. venatrix* differs in (1) the narrower anterior portion of the head, and correspondingly a proportionately wider posterior portion; (2) the differently shaped clypeus; (3) the longer mandibles; (4) the different pilosity, particularly on the head. From *S. creightoni,* which it closely resembles in the shape of the head and mandibles, *S. venatrix* differs in (1) its entire and rounded clypeal borders; (2) the very different pilosity, especially on the vertex of the head and on the thorax.

Described from a colony containing about 60 workers.

Eight colonies and occasional scattered workers have been taken in Pike, Lawrence, Scioto and Adams Counties. The species is definitely a soil or humus dweller and forages for Collembola under the leaves and dead vegetable matter on the surface of the ground. So far as we can tell, it is not associated with other species for the purpose of obtaining the Collembola about their nest. Specific examples of the colonies may give a better idea of the habitus. A colony was found in a small opening near the edge of some young oak woods on a rather dry, gently-sloping hillside. The soil was a sandy clay. Several workers were first observed around a light cover of dead leaves. One of these, carrying a springtail in its mandibles, led to the nest, the entrance of which, was a tiny hole under a flake of stone in the middle of a small bare area 30 sq. cm. in extent. Just below the surface, this hole widened out into a spacious, elongate chamber 5 to 10 mm. in diameter and 10 cm. in length, which appeared to be the hollow interior of a dead and decayed root. Another colony was found in the grassy humus on the edge of a bushy thicket in a field. A colony of *Aphaenogaster fulva* was under an adjacent stone. Four colonies, including the type, were found in a grassy clearing in some dry, open woods. Two of these colonies were on the surface in the

tangled roots of the grass, while the other 2 were in the soil
2 to 8 cm. below the surface. Galleries of *Camponotus cas-
taneus* subsp. *americanus* Mayr ran close to one nest, but
we were unable to find any connection between the two.
Two colonies were found in the cedar thicket described
above under *S. missouriensis*. One of these was nesting in
an opening at the bottom of the humus, the other in a small
cavity at the base of an old rotted cedar stump. Stray
workers in these and other places were often found by pull-
ing back the top cover of the humus in places where springtails were abundant.

Strumigenys (Cephaloxys) abdita, sp. n,

Worker: (Pl. 3, fig. 6) : Length, 2 mm.

Head, exclusive of mandibles, 1.3 times as long as the
greatest width across the occipital lobes, 2.4 times as long
as the greatest width of the clypeus; sides of anterior portion of head very slightly convergent; clypeus short and
broad, the anterior border strongly flattened or truncate but
not so as to make the head appear sharply rectangular; mandibles rather long and slender, compressed dorso-ventrally,
$\frac{1}{4}$ - $\frac{1}{5}$ the length of the head alone, the internal border
nearly straight, the external border straight on the basal
half, gently convex on the apical half; mandibles with a pair
of large basal teeth partially concealed by the clyeus when
the mandibles are closed; basal teeth followed by a toothless
space $\frac{1}{3}$ the length of the portion of the mandibles anterior
to them; terminal teeth comprising a compact row of 4 or 5
pair of large acute teeth, the second largest, the rest decreasing somewhat in length anteriorly, meeting and merging
with little interruption into the apical series of a number of
small teeth on the deflected tip of the mandibles; antennal
scapes slightly angulate basally; first joint as long as the
fourth; terminal joint $1\frac{1}{4}$ times as long as the rest of the
funiculus. Humeri prominent, broadly angulate; median
dorsal carina of thorax obsolescent; prominent lateral
carinae present on base of epinotum terminating in the
epinotal spines; epinotal spines somewhat longer than broad
at the base, acute, flattened; infraspinal lamellae moderately
wide dorsally, each suddenly expanding ventrally into a wide,

rounded plate; mesoepinotal suture distinct, slightly constricted.   Node of petiole in profile rather strongly convex
above.

Head, thorax and petiole reticulate-punctate, subopaque,
the sculpture on the clypeus decidedly finer than on the rest
of the head; frontal area, sides of the mesonotum, meso-
and metapleura, dorsum of the postpetiole and gaster smooth
and shining, first gastric segment with numerous coarse
longitudinal striae on the basal ⅓.

Hairs on the clypeus numerous, moderately long, somewhat irregular, erect, the tips spatulate and curved horizontally, numbering about 30 on the dorsal surface, the border
with 10 or 12 similar hairs curved anteriorly, the whole
effect giving the clypeus a woolly appearance when viewed
under low magnification.   Pilosity of the rest of the head
sparser, more curved and narrowly squamose; across the
posterior border of the head is a transverse row of 4 evenly
spaced, very long, thin, erect hairs; although 1 or 2 of these
is sometimes missing, the position of the others is not altered.   Antennal scapes with 5 or 6 irregular, moderately
long, erect, narrow, squamose hairs on the external border,
4 or 5 similar but much shorter hairs on the dorsal surfaces.
Thorax with sparse, moderately long, clavate, subappressed
hairs and 1 or 2 much longer erect, thin hairs confined principally to the dorsum of the mesonotum.   Node of petiole
with numerous rather short, curved, blunt or clavate hairs.
Postpetiole and gaster with very few long, slender, nearly
straight hairs.

Color ferruginous; gaster darker.

Type locality: Jackson, Ohio.

Described from 3 workers found under a board and pieces
of slate in a shaded spot in a backyard in Jackson.   We did
not succeed in locating the colony.   It may be noted that of
the 4 species of *Strumigenys* (*pergandei, rostrata, reflexa,
abdita*) found in this yard, 2 were undescribed.

In order to facilitate the separation of the 6 new forms
described above, we have modified Smith's key[5] to include

[5]Smith, M. R., 1931, Revision of the Genus Strumigenys of America
    North of Mexico, Based on a Study of the Workers, Ann. Ent. Soc.
    Amer., 24, pp. 686-710.

them, as well as several other species described[6] since the
publication of Smith's paper.

*Key to Workers of Strumigenys, subgenus Cephaloxys of the
United States.*

1. Dorsal surface of first gastric segment clearly shagreened, subopaque; infraspinal lamella absent ....
   .... *margaritæ* Forel.
   Dorsal surface of first gastric segment smooth and
   shining; infraspinal lamella present 2

2. Prothorax not only flattened, but also very strongly
   marginate laterally; head almost destitute of pilosity
   except for a pair of short, more or less erect, club-
   like hairs on the vertex. ....
   .... *membranifera simillima* Emery
   Prothorax not as above; head covered more or less
   abundantly with varied types of pilosity 3

3. Sides of head as viewed from the front evenly and
   smoothly converging to the apices of the mandibles.
   4
   Sides of head subparallel or only slightly converging;
   external border of mandibles not lying on an anterior projection of the sides of the head 15

4. Clypeus very acute anteriorly; clypeal hairs few, long,
   erect, thickened, confined principally to the median
   anterior portion of the disk .... *deitrichi* M. R. Smith
   Clypeus distinctly not as above 5

5. Clypeus smooth and shining 6
   Clypeus opaque or subopaque 8

6. Clypeal hairs short, curved, apically enlarged ....
   .... *brevisetosa* M. R. Smith

[6]Kennedy, C. H., and Schramm, M. M., 1933, A New Strumigenys with
Notes on the Ohio Species, Ann. Ent. Soc. Amer., 25, pp. 95-104.
(*S. ohioensis*)
Weber, N. A., 1934, A New Strumigenys from Illinois, Psyche, 41,
pp. 63-65. (*S. talpa*)
Smith, M. R., 1935, Two New Species of North American Strumi-
genys, Ann. Ent. Soc. Amer. 28 pp. 214-216. (*S. rohweri, S.
brevisetosa*)

Clypeal hairs long, ½ to ⅓ times the width of the clypeus 7

7.   Edge of clypeus in profile entire; clypeal hairs straight, thin, abundant; hairs on vertex sparse, hardly clavate .... *clypeata* var. *laevinasis* M. R. Smith

   Edge of clypeus in profile deeply grooved; clypeal hairs sparse, curved, slightly enlarged apically; hairs on vertex numerous, shorter, clavate (Pl. 3, fig. 2) ....
   .... *bimarginata* sp. n.

8.   Clypeus with a few, long hairs, very much enlarged apically and principally on the anterior portion of the disk and also a pair of long, thick, recurved, but not suddenly enlarged hairs, posteriorly *ornata* Mayr

   Clypeal pilosity distinctly not as above 9

9.   Clypeal hairs straight, imperceptibly or not at all enlarged 10

   Clypeal hairs curved, distinctly clavate or squamose 11

10. Clypeal hairs short, not over ⅛ as long as the width of the clypeus .... *ohioensis* Kennedy and Schramm

   Clypeal hairs long, ⅓ to ½ the width of the clypeus....
   .... *pilinasis* Forel

11. Clypeal hairs short, squamose, appressed 12

   Clypeal hairs longer, more or less erect, clavate or narrowly squamose 13

12. Clypeus broadly and evenly rounded; the surface in large part concealed by the squamose hairs ....
   .... *clypeata* Roger

   Clypeus very broadly rounded, appearing somewhat truncate; clypeal surface almost entirely concealed by the spatulate hairs .... *rohweri* M. R. Smith

13. Clypeus rather sharply truncate in appearance; mandibles ¼ the length of the rest of head (Pl. 3, fig. 3)
   .... *manni* sp. n.

   Clypeus broadly rounded, not truncate; mandibles shorter 14

14. Head broader; mandibles less than ⅕ the length of the rest of the head; posterior border of head shallowly excised; toothless space of mandibles distinct
   talpa Weber

Head narrower; mandibles slightly more than ⅕ the
length of the rest of the head; posterior border deeply excised; toothless space of mandibles small and indistinct. (Pl. 3, fig. 1.) .... *medialis* sp.n.

15. Mandibles longer, ⅓ the length of the rest of head,
clypeus truncate or emarginate or very broadly flat-
tened anteriorly 16

Mandibles shorter; clypeus variable 17

16. Clypeus decidedly truncate anteriorly, thus giving the
head a subrectangular appearance; antennal scapes
not only short but very strongly angulate basally ....
.... *angulata* M. R. Smith

Clypeus, although moderately truncate anteriorly, not
enough to give a decidedly subrectangular appearance to the head; scapes longer and less angulate
basally .... *pergandei* Emery

17. Clypeus truncate or subtruncate in front 18

Clypeus broadly rounded in front 21

18. Mandibles with large coarse teeth on their entire inner
borders; clypeus broadly truncate or slightly emarginate .... *rostrata* Emery

Mandibles toothed on only a part of their inner border; clypeus truncate but never emarginate 19

19. Mandibles longer, ¼ to ⅕ the length of the rest of
head; clypeus very short and broad, the sides gently
convergent (Pl. 3, fig. 6) .... *abdita* sp.n.

Mandibles shorter, ⅙ the length of the rest of head;
clypeus longer, the sides more strongly convergent
....20

20. Hairs on head rather abundant, distinctly squamiform
.... *creightoni* M. R. Smith

Hairs on head less abundant, longer, and, although
slightly enlarged apically, not squamiform ....
.... *sculpturata* M. R. Smith

21. Sides of anterior portion of head gently and evenly
convergent to the very broadly rounded clypeus;
mandibles nearly ⅕ the length of the rest of head
Pl. 3, fig. 5) ....*venatrix* sp.n.

LEGEND FOR PLATE III.

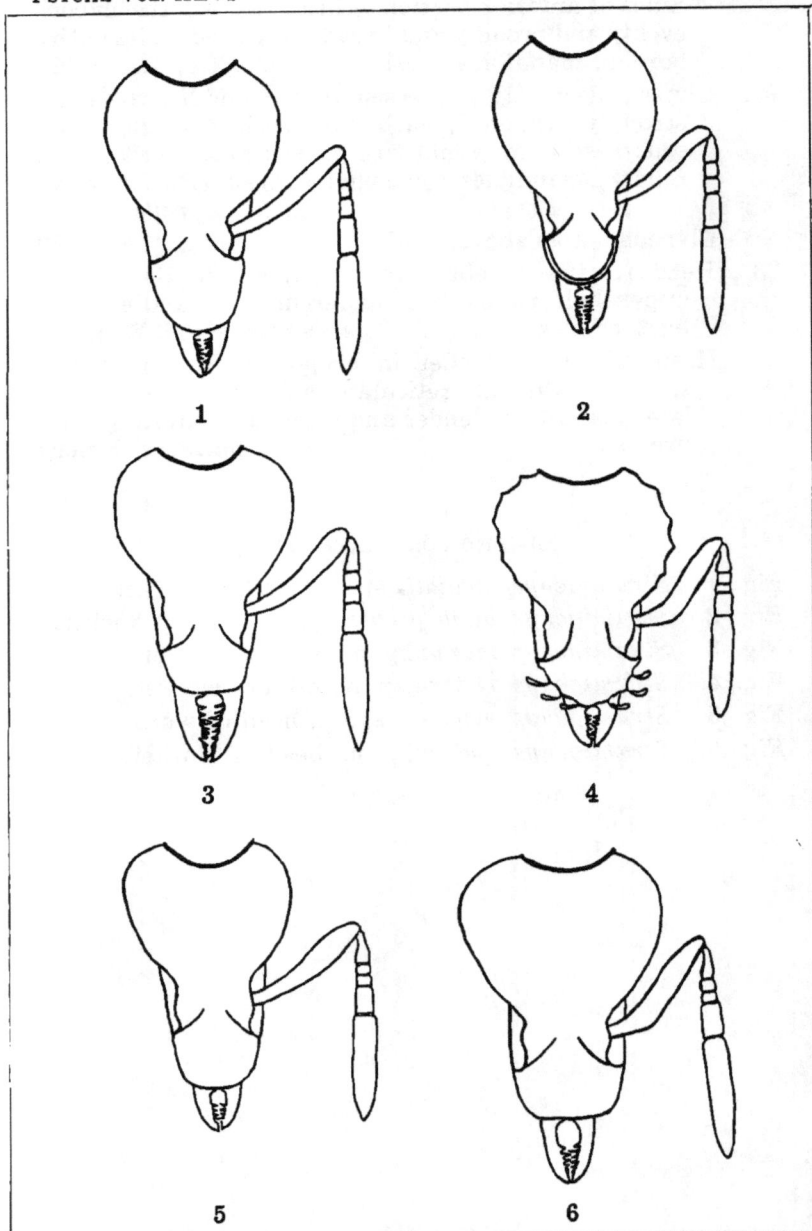

Wesson — Strumigenys

PIN-LABELS IN MULTIPLES OF 1000, ALIKE

One Dollar Per Thousand

Smallest Type. Pure White Ledger Paper. Not over 4 Lines nor 30 Characters (13 to a line) Additional Characters, 3 cents each, in total and per line, per 1000. Trimmed so one cut makes a label.

C. V. BLACKBURN, 7 Emerson St., STONEHAM 80, MASS.

CAMBRIDGE ENTOMOLOGICAL CLUB

A regular meeting of the Club is held on the second Tuesday of each month (July, August and September excepted) at 7.45 p.m. in Room B-455, Biological Laboratories of Harvard University, Divinity Ave., Cambridge. Entomologists visiting Boston are cordially invited to attend.

WARD'S ENTOMOLOGICAL SERVICES

Entomological Supplies and Equipment
Carefully designed by professional entomologists. Material of high quality at low prices. **Send for Supply Catalog No. 348.**

Insect Preparations
Life Histories, Type Collections, Collections of Economic Insects and Biological Insect Collections. All specimens are accurately determined.

Insects for the Pest Collection
We have in stock over three hundred species of North American Insect Pests. **Send for Price List No. 349.**

Ward's Entomological Bulletin
A monthly publication sent free to all entomologists requesting it.

Information for the Beginner
Send for **"Directions for Collecting and Preserving Insects"** by Dr. A. B. Klots. A mine of useful information. Price 15 cents.

WARD'S NATURAL SCIENCE ESTABLISHMENT, Inc.
P. O. Box 24, Beechwood Station
Rochester, N. Y., U. S. A.
The Frank A. Ward Foundation of Natural Science of the University of Rochester

BACK VOLUMES OF PSYCHE

The Cambridge Entomological Club is able to offer for sale the following volumes of Psyche. Those not mentioned are entirely out of print.

Volumes 2, 3, 4, 5, 6, 7, 8, 9, 10, each covering a period of three years, $5.00 each.

Volumes 12, 14, 17, each covering a single year, $1.00 each.

Volumes 18, 19, 20, 21, 22, 23, 24, 25, 26, each covering a single year, $1.50 each.

Volumes 27, 28, 29, 30, 31, 32, 33, 34, 35, 36, 37, 38, 39, 40, 41, 42, 43, 44, 45, each covering a single year, $2.00.

Orders for 2 or more volumes subject to a discount of 10%.

Orders for 10 or more volumes subject to a discount of 20%.

A set of all the volumes available (40 in all) will be sold for $81.00.

All orders should be addressed to

F. M. CARPENTER, Associate Editor of Psyche,
Biological Laboratories,
Harvard University,
Cambridge, Mass.

PSYCHE

A JOURNAL OF ENTOMOLOGY

ESTABLISHED IN 1874

VOL. XLVI   DECEMBER, 1939   No. 4

TABLE OF CONTENTS

CAMBRIDGE ENTOMOLOGICAL CLUB

OFFICERS FOR 1939-1940

President .	C. H. Blake
Vice-President	F. M. Carpenter
Secretary	C. T. Parsons
Treasurer	Richard Dow

	T. Barbour
Executive Committee	C. H. Blake
	R. T. Holway

EDITORIAL BOARD OF PSYCHE

EDITOR-IN-CHIEF
C. T. Brues, Harvard University

ASSOCIATE EDITOR
F. M. Carpenter, Harvard University

CONSULTING EDITORS

Nathan Banks,
Harvard University.

A. E. Emerson,
University of Chicago.

Thomas Barbour,
Harvard University.

A. L. Melander,
College of the
City of New York.

Richard Dow,
New England Museum of
Natural History,
Boston, Mass.

J. G. Needham,
Cornell University.

PSYCHE is published quarterly, the issues appearing in March, June, September, and December. Subscription price, per year, payable in advance: $2.00 to Subscribers in the United States; foreign postage, 25 cents extra, Canada 15 cents. Single copies, 65 cents.

Cheques and remittances should be addressed to Treasurer, Cambridge Entomological Club, Biological Laboratories, Harvard University, Cambridge, Mass.

Orders for back volumes, missing numbers, notices of change of address, etc., should be sent to Professor F. M. Carpenter, Biological Laboratories, Harvard University, Cambridge, Mass.

IMPORTANT NOTICE TO CONTRIBUTORS

Manuscripts intended for publication, books intended for review, and other editorial matter, should be addressed to Professor C. T. Brues, Biological Laboratories, Harvard University, Cambridge, Mass.

Authors contributing articles over 8 printed pages in length will be required to bear a part of the extra expense, for additional pages. This expense will be that of typesetting only, which is about $2.00 per page. The actual cost of preparing cuts for all illustrations must be borne by contributors; the expense for full page plates from line drawings is approximately $5.00 each, and for full page half-tones, $7.50 each; smaller sizes in proportion.

AUTHOR'S SEPARATES

Reprints of articles may be secured by authors, if they are ordered before, or at the time proofs are received for corrections. The cost of these will be furnished by the Editor on application.

Printed by the Eliot Press Inc., Jamaica Plain, Mass., U. S. A.

PSYCHE

VOL. XLVI DECEMBER, 1939 No. 4

A KEY TO THE MOSQUITOES OF MASSACHUSETTS

By GEORGE S. TULLOCH, Chief Entomologist[1]

Massachusetts Department of Public Health
Boston, Massachusetts

During the summer of 1939 the Department of Public Health of the State of Massachusetts conducted a state-wide mosquito survey with the cooperation of the Works Projects Administration. This survey was one phase in the program of a study of the general problem of encephalitis. It was initiated following an outbreak of encephalitis in man in 1938 which was traced to the eastern virus of equine encephalomyelitis. The identification of biting mosquitoes was made by using a key compiled by Tulloch (1930) which was taken from Dyar (1922) and Matheson (1929) and modified to include those species reported from New England. The present key is a revision of the earlier one which has been enlarged to include the non-biting as well as the biting mosquitoes and is based on the examination of over 100,000 specimens. Although this key is restricted to the species which may be found in Massachusetts it is sufficiently inclusive for use in any of the New England states. It is accompanied by illustrations of many of the characters of taxonomic importance and by a summary of the species of Culicidæ which have been taken in Massachusetts.

[1] Grateful acknowledgment is made to the following for assistance: Dr. R. F. Feemster, Director, Division of Communicable Diseases, Massachusetts Department of Public Health; Dr. V. A. Getting, Technical Director, Massachusetts Mosquito Survey; Prof. J. C. Bequaert, Consulting Entomologist; V. A. Bell, R. P. Holdsworth, Jr., C. E. Elliott, Dr. B. W. Parker, Dr. J. W. Hawkins, G. C. Tower, H. D. Rose, and R. O. Bohm, Entomologists and to Mr. J. Milano for preparation of the plates.

The material for this key has been modified from the works of many authors, notably Smith (1903), Headlee (1921), Dyar (1922, 1928), Dyar and Shannon (1924), Matheson (1925, 1929), Bradley (1936), Edwards (1932), Johannsen (1903, 1923, 1934), Marshall (1938) and King, Bradley and McNeel (1939).

Mosquitoes are small two-winged insects belonging to the order Diptera, family Culicidæ. The Culicidæ are separated from all other Diptera by a characteristic wing venation which is outlined by Edwards (1932) as follows: Subcosta (Sc) long and reaching costa; radius 4-branched, R_{2+3} forked, R_{4+5} simple, no cross vein connecting R_1 and R_2; media two branched; cross veins r-m and m-cu both present; cubitus forked; anal vein long and reaching wing margin; axillary vein absent or very faint (Fig. 5). There is no other single character which separates the family from other Diptera. Other common family characters are (1) the small or rudimentary first antennal segment and the more or less enlarged second segment, (2) the completely divided pronotum, the posterior divisions of which appear to form part of the pleuræ. These characters, however, are not distinctive since they are shared by one or more families of Diptera.

The larvæ of the Culicidæ are distinguished from all other dipterous larvæ by the presence of a complete head capsule and of only one pair of functional spiracles situated dorsally on the eighth abdominal segment opening free to the surface (Fig. 19) or into an air tube or by the presence of a complete head capsule and air sacs in the thorax and seventh abdominal segment (Fig. 17) (*Chaoborus*).

Key to Subfamilies of Culicidae

Adults

1. Antennal flagellum 14 segmented; vein Sc ending above or before base of Rs (Fig. 5). Mouthparts short, wings without scales: ....*Dixinæ*

   Antennal flagellum 13 segmented; vein Sc ending much beyond base of Rs. Wings with scales at least on fringe 2

2. Mouthparts short, palpi incurved; scales almost confined to wing fringe: ....*Chaoborinæ*

   Mouthparts modified to form a long proboscis, palpi not incurved; wing veins and legs scaly: ....*Culicinæ*

Larvæ

1. Thorax narrow with distinct segmentation; prolegs on the first 2 abdominal segments; tracheæ ending in a pair of discs on eighth abdominal segment (Fig. 21) : _____*Dixinæ*
   Thorax distinctly broader than abdomen, without distinct segmentation, paired prolegs lacking_____2

2. Antennæ prehensile, with long and strong apical spines (Fig. 17) : _____*Chaoborinæ*
   Antennæ not prehensile (Fig. 8) : _____*Culicinæ*

Subfamily Dixinæ

This group is represented by the single genus *Dixa*.

KEY TO THE GENUS DIXA

Adults

1. Tips of hind tibiæ noticeably enlarged, deep black, sharply contrasting with the remainder of the member; wing veins with clouded margins; proboscis black, halteres yellowish, scutellum fuscous testaceous; terminal clasper segment tapering, mesal process of the basal segment simple, elongate:_____*clavata*
   Tips of hind tibiæ not so sharply differentiated_____2

2. Petiole of R_{2+3} (measured on a straight line from its base to base of fork) less than $\frac{3}{8}$ as long as R_3; proboscis, scutellum, and knob of the halteres yellow; crossvein of wing very feebly clouded, r-m crossvein slightly distad of the base of R_{4+5} :_____ *terna*
   Wing with other characters_____ 3

3. Wing with one distinct spot_____ _____ 4
   Wing spot very indistinct or wanting_____ 5

4. Petiole of R_{2+3} and R_3 subequal in length; proboscis and scutellum blackish: _____ _____ _____*centralis*
   Petiole shorter; proboscis and scutellum yellowish:_____
   _____ *notata*

5. Dorsum of the thorax as well as the upper part of the pleura black; proboscis, halteres and scutellum dark:
   _____ *fusca*
   Dorsum of the thorax yellowish with thoracic darker

stripes which may be more or less confluent; palpi
dark _____6

6. First tarsal joint of fore leg about ⅔ as long as the
   tibia: _____*cornuta*
   First tarsal joint of fore leg about ¾ as long as the
   tibia _____7

7. Apical segment of the clasper of the male fully as broad
   beyond the middle as at the base; Sc ends about
   opposite the base of Rs; distance between the cross-
   veins measured on the media usually not exceeding ½
   the length of the m-cu crossvein: _____*modesta*
   Apical segment of the clasper of the male tapering; Sc
   ends distinctly proximad of the base of Rs; distance
   between the crossveins about equal to the length of
   the m-cu crossvein: _____*similis*

Larvæ

Only two of the species given in the key above are known
in the larval stage, *D. modesta* Joh. and *D. cornuta* (Joh.)
which may be separated by using the key by Johannsen
(1934).

Subfamily Chaoborinæ

KEY TO GENERA

Adults

1. Clypeus small and nearly bare; R_1 ending far from tip of
   R_2: _____*Corethrella*
   Clypeus larger and very hairy; R_1 ending close to tip
   of R_2 _____2

2. First tarsal segment much shorter than second:_____
   _____ *Mochlonyx*
   First tarsal segment longer than second_____3

3. Clypeus as long as head; claws larger and toothed:_____
   _____ *Eucorethra*
   Clypeus shorter than head; claws small and simple:_____
   _____ *Chaoborus*

Larvæ

1. Eighth abdominal segment with an elongate single dorsal respiratory siphon or air tube_____2

Eighth abdominal segment without an elongate single
dorsal air tube; with a flattened spiracular disc on
the eighth segment or with air sacs in the thorax and
the seventh abdominal segment_____3

2. Antennæ inserted close together, folding outwardly and
fitting into grooves on the head (Fig. 20) :_____
_____ *Corethrella*
Antennæ inserted far apart, pendent in resting position (Fig 18) : _____*Mochlonyx*

3. Air sacs present in thorax and seventh abdominal segment (Fig. 17) : _____*Chaoborus*
Air sacs absent, a well-developed spiracular disc on
eighth abdominal segment (Fig. 19) : _____*Eucorethra*

KEY TO THE GENUS CHAOBORUS

Adults

1. Wings spotted or clouded_____2
Wings without spots or clouds_____4

2. Width of hind marginal wing fringe nearly as great as
distance between cubitus and hind margin_____3
Hind marginal wing fringe less than half the distance
between cubitus and hind margin : _____ _____*trivittatus*

3. Femora and tibiæ with numerous distinct spots :_____
_____ _____ *punctipennis*
Femora and tibiæ without distinct spots except at bases
and apices : _____ _____*albatus*

4. Mesonotum with dark longitudinal bands : __ *americanus*
Mesonotum with yellowish red longitudinal bands :_____
_____ *albipes*

*Larvæ**

1. Pre-labral leaf-like appendages very narrow and lan-
ceolate : _____*punctipennis*
Pre-labral leaf-like appendages less than seven times
as long as broad _____2

2. Mandibular fan with 25 or more rays :_____*americanus*
Mandibular fan with not over 18 rays_____3

3. Mandibular fan with 16-18 rays : _____*trivittatus*
Mandibular fan with not more than 12 rays :____*albipes*

* Larva of *C. albatus* is unknown.

KEY TO THE GENUS MOCHLONYX

Adults

1. Wing vestiture entirely pale yellow............................2
   Wing vestiture black and yellow: ....*cinctipes*
2. Scutellar setæ numerous, arranged in two or three irregular rows: ....*karnerensis*
   Scutellar setæ sparse, arranged in a single row: ....
   .... *fuliginosus*

*Larvæ**

1. Clypeal and frontal spines barbed from base to a little
   beyond middle: ....*karnerensis*
   These spines with long barbs beyond middle: ....*cinctipes*
*   The larva of *M. fuliginosus* is unknown.

The following genera of the Chaoborinæ are represented
by single species: *Corethrella brakeleyi* Coquillett and *Eucorethra underwoodi* Underwood.

Subfamily Culicinæ

KEY TO GENERA

Adults

1. Postnotum with a median tuft of setæ located near the
   posterior margin (Fig. 2): ....*Wyeomyia*
   Postnotum without a tuft of setæ.........................2
2. Wings with the second marginal cell not half as long as
   its petiole (Fig. 5): ....*Uranotænia*
   Wings with the second marginal cell more than half as
   long as its petiole...3
3. Scutellum rounded or crescent-shaped with an even
   fringe of marginal setæ (Fig. 3): .... *Anopheles*
   Scutellum distinctly trilobed (Fig. 4) with marginal
   setæ aggregated on the lobes 4
4. Spiracular bristles present (Fig. 2) 5
   Spiracular bristles absent........ 6
5. Post-spiracular bristles present (Fig. 2); abdomen of
   female with the eighth segment wholly retractile: ...
   .... *Psorophora*
   Post-spiracular bristles absent; cross veins of wings

tending to lie in line, or mesonotum with bare areas
devoid of scales or both: ....*Theobaldia*

6. Pronotal bristles only two stout setæ (Fig. 2) ; proboscis
   with black and white scales so arranged as to form
   longitudinal striæ; mesonotum with six longitudinal
   lines of white scales: ....*Orthopodomyia*
   Pronotal bristles more than two, generally a prominent
   row; proboscis without longitudinal striæ; mesonotum
   without six longitudinal lines of white scales............7

7. Wings with scales distinctly large and broad; first joint
   of all tarsi with broad median rings; all of the other
   tarsal joints black with basal half white scaled:.........
   .... *Mansonia*
   Wings with scales normal; tarsi not as above............8

8. Post-spiracular bristles present; female usually with
   the abdomen pointed and the cerci exserted or tarsi
   with white rings on both ends of joints: ....*Aedes*
   Post-spiracular bristles absent; female with a blunt abdomen; tarsi without white rings involving both ends
   of joints: ....*Culex*

Larvæ

1. Eighth segment of abdomen provided with a distinct,
   elongate respiratory or air tube (Fig. 8)....................2
   Eighth segment of abdomen without a distinct, elongate
   respiratory or air tube (Fig. 9) : ....*Anopheles*

2. Air tube without a pecten (Fig. 12)....................3
   Air tube with a pecten (Fig. 8)........................5

3. Air tube about twice as long as wide, the apical portion sharply attenuated and provided with saw-like
   teeth dorsally for penetrating into plant tissues (Fig.
   12) ; larva found attached to the roots of certain
   aquatic plants: .... *Mansonia*
   Air tube about three times as long as wide, tapering
   more or less uniformly to the apex....................4

4. Air tube with many short single hairs; larva found in
   the water of the pitcher plant: ....*Wyeomyia*
   Air tube without scattered single hairs but with a
   large pair of hair tufts before the middle; abdomen

with dorsal chitinous plates on the sixth, seventh and
eighth segments: _____*Orthopodomyia*

5. Head elongate, elliptical; head hairs single, stout like
heavy spines: _____*Uranotænia*
Head nearly circular or transverse; head hairs not like
heavy spines _____6

6. Air tube with several pairs of ventral tufts: _____*Culex*
Air tube with a single pair of ventral tufts or with a
single pair of tufts and a median ventral row of 10
to 12 unpaired tufts or without any paired ventral
tufts _____7

7. Air tube with the paired hair tufts placed close to the
base between the pecten rows: _____*Theobaldia*
Air tube with the paired hair tufts placed near or beyond the middle _____8

8. Anal segment ringed by the dorsal plate, with tufts of
the ventral brush piercing the ring: _____*Psorophora*
Anal segment not ringed by the dorsal plate, or if ringed,
the tufts of the ventral brush posterior to the ring: ____
_____ *Aedes*

KEY TO THE GENUS AEDES

Adults

1. Proboscis of female ringed with white (Fig. 1)_____ 2
Proboscis of female not ringed with white_____3

2. Abdomen with a pale longitudinal dorsal stripe (Fig. 1);
wings with black and white scales: _____*sollicitans*
Abdomen without a pale longitudinal dorsal stripe;
wings with black scales: _____*tæniorhynchus*

3. Tarsi with white rings on at least some of the segments
(Fig. 1) _____4
Tarsi without white rings _____11

4. White tarsal rings involving both ends of segments_____ 5
White tarsal rings basal only_____7

5. Wings scales markedly bicolored: _____*dorsalis*
Wings scales uniformly dark, or nearly so_____6

6. Mesonotum uniformly reddish brown, or nearly so:_____
_____ *canadensis*
Mesonotum pale with a broad dark medium stripe; abdomen rather bluntly rounded: _____*atropalpus*

7. Tarsi with pale broad rings especially on hind legs; wings scales bicolored_____ _____8
   Tarsi with narrow rings; wing scales uniformly dark or nearly so_____10

8. Lower mesepimeral bristles absent: _____ *excrucians*
   Lower mesepimeral bristles present (Fig. 2) _____ 9

9. With three to five lower mesepimeral bristles; mesonotum bronzy-brown on the disc, the scales on the antescutellar space, lateral margins and a sub-dorsal line each side of the disc whitish:_ _____. *stimulans*
   With two lower mesepimeral bristles; mesonotum with a broad median stripe of yellowish brown scales, the anterior edge, the sides of the disc and antescutellar space with yellowish white to white scales:__ *fitchii*

10. Last two abdominal segments nearly entirely white scaled, venter entirely yellowish white: _____*cantator*
    Last two abdominal segments with apical and basal bands; venter with each segment with a median black spot or stripe which may be joined to lateral black spots forming a Y: _____*vexans*

11. Lower mesepimeral bristles absent_____12
    Lower mesepimeral bristles present_____ 17

12. Mesonotum with silvery scales____ _____13
    Mesonotum without silvery scales_____ 15

13. Mesonotum silvery on the sides with a dark brown median stripe which widens behind the middle and which is divided by the antescutellar space, the antescutellar space is margined by silvery scales: _____
    ____ _____ _ _____ _____ *triseriatus*
    Mesonotum with a medium silvery stripe reaching scutellum or entirely silvered_____14

14. Mesonotum with a broad well-defined median silvery stripe: _____ _____ _____ _____ _ *atlanticus*
    Mesonotum with a narrower poorly defined or diffuse median stripe; mesonotum of male entirely silvery; a very small blackish species: _____*dupreei*

15. Abdomen with a continuous lateral white line; mesonotum uniformly colored with golden-brown scales, paler about the antescutellar space: _____ *cinereus*
    Abdomen without a continuous lateral white line; me-

sonotum with a median dark band_____16

16. Mesonotum with two yellow or yellowish-white stripes separated by a narrow, dark brown median band; sides dark brown to black: _____*trivittatus*

Mesonotum with the golden brown median stripe slightly constricted at the middle; with two short sublateral stripes posteriorly: _____*hirsuteron*

Mesonotum with the median band widening posteriorly; apical margins of abdominal segments with fine long brownish hairs: _____ _____*aurifer*

17. With one to three small mesepimeral bristles; mesonotum with brownish-yellow scales uniformly distributed: _____*intrudens*

With three or more stout mesepimeral bristles; mesonotum with a median stripe or paired brown median lines _____18

18. Mesonotum with paired brown median lines_____19

Mesonotum with a median brown stripe_____20

19. Mesonotum yellow or bronzy with a pair of black median lines, often joined into a median stripe; legs deep black: _____*diantæus*

Mesonotum with paired median lines separated by a broad golden brown line: _____*impiger*

Mesonotum with paired median lines separated by a narrow yellow line; sides grayish: _____*communis*

20. Mesonotum with the median band laterally expanded near the middle: _____*trichurus*

Mesonotum with the median band only slightly darker than the lateral margins: _____*punctor**

_____ _____ _____ _____*implacabilis**

*There are no satisfactory characters with which to separate these species. In *A. punctor* the median band of the mesonotum may in some cases have a middle line of slightly paler scales. The last abdominal segment of *A. implacabilis* is usually pale scaled whereas in *punctor* it has a V-shaped dark area.

Larvæ

1. Air tube with tuft within pecten_____2

Air tube with tuft beyond pecten_____3

2. Air tube with several dorsal hair tufts, anal gills normal: _____*trichurus*
   Air tube without several dorsal hair tufts, anal gills large and inflated: _____*atropalpus*

3. Pecten with detached teeth outwardly (Fig. 15)_____4
   Pecten without detached teeth outwardly (Fig. 16)____9

4. Antennæ enlarged basally: _____*aurifer*
   Antennæ not enlarged basally_____5

5. Antennæ as long as head: _____*diantæus*
   Antennæ not as long as head_____6

6. Both pairs of head hairs (Fig. 8) double: _____*excrucians*
   Both pairs of head hairs not double_____7

7. Lateral abdominal hairs (Fig. 8) single beyond second segment _____8
   Lateral abdominal hairs not single beyond second segment: _____*vexans*

8. Air tube 2½ to 3 times as long as wide, tuft on air tube large: _____*intrudens*
   Air tube 3½ to 4 times as long as wide, tuft on air tube small, located on outer third of tube: _____*cinereus*

9. Comb scales in a single or in an irregular single row____10
   Comb scales in a triangle_____13

10. Anal segment ringed by plate _____11
    Anal segment not ringed by plate: _____ *triseriatus*

11. Air tube five times as long as wide: _____ *dupreei*
    Air tube 2 to 3½ times as long as wide_____12

12. Dorsal brush of anal segment consisting of two pairs of long hairs: _____ *implacabilis*
    Dorsal brush of anal segment consisting of a pair of long hairs and a pair of dorsal tufts: _____ *atlanticus*

13. Anal segment ringed by plate_____14
    Anal segment not ringed by plate_____ 17

14. Upper and lower head hairs double: _____*punctor*
    Upper and lower head hairs single_____ 15

15. Anal gills at least as long as anal segment:___ *trivittatus*
    Anal gills shorter than anal segment_____16

16. Lateral abdominal hairs double on segments two to five; scale of comb with a stout apical spine: _____*sollicitans*

Lateral abdominal hairs triple on segments three to five;
scale of comb with a fringe of spines of approximately
equal length: ....*tæniorhynchus*

17. Air tube at least four times as long as wide: ....*fitchii*
    Air tube three times or less as long as wide.............18

18. Head hairs single...19
    Head hairs double or multiple.......................................21

19. Anal gills at least as long as anal segment....................20
    Anal gills much shorter than anal segment: ...... *dorsalis*

20. Scale of comb with broad apex bearing four to seven
    stout spines: .... *communis*
    Scale of comb with single stout spine: ....*impiger*

21. Both pairs of dorsal head hairs multiple.......................22
    Both pairs of dorsal head hairs not multiple.............23

22. Anal gills budlike; found in salt water: ....*cantator*
    Anal gills well developed: ....*canadensis*

23. Lower head hairs double, upper triple:......*hirsuteron*
    Lower head hairs single, upper double: ....*stimulans*

KEY TO THE GENUS THEOBALDIA

Adults

1. Tarsi with poorly defined yellowish white rings at both
   ends of some of the joints: .... *morsitans*
   Tarsi without rings on any of the joints........................2

2. Scales of the wings mixed, black or brown and white
   especially along the costal margin; proboscis with
   intermixed black and white scales: ....*inornata*
   Scales of the wings all brown or black..........................3

3. Mesonotum brown marked with yellowish lines or spots;
   wings with some of the scales slightly aggregated
   along the third vein; a large species: ...... *impatiens*
   Mesonotum entirely reddish brown; wing scales normal;
   each abdominal segment with an apical row of coarse
   yellow hairs; a small species (4 mm.) : ...... *melanura*

Larvæ

1. Pecten produced into long hairs on outer half (Fig. 13)
  2
   Pecten not produced into long hairs on outer half........3

2. Both pairs of head hairs consisting of tufts having approximately six hairs, all of about equal length:......
.... *impatiens*
Lower head hairs of three or four long hairs, upper head hairs multiple and shorter than the lower hairs:......
.... *inornata*

3. Comb scales in a single row; air tube with a row of 10-12 median unpaired tufts along the ventral side beyond the pecten: ....*melanura*
Comb scales in a triangle; air tube without unpaired median ventral tufts beyond the pecten: ..... *morsitans*

KEY TO THE GENUS PSOROPHORA

Adults

1. Mesonotum brown with a median longitudinal stripe of brilliant golden curved scales bordered by narrow bare stripes ....*ciliata*
Mesonotum uniformly colored................................ 2

2. Claws of the female toothed (Fig. 6); wing scales dark:
.... *posticata*
Claws of the female not toothed (Fig. 7); wings uniformly marked with black and white scales: *columbiæ*

Larvæ

1. Both pairs of head hairs single, upper pair very short:
.... *ciliata*
Both pairs of head hairs not single..... 2

2. Upper and lower pairs of head hairs multiple; pecten of three to five teeth widely separated on the basal half of the tube (Fig. 14): ....*columbiæ*
Upper and lower pairs of head hairs double; pecten of three to four teeth on the basal fifth of tube; tuft of air tube absent: ....*posticata*

KEY TO THE GENUS ANOPHELES

Adults

1. Palpus with white markings.................................... 2
Palpus without white markings 3

2. Apical segment of palpus entirely white scaled; anal vein with three dark spots separated by white (two spots in the male): ....*crucians*

Apical segment of the palpus white-tipped; anal vein
entirely dark without spots: _____*walkeri*

3. Costal margin of wing with two white or yellowish-white
spots, a large one beyond the middle and a small one
at the apical end: _____ _____ _____ _____ *punctipennis*
Costal margin of wing without white or yellowish-white
spots _____4

4. Fringe at apex of wing with a distinct light yellow to
coppery spot: _____*maculipennis*
Fringe at apex of wing without a distinct light yellow to
coppery spot _____ _____ _____ 5

5. Wing with dark scales uniformly distributed: ___ *barberi*
Wing with the dark scales definitely aggregated to form
dark spots at the base of the radical sector, at cross-
veins r-m and m-cu, at fork of R_2 and R_3 and at fork
of M_{1+2} and M_{3+4} : _____ *quadrimaculatus*

Larvæ

1. Abdomen with plumose lateral hairs (Fig. 9) on first
six segments; head hairs simple: _____ _____ *barberi*
Abdomen with plumose lateral hairs on first three segments; head hairs plumose_____ 2

2. Abdominal segments 4 and 5 with two conspicuous
tufted hairs (Fig. 11) (hair 0 and the antepalmate or
hair 2) anterior to the palmate tuft, these hairs
usually approximately equal in size and with four to
nine branches; fresh water form: _____ *crucians*
Abdominal segments 4 and 5 with but one conspicuous
hair (antepalmate or hair 2) anterior to the palmate
tuft, this hair may be single or with two or three
branches _____,_____3

3. Abdomen with the palmate tufts on segments 3 to 7
inclusive, of similar form but those on segments 3 and
7 distinctly smaller than the others; posterior clypeal
hairs (Fig. 10) long and usually single; tubercles of
inner anterior clypeal hairs (Fig. 10) wide or close;
brackish water form: _____*crucians*
Abdomen with the palmate tufts on segment 3 approximately equal in size to those on the succeeding segments _____ _____ _____4

4. Tubercles of inner anterior clypeal hairs separated by at least the width of one of these tubercles; antepalmate hairs on segments 4 and 5 usually single; palmate tufts on segment 2 usually well developed: _____ _____ *quadrimaculatus*
   Tubercles of inner anterior clypeal hairs so close together that another tubercle of similar size could not be placed between them_____ 5

5. Inner anterior clypeal hairs not minutely feathered toward tip; antepalmate hairs of abdominal segments 4 and 5 usually double or multiple_____ 6
   Inner anterior clypeal hairs minutely feathered toward tip; antepalmate hairs of abdominal segments 4 and 5 usually single: _____*walkeri*

6. Antepalmate hairs of abdominal segments 4 and 5 usually with 2 branches, rarely 1 or 3; posterior clypeal hairs usually with 2 branches from near base; inner anterior clypeal hairs single, unbranched: _____ _____ *punctipennis*
   Antepalmate hairs of abdominal segments 4 and 5 usually with 3 branches, rarely with 2 or 4; posterior clypeal hairs usually long with apical branching; inner anterior clypeal hairs unbranched or with 2 or 3 branches beyond middle: _____*maculipennis*

KEY TO THE GENUS CULEX

Adults

1. Abdominal segments with transverse apical white bands: _____ *apicalis*
   Abdominal segments with basal white bands or none:. 2

2. Abdominal segments with basal white bands_____ 3
   Abdominal segments without basal white bands: _____
   _____ *salinarius*

3. Basal white band of the second abdominal segment triangularly produced medially: _____*pipiens*
   Basal white band of the second abdominal segment transverse: _____ *territans*

Larvæ

1. Antenna with the tuft at or before the middle____*territans*
   Antenna with the tuft beyond the middle_____2

2. Both upper and lower head hairs multiple_____ _____3
   Both upper and lower head hairs not multiple, usually
   single but with all variations between the complete
   single and complete double condition, rarely with one
   or two head hairs triple: _____*apicalis*
3. Air tube long and slender, about seven times as long
   as broad, slightly expanded before the apex; subdorsal
   hairs on segments three to six multiple: __ *salinarius*
   Air tube not over five times as long as wide tapering
   uniformly toward the apex; subdorsal hairs double on
   segments three to six: _____ *pipiens*

The following genera of Culicinæ are represented by single
species; *Mansonia perturbans* (Walker), *Orthopodomyia
signifera* (Coquillett), *Uranotænia sapphirina* (Osten
Sacken), *Wyeomyia smithii* (Coquillett).

SUMMARY OF SPECIES OF CULICIDAE REPORTED FROM
MASSACHUSETTS

The following species of mosquitoes were reported by
Johnson (1925):

Subfamily Dixinæ

Dixa centralis Loew
D. clavata Loew
D. cornuta Johannsen
D. modesta Johannsen
D. notata Loew

Subfamily Chaoborinæ

Mochlonyx cinctipes Coquillett as *Corethra cinctipes*
Coquillett
M. karnerensis Felt as *Corethra culiciformis* (DeGeer)
M. fuliginosus Felt as *Corethra fuliginosus* Felt.
Chaoborus albipes (Johannsen)
C. americanus Johannsen as *C. crystallina* DeGeer
C. albatus Johnson
C. punctipennis Say
C. trivittatus Loew

Subfamily Culicinæ

Wyeomyia smithii (Coquillett)

Erratum

page 129, first line, above *Culex apicalis* insert :
Culex pipiens Linnæus

Culex apicalis Adams as *C. testaceus* Van der Wulp
C. *territans* Walker
C. *salinarius* Coquillett
Theobaldia melanura (Coquillett) as *Culex melanurus* (Coquillett)
T. *morsitans* (Theobald) as *Culiseta dyari* (Coquillett)
T. *inornata* (Williston) as *Culiseta inornatus* (Williston)
Mansonia perturbans (Walker) as *Taeniorhynchus perturbans* (Walker)
Psorophora ciliata (Fabricius)
P. *posticata* (Wiedemann) as *P. sayi* Dyar and Knab
Aedes trivittatus (Coquillett)
A. *aurifer* (Coquillett)
A. *punctor* (Kirby)
A. *intrudens* Dyar
A. *hirsuteron* (Theobald)
A. *communis* (DeGeer) as *A. lazarensis* (Felt and Young)
A. *dorsalis* (Meigen)
A. *canadensis* (Theobald)
A. *stimulans* (Walker)
A. *cantator* (Coquillett)
A. *fitchii* (Felt and Young)
A. *trichurus* (Dyar) as *A. cineroborealis* Felt and Young
A. *atropalpus* (Coquillett)
A. *excrucians* (Walker)
A. *taeniorhynchus* (Wiedemann)
A. *sollicitans* (Walker)
A. *triseriatus* (Say)
A. *vexans* (Meigen)
A. *cinereus* (Meigen)
A. *impiger* (Walker)
Uranotænia sapphirina (Osten Sacken)
Anopheles punctipennis (Say)
A. *quadrimaculatus* (Say)
A. *maculipennis* (Meigen)
A. *walkeri* (Theobald)

In 1930 one additional Culicine was reported by Tulloch:

Aedes implacabilis (Walker) or *Aedes abserratus* (Felt and Young)

Several species new to Massachusetts have been recovered during the present survey. They are as follows:

Subfamily Chaoborinæ

Eucorethra underwoodi Underwood—Yarmouth, July 27, 1939, Armstrong

Corethrella brakeleyi Coquillett—Taunton, July 20, 1939, Collector M. W. Chambers

Subfamily Culicinæ

Psorophora columbiæ Dyar and Knab—Northampton, July 18, 1939, Collector W. J. Neunier

Orthopodomyia signifera (Coquillett)—Sudbury, August 28, 1939, Collector W. J. Normandin

Anopheles crucians Wiedemann—Orleans, August 29, 1939, Collector J. L. Drew

LITERATURE CITED

Bradley, G. H., 1936. On the identification of mosquito larvæ of the genus Anopheles occurring in the United States (Diptera, Culicidæ). South. Med. Jour. 29: 859-861 illus.

Dyar, Harrison G., 1922. The mosquitoes of the United States. U. S. Natl. Mus. Proc. 62, art. 1, 119 pp.

——1928. The mosquitoes of the Americas. Carnegie Inst. Wash. Pub. 337, 616 pp. illus.

Dyar, Harrison G. and Shannon, Raymond C., 1924. The American Chaoborinæ. Ins. Ins. Mens. 12: 201-216.

Edwards, F. W., 1932. Diptera, Fam. Culicidæ. 258 pp. illus. Bruxelles. In Wytsman, P., Genera Insectorum, fasc. 194.

Headlee, Thomas J., 1921. The mosquitoes of New Jersey and their control. N. J. Agr. Exp. Sta. Bull. 348. 229 pp. illus.

Johannsen, O.. A., 1903. Aquatic insects in New York State. N. Y. State Mus. Bull. 68, part 6: 328-441. illus.

——1923. North American Dixidæ. Psyche 30: 52-58. illus.

——1934. Aquatic Diptera, Part 1. Nemocera, exclusive of Chironomidæ and Ceratopogonidæ. Cornell. Univ. Agr. Exp. Sta. Memoir 164. 71 pp. illus.

Johnson, Charles W., 1925. Fauna of New England 15, List of the Diptera or two-winged insects. Boston Soc. of Nat. Hist. 7. 326 pp. illus.

King, W. V., Bradley, G. H., and McNeel, T. E., 1939. The mosquitoes of the southeastern States. U. S. Dept. Agr. Misc. Pub. 336. 90 pp. illus.

Marshall, J. E.. 1938. The British Mosquitoes. 341 pp. illus. William Clowes and Sons, Ltd. London and Beccles.

Matheson, Robert, 1925.   Notes on Chaoborinæ (Diptera, Culicidæ).
      Can. Ent. 57: 159-160.
——1929.   A handbook of the mosquitoes of North America.   268 pp.
      illus.   Springfield, Ill. and Baltimore, Md.
Smith, John B., 1904.   Report of the New Jersey State Agricultural
      Experiment Station upon the mosquitoes occurring within the
      state, their habits, life history, etc.   482 pp.   illus.   Trenton.
Tulloch, George S., 1930.   A key to the biting mosquitoes of New Eng-
      land.   Psyche 37: 234-244.   illus.

EXPLANATION OF PLATES

PLATE 4

1. Female mosquito (after John B. Smith).

PLATE 5

2. Side view of thorax showing bristle areas.
3. Dorsal view of crescent-shaped scutellum.
4. Dorsal view of trilobed scutellum.
5. Generalized wing of a mosquito.
6. Tarsus with toothed claws.
7. Tarsus with simple claws.

PLATE 6

8. Larva of *Aedes* (after Marshall).
9. Larva of *Anopheles* (after Marshall).

PLATE 7

10. Head of *Anopheles* larva (after Marshall).
11. Dorsal view of segments 4 and 5 of *Anopheles* larva.
12. Air tube sharply attenuated without a pecten.
13. Air tube with some of the pecten teeth produced into long hairs.
14. Air tube fusiform with small tuft (after Dyar).
15. Air tube with pecten teeth detached outwardly.
16. Air tube with pecten teeth not detached outwardly.

PLATE 8

17. Larva of *Chaoborus* (after Johannsen).
18. Larva of *Mochlonyx* (after Johannsen).
19. Larva of *Eucorethra* (after Johannsen).
20. Larva of *Corethrella* (after Johannsen).
21. Larva of *Dixa* (after Johannsen).

Psyche, 1939 VOL. 46. PLATE IV.

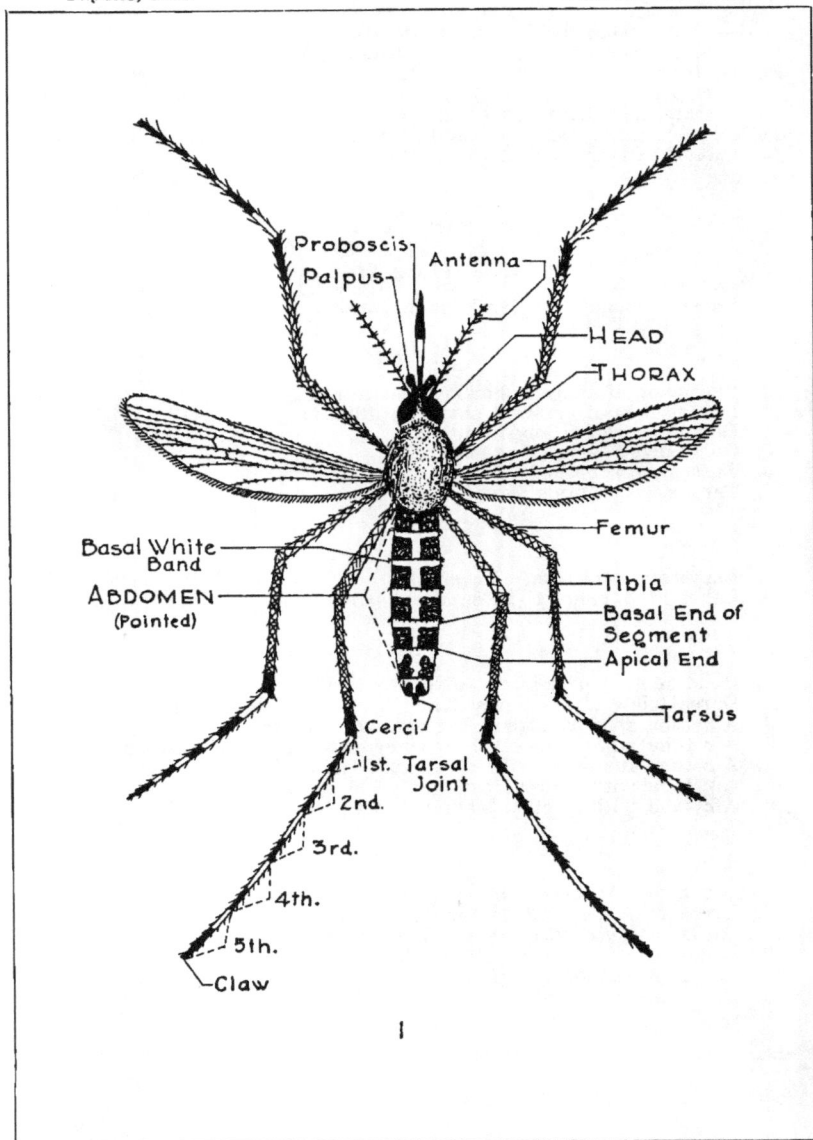

Tulloch — Mosquitoes of Massachusetts.

Psyche, 1939   VOL. 46, PLATE V.

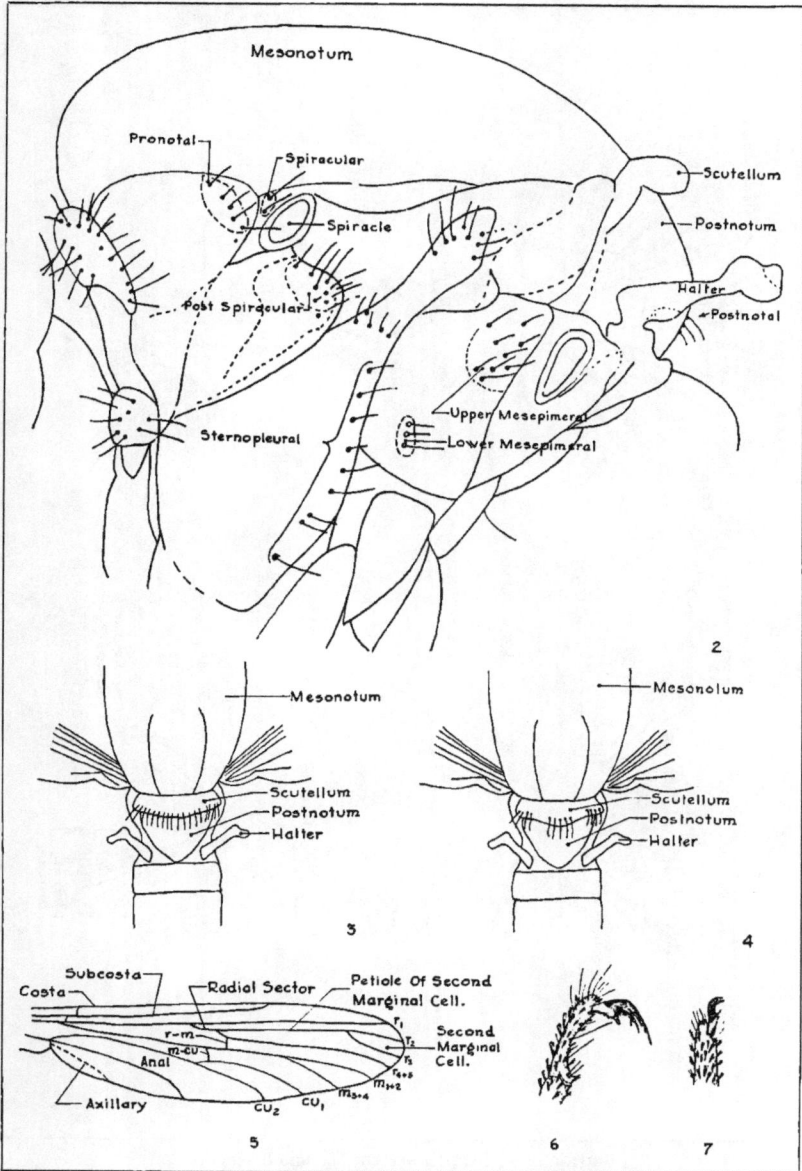

Tulloch — Mosquitoes of Massachusetts.

Psyche, 1939 VOL. 46, PLATE VI.

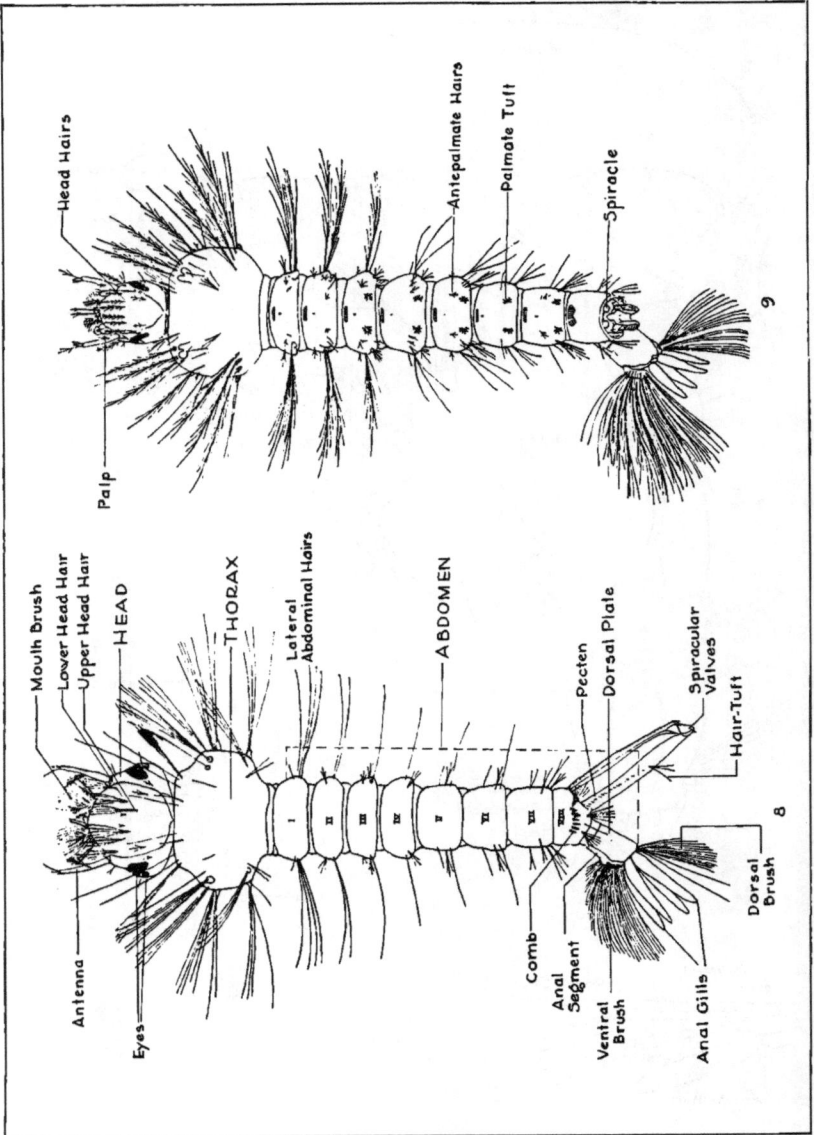

Tulloch — Mosquitoes of Massachusetts.

Psyche, 1939   VOL. 46, PLATE VII.

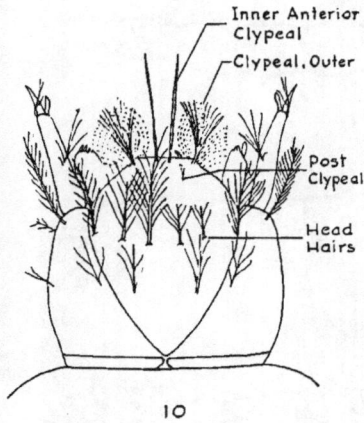

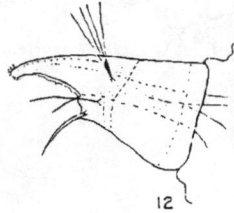

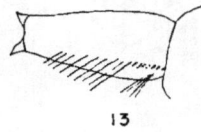

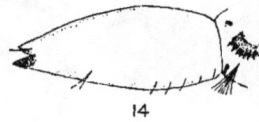

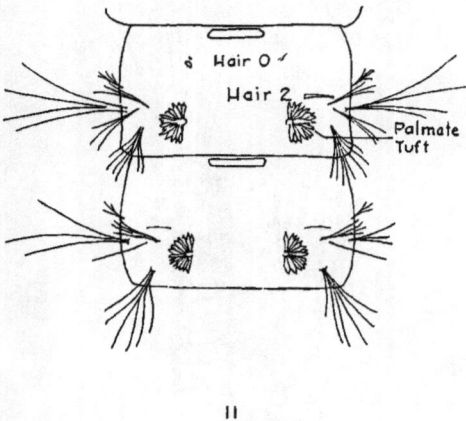

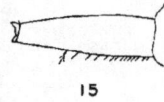

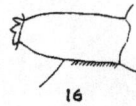

Tulloch — Mosquitoes of Massachusetts.

Psyche, 1939 Vol. 46, Plate VIII.

17

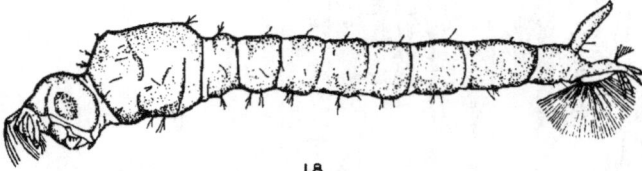

18

19

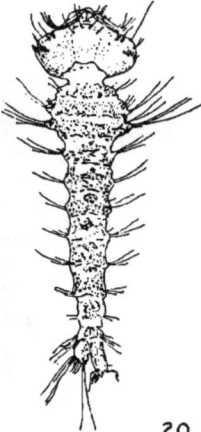

20

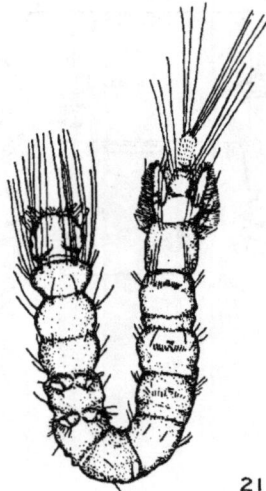

21

Tulloch — Mosquitoes of Massachusetts.

A NEW SUBSPECIES OF *CREMATOGASTER MINUTISSIMA* WITH REVISIONARY NOTES CONCERNING THAT SPECIES. (HYMENOPTERA:FORMICIDÆ)

By William S. Creighton

College of the City of New York.

In 1895 Carlo Emery published the second half of his monograph dealing with North American ants. A considerable proportion of the material on which this work was based had come to Emery from Pergande who was, at that time, connected with the National Museum. As a general rule Pergande gave no names to the ants which he sent to his colleague probably because, in most cases, he was not sure as to what was new. In the instance which I wish to discuss here, however, Pergande had not only recognized the form as new but had selected the name which it now bears. There seems to be no other interpretation which can be placed upon Emery's treatment of *Crematogaster victima* subsp. *missouriensis*. Emery attributed this form to Pergande, stating that the latter had used the name *in litteris*. There is no method whereby one can determine whether Pergande was actually preparing to publish a description of *missouriensis* and it makes very little difference if he was. Emery accompanied his citation of the form with a brief characterization permitting its recognition. This, of course, is the original description of *missouriensis*, which is to be attributed to Emery and not Pergande. I do not doubt that many would regard this as a flagrant case of name-grabbing but it is by no means certain that such was the case. It is difficult to believe that Emery supposed that he could give *missouriensis* to Pergande by merely citing him as author. It seems more probable that Emery was under the impression that Pergande would publish the description of the new form before the appearance of his (Emery's) monograph and that he inad-

vertently let slip into print a manuscript notation which was
to have been subsequently altered. It is easier to be tolerant
of this mistake than it is to agree with Emery's treatment
of the taxonomic status of *missouriensis*. I can see no reason
why he should have assigned it to *victima* instead of to
Mayr's *minutissima*. In 1870 Mayr had published a key to
the New World species of *Crematogaster* in which he clearly
distinguished between the characteristics of Smith's *victima*
and his own *minutissima*. Emery must surely have employed
Mayr's key and just as surely he should have been aware
that *missouriensis* is more closely related to *minutissima*
than to *victima*. The distinct areas of cephalic punctures
which are present in *victima* are absent in the other two
forms. In recent years the recognition of a number of additional subspecies has considerably expanded the specific
limits of *victima*. Even so the above contention can be de-
fended. Still more peculiar is Emery's disregard for zoögeo-
graphical considerations. When he assigned *missouriensis*
to *victima* the latter species was known only from Brazil.
It would certainly have seemed more logical to consider the
possibility of relationship with a species which had been
found in the Gulf Coast region. As far as I can determine no
one has ever questioned Emery's judgment in the matter.
Despite this I believe that *missouriensis* should be regarded
as a northern race of *minutissima*. In addition there is a
western race which is described below.

Crematogaster (Orthocrema) minutissima thoracica
subsp. nov.

The subspecies *thoracica* differs from the typical form and
the subspecies *missouriensis* in its distinctly more shining
thoracic dorsum. In both the other two forms the dorsum
of the promesonotum bears, in addition to longitudinal
rugæ, a number of fine and fairly close-set punctures. These
punctures, while not dense enough to produce an opaque
appearance, dull the surface to a considerable extent. They
are not present in the subspecies *thoracica*. In addition
thoracica usually lacks longitudinal rugæ on the pronotum
and, when they are present, they appear to form a wavy
border at the extreme edge of the pronotum. The longi-

tudinal rugæ in the typical *minutissima* are well developed and at least two of them lie well in towards the center of the pronotum. In *missouriensis* the rugæ are variable in position but when they occur at the edge of the thorax, as frequently happens, they are more prominent than in *thoracica*. The shape of the petiole seen from above is usually quite characteristic in *thoracica*. The sides gently diverge behind so that the petiole is widest at the rear. The difference is not great but the wedge-like appearance is rather different from that of the other two subspecies, where the petiole is more quadrate with the sides subparallel and widest, if there is much difference in width, at the middle. The epinotal spines of *thoracica* are short like those of the typical form. In other respects *thoracica* is very similar to the typical *minutissima*.

Described from a series of workers taken by W. M. Mann in Miller Canyon, Huachuca Mountains, Arizona (elevation 6000 ft.). In addition to this type series I have seen other specimens also secured by Dr. Mann, in Ramsey Canyon (elevation 5800 ft.) in the Huachucas.

Holotype (worker) and a series of paratypes in the collection of the Museum of Comparative Zoölogy. Additional paratypes in the collection of the American Museum of Natural History and the collection of the writer.

The three subspecies of *minutissima* and our single remaining species in the subgenus *Orthocrema*, Cr. (*O.*) *arizonensis*, may be separated as follows:

1. Tip of the antennal scape in repose notably surpassing the occipital border; color yellow; the gaster clothed with abundant long hairs _____2

   Tip of the antennal scape in repose failing to reach the occipital border; color piceous brown; the erect hairs of the gaster short and sparse: _____*arizonensis*

2. Dorsum of the promesonotum very smooth and shining; rugæ, if present, feeble and confined to the edge of the pronotum: _____*minutissima thoracica*

   Dorsum of the promesonotum finely punctate in addition to the longitudinal rugæ, the surface feebly shining; rugæ well-developed and often placed towards the center of the thorax__ _____ _____3

3. Epinotal spines about one-half as long as the distance which separates their bases and rather strongly directed upward; pronotum with the rugæ usually lateral in position: _____ _____ *minutissima missouriensis*

   Epinotal spines less than half as long as the distance which separates their bases and directed more backward than upward; pronotum with two prominent rugæ near the middle: _____ *minutissima minutissima*

THREE NEW NEOTROPICAL COPROPHAGOUS COLEOPTERA

BY RENAUD PAULIAN

Laboratoire d'Entomologie du Museum, Paris

The three new species described herein were sent me for study, together with a long series of unnamed coprophagous Coleoptera, mostly from the Neotropical region, by the Museum of Comparative Zoölogy of Harvard University. I am glad of this opportunity to thank Dr. P. J. Darlington, Jr., for the most interesting material he sent me and for his generosity in allowing me to keep paratypes of the new species.

Besides the new species, the material sent to me contained a long series of species of Canthidium. For the most part they were probably new, at least the species were neither in the Paris Museum, the British Museum, nor in my own collection. But it should be necessary, before describing new species of this genus, and of the closely allied Choeridium, to make a general revision of the species, as Harold's monographs are old and rather inadequate.

I take this opportunity to indicate that *Uroxys productus* Arrow, described from an old specimen without locality label, has been collected by Dufau (in coll. Fleutiaux) under stones at Trois Rivieres, Guadeloupe Is., West Indies. It appears to be rare and found only in unique specimens.

Canthon darlingtoni n. sp. (fig. 1, 2, 7)

Type: One specimen from Colombia: Santa Marta (P. J. Darlington). Museum of Comparative Zoölogy, no. 23,693.

Paratypes: A small series of specimens from the same locality in my collection and the Museum of Comparative Zoölogy.

Length: 4.75-5.5 mm., breadth: 3-3.5 mm.

Body convex, orbicular, very broad, shining but minutely shagreened above. Head brown-red; thorax pale testaceous

with a large median anterior dark red patch; this patch
touches the anterior margin, which is slightly darkened, as
are also the lateral margins and the small lateral foveæ;
middle of base with a vaguely rectangular dark patch. Elytra
pale testaceous, with a dark transverse patch along the base;
this patch broader at the sides, the sutural interstriæ darkened, a broad transverse patch about the middle, and on each
elytron a small dark apical patch. Antennal club piceous, tro-
phi yellow; legs red, with the femora largely testaceous in
the middle, tarsi only slightly paler than the tibiæ. Underside red, with a small testaceous patch at the sides of the
abdominal segments, this patch much larger on the last segment; pygidium reddish at the base, yellow at the apex.

Head rather broad, part of the eyes visible from above
small and narrow; sides of the clypeus slightly raised, the
anterior part impressed between the two anterior teeth; vertex with a slight median impression; anterior clypeal teeth
curving upwards, rather long, parallel, rounded at apex;
sides of the clypeus only very feebly sinuate between these
teeth and the clypeogenal suture, which is very slightly
marked; genal sutures feeble; genæ rounded, their greatest
breadth at the middle. Head without any puncturation.

Thorax transverse, anterior angles acute, sides straight
between those angles and the median angles, which are
rounded and protrude very slightly behind. Posterior half
of the sides gently rounded to the hind angles which are very
slightly protruding behind, the sides of the base being feebly
emarginated just inside these angles. Lateral margin a little
more marked at the anterior angles; anterior margin complete; base gently rounded, with only a very slight angular
protuberance in the middle; no scutellar impression. Puncturation very feeble and sparse, slightly stronger behind.

Elytral margins nearly straight, strongly curved behind;
elytra convex, depressed along their apical margin; interstriæ flat, regular, only very sparsely and very feebly punctured; striæ distinct, not deep, distinctly punctured; scutellar impression very deep; elytral striæ ending anteriorly
in small, basal, longitudinal foveæ; external epipleural margin very sharp, epipleura broad.

Pygidium nearly smooth, very short and broad, not margined at the base. No prosternal carina; mesosternum very

short; metasternum with a broad, arcuate fovea, smooth.
Anterior tibia broad, with three very sharp and long marginal teeth; median and posterior tibiæ slightly arcuate and
strongly carinate. Tarsi long, equal to ¾ of the tibial length,
compressed, metatarsus much shorter than the second joint.
Hind femora slightly clavate, not margined.

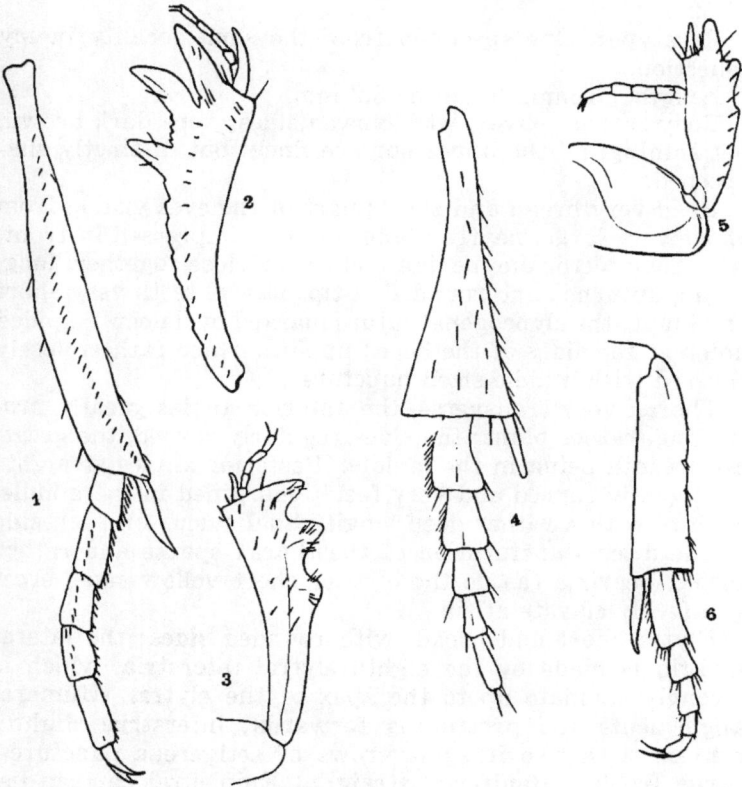

Fig. 1. *Canthon darlingtoni* n. sp., posterior leg.
Fig. 2. *id.*, anterior leg.
Fig. 3. *Croxys pygmaeus*, anterior leg.
Fig. 4. *Bdelyrus bowditchi* n. sp., posterior leg.
Fig. 5. *Onthocharis panamensis* n. sp., anterior leg.
Fig. 6. *id.*, posterior leg.

This very pretty little species belongs to the group *cyanocephalus* Har. but it is quite peculiar by its colour pattern and its broad form.

Bdelyrus bowditchi n. sp. (fig. 3, 4)

Type: From British Honduras: M-tee district, F. C. Bowditch Collection. Museum of Comparative Zoölogy no. 23,694.

Paratype: One specimen from the same locality in my collection.

Length: 5 mm., breadth: 3.2 mm.

Body rather convex, with curved sides; very dark brown, not shining, all the upper surface finely but distinctly shagreened.

Head very broad and short; part of the eyes visible from above very large, nearly round; clypeus impressed in front, with four teeth, the median teeth very close together, long, broad, upturned and rounded at tip; lateral teeth very short and blunt; the clypeogenal suture marked by a deep, rounded notch at the sides of the head; upper surface rather closely covered with middle-sized punctures.

Thorax very transverse, the anterior angles greatly protruding, rather blunt; the sides regularly curved, the greatest breadth being in the middle. Posterior angles straight; base gently curved and very feebly margined in the middle. Thorax with a rather deep longitudinal sulcus on each side of the disc. Puncturation of the thorax sparse and rather feeble, bearing (as do the elytra) short yellow setæ, erect and feebly clavate at tip.

Elytra short and broad, with rounded sides; the lateral margin is made by the eighth elytral interstria, which is strongly carinate up to the apex of the elytra. Humeral angle acute and protruding forwards; interstriæ slightly convex, with two irregular rows of setigerous punctures. Striæ feeble, cateniform, straight. Epipleural carinæ distinct.

Pygidium horizontal, short and small, with a strong annular groove. Mesosternum rather long. Prosternum strongly excavated under the front angles. Anterior tibiæ truncate at apex, short and broad; posterior tibiæ greatly enlarged at the tip. Tarsal joints triangular.

This new species appears at first sight as nearer to *Canthochilum* Chap. than to *Bdelyrus* Har. but the structure of the elytra ranges it decidedly in this last genus. *B. bowditchi* n. sp. is quite different from *B. seminudus* Bates (from Costa Rica and Ecuador) by the puncturation, the shagreened upper surface and the quadridentate clypeus. *B. lagopus* Har. from Brazil, the genotype, is unknown to me but nothing in its description differentiates it from *B. seminudus*, which, by the way, Bates placed in *Aphengium*.

Onthocharis panamensis n. sp. (fig. 5, 6, 8)

Type: From Panama Canal Zone: Barro Colorado Island, K. W. Cooper. Museum of Comparative Zoölogy no. 23,695.

Paratype: A specimen from the same locality in my collection.

Length: 3.5 mm., breadth: 1.5 mm.

Body parallel, elongate, very shining, very convex, metallic green.

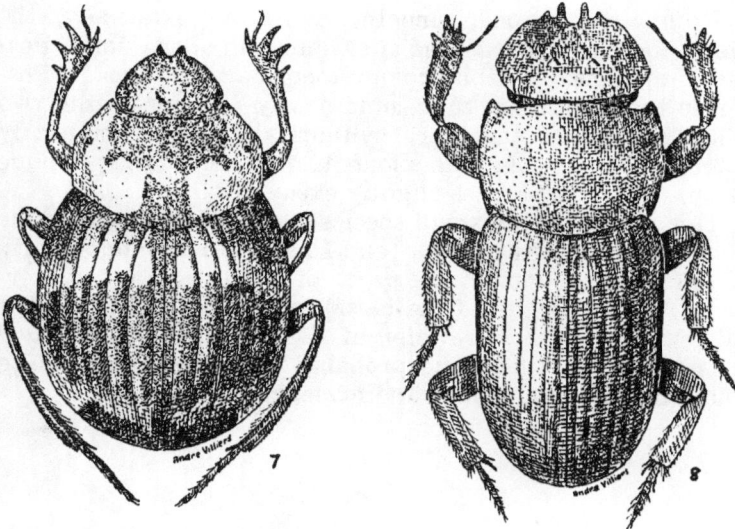

Fig. 7. *Canthon darlingtoni* n. sp.
Fig. 8. *Onthocharis panamensis* n. sp.

Head very broad, clypeus depressed in front, sex-dentate, the lateral teeth very short, broad and rounded; the median teeth long, slender, rounded at the apex. Part of the eyes visible from above very narrow. Vertex with two small, rounded tubercles. All the head covered with a sparse and rather strong puncturation.

Thorax very convex, parallel-sided in the first four-fifths, slightly sinuate behind; posterior angles strongly protruding behind; base strongly emarginate inside the posterior angles, a strong oblique depression in front of this emargination; base gently and regularly rounded; disc of thorax with a short median longitudinal sulcus on the posterior half, this sulcus not touching the base; front angles acute; puncturation rather strong and sparse.

Elytra parallel, with a feeble scutellar impression, interstriæ slightly convex, very feebly and sparsely punctured; striæ rather strong, not closely punctured. Pygidium very convex and shining, rather long, strongly margined, the margin slightly angular in the middle, sparsely and finely punctured.

Front tibiæ broad, smooth, tridentate externally, the apical tooth in line with the lateral margin of the tibiæ. Posterior and median tibiæ compressed, parallel, broad. Posterior tarsi with the first joint nearly as long as the two following taken together, cylindrical. Abdomen nearly smooth. Prosternum with a long, transverse, slightly oblique carina; the front angles slightly excavated.

This new and very small species is quite distinct from the known species of the genus (and I have had the opportunity of studying in London the types of Westwood and Waterhouse) by the length of the tarsal joints and their cylindrical form. A general revision of the genus is much needed as many unidentified, and probably new, species are to be found in many collections and museums.

METAMORPHOSES OF CUBAN HESPERIINÆ

By V. G. Dethier

Biological Laboratories, Harvard University

INTRODUCTION

As is generally the case when the life histories of skippers are studied, members of the subfamily Pyrginæ receive most attention while the Hesperiinæ are almost totally neglected. This situation is difficult to understand for though larvæ of the Pyrginæ are admittedly more spectacular and more frequently encountered in the field, a satisfactory treatment of their life histories is rendered difficult by several factors not the least of which is the fact that gravid females do not readily oviposit in captivity. Again, in many instances the food plant is unknown. On the other hand, Hesperiinæ oviposit on the least provocation, and the larvæ can be reared practically upon any grass. It is all the more surprising that the metamorphoses of Cuban Hesperiinæ have suffered neglect since all species can undoubtedly feed on sugar cane. Those species treated in this paper readily did so and the Hesperiinæ include not a few potential sugar cane pests.

Of the twenty-two species listed in this subfamily by Bates (1935) the life histories of but half are now known. Species which also occur in the United States have been studied by workers there. Gundlach (1881) recorded two additional species, and six species are treated below.

This work was made possible by my receiving a Harvard University Fellowship to study at the Atkins Institution of the Arnold Arboretum at Soledad, Cuba. The incompleteness of some of the life histories is due in part to the limited time available for study in Cuba. Color descriptions are based on a comparison with Ridgway's (1920) color charts.

It is a pleasure to acknowledge the generosity of Professor Thomas Barbour and the cheerful assistance of Mr. Frank Walsingham.

Polites baracoa (Lucas)

Egg.

Height .5 mm. Greatest diameter .7 mm. Yellow when laid, later becomes flesh color due to the appearance of blood red coloring in the fine raised reticulation present over the surface of the egg.

First Instar.

Head height .4 mm.; head width .37 mm. Head deep piceous. Shallowly punctate. Shield same color. Length of body 1.5 mm. Body yellow at emergence; after eating, tinged with grass green. Clothed with short distinctly clavate hairs. Anal segment with two pairs of long forwardly recurved hairs and a shorter pair of backwardly decurved hairs. Spiracles very faint fuscous. Legs fuscous.

Second Instar.

Head height .7 mm.; head width .6 mm. Head lighter piceous than before, with more numerous short colorless hairs. Head roughly punctate. In some specimens there are light areas in the regions of the epicranial and adfrontal sutures. Body length 2.4 to 4 mm. Body light green covered with many short colorless to brown hairs. Anal plate gray.

Third Instar.

Head height .9 mm.; head width .85 mm. Head roughly punctate. Slight evidence of light areas characteristic of later instars (cf. Fig. 10). Length of body 5.5 mm. Green dorsally, yellow laterally and ventrally. Covered with numerous short black hairs. Anterior two thirds of anal plate gray with a roughly spherical light area on either side of the median line. Posterior third of anal plate a much lighter gray.

Fourth Instar.

Head height 1.1 mm.; head width 1.1 mm. Head coarsely shagreened. Characteristic piceous design on a very light fuscous background (Fig. 10). Margin of foramen magnum piceous. Body length 6.5 to 8 mm. Mid-dorsal line dull green. Paradorsal lines mottled with light and dark green. Intersegmental areas brownish. Spiracles light cream. Short hairs covering body arising from small black warts. Dark

gray area of anal plate of greater extent. Light spots more
elongate.

Fifth Instar.

Head height 1.4 mm.; head width 1.5 mm. Piceous design
reduced in area. Ground color Old Gold except for a white
band on either side of the epicranial suture and a white spot
in the region of the ocelli. Rim of foramen magnum black.
Body length 10 mm. Narrow irregular mid-dorsal line Argus
Brown. Lateral line same but wider. Body Vinaceous-Buff,
lighter on borders of lateral line and spotted with few irregular spots of Argus Brown. Stigmatal line a faint suggestion
of darker background. Areas between dorsal line and lateral line more heavily spotted than elsewhere. Scattered colorless hairs over body. Spiracles cream. Black and white
design on anal plate as in Fig. 4.

Eggs laid May 10 and 11 hatched May 17 seven days having elapsed. Moulting into the second instar took place on
May 22 the first instar being of five days' duration. The
second instar was of four to five days' duration moulting
having occurred May 26. The third instar consumed five
days with moults May 31. The fourth and fifth instars likewise were of five days' duration each.

Catia misera (Lucas)

Egg.

Height .75 mm. Greatest diameter .82 mm. Egg white,
covered with a raised reticulation forming polygonal areas
as is usual with the eggs of Hesperiinæ.

First Instar.

Head height .5 mm.; head width .45 mm. Head black,
shiny, very faintly punctate. Few very small whitish hairs.
Body length 2 to 3.8 mm. Body light Vinaceous-Buff spotted evenly with Fawn Color spots, more distinct on the
posterior segments. Becomes slightly grass green especially
at the anterior end after eating. Few scattered hairs on
body bulbous at tip. Two pairs of long forwardly recurved
hairs on anal segment. Also a pair of shorter backwardly
decurved hairs. Claws of first pair of legs slightly fuscous.

Second Instar.

Head height .72 mm.; head width .70 mm. Head shiny black with faintly raised reticulations also shiny. Thoracic legs fuscous. Length of body 4.5 to 5 mm. Body dull grass green thickly mottled with maroon and white. Dull greenish mid-dorsal line. Under side of body dull greenish. Bright orange spot on each segment, segments one and two excepted, at stigmatal line. Short hairs covering body. Those on anal plate longer.

Third Instar.

Head height .8 mm.; head width .78 mm. Head roughly shagreened. Characteristic black and white design of head with greater percentage of black than in following instars (cf. Fig. 13), that is, white bands not so broad. Body length 5 to 7 mm. Body mottled white and dark ferruginous on dull background. Orange spots same as above. Many short black hairs from black tubercles. Legs fuscous.

Fourth Instar.

Head height 1.2 mm.; head width 1.0 mm. Head design as in Fig. 13. Body length 7 to 10 mm. Not much change from previous instar, general effect darker.

The egg stage lasted from seven to ten days. Eggs laid May 6, 7, and 8 hatched May 16; those laid May 9 to 11 hatched May 18; those laid May 19 and 20 hatched May 26 and 29. The first instar was of five to six days' duration with moults occurring in the above three groups May 23, 23, and 31 respectively. The second instar was of four to eight days' duration. The third and fourth instars were of seven days' duration each.

Poanes radians (Lucas)

Egg.

Height .5 mm.; greatest diameter .75 mm. Pearl white when laid. Later acquires a bright pink design which consists of an irregular circumpolar band and a slightly wider irregular equatorial band. The usual reticulation is present.

First Instar.

Head height .5 mm.; head width .52 mm. Head shiny black, faintly pitted. Body length 2 to 3.5 mm. Claws of thoracic legs fuscous. Body light Baryta yellow; light green after eating. Two pairs of long forwardly recurved hairs of approximately equal length on anal segment.

Second Instar.

Head height .72 mm.; head width .7 mm. Head dull black, raised reticulations darker than ground work. Lighter in region of epicranial suture. Length of body 4.5 mm. Body yellow green covered with minute black hairs. Dorsal line slightly darker green. A conspicuous black stellate spot on each side of the median line of the anal plate.

Third Instar.

Head height .87 mm.; head width .8 mm. Characteristic brown to piceous head design on yellowish background (cf. Figs. 7 and 9) first appears in this instar. Areas bordering the epicranial and adfrontal sutures are white. Body length 5.5 to 9 mm. Body grass green with many short black hairs. Dull green mid-dorsal line. Spots on anal segment now usually four (Fig. 1).

Fourth Instar.

Head height 1.25 mm.; head width 1.10 mm. Head as in Figs. 7 and 9. Body length 9.5 mm. Similar to foregoing instar.

Eggs laid May 6 to 8 emerged May 13, five to seven days having elapsed. The first instar consumed six days moulting having occurred May 19 and 20. The second instar was of five to twelve days' duration with moulting May 31. The third and fourth instars required ten days each.

Lerodea tripuncta (Herrich-Schäffer)

Fourth Instar.

Head height 1.5 mm.; head width 1.35 mm. Head with a rough raised reticulation and the same characteristic fuscous design on whitish background as in the following instar. Body light green covered with short whitish to brownish hairs.

Fifth Instar.

Head height 1.9 mm.; head width 1.5 mm. Head as in

Fig. 5. Roughly shagreened and covered with many short white hairs. Body length 22 mm. Light green.

Chrysalis.

Length 18 mm. Narrow and generally cylindrical in shape. Anterior end acute. Cremaster long and pointed. Tongue case same length as chrysalis but free from base of wing pads to end. Surface of chrysalis smooth. General color light green. Free portion of tongue case with slight pinkish tinge. Cremaster transparent and colorless at its tip.

Prior to emergence of the adult the dark color of the wings becomes visible as does also the brilliant red of the eyes. The duration of the chrysalis stage is eight days.

Prenes nero sylvicola (Herrich-Schäffer)

Egg.

Height .5 mm. Greatest diameter .75 mm. The eggs range in color from bone white to flesh. The surface is adorned with a raised reticulation forming polygonal cells.

First Instar.

Head height .5 mm.; head width .6 mm. Head piceous, shiny, punctate, and with few whitish hairs. Body length 2 to 4 mm. Yellow on emergence, light green after eating. Covered with a few short brown clavate hairs. Anal plate with two pairs of very short (for this position) recurved hairs.

Second Instar.

Head height .75 mm.; head width .6 mm. First appearance of characteristic head pattern (cf. Fig. 11). Head with raised reticulation and short brownish to colorless hairs. Ground color light yellowish to greenish. Length of body 4.5 mm. Body clear grass green with a dark green mid-dorsal line bordered by a narrow white line. Also thin white paradorsals. Body covered with minute black hairs.

Third Instar.

Head height .9 mm.; head width .9 mm. Dark areas of head pattern more extensive than in following instar (Fig. 11). Minute black hairs covering head. Length of body 6 to 13 mm. Design as in previous instar but more pronounced. Faint indication of a white substigmatal line.

Fourth Instar.

Head height 1.6 mm.; head width 1.5 mm. Head as in Fig. 6. Body length 15 mm. Similar to previous instar.

Eggs laid May 11 to 13 emerged May 15 and 16 three to five days having elapsed. The first instar consumed from four to eight days with moults May 19 and 23. The second instar required five days with moults May 28. The third instar was of four days' duration.

Prenes nyctelius coscinia (Herrich-Schäffer)

Second Instar.

Head height 1.6 mm.; head width 1.5 mm. Head with raised reticulations and the characteristic design seen in all the following instars (cf. Fig. 8). Body green covered with minute brown hairs.

Third Instar.

Head height 2.1 mm.; head width 2.0 mm. Roughly punctate, otherwise similar to previous instar. Body length 12 mm. Body covered with many short black hairs. First four segments Sorrento Green. Remainder of body Opaline Green. Stigmatal line Opaline Green.

Fourth Instar.

Head height 2.6 mm.; head width 2.5 mm. Similar to previous instar. Body length 18 to 20 mm. Same as above.

Fifth Instar.

Head height 3.2 mm.; head width 3.0 mm. Head roughly punctate. Design as in Fig. 8. Dark areas fuscous; light areas Reed Yellow. Body length 25 to 28 mm. Body Water Green.

Chrysalis.

Length 21 mm. Covered with short brown hairs except on head and dorsal areas where the hairs are considerably longer, those on head being the longest. Tongue case reaches only to sixth abdominal segment. It is free only at the last segment. Cremaster short and blunt. General ground color dead grass yellow. Eyes, mouthparts, cremaster, and tip of tongue case light brown. Two brown spots on pronotum.

When about to pupate the mature larva becomes dead grass yellow and spins a loose cocoon in the grass. Larvæ which pupated May 18 emerged May 27 nine days having elapsed.

CLASSIFICATION

Although the extent of our knowledge of larval Hesperiinæ in Cuba does not yet permit of a workable key to the different species, it already holds more than fair promise for one at a later date.

All of the forms now described may be identified by the characteristic head pattern or the color of the head of the later instars. For this the moulted head capsule is adequate.

It will be found that the larvæ may be divided into two groups, those with a color pattern on the head and those without. The patterns are sufficiently constant within the species to enable one to separate them by referring to Plate IX. *Polites baracoa* and *Poanes radians* may further be identified by the color pattern on the anal plate. *Catia misera* is characterized by dark ferruginous mottling. In this respect it closely resembles *Catia otho*. Two species are known in which the head lacks any definite pattern. One, *Calpodes ethlius*, may be distinguished by its dark orange head; *Hylephila phyleus*, the other, by its dark brown to black head.

LITERATURE CITED

Bates M., 1935. The butterflies of Cuba. Bulletin of the Museum of Comparative Zoölogy, 78 (2) : 61-258.

Gundlach, J., 1881. Contribución á la entomología cubana. (Vol. 1, Lepidoptera). Havana.

Ridgway, R., 1920. Color standards and color nomenclature. Washington, D. C.

Psyche, 1939 VOL. 46, PLATE IX.

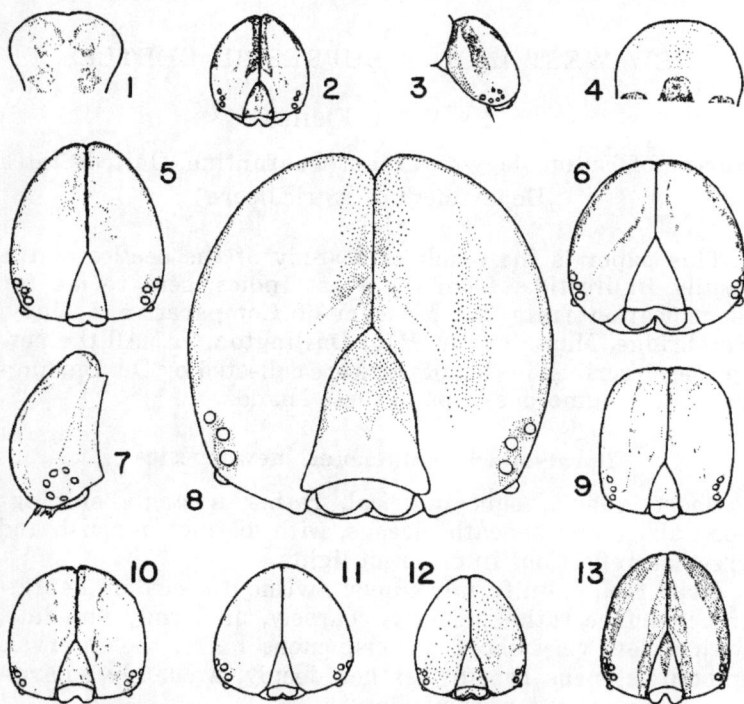

Fig. 1. Color pattern on the dorsal side of the anal segment of *Poanes radians* (Lucas).
Fig. 2. Front view of the head of *Lerodea eufala* (Edwards).
Fig. 3. Lateral view of the same.
Fig. 4. Color pattern on the dorsal side of the anal segment of *Polites baracoa* (Lucas).
Fig. 5. Front view of the head of *Lerodea tripuncta* (Herrich-Schäffer). Last instar.
Fig. 6. Front view of the head of *Prenes nero sylvicola* (Herrich-Schäffer). Fourth instar.
Fig. 7. Lateral view of the head of *Poanes radians* (Lucas). Fourth instar.
Fig. 8. Front view of the head of *Prenes nyctelius coscinia* (Herrich-Schäffer). Last instar.
Fig. 9. Front view of the head of *Poanes radians* (Lucas). Fourth instar.
Fig. 10. Front view of the head of *Polites baracoa* (Lucas). Fourth instar.
Fig. 11. Front view of the head of *Prenes nero sylvicola* (Herrich-Schäffer). Third instar.
Fig. 12. Front view of the head of *Hylephila phyleus* (Drury).
Fig. 13. Front view of the head of *Catia misera* (Lucas). Fourth instar.

NEW WEST INDIAN BUPRESTID BEETLES

By W. S. Fisher

Bureau of Entomology and Plant Quarantine, United States
Department of Agriculture

This paper is the result of a study of the beetles of the family Buprestidæ from the West Indies, sent to me for identification from the Museum of Comparative Zoölogy, Cambridge, Mass., by Dr. P. J. Darlington, Jr. All the new species described in this paper were collected by Dr. Darlington on his numerous trips to these islands.

Paratyndaris antillarum, new species

Short, robust, subcylindrical, rather strongly shining; body above and beneath piceous, with distinct purplish and greenish reflections in different lights.

Head feebly, uniformly convex, without a median depression; surface rather densely, coarsely, uniformly punctate, with a few very short, inconspicuous hairs, the intervals smooth; clypeus broadly, rather deeply, arcuately emarginate in front; antennæ missing.

Pronotum strongly, uniformly convex, one-third wider than long, distinctly narrower at apex than at base, widest at middle; sides strongly arcuately rounded; lateral margin, when viewed from the side, entire, and slightly arcuate; anterior margin truncate; base vaguely, transversely sinuate; disk without depressions or smooth lines; surface finely, transversely striolate, and asperate at middle, coarsely, rather densely punctate, and more or less rugose toward the sides, sparsely clothed with short, inconspicuous hairs. Scutellum glabrous, elongate-triangular.

Elytra as wide as pronotum at base; sides nearly parallel from humeral angles to behind middle (feebly constricted along basal fourth), then arcuately converging to the tips, which are separately broadly rounded, with a distinctly elevated, sinuate, preapical carina; lateral margins coarsely, irregularly serrate; disk uneven, and each elytron with a transverse depression along base, an oblique depression in front of middle, and a feeble, median gibbosity at apical third; surface irregularly striate, coarsely, irregularly punctate, more densely basally, and sparsely, irregularly clothed with moderately long, recumbent, whitish hairs.

Abdomen beneath coarsely, rather sparsely, uniformly punctate, sparsely clothed with very short, inconspicuous hairs; second sternite with the posterior margin truncate, without a distinct plate extending over the third sternite; last visible sternite terminating in an acute spine.

Length 7 mm., width 3 mm.

Type locality.— South side of Lake Enriquillo, Dominican Republic.

Type.— In the Museum of Comparative Zoölogy, Cambridge, Mass. Type no. 23,696. Paratype in the United States National Museum.

Described from two specimens (one type) found dead at the type locality during September 1938 by P. J. Darlington, Jr.

The type is probably a female but has not been dissected. Both specimens are more or less broken and the head is missing from the paratype. The paratype has a very small plate at posterior margin of second sternite.

This is the first species of *Paratyndaris* to be recorded from the West Indies. It resembles *P. acaciæ* Knull, but differs from that species in being shorter and more robust, in having the elytra uneven, uniform in color, and the lateral margin without two distinct teeth near apex, the second sternite without or with only a feebly indicated plate at the posterior margin, and in not having the pronotum sulcate at the middle.

Buprestis hispaniolæ new species

Female.— Broadly elongate, moderately convex above, strongly shining; pronotum brownish cupreous, with a more or less distinct greenish reflection, and ornamented with reddish yellow as follows: A rather broad vitta on each side along lateral margin extending from apical angle to near posterior angle, a narrow fascia on each side on anterior margin, three round spots along base, and a rounded spot at middle near anterior margin; elytra purplish brown, each elytron with two broad, irregular, reddish-yellow vittæ, the lateral one extending from humeral angle to near apex, and the sutural one from near base to apical fifth; body beneath brownish cupreous, with the prosternum, median parts of metasternum and mesosternum, femora in part, and transverse fasciæ on the sternites, reddish yellow.

Head nearly flat, purplish brown, with a transverse yellow spot on each side at vertex and several irregular yellow spots behind the clypeus, and with a short carina on the front; surface coarsely, irregularly, confluently punctate, sparsely clothed with short, erect, inconspicuous hairs; eyes feebly converging above; clypeus broadly, arcuately emarginate in front.

Pronotum twice as wide as long, distinctly narrower at apex than at base, widest near base; sides sinuate and strongly, obliquely diverging from apical angles to near posterior angles, which are broadly rounded; anterior margin broadly, arcuately emarginate, with the median lobe broadly, feebly rounded; base transversely sinuate; surface slightly uneven, coarsely, deeply, irregularly punctate, with a few short, inconspicuous hairs at posterior angles, the intervals smooth. Scutellum quadrate, truncate in front, broadly rounded behind.

Elytra slightly wider than base of pronotum; sides feebly expanded behind the humeri, feebly converging to apical third, then strongly, arcuately converging to the tips, which are separately transversely truncate, with a small tooth at each angle; surface striato-punctate, the striæ not deeply impressed, the punctures fine and closely placed in the striæ; intervals feebly convex, coarsely, irregularly punctate, and the intervals toward the sides more or less rugose.

Abdomen beneath coarsely, irregularly punctate, sparsely clothed with short, semierect, white hairs, the intervals obsoletely granulose; first sternite longitudinally flattened at middle; last visible sternite sinuately rounded at apex. Prosternum coarsely, sparsely punctate, sparsely clothed with short, recumbent, whitish hairs; prosternal process

flattened at middle, obliquely expanded from anterior coxal
cavities to the apex, which is acute.

Length 18-20 mm., width 7-7.5 mm.

Male.— Unknown.

Type locality.— Between Constanza and Jarabacoa, at an
altitude of 2,000 to 4,000 feet, Dominican Republic.

Type.— In the Museum of Comparative Zoölogy, Cambridge, Mass. Type no. 23,697. Paratype in the United
States National Museum.

Described from two females (one type) both collected by
P. J. Darlington, Jr. The type was collected at the type locality during August 1938, and the paratype was collected in
the foothills of the Cordillera Central, south of Santiago,
Dominican Republic, during June 1938.

This species resembles *Buprestis lineata* F., but it differs
from that species in having the pronotum and underside of
body ornamented with reddish-yellow spots. The reddish-
yellow spots on the underside of the body in the two specimens examined are more or less variable in shape.

Peronæmis insulicola, new species

Male.— Rather narrowly agriliform, rounded in front,
more acuminate behind, glabrous, rather strongly shining;
head bluish green in front, becoming violaceous on occiput;
pronotum dark green, with a more or less distinct violaceous
tinge on certain parts; elytra dark violaceous green, bronzy
green along sutural margins; body beneath green, with a
golden reflection on abdomen, more strongly shining than
above, and the legs in part bluish green.

Head nearly flat in front, with a vague, longitudinal carina
on occiput; surface coarsely, deeply, densely, uniformly
punctate, the intervals finely granulose; clypeus wide between the antennal cavities, feebly, transversely concave,
broadly, shallowly, angularly emarginate in front.

Pronotum rather strongly convex, strongly deflexed at
sides, one-third wider than long, slightly wider at base than
at apex, widest at middle; sides feebly, arcuately rounded;
anterior margin feebly sinuate, with a feeble, broadly
rounded, median lobe; base nearly transversely truncate;
lateral margin when viewed from the side sharply defined,

arcuate, extending from base to near apical angle; disk with three large, deep, basal depressions, the median one not extending to middle, with a deep fovea in front of scutellum, the lateral ones extending to middle of pronotum; surface coarsely, deeply, densely, uniformly punctate, the intervals finely, densely granulose. Scutellum twice as wide as long; sides feebly rounded; surface nearly smooth.

Elytra as wide as pronotum at base; sides broadly, angularly expanded behind humeral angles, nearly parallel to middle, then strongly, obliquely converging to the tips, which are acute; lateral margins coarsely, irregularly serrate; basal depressions rather deep and broadly transverse; surace irregularly striato-punctate, more or less rugose basally, the intervals finely, densely granulose, with a few coarse punctures intermixed.

Body beneath coarsely, rather densely, irregularly punctate, finely granulose, sparsely clothed with moderately long, erect, inconspicuous hairs; last visible sternite feebly, arcuately emarginate at apex.

Length 10 mm., width 3.25 mm.

Female.— Unknown.

Type locality.— Between Constanza and Jarabacoa, at an altitude of 2,000 to 4,000 feet, Dominican Republic.

Type.— In the Museum of Comparative Zoölogy, Cambridge, Mass. Type no. 23,698.

Described from a unique male collected at the type locality during August 1938 by P. J. Darlington, Jr.

This species is allied to *Peronæmis monticola* Fisher, but it differs from that species in being of a more uniform color above, in having the pronotum rounded at the sides, the elytra strongly angulated behind the humeral angles, and in not having a finely punctured vitta along the sutural margins of the elytra.

Enbrachys gibbipennis, new species

Male.— Ovate, nearly twice as long as wide, broadly rounded in front, more attenuate posteriorly, strongly shining, glabrous; head and pronotum green, more or less bronzy, the latter with the elevated median part piceous; elytra uniformly piceous; body beneath piceous, with an indistinct purplish tinge.

Head moderately convex, broadly, longitudinally depressed in front, with a narrow, longitudinal groove extending from clypeus to middle of front, deeply, narrowly, transversely depressed behind clypeus, with three deep foveæ in the depression, one median and two lateral; surface densely, coarsely granulose, with numerous coarse, shallow punctures intermixed; antennal cavities nearly contiguous in front.

Pronotum nearly three times as wide as long at middle, considerably narrower at apex than at base, widest near base; sides parallel along basal third, then strongly, obliquely converging to the apical angles, which are acute; posterior angles subrectangular; when viewed from the side the lateral margin is straight anteriorly, arcuate near posterior angle for the reception of the anterior leg; anterior margin deeply, broadly, arcuately emarginate; base transversely sinuate on each side, the median lobe strongly produced, and broadly truncate in front of scutellum, disk with the antero-median part strongly, transversely convex, narrowly flattened along base, and very broadly flattened and uneven at the sides; surface coarsely, sparsely punctate on convex median part, densely granulose, with a few coarse punctures intermixed on the flattened areas. Scutellum triangular, distinctly wider than long.

Elytra nearly as wide as pronotum at base; humeral angles broadly rounded; sides parallel from humeral angles to middle, then obliquely converging to the tips, which are conjointly broadly rounded; lateral margins feebly serrate; surface very uneven, coarsely, sparsely, shallowly, irregularly punctate, and each elytron with moderately elevated, broadly rounded gibbosities as follows: An oblique one on humerus, an elongate one along sutural margin behind scutellum, a rounded one near lateral margin just behind the middle, and an elongate one near apex.

Abdomen beneath vaguely granulose or reticulate, with a few shallow, inconspicuous punctures intermixed; last visible sternite broadly rounded at apex, the apical groove deep, and following outline of lateral margins. Prosternum feebly reticulate, sparsely, coarsely, shallowly punctate; prosternal process broad, the sides obliquely converging to the apex, which is broadly rounded.

Female.— Differs from the male in being uniformly pice-ous, with a more or less distinct cupreous reflection, and in having the last visible sternite more broadly subtruncate at apex.

Length 2.75 mm., width 1.5 mm.

Type locality.— Mt. Diego de Ocampo, at an altitude of 3,000 to 4,000 feet, Dominican Republic.

Type and allotype.— In the Museum of Comparative Zoöl-ogy, Cambridge, Mass. Type no. 23,699. Paratypes in the United States National Museum.

Described from four specimens, two males and two fe-males (one male type), all collected at the type locality dur-ing July 1938 by P. J. Darlington, Jr.

This species resembles *Enbrachys otero* Fisher, from which it differs in having the front of the head more shal-lowly depressed, the sides of the pronotum more strongly flattened, and in not having the gibbosities on the elytra so abruptly elevated.

Leiopleura darlingtoni, new species

Oblong, rather strongly convex above, broadly rounded in front, more strongly narrowed posteriorly; head yellow-ish cupreous; pronotum reddish cupreous on convex median part, bronzy green on flattened area at sides; scutellum bright blue; elytra opaque olivaceous green, with a quadrate, opaque, blue spot behind the scutellum, a large, shining, piceous area on each side along lateral margin behind hu-merus, and a similar area in front of scutellum, common to both elytra; body beneath black, with a faint purplish re-flection, and strongly shining.

Head strongly, uniformly convex, with four deep, round foveæ behind the clypeus; surface densely, coarsely reticu-late, with a few shallow, indistinct punctures intermixed; antennæ uniformly piceous, nearly contiguous at bases.

Pronotum twice as wide as long, distinctly narrower at apex than at base, widest along basal half, strongly, uni-formly convex on antero-median part, strongly flattened along base and on each side along lateral margin; sides strongly, arcuately diverging from apical angles to middle, then parallel to the posterior angles; anterior margin sub-truncate; base transversely sinuate on each side, the median lobe feebly produced and broadly truncate in front of scutellum, surface coarsely, densely reticulate, with a few shallow, inconspicuous punctures intermixed. Scutellum triangular, nearly twice as wide as long, densely granulose, the granules flattened on top, resembling round, microscopic scales.

Elytra slightly wider than base of pronotum, rather strongly convex, broadly depressed along lateral margins behind humeri; humeral angles obtusely rounded; sides parallel and feebly sinuate from humeral angles to middle, then arcuately converging to the tips, which are conjointly broadly rounded, the lateral margins not distinctly serrate; humeri strongly elevated; surface densely granulose and sparsely, coarsely punctate on the olivaceous-green and bright-blue areas, the granules similar to those on the scutellum, and sparsely, coarsely punctate on the shining piceous areas.

Abdomen beneath densely, obsoletely reticulate, with a few inconspicuous punctures intermixed; last visible sternite broadly rounded at apex. Prosternum obsoletely reticulate, with a few coarse punctures intermixed, the groove for the insertion of the antenna short and shallow. Metasternum shallowly emarginate in front.

Length 2 mm., width 0.8 mm.

Type locality.— Labeled "R. Froide, Port-au-Prince, Haiti."

Type.— In the Museum of Comparative Zoölogy, Cambridge, Mass. Type no. 23,700.

Described from a single specimen collected at the type locality October 3, 1934, by P. J. Darlington, Jr., to whom I take great pleasure in dedicating the species.

This species differs from all the known species of *Leiopleura* in having the peculiar scale-like sculpture on the elytra and scutellum.

Micrasta puertoricensis, new species

Male.— Oblong oval, equally rounded in front and behind, moderately shining, glabrous; uniformly black, with an indistinct bronzy tinge above; body beneath black, with a faint purplish reflection, the tarsi yellowish, with the tarsal lamellæ whitish.

Head feebly convex, when viewed from above forming a

regular arc with the pronotum; surface densely alutaceous, sparsely, coarsely, shallowly punctate; front with the sides parallel; clypeus not transversely depressed, feebly constricted between the antennal cavities, feebly, broadly emarginate in front. Antenna extending beyond base of pronotum, sparsely clothed with long, erect, whitish hairs; first and second segments globuse, subequal in length; third distinctly narrower, feebly expanded at middle, subequal in length to the second; the following segments rather robust, subequal in length, slightly triangular, the last segment longer than the tenth, and acute at apex.

Pronotum strongly, uniformly convex, feebly, transversely flattened along base, twice as wide as long, distinctly narrower at apex than at base, widest behind middle; sides strongly, arcuately converging anteriorly, slightly converging near posterior angles; when viewed from the side the marginal and submarginal carinæ feebly arcuate, widely separated for nearly their entire length, and united at base, the marginal carina more or less obsolete anteriorly; anterior margin feebly, arcuately emarginate; base transversely truncate; surface feebly alutaceous, sparsely, coarsely, shallowly punctate. Scutellum triangular, acute at apex.

Elytra as wide as pronotum at base; sides parallel from humeral angles to apical third, then arcuately converging to the tips, which are conjointly broadly rounded; humeri not prominent; disk uniformly convex, with a shallow, transverse depression at base of each elytron; surface feebly, sparsely punctate, the intervals nearly smooth.

Abdomen beneath feebly convex, feebly reticulate, vaguely punctate, clothed with a few short, erect, inconspicuous hairs; basal sternite with a round, median depression, which is densely clothed with long, erect hairs; last visible sternite broadly rounded at apex. Prosternum moderately convex, coarsely, sparsely punctate; anterior margin subtruncate; prosternal process broad, the sides parallel, and broadly truncate at apex. Femora moderately robust. Tibiæ straight and slender.

Length 1.25 mm., width 0.6 mm.

Type locality.— Maricao Forest, at an altitude of 2,000 to 3,000 feet, Puerto Rico.

Type.— In the Museum of Comparative Zoölogy, Cambridge, Mass. Type no. 23,701. Paratype in the United States National Museum.

Described from two males (one type) collected at the type locality between May 30 and June 2, 1938, by P. J. Darlington, Jr.

This species resembles *Micrasta oakleyi* Fisher, but differs from that species in being uniformly black with an indistinct bronzy-green tinge, in having the marginal carina on the pronotum more or less obsolete anteriorly, the pronotum feebly, transversely depressed along the base, the scutellum acute at the apex, the surface of the elytra more feebly punctured, and in not having the clypeus transversely depressed.

Micrasta subcylindrica, new species

Female.— Differs from *Micrasta puertoricensis* Fisher as follows: Elongate, subcylindrical, and strongly convex above, strongly shining, piceous; pronotum more coarsely punctured, widest at middle, with the sides arcuately rounded; head coarsely, sparsely punctate, feebly, longitudinally depressed at middle; scutellum longer than wide, acute at apex; each elytron with a broad, triangular depression at base; abdomen and prosternum coarsely, densely punctate, the basal sternite without a round, median depression clothed with long hairs (this is a male sexual character); and the tarsi and apical halves of tibiæ yellowish.

Length 2 mm., width 0.75 mm.

Type locality.— Soledad (Cienfuegos), Cuba.

Type.— In the Museum of Comparative Zoölogy, Cambridge, Mass. Type no. 23,702.

Described from a unique female collected during May 1936 by P. J. Darlington, Jr.

Micrasta monticola, new species

Male.— Differs from *Micrasta puertoricensis* Fisher in being more robust, more strongly convex above, strongly shining, uniformly bronzy brown, and in having the pronotum and elytra coarsely, rather densely punctate, with the intervals smooth, pronotum widest along basal half, with the sides nearly parallel posteriorly, scutellum longer than wide, and acute at apex, elytra with the sides parallel from humeral angles to middle, and each elytron with a distinct, rather broad, transverse groove at base, the last visible sternite broadly rounded at apex, and in having the intermediate sternites narrowly, transversely grooved at the middle.

Length 2 mm., width 1 mm.

Type locality.— Mt. Diego de Ocampo, at an altitude of 3,000 to 4,000 feet, Dominican Republic.

Type.— In the Museum of Comparative Zoölogy, Cambridge, Mass. Type no. 23,703.

Described from a unique male collected during July 1938 by P. J. Darlington, Jr.

Micrasta hispaniolæ, new species

Female.— Differs from *Micrasta monticola* Fisher in being uniformly bluish black, subopaque, in having the pronotum widest at the middle, with the sides arcuately converging posteriorly, and the surface rather densely, coarsely punctate, with the intervals distinctly alutaceous, and in having the sides of the elytra parallel from humeral angles to apical third. It also resembles *Micrasta puertoricensis* Fisher, but it differs from that species in being more robust, more strongly convex above, subopaque, in having the pronotum and elytra rather densely, coarsely punctate, with the intervals distinctly alutaceous, and in having a distinct, broad, transverse depression at the base of each elytron.

Length 2 mm., width 1 mm.

Type locality.— Foothills of the Cordillera Central, south of Santiago, Dominican Republic.

Type.— In the Museum of Comparative Zoölogy, Cambridge, Mass. Type no. 23,704.

Described from a unique female collected during June 1938 by P. J. Darlington, Jr.

It is just possible that this may be the female of *monticola* Fisher, but on account of the differences given and without additional notes on their habits it seems advisable to consider them to be two distinct species. There does not seem to be a good series of any of the described species of this genus available for study, so it is impossible to decide what variation occurs in the species.

CONCERNING CHLOROPERLA (PERLIDÆ)

BY NATHAN BANKS

Museum of Comparative Zoology.

Recently there has been discussion by Frison and Ricker, the latter quoting Claassen, as to whether this name should replace Alloperla. When I made the Classification of the Perlidae in 1906, I had no European collection, and there was then no literature on the European forms of prime value. So I accepted Hagen's use of Isopteryx based on the lack of a folded anal area to the hind wing which is true for our form that he identified as *cydippe* Newm. I showed that the genus Chloroperla should replace Isopteryx. Since then I have not treated this group, but others have. Enderlein in 1909 applied my classification to the European and exotic forms known to him. Seeing that some of the European species had a small anal area, he wisely used another and more definite character, the fact that the second anal vein of the fore wings is unbranched in all the species, except *I. serricornis*, for which he made a new genus, Isoptena.

In 1912 Okamoto in his revision of the Japanese Plecoptera also uses this unforked second anal as the character of Chloroperla. In 1936 Kimmins reviewed the facts concerning Chloroperla and Isopteryx and agreed with me that the latter is a synonym of the former. He lists three species of Chloroperla in the British fauna, *torrentium, tripunctata,* and *apicalis*. The first two have a small anal area to hind wings, the third lacks it. So Kimmins evidently is using the unforked second anal as the generic character. But Needham, Claassen, Frison, and Ricker seem unaware that the unforked second anal has ever been used as the generic character, although they list Enderlein's paper in their bibliographies. Moreover, Needham and Claassen in their description of Chloroperla state that the second anal is branched, and put it under this heading in their synoptic table; however, their figure on Plate 14 shows the second anal unbranched. It was doubtless this mistake that led Ricker to describe his Hastaperla. Using the unbranched second anal vein as the generic character, our species (*brevis*) belongs to Chloroperla as truly as *apicalis* and *tripunctata.*

In 1912 when I saw the type of *C. cydippe* Newm. I noted it had a small anal area with one longitudinal vein; recently Ricker has seen it and says the second anal is forked, so this species is doubtless an Alloperla.

Kimmins considers that the genotype of Chloroperla (*lutea* Latr. is a synonym of *tripunctata.* I cannot agree. Latreille says of *lutea,* "extrémité des antennes noires"; and Newman says of *apicalis,* "extreme portions of the antennæ intensely black". Neither mention any black border to the pronotum.

Scopoli does not mention antennæ in his description of *tripunctata,* which, he says, agrees except in some points with *grammatica.* Of *grammatica* he says, "antennæ basi flavæ, extrorsum fuscæ". Klapalek in Süsswasserfauna Deutschlands (1909) says for *tripunctata* that the basal third of the antennæ is yellow, rest black, and that the pronotum is bordered with a black line.

In specimens here (Hagen coll.) *tripunctata* has mostly brown to black antennæ except basal third or less, while in *apicalis* (even specimens at least 90 years old) there is a greater part yellow and beyond "intensely black". Since *lutea* agrees with *apicalis* in both antennæ and pronotum and in neither with *tripunctata,* it is evident that *lutea* Latr. will replace *apicalis.* In either case *brevis* belongs to Chloroperla, and Chloroperla is distinct from Alloperla.

PSYCHE

INDEX TO VOL. XLVI, 1939

INDEX TO AUTHORS

INDEX TO SUBJECTS

All new genera, new species and new names are printed in SMALL CAPITAL LETTERS.

PIN-LABELS IN MULTIPLES OF 1000, ALIKE

One Dollar Per Thousand

Smallest Type. Pure White Ledger Paper. Not over 4 Lines nor 30 Characters (13 to a line) Additional Characters, 3 cents each, in total and per line, per 1000. Trimmed so one cut makes a label.

C. V. BLACKBURN, 7 Emerson St., STONEHAM 80, MASS.

CAMBRIDGE ENTOMOLOGICAL CLUB

A regular meeting of the Club is held on the second Tuesday of each month (July, August and September excepted) at 7.45 p.m. in Room B-455, Biological Laboratories of Harvard University, Divinity Ave., Cambridge. Entomologists visiting Boston are cordially invited to attend.

WARD'S ENTOMOLOGICAL SERVICES

Entomological Supplies and Equipment
Carefully designed by professional entomologists. Material of high quality at low prices. **Send for Supply Catalog No. 348.**

Insect Preparations
Life Histories, Type Collections, Collections of Economic Insects and Biological Insect Collections. All specimens are accurately determined.

Insects for the Pest Collection
We have in stock over three hundred species of North American Insect Pests. **Send for Price List No. 349.**

Ward's Entomological Bulletin
A monthly publication sent free to all entomologists requesting it.

Information for the Beginner
Send for **"Directions for Collecting and Preserving Insects"** by Dr. A. B. Klots. A mine of useful information. Price 15 cents.

WARD'S NATURAL SCIENCE ESTABLISHMENT, Inc.
P. O. Box 24, Beechwood Station
Rochester, N. Y., U. S. A.
The Frank A. Ward Foundation of Natural Science of the University of Rochester

BACK VOLUMES OF PSYCHE

The Cambridge Entomological Club is able to offer for sale the following volumes of Psyche. Those not mentioned are entirely out of print.

Volumes 2, 3, 4, 5, 6, 7, 8, 9, 10, each covering a period of three years, $5.00 each.

Volumes 12, 14, 17, each covering a single year, $1.00 each.

Volumes 18, 19, 20, 21, 22, 23, 24, 25, 26, each covering a single year, $1.50 each.

Volumes 27, 28, 29, 30, 31, 32, 33, 34, 35, 36, 37, 38, 39, 40, 41, 42, 43, 44, 45, 46, each covering a single year, $2.00.

Orders for 2 or more volumes subject to a discount of 10%.

Orders for 10 or more volumes subject to a discount of 20%.

A set of all the volumes available (40 in all) will be sold for $83.00.

All orders should be addressed to

F. M. CARPENTER, Associate Editor of Psyche,
Biological Laboratories,
Harvard University,
Cambridge, Mass.

www.ingramcontent.com/pod-product-compliance
Lightning Source LLC
Chambersburg PA
CBHW022127020426
42334CB00015B/792